Kinship in Neckarha

This work analyzes shifts in the relations of families, households, and individuals in a single German village during the transition to a modern social structure and cultural order. Sabean's findings call into question the idea that the more modern society became, the less kin mattered. Rather, the opposite happened. During "modernization," close kin developed a flexible set of exchanges, passing marriage partners, godparents, political favors, work contacts, and financial guarantees back and forth. In many families, generation after generation married cousins. Sabean also argues that the new kinship systems were fundamental for class formation, and he repositions women in the center of a political culture of alliance construction. Modern Europe became a kinship "hot" society during the modern era, only to see the modern alliance system break apart during the transition to the spostmodern era.

This book is one of a series of monumental local studies coming out of the Max Planck Institute for History in Göttingen. It is the most thoroughgoing attempt to work between the disciplines of social and cultural history and anthropology, and it demonstrates successfully the power of microhistory to reconceptualize general historical trends.

Kinship in Neckarhausen, 1700–1870

DAVID WARREN SABEAN
University of California, Los Angeles

PUBLISHED BY THE PRESS SYNDICATE OF THE UNIVERSITY OF CAMBRIDGE
The Pitt Building, Trumpington Street, Cambridge CB2 1RP, United Kingdom

CAMBRIDGE UNIVERSITY PRESS
The Edinburgh Building, Cambridge CB2 2RU, United Kingdom
40 West 20th Street, New York, NY 10011-4211, USA
10 Stamford Road, Oakleigh, Melbourne 3166, Australia

First published 1998

Printed in the United States of America

Typeset in Ehrhardt

Library of Congress Cataloging-in-Publication Data

Sabean, David Warren.
Kinship in Neckarhausen, 1700–1870 / David Warren Sabean.
p. cm.
Includes bibliographical references (p.) and index.
ISBN 0-521-58381-0 (hb). – ISBN 0-521-58657-7 (pb)
1. Kinship – Germany – Neckarhausen (Nürtingen). 2. Family – Germany – Neckarhausen (Nürtingen). 3. Ethnohistory – Germany – Neckarhausen (Nürtingen). 4. Neckarhausen (Nürtingen, Germany) – Social life and customs. I. Title.
GN585.G4S33 1997
306.83'0943'46 – dc21 97-34087
CIP

A catalogue record for this book is available from the British Library.

ISBN 0 521 58381 0 hardback
ISBN 0 521 58657 7 paperback

to George L. Mosse
who taught us all about teaching

In Ersilia, to establish the relationships that sustain the city's life, the inhabitants stretch strings from the corners of the houses, white or black or gray or black-and-white according to whether they mark a relationship of blood, of trade, authority, or agency. When the strings become so numerous that you can no longer pass among them, the inhabitants leave: the houses are dismantled; only the strings and their supports remain.

From a mountainside, camping with their household goods, Ersilia's refugees look at the labyrinth of taut strings and poles that rise in the plain. That is the city of Ersilia still, and they are nothing.

They rebuild Ersilia elsewhere. They weave a similar pattern of strings which they would like to be more complex and at the same time more regular than the other. Then they abandon it and take themselves and their houses still farther away.

Thus, when travelling in the territory of Ersilia, you come upon the ruins of the abandoned cities, without the walls which do not last, without the bones of the dead which the wind rolls away: spiderwebs of intricate relationships seeking a form.

–Italo Calvino, *Invisible Cities*

Contents

Tables

Tables

Abbreviations

B	brother
BM	Bürgermeister
D	daughter
F	father
fl	Gulden (florin)
FRKN	Frickenhausen
GRBTLG	Grossbettlingen
GRTZ	Grötzingen
H	husband
M	mother
NH	Neckarhausen
NTLF	Neckartailfingen
NRTG	Nürtingen
OBBHNG	Oberboihingen
OBENSG	Oberensingen
RDWG	Raidwangen
S	son
UNENSG	Unterensingen
W	wife
WLFS	Wolfschlugen
x	step
Z	sister
ZSHN	Zizishausen

Note: All dates follow German usage: day, month, year (12.2.1796 = 12 February 1796).

Abbreviations of sources

Gericht	Gerichts- und Gemeinderatsprotocolle, Neckarhausen
HSAS	Hauptstaatsarchiv Stuttgart
KB	Kaufbücher
Kirchenkonvent	Kirchenkonventsprotocolle, Neckarhausen
LKA	Landeskirchliches Archiv, Stuttgart
Nürtingen Stadtgericht	Stadtgerichtsprotocolle, Nürtingen
Oberamtsgericht	Nürtingen Oberamtsgerichtsprotocolle, STAL
Reyscher	August Ludwig Reyscher, ed., *Vollständige historisch und kritisch bearbeitete Sammlung der württembergischen Geseze*
RPTK	*Realenzyklopädie für protestantische Theologie und Kirche*
Schultheissenamt	Schultheissenamtsprotocolle, Neckarhausen
STAL	Staatsarchiv Ludwigsburg
Vogtruggericht	Vogtruggerichtsprotocolle, Neckarhausen (Bescheid- und Rezessbuch)

On reading kinship diagrams

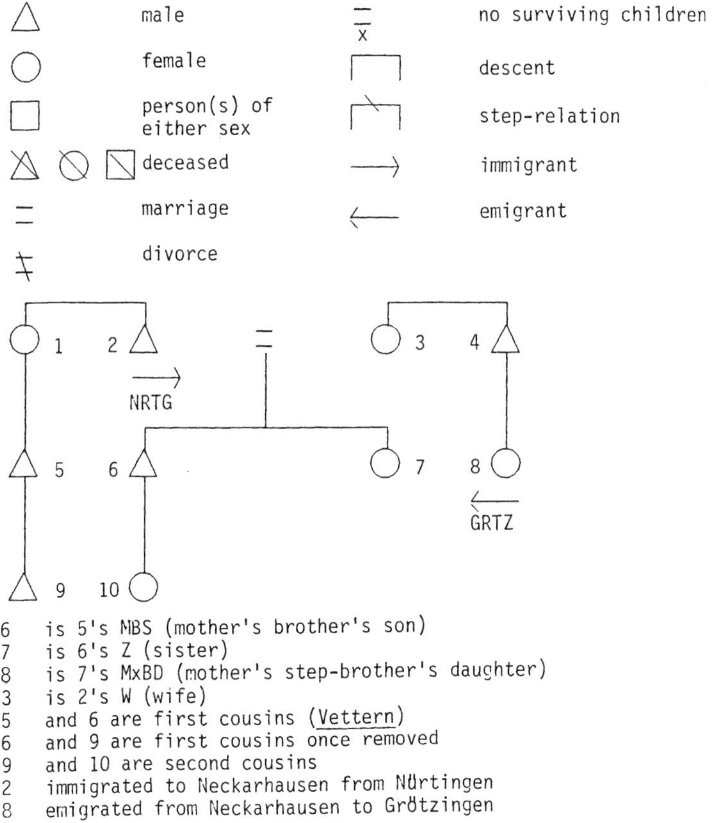

6 is 5's MBS (mother's brother's son)
7 is 6's Z (sister)
8 is 7's MxBD (mother's step-brother's daughter)
3 is 2's W (wife)
5 and 6 are first cousins (<u>Vettern</u>)
6 and 9 are first cousins once removed
9 and 10 are second cousins
2 immigrated to Neckarhausen from Nürtingen
8 emigrated from Neckarhausen to Grötzingen

Glossary

German words are italicized when they occur for the first time in the volume or when attention is focused on their use.

affinal related by marriage
agnatic relations reckoned through father
Amt bureau; district
Amtmann officer, official, administrator
Amtsverweser temporary incumbent of an office
Bauer agricultural producer, peasant
Beständer contractor; farmer
Blutsfreundschaft kin or kinship by blood
Blutschande incest
Bürger enfranchised member of a locality, citizen
Bürgerauschuss committee representing locality inhabitants
Bürgermeister chief financial officer of a locality
Bürgerrecht citizenship, full rights in a locality
Bürgerschaft citizens of a locality
Bürgschaft pledge, bond, surety
clan group of people related through descent
cognatic relations reckoned through both parents
consanguineal related by blood
Conventsrichter church consistory elder
cross cousins cousins reckoned through parent's different sex sibling
dot dowry
Döte godfather (relation to child)
Dote godmother (relation to child)
Ehesuccessor marital successor (spouse's subsequent spouse)

endogamy marriage inside the group
exogamy marriage outside the group
Familie family; kin-group
Freund friend; relative
Freundschaft kinship; affinity
Gant bankruptcy
Gegenschweher co-(rresponding)-parents-in-law
Gemeinderat local council; member of local council
Gemütlichkeit comfort
Gericht court
Gerichtsschreiber court clerk, recorder
Gerichtsverwandter Richter; member of the court; justice
Geschwister siblings
Geschwisterkind cousin
Gevatter(in) godfather (mother) (relation to parents)
Gevatterkind godchild (relation of parent to godparent)
Gevattermann godfather (relation to parent)
Gevattersohn godson (relation of father of child to godparent)
Grad degree
Güterpfleger warden, property overseer, or administrator
Hausmacht political influence of a family
Herrschaft lordship; authority, domination, dominion, rule; power; domain; seigneury
herrschaftliche Interesse fiscal interests of the prince
heterogamy marriage of unequals
Hofbauer farmer; tenant of a large farm
homogamy marriage of equals
hypergamy marriage upward (by women)
isonymy matching names
kindred group of relatives related to an individual
Kindskind(er) second cousin(s)
Kirchenkonvent church consistory
Kirchenordnung ecclesiastical code
Kriegsfrau court ward (woman); correlative to Kriegsvogt
Kriegsvogt curator ad litem; gender tutor; representative
Kriegsvogtschaft gender tutelage
Landschaft parliament, estates
Markung territory of a locality
matrifocal relationships centered on or constructed by a senior woman
matrilateral relationship reckoned through mother
matriline descendants through females of a common progenitrix
Mütterliches maternal inheritance
Mundtod incompetent, in state of civil death
neolocality residence not defined by parents' residence

neonymy creation of a novel name
Nutzniessung usufruct
Oberamt district
Oberamtmann chief district officer (see Vogt)
ousta household
parallel cousin cousin reckoned through parent's same-sex sibling
Partei faction
Parteilosigkeit neutrality
patrilateral relationship reckoned through father
patriline descendants through males from a common progenitor
patrilocality residence according to father's kin
Pflegekind ward
Pfleger guardian
Pflegschaft guardianship
Pförch sheepfold
Rat council; member of council
Richter justice; member of the court (Gericht)
Schichten social strata
Schultheiss chief administrative officer of a village
Schultheissenamt Schultheiss bureau
Schwägerschaft affinity
Scribent lower clerk
Sippe kindred
Stadtknecht town baliff
Stamm root; progenitor
Stammgut ancestral home; estate belonging to the chief line
Stand, Stände corporate group(s); status; class(es)
teknonymy naming by occupation or trade
Unteramtmann deputy to the Amtmann
Untervogt deputy to chief regional official
uterine relations reckoned through mother
uxorilocality residence according to mother's kin
Väterliches paternal inheritance
Verein club; association
Vetter cousin; earlier usage: uncle
Vetterle Swabian dialect form for Vetter (diminutive)
Vetterlesgericht a court full of relatives
Vetterleswirtschaft nepotism; corruption
Vogt chief regional official; representative; guardian
Waisengericht orphan's court
Waisenkind orphan
Waisenrichter justice of the orphans' court
Waldmeister forest administrator

Preface

George Mosse once explained to his graduate students how to put a book together: take notes until the shoe box is full, throw the box out the window, and write. Ah, but we were young, and the smell of revolution was in the air. Social history, with its need for stakhanovite heroes, beckoned and promised to overturn our understanding of the past. We were to spend long hours in the archives, years filling out family reconstitution forms, and more years figuring out what to do with them, all the while (although we did not suspect it at the time) shunting data from one outmoded technological system to another. Today I see more clearly how astute the practical advice was, but I also see how much I was building on the sure foundations George had already provided and how pervasive his influence has been. He taught me to pay close attention to the symbols and ideas that have moved people in the past. There was no great leap, apart from methodological razzle-dazzle and less readable prose, from his kind of cultural history to my kind of social history. Most important were his broad understanding of what constituted political practice and his sympathetic grasp of concrete existence. He understood that just those areas of life that people develop to avoid power, flee self-interest, and obtain distance are as much inflected with politics and with material culture as anything else. He was practicing critical history long before there was a word for it. When I look back on my intellectual development, I think that George taught me above all else two essential things: history writing as the practice of irony and history teaching as a high calling, demanding discipline, care, and a great deal of humor. I recently had the chance to hear George lecture once again after more than thirty years, this time in Los Angeles. The audience was full of students from Madison in the '60s – all of us reminded of an almost forgotten intensity of intellect and moral commitment. I want to dedicate this book to one of America's most successful teachers. No one who failed to hear Mosse lecture in the early '60s can experience history quite in the manner that we still do.

I have a second major debt, one that came later as I was puzzling out ways to incorporate social anthropology into the practice of history. During the academic year 1972–3, I had a Social Science Research Council postdoctoral fellowship to Cambridge University, where I spent the time in daily exchange with Jack Goody. Jack introduced me to that powerful and coherent school of British anthropologists who had studied and worked with Bronislaw Malinowski and A. R. Radcliffe-Brown. In conversations with Jack and his wife Esther, I worked out ideas about social reproduction and about the usefulness of a relational concept of property for historical and social analysis. Jack's broad vision of kinship, his elemental good sense, and his interest in historical process have all had a profound effect on how I have thought through the problems in this book. He has always been far more interested in building on past scholarship than on novelty for its own sake. I think he got it right recently when he remarked, "It is an impoverished field that sees itself as having to discard its predecessors at each generation instead of critically building on their achievements."[1]

Like M. Jourdain, who found out that he had been speaking prose for forty years without knowing it, I had been practicing "microhistory" without being aware that it might have a name. I have left it to my former and present colleagues, Hans Medick and Carlo Ginzburg, respectively, to explain the assumptions behind the methodology.[2] Simply put, I set out to examine kinship as an analytically distinct issue that required my data base to be restricted to a single locality in order to reach the details that could not be had any other way. I found that kinship was an inordinately useful starting place for elucidating a social order and that the study of one locality was a most powerful heuristic device. Tracking everyday aspects of intra- and interfamilial exchange, patterns of marriage, care for orphans, cooperation in agriculture, habitual ways of doing things, and the promotion and placing of children connects kinship to matters of gender, politics, production, and culture. I found that a number of fundamental historical issues could not be made sense of without understanding kinship and without starting the inquiry in a controlled and restricted location. Take, for example, the problem of class. If class is about anything, it is about the coordinated and managed access to property. Just for that reason, property, and indeed class, remain incoherent in the absence of kinship. And seeing how they are connected requires a patient attention to small details. Fundamental matters such as the nature and composition of households, the social division of labor, the distribution of authority,

[1] Jack Goody, *The Expansive Moment. The Rise of Social Anthropology in Britain and Africa 1918–1970* (Cambridge, 1995), pp. 144–5.

[2] See the introduction, "Entlegene Geschichte? Lokalgeschichte als mikro-historisch begründete allgemeine Geschichte," to Hans Medick, ed., *Weben und Ueberleben in Laichingen 1650–1900. Lokalgeschichte als allgemeine Geschichte* (Vandenhoeck und Ruprecht: Göttingen, 1996). See also Carlo Ginzburg, "Microhistory: Two or Three Things That I Know about It," *Critical Inquiry* 20 (1993): 10–35.

the dynamics of social hierarchy, and the arrangement of political practices within gender-constructed milieus, all remain unintelligible without a thoroughgoing analysis of kinship. Furthermore, the more distanced the viewpoint, the easier it is to fail to grasp kinship as a coherent system. But the methods of microhistory have to tack continuously with those of comparative history in order to bring lives as they really are lived – locally, on the ground – into recognizable and discussable shape, not as generalized information but as alternative logics of patterned reciprocity. Comparison in its turn cannot be done in bits and pieces but involves a careful reading of complex social structures against each other, looking for variations in strategical coherence or unexpected consequences of different social dialectics.

In an earlier work on the village, *Property, Production, and Family in Neckarhausen 1700–1870,* I looked at internal family and household dynamics, examining relations between husbands and wives and parents and children. I argued that toward the end of the eighteenth century the opening up of the village to outside markets, the reconfiguration of agricultural output, and the intrusion of capital profoundly altered the sexual division of labor, relations between husbands and wives, the structure and ideology of the house, intergenerational distribution and control of wealth and productive resources, the patterns of authority, and the way property mediated relationships among family members. The fact that the more fluid economy of the village shifted interactions within and between families poses new questions for studying kinship in other places and at other social levels during the process of modernization. Just as in the earlier book I argued for a reworking of the theme of family and modernity, here I am arguing for a reconceptualization of gender and class in terms of sharply focused attention on kinship as a modern construction.

This book therefore takes as its theme the set of familial relations among individuals and households. Sometimes kinship studies confine themselves to marriage exchanges, but I am concerned throughout with the encompassing patterns of reciprocity as well as with their reverse side – with forms of behavior that refuse exchange, establish lines of fission, or set up practices of exclusion. Kinship is very much about identity, for, after all, within its dynamics people are socialized, recognized, and ordered into intelligible hierarchies. Thus the examination of kinship promises to link issues of pressing current concern about subjectivity to older ones of social practice. Thinking about both identity and kinship prompts, as I will show, consideration of parallel problems of memory and narrative construction. Kinship is based on recall, commemoration, and remembering old debts, and its basic working procedure explicitly or implicitly operates from within a repertoire of mutually constructed stories. Kinship displays recurring patterns, and even though in my analysis I constantly endeavor to tease out form and structure, I am well aware that they are the result of numerous everyday practices – activities such as getting together a plow team, competing for a young girl's favor, discussing the fair allocation of building wood, or bidding on a village contract. Despite being embedded in mundane practices and produced within them, kinship proves to be systemic. Although it is constructed in the give and take of daily life, in the end it offers a system of patterned expectations, a coherent set of constraints, and an arena in which claims and obligations can be negotiated with strategic intent and greater or lesser degrees of tactical finesse.

Opening up kinship reveals a largely unexplored terrain of political activity. In the analysis of the history of Neckarhausen, the rise of a market in land and the massive influx of capital for agricultural intensification provided an explanatory entry into the problem of reordered relations among kin. In a parallel fashion in the larger society, the processes of bringing together capital and distributing it cannot be grasped outside the politics of kinship. In nineteenth-century Europe, strategic support for families in crisis, in bankruptcy, and at stress points in the life cycle called upon the calculated if intermittent intervention of kin. Skilled negotiations among existing and potential kin were necessary to maintain entrances to and exits from social milieus and to police cultural and social boundaries. Within the dynamics of family occurred a large part of the ludic, festive, competitive, and charitative activities that configured political cultures. Part of the reason that kinship has not been systematically brought into the conceptual framework of the political has to do with the central place of women for configuring alliances between subpopulations, for maintaining the practices of code and symbol recognition so crucial for sexual and cultural attraction, and for training rules and practices into bodies. Class habitus grew out of the interplay among kin, the setting of which in the nineteenth century was staged mainly by women. Connubium was at the heart of class formation, and alliances were continually configured around the negotiating activities of women. Politics is not only about ideology formation and party struggles, but it is also about cultural struggles: fashioning mannered discourses, patterning everyday forms of social intercourse, and configuring the aesthetics of distinction. To get at such issues, I consider the finely spun networks of social interaction, the complex interplay of reciprocities, and the links between familial intercourse and social imagination. Both kinship and politics are about building the ties that bind, and much of what this book is about is understanding cultures of obligation. The argument that emerges here is the reverse of older understandings of the relationship between politics and class. Rather than social differentiation and class articulation leading to certain forms of intervention in the political sphere, power is far more autonomous and politics is an active force in configuring class formation and ordering relations between classes.

* * *

I have many, many people to thank for helping me with this book. The initial lessons in social anthropology came from Robert Groves and George Bond during my first academic appointment at the University of East Anglia from 1966 to 1970. In 1968 Christopher Turner and I taught an interdisciplinary course on the history of the family and kinship in which I first outlined the problematic of this book. Many of the early methodological discussions took place at the University of Pittsburgh from 1970 to 1976, where Sam Hayes had brought together a remarkable group of innovative social historians. Larry Glasco talked me into using the computer to create a data base. With Jonathan Levine, the editor of *Historical Methods,* I discussed methodological practice for hours, and the happy occasion of long visits by Emmanuel Le Roy Ladurie and Edward Thompson strengthened my resolve to experiment with new ways of getting at things. Members of the peasant studies group at Pittsburgh encouraged me to read widely in comparative approaches to rural life. I also had help from a number of assistants. Sandy Dumin and Ella Jacobs keypunched and verified all of the parish register forms I had filled out. Eva Savol and Raymond Monahan prepared some of the tax records and inventories for keypunching by Lena Crnovic.

From 1976 to 1983, I was a fellow at the Max-Planck-Institut für Geschichte in Göttingen. The director, Rudolf Vierhaus, presided over an innovative, *eigensinnige* group of social historians concerned with the history of protoindustrialization, working class culture, and rural society. He was still a firm believer in basic research as the central role of such an institution, and I think that the recent publications of his group show that that form of ground-breaking scholarly pursuit is compelling and cannot be rushed. I found Alf Lüdtke's interests in power and everyday life crucial for my own formulation of the issues. Peter Kriedte offered a superb knowledge of agrarian institutions. Jürgen Schlumbohm read and commented on every word I wrote. He has proved a constant friend. His own book on the parish of Belm is a model study of demographic and social analysis, one of the most profound works of microhistory I know. Hans Medick chose to work on a Swabian village not far from Neckarhausen. We spent an intense seven years discussing the ins and outs of sources, the uses of anthropology for historical work, and the meaning and practice of microhistory. Although I do not think I ever convinced him of the central importance of kinship, the argument owes as much to his skepticism as anything else. Loli Diehl and Gerlinde Müller redacted the complex marriage and estate inventories onto forms, which Kornelia Menne entered on the computer. The computerization of the entire data base was made possible by the system "Kleio," developed by Manfred Thaller.

Many visitors to the Max-Planck-Institut helped me think through the issues: David Gaunt, David Levine, Jonathan Knudsen, Vanessa Maher, Gerald Sider, and Robert Berdahl. Above all, William Reddy was a congenial visitor. He has thought more profoundly than anyone else about how anthropology and history can speak to each other. He eventually read the first version of the manuscript, and his comments led me to recast the argument completely. He has also offered penetrating comments on the current version. Various members of the continuing seminar on family history and the Round Table in Anthropology and History discussed issues of family and kinship with me: Barbara Duden, Michael Mitterauer, Heidi Rosenbaum, and Regine Schulte. Karin Hausen at the Technical University in Berlin has been especially important in approaching my work with good humor and the right touch of ironic detachment. She introduced me to the Ernst Brandes texts, gave me leads to many sources, and prompted me to write the concluding two chapters. She has always been an engaged critic of my work, and many of the questions I have asked have grown out of conversations between us. I have gained many insights about Württemberg history over the years from talks with Carola Lipp and Wolfgang Kaschuba. I also learned a great deal from younger scholars at the Institute: Gadi Algazi, Michaela Hohkamp, and Peter Becker. I am particularly grateful to Bernhard Jussen for helping me think through the issues of godparentage.

Such a work as this could never have been written without the gracious and patient help of the staffs of various archives. For many years, the Württembergisches Hauptstaatsarchiv in Stuttgart was a home away from home. I want to thank the staff there, as well as at the Staatsarchiv in Ludwigsburg for establishing excellent working conditions and a professional atmosphere. Dr. Dietrich Schäfer at the Landeskirchlichesarchiv in Stuttgart offered welcome encouragement and assistance in getting the Neckarhausen parish material microfilmed. I have also benefited from assistance in Neckarhausen. When I first arrived in 1967, Bürgermeister Schwarz gave me permission to use the sources in the Rathaus, and Gemeindepfleger Hagenlocher arranged to let me have them microfilmed. The present Gemeindevorsteher, Willi Knapp, continued to allow access to the material and microfilming privileges.

During my years at the University of California (from 1983 to 1988, and since 1993) and at Cornell University (from 1988 to 1993), many colleagues and students have encouraged me and offered valuable critical readings. William Clark went through the first version as well as the current one line by line and offered brilliant structuralist readings. Scott Waugh thought it was important to keep the details. Isabel Hull read every word and gave me sensible ideas about how to revise and encouraged me to finish up. She was a delightful colleague and a major reason for missing Ithaca. Erik Monkonnen liked the diagrams and all the details. Bernard Heise gave me amused comment and insisted on clarity. Christopher Johnson explained why my arguments were important. Ever since we started out in graduate school together, he has offered the challenging perspective of a socially committed historian.

I want to thank Frank Smith once again for being an encouraging and patient editor. Vicky Macintyre did a superb job reading her way into the rhythms of my prose and saving me from many inconsistencies. I was very pleased that she was willing to take on another monster manuscript from me.

All through the many years, my wife, Ruth, has been striding ahead into the informational future, while I have been making forays into the more settled terrain of the past. Twenty-five years ago, a graduate student remarked that we both seemed so spry. Now that the term might have some meaning, I have visions of us skipping off into the new age, continually wrangling about the gains and losses of the new technology.

INTRODUCTION

1

An introduction to kinship

We need only as much theory as necessary.

– Jack Goody, *Expansive Moment*

During the three decades it took to put this study together, visions of Casaubon danced in my head, while all about me scholarly interest in population studies and in kinship analysis was on a steep decline.[1] With the recent loss of faith in social analysis, the basic weapons of the social historian's armament, such as "class," have been blunted or tossed aside. Yet I still find "class" a useful instrument, and in one way or another this book beats its way toward an argument that explains how kinship and class have interacted with each other during the modern era. The fact that these two concepts have been replaced in many disciplines by "identity" and "selfhood" has left me with the quixotic task of breaking a social-historical lance on the windmills of subjectivity.

In 1968 I set out to look at a relatively simple question arising from the widely held view among social scientists that modernization had fundamentally altered the nature of the family in Western civilization and that each social epoch was characterized by a dominant form of familial relations. People in Europe, so the story went, had once constructed their lives within a dense network of kin. Industrialization, urbanization, and monetization of social relations had allowed individuals and families to free themselves from traditional ties and enter into rationally calculated entrepreneurial activities or, by moving whenever necessary, to take up the opportunity to sell their labor in a free-wage market. Experts in development offered this successful transition in the West as a model for backward countries to emulate. In a future world economy premised on the tactical

[1] See Signe Howell and Marit Melhuus, "The Study of Kinship; The Study of Person; A Study of Gender," in Teresa del Valle, ed., *Gendered Anthropology* (London, 1993), pp. 38–53, here p. 39; and Jane Fishburne Collier and Sylvia Junko Yanigisako, "Introduction," in Collier and Yanigisako, eds., *Gender and Kinship: Essays towards a Unified Analysis* (Stanford, 1987), pp. 1–13, here p. 1. All of these authors want to revitalize kinship in the light of new understandings about gender, a point that will be partly documented in this book.

versatility of the nuclear family, obligations to extended kin were seen as a liability.

My question was twofold. First, I wanted to know if the generally accepted account of the European past was correct and what specific form the transition had taken – I was skeptical about offering an ill-conceived and little-understood model for underdeveloped areas of the world to emulate. Second, I wanted to know how the connections between and among families were patterned during the long pretransition period in which relations between people were supposed to have been dominated by a web of kinship. In a certain sense, where everyone is kin, no one is kin; that is to say, all the connections between kin could hardly carry the same meaning, moral exigency, or attitude. So the problem was to find a way to map the territoriality of kin in some particular context where there was enough detail to be specific about the degree to which people shaped their everyday lives with and without family and relatives.[2] There was also a complex hermeneutic problem to be solved, which Françoise Zonabend has effectively sketched: "Ethnologists have shown that in those societies called archaic, people 'disguise social and political maneuvers under the cloak of kinship' [in the words of Lévi-Strauss]. We could ask whether our societies, called modern, do not attempt to disguise the genealogical imperatives of alliance under the cloak of politics and economics."[3] I came to see in the course of this study that the distribution of property cannot be explained without an understanding of kinship, and that the same is true of the structure of households, the division of labor, and the deployment of authority. I also found that a thoroughgoing analysis of kinship could help rehabilitate class and lead to a subtler understanding of women's political practice, especially in the nineteenth century, which was when women supposedly disappeared into the realm of the private and therefore became effectively cut off from activity in the public sphere, the only "true" arena of political engagement.

In the late 1960s there were two tools at hand for investigating the kinds of questions that family and modernization posed. One consisted of parish registers. A decade earlier Etienne Gautier and Louis Henri had developed a method for examining demographic behavior at the village level that involved "reconstituting" individual families by a systematic exploitation of baptism, marriage, and burial registers.[4] I thought that it might be possible to develop just such a grid

[2] Since I began this study, there has been a great deal of research on family ideology, on the structure of households, and on demographic patterns. Accounts of the literature can be found in Tamara Hareven, "The History of the Family and the Complexity of Social Change," *American Historical Review* 96 (1991): 95–124; and Richard L. Rudolph, "The European Peasant Family and Economy: Central Themes and Issues," *Journal of Family History* 17 (1992): 119–38.

[3] Françoise Zonabend, "Le très proche et le pas trop loin: Réflexions sur l'organisation du champ matrimonial des sociétés structures de parenté complexes," *Ethnologie française* 11 (1981), pp. 311–18, here pp. 316–17.

[4] Etienne Gautier and Louis Henry, *La population de Crulai, paroisse normande: Etude historique,* Institut national d'études demographique, Travaux et Documents, Cahiers 33 (Paris, 1958). See also Louis Henry, *Manuel de démographie historique,* Hautes études medievales et modernes, 3 (Geneva, 1967). Cf. D. E. C. Eversley, Peter Laslett, and E. A. Wrigley, eds., with contributions by

in this study, but that I should add to it tax and land registers, debt and sale records, mortgage files – all kinds of lists – as well as minutes and protocols from police investigations and judicial hearings. As Jacques Dupâquier and Tony Wrigley later suggested, and as Hans Medick now has brilliantly demonstrated, expanded family reconstitutions could provide social historians with their own microscopes.[5] The second tool was a "genealogical" method that social anthropologists employed in their rich and fascinating literature on kinship. This method offered the necessary conceptual instruments and suggested the paths to follow in parsing the syntax of linkages turned up by family reconstitution.[6] The fact that anthropology was usually based on close observation of everyday life in small localities offered a genial complement to a social-historical strategy based on records from a single village. By blending the practices of these two disciplines, I felt that the microhistorical approach of this study would surely produce exciting results.

Locating a suitable community to examine did not take a great deal of time. I wanted to find a village in southern Germany, since I was already familiar with the sources and archives in that area. I also wanted to find a village with traditional three-field agriculture and mixed stock and grain production, one of strong peasant character and not affected very much, at least in the eighteenth century, by protoindustrialization.[7] The village had to be large enough to offer a variegated social life but small enough – so I thought – not to overwhelm the researcher with source material. But in the case of Neckarhausen, the Württemberg village I naively stumbled across, there happened to be between 300,000 and 500,000 pages of documents, far more, it turned out, than I had bargained for or could ever hope to exploit.

W. A. Armstrong and Lynda Overall, *An Introduction to English Historical Demography from the Sixteenth to the Nineteenth Century* (London, 1966).

5 See the references in Hans Medick's introduction to *Weben und Ueberleben in Laichingen 1650–1900. Lokal geschichte als allgemeine Geschichte* (Vandenhoeck and Ruprecht: Göttingen, 1996): "Entlegene Geschichte? Lokalgeschichte als micro-historisch begründete allgemeine Geschichte." For an introduction to kinship analysis with historical materials, see Andrejs Plakans, *Kinship in the Past: An Anthropology of European Family Life 1500–1900* (Oxford, 1984).

6 The term goes back to W. H. R. Rivers, "The Genealogical Method of Anthropological Enquiry," *Sociological Review* 3 (1910): 1–12, repr. in *Kinship and Social Organization*, London School of Economics Monographs on Social Anthropology, 34 (London, 1968). Ernest Gellner, "The Concept of Kinship, With Special Reference to Mr. Needham's 'Descent Systems and Ideal Language,' " *Philosophy of Science* 17 (1960): 187–204, sees kinship structure as the manner in which a pattern of physical relationships is made use of for social purposes. Although his position has been challenged by Needham and others, I cannot see how kinship can mean anything if it does not mean at least this.

7 After working on Neckarhausen for a decade, I joined a research group devoted to microhistorical approaches to protoindustrialization at the Max-Planck-Institut für Geschichte in Göttingen. The three community studies that came out of the project demonstrate the fruitfulness of the approach. See Jürgen Schlumbohm, *Lebensläufe, Familien, Höfe: Die Bauern und Heuersleute des Osnabrückischen Kirchspiels Belm in proto-industrieller Zeit, 1650–1860,* Veröffentlichungen des Max-Planck-Instituts für Geschichte, 110 (Göttingen, 1994); Peter Kriedte, *Eine Stadt am seidenen Faden. Haushalt, Hausindustrie und soziale Bewegung in Krefeld in der Mitte des 19. Jahrhunderts,* Veröffentlichungen des MPI für G., 97 (Göttingen, 1991); Hans Medick, *Weben und Ueberleben.*

I dealt with the economic and institutional history of the village in an earlier study, *Property, Production, and Family in Neckarhausen.* That book considered the "internal" workings of the family – relations between husbands and wives and parents and children – in the context of traditional farming and the exigencies of the agricultural revolution, inheritance, the domestic estate, and a developing market for land. This book deals with the relationships between households and between individuals beyond the nuclear family, and with the "external" workings of the family in the larger network of kin. The original intent was to follow kinship patterns from the beginnings of parish registers in the 1550s to the end of the eighteenth century, but richer source material and the chance to follow issues across the "traditional" and "modern" divide shifted the focus to the period between 1700 and 1870. The ability to study genealogies at a suitable depth has been made possible by a family reconstitution from 1558 to 1869, which provides a genealogical grid of more than 4,000 families.[8] Such a study may look like a natural candidate for computer analysis, but that is not as straightforward as it may seem.

I began the study at a time when computers were more adept at processing the data of physicists than of poets. Conceptually and physically, all that a social historian could hope for then was fixed-format keypunching of a set of variables onto holerith cards. In the hope of future developments in computer technology and systems analysis and with the help of various programmers, I devised a free-format entry system that took hours of computer time on large university installations. Eventually, the machine-readable data were transferred from the punch cards to magnetic tapes, then to central-facility fixed disks, and finally to personal computer floppy, laser, and hard disks, which became part of an experiment to develop the historical database "Kleio" at the Max-Planck-Institut für Geschichte in Göttingen.[9] During each of these stages, however, my interest was fixed on the ever-growing amounts of data and their analysis and not on the rapidly changing computer technology. The consequences and limitations of that choice, as well as many of the presuppositions of the analysis, are discussed in the appendix. Although all of the data are machine readable and although while in Göttingen I was able to generate several hundred genealogies by computer, I have not mastered the technology that would allow me simply to sit at a desktop computer and create any particular genealogy. Rather than invest long periods of time to make that possible, I always found it preferable to work out a table or follow a genealogy by hand through the printed-out family reconstitution to answer the burning question of the moment. I do not want to devote further space here to the technical details but merely wish to indicate the scope of the study and its intellectual cast: this is hard-core social history, and the reader

[8] An account of the set of sources can be found in the appendix.

[9] The system was developed by Manfred Thaller. For an introduction, see Peter Becker and Thomas Werner, *Kleio. Ein Tutorial,* Halbgraue Reihe zur historischen Fachinformatik, Serie A: Historische Quellenkunde, Band 1, 2d ed. (St. Katharinen, 1991).

should be warned before proceeding that he or she will not come out of the experience unaroused.

The original intent of this study was simply to map the set of kin relations for a particular "premodern" European population. (Categories of "modern," "traditional," and the like became radically destabilized in the course of the undertaking, even though they did not altogether disappear.) The conceptual tools and ways of thinking about kinship were developed primarily through considerable reading of British social anthropology, and in one way or another the strongest line of influence came from A. R. Radcliffe-Brown and Meyer Fortes, mediated through the work of and conversations with Jack and Esther Goody. The strength of that tradition seems to lie in its stress on "jural" relations, ranging from the social implications and cultural meanings of formal inheritance systems to both the institutionalized and the informal realms of rights, duties, claims, and obligations.[10] A great deal of the social world can be encompassed when one can give a systematic account of the claims people make on one another and the obligations they assume.[11] I do think that one needs to start there and not assume that kinship encompasses a particular domain, with particular properties in its own right.[12] Kinship is embedded in a range of economic, political, and cultural phenomena and does not have an inherent meaning or a particular field of activity subject to its own rules or norms. Like Edmund Leach in his study of Pul Eliya, I usually view kinship in Neckarhausen as essentially "another way of talking about property relations," but perhaps it is best to take a less preprogrammed view and regard kinship as an "idiom" through which a great many relations are conceptualized and a great many transactions are negotiated.[13]

[10] Jane Fishburne Collier and Sylvia Junko Yanigisako, "Toward a Unified Analysis of Gender and Kinship," in Collier and Yanigisako, eds., *Gender and Kinship,* pp. 14–50, here p. 29, want to support the notion that gender and kinship studies are concerned with understanding rights and duties that order relations between people defined by difference.

[11] The kind of detailed ethnography that Meyer Fortes presents in *Web of Kinship among the Talensi: The Second Part of an Analysis of the Social Structure of a Trans-Volta Tribe* (Oxford, 1949), or work of the caliber of J. van Velson's *Politics of Kinship: A Study in Social Manipulation Among the Lakeside Tonga* (Manchester, 1964) fulfills, I think, Pierre Bourdieu's injunction to treat kinship as something people make and with which they do something. He suggests looking at kinship in terms of the practices kin produce: *Outline of the Theory of Practice,* trans. Richard Nice (Cambridge, 1977), pp. 35–6. The emphasis on rights and obligations keeps power as a central aspect of kinship. The tradition here ultimately traces back to Maine: see Elman R. Service, *A Century of Controversy: Ethnological Issues from 1860 to 1960* (Orlando, 1985), p. 5.

[12] Collier and Yanigisako, "Toward a Unified Analysis," p. 35, argue against asking how rights and obligations are mapped onto kinship bonds and instead suggest asking how specific societies recognize claims and allocate responsibilities.

[13] Edmund Leach, *Pul Eliya: A Village in Ceylon* (Cambridge, 1961), p. 305, argues that the reality of kinship where he carried on research is found in its relationship to land and labor. Pierre Bourdieu, *Outline,* p. 35, makes the point that genealogical relations are never strong enough to determine relations between individuals on their own. There has to be shared interest or a "common possession of a material and symbolic patrimony." David M. Schneider, *A Critique of the Study of Kinship* (Ann Arbor, 1984), p. 8, insists that the "arbitrary segregation of a rubric like 'kinship', taken out of the context of the whole culture, is not a very good way to understand how

Scholars tend to judge the extent to which kinship dominates a society from the range of overlap between a particular set of genealogical relations and some other set of functions. In Württemberg rural society, for example, in the course of the eighteenth century peasants were increasingly forced to seek credit to capitalize their holdings and to pay for ever more expensive new parcels of land. Mortgage money did not come from fellow villagers but from outside investors: merchants, pastors, officials, rentiers, and widows. It might be possible to argue that the function of credit was disentangled from kinship and to tally all such functions to determine roughly how much or how little kinship counted. But the problem is not so easily solved. In this example, it turns out that all mortgage applications went through a village mortgage committee composed of several members of the court (*Gericht*), and later the village council (*Gemeinderat*). The linking up of a particular landholder with outside capital was always monitored and controlled by village officials charged with judging the creditworthiness, solvency, and honor of their fellow villagers and was made possible by other members of the community who were prepared to risk their own property by guaranteeing payment of a loan. Through this kind of institutional arrangement, kinship and the hierarchy of familial reputation played a fundamental role in villager access to outside funds. Furthermore, it was quite possible for kin to manipulate the relationship through a variety of strategies, some of which are discussed in this book. The point is that kinship is not a special domain of obligations and rights (in this case, the obligation of kin to lend to one another), of emotional commitment and "amity," but is itself a set of connections that vary not only from society to society but within each society itself.[14] But this view of kinship does not put to rest all the issues. Each society has different systems or bundles of relations, which set up coherent patterns of their own. Pierre Bourdieu conceptualizes such sets in spatial

a culture is structured." Hildred Geertz and Clifford Geertz, *Kinship in Bali* (Chicago, 1975), p. 3, think of kinship as an "idiom," not an autonomous system. Schneider, *Critique*, p. 19, uses the concept as well. For my argument about property, see "Aspects of Kinship Behaviour and Property in Rural Western Europe before 1800," in Jack Goody, Joan Thirsk, and E. P. Thompson, eds., *Family and Inheritance: Rural Society in Western Europe, 1200–1800* (Cambridge, 1976), pp. 96–111; "Unehelichkeit: Ein Aspekt sozialer Reproduktion kleinbäuerlicher Produzenten: Zu einer Analyse dörflicher Quellen um 1800," in Robert Berdahl et al., eds., *Klassen und Kultur: Sozialanthropologische Perspektiven in der Geschichtsschreibung* (Frankfurt, 1982), pp. 54–76; (with Hans Medick) "Interest and Emotion in Family and Kinship Studies: A Critique of Social History and Anthropology," in Hans Medick and David Warren Sabean, eds., *Interest and Emotion: Essays on the Study of Family and Kinship* (Cambridge, 1984), pp. 9–27; *Property, Production, and Family in Neckarhausen, 1700–1870* (Cambridge, 1990), pp. 17–19, 31–4, 422–7.

[14] The notion of "amity" comes from Meyer Fortes, "Kinship and the Axiom of Amity," in *Kinship and the Social Order. The Legacy of Lewis Henry Morgan* (Chicago, 1966), pp. 219–49. The point I am making here is similar to Maurice Bloch's Madagascar example in "The Long Term and the Short Term: The Economic and Political Significance of the Morality of Kinship," in Jack Goody, ed., *The Character of Kinship* (Cambridge, 1973), pp. 75–87. In this situation, moral commitment constitutes kinship, and kin can be relied upon over the long haul. In order to maximize the group of contacts, however, people put a great deal of work into relations with nonkin on a day-to-day basis, working with short-term balanced reciprocity.

terms, suggesting that each has its own habitual behavior and strategic possibilities, which overlap and reinforce the others at various points.[15] Whatever patterns of relations and moral commitments a particular society establishes among kin provides a set of values and an arena of discourse in which an individual can negotiate.[16] Claims made on others on the basis of kinship have to be understood both in terms of the internal coherence of the kinship system in a particular context and in terms of the connection of kinship to other patterns of social and cultural life.[17]

The major alternative to the British functionalist school (Malinowski, Radcliffe-Brown, and their students) in the 1960s was offered by the French structuralists, who were little concerned with the practical everyday web of social and familial relations. Edmund Leach took Lévi-Strauss to task for this: "The reciprocities of kinship obligation are not merely symbols of alliance, they are also economic transactions, political transactions, charters to rights of domicile and land use. No useful picture of 'how a kinship system works' can be provided unless these several aspects or implications of the kinship organization are considered simultaneously."[18] Building on Marcel Mauss's essay on the gift and taking a cue from Saussurian linguistics, Lévi-Strauss developed a theory of exchange that focused the discussion of kinship on marriage and marriage alliance.[19] In some ways, his work was an elaborate theory of communication based on the idea that women circulate between groups of men in accordance with patterned systems of reciprocity. Other anthropologists were quick to point out that the exchanging groups are frequently composed of men and women together and that it is not always young women who are exchanged.[20] It seems a mistake to abstract one moment out of a larger context of exchanges and isolate exchange itself from production and property relations. Furthermore, in structuralist ac-

[15] See, e.g., Pierre Bourdieu, "The Social Space and the Genesis of Groups," *Theory and Society* 14 (1985): 723–44.

[16] See Collier and Yanigisako, "Introduction," p. 6. Geertz and Geertz, *Kinship in Bali,* p. 31, view kinship as "only one mode of ordering rights and duties which must adjust to counterbalancing pressures and pulls of other modes."

[17] Geertz and Geertz, *Kinship in Bali,* p. 156, argue against the notion of a "kinship system" because it assumes that the "ordering principles of a society are partitionable into natural kinds only adventitiously connected." Bourdieu would respond that the adventitious connection is the advantageous point. But he would agree with their idea that the importance of kinship symbolization varies from society to society. Furthermore, he would argue against Geertzian cultural holism and suggest that the variation is from class to class and family to family; see Bourdieu's "Social Space." See also Collier and Yanigisako, "Introduction," p. 6.

[18] Edmund R. Leach, *Rethinking Anthropology,* London School of Economics Monographs on Social Anthropology, 22 (London, 1961), p. 90.

[19] On this point and the contrast between Lévi-Strauss and Radcliffe-Brown, see Service, *Century of Controversy,* pp. 89–97.

[20] Jack Goody, "Marriage Prestations, Inheritance and Descent in Pre-Industrial Societies," *Journal of Comparative Family Studies,* 1 (1970): 37–54. For a summary of the problems, see also Christine Gailey, *Kinship to Kingship: Gender Hierarchy and State Formation in the Tongan Islands* (Austin, 1987), pp. 10–15.

counts, young women were not treated as right-bearing persons.[21] As Christine Gailey notes:

> Marriage exchanges, like household arrangements, are not the "core" of any kin-based culture. Even in patrilineal societies where women do leave their natal groups upon marriage, ties to the natal group are not necessarily broken with marriage: they can be transformed, expanded, or activated at strategic times. The claims established with marriage are far more complex than structuralists have indicated. . . . To reduce this complexity to women mediating men's communication does not help our understanding of this range of claims.[22]

In the view of Radcliffe-Brown, social relations among kin are extensions of relations among siblings. The principle of the "unity of the sibling group" allows for different configurations of sibling pairs according to birth order, age, and gender, but whatever the constellation of emotional attachments, they provide foundations for the extension of sentiment to other kin.[23] Without subscribing to his psychological assumptions about kinship construction, we might well find that sibling relations provide essential building blocks for structuring kinship.[24] In eighteenth-century Neckarhausen, for example, productive, market, and political processes appeared to crystallize out of the web of kin a particular emphasis on brothers – which provided the agnatic twist (emphasizing relatives through the father's side) inside a cognatic system (emphasizing relatives through both

[21] This is one of the essential insights running through the work of Jack Goody.

[22] Gailey, *Kinship to Kingship*, p. 13.

[23] Françoise Héritier, *L'exercice de la parenté* (Paris, 1981), pp. 36–53, took up this point and adapted it to structural analysis, arguing that the identity of siblings of the same sex and the difference of siblings of the opposite sex lie at the origin of the fundamental mechanisms of alliance. Jack Goody, *The Development of the Family and Marriage in Europe* (Cambridge, 1983), p. 136, sees the "unity of the sibling group" as a fundamental underlying feature of Germanic kinship reckoning. In *The Oriental, the Ancient, and the Primitive: Systems of Marriage and the Family in the Pre-Industrial Societies of Eurasia* (Cambridge, 1990), p. 10, he questions the extension of sentimental bonds as the explanation for structural features of a system (vs. Fortes) and places the emphasis on property.

[24] Marilyn Strathern, *After Nature: English Kinship in the Late Twentieth Century* (Cambridge, 1992), p. 134, suggests that the assumption that lies behind English understanding of kinship is that relatedness is about being close. But what one finds among coordinated kin in the nineteenth-century German middle classes, for example, does not suggest that emotional proximity was at all necessary (see Jürgen Kocka, "Familie, Unternehmer und Kapitalismus. An Beispielen aus der frühen deutschen Industrialisierung," *Zeitschrift für Unternehmergeschichte* 24 (1979): 99–135, here p. 124). Jill Dubisch, "Gender, Kinship and Religion: 'Reconstructing' the Anthropology of Greece," in Peter Loizos and Evthymios Papataxiarchis, eds., *Gendered Identities: Gender and Kinship in Modern Greece* (Princeton, 1991), pp. 29–46, here pp. 39–40, looking at a different dyad – mother/daughter – regards the relationship as culturally constituted and not based on sentiment. J. D. Freeman, "On the Concept of the Kindred," *Journal of the Royal Anthropological Institute* 91 (1961): 192–220, here p. 209, wrote: "Kindred relations cannot, I believe, be accounted for as simple extension of the sentiments which develop in the nuclear family. . . . What is basic is the fact that relations between kindred are governed by a special morality arising from the recognition of common descent." For a recent account that builds on Radcliffe-Brown's notion of sentiment and incorporates Lacan, see Margaret Trawick, *Notes on Love in a Tamil Family* (Berkeley, 1990), pp. 141–2, 152–4.

parents). In the course of the nineteenth century, the core relations inside the sibling group came to be centered on the brother/sister (B/Z) constellation, which moved women into a central position in the practical construction of kin relations.[25] But the shift presents a more general problem, since the brother/sister became the key sibling dyad throughout the property-holding classes around 1800.[26] It may well be that we cannot provide a completely satisfactory explanation for such broad cultural shifts, but we can explore their consequences and compare the shape of social relations from class to class.

During the eighteenth and nineteenth centuries, kinship articulated with political processes and with the state in ever changing ways. In the eighteenth century, states went to considerable trouble to relax marriage rules prohibiting cousins and brothers and sisters-in-law from marrying one another, which left those families closely tied up with state service – among others – free to create tightly overlapping bonds of reciprocity and long-enduring alliances. At the same time and parallel to this development, an ever sharper discourse condemned the peculiar form of nepotism built around networks of cousins (*Vettern*). I will argue that these two things are closely related. In Neckarhausen and throughout Württemberg villages, the critical term *Vetterle* appeared in the 1740s, precisely at the time that politically powerful groups in the village began to marry their second cousins, thereby creating interlocking syndicates to control the distribution of village resources more tightly. What went on at the village level was paralleled at the regional and state level. By the end of the eighteenth century, with the most prosperous elements of the society in the vanguard, closer forms of exchange had developed between allied families, while the critique of corruption – the illegitimate intermingling of private and public concerns – had reached a peak.[27] The political battle seems to have come to a head during the 1820s. After that date most of the stories told by historians cease to concern themselves with corruption and nepotism, and consequently with kinship. Once the crucial distinction between public and private became part of the basic assumptions of the politically active classes, interest in the private practices of families, except for

[25] Héritier, *L'exercice*, p. 38, argues that the cross-sex sibling solidarity is never so strong as the parallel-sex one. But the shift to the B/Z attachment in Europe during the Romantic period belies this generalization.

[26] See David Warren Sabean, "Fanny and Felix Mendelssohn-Bartholdy and the Question of Incest," *Musical Quarterly* 77 (1993): 709–17. See also Leonore Davidoff, "Where the Stranger Begins: The Question of Siblings in Historical Analysis," in *Worlds Between: Historical Perspectives on Gender and Class* (Oxford, 1995), pp. 206–26.

[27] I want to take the private/public distinction in the nineteenth century as constitutive of the kinship system that emerged during that period. The problem anthropologists now deal with has to do with the distortions of that legacy for current analysis. Rayna Reiter has made this point – see Collier and Yanagisako, "Toward a Unified Analysis," p. 19. See also Marilyn Strathern, *After Nature*, pp. 188–90. John Camaroff, "*Sui genderis*: Feminism, Kinship Theory, and Structural 'Domains,' " in Collier and Yanigisako, eds., *Gender and Kinship*, pp. 53–85, here p. 65, associates suggestively the public/private dichotomy with class formation, a point I will take up in the conclusion.

sexual pathologies and effective establishment of patriarchy, more or less disappeared.[28] Yet there was a great deal of activity in the private realm that was not unrelated to the old problem of succession to office. No family could any longer openly act as if it had the right to a particular position in the state and to the spoils of office. And yet families were just as interested as before in promoting their young and placing them in strategic positions. I will argue that this called for a reconfiguration of the networks connecting families with one another and for forms of alliance that simultaneously created the possibilities of close enough integration to support coordinated activities and a proliferation of connections to other families. The increasing incidence of repeated marriages among consanguineal (related by blood) and affinal (related by marriage) kin was part of this two-pronged strategy for developing both strong and extensive kinship ties. The public/private distinction also masked the work women performed in kinship construction in the nineteenth century and hid the structural importance of their networks from social observers. The ideology of the nineteenth century continually contrasted structure (male) and sentiment (female). But as Jill Dubisch has argued, sentimental relationships are culturally constructed and bear "a structural significance which may be equal to (if not in some respects greater than) that of relationships between men." "Moreover," she goes on to say, "if kinship relations are not seen as confined to the domestic unit alone . . . then the broader role of women in kinship structures becomes more clear."[29]

As the following chapters show, a parallel process was also taking place in the economic realm, the logic of which is captured in the shift from a concern with caring for a patrimony to making strategic moves in a developing capitalist economy. In a village like Neckarhausen, for example, a person's wealth and position at the beginning of the eighteenth century was determined for the most part by inheritance. It could be argued that throughout European society up to about that time social dynamics were dominated by a concern to inherit, maintain, and pass on an estate, a monopoly, or a craft. By the early nineteenth century, the nature of the game had already changed. In Neckarhausen, for example, a lively market in land altered the way resources were allocated in the village. Different kinds of networks were necessary if the land-holding classes were to dominate or impose some kind of control on the market. Similar shifts can be seen throughout German society. Heinz Reif has shown how the Westphalian nobility con-

[28] Bourdieu, *Outline*, p. 41, suggests in a parallel situation that the opposition of public and private reduces the activities of women in kinship politics to the "shameful, secret, or at best unofficial." In Germany, as I will argue in the conclusion, the "private" became reduced to the domestic, a realm of women's activity that was embarrassing for men commenting on politics and public matters.

[29] Dubisch, "Gender, Kinship, and Religion," p. 40. She finds the contrast of sentiment and structure not convincing. On this point, see Hans Medick and David Warren Sabean, "Interest and Emotion in Family and Kinship Studies: A Critique of Social History and Anthropology," in Medick and Sabean, eds., *Interest and Emotion: Essays on the Study of Family and Kinship* (Cambridge, 1984), pp. 9–27.

verted from a caste that controlled public office to one that functioned as a regional elite.[30] In Prussia the new age brought an active market in Junker estates and economic difficulties for many aristocratic families. Over a series of generations, opportunity for entrepreneurs along the Rhine recentered economic activity around the expansion of firms in mining, metallurgy, and commerce away from the protective care of stable or scarce resources. Generating capital, obtaining access to credit, coordinating management skills, rescuing bankrupt families, and securing succession to office all took place in a reconfigured alliance system.

This alliance system created dense, overlapping, criss-crossing networks that played key roles in socialization, cultural integration, class formation, business networking, and the coordination of political opinion. Persistent alliances between families stressed horizontal relations and a reiterated integration through homogamy (marriage of equals). Perhaps the single most symbolic act both to acknowledge the social hierarchy and police the boundaries of class was marriage.[31] And an increasing regulator of marriage alliance in the nineteenth century was the dowry, whose inflation can be chronicled over the period. But marriage had two goals: first, to integrate and tighten the bonds with equals and second, to increase strategic alliances with neighboring classes. Throughout nineteenth-century society, homogamy was coupled with hypergamy (the marriage of women upward in the social hierarchy). A key mechanism here was the dowry, which allowed wealth to pass from classes that generated it to classes of higher status but with more fixed resources.[32] The history of hypergamy in Europe has not yet been written, but observers throughout the century and beyond have descried holy or unholy alliances between the wealthy middle classes and the aristocracy, and a much older process when observed for the 1880s and 1890s has come to be thought of as a feudalization of the German bourgeoisie.[33] What needs to be analyzed is the systematic passage of women upward in the social hierarchy, their assimilation into their new social stations, and their crucial political activities in

[30] Heinz Reif, *Westfälischer Adel 1770–1860: Vom Herrschaftsstand zur regionalen Elite* (Göttingen, 1979). For a brilliant analysis of kinship among a regional German nobility in the seventeenth and eighteenth centuries, see Christoph Duhamelle, "La noblesse d'église. Famille et pouvoir dans la chevalerie immediate rhenane, xviie–xviiie siècles," Thèse d'histoire, Université de Paris-1 (29 November 1994), MSS.

[31] Nur Yalman, *Under the Bo Tree: Studies in Caste, Kinship, and Marriage in the Interior of Ceylon* (Berkeley, 1967), p. 180, makes a similar point: "The refusal to give women is the most forceful public statement that the other group is considered to be of lower rank." He also argues that the practices of endogamy of local groups are the mechanisms by which larger ones – in his example, castes, but for nineteenth-century Europe, we could read "class" – without formal organization remain demarcated (pp. 205–9).

[32] For a comparative South Asian example of the connection between dowry and hypergamy, see Yalman, *Under the Bo Tree,* pp. 172–80.

[33] These issues will occupy our attention in Chapter 22. Ladislav Holy, *Kinship, Honour and Solidarity: Cousin Marriage in the Middle East* (Manchester, 1989), p. 113, argues that hypergamy is actually tied to lineage solidarity – in our context, read "class solidarity" – by ensuring that wives are not of higher status, which would cause children to identify with matrilateral kin. We will see that in nineteenth-century Europe group membership had a strong agnatic bias.

mediating between their kin.[34] We will find evidence of hypergamy in Neckarhausen and will look at the issue in comparative perspective in concluding chapters.

The texture and architecture of the book

The central argument of this study unfolds through the exegesis of a series of kinship diagrams. Not everyone is particularly interested in reading such schematic pictures, and hardly anyone would certainly want to read a great many of them. I have piled them up at considerable length partly out of a desire to explore the issues sufficiently and partly out of an impulse to substantiate my case, as any historian is wont to do. As I put the argument together over the years, I continually had to ask whether the patterns I was finding were significant, and if they were, then what was their meaning? I had no idea that the simple question I set out to answer would take so long to fathom. The manuscript went through many unreadable permutations, and this final text is considerably stripped down, with many dozens of diagrams set aside to spare the reader my own obsessions.

My basic approach here is to select a particular institutional arrangement (such as marriage or godparentage) or a recurring set of transactions (such as buying and selling land) and to systematically inquire about the degree to which kin interacted with one another.[35] This entailed selecting a succession of pairs of people who had transacted some kind of business together and seeing if they could be located in one another's kinship universe. By working with a large enough sample of such dyadic relationships, I sought to map how people utilized, engaged, and cooperated with kin. I also wanted to know where the breaks and fissures in the community ran, when people disengaged themselves from or ignored one another, and how often people constructed relationships without taking kinship into consideration.

The available documents showed a number of connections that could be studied systematically over most of the period between 1700 and 1870. Needless to say, the decision as to which relationships needed to be examined had to do with the very nature of the sources. Nonetheless, each series of connections points up different aspects of patterned behavior and systemic regularities. The "indicators" that I can track are marriage alliance, godparentage, naming, guardianship, *Kriegsvogtschaft* (until 1828 women in any business had to be accompanied before a court by a *Kriegsvogt*), loan guarantees and performance bonds, and property transactions (handled at length in *Property, Production, and Family in Neckarhausen*). By studying these as an interlocking system for any period, we can establish

[34] See Sherry Ortner, "The Virgin and the State," *Feminist Studies* 3 (1978): 19–35, here pp. 31–2. Ortner argues that the context of hypergamy is the orientation toward upward mobility through the manipulation of marriage. Dowry enhances the girl's value for a higher-status spouse.

[35] The project was first outlined in "Verwandtschaft und Familie in einem württembergischen Dorf 1500 bis 1870: einige methodische Ueberlegungen," in Werner Conze, ed., *Sozialgeschichte der Familie in der Neuzeit Europas* (Stuttgart, 1976), pp. 231–46.

many of the structural parameters of kinship. But what we locate is the sedimentation, so to speak, of practices that are difficult to study directly. We may find, for example, that people begin to marry their cousins at a certain period or to construct names for their sons out of a combination of those of their paternal and maternal uncles, but we seldom, if ever, locate any explicit commentary on such matters in our sources. This explains in part the painstakingness of my approach. Much remains based on inference and the very fact of pattern and regularity. Throughout, I have sought to attain what mathematicians would call an "elegant" solution to the trail of calculation, which balances, I hope, the close attention demanded by the text.

The costs of developing a large number of genealogies to enough depth to carry out the exercises I set for myself were considerable. In order to make the project feasible, I decided to look at the interlocking structures of a series of cohorts evenly spaced throughout the period under consideration. Beginning with 1700, I chose five cohorts covering ten years each, spaced forty years apart. The size of each sample and the nature of the selection of data are discussed in the appendix, which also presents a complete set of tables for each cohort. There were quite dramatic shifts in the structure of kinship over the period considered in this book, but I found the repetition of the same method of representation for each cohort too unrelieved to maintain a reader's attention. I also wanted to experiment with different ways of getting at kinship practice and with different forms of narrative construction.[36] As a result, the text presents the complete structural exercise for only the first (1700–1709), third (1780–9), and fifth (1860–9) cohorts. For the second (1740–9) and fourth cohorts (1820–9), I summarize the trends and then go on to tell stories. For cohort II, I recount an investigation into malfeasance in office by the *Schultheiss* (village headman) Johann Georg Rieth III, and for cohort IV, I narrate a series of thirteen short, interlocking biographies. In both of these sections I address social practice and ask how different people developed different tactics inside a larger, structured context of patterned kinship behavior. Before moving to the main body of the work, however, I discuss the political discourse about kinship prevalent in the eighteenth century and the political issue of "incest," particularly the way in which the state allowed or prevented various forms of alliance. The analysis concludes with a broad discussion of the context in which Neckarhausen kinship structures emerged, the conceptual and theoretical issues that this study raises, and the intersection of kinship with class and gender both in and beyond the village.

At this point, I need to provide a few guidelines for the reader. Kinship diagrams can be very off-putting to say the least, and the more complicated they

[36] An early example is found in "Young Bees in an Empty Hive: Relations between Brothers-in-Law in a South German Village around 1800," in Medick and Sabean, eds., *Interest and Emotion*, pp. 171–86.

become, the more head-splitting they can be. But they cannot easily be dispensed with, since they so eloquently and trenchantly summarize a great deal of information. Nevertheless, they do not speak for themselves and sometimes require a great deal of explanation. I find myself caught between two different readerships: older anthropologists will find my dogged approach irritating (younger ones who no longer take an interest in kinship will be irritated anyway), and social historians will be mystified by explanations that seem too telescoped. I suggest that a reader who has difficulty with pictorial schemata of the kind that repeat themselves endlessly throughout this text take one of the longer examples in the first cohort and learn to trace out all the connections. That exercise can act as a tutorial in pictogram exegesis. In much anthropological work, such diagrams are used to summarize the results of an investigation, but here they are used almost exclusively as research instruments, as a means of locating those relationships that form the center of the investigation. This inductive approach is dictated in part by the nature of the sources and in part by the need for me to overcome my own skepticism about the results.

The basic conventions followed in kinship diagrams are explained in a note at the front of the book. There the reader will also find a key to the notations used, each of which should be read in its complete form whenever it is encountered. "FBSWZ," for example, should be read as "father's brother's son's wife's sister [cousin's sister-in-law]." Note that since "S" is reserved for "son," "Z" is used for "sister." Because it takes time to become familiar with these notations, reading them in full helps to demystify them. Even after receiving these helpful hints, some readers may not want to work through all of the examples. I have therefore tried to be clear, at the beginning of the more complicated cases, about what the reader can expect to find. The monographic description of the example is italicized, to allow the harried and hurried to skip over the detailed explanation. Nevertheless, one should try to work through enough examples to understand how the exercises have been carried out and to become familiar with the symbols and procedures. Each italicized passage is followed by a summary of the conclusions at that stage of the argument, which allows the reader to follow its gist apart from the demonstrations themselves. Scholars who become caught up in the representational possibilities of kinship diagrams and want to construct their own diagrams can find ample material on the subject in the appendix.

The main body of the text deals with various forms of social interaction, such as godparentage, but I am unable to say much there about the conceptual issues that each such indicator raises, nor am I able to highlight some of the overarching aspects of institutional arrangements. In the remaining part of this chapter, I want to outline some of these considerations. The unsuspecting social historian should be prepared to immediately plunge into a sea of arcane knowledge, while suspicious anthropologists should be forewarned that I will be treating in an all too brief and schematic manner matters with which they are all too familiar or have long since forgotten.

Marriage alliance

Marriage is only one aspect of a system of kinship and only part of a larger set of reciprocities. Nevertheless, it establishes more or less fixed lines that divide people from and connect people to one another. Marriage binds individuals together in a network of in-laws (affines), and it provides the foundation for charters of inheritance, succession, and identity. In particular societies, structural persistence can be established in other ways. In Neckarhausen, long-term ties were set up through godparentage, or what some anthropologists call "ritual coparenthood." I do not know of anyone who has attempted to give a formal account of godparentage, but the literature abounds in attempts to account for systemic marriage patterns, and one of my tasks in this study has been to investigate whether marriage alliances in Neckarhausen lend themselves to formal analysis.

In their studies of kinship and marriage in the European past, French ethnographers and historians have frequently used elements of exchange theory developed by the structuralist Lévi-Strauss. Chapter 20 discusses at length the brilliant work in this regard by Gérard Delille, Pierre Lamaison and Elisabeth Claverie, and Martine Segalen. The issues raised there and their relevance to the analysis of Neckarhausen cannot be understood, however, without some knowledge of the basic principles and vocabulary of the structuralist approach.

One such principle, formulated by Lévi-Strauss, is that kinship systems can be divided into "elementary" and "complex" (and "semicomplex") types, depending on whether or not formal rules dictate the choice of a spouse.[37] Elementary types are found in simple, undifferentiated societies in which groups recruit their members according to the dynamics of lineal succession. Such societies prescribe certain kinds of choices for people on the basis of genealogical reckoning, and material interest is of decidedly secondary importance, if it is considered at all. By contrast, complex systems – such as our own – which are marked by social differentiation, set up negative (rather than positive) rules forbidding marriage within certain boundaries and subjecting it to calculations of wealth, class, education, sentiment, and the like.[38] Because complex systems disallow alliance with the same set of relatives that the parents married into, marriages linking together one family in a particular generation cannot be the basis for reciprocity in the next. In fact, the decision to ally with some group

[37] See Claude Lévi-Strauss, *The Elementary Structures of Kinship*, rev. ed., trans. James Harle Bell, John Richard von Sturmer, and Rodney Needham, ed. Rodney Needham (Boston, 1969). The first edition appeared in French in 1949, and the second in 1967. An overview and comparison with Meyer Fortes and G. P. Murdock can be found in J. A. Barnes, *Three Styles in the Study of Kinship* (London, 1971). A handy introduction to the whole problem is provided by Robin Fox, *Kinship and Marriage: An Anthropological Perspective* (Harmondsworth, 1967). For a sympathetic development of Lévi-Strauss's ideas, which integrates some of the important criticism into a basically structural account, see Trawick, *Notes*, esp. pp. 117–86.

[38] Goody, *Oriental*, p. 11, questions the very idea of kinship-dominated societies and finds it difficult to point to a kinship domain that is not also economic, political, and religious.

in one generation positively indicates that a new alliance with that group is to be forbidden for many generations (in the Protestant regions of early modern Europe, as we shall see, the span is three generations, and in Catholic regions it is four).

In elementary kinship systems, marriage can be "restricted" (within the bounds of direct reciprocity) or "generalized" (in the sense that wife givers and wife takers do not belong to the same groups). The classic form of restricted exchange is a marriage with the father's sister's daughter (FZD) where lineage A gives a bride to lineage B in one generation and in the next generation receives a bride in return (Figure 1.1). In such a situation, Lévi-Strauss argues, a society can be divided into as few as two lineages (moieties) to make the system work. The classic form of generalized exchange is a marriage with the mother's brother's daughter (MBD). Here, lineage A cannot receive brides back from lineage B but only from a third, fourth, or some other lineage. Such a system involves at least three lineages and the marriage form: A marries B marries C marries A (Figure 1.1). These two forms – FZD and MBD – are called "cross-cousin" systems because they are reckoned through parents' siblings of the opposite sex and signal the alliance of different lines or lineages. The other kinds of cousin systems – parallel, FBD, MZD – do not suggest systematic reciprocity, and in the case of the FBD, argues Lévi-Strauss, imply its positive refusal. Cross-cousin marriages, by recognizing the practice of finding spouses outside the lineage group, are "exogamous," while parallel cousin marriages are "endogamous."[39]

All the elementary forms of marriage exchange in the structuralist account arise in contexts of clear rules for lineage recruitment and the marking of people as belonging unambiguously to this or that lineage according to specified principles.[40] Since in European societies the only rule is that one cannot marry anyone related to oneself – at least as far as effective social memory goes – systematic, continuing alliances cannot take place between groups, and neither restricted nor generalized forms of exchange are possible. Although there are ways for families to reinforce alliances during one generation (two siblings can marry two siblings, for example), the same man or woman cannot marry a second time into the same group, since the prohibitions concerning marrying relatives of a deceased spouse are as extensive as those against marrying one's own relatives.

Lévi-Strauss's distinction between elementary and complex systems of kinship rests on the assumption that whole societies are characterized more or less uniformly by a particular system of rules.[41] Demographically, it may be impossible

[39] Note that in formal kinship analysis "exogamy" and "endogamy" are referenced to groups composed by descent. But the terms can be used more generally for marriages inside or outside villages, regions, status groups, occupational groups, wealth strata, classes, and the like. In the situation of ego-focused kindred, where one makes a distinction between near and far kin, endogamy can refer to marriage with near kin, and the like.

[40] Goody, *Oriental,* p. 9, objects to ascribing inherent meaning to cross-cousin marriage. It takes different forms in different cultures.

[41] See Ladislav Holy's objection to this in *Kinship,* p. 62. Luc de Heusch, *Why Marry Her?: Society*

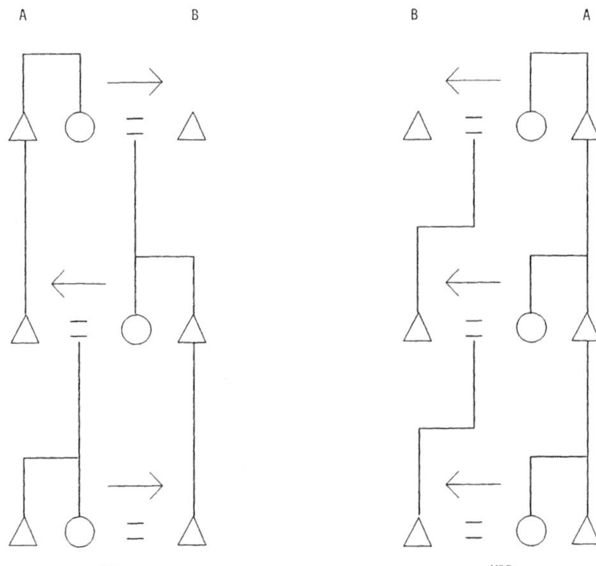

Figure 1.1

for every man in a society to marry a MBD, but the answer to that problem lies in classification. All the women of the proper generation of a particular lineage that can or should provide wives can be ascribed the genealogical position of matrilateral cross first cousins (MBD) despite the fact that many of them are not linked to their prospective husbands by such direct genealogical paths.

Given the theoretical distinctions established by Lévi-Strauss, it comes as a surprise that ethnographers and historians have been finding in Europe patterns of marriage that in their formal characteristics imply the elementary forms of either restricted or generalized exchange. The difference is that the marriages of a group of siblings display now this and now that principle of exchange, and there is no uniform practice throughout a village, region, or social class.[42] Pierre Bourdieu made precisely this objection to Lévi-Strauss's structuralism, arguing that any particular marriage could be seen as meaningful only in relation to the totality of possible marriages. Some marriages can integrate groups more tightly by reinforcing ties already established, whereas others can go outside already beaten pathways to expand

and Symbolic Structures, trans. Janet Lloyd (Cambridge, 1981), p. 13, remarks that different elementary forms belonging to a single structural family may exist within the same cultural region. Trawick, *Notes*, pp. 121–8, argues that in South India there can be matrilines or patrilines within a single marriage system.

[42] Trawick, *Notes*, p. 128, points out that most analyses of marriage exchange are essentialist and ascribe one cause for one effect. But different actors in different social situations may be involved in marriage for conflicting reasons.

the possible alliances of a family.[43] The question is whether it is meaningful to analyze a "bricolage" composed of bits and pieces of elementary systems (MBD, FZD, MFBSD, etc.) in terms of formal exchange principles. Bourdieu's categories of "integration" and "expansion" leave open that possibility by framing the issue in terms of the tensions set up by repeated reciprocities.

Throughout the study of Neckarhausen and the treatment of comparative material, I find two quite distinct periods, which may be labeled "classical" (the early modern period) and "modern" (the "long" nineteenth century). In the former, Lévi-Strauss's characterization of society as "complex" applies, at least as a point of departure. There were no prescriptive rules of marriage, only the negative injunction precluding marriage within a more or less extended range of kin. Dispensations were exceptional, and the state/church with its increasingly long runs of baptism and marriage registers could enforce conformity to the rules. Nevertheless – as I shall show and as Delille, Merzario, and others have also demonstrated – there were forms of marriage among affines that conform to patterns of exchange found in Lévi-Strauss's exegesis of elementary structures. It seems useful therefore to apply formal analysis of reciprocity to recover such mechanisms. In the second period – the modern – many of the previous marriage restrictions disappeared, and subsequently repeated exchanges among close consanguineal kin were allowed, as indicated by the occurrence of cross-cousin marriages among first and second cousins of all kinds. This development suggests new possibilities for reciprocity and alliances prohibited in the "classical" era. But one also sometimes finds examples that, according to Lévi-Strauss, deny alliance. These forms include marriage with the father's brother's daughter (FBD), in which case a young man finds a spouse in his own lineage instead of an allied group.[44] Rather than being characterized by a single principle of alliance, the society contains shards of elementary forms joined with one another in such a way as to provide an interlocking system of alliance. Nevertheless, European kinship in the nineteenth century was strongly oriented toward exogamy in the technical sense that cross cousins were preferred over parallel cousins.[45] Such a system puts a "high value on affinity," on those ties that integrate people together within broadly equal social and cultural strata.[46] Only by recogniz-

[43] Pierre Bourdieu, *Outline of a Theory of Practice*, p. 57: "The choice between fission and fusion, the inside and the outside, security and adventure, is posed anew with each marriage." See also *Logic*, p. 187, and also the entire chapter, "The Social Uses of Kinship," pp. 162–99.

[44] There is considerable interest in patrilateral parallel-cousin marriages (FBD) for the Middle East. The complex literature is brought together and analyzed carefully in a fine book by Ladislav Holy, *Kinship*, which also contains a complete bibliography. Carroll Pastner argues that one should not see the FBD marriage as an isolated trait but as one part of an overall set of patterns: "Cousin Marriage among the Zikri Baluch of Coastal Pakistan," *Ethnology* 18 (1979): 31–47, here p. 31.

[45] Ladislav Holy, *Kinship*, pp. 4, 31, 38, 62, 69, 110, argues against seeing a particular form as serving the same pragmatic function under different economic, political, social, and cultural conditions.

[46] See Ladislav Holy, *Kinship*, p. 117. Jack Goody, "Evolution of Kinship," Edinburgh Lectures, MS, n.d., has an interesting observation. He points out that Lévi-Strauss sees cross-cousin marriages as creating ties of solidarity between social groups and as being characteristic of simple societies. Goody argues that cross-cousin marriages are more likely bimodal and articulate with class in marriage regulated by considerations of property.

ing those ties can a formal analysis penetrate the systemic qualities of modern European kinship.

Another point to note is that anthropologists distinguish between unilineal and bilateral (or agnatic/uterine and cognatic) systems. The distinction has to do with whether and how people are recruited to groups on the basis of descent. Even though British, in contrast to French, anthropology is associated with the notion of unilineal descent groups, Lévi-Strauss's principles of exchange assume a set of lineages based on unilineal descent through either the father (agnatic) or the mother (uterine). These are precisely the groups that enter into relations of repeated reciprocity.[47] In Europe, for the most part, such recruitment is not possible, since descent does not privilege the transmission of rights through exclusively male or female lines but recognizes claims bilaterally through both father and mother. In a "cognatic" system such as this, which recognizes relatives equally from both sides, the lines of descent continually converge only on groups of siblings.[48] And the rules of marriage, since they are negatively stated, are said to be "ego-focused": an individual cannot find a spouse from among those equally related through either parent. The "kindred," thought of as a group of relatives emanating outward from an individual, cannot be conceptualized as a bounded group, since different individuals have different kindreds, and even cousins cannot be said to be members of the same collectivity.[49] Therefore one problem in applying structuralist notions of reciprocity to kinship analysis is the absence of groups that might exchange with one another.[50] In certain areas, characterized by farms that descend unbroken to a line of descendants, the "patrimony" might, however, provide just such an organizational node for reciprocity. Some historians have adapted the notion of patrimonial lines to this purpose and analyzed the circulation of dowries in terms of restricted and generalized exchange patterns. In the case of the Gévaudan, considered by Lamaison and Claverie, farm units provided structure in a cognatic system of kin reckoning where farms frequently fell to daughters instead of sons.[51]

[47] Marilyn Strathern, "Parts and Wholes: Refiguring Relationships in a Post-Plural World," in Adam Kuper, ed., *Conceptualizing Society* (London, 1992), pp. 75–104, here pp. 86–91, shows that England and Europe became "prototypes" for societies without unilineal descent groups. Cognatic systems became "marginalized" in anthropological discourse and seemed either totally uninteresting or so familiar that they could not be successfully analyzed. Adam Kuper, *The Invention of Primitive Society: Transformations of an Illusion* (London, 1988), has written off lineage altogether.

[48] Strathern, "Parts and Wholes," p. 90, points out that tracing cognatic kinship in Europe has not produced groups or a "sense of convention or society." Researchers find only an "endless recombination of elements devolved from and focusing on individuals."

[49] Strathern, "Parts and Wholes," p. 91, argues that the difficulty in dealing with Western kinship is that it is conceptualized as cognatic and is therefore "profoundly uninteresting." "It disappears in studies of local communities or class or visiting patterns."

[50] Yalman, *Under the Bo Tree*, p. 223, provides a South Asian example in which descent groups do not exist. He argues – and this would go for Neckarhausen – that the more the endowments of women resemble those of men in kind and size, the weaker the cohesion of the descent group is likely to be.

[51] Pierre Lamaison and Elisabeth Claverie, *L'impossible mariage. Violence et parenté en Gévaudan, xviie, xviiie, xixe siècles* (Paris, 1982). See the discussion of their work in Chapter 20.

Apart from structural principles of impartible inheritance, no other tools have been available to allow historians to model reciprocity in the absence of lineage recruitment to groups. Ethnographer Martine Segalen has therefore attempted to refashion the notion of kindred for this purpose, suggesting that the interweaving of networks and overlapping of personal kindreds in southern Brittany gives a degree of recognizable structure to a system of open-ended groups.[52] In the classic statement on the subject, J. D. Freeman argued that a repeated interweaving of kin through marriage could offer a fundamental coherence to recognizable kindreds:

> If the marriage of cousins is continued generation by generation this results in a continuing consolidation of stocks and produces a closer cognatic network than in societies where the marriage of close cognates does not occur. This, I would suggest, is a most significant feature of some bilateral societies, for while they lack the large-scale descent groups of unilineal societies, their cognatic networks are close and cohesive and so of great importance in the multiplex relations of social life.[53]

In Neckarhausen, where children of both sexes inherited equal amounts of land and farm complexes were broken up in each generation, the notion of patrimonial lines seems of limited use. Furthermore, the kind of regional kindreds analyzed by Segalen does not coincide with the large nucleated village settlement typical of Württemberg, at least before the nineteenth century. The church stressed cognatic kin reckoning in its table of marriage prohibitions, and the practical everyday interactions of people took place in recognition of kin traced in a balanced way through both parents. People talked about "lines" of property devolution but gave equal weight to property descending through maternal and paternal lines. Although inheritance, exogamy, and everyday behavior all suggest a completely cognatic system, some generations in Neckarhausen placed a systematic emphasis on agnatic relations (those traced through fathers), and on the "patrilineal" reckoning of kin, whereas other generations stressed uterine relations (those traced through mothers), with a "matrifocal" turn in alliance construction.[54] But even then, one

[52] There is a similar analysis by Nur Yalman, *Under the Bo Tree*, pp. 189–90. In his Ceylon example, interconnectedness is reinforced repeatedly among people with many kinship links in common among themselves but few with other kindreds. Richard Feinberg, "Kindred and Alliance on Anuta Island," *Journal of the Polynesian Society* 88 (1979): 27–48, here pp. 328, 343–4, suggests that alliance reinforces integration. There is a cooperation between ritual, consanguineal, and affinal principles whereby people work out a set of cooperating, reciprocating, exchanging relationships. People constantly reach out and marry distant kin and thereby reinforce the weakest bonds. In his example, each generation composes different alliances from the last.

[53] J. D. Freeman, "On the Concept of the Kindred," *Journal of the Royal Anthropological Institute* 91 (1961): 192–220, here p. 207. For a historical analysis, see Duhamelle, "Noblesse d'église."

[54] Martine Segalen, "Parenté et alliance dans les sociétés paysannes," *Ethnologie Française* 11 (1981): 307–9, here p. 307. Peasant France stresses "line" instead of "lineage" or "clan." Modes of devolution differentiate peasant areas. Zonabend, "Le très proche," p. 312, thinks that where partible inheritance exists, there can be no patrilineal or matrilineal lines, but will show that in partible-inheritance Neckarhausen, patrilines developed.

must understand exchange without constituted groups.[55] What developed in Neckarhausen and in most of Europe during the same period under consideration here were dense networks that offered cohesion and coherence, with a certain degree of open-endedness.[56] Freeman emphasized the flexibility of such relationships, pointing out that the kindred in bilateral "societies present an individual with a wide range of optative relationships – relationships which, in the absence of any binding descent principle, it is possible for him to accentuate as he pleases or as suits his special interests."[57] I do not want to follow Freeman too far here, because he seems to be moving toward assumptions of pure manipulation, although I do not believe that was his intention. As Emrys Peters has stressed, interlocking relationships imply by necessity interdependence and therefore "structure of some sort."[58]

In their analysis of rural French society, Tina Jolas, Yvonne Verdier, and Françoise Zonabend proposed the notion of "rechaining" to explain the pattern of marriage just at the point where bonds become weak.[59] And others have presented elegant descriptions of systemic exchange that follow the construction of mutual obligation in the circulation of restricted goods, such as marriage endowments between families and homesteads, over many generations. But the problem with the notion of exchange developed in the structuralist account and refitted for historical analysis in European societies is that it abstracts a particular set of circulating goods – women, bridewealth, dowries – from the total set of prestations, exchanges, and property relations and from productive processes and the larger context of social reproduction.[60]

The present account of Neckarhausen not only looks at the formal aspects of marriage alliance but also integrates marriage into the larger system of exchange. The purpose here is not to reify structures but to uncover the underlying practices that produce systemic regularities. The analysis remains structuralist in the sense that it is "about patterns [and] relations between relations."[61] But it is also about the underlying nature of practical, everyday transactions between people. Margaret Trawick describes the problem of marriage alliance in this way: "The continuity of a kinship strategy such as cross-cousin marriage may be attributed to a dynamic of unresolved tensions and unfulfilled desires as much as to the fulfillment of some function or the resolution of some conflict. . . . [W]e can see

[55] Héritier, *L'exercice.* pp. 99–100, does not find groups pertinent to the operation of alliance. The only thing that matters is the redoubling of an earlier alliance – a marriage with a MBD, and so on.

[56] Sperber distinguishes between systems that imply groups that exchange and those that set up "privileged" networks of matrimonial relations through "preferential" marriage. The latter are more fluid. See Luc de Heusch, *Why Marry Her?*, p. 32.

[57] Freeman, "Concept of Kindred," pp. 210–11.

[58] Emrys Lloyd Peters, "Aspects of Affinity in a Lebanese Maronite Village," in J. G. Peristiany, ed., *Mediterranean Family Structures* (Cambridge, 1976), pp. 27–80, here pp. 67–9.

[59] Tina Jolas, Yvonne Verdier, and Françoise Zonabend, " 'Parler famille,' " *L'homme* 10 (1970): 5–26, here pp. 17–22.

[60] See Goody, *Oriental,* pp. 9–10. He stresses that the meaning of exchange varies from cultural area to cultural area.

[61] Trawick, *Notes,* p. 135.

kinship strategies as played out from the emotional habitus acquired in early childhood within the domestic family."[62] This way of putting the matter suggests that the larger context of reciprocity in which children grow up provides the foundation for strategies of alliance construction through marriage. It also suggests that kinship is central to current theoretical discussions about "identity."

Godparentage

The analysis of godparentage in Neckarhausen remains rather schematic in this volume, largely because there is little direct evidence in the village court protocols about what godparents did for their godchildren or how they acted with regard to the parents they sponsored. I begin the analysis in each cohort by asking the simple question that lies at the heart of the book: did parents choose kin or "strangers" to be godparents for their children, and if they did choose kin, which ones? The answers to that question complete important parts of the map of kinship relations and offer another step in the assessment of the extent of the field of recognized blood ties or ties between people connected through marriage. This mapping exercise is of crucial importance and will be the chief analytical concern for each cohort. As each feature is delineated, the empty areas in the map will be gradually filled in, so that contiguities, overlaps, and uncharted areas can be assessed with greater precision.

In the literature, godparentage has been discussed in terms of a great many social relationships, but at least three of its functions seem fundamental. To begin with, godparentage extends kinship recognition and special friendship beyond those relationships already established by blood and marriage.[63] Second, it appears to have a co- (or anti-)parental function.[64] The godparent has certain ritual, spiritual, or (anti-)parental functions for a child and may substitute for a parent in a crisis situation, perhaps becoming the child's guardian, or may be the practical or symbolic pole that attracts a child away from the family. Third, the relationship can carry an element of asymmetry, hierarchy, or power, with the godparent acting as a patron for a client.[65]

How godparentage is modeled here depends on the basic terms used to express the godparent relation in Württemberg: *Gevatter(in)* and *Döte* (fem.: *Dote*). The former term was the one used by parents for the godparent of their child or children. Döte was used by the child for his or her godparent, and this term could be used reciprocally; that is, the godparent could refer to the child in the

[62] Trawick, *Notes,* p. 154.

[63] See Bernhard Jussen, *Patenschaft und Adoption im frühen Mittelalter: Künstliche Verwandtschaft als soziale Praxis,* Veröffentlichungen des Max-Planck-Instituts für Geschichte, 98 (Göttingen, 1991), pp. 26–7.

[64] Julian Pitt-Rivers, "Ritual Kinship in the Mediterranean: Spain and the Balkans," in J. G. Peristiany, ed., *Mediterranean Family Structures* (Cambridge, 1976), pp. 317–34, here pp. 319–21.

[65] See the analysis in Hugo V. Nutini, *Ritual Kinship: Ideological and Structural Integration of the Compadrazgo System in Rural Tlaxcala,* vol. 2 (Princeton, 1984), p. 68. See also, Donn V. Hart, *Compadrinazgo. Ritual Kinship in the Philippines* (DeKalb, 1977), p. 19.

diminutive as Dötle. A distinction must also be made between those terms expressing a relation and those used as a form of address. I have found only one text – from another village from the 1740s – in which Gevatter or *Gevattermann* was used as a term of address.[66] In that case, the social difference between the two individuals was significant, and the use of Gevatter expressed both moral asymmetry and an element of patronage. This kind of interaction could exist as long as a godparent was significantly older, wealthier, or better placed politically. But if godparents were chosen from close relatives or from the same age set, vertical relationships might be replaced by horizontal ones. And perhaps Gevatter as a term of address would be dropped. Over the course of Neckarhausen history, godparentage did not have a stable meaning. During the "classical" period, when marriage partners were chosen from outside an extensive range of kin, so were godparents. When endogamy developed, godparents then also came to be chosen from among close kin. In the first situation, godparents could function as patrons, whereas in the second that role was hardly possible. As indicated in my first volume on Neckarhausen, early in the eighteenth century godparents frequently acted as go-betweens in property transactions involving unrelated buyers and sellers and thus appeared to play an important mediating role. By the end of the eighteenth century, such a role in the economic life of the village had disappeared.

Throughout the period under consideration, Neckarhausen utilized godparentage to stress intensive rather than extensive relations. Although in a family with several or many children, ritual co-parentage offers the opportunity to construct a fairly extensive network, in Neckarhausen this possibility was not taken up. Once chosen, godparents continued to serve for each successive birth. This means that the relationship was continually reemphasized over the entire child-bearing phase of a family's life and well beyond. Quite often, of course, a particular person ceased to be a godparent, sometimes because of a quarrel but most often as a result of death or emigration. In such a case, the usual practice was to take on the son or daughter or another close relative of the godparent to continue in the position, maintaining as strict a continuity as possible. And another form of perpetuation provided stable relationships over long periods of time: frequently, upon remarriage of a parent, the same people acted as godparents who were godparents in the previous marriage. There are even examples in which, after the deaths of both of the original spouses, their "successors" in the household continued with the original godparents despite being completely unrelated to them.

These considerations throw light on the function of godparents for parents. Julian Pitt-Rivers suggests an "antiparental" aspect to godparents, arguing that parents attach the children to the family and to the past while godparents care for the individual child, for its spiritual particularity, and open the child up to the larger society.[67] But the fact that godparents stood for all the children casts

[66] David Warren Sabean, *Power in the Blood* (Cambridge, 1984), p. 155.
[67] Pitt-Rivers, "Ritual Kinship," pp. 319–21.

doubt on that interpretation here. The children of each marriage had quite separate sets of rights, and a great deal of inventory making and assigning of guardians was organized around this fact. However, godparentage does not seem to have been used to emphasize the individual children of each marriage in their divergent interests but in fact underlined the continuity of the house. The expectation that godparents might substitute for parents in the case of death is also not borne out. As explained later in the book, it was very unusual for godparents to take on the function of guardians. In the mid nineteenth century, a couple might choose a sibling or a cousin as a godparent, and another sibling or cousin as guardian, but no relatives ever held both offices for the same household.

All the evidence here suggests that the weight of the institution in Neckarhausen fell on the Gevatter relationship rather than on the Döte/Dote relationship. This would help explain a remark of Sebastian Franck in the sixteenth century suggesting that the Gevatter was a guarantor (*Bürge*) before God. It is the same word that is used to designate underwriting a loan or guaranteeing a person's conduct. The idea is that a guarantor suffers if the contracting party fails to fulfill his obligation. The notion of *Bürgschaft* has nothing directly to do with the child; rather, it is the task of representing the parents before the community as honorable, or perhaps guaranteeing the social conditions of paternity. But the point about Bürgschaft has other dimensions and in Neckarhausen leads once again to a reversal of expectations. In the nineteenth century the practice of underwriting loans and guaranteeing performance expanded with peasant indebtedness and increased mobility in the building trades. While godparentage may have been incompatible with guardianship, it was not at all incompatible with Bürgschaft. But in all of the examples I have been able to find, couples underwrote their own Gevattern. Rather than the godparent appearing as patron, he or she appears here as client. Bürgschaft in the two meanings of the term set up a direct reciprocity between social and material functions, reversing their direction in unexpected ways.

Godparentage appears to have been a diffuse, multifunctional institution, with an unstable valance and different meanings, not just over time but for different families. Like any kind of kinship connection, it carried moral weight – claims and expectations – and for that reason was subject to strain. In fact, there is a Swabian saying that attests to the possibility of conflict: "If you want to make someone your enemy, you must first get him to be your Gevatter."[68] In a way, godparentage is a kind of argument about crucial social relations, claims to resources, and logical connections. As much as it was subject to individual strategy and flexible practice, as an institution it demonstrates many regularities and structural features. The choice of a godparent set up an enduring relationship and was all the more important because at the same time it excluded all those people not chosen. Since the shifts in the structure of godparentage correlate so closely with shifts in marriage alliance, as we shall see, despite the spareness of references

[68] Art, "Gevatter," in Hermann Fischer, *Schwäbisches Lexikon* (6 vols., Tübingen, 1904–36).

in those sources that could offer clues to its discursive meaning, its study will prove richly rewarding.

Naming practices

Childnaming is a significant, although largely ambiguous, aspect of kinship practice. Until recently, very little was known about the range of customs in Western Europe, and studies in the United States are just beginning.[69] There are difficult theoretical and methodological issues to resolve in this field of study, even when the data seem straightforward. To begin with, a name recorded by officials may not be the name that the parents have given a particular child. Or the name given at birth may never be used or intended to be used in the form recorded. In Neckarhausen, Hans Jerg or Jerg will be recorded as Johann Georg, Burga as Waltburga, Catharina as Anna Catharina. Consideration of the difference between village usage and the practices of literate elites makes a general point: names have different meanings in different contexts. They can be used to differentiate individuals or to order people into higher entities of families, station, class, or age cohort. Inside a family, a name, such as Mark, differentiated one child from another in Western society of the early 1980s, but in the school classroom it served to connect the individual with the middle-class cohort born in the 1960s and frequently required a surname to distinguish among different boys. This was the case whether the child was attending school in England, France, Germany, or the United States. This very problem of individuation and classification is the first one to be considered in this book and is the one most frequently discussed by historians.

Naming is not an unambiguous act connecting or differentiating people in such a way that statistical changes point directly to changing patterns of family relations. Arbitrary meanings – such as extension of the lineage, recognition of the cohesion of kinship, denial of uniqueness – must not be assigned to the act of a father naming a son after himself. It would be just as easy to consider the practice a recognition of fundamental opposition, of the turnover of generations, as the first step of the father on the way to death. Just as the father and son will struggle over the property and the father will inevitably be the loser, so they will struggle over the name and the outcome will be the same. Attaching oneself or another to the past is a present social act that has meaning in the present struggle for symbols of power. But giving priority to the father's name may be symbolic of the shallowest genealogical tracing, of a break between adult siblings, of the stress of each nuclear family as a productive unit. It is not a denial of the "uniqueness"

[69] See Michael Mitterauer, *Ahnen und Heilige: Namengebung in der europäischen Geschichte* (Munich, 1993). Daniel Scott Smith has written a pioneering article: "Child-Naming Patterns and Family Structure Change: Hingham, Massachusetts 1640–1880," *Newberry Papers in Family and Community History*, Paper 76–5 (January, 1977). For a critique, see David Warren Sabean, "Exchanging Names in Neckarhausen around 1700," in Peter Karsten and John Modell, eds., *Theory, Method, and Practice in Social and Cultural History* (New York, 1992), pp. 199–230.

of the son but a marking out of a social field and a set of power relations or a move in the struggle for symbolic meaning.[70]

In Lévi-Strauss's account, names of different types – unique versus class – do not say anything about a difference in the object.[71] Proper names and classificatory names are for Lévi-Strauss logical transformations of one another. At the one extreme, one is classifying the object, at the other oneself. For Lévi-Strauss, naming that classifies the child as member of this or that moiety, ramage, patrilineage, or household cannot be compared in quantitative fashion with naming that finds unique terms for each child in a society. That is because the first exercise is concerned with the name-receiver – the object – whereas the second is concerned with the name-giver – the subject. So one should not simply use statistical series to compare situations that cannot be compared, that are indeed logical transformations of each other.

In general my analysis of naming practices draws on reconstituted families giving the actual names bestowed on children and a map of the existent set of names in the kin network at the time of the child's baptism. Although one can derive statistics of name matching and show changes over time, the complex set of forces in play is difficult to discern here. It is important to understand, even when the facts seem to point in no particular direction, that naming itself does not mean the same thing from time to time and in different family constellations and class situations.[72] It is not just that different people may take part in the decision but that different acts can be taking place altogether. In my consideration of naming, I try to examine the structure as it occurred at a particular time and to fit it into what is already known about other family practices. This in turn will provide a basis for further exploration of the dynamics of kinship. Some of the meaning of giving names to children will emerge only in later analysis.[73]

The names given to children at baptism were only part of a larger structure of naming in the village of Neckarhausen. In the first place, people were often not called by the names given in the baptismal register. This is clear from the register itself in the early years before the Thirty Years' War. Take the case of Catharina Stoll, who was baptized in 1588. Her father was given as Bastian, her mother as Margaretha, her godfather as Theus, and her godmother as Barbla. That is, her name was given in Hochdeutsch (or Latin), whereas those of her father, godmother, and godfather were entered in the manner by which they were probably called: Bastian (later Basten) instead of Sebastian, Theus instead of Matheus, and Barbla, instead of Barbara. The mother's name was recorded as Margaretha, but the next time a child was born, she appeared as Gretha. The

[70] A fascinating study of naming and social power is provided by Bernard Vernier, "Putting Kin and Kinship to Good Use: The Circulation of Goods, Labour, and Names in Karpathos (Greece)," in Medick and Sabean, *Interest and Emotion*, pp. 28–76.

[71] Claude Lévi-Strauss, *The Savage Mind* (London, 1966), pp. 182–88.

[72] As Lévi-Strauss says: "the same term can, depending only on its position in a context, play the part either of a class indicator or of an individual determinant." *The Savage Mind*, p. 188.

[73] We must also keep in mind that the act of naming can sometimes be more important than the name itself: David Maybury-Lewis, *Akwe-Shavante Society* (New York, 1974), p. 235.

father also had a nickname – Glemer or Glemser. These differences reflect distinctions between names as recognized by officials, those recognized by the family, and those current in the village. Different names might also be used to distinguish people at different levels and in different contexts.

By the sixteenth century surnames had already come to be largely fixed and seemed to designate people as a member of this or that family. From the beginning of my documentation (1560s), names were binomial, consisting of a family designation and a Christian name. Naming at baptism was only part of a larger context of naming, and it was not necessary for the villagers to know all the possible names available for an individual in all contexts. In some present-day situations, for example, in Spain and Cyprus, villagers are often completely unaware of surnames of people they know very well.[74] Names used in transactions with outsiders are not necessarily those used in everyday communal social relations. In a village such as Neckarhausen, there was considerable overlap of names. Individual families did not take care to see that no other child in the village had the same name. Distinguishing among men with the same name was done by descent (i.e., by referring, for example, to "Hans Hentzler, son of Salomon"), or by occupation (Hans Hentzler, Weber), or by age or precedence (*Jung* Hans Hentzler, *Alt* Hans Hentzler). The use of "jung" and "alt" – occasionally "jung jung" or in combination with teknonymy – took place without regard to whether two individuals were father and son: they might not have been closely related at all. Above all, this way of naming underlines the generational shallowness of names.[75] When Alt Hans died, the next oldest Hans became Alt Hans. In a similar fashion, a man differentiated from another man by incorporating his occupation into his name had no distinguishing mark to maintain him in village memory. There was a jumble of Hans Jerg Bauknechts kept track of by seniority, occupation, and filiation. After one of them died, the group names were reshuffled, and his name was replaced by that of a living person. As a result, villagers lost the ability to refer to him. As each generation succeeded the previous one, the stock of names was appropriated by the living adults just as land and houses were. Naming a son after a father rather than attaching a child to a long line of kin in fact makes the dead quickly indistinguishable from one another. The "struggle" over the name between father and son is one aspect of a larger struggle of several adults who share the same surnames and Christian names. Everything suggests that villagers developed sufficient marks to distinguish among active adults but not to distinguish between the living and the dead. As shown throughout the book, the names of the grandparent generation were seldom utilized for naming children, another argument for shallow generational reckoning.

One topic of primary interest here is the way that name giving in Neckarhausen

[74] Peter Loizos, *The Greek Gift: Politics in a Cypriot Village* (Oxford, 1975), p. 96; Julian Pitt-Rivers, *The Fate of Schechem or the Politics of Sex: Essays in the Anthropology of the Mediterranean* (Cambridge, 1977), p. 59.

[75] A similar point is made by Geertz and Geertz, *Kinship in Bali*, p. 91.

reflects salient features of the social fabric – or the structural fault lines between families and generations. The analysis proceeds on the assumption that naming a child can carry several meanings within itself. It is part of the structure of everyday relations among adults active in the struggle for consideration, honor, and esteem. Naming a child arises from the reproductive strategies of adults considered in the broadest possible way. Lévi-Strauss's point, that one never names but classifies, suggests that giving a name is an act of tracing present lines of social force – a statement about or a move in the present social struggle. But, as he also notes, giving a name is usually a complex operation – not just about the subject or the object exclusively but about both at once. Forces of individuation and categorization can be in play with respect to the object – the godparent symbolically representing the child against the parents and the society – although exactly which parts of the contending aspects of social reality are represented by parents and godparents is open to discussion.[76]

A reportedly common practice in Württemberg at the end of the nineteenth century was for a boy to receive his first pair of pants or a girl her first dress from the person after whom they were named.[77] Such a practice implies that the namesake was expected to be alive and maintain an active relationship with the family. It also fits into my argument about naming and generational rotation. It is precisely the namesake who marks a crucial step toward adulthood and the supplanting of the parents.

Guardianship

One of the obvious roles that kin play is that of guardian for orphans. In Württemberg villages, a guardian was appointed to defend a child's interests and to look after his or her inheritance rights whenever at least one parent died. Although it seems to have been more usual to refer to a child as an "orphan" (*Waisenkind*) when the father was dead, whether or not the mother was still living, institutionally there appears to have been little difference. A guardian (*Pfleger)* was appointed to ensure that the property of a deceased parent was properly inventoried and that the rights of the children in relation to the surviving parent

[76] Ramos compares the Truk Islanders studied by Goodenough, the Lakalai, and the Sanumá indians of Northern Brazil. According to Goodenough, naming practices and modes of address counterbalance other aspects of the social system. For example, on the Truk Island where group action is stressed at the expense of the individual, it is precisely the naming system that provides individual identity – there are no two individuals with the same name. Among the Lakalai, by contrast, individuals are not so bound up with group obligations and have ample opportunity to express themselves individually inside parameters of the social system. As a result, the naming system does not have to be used to express individuality and operates with cyclical patterns that emphasize specific social relations. Among the Sanumá, whose people often have three or four names, both individuation and categorization can be expressed at different times over a person's lifetime. Ward H. Goodenough, "Personal Names and Modes of Address in Two Oceanic Societies," in Melford E. Spiro, ed., *Context and Meaning in Cultural Anthropology* (New York, 1965).

[77] Karl Bohnenberger, ed., *Volkstümliche Ueberlieferungen in Württemberg: Glaube – Brauch – Heilkunde* (Stuttgart, 1980; original 1904ff.), p. 87.

were duly respected. The guardian stood by while the property was inspected and inventoried and saw to it that at each stage of their development the wards (*Pflegekinder*) were treated according to the law. Of course, the duties of the *Pflegevater* were greater when both parents were deceased, since he had to see that expenditures for the children were properly made, property sold or entrusted to a lessee, money invested, and rents or interest collected. All of these activities were recorded in proper accounts, which theoretically at least were read and inspected periodically before the "orphan's court" (*Waisengericht*) of the village. The guardian was in many respects a "co-parent," since he was responsible for the child's inheritance, care, education, and marriage plans, and in many cases where both parents were deceased took over the entire duties of a child's parents. In any event, it appears that when one parent survived, the Pfleger could be a real co-parent even if not concerned with the day-to-day situation of living together as a family group.

In general, a young person who had lost a parent was entrusted with a Pfleger until reaching adulthood. Technically, this occurred on one's twenty-fifth birthday. But anyone marrying before that age became fully responsible for his or her own affairs. Even after twenty-five, a young person who was not yet married often stayed under the care of a guardian. This would happen, for example, if a young artisan was off on his Wanderjahr, or was in the army, or temporarily absent or living elsewhere. By the mid nineteenth century, many young people emigrated to America and their Pfleger administered whatever property they left behind. In the eighteenth century, women remained in wardship (*Pflegschaft*) until they married, after which they came under the administration of their husbands with a Kriegsvogt appointed by the court to represent them in any situation in which the husband was selling or encumbering family property. In the nineteenth century, young unmarried women were allowed to administer their own affairs (*verwaltungsfähig*) after the age of twenty-five and could declare their independence before the court.[78]

A problem that sometimes arose in these cases had to do with the interests of the Pfleger himself. In many instances, especially when the children were young, it was possible for him to use the resources of the wardship. At times the Pfleger could take over the lease of a property himself. On the principle that a Pfleger should not be indebted to his Pflegschaft, this presented a problem, and may have caused the authorities to disallow the direct leasing of land by a guardian or to bring it under tighter control: in any event, certain conflicts of interest were done away. By way of example, Schultheissen who had frequently acted as Pfleger in the eighteenth century were denied that right in the nineteenth century because of widespread abuse of the institution.

The chief interest in being a Pfleger was probably that it enabled one to do favors for others. A guardian could decide who should lease land and on what conditions. In this way one could receive monetary rewards or win friends by

[78] *Gericht*, vol. 13, fol. 32 (23.11.1838) for an example. See Sabean, *Property*, pp. 209–18.

dispensing patronage. At the same time, the Pfleger had to chase debts, a continual problem.[79] It was one of the forms of Schultheissen power until the early years of the nineteenth century. Various court members functioned as Pfleger and because of their official status could gather small spheres of interest around themselves, which were especially important if individuals under guardianship had no close kin to protect them. Depending on the personal situation of the Pfleger and his kinship relation to his charge, claims on and obligations to the children could be in tension or divided up in various ways.

From many texts, it is clear that Pfleger were elected or selected by the Gericht.[80] If there were no close relatives exercising claims, a member of the Gericht was named to the position. At times, the candidate had to meet specific criteria; the ability to write, for example, was a common requirement, especially where the liquidation of an estate was at issue.[81] Since the Pfleger was required to keep a notebook (*Rapiat*) or ledger (*Tabelle*), it would seem that being able to write was increasingly taken for granted. Because he would have many court appearances, it was also usually necessary to be a local resident. In the nineteenth century, a guardian appeared whenever the court called for a birth certificate or character attestation, say, because a young person wished to settle in another place, or marry outside the village, or take on any kind of responsibility such as a job as a builder. At times a guardian would have to put up caution money, which of course placed his own property in jeopardy. This practice seems to have increased in the nineteenth century, which meant that, given the risks involved, a man was likely to take on the job only because of kinship obligation, official responsibility, or profit.[82]

Although the law promulgated in the sixteenth century already stated that the property of a Pfleger was tacitly pledged, unless adequate records were kept, the authorities found it exceedingly difficult to check up on anyone who took on the responsibility.[83] The very fact that the Schultheiss could be a Pfleger in the eighteenth century suggests that money and social credit were to be gained from the institution. A big step toward bringing the practice under control was a move to deny the Schultheiss the right to become party to something he was supposed to regulate. In any event, various ordinances in the eighteenth and early nineteenth centuries openly admitted that the rules of Pflegschaft had often been violated, that receipts had not been properly recorded, that village officials did not oversee all the wardships, that accounts were not properly kept or periodically inspected.[84] They implied that many Pfleger could not even read and noted that it was usual for guardians to treat cash receipts from their own wardships as their personal income. In the final decades of the eighteenth century, one of the

79 *Gericht*, vol. 11, fol. 98 (4.4.1828).
80 *Gericht*, vol. 11, fol. 154 (29.10.1829), fol. 190 (19. 8. 1830).
81 *Gericht*, vol. 6, fol. 94 (11.6.1805).
82 *Gericht*, vol. 11, fol. 132 (23.3.1829).
83 Reyscher, *2. Landrecht*, vol. 4, p. 320.
84 Reyscher, General Rescript (18–24.12.1748), vol. 6, p. 491, (10.9.1803), vol. 6, pp. 1788–91.

major tasks of officials from Nürtingen was to see that every Pflegschaft was properly registered, that the village court as a whole and not just the smaller orphan's court appointed guardians, and that all accounts were inspected at the end of the first year. They also made sure that the village magistrates saw to it that outstanding debts to Pflegschaften (quitrents, interest, principal due) were paid annually or secured by third parties. Each guardian was to be given a ledger in which to keep accounts presentable to the orphan's court for inspection.[85] According to the law codes, close relatives were expected to be appointed as Pfleger or to be part of the selection process.[86] Selection could also be made by testament, although I have not yet found any written examples for Neckarhausen. Since there is occasional mention of parents choosing Pfleger, the will of a deceased parent may have been known to the court and thus would have been taken into consideration.

The evidence suggests that there were fewer effective controls on Pflegschaften in the eighteenth century and that guardians often took kickbacks, purchased land in disguised fashion, lined pockets while liquidating estates, and treated regular income as a personal perquisite. The emphasis would have been on the *right* of close relatives to hold wardships, with other relatives looking on jealously to protect their own interests. Relatives of the deceased parent would be intimately concerned about the fate of property that their kin had brought to the marriage. It would tend to create a bond between the maternal uncles and sister's children in the interchange between Pfleger and father, or conversely, between the Pfleger and children against the mother's male kin, who might wish to use their connection against those who rented a woman's property or cultivated it for shares. When the matter is examined statistically, one finds close relations among children with both sets of uncles and aunts, but which set entered structurally into which relationships all depended on what the history of the family had been. For example, when a father died, the mother's property and that of the children was left in usufruct. If the boys were old enough and physically present, they could do the plowing, harrowing, and other physically demanding and skilled agricultural tasks. However, the physical care of animals and the responsibility for complex agricultural organization was not usually taken on by the very young: all the sources suggest a prolonged adolescence. When the children were too young, the mother, if she did not marry immediately, might naturally accept her brothers and sisters' husbands as people capable of running her fields, leasing them, or plowing, harrowing, and doing other heavy work. There were many carting jobs, such as carrying grain to be milled, which were strictly done by men. Whether this is seen as mutual aid or exploitation is not the point. Male work was necessary, and it was not done for free. The Pfleger, one would expect, would come from the deceased father's side of the family. In supporting the property interests of the deceased husband and his children, he had to deal

[85] Reyscher, General Rescript (2.6.1788), vol. 6, p. 669.

[86] Reyscher, "Staat und Unterricht für Vormünder (1776)," vol. 6, pp. 605–14.

with the fact that all of the property was in the wife's usufruct. Thus the children's set of relatives consist of the mother and male relatives of the mother (MB) in the role of labor exploitation, control of the product, and a mixture of trust and suspicion. The father's male relatives in such a situation were expected to solicit on behalf of and represent the father's lineage interest – to see that sufficient manure was spread, the fields plowed often enough and with sufficient care to kill the weeds, the harvest kept dry, and all the grain accounted for. The number of ways to cut corners were enormous and called for a watchful eye and constant intervention. In this scenario, the FB would emerge as the figure of care, while the MB's role would be filled with tension. In cases where the father survived, however, he could do his own male work. There was no comparable tension-filled role for his male relatives equal to that of the MB in the first example. Since the male relatives of the mother were the ones to oversee the activities of the father, tensions would be distributed differently, according to whether the father remarried. The MB would be a key supporter of children against the new wife and her relatives or could act as an interloper where a father did not marry and all of his labor would pay off in inheritance for the children. In this bilateral system, where property fell equally to women and men, the role of the maternal uncle seems a possible source of tension. As discussed in later chapters, there was a bias, especially in the eighteenth century, toward naming children from the father's side of the family and a bias in continuing extended kin relations on the father's side. This tendency may be explained in part by the problem of caring for orphans and gives added force to the term "orphan" when used for children without fathers as well as for children with no parents at all.

In the nineteenth century, the bureaucratization of wardships gave less opportunity for exploiting opportunities offered by the system. In the first place, more of the agricultural work fell to women anyway, and the preparation of fields played less of a role in the total agricultural round.[87] In turn, women cared in essential ways for cattle and could offer one part of a yoke in exchange for having a field plowed. In any event, they were better placed to pay a "wage" for a job such as plowing rather than turn over the care of a field in return for a rent or part of the produce. A widow, however much she might rely on male relatives, was less likely to be the object of their claims. For a little paid plowing, a brother-in-law was as good as a brother. A woman was also capable now of trading her labor for male labor. The very fact that peasant women were able to exercise some independence in this area is shown by the increased number in this group who remained widows and kept ownership of land or usufruct rights in their own hands well into old age. The sale of land to women also points in the same direction. Whatever tensions there might have been between guardians and widows most likely pertained to her own competence as agriculturalist and householder – whether she was properly maintaining the property inherited by herself and her deceased husband, which in turn was to be passed on to the children.

[87] For changes in the sexual division of labor, see Sabean, *Property*, pp. 148–56.

Because a wardship offered less opportunity for exploitation and placed the Pfleger more at risk in the nineteenth century, it became something of a burden, more an *obligation* than a *right*. The Pfleger was often there to run interference for his charges, to petition for gifts from the village court, to solicit good testimonials to obtain a job or effect a marriage, to get financial support to emigrate. All of these tasks were ones of connection and political manipulation and suggest close coordination between male relatives of the mother and her in-laws, the blood relatives of her deceased husband. The surviving widower was in a slightly different position. He needed female labor or a substitute. Such labor could come from the children, a second wife, or female servants, but child labor became as important to the system as female labor. (That is the memory of many of the oldest villagers today – unremitting hoeing in the fields as children). The heavy inputs of sacrificial labor of a deceased mother would have been sorely missed, and close attachment would have developed for anyone mitigating the effects of a father's drunkenness, violence, or wastrel life. In such a situation, the role of MB or even of FB could have been important. The intervention of guardians is repeatedly to be found in the sources from the nineteenth century. Whether in cooperation or in tension with the father, the "political" connections of Pfleger and the pool of relatives from which they were chosen were important considerations.

Kriegsvogtschaft

Until the third decade of the nineteenth century, married women and widows were represented in all official business by a Kriegsvogt.[88] The term is derived from legal vocabulary, where the parties in a trial were considered to be "at war" (*Krieg*) with one another. *Vogt* has many applications but in general refers to a representative who is empowered to speak for, or represent, an institution or person. In this case, a Kriegsvogt "represented" his charge before the local court and in the conduct of legal business. The reciprocal term, *Kriegsfrau,* expressed an adult relationship in contrast to guardianship, where the reciprocal terms were Pfleger/Pflegekind (Pflegesohn, Pflegetochter).[89] Until 1828, when the legal situation changed (see Volume I), a woman remained a ward essentially until she married if either of her parents were deceased.[90] Legal business was carried on for her by her father or her guardian, or both together. Upon marriage, she came under the administration of her husband, but whenever any business was conducted that could affect her property situation, a court-appointed Kriegsvogt had to be present. The Kriegsvogt, selected by the woman herself, had to be formally installed before the Gericht, which often took place the first time a couple wanted

[88] See David Warren Sabean, "Soziale und kulturelle Aspekte der Geschlechtsvormundschaft im 18. und 19. Jahrhundert," in Ute Gerhard, ed., *Handbuch für die Rechtsgeschichte der Frau* (Beck Verlag: München, forthcoming [1997]).

[89] See, e.g., *Gericht,* vol. 1, fol. 141 (7.7.1762).

[90] Sabean, *Property,* pp. 148–56.

to borrow money or sell or purchase a strip of land.[91] The Kriegsvogt was empowered to act on his Kriegsfrau's behalf in all matters and was called upon to take a formal oath of office.[92] In general, Kriegsvögte represented those who were legal adults but who could not independently carry on legal business. They stood against the husband or against the Pfleger of the children, so that in any court situation antagonisms and potentially conflicting interests were formally recognized.

When a married couple appeared before the court, the job of the Kriegsvogt was to read all legal documents to the woman, explain their meaning, and obtain her consent. She was reminded of her "female liberties," which she could renounce, making her property attachable in case of debt or bankruptcy. When marital tensions arose, the Kriegsvogt was there to represent the wife, of course. The Kriegsvogt would be present at all divorce or separation proceedings, just as the Pfleger would be present for the children.[93] Although mutual observation and control might have taken place between friends, kin, and neighbors, institutional concreteness was established in the figure of the Kriegsvogt. Kriegsvögte, Pfleger, and "close relatives" hedged in action or cooperated to create new opportunities.

Pledging

Little information is available on the way people stood surety for one another. There are enough texts from the eighteenth century to suggest that it was a common enough practice to back a loan or a mortgage with a guarantee from a third party. However, it is only in the early nineteenth century that the documentation becomes sufficient. The very fact that guarantees (*Bürgschaften*) were increasingly mentioned in official texts suggests greater control and an extension of the system, but certain kinds of documentation by and large escaped public notice. A letter of debt exchanged by two people might well be backed up by a third-party guarantee, but the facts are only hinted at when there is a dispute over a signature or the third party himself went bankrupt.

In the nineteenth century, it was increasingly necessary for purchasers of land at auction to post a bond by a third party. Therefore lists of names of guarantors (Bürgen) can be obtained from the register of land sales. The need for such assurances was compounded by the rash of bankruptcies in the 1810s and 1820s and by the high capital demands associated with agricultural intensification at the beginning of the nineteenth century. In addition, with more people working outside the village (taking on contractual work in road building, canals, carpentry, masonry and the like), guarantees were ever more necessary to ensure that the worker was both honest and competent. As the mobility of workers and con-

[91] E.g., *Gericht*, vol. 1, fol. 30 (26.5.1750).
[92] E.g., *Gericht*, vol. 1, fol. 132 (26.3.1761).
[93] *Gericht*, vol. 4, fol. 18 (30.4.1785).

tractors increased and they began negotiating in a larger market network, the migrant workforce became more tightly bound to the capital resources of the village. The wealth of Neckarhausen residents was put at risk every time a village carpenter repaired a roof in another village, a pavior put in a series of drains, or a trader sold butter door to door in another village or town. Changes in the nature of the economy, greater fluidity, and more contacts with the outside all forced people to cultivate relationships that would spread the risks. In their struggle to meet these challenges of the volatile land market and economic diversification, villagers grew more and more dependent on one another. They accepted risk for each other but at the same time acted as powerful restraints on each other's behavior. Practically every time people entered into new social or economic relations, village guarantees were sought. If a girl contracted to marry in another village, someone in Neckarhausen pledged his or her entire property that her dowry and savings were correctly stated. When a father took over his children's maternal inheritance in usufruct, he had to pledge his own property as a guarantee that he would maintain theirs. Upon migrating to America, a young person got someone to guarantee that he or she would not return as an impoverished burden on the community or that the money the village advanced would actually be used for the boat fare.

* * *

Together, marriage, godparentage, naming, guardianship, transacting property, Kriegsvogtschaft, and pledging provide a means of determining how some of the interlocking ties of kinship created structure at different points in time. Such "indicators" allow particular aspects of reciprocity to be looked at synchronically, in their systemic interdependence, and diachronically, as they shift in the way they tack with one another over time. But structure does not lock individuals into specific kinds of behavior. Statistically at a particular moment, for example, many people might be looking to cousins for spouses, godparents, guardians, and the like, but this does not mean that everyone did so even when such candidates were available. Strategies were developed with continual observation and consideration of how other people made claims on one another. As one tries to take a measure of the system, one finds many kinds of reciprocal transactions that cannot be considered in terms of their everyday importance: aid in childbirth, plowing, support in tavern brawls, arranging work teams, offering job contacts, votes, advice regarding a sick cow, and so forth. Sometimes it is best to view how such things hold together through the prism of particular life histories. Precisely because no one methodology is able to capture the complexity of the subject, this volume approaches kinship through a variety of representational and narrative strategies. But before the systematic inquiry begins, it is essential to see how kinship became a central element of local political discourse in the eighteenth century and how a theological dimension of statecraft impinged upon the capacity of villages to configure certain modes of kin interaction.

2

Vetterleswirtschaft: Rise and fall of a political discourse

This study deals with a period of Württemberg rural history when a particular aspect of kinship became a charged political issue. The term "Vetter" (cousin) reverberates throughout the texts from the 1740s through the 1820s, usually in the context of social or political controversy. There are indications that by the second half of the eighteenth century oligarchical structures, coordinated through familial alliances, dominated the chief civil and ecclesiastical institutions of the country as well as county (*Oberamt*) and local government. In this chapter, I consider the origins of the specific discourse about cousins and differentiate the kinship logic of that period from what went before and after. My central concern is the formation of the particular language of kinship that accompanied a redeployment of power at the level of the village magistrates. People frequently referred to a local court as a *Vetter-Gericht* or *Vetterlesgericht,* alluding to the fact that its members were all closely related and acted as a tightly organized syndicate to coordinate the use of village resources, to dispense patronage, to channel various emoluments to themselves, and to defraud the central government of taxes, tithes, and other sources of income. The different ways kinship was talked about from period to period reflected considerable differences in social practice and the constitution of authority and power in village life. Although my focus – or starting point – is the village, much of what I have found is consistent with what others have found in towns, regions, courts, and capitals. The local setting allows me to observe the issues in a controlled environment and thus to speculate from a broader perspective about the links between more familiar social and political discourses and the arcane features of village and family life.

A good example of the situation at its height comes from the second decade of the nineteenth century. In 1817 the Württemberg king sent Friedrich List to Heilbronn to question a group of subjects who had decided to leave the country for the new world.[1] They offered many reasons for doing so and reflected at length on the conditions that had made life impossible in their home villages. Burdensome taxes were high on the list, of course, but there were a host of other complaints as well. Politically, a central issue was faction – their term being *parteiisch* – but they described the situation in terms that List would overlook when he later reflected on his interviews.[2] They talked about networks of *family* faction, nepotism, and coordinate groups of *cousins* (Vettern).[3] Jacob Hampp from Egolsheim put the matter simply: "The Schultheiss and Bürgermeister support each other because they are cousins and the other magistrates also cooperate because they are related together."[4] Johann Jacob Strähle, also from Egolsheim, concurred: "The magistrates are one family . . . at road repairs and other village jobs, bread is taken out of the mouths of the villagers."[5] In a similar vein, Sebastian Baumgart and others from Dahnenfeld reported: "The officials are related together and are simply one chain."[6] Also Christian Schwarz from Sulzbach mentioned: "My village headman himself made the suggestion that I should move to America because his own son-in-law has property bordering mine."[7] And two Bürger from Wilsbach warned about influence and collusion: "When a commissioner comes, he should be told that he is not allowed to lodge at the inn, because the innkeepers are magistrates and brother[s]-in-law to the Bürgermeister."[8]

Several connections made by the witnesses and the way they actually put the issues shed important light on the political dynamics of village life. Besides taxes and inflation, matters such as tithe corruption, bullying, packing seats on the village council, controlling credit, self-serving cooperation with higher authorities, irregularities in financial operations, and unfair allocation of taxes were all

[1] Some of the issues are handled in an earlier discussion, "Social Background to Vetterleswirtschaft: Kinship in Neckarhausen," in Rudolf Vierhaus and Mitarbeitern des Max-Planck-Institut für Geschichte, eds., *Frühe Neuzeit – Frühe Moderne? Forschungen zur Vielschichtigkeit von Uebergangsprozessen,* Veröffentlichungen des Max-Planck-Institut für Geschichte, vol. 104 (Göttingen, 1992), pp. 113–32. See also my *Property, Production, and Family in Neckarhausen, 1700–1870* (Cambridge, 1990), p. 48, n. 53.

[2] See, e.g., his essay from 1842, "Die Ackerverfassung, die Zwergwirtschaft und die Auswanderung," in *Friedrich Lists Kleinere Schriften,* ed. Friedrich Lenz, vol. 1 (Jena, 1926), pp. 437–554.

[3] Günter Moltmann, ed., *Aufbruch nach Amerika. Friedrich List und die Auswanderung aus Baden und Württemberg 1816/17. Dokumentation einer sozialen Bewegung* (Tübingen, 1979). Kinship also played a role for those who were leaving. Michael Munz from Möglingen testified: "I have news from relatives (*Verwandten*) in America, who have it good there. A cousin (*Vetter*), who is traveling with me, provided me with money" (p. 135). For examples of letters from "cousins" in America, see p. 149.

[4] Moltmann, *Aufbruch,* p. 131: "Der Schultheiss und Bürgermeister halten zusammen, denn sie sind Vetter und die andern MagistratsPersonen halten auch mit, weil sie zusammen verwandt sind."

[5] Moltmann, *Aufbruch,* p. 132: "Der Magistrat ist eine Familie . . . bei Strassen-und Akkorden ist . . . den Bürgern das Brod vor dem Munde weg."

[6] Moltmann, *Aufbruch,* p. 166: "die Beamte zusammen verwandt, und nur eine Kette sind."

[7] Moltmann, *Aufbruch,* p. 158: "mein Ortsvorsteher selbst hat mir den Vorschlag gemacht, nach Amerika zu ziehen, weil sein eigener Tochtermann Güter neben mir liegen hat."

[8] Moltmann, *Aufbruch,* p. 165: "wenn ein Commissarius komme, demselben noch aufzugeben wäre, dass er nicht im Wirtshaus logiren dörfe, weil die Wirthe Magistratspersonen und Schwagher zu dem Bürgermeister seyen."

coupled with the coordination of political practice through kinship. But in List's assessment of the situation, stress was put less on kinship than on class.[9] He referred to factionalism, to a struggle between rich and poor, but completely suppressed any mention of political or social formations driven by kinship considerations. Such an interpretation would not have been out of line with the emerging social sciences, which were just beginning to adopt class as the key analytical concept for representing advanced societies.[10] Kinship became something archaic, a principle ordered in terms of historical progress, a social formation fitting an earlier stage of human development, and a concept that was found inadequate for social analysis.

The political language of cousinship

An important question raised by the testimony of List's commission is whether such familial ties had always been part of village social and political dynamics. The answer is, family and kinship were indeed significant before the middle decades of the eighteenth century, but they were structured quite differently. The details of the two systems are the subject of the first two sections of this book, but in this chapter the aim is to introduce the issues as they were articulated in political language in many villages throughout Württemberg. The earliest text I have found that uses the word "Vetter" in a political dispute comes from 1755. Several inhabitants from the village of Ditzingen had brought charges against the Schultheiss, alleging that the chief magistrates made up a *Vetterlensgericht* (cousins' court).[11] The actual relationships that were detailed involved an uncle and nephew (brother's son) and two men described as "co-parents-in-law" (*Gegenschweher* – men whose children were married to one another), while the Schultheiss's only connection to the members of the Gericht was through godparentage. The key figure in this case was Hans Jerg Rocher, the previous Schultheiss, whose nephew had sat on the Gericht before Rocher resigned as Schultheiss and rejoined it himself. He was the one with the co-parent-in-law

9 See Moltmann, *Aufbruch,* p. 140. After a day of testimony, List summarized the issues in terms of political freedom, speaking of "all kinds of oppression that arose from civil conditions." In his final report, he remarked in general on repression, a lack of civil freedom, and pietist fanaticism but identified the concrete causes of emigration as high taxes, direct harassment by local officials, high costs of official records, delays in court, oppression by forest officials, and problems with landlords in the border areas of the kingdom. The recent harvest failures and inflation of food prices exacerbated the problems, he said. Interwoven in his account is a struggle between rich and poor (pp. 175–86).

10 For an excellent introduction to the historical development of the concept "class," see Otto Gerhard Oexle, Werner Conze, and Rudolf Walther, art. "Stand, Klasse," in *Geschichtliche Grundbegriffe,* ed. Otto Brunner, Werner Conze, and Reinhard Koselleck, vol. 6 (Stuttgart, 1990), pp. 155–284. It would not be fair to say that List's analytical concept of "class" was as articulated as that of Karl Marx, Lorenz von Stein, or Max Weber, but his whole approach makes class implicit, and the term itself occurs in such works as "Ackerverfassung."

11 Hauptstaatsarchiv Stuttgart (HSAS), A214, Bü 517, "Dizingen. Die von Johannes Wielanden et cons. gegen den Schultheissen Johann Jacob Schweizer immediato angebrachte Delata, welche von dem Canzley Advocato Ord. Frommen als Commissario untersucht worden, betr" (1755–56).

on the court and was godparent to the new Schultheiss. According to the villagers who brought the complaint, the corruption led by both Schultheissen had been made possible by coordination among kin on the Gericht.

The use of the term "Vetter" in this case points to relationships that were not actually based on cousinship. In fact, the word was used to designate all kinds of close relatives and could be extended to wider kin whose connection to the speaker was only vaguely known, or to anyone in a situation where one wanted to suggest a spirit of close familial cooperation.[12] Such use of the word "cousin" is much older, of course, and historians are familiar with the long practice of nobles addressing each other as "Vetter" in letters. Nonetheless, after diligent search through the several hundred cases of village conflict contained in the commission reports in the Württemberg State Archives, I can find no political use of the word before the 1750s. It became fashionable to designate kin of all kinds in this manner just about the time that cousins came to play an important mutual role in a variety of social situations where they had not done so before. In other words, cousins became the structurally central element in the new kinship system, the beginnings of which, as I shall show throughout this book, are traceable to the 1740s and 1750s. The way the word "cousin" came to be extended to all kinds of relatives is parallel, of course, to the similar use of the term "nepotism," which literally, at least, designates nephews. In the Middle Ages, where the mother's brother acted as patron to the sister's son or the celibate churchman played a special role for his nephews, the key structural element of uncle and nephew made "nepotism" the apt phrase for kinship-centered politics as such.[13] In the eighteenth and nineteenth centuries, the ordering of such politics around "Vettern" suggests that the coordinates of the system were the children and grandchildren of siblings.

Each village in Württemberg proceeded at its own pace in these matters and

[12] See the article "Vetter" in *Grimms Wörterbuch*. The word is derived from "Vater" (father) and originally denoted the father's brother and later the mother's brother (*Oheim*) as well. It is hard to date the shifts in meaning from Grimms's article, but it appears that by the sixteenth century at least, "Vetter" had come to refer to cousins (*Geschwisterkinder*) and in a more general sense any male relative. Fischer's *Schwäbisches Wörterbuch* gives a similar etymology. Fischer discusses the Swabian use of "Vetterle" in the context of nepotism: "Vetterlesschaft," "Vetterleswirtschaft," "Vetterleswesen." A "Vetterlesgericht" is one dominated by nepotism. Mack Walker is one of the few modern scholars to follow "Vetterle" as a political concept, but he consistently derives the meaning from the uncle relationship and does not sufficiently take into account the semantic shift that seems to have occurred, at least in southern Germany, by the early eighteenth century. By keeping with "uncle," he gives a benign cast to the institution and introduces a generational connotation to the system in the eighteenth century that I do not think is there: see Walker, *German Home Towns: Community, State, and General Estate 1648–1871* (Ithaca, 1971), pp. 56–63. Cf. the careful dating of the semantic shifts in Robert T. Anderson, "Changing Kinship in Europe," *Kroeber Anthropological Society Papers* 28 (1963), pp. 1–48, here 18–20.

[13] On the uncle/nephew relationship in the Middle Ages, see C. H. Bell, "The Sister's Son in the Medieval German Epic. A Study in the Survival of Matriliny," *University of California Publications in Modern Philology*, 10 (1920): 67–182; G. Duby, "In Northwestern France: The 'Youth' in Twelfth Century Aristocratic Society," in F. L. Cheyette, ed., *Lordship and Community in Medieval Europe* (New York, 1968), pp. 198–209.

few villages were likely to have been dominated politically by a cousin system throughout the whole period in which such politics were frequently commented upon. Nonetheless, there does seem to have been a general shift in concern and a change in the nature of the argument around 1740. The best and most extended text for the transition period that I have seen – provided for me by Hans Medick – comes from the village of Laichingen in 1738. The head magistrate wrote agitatedly and somewhat confusedly in his protocol book that people were not to address him familiarly as a relative. The passage is worth quoting in full because it demonstrates some of the linguistic strategies made possible by cousinship.

> In this village, the bad practice of calling the chief officer, as well as other officials and strangers on official business, cousin, not at all to their credit, has gotten out of hand. [This happens] when one or another villager, whether closely or distantly related to him, comes to the bureau or court or to some other proceedings with an outsider or fellow villager [and] calls him cousin. Thereby it often happens that the other party is intimidated and considers the term to be partisan. In order to prevent this and do away with it, it is positively forbidden to anyone by a fine of one Gulden to call the officer cousin when he sits in his office or court and officially represents the person of his gracious prince and lord, since I am neither father, son, brother, brother-in-law, nor cousin in office and court. Therefore one should take heed and abstain from unnecessary cousin discourse.[14]

There is nothing in the quotation to suggest that the practice of calling the chief official of the town "Vetter" was new. But at least there was a new sensitivity about the inappropriateness of such an address. Certainly the various opponents in business before the court interpreted the use of such language as partisan, and the term "parteiisch" is the one most often coupled with complaints about familial politics.[15] Kin were understood to provide fundamental ties for coordinate interests and to provide the core personnel for local syndicates. And clearly townspeople were making a subtle or not so subtle claim for favor by adopting the term of address for the chief magistrate. A clear understanding of the precise situation here can help clarify the structure of kin transactions before the shift to a new political culture in the 1740s.

Constitutionally, Laichingen was a peculiar place. It had the characteristics of

[14] Stadtarchiv Laichingen, *Ruog-Gerichts-Protokolle, 1734–43* (2 December 1738), pp. 129–30 : "[Es] hat dieses Orths die üble, Amtmann bey herrschaftlichen Geschäften sowohlen als andere Beamten und frembden Leuthen zu kainer Ehre gereichende Gewohnheith, also überhand genommen, dass wann ein oder andre Burger, der waith oder nahe mit demselben verwandt, vor Amt, Gericht, oder sonstige Verhandlung mit Frembden oder seinen Mitburger kommt, ihne einen Vetter heisset, wodurch manchmal geschiehet, dass eines solchen gegen Part abgeschröckt und den Spruch vor partheyisch hält: diesem aber zu begegnen und abzukommen wird hiemit ernstlich und bey einem Gulden Straf einem jeden verbotten, Amtmann, wann er im Amt oder Gericht sizet und als ein Diener die Persohn seines geehrten Fürsten und Herrn präsentiert, keinen Vetter zu heissen, massen ich weder Vatter, Sohn, Bruder, Schwager oder Vetter im Amt und Gericht bin, dahero man sich dessen wohl in Acht zu nehmen und des ohnnöthige Vetterlens Reden unterlassen hat."

[15] On the development of the notion and reality of "party," see Paul Nolte, "Gemeindeliberalismus: Zur lokalen Entstehung und sozialen Verankerung der liberalen Partei in Baden 1831–1855," *Historische Zeitschrift* 252 (1991): 57–93.

both a large village and a small town, but with a good degree of autonomy.[16] Somewhat isolated on the Swabian Alb, it had a large territory (*Markung*) with extensive agriculture but was also important as a weaving village. Hence there was constant tension between Laichingen and the town of Urach, the site of the linen-cloth trading monopoly. It was also a hotbed of radical pietism, sending missionaries as far away as Pennsylvania, Labrador, and the West Indies. If it had been a mere village, it would have had a Schultheiss elected from among its own ranks as its chief official. But a town – which usually also functioned as the center of an administrative district – would have had a *Vogt* or *Amtmann* appointed by the duke. At this period in its history, Laichingen had a subprefect, or *Untervogt* (*Unteramtmann*). In 1738 the office was filled by Philipp Jacob Waiblinger, who not only came from the town, but was also son of the pastor. One brother was a corrupt toll collector and another succeeded him in office. Philipp's uncle was the schoolmaster, married into the pietist Mack family, whose members were prominent town officials. Both families were linked through pietism and provided missionaries for the Moravian Brethren. Here is an illustration of the anthropological commonplace that the powerful and rich have more kin than the weak and poor. It is not just that powerful persons use their position to create lines of dependence and patronage in order to buttress their authority or extend their power; they also act as a dynamic center upon which people make claims and constitute themselves as part of the powerful individual's kinship orbit. Whether Untervogt Waiblinger was conscious of the irony when he spoke of *unnecessary* cousin discourse can be left to an estimation of his pietist gravity.

The situation in this example was typical for the period before the 1740s, although the text was formulated precisely in the context of a reconfiguration of kinship and village politics. Every case that I have examined from the second half of the eighteenth century and the List commission protocols show an *interlocking set of magistrates* who coordinated their interests through kinship. Before the 1740s and 1750s, however, a partisan group existed within the village or town population as a whole, coordinated through its connection to one or more of the magistrates. The group of relatives connected to a particular individual made up his or her *Freundschaft*, an institution that has sometimes been thought of as a clan (*Sippe*), although the term "clan" implies rather too much. In the anthropological literature, clan denotes an association whose membership is recruited through inheritance and marriage and whose activities are coordinated through hierarchies based on age, or wealth, or ascriptive rules.[17] And the members of a clan are conscious of themselves as a group. But the examples from Württemberg show no evidence of kinship consciousness beyond the networks developed by individuals out of various strands of patronage and ties of blood and marriage.

[16] The "village" is subject to an extended and subtle treatment by Hans Medick in his 1992 Habilitationsschrift, *Weben und Ueberleben in Laichingen 1650–1900. Lokalgeschichte als allgemeine Geschichte* (Vandenhoeck & Ruprecht: Göttingen, 1996).

[17] See George P. Murdock, *Social Structure* (New York, 1949), pp. 65–78.

Rather than an institutionalized clanlike collectivity, a Freundschaft was a shifting set of people in a particular person's orbit, and this set constituted an "ego-focused" network peculiar to that individual. The distinction between ego-focused networks and more or less bounded groups recruited on the basis of descent is a central one throughout this book. Such networks are less stable than descent groups and are continually being reconfigured according to the social, economic, and political fortunes of the person at the center. They constantly have to be reproduced, as is reflected in the modern term "networking." Sometimes the interlocking, overlapping intensity of a series of networks, together with the long-term association of families, "houses," and individuals as patrons and clients of one another justifies the word "clan" in the European literature on kinship, although for reasons given in Chapter 1, I prefer "kindred."[18]

Early eighteenth-century kindreds

The Württemberg commission investigations from the early eighteenth century illustrate clearly how a magistrate or two could build a political position or create a following on the basis of kinship connection.[19] In the village of Nehren, with a population of just under 500, the Schultheiss was removed from office for corruption, and in 1714 the villagers elected a member of the Gericht, Martin Dürr, to replace him. Dürr received a slight majority of the votes; however, several people petitioned to annul the election on the grounds that he had a very large kindred (Freundschaft) in the village. Predicting unrest and perhaps an open rebellion unless someone who did not have so many "friends" was chosen, they boosted the losing candidate whose votes had come from purely "unpartheyischen Persohnen." And in a document listing all his relatives in the village, Dürr's opponents concluded that his Freundschaft was steadily encompassing more and more people: "From this previously described kindred, it is to be considered how much this will spread among the villagers and increases indeed every day, although already complaints had been made about it many years ago."[20] In his report, the commissioner pointed out that it had been precisely the

[18] See also Martine Segalen's use of "kindred" in *Fifteen Generations of Bretons: Kinship and Society in Lower Brittany 1720–1980* (Cambridge, 1991), pp. 114–20. On the complex linkages between houses that constitute "clans," see Elisabeth Claverie and Pierre Lamaison, *L'impossible mariage: Violence et parenté en Gévaudan 17ᵉ, 18ᵉ, et 19ᵉ siècles* (Paris, 1982), pp. 272–8. See the contrasting notion of "lineage," in Gérard Delille, *Famille et proprieté dans le royaume de Naples (xvᵉ–xixᵉ siècle),* Bibliothèque des écoles françaises d'athènes et de rome, 259 (Rome and Paris, 1985), pp. 42–5; on lineage quarters, pp. 89–97. I will come back to these issues in Chapter 21.

[19] HSAS, A214, Bü 921, "Nehren. Georg Krauss gegen den Schultheissen Hans Hauser und Cons. wegen Injurien" (1714–18). There is a fascinating discussion of kinship dynamics and politics in Nehren by Carola Lipp in F. A. Köhler, *Nehren: Eine Dorfchronik des Spätaufklärung,* ed. Carola Lipp, Wolfgang Kaschuba, and Eckart Frahm, Untersuchungen des Ludwig-Uhland-Instituts der Universität Tübingen, vol. 52 (Tübingen, 1981), pp. 164–6. Lipp provides the best introduction to date on "Vetterleswirtschaft" – though she does not take up the question of changes in kinship organization over time.

[20] HSAS, A214, Bü 921: "Auss diser vor geschribene Freindschafft ist zu Erachten, wie wirdt Es

large Freundschaft of the previous Schultheiss that had been the cause of all the troubles. From the commissioner's viewpoint, the well-integrated kinship group had enabled the chief magistrate to cheat various ducal and village accounts dealing, among other things, with wine, excise taxes, tithes, threshing, and sheep-herding. During the 23 years that the newly elected Martin Dürr had served on the court, his Freundschaft had increased considerably. The entire report expressed the problem as one of the *extension* of kinship connection by an official *into the community*. Interlocking politics among the magistrates were not considered an issue, despite the fact that building a party within the Bürgerschaft had to include some fellow partisans from among the ruling officials.

The situation described here was similar to one in Schönaich near Böblingen from the early 1720s.[21] *There the Schultheiss had been dismissed because of his disastrous conduct of office and many personal debts. The regional official (Vogt) had considerable problems finding a replacement, since a similar situation of partisanship built on kinship was to be feared: "He almost did not know where he could select a competent subject, since everyone hung together as one chain because of close relatives."*[22] *In this early case, there had indeed been a packed court. The newly elected Schultheiss, Jacob Bender, was the niece's husband of the old one, whose corruption had led to a village rebellion and the arrival of troops. Bender's stepgrandfather was Bürgermeister, and his brother-in-law was on the Gericht. The Vogt referred to the situation as "deeply rooted nepotism and destructive collusion." The earlier Schultheiss, Jacob Rebmann, had helped elect his son and half-brother to the Bürgermeister offices, and the closest relatives of the Schultheiss held all the best village jobs. As often occurs in such cases, one villager could not remember any accusations against the Schultheiss, "without doubt because he was an intimate of the Schultheiss, and his cousin."*[23] *The Schultheiss pursued his office with "vengeance" (Rachgier) and "violence."*

In some instances, a particular kingroup saw a magistrate position as belonging to themselves. In 1732 in Neckartailfingen, the Familie of the previous Schultheiss, having failed to have the successor elected from among their own ranks, "stood in hate against" the new one.[24] *The major opponent of the old Schultheiss, Michael Bliem, had been coopted onto the Gericht in order to silence him after the Heinrich Familie and their supporters "sought in every way and manner to bring him into their party."*[25] *And the Heinrich family tried to work their influence by bringing charges against the*

sich under der Burger Schafft Ein raisset, und also noch daglich vermehret, da doch schon vor viehlen Jahren darüber ist geclagt worden."

21 HSAS, A214, Bü 184, "Schönaich (Böblingen). Untersuchung der mehrfaltigen Klagen der Bürgerschaft gegen den Schuldheissen Jacob Rebmann, Unbottmässigkeit der Bürgerschaft und militarische Execution" (1721–43).

22 HSAS, A214, Bü 184: "dass er fast nicht wisse, wo er zu Schonaich ein recht tüchtiges Subjectum nemen sollte, massen alles um der nahen anverwandtschafft willen wie eine kette zusammen hange."

23 HSAS, A214, Bü 184: "ohne Zweifel weilen er dess Schultheissen intimus und mit ihme Geschwisterkind."

24 HSAS, A214, Bü 739, "Neckartenzlingen. Commissions Acta über den Schultheissen Johannes Mayer" (1732–40).

25 HSAS, A214, Bü 739: "auf alle weiss und weg ihne in Ihre Partie einzubringen gesucht."

new Schultheiss. At the beginning of their efforts, the son-in-law of the deceased Schultheiss visited the schoolmaster, Rommel, to get him to write up a few complaints. When that failed, they put pressure on his cousin to persuade him to cooperate. As Rommel put it: "Because the Schultheiss position escaped the Heinrich family, that is why so much trouble has arisen in the locality, since it has taken every opportunity . . . and gathered whatsoever was possible against the Schultheiss.[26]

This case from Schönaich again reveals village politics organized around interlocking kindreds that solidified their position through connection to one or more officeholders. The story is filled with bloody street battles between factions, attempts to seduce enemies through bribes, and violence and intimidation on the part of the chief magistrate. The stakes were high: they consisted of both honor and livelihood. Despite the fact that different village strata were competing with one another here, the forces at play cannot be described as class politics. A poor relative of the Schultheiss was looking for pickings as a cowherd or field guard, or a well-connected carpenter would expect to get the sheep-barn repair contract. Kinship groups were vertically organized and frequently maintained their integrity by violent confrontation with competing "families." And it was a high-risk game to attempt to topple a Schultheiss. In Oeschingen in the 1730s, the plaintiffs had to sell their property to pay for the stiff fines and investigation costs for their failed attempt.[27] Indeed, the Schultheiss profited by buying up some of the condemned property of his enemies.

A new alliance system

How did the political structure of kinship change after the 1740s, during the period of "Vetterleswirtschaft"? In the main, there was a decline in the prevalence of kindred or Freundschaften coordinated by one or two figures strategically placed among the magistrates – the Schultheiss, Gericht (from which the Bürgermeister were usually chosen), and Rat. Instead, the members of the magistrates, representing different families, systematically created alliances with each other. Men already on the court drew closer together by arranging the marriage of their children (thereby becoming Gegenschweher or co-parents-in-law) or by becoming in-laws of one another – one married the other's sister, wife's sister, brother's widow, or the like. Similarly, men coopted their sons-in-law, stepsons, and occasionally, either illegally or with a formal dispensation, their sons and nephews onto the court. Prominent, of course, were cousins who served with one another. Although it was illegal for close kin to serve on the Gericht together, each institution – Schultheiss, Gericht, and Rat – was treated separately, so that,

[26] HSAS, A214, Bü 739: "und weil dann die Schultheissen Stelle von der Heinrischen Familie gefallen, so sey bissher alles ohnheil in dem Flecken entstanden, da sie allerhand gelegenheit gesucht . . . und was immer moglich gewesen, wider den Schultheissen gesammelt."

[27] HSAS, A214, Bü 926, "Oeschingen. Untersuchung der klagen der Bürgerschaft gegen den Schuldheissen, Georg Friedr. Mök daselbst so wie auch der Unbotmässigkeit der Bürgerschaft" (1716–39).

for example, there was no legal impediment to having three brothers among the magistrates so long as one was Schultheiss, one was on the Gericht (and eligible to be Bürgermeister), and one was on the Rat. Many charges brought against a village political establishment suggested that the magistrates had become a syndicate of allied families. But the investigating officers frequently threw out the charges because there was no violation of the letter of the law. Nonetheless, for the purposes of this discussion, the list of relationships provided by the villagers indicates their views about which relatives were likely to act together in collusion.

Before moving on to the villagers' notions about close relatives, I want to document briefly my contention about kin politics during the second half of the eighteenth century. This is just the first step in the argument, however: the complexities of kinship alliance will be the subject of the rest of the book. Unfortunately, the richly rewarding commission reports available for the eighteenth century do not exist for the nineteenth, so it is difficult to determine how long the system of Vetterleswirtschaft dominated rural Württemberg life. Elements of it are probably still alive today, and certainly it can be shown that the alliance system put into place around the mid-eighteenth century was still going strong through the 1860s. Yet the tight oligarchical control of village institutions by allied families does not seem to have survived past the mid nineteenth century and was already challenged significantly earlier. The question of when the system broke apart will be taken up later. First, it is important to understand how villagers talked about kinship and power during the second half of the eighteenth century.

A typical case comes from Bissingen in 1756.[28] In this instance, when members were elected to the Gericht they were not yet related, at least not as closely as they eventually were. The Schultheiss and one of the Richter subsequently became co-parents-in-law (Gegenschweher), and two of the Richter also became Gegenschweher. Two others were actually first cousins (*Geschwisterkind*, literally: siblings' children), but during their tenure became brothers-in-law, and two others who were more extended (*etwas weitläuffer*) cousins also became brothers-in-law. The tax estimator was son of the Schultheiss, and the court clerk (*Gerichtsschreiber*) was his father-in-law. In this particular case, charges had been brought by one disgruntled villager who wanted the court clerk's job, but most of the villagers had no complaint about the interlocking alliances of the magistrates. Such alliances were constantly being constructed: people with power arranged for their children to marry, and cousins sought to reinforce their interconnections by marriage.

There are many similar cases from the 1750s, when these political alliances were first being constructed.[29] The coordinated adm nistration of a village

[28] HSAS, A214, Bü 479, Bissingen (Kirchheim unter Teck). "Commissions-und Inquisitions-Acta über den Schultheissen Bunz" (1756–9).

[29] HSAS, A214, Bü 1037, "Enzweyhingen. Schultheiss Böhmler. Commissions und Inquisitions Acta" (1755–8); Bü 1111, "Lauterbach. Winnenden. Untersuchung . . . gegen Schultheiss und Richter" (1755–6); Bü 479; Bü 517; Bü 518, "Gerlingen. Commisarische Untersuchung verschie-

through kin could occasion complaints from disgruntled and disaffected individuals, or it could become the target of an opposition syndicate. In most cases the Schultheiss worked in collusion with the regional Vogt, or Oberamtmann, who quite frequently dismissed any charges brought by disaffected villagers. Only a more serious rebellion brought an investigation by an outside commissioner, who sometimes probed the connection between the village magistrates and county (*Amt*) officials. On many occasions, the issue was left vaguely understated: in Oberlenningen, several members of the magistrates "stand in rather close affinity and consanguineal relation, whereby it is indeed possible that the village has not exactly managed its income for the best."[30]

The density of relations is illustrated by a 1771 case from Weinsheim near Maulbronn, where the "whole Rathaus was composed from one kindred."[31] *The Schultheiss and a Richter (member of the Gericht) were first cousins. Two other Richter were the Schultheiss's brothers-in-law. Two of the Richter were co-parents-in-law. A member of the Rat was the Schultheiss's brother, and another the nephew of a Richter. The village of Dusslingen (1765) had a clear "Vetter Gericht," containing the son and brother-in-law of the Schultheiss.*[32]

The politics of village magistrates

What accounts for the systematic construction of alliances among village magistrates from the late 1740s onward? As genealogical evidence for Neckarhausen shows, the leaders in the redeployment of kinship were the magistrates themselves, who utilized both innovative marriage and ritual kinship strategies to coordinate their own interests and to refashion the village's intercourse with the state. Not until a whole generation or two later (1780s) would the wealthier landholders as a group adopt the same politics of alliance formation. The system, which eventually acted as a kind of matrix for class formation, was not in the first instance prompted by class interests or by class dynamics: during the first half of the eighteenth century both landholders and artisans were represented among the magistrates of a village such as Neckarhausen, and artisans were only

dener Beschwerden des Christoph Bokel u. cons. gegen der Commun Vorstehern" (1755–6); Bü 550, "Ossweil. Ludwigsburg. Commissarische Untersuchung . . . wider den Schultheiss Trostel" (1756–9); Bü 551, "Asperg. Commissions-und Inquisitions Acta den gewesenen Schultheissen Adam Renz allda enthaltend" (1756–63); Bü 925, "Oeschingen. Untersuchung der Delata des Johann Heinrich Rudolph gegen den Schultheissen und die Commun Vorsteher daselbst" (1755–61).

30 HSAS, A214, Bü 481, "Oberlenningen. Untersuchungs Commission . . . wider . . . Johannes Gollmer" (1755–7): "in zimlich genau-und naher Freund und Verwandtschafft stehen, dahero freylich auch kommen mag . . . dass der *Commun* eben nicht zum besten, mit denen *Revenu* gehausset worden."

31 HSAS, A214, Bü 559, "Weinsheim. Maulbronn. Untersuchung der Klagsachen . . . gegen den dasigen Schuldheissen Matth. Benzinger u. cons." (1771–3): "dass das ganze Rathhaus zu Weinsheim aus einer freundschafft bestehe."

32 HSAS, A214, Bü 930, "Dusslingen. Untersuchung der von der Bürgerschaft gegen den Amtmann Bührer daselbst vorgebrachten Klagen und die unter der Bürgerschaft entstandene Unruhe betr" (1765–84).

squeezed out of power during the ensuing decades. And although wealthier members of the village had greater opportunity to join the Gericht or become Schultheiss, the exclusive oligarchical monopoly of office by the village well-to-do characteristic of the later period was by no means evident around 1700. The beginnings of cousin alliances were worked out among the political leaders of the village, who included peasant proprietors and artisans, as well as both wealthy and more modest members of the village. Cousins could, of course, be important for people before the 1740s, as in the examples from Schönaich, where a man seemed ready to perjure himself for his Schultheiss cousin, and from Neckartailfingen, where a faction tried to corrupt a schoolmaster through a cousin.[33] In both these instances, the reporting commissioner noted the details about the cousin connection because he knew his audience would immediately understand that the relationship established claims of support between people. After 1740 or so, villagers constructed a new alliance system through marriage, ritual kinship (godparentage), crisis kinship (guardianship), gender tutelage (*Kriegsvogtschaft*),[34] property transactions, cooperation in production, and political coordination out of consanguineal relationships that had always been marked as potentially supportive but that were redeployed in a new network of social connectors, which redirected the flow of resources, emotions, and commitments. All of this remains to be demonstrated in subsequent chapters.

Every village had many resources to manage, whose distribution could affect the levels of subsistence of its members and the possibilities for accumulation. Any community with forestland provided ample opportunity for significant favoritism, but there were many other ways to give an edge to someone politically connected to the village administration – extra animals in the sheep or cowherd, a few days' sheepfold on arable strips, pasture rights, a roof-repair contract for the Rathaus, inflated receipts, favorable real estate assessments, a good credit rating, or assignment of a wardship. But by far the most significant way to pursue advantage in a village was no doubt to gain control of the resources flowing out

[33] In the case from Nehren just discussed (HSAS, A214, Bü 921), the plaintiffs objected to the election of Dürr because of his considerable Freundschaft in the village. The list of Freunde includes, among others, five brothers, a father-in-law, a son-in-law, three first cousins (Geschwisterkind), a brother-in-law's nephew, a sister's daughter's husband, a brother's daughter's husband, a brother's son, a sister's husband, a sister's husband's brother (the previous Schultheiss), and a cousin's husband, together with the closest relatives (*nechster Befreind*) of his wife – her three brothers-in-law, two husbands of her brothers' widows, four first cousins (Geschwisterkind), and husband of her brother's daughter. The couple also were connected to many people through godparentage. This list includes blood relatives up to nephews, the husbands of nieces, and cousins, and various affinal kin up to sister's husband's brother, cousin's husband, and the marital successors of brothers (brother's widow's husband). Marriage brought a man the potential support of his wife's kin, and successive marriages could be used to build a very large kindred.

[34] On the institution of Kriegsvogtschaft, see Chapter 1 in this volume, and Sabean, *Property*, pp. 211–18. Whenever adult women appeared before a court to transact business, they were assigned a Kriegsvogt to assist them, to read and explain all documents, and to attain their consent. See also David Warren Sabean, "Soziale und kulturelle Aspekte der Geschlechtsvormundschaft im 18. und 19. Jahrhundert," in Ute Gerhard, ed., *Handbuch für die Rechtsgeschichte der Frau* (Beck Verlag: Munich, forthcoming [1997]).

of it, that is, the taxes, tithes, and rents appropriated in one way or another by the prince and state officials. A glance at the many commission investigations of local magistrates for corruption and malfeasance in office reveals that the internal politics of most villages came to revolve around the organization of deliveries of state levies, those payments collected under the rubric *herrschaftliche Interesse*: tithes on grain, straw, hay, and wine; excise taxes on wine and schnapps; tolls; duties on livestock sales; and rents on land held in tenure from the duke or some ducal institution, a large proportion of which were collected in kind.

Any village that hoped to shave some percentage points off the deliveries to outside institutions had to organize its responsible agents tightly. And, of course, a great proportion of the production of a village was at stake: some 20 percent of the grain and wine harvest was channeled to state storage barns and cellars, along with considerable amounts of straw and hay. All these deliveries were organized by village officers under the control of the busy and often corruptible county Vogt or cameral officials. There were ample opportunities to falsify the count of tithe sheaves on the field or to overlook a certain number of barrels of wine going into people's cellars. Good, clean straw frequently left a village only to arrive inexplicably at the prince's barns wet and sour. Many Schultheissen kept separate account books for threshed grain, one to keep track for themselves and another to present to cameral officers. All of this "fraud" – and I have indicated only a few of the myriad ways it could be carried out – could only have been successful in the presence of widespread collusion. The accountable village officers either had to have the cooperation of those in the know or must have been able to intimidate them sufficiently. Moreover, the system was clearly easiest to operate with the connivance of county officials, although villagers had to balance their own interests against those of outsiders. Even when a Vogt received payoffs for colluding in this or that fraudulent delivery, he did not know everything that was going on.

At the time, villages were greatly interested in minimizing what was appropriated by the prince and the state. But there was also an internal differentiation of those who profited from a conspiracy. Village members frequently gave tacit assent to cooperation among the magistrates, whose success brought many of them some kind of reward. Yet jealousy and dissatisfaction with the distribution of the spoils could lead to quarrels and the betrayal of village secrets to state officials. Furthermore, if the village was large enough, the disaffected parties could develop into contending factions that either peacefully alternated in dividing up the spoils or fought it out over the question of rights to participate in the system of corruption. By the mid eighteenth century, the whole situation had changed. The very fact that so many investigations of corruption were launched in 1755 indicates the state had mobilized to make the collection of dues more efficient. During that decade a reorganization, streamlining, and regulation of the village constitution was incorporated in a detailed handbook for village magistrates – the new *Commun-Ordnung* – which put into place an elaborate auditing system designed to balance and check local against county officials and administrative, clerical, and financial officials against one another.[35] In the face of aggressive state monitoring of the flow of village tribute, villagers could protect themselves only by tightening the coordination of their resistance – and for that, the one effective instrument at hand was the close alliance of magistrates among themselves: through marriage if possible; through cooperation with uncles, nephews, and cousins; and through the flexible vehicle of ritual kinship.

The state's more efficient collection was only part of the equation, however. A great deal more produce was now moving from the village to the ducal granaries, barns, and cellars, and new amounts of grain and the like were available for exploitation. The eighteenth century saw an expansion of viniculture and the extension of arable crops onto newly cleared or drained land. More careful measuring of the territory of each village made it possible to monitor the quality of arable and meadowland with increasing precision.[36] The state also moved to develop a grain storage system and to this end called on every villager to contribute a certain amount of the harvest, which would provide reserves to draw on in case of a harvest failure. With the settling down of conditions after the Thirty Years' War and a refilling of the villages with a dense population by the 1740s and 1750s, the traditional system of agricultural exploitation reached its height. A better-regulated and expanded bureaucratic apparatus was in a more advantageous position to see that such forms of surplus extraction as tithes yielded closer to their maximum return.

The grain tithe clearly illustrates the way in which village magistrates and coordinated syndicates were able to hold back some of the produce bound for state granaries. Until well into the eighteenth century, the characteristic manner of levying the tithe was to auction it off to the highest bidder after the village magistrates and county officials had estimated the return shortly before the harvest. Already in 1604 an edict from the duke mentioned "Parteien" who had conspired to rig the bidding.[37] In 1660 a regulation spelled out how villagers managed to control the annual tithe auction: "Subjects secretly divide themselves up, making two, three, or more gangs, and come to an arrangement with one another to the effect that if one party this year leases the tithe, the next year that one steps back and gives place to the others in the queue."[38] This system of

[35] "Commun-Ordnung, vom 1. Juni 1758," in Reyscher, vol. 14, pp. 537–777. See the discussion of the state auditing system in David Warren Sabean, *Power in the Blood* (Cambridge, 1984), pp. 19–20.

[36] During the 1720s and 1730s, officials undertook a revision of the tax valuation system for each village, measuring each plot of land and classifying it according to its productivity. The *Steuerrevisionsakten* are in HSAS, A261.

[37] Reyscher, vol. 16, p. 205: "Generalrescript in Betreff der Behandlung der Fruchtzehentverleihungen" (6.6.1604). See also "Generalreskript in Betr. der Beschränkung der Fruchtpacht-Nachlässe" (3.6.1605), p. 207. The "Zweite Zehend-Ordnung" refers to collusion (27.6.1618), p. 213. Also "Allgemeines Verbot von Parteilichkeiten bei dem Verkauf von Früchten auf den herrschaftlichen Kästen" (24.3.1623), p. 359; "Generalreskript die sorgfältigere Wahrnehmung des herrschaftlichen Interessen beim Geldeinzug . . ." (20.1.1624), p. 361.

[38] "Anordnung gegen die heimlichen Uebereinkünfte bei Zehendverleihungen" (24.4.1660), in

conspiratorial bidding always had required some organization, but in the face of greater pressure from outside officials, and perhaps also because of the greater stakes, villagers had to coordinate their activities in a more integrated way, which gave rise to a new alliance system. In fact, the first mention in an edict of kin playing a role in collusive bidding occurs in 1735.[39]

In Neckarhausen, the reordering of the system took place around 1750, and control of the tithe deliveries was the chief motive prompting oligarchical collusion, although administration of the grain reserves and wine excise taxes also offered occasions for political maneuvering.[40] As far as the tithe lease was concerned, when village magistrates worked out a deal with the Nürtingen Vogt involving kickbacks in exchange for greater village autonomy, some villagers were squeezed out of the spoils. It was in this context that in 1751 two villagers, Adam Falter and Hans Jerg Speidel, were censured and fined by the Vogt – Sattler by name – for calling some of the partners in the annual tithe lease "scoundrels" (*Schelmen*) and suggesting that the tithe auction was dishonest.[41] The Vogt told them "in the future to keep a better lock on their well-known, constantly too wide-open mouths."[42] It is significant that the term "Vetterle" appears in the records about the same time that villagers were commenting on issues having to do with the tithe lease and that various officials were being disciplined for fraudulent handling of grain reserves and wine excises. In 1749 Johannes Waldner was very upset because he had not been coopted onto the Gericht, especially after he

Reyscher, vol. 16, pp. 410–11: "Undertanen . . . sich heimlich separiren, zwo, drei oder mehr Rotten machen, und sich dergestalten mit einander vergleichen, dass wenn die eine Parthey dises Jahr den Zehenden bestanden, selbige Künfftiges Jahr zuruck gehen, und die andere Anstehen müssen."

39 "Allgemeine Vorschriften hinsichtlich der genaueren Wahrnehmung des herrschaftlichen Interesse bei der Frucht-und Wein-Verwaltung" (15.5.1735), in Reyscher, vol. 16, p. 591. See also "Allgemeine Vorschriften die Wahrung des herrschaftlichen Interesse bei Zehen-und Gulten-Verpachtungen betr." (19.7.1736), p. 591. The "Generalreskript des diesjährigen Ernd-Generale betr.," vol. 16, Abt. 2, p. 16: "Die heimliche- und in Vorausverabredete Gemeinschaft eines Zehend-Pachts, welche sich öfters ganze Gemeinden, oder nach einem unter ihnen festgesetsten Turnus abwechslungsweise einzelne Parthien der Orts-Einwohnerschaft, zu offenbarem Schaden." And see finally the "Ernd-General-Rescript für das Jahr 1808 . . ." (17.6.1808), p. 93.

40 There was an order from the Vogt to ensure that every villager maintain a portion of grain in the village reserve barn; *Vogtruggericht,* vol. 1, f. 23 (3.2.1750). It was pointed out that at the 1749 wine harvest villagers had refused to take their grapes to the duke's wine cellar to be pressed but took them home. The Schultheiss was told to fine the whole village if necessary; f. 22 (3.2.1750). The next year a Richter was fined and severely reprimanded for stealing two bunches of grapes from a neighbor's vineyard. Although the offended party had only wanted a reprimand, the Vogt insisted on a fine because the *herrschaftliche Interesse* (tithe and excise tax) had been defrauded. By the end of the year, he had even been suspended from his position on the Gericht; f. 28 (15.2.1751); f. 30 (14.12.1751).

41 *Vogtruggericht,* vol. 1, f. 29 (14.12.1751): "es gehe schelmisch zu."

42 *Vogtruggericht,* vol. 1, f. 29 (14.12.1751): "ihre wohlbekannte immer zu weit aufsperrende Mäuler besser zäumen." During that same year there was a case in which the tithe lessee and the Schultheiss had various sheaves and threshed grain delivered by one of the laborers to their own barns instead of the tithe barn: vol. 1, f. 27 (15.2.1751). On that same date the Bürgermeister, Fridrich Schober, was fined for not entering the sale of part of the village grain reserves into the account book: f. 25.

had bought everyone drinks during his campaign: "It is now a right cousins court."[43]

In 1755 the Vogt in Nürtingen was removed from office for, among other things, colluding with the Neckarhausen Schultheiss over the tithe lease, and while still under investigation, he committed suicide.[44] Contrary to ducal regulations, he had worked out a deal with the Neckarhausen magistrates to allow each villager to take his or her own tithe sheaves home instead of leaving them in the field to be collected. From then on, the tithe was to be reckoned according to the dimensions of a parcel, not as before by counting out every tenth sheaf as it stood on the field. According to the investigating officer, this form of collection inclined bidders to be cautious. Not only did the best land end up with a tithe as low as the worst land, but people also delivered their worst grain. As a result, the duke ended up with less grain of poorer quality. Furthermore, there were rumors that the lessees had substituted even worse-quality grain than they had collected. The partners in the tithe lease were not put on oath, and they kept private accounts not subject to public review. They deducted various costs for meals, wages, and honoraria from the gross. And they produced accounts that estimated the size of the fields downwards and "sinfully" miscalculated the assessments. The whole system had been tried out in 1751/52, precisely when Adam Falter and Hans Jerg Speidel had spoken up, and the investigation of Sattler in 1755 alluded to considerably more conflict than had come before the local court. In his defense, Sattler said that Neckarhausen was a three-quarter-hour trip to Nürtingen and that many of the tithe sheaves disappeared on the way. He had left the entire responsibility to the Neckarhausen Schultheiss, who oversaw the collection registers and monitored each producer's share by himself. Sattler only carried out an estimation before the harvest and stood by as the tithe lease was auctioned in the presence of the entire Bürgerschaft. As far as the investigating commissioner was concerned, all of the evidence suggested that Vogt Sattler had been taking bribes from the lessees.[45]

Neckarhausen fits into this general picture of political conflict in the various villages of the duchy. During the late 1740s, a *Vetterlesgericht* was established, just about the same time that a collusive system of tithe collection was worked out. The Schultheiss and Vogt collaborated with each other, and the Vogt used his office to suppress dissent in the village. He selectively proceeded against various villagers and made a great show out of protecting the "herrschaftliche Interesse" at the same time that he was helping set up a cartel in the village and taking bribes. Of course, he may have been more honest than he appeared and his suicide may have been the result of deep despair over unjust accusations. But

[43] *Vogtruggericht*, vol. 1, f. 12 (10.2.1749): "Es seye jetzo ein recht Vätterlens Gericht." He was warned not to slander the village magistrates to whom he owed obedience and respect.

[44] HSAS, A214, Bü 740, "Inquisitions Commissions Acta über die . . . selbst entleibten Rath und Vogt Sattler zu Nürtingen" (1755).

[45] This case and the politics of village kinship will be discussed in greater detail in Cohort II, Chapter 10.

in that reading of the evidence, he had been used as a more or less willing tool by a newly established, clever, well-coordinated village oligarchy, led by the Schultheiss. In any event, issues of tithe collection made their way into the records for a few years early in the 1750s but then there followed many years of silence. It was only with the establishment of a system of tight coordination of kin around the village Gericht that corruption was openly talked about and entered the public record. Within a few short years, the oligarchy had commanded silence. The context of all of this will be investigated closely later on, but it should be recognized here that Neckarhausen constructed its Vetterle system about the same time that other villages across the duchy were doing so and that that system was closely bound up with the politics of surplus extraction.

The view from inside a village about what constituted an improperly packed court – a Vetterlesgericht – differed from that of state officials, who considered the matter not in terms of effective coordination of interests or the dynamics of alliance but from the letter of the law. Even then, individuals could petition for a ducal dispensation from its provisions, sending the plea through the county Vogt, whose backing was almost always approved in Stuttgart. Frequently, however, the Vogt simply accepted an election and reported on its results to the ducal council without mentioning the fact that relatives illegally sat together. Beginning with the law codes of the sixteenth century, the duchy forbade close relatives from sitting on the Gericht together, although there was never, as already pointed out, a problem with having relatives in the three parts of the magistrate system – Schultheiss, Gericht, and Rat. The principle throughout the eighteenth century was that court members could not be related up through second cousins, or as in-laws up to first cousins.[46] Toward the end of the century, edicts were prom-

[46] The Württemberg laws had always forbidden close relatives to sit on the magistrate assemblies together, although there had always been the possibility of a dispensation. There does not seem to have been too much practical control until the second and third decades of the nineteenth century. See "3. Hofgerichtsordnung" of 1557, in Reyscher, vol. 4, p. 109. The "2. Landrecht" of 1567 objected to people serving on a Gericht who were related by blood, vol. 4, p. 192. In the "3. Landrecht" of 1610, vol. 5, pp. 3–358, it was forbidden to have two members of a Gericht who were related to each other as second cousins or as in-laws up to first cousins (3. Grad Blutsfreundschaft, 2. Grad Schwägerschaft). According to the "General Reskript, die unstatthafte Verwandtschaft der Stadt-und Amtsschreiber mit den Ober-und Stabsbeamten betr." (25.7.1786), vol. 6, p. 668, these officials were not allowed to be, or become, closely related. This was specified more closely six years later in the "General Reskript, die unstatthafte Verwandtschaft der Stadt-, Amts-, und Kloster-Schreiber mit den Ober-und Stabs-Beamten betr." (19. 3. 1792), ibid., pp. 686–7, which said that they were not allowed to be related in the collateral line in the second degree of Verwandtschaft or Schwägerschaft. The "General-Reskript, die Beschränkung der Dispensationen von der Verwandtschaft zwischen Magistrats-Personen betr." (13. 6. 1795), vol. 14, p. 1103–4: "Die Magistrate . . . zum Theil aus mehreren Personen bestehen, welche mit einander gegen die Verordnung unsers Landrechts . . . verwandt sind." Such people were supposed to get dispensations, which were not to be given out lightly. The "K. Verordnung, die Dispensation von dem Verbot der Verwandtschaft unter den Mitgliedern der Gemeinde-Räte betr." (19. 8. 1819), in ibid., p. 1202, said that to get a dispensation, the person had to be of excellent quality and win an absolute majority of votes. "See also the "Erlass des K. Justiz-Ministerium an den Pupillensenat des K. Obertribunals und Gerichtshofs in – betr. die Dispensations-Erteilung von zu nahe Verwandtschaft, zum Behuf der Aufnahme in das Waisengericht oder in das Oberamts-Gericht" (4. 3. 1823), vol. 7, p. 1125. This contains a form for seeking a dispensation.

ulgated to restrict the possibility of dispensations, but as late as 1795 the wording makes clear that the principles were honored only in the breach. In 1819 the lawgivers still allowed dispensations where a candidate had won an absolute majority of the votes and was "well qualified."

The villagers' viewpoint

It would be useful to look at all the cases in which villagers perceived improper kinship combinations among village magistrates in order to determine which kinds of relatives, from their point of view, were thought to have coordinate interests.[47] For the second half of the eighteenth century, I have found twelve

[47] In Enzweihingen in 1755, the Schultheiss and Bürgermeister were brothers-in-law (*leiblich geschwägert*), which was quite within the letter of the law, since there was no regulation against the Schultheiss being related to members of the Gericht, from which the Bürgermeister were chosen; HSAS, A214, Bü 1037. They "directed everything in the village, and the rest of the Richter were permitted to say practically nothing, but were there only to give their signatures." In Buch near Winnenden in 1755, the Schultheiss and a Richter were brothers-in-law; HSAS, A214, Bü 1114, "Buch. Winnenden. Untersuchung . . . gegen Vogt Pistorius . . . und Schultheiss und Richter . . ." (1755–9). Although all the Gericht and Rat members in Weilimdorf (1755) were closely related, only three members of the Rat were within the forbidden degrees as second cousins – which was not illegal because the law covered only the Gericht; HSAS, A214, Bü 276, "Weyll im Dorff. Commissions und Inquisition Acta . . ." (1755–8). In Bissingen near Kirchheim/Teck (1756), upon election, none of the magistrates had been related; HSAS, A214, Bü 479. Now the Schultheiss was a co-parent-in-law (Gegenschweher) with the most senior Richter. Two other Richter were also Gegenschweher, and two were distant cousins who became brothers-in-law. Apparently two others were first cousins. Various officers of the village were close relatives of the Schultheiss, who had appointed his son as tax assessor and his brother-in-law as court clerk (*Gerichtsschreiber*). The "Vetterlensgericht" in Ditzingen (1755) mentioned earlier contained a co-parent-in-law, and uncle and nephew (*Bruderssohn*), and a man and his godparent (*Gevatter*); HSAS, A214, Bü 517. A nice example of in-law connections is provided by Gerlingen (1755); A214, Bü 518. One Richter's grandson married the Bürgermeister's daughter, and the Bürgermeister's son married a Richter's daughter. Two Bürgermeister were married to two sisters, and one Richter was married to the Schultheiss's wife's sister. The two tax assessors, one being the Schultheiss, were brothers. In Asperg (1756), the Bürgermeister was a brother-in-law (*leiblicher Schwager*) of the Schultheiss; HSAS, A214, Bü 551. Various plaintiffs in the village of Oeschingen were concerned about the Freundschaft among the magistrates; HSAS, A214, Bü 925. The son-in-law of the Schultheiss sat on the Gericht and had taken over many village offices, including the sheepfold accounts, fire and building inspection, and fire and building wood conveyance (*Holtzgeber*). He in turn was the brother-in-law of the court clerk, who was a member of the Rat. Two first cousins (*Geschwisterkind*) were Bürgermeister (and therefore also on the Gericht). Each of them had a son-in-law on the Rat. Various members of the magistrates were co-parents-in-law. With regard to the "Vetter Gericht" in Dusslingen (1765), the Schultheiss's son and brother-in-law were on the Gericht "wherein otherwise various prohibited degrees were also to be met with"; HSAS, A214, Bü 930. "In Weinsheim the whole Rathaus consisted of one Freundschaft" (1771); HSAS, A214, Bü 559. The Schultheiss and one Richter were first cousins, and with two others he was brother-in-law. One brother-in-law had a co-parent-in-law on the Gericht with himself. A brother of the Schultheiss was on the Rat, and another Rat member was nephew of a Richter. According to the Schultheiss, some of these people became related to each other only after elected, while the others got dispensations. In Neckarrems (1785) a father and son served on the Gericht; HSAS, A214 Bü 1059, "Neckarrems. Commissions-Acten . . . in Klagsachen gegen Schultheiss Rösch . . ." (1785–7). Freundschaft and Anverwandtschaft among the magistrates were the foundation of serious corruption in Undingen (1791); HSAS, A214 Bü 1023, "Undingen: Delation gegen Schultheiss Bulach . . ." (1791–1805). There the Schultheiss was brother-in-law to one of the orphan's court

cases in which villagers complained about their magistrates being too closely related or expressly referred to a Vetter-Gericht. Direct cousins played some role, especially between the Schultheiss and Gericht or Rat, the Gericht and Rat, and even among Rat members – all such relations being legal. But among Richter there were also a few first and second cousins, in principle subject to ducal permission. In one instance, distant cousins had drawn closer to one another through marriage. It is clear from the evidence (altogether nine instances) that the chief way of constructing an interlocking clique between the Schultheiss and the Gericht and Rat was through brothers-in-law. And villagers found a strategy of two men marrying two sisters to be prima facie evidence of collusive activity. Among Richter, the most frequent form of alliance was that of co-parent-in-law, where two older men cemented their relationships by arranging for the marriage of their children (seven instances). Here again there was nothing illegal, nor was there in the example of two men married to two sisters, or of a man serving with his brother's son-in-law. But such relationships all elicited local complaints of "Vetter-Gericht." And magistrates were also all criss-crossed with godparents.

A good example of the construction of alliance and the dynamics of village politics comes form Kleinheppach near Waiblingen (1791).[48] *The conflict there arose over the issue of coopting a new Richter who was related to other Richter already in office. In fact, he had two "brothers-in-law" and three "cousins" already serving, which gave him five of the seven votes. A deputation of the community spoke of an "increase [Vergrösserung] of our local Vetter-Gericht." They complained that whenever a village position was open these cousins got together and selected the candidate. Whenever any matter came before the Gericht, this Familie made up the majority and always voted for its own Privat-Interesse. The Bürger were unable to change matters through protestations, especially because the Schultheiss failed in authority and Parteilosigkeit. Since he was a tippler and needed cash, he and his five cronies continually voted for some task to carry out that could earn him a day's wage. The results of all this were clearly felt in every householder's tax bill.*

It was not, of course, simply that the new candidate was related to some of the Richter. They already were related to each other in multiple ways. Two of them were stepbrothers-in-law. One Bürgermeister was the uncle (mother's brother) of the other, one of whom in turn had two "fourth-degree" in-laws on the Gericht. Two Richter were sons-in-law of a Bürgermeister's brother. Two more were co-parents-in-law, and two were brothers-in-law. The commissioner pointed out that there was little legal problem with any of this. Although brothers-in-law could not serve together, stepbrothers-in-law could. It was not known if the uncle and nephew had obtained a dispensation, but they had served together for so long that they might as well continue to do

Richter and had another brother-in-law, a stepson, and a first cousin on the Gericht. Two members of the Rat were brothers. A Richter had a brother-in-law on the Rat, who was also a cousin to the Schultheiss and two other Richter. Two of the men responsible for investigating boundaries (*Untergänger*) were uncle and nephew.

48 HSAS, A214, Bü 1061, Kl. Heppach (Waiblingen). "Untersuchung . . . gegen den . . . Magistrat . . ." (1791–9).

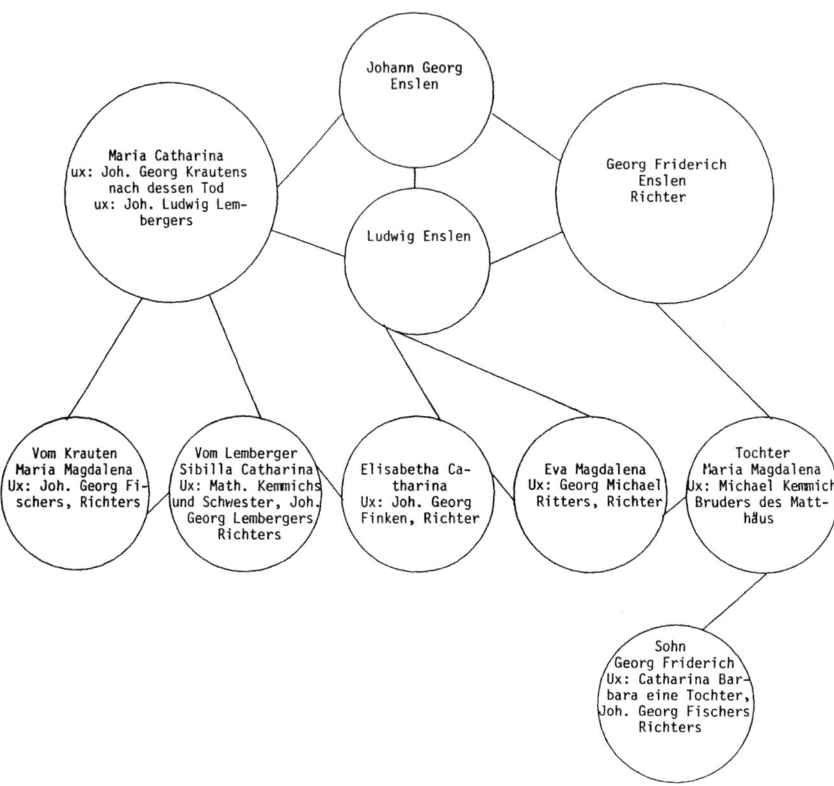

Figure 2.1

so. Fourth-degree affinity was not a legal impediment. The two men who were brothers-in-law of a third were only in the third degree of affinity, which was not illegal. Co-parents-in-law were also not contrary to regulations. Although there was no indication that the two brothers-in-law had received dispensations, the matter was to be left alone, since they had served together for several years; however, the newly elected member was disqualified because he had a brother-in-law on the Gericht. I have represented here the kinship diagram drawn up for the investigation and redrawn it, so that the interlocking kinship ties can be clearly delineated (Figures 2.1 and 2.2).

Young Michael Kemmich was the man newly elected to the Gericht. His deceased father had served for eighteen years, and while there had allied with Georg Friedrich Enslen through the marriage of their children. The description of Kemmich's connections with the Gericht members was not entirely accurate. The three cousins were actually husbands of cousins of his wife. With one of these men, Johann Georg Fischer, he had reinforced the connection through a marriage of their children. His father-in-law, Georg Friedrich Enslen, served on the court, but his affinity with Lemberger (also a cousin of his wife) was indirect – a brother of his brother's wife. What appeared to

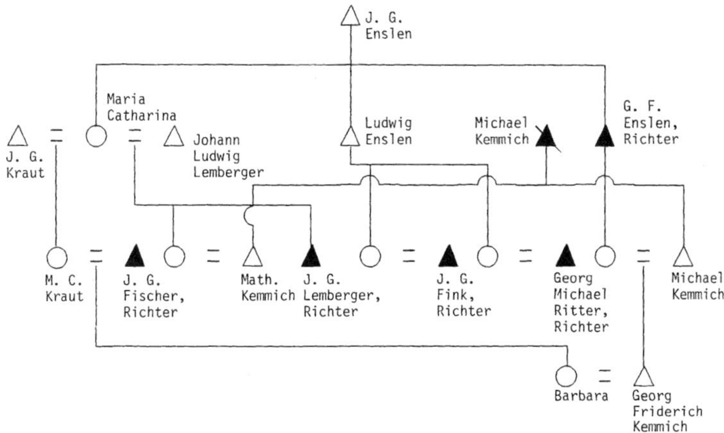

Figure 2.2

the villagers as a "Vetter-Gericht" did not involve any people directly related by blood, although men were undoubtedly understood to be capable of building alliances through their wives' cousins. And men associated with each other took the opportunity of second and third marriages to construct affinal ties. Or they arranged for the marriage of their children. Michael Kemmich, himself the object of such a strategy, in turn arranged for the marriage of his son with the daughter of his wife's cousin and one of his closest supporters on the Gericht.

The state's viewpoint

From the language and perception of "cousin" politics reflected in commission reports, it is clear that by the end of the eighteenth century the system had developed a remarkable degree of integration. As I have shown in my first study of Neckarhausen, certain aspects of cousin politics remained strong through the 1860s. The sale of land to cousins, which was already a central aspect of the property market early in the nineteenth century, continued to grow throughout the next seven decades.[49] Nonetheless, it does seem to be the case that village courts packed with cousins played a smaller role after the 1830s, although it is difficult to gather evidence from scattered references. Certainly the situation as List found it in 1817 was widespread throughout the realm. An article by a village delegate from Lauffen in the *Württembergischer Volksfreund* in 1818 complained that the "chief difficulty in the great disorder in our village of Lauffen is . . . the chain of in-laws and cousins within the magistrates."[50] An anonymous writer in

[49] Sabean, *Property*, pp. 401–10.

[50] "Christoph Nellmanns zweiter Zuruf an die Gemeinds-Deputierten zu Lauffen, in *Der Württembergische Volksfreund. Ein Wochenblatt für Recht und bürgerliche Freiheit* (Stuttgart, 26.3.1818): "Der Hauptgegenstand des grossen Unwesens in unserem Ort Lauffen ist, wie Euch allen bekannt, die

the *Württembergisches Archiv* argued that in all of the local magistrates an "unlimited and continuous aristocratism rules," which was subject to no control outside of itself and through cooptation steadily replenished its ranks.[51] In 1824 the parliamentary deputy von Seeger suggested that a village Schultheiss could hardly avoid administering his office through family. In the rare instances where a communal headman saw the evils in nepotism, his own family would stand in his way. The interests of a single member were always protected by the coordinated politics of all the relatives.

> The family ties of the village chief magistrate are usually considerable before he takes office, but they increase through grown sons and daughters, who graft still more branches onto the already strong trunk through marriage. These family chains have the most disadvantageous consequences for public offices. In them lies the principal reason why order and policing so seldom can be found in the village.[52]

All of the liberal writers in the two decades or so after the founding of the kingdom in 1805 found fault with the organization of village political life by familial factions. But the issue went well beyond the local level: it can be shown that Vetterleswirtschaft as a system of political organization developed at the level of state institutions and among the middle classes, at about the same time and at the same pace as this occurred in Württemberg villages.[53] Tight oligarchal control had evolved within the ducal privy council and the executive committee of the Estates (*Landschaft*) in a series of stages.[54] In sharp contrast to seventeenth-century government, the privy council came to be dominated by a few families tied closely to court politics after 1712: "The favorite with her faction had so boldly taken control of all positions that sister [*sic*], brother, and son sat together in the Privy Council."[55] By the 1740s, this kind of familial control extended itself throughout the organs of government. "Corruption" had spread like an "incred-

Kette von Schwägerschaften und Vetterschaften in unserem Magistrate, gegen deren nachtheilige Folgen ich schon so vielfältig, aber leider vergebens, geklagt und gekämpft habe" (p. 134). A copy exists in the Göttingen Universitätsbibliothek under the call number: 8° H. Württ., 273. It contains many local petitions and notes about village and town conditions.

51 "Kritik des Verfassungs-Entwurfs der württembergischen Stände-Versammlung," in *Württembergisches Archiv,* 2 (1817), pp. 27–8. This liberal newspaper was printed in Heidelberg and reached three volumes from 1816–18. A copy exists in the Göttingen Universitätsbibliothek under: 8° H. Württ., 270.

52 "Vortrag des Abgeordneten v. Seeger die lebenslängliche Dauer der Gemeinde-Aemter betreffend" (1824), pamphlet, n.p., n.d. This 17-page pamphlet reproduced a speech given in 1824. A copy is to be found in the Göttingen Universitätsbibliothek: 8° H. Württ., 1005.

53 See the discussion in Walker, *Home Towns,* pp. 56–63.

54 *Ludwig Timotheus v. Spittler,* "Entwurf einer Geschichte des engern landschaftlichen Ausschusses" (1796), in *Vermischte Schriften über deutsche Geschichte, Statistik und öffentliches Recht,* vol. 3 of *Sämmtliche Werke,* ed. Karl Wächter, 13 vols. (Stuttgart and Tübingen, 1837), pp. 16–156.

55 Spittler, "Entwurf," p. 132.

ible cancer," and people complained about the "spreading disorder of familial aristocracy."[56]

Cousin politics in and beyond the village

Several general trends in the constitutional history of Württemberg in the eighteenth and nineteenth centuries should be mentioned at this point. During the eighteenth century, there emerged a system of kin-coordinated politics that encompassed court, parliament, and urban and county governments.[57] One of its main components was a self-conscious, well-articulated middle class of officials closely tied up with a politics of marriage and family alliance. But toward the end of the century, liberal thought began to make a clear distinction between public and private interest. Everything that had previously been ordered according to familial and kinship concerns came to be seen as "corrupt": Hegel dismissed the entire structure of family-coordinated government as a "fodder barn."[58] In his view, the development of the state should proceed as a dialectical working out of rationality, which would increase to the degree that the private possessions of the prince became public property and officials moved from being administrators of private property to administrators of state law.[59] This distinction between "private" and "public" became the crucial analytical instrument for Robert von Mohl, Gustav Schmoller, and other nineteenth-century commentators on the development of the Württemberg state.[60] At the heart of the constitutional battles after 1815, between political factions rooted in "old corruption" and the liberals or the champions of a revised administrative monarchy, was the issue of the relation of private interest to public exercise of office. The liberal reformer Kerner (himself the product of old ruling-family connections) dismissed Ludwig Uhland and his party of "Altrechtler" precisely because they were coordinated through kinship and defended the conditions that made their familial alliances possible: "They are all allied together through marriage (*verschwägert*) and grown together like dreadlocks (*Weichselzopf*) with the old system."[61]

Under King William I (1816–64), systematic steps were taken to develop an

[56] Spittler, Geschichte des württembergischen Geheimen-Raths-Collegiums," in *Vermischte Schriften,* pp. 279–452, here p. 428.

[57] See, e.g., Erwin Hölzle, *Das alte Recht und die Revolution. Eine politische Geschichte Württembergs in der Revolutionszeit 1789–1805* (Munich and Berlin, 1931), pp. 29, 104, 110–2.

[58] G. W. F. Hegel, "Ueber die neuesten innern Verhältnisse Württembergs besonders über die Gebrechen der Magistratsverfassung" (1798), in Georg Lasson, ed., *Hegels Schriften zur Politik und Rechtsphilosophie,* in *Sämtliche Werke,* vol. 7 (Leipzig, 1913), pp. 150–4.

[59] "Verhandlungen in der Versammlung der Landstände des Königsreichs Württemberg im Jahre 1815 und 1816," in *Hegels Schriften,* pp. 157–281, here, p. 173.

[60] Gustav Schmoller, "Der deutsche Beamtenstaat vom 16. bis 18. Jahrhundert," in *Untersuchungen zur Verfassungs-, Verwaltungs- und Wirtschaftsgeschichte* (Leipzig, 1898), pp. 289–313. See also Alfred Dehlinger, *Württembergs Staatswesen in seiner geschichtlichen Entwicklung bis heute,* vol. 2 (Stuttgart, 1951, 53), pp. 920–63.

[61] Quoted in Hartmut Froeschle, *Ludwig Uhland und die Romantik* (Cologne, 1973), p. 131.

administrative apparatus completely divorced from private familial interests. The constant danger according to Schmoller – another descendant of Württemberg "old corruption" – was corruption and inertia: "In every larger body of officials, the danger always continues to arise, that it develop into a Vetternclique, that patronage corrupt it, that too many lazy sinecure chasers infiltrate, who with little work want to pamper themselves and get rich, and that routine becomes master over fresh initiatives and self-sacrificing devotion."[62]

Every political history of Württemberg covering the first half of the nineteenth century mentions a radical structural change in the ten years or so after 1815. After that, one no longer hears about Vetterleswirtschaft. That was the old system, soundly defeated in the series of reforms under the new monarchy and the organization of political life around parties, driven in part at least by ideological concerns. In a system where kinship became something of an embarrassment, strictly relegated to the private realm, and difficult even to conceptualize, let alone treat as a subject for sociological investigation, the term "Vetterleswirtschaft" itself lost its familial moorings. Today it is used to refer to provincial corruption as such, the system of favors spread among local businessmen and politicians who have no necessary kinship connection at all.

In the village under study here, the relationship of kinship to political and administrative life gradually changed over time in part because the village was never an isolated unit. There was a steady interchange between it and the political institutions of the duchy and later the kingdom. Around 1740 – when Neckarhausen and many villages of the territory witnessed the rise of new familial alliances and the coordination of kin in new ways among their magistrates – the court, church, bureaucracy, and cities were subject to the same dynamics.[63] Indeed, many a regional official, exercising his position within a well-articulated system of familial alliance, aided and abetted the establishment of coordinated practices of family and government in the villages under his charge. After the close of the Napoleonic Wars, the attack on the politics of kinship expanded from the bureaucracy and state government to the villages. In Neckarhausen the uncoupling of family from village government took place in stages over many decades and was replaced step by step by class politics. And yet class formation in the nineteenth century was closely tied up with kinship dynamics. Because systems of familial endogamy and class endogamy came to overlap and reinforce each other, it is now difficult to distinguish activity in one area from activity in the other. The more the government of the village became divorced from "private" interest, the tighter and more frequent became the ties between kin. The

[62] Schmoller, "Beamtenstaat," p. 307.

[63] On the development of alliances among Württemberg pastoral families, see Martin Hasselhorn, *Die altwürttembergische Pfarrstand im 18. Jahrhundert,* Veröffentlichungen der Kommission für geschichtliche Landeskunde in Baden-Württemberg, Series B: Forschungen, vol. 6 (Stuttgart, 1958). For political culture as a whole, see Clemens Theodor Perthes, *Politische Zustände und Personen in Deutschland zur Zeit der französischen Herrschaft,* 2d ed. (Gotha, 1862), pp. 471–3.

more invisible family concerns became – as their role in providing entry to wealth and position grew less "public" – the more crucial they became in the everyday practice of class culture. These themes will occupy us throughout the book.

Gustav Schmoller quite rightly saw in the development of a rationalized, self-conscious, educated, and inner-directed bureaucracy a key to the effective separation of public and private (familial) concerns. He argued that over time a series of different aspects together created a "caste" of neutral officials whose only concern was the efficient and rational running of the state. Hence they devoted their attention to money wages, clear rules, instructions and controls, disciplinary statutes, a well-articulated hierarchy of offices, recruitment from various social classes, education, and established concepts of obligation and honor.[64] In Neckarhausen, increased familiarity with handling bureaucratic documents, a differentiation of functions and professionalization of record keeping, the stabilization and regulation of magistrate wages, and the integration of the Schultheiss office into a more clearly articulated official hierarchy played a similar role. Already in the second decade of the nineteenth century, the county (*Oberamt*) court in Nürtingen became the court of first instance for many misdemeanors that had once been dealt with by the village magistrates. By the 1840s judicial and administrative matters had been divorced. The Schultheiss acted more as a court recorder than a judge, overseeing complaints, which were sent on to Nürtingen. In the 1820s the village hired a professional accountant from the outside to take up residence and maintain the mortgage and real estate records and to keep the various accounts that used to fall to the village Bürgermeister.[65] By the 1860s the villagers actually elected such an accountant as their Schultheiss, who a few years later was succeeded by one appointed by the state.[66] Until 1820, the Gericht and Rat were self-coopting, so it was possible to put family concerns openly in first place. The communal reform law replaced the Gericht with a Gemeinderat, whose members were elected at large in the first instance for five-year terms.[67] Only after winning a second election did the incumbent assume a lifetime position. In a much larger village, with only three or four positions falling vacant each decade, the dynamics of village-wide elections based on neighborhood factions, occupational concerns, and differences in wealth determined succession to office.[68] In such a situation, families had to mobilize parties and set up coalitions

[64] Schmoller, "Beamtenstaat," p. 307.

[65] *Gericht*, vol. 11, f. 104 (29.6.1828); f. 131 (20.2.1829). Earlier the financial officers of the village had taken their receipts and notes to a county clerk (*Substitut*) in Nürtingen to be drawn up into proper accounts; *Gericht*, vol. 2, f. 65 (21.1.1774); vol. 3, f. 66 (7.6.1781); *Vogtruggericht*, vol. 1, f. 136 (22.11.1786).

[66] *Gericht*, vol. 18, f. 206 (19.10.1868).

[67] *Gericht*, vol. 9, f. 88 (3.6.1819). Later the first term of office was for two years.

[68] In 1850 a villager complained that three men had been elected to the Gemeinderat from the "Upper Village" (where the poorer artisans and farm laborers lived); *Gericht*, vol. 15, f. 62 (25.11.1850). A year earlier, a mason complained that another man had said that "beggar boys" (Bettelbuben) from the Oberdorf had been elected to the Gemeinderat; *Schultheissenamt*, vol. 2, f. 202 (27.8.1849).

to capture votes. In the long run and by the close of this study, village faction, with its hidden familial dynamics, had crept into regional and national party politics.[69]

"Vetterleswirtschaft" has always been viewed as the opposite of the modern, rational, and efficient form of bureaucratic and party political government. For the most part, it has been seen as a sure foundation for corrupt rule, and as an illegitimate confusion of private and public concerns. In this study, it is examined in the context of a particular political economy – through the links to property holding, agricultural and craft production, and state dynamics of surplus extraction. Such an approach not only opens a window onto kinship construction, but also draws attention to issues of class culture and class formation that extend beyond the period in which "cousins" openly constituted the public realm.

As this chapter has shown, kinship has been connected to political processes and structure in different ways at different times. But in the region under consideration, kinship was never a static set of principles or way of joining people together. Indeed, the very possibility of families allying with one another changed radically from period to period. The state created formidable rules that governed the kinds of alliances that could be entered into. At the same time, popular culture also established boundaries for licit and practical solutions to familial strategic aims. The early modern state was very much concerned with who could marry whom, and it connected and disconnected people through a "symbolics of blood."[70] Thus the next logical step in this analysis is to examine the rules of incest.

[69] See Paul Nolte, "Gemeindeliberalismus." An important analysis of kinship and politics in a nineteenth-century Württemberg village is offered by Carola Lipp in Wolfgang Kaschuba and Carola Lipp, *Dörflisches Ueberleben: Zur Geschichte materieller und sozialer Reproduktion ländlicher Gesellschaft im 19. und frühen 20. Jahrhundert,* Untersuchungen des Ludwig-Uhland-Instituts der Universität Tübingen, vol. 56 (Tübingen, 1982), pp. 572–98. She works with a concept of descent rather than alliance. Her analysis underplays the political effect of class formation. Cf. Chapter 16 in this volume.

[70] Michel Foucault has grasped the theoretical importance of "alliance" for social reproduction and the indispensability of incest rules for alliance formation in *History of Sexuality,* vol. 1, *An Introduction,* trans. Robert Hurley (Harmondsworth, 1978), pp. 106–9.

3

The politics of incest and the ecology of alliance formation

The early modern state was greatly concerned with the kinds of alliances that its subjects could enter into. During the second half of the sixteenth century, when princes consolidated their power through the detailed elaboration of codes of law, every Protestant territory in Germany issued a precise and long list of prohibited marriage partners and decreed that the table of prohibited degrees should be read periodically in each parish church. In many of the ecclesiastical ordinances (*Kirchenordnungen*), more space was given to the issue of marriage interdictions than any other matter.[1] Catholic territories remained under the rules established in canon law, but theologians and lawyers in that tradition were as busy as their Protestant counterparts elaborating the specifics and providing a theoretical justification for each detail.

The state, of course, was not a unified entity, even though the system of rules it provided established a uniform code for its inhabitants. Different discursive groups fed off separate traditions and texts, promoted alternative rules, and developed specialized vocabularies and systems of logical inference. The most elaborate schemas were worked out by theologians and jurists in competition with each other and with cross-references and rhetorical borrowings. But rulers frequently developed their own perspectives quite outside the exigencies of learned discourse. In this matter, as in most others, little work has been done on the degree to which the state responded to attitudes and values articulated within the cultures of different strata of the population, and it is quite possible that the conservatism evidenced in the law codes reflected a popular malaise prompted by initial Reformation tampering with incest prohibitions.[2]

[1] The ordinances are published in a remarkable series: Emil Sehling, ed., *Die evangelischen Kirchenordnungen des XVI Jahrhunderts*, 15 vols. (vols. 1–5, Leipzig, 1902–13; and vols. 6–15, Tübingen, 1955–77).

[2] The issue is usually put in terms of an unwillingness to provoke the emperor or scandalize potential

The Kirchenordnungen

With certain modifications, the system of marriage prohibitions established in Germany in the sixteenth century remained in force almost everywhere until the eighteenth century and continued to determine the conceptual schema in states such as Württemberg throughout most of the nineteenth. Despite their desire to differentiate themselves from medieval canon law, Protestant scholars and administrators kept a broad set of restrictions, which had considerable consequences for the kinds of alliances that families and households in cities and the countryside could make with each other. In general, the new laws forbade marriages between a wide range of people related by blood (in many states extending out to second cousins) or by marriage (here again extending out to second cousins of a former spouse or even sexual partner). Each rule in the ordinances was supported by some sort of an explanation, often reflecting the particular scholarship of the responsible theologians or jurists. They frequently culled their arguments from ancient texts to support positions already decided upon, and when taken together, their justifications demonstrate a number of tensions and an overall lack of coherence.

Some scholars relied on Augustine, who had suggested that the purpose of divine law was to force families to open themselves out to the larger community, to extend the circle of friends or the bonds of love between people – an early formulation of Lévi-Strauss's principle of exchange.[3] Others thought the system of marriage prohibitions was a means of preventing certain families from concentrating property in their own hands.[4] But neither of these arguments was elaborated at great length.[5] I doubt that any state officials were referring to em-

political supporters, but cultural conservatism in the broad mass of the population is as likely to have helped push the Reformers back from their original liberality. Recent work on family, gender, and age hierarchies has shown that reformed moral codes and institutions of social discipline found a considerable number of backers. See, e.g., Hans Medick, "Village Spinning Bees: Sexual Culture and Free Time among Rural Youth in Early Modern Germany," in Hans Medick and David Warren Sabean, eds., *Interest and Emotion: Essays on the Study of Family and Kinship* (Cambridge, 1984), pp. 317–39; Thomas Robisheaux, *Rural Society and the Search for Order in Early Modern Germany* (Cambridge, 1989), pp. 95–100; Lyndal Roper, *The Holy Household: Women and Morals in Reformation Augsburg* (Oxford, 1989), pp. 27–49.

3 "Kurpfalz Eheordnung 1583," in Sehling, *Evang. Kirchenordnungen,* vol. 14, p. 312: "so that love and friendship among people and subjects will be extended all the more, more deeply planted, and more strongly maintained." See Claude Lévi-Strauss, *The Elementary Structures of Kinship,* rev. ed., trans. James Harle Bell, Johan Richard von Sturmer, and Rodney Needham (Boston, 1969), pp. 29–41.

4 "Hesse Reformationsordnung 1572," in Sehling, *Evang. Kirchenordnungen,* vol. 8, pp. 404–5: "Because among the common folk it is more common that those who are related to each other through blood or affinity undertake to marry because of their property and other matters."

5 The latter, a commonplace since the ancient world, has seldom been worked out for any concrete social system of property holding. A variation of the argument has been elaborated by Jack Goody, in *The Development of Family and Marriage in Europe* (Cambridge, 1983), pp. 88–156. In Goody's view, the practical logic of clerical exogamy rules in the early Middle Ages was to reduce the claims on familial property to ease transference of title to the church. Objections that cast doubt on a broad coordinated strategy for such a complex institution over such a long time seldom give much

pirical facts whenever they brought up this issue. But Augustine's formulation was likely to have met with approval among particular social groups in sixteenth-century society. For many people, the strategy of extending the maximum number of people related to themselves made good social and political sense. In general, the degree of respect any individual of a particular social milieu received from the prince and his officials was governed by the size and coherence of his "Sippe," or kindred. Felons could even be released from punishment for serious crimes to the bond of their relatives and "friends." The roles that siblings and collateral relatives played for one another as guardians, given the demographic problems of the age, coupled with the rudimentary administrative capacities of the state, made it necessary to define a fairly large exogamous unit – that group so intimately tied up in multiple ways with one another as residual heirs, crisis administrators, and so on, that marriage within the group was precluded.[6] Furthermore, although there has not been any analysis of kinship extension in the sixteenth century, anecdotal evidence and reference to the marriage registers for Neckarhausen suggest that the geographic area covered by marriages among rural folk, at least, was much larger than for any period before the second half of the nineteenth century.[7] Exogamy rules enforcing marriage outside of a fairly extended set of relatives were in keeping with the practices of dominant members of rural communities, who maintained extensive and coherent networks of relatives well beyond the confines of a town or village.[8]

The ecclesiastical ordinances emphasized two concerns in particular: proper relations in the "house" and the avoidance of pollution. Both of these concerns grew out of Lutheran theology, supported by academic philosophy and jurisprudence. Religious texts abounded with tension between Luther's emphasis on incest prohibitions based on patriarchal authority in the household and parental respect and canon law notions of blood and pollution, both of which found support in pastoral rhetoric inspired by the Old Testament.[9] According to Luther,

thought to how practices are formed within culture. It seems quite probable that a link exists between cultural norms and property strategies. I find less convincing the thesis that endogamy is a realistic means in most property systems for concentrating the ownership and management of property. Discussions along these lines tend to be vague at best. Germaine Tillion, *The Republic of Cousins: Women's Oppression in Mediterranean Society,* trans. Quintin Hoare (London, 1983; first published in France, 1966), p. 104, contests the idea that endogamy can be explained by the desire to "avoid excessive sub-division of family holdings." Ladislav Holy has recently looked at the arguments proposed for cousin marriage in the Near East and shown that the notion that the system is based on a desire to concentrate property does not explain very much. See *Kinship, Honour and Solidarity: Cousin Marriage in the Middle East* (Manchester, 1989), chap. 1.

6 On this point, see Martine Segalen, *Fifteen Generations of Bretons: Kinship and Society in Lower Brittany 1720–1980,* trans. J. S. Underwood (Cambridge, 1991), pp. 123–8.

7 The extant *Urpheden* (signed documents accepting a court judgment or sentence) from the sixteenth century in the Württemberg archives attest to a significant movement of families and family members over a considerable territory.

8 Robisheaux, *Rural Society,* pp. 95–100, has shown that certain features of the Lutheran ideology of marriage found ready acceptance among village patriarchs. Extensive exogamy rules were likely to agree with their practices as well. In this case Luther argued for a reduction in the extensiveness of such rules but was very quickly overruled.

9 Concerned to find unifying Reformation principles in the new laws, Karl August Moriz Schlegel,

divine and natural law prescribed a fundamental power relationship between parents and children (*respectus parentelae*), which expressed itself in strong hierarchies of age and gender.[10] Certainly these ideas left their stamp on many of the formulations in the Ecclesiastical Ordinances, especially in those passages dealing with sexual relations between direct ascendants and descendants and seniors and juniors. The symbolics of this grid created such fundamental categorical oppositions that theologians always had more trouble with the marriage of a man with his same-age aunt than with his same-age niece.[11] Although such commentators as Karl Schlegel were quite right that the ordinances adopted the new principle of paternal respect, they underplayed the degree to which other notions determined the arguments in the ordinances and the two centuries of controversy that followed.[12] Luther himself, very early on in his reforming career (1522), totally rejected canon law reckoning of the prohibited degrees and their extension beyond Mosaic specifications as based on non-biblical principles and rooted in papal greed for cash payoffs to dispense them.[13] He, as well as a small number of writers up to the eighteenth century, interpreted the Mosaic prohibitions listed in Leviticus 18 and 20 (which will be discussed later in this chapter) as an enumeration without any inherent logical principles for extension. The list referred strictly to the itemized persons. Canon lawyers had adopted a reckoning by "degrees," creating a balanced computation according to the substance any two people shared by descent (indeed, as will be seen, by marriage as well). Despite Luther's forthright condemnation of such meddling with divine commandments, all of the Lutheran churchmen-administrators reintroduced the ca-

the most thorough student of Protestant marriage restrictions, suggested that the *Kirchenordnungen* all rejected medieval explanations for incest rules based on blood pollution in favor of ones rooted in the exigencies of the patriarchal house; *Kritische und systematische Darstellung der verbotenen Grade der Verwandtschaft und Schwägerschaft bey Heirathen* (Hannover, 1802). For a quick overview derived largely from his work, see the article, "Eherecht," in the *Realencyklopädie für protestantische Theologie und Kirche* (Leipzig, 1898), vol. 5, pp. 198–227. A good overview of the development of canon law can be found in the *New Catholic Encyclopedia,* s.v. "Affinity" (vol. I, pp. 167–70) and "Consanguinity" (vol. 4, pp. 192–96). A recent discussion with the acute insight of a social anthropologist is Jack Goody's *Development of Family and Marriage in Europe,* esp. 48–68 and 134–46.

[10] "Wolfenbüttel Kirchenordnung 1569," in Sehling, *Evang. Kirchenordnungen,* vol. 6/1, pp. 219–20: "Warning: the fourth commandment of God (Exodus 20:12), you should honor father and mother. There can however be no greater and horrifying dishonor of father and mother and all those who are to be considered in the place of our fathers and mothers done by children than to be violated by them through incest (*Blutschande*) and polluted"; "Preussen Consistorial Ordnung 1584," in vol. 4, p. 133; "Rostock Ehesachen 1581," in vol. 5, p. 293: "If Adam were still alive, he could not come courting because he is the father of all people"; "Kurpfalz, Von der Ehesachen 1556," in vol. 14, p. 223: "for such persons are among themselves as father and sons, mother and daughters. Therefore it is the case that if Adam lived today, because all women come from him and are reckoned as his daughters, he would not be allowed to take a wife from among them to marry"; "Emden Eheordnung 1596," in vol. 7/1, p. 528: the passage argues that an uncle and aunt are to be regarded as being in the place of father and mother.

[11] There was the additional problem that the Leviticus texts expressly forbade marriage with the father's sister and mother's sister but not with the brother's daughter or sister's daughter.

[12] Schlegel, *Darstellung,* pp. 42–5.

[13] "Welche Personen verboten sind zu ehelichen," in *Vom ehelichen Leben* (1522), in Otto Clemen, ed., *Luthers Werke in Auswahl,* vol. 2 (Berlin, 1950), pp. 335–59.

nonical rules, even if in slightly modified form, as well as the manner of reckoning, as they began to institutionalize the Reformation in civil and ceremonial law. I want to go into the laws of marriage prohibition because they were important for preventing or allowing certain marriage configurations I will be discussing in the study of Neckarhausen kinship and in the comparative excursus in Chapters 20 and 21.

The Kirchenordnungen made a clear distinction between incest proper and the wider set of marriage prohibitions. Although the wording was not always consistent, incest (*in-castus* impure, polluted, unholy) referred to divine or natural law prohibitions, neatly summarized in the Leviticus lists, whatever trouble scholars had in understanding the inclusion or exclusion of any particular relationship. The enumeration could be extended logically to include similar relatives, but beyond that the state had the right to include even more people – no longer to prevent incest directly but to discipline the population, raise their cultural level, or provide a protective zone around the essential incestual core.

Lutheran pastoral rhetoric was built around a notion of collective retribution, with Old Testament examples woven throughout the texts. Certain kinds of sin made the "land and people" subject to the full force of God's wrath, and the motif of being driven from the land for the corruption of even one person was everyday stuff for sermon material and frequently made its way into the imagery of the Kirchenordnungen.[14] Indeed, the Merseburg Church Ordinance warned that God had "often allowed whole kingdoms and princedoms, land and people, to be horribly ravaged and laid waste" for incest. Reaching back to Talmudic sources, theologians argued that the state had to build a buffer zone around the Leviticus prohibitions in order to ensure that no one would penetrate the barrier.[15] State officials thought that the fundamen-

[14] "Pommern Kirchenordnung 1542," in Sehling, *Evang. Kirchenordnungen,* vol. 4, p. 368; "Merseburg Kirchenordnung 1548," in vol. 2/1, p. 29: "none should commit this horror so that the land will not spit you out if you pollute it"; p. 34: "indeed do not pollute the land and people with such sins and lead [them] into misery and destitution as is taught us in the Holy Word as a horrible example, wherein we can see how hard God punishes incest (*Blutschande*) and fornication at all times."; "Brandenburg Visitations- und Consistorialordnung 1573," in vol. 3, p. 126: talks about land and people brought into misery because of horrible sins. God always punishes incest and fornication before other sins; "Mecklenburg Kirchenordnung 1557," in vol. 5, p. 231: terrible punishment brings good fruit; "Hohenlohe Eheordnung 1572," in vol. 15, p. 186: incest is a pollution and brings land and people into misery; "Grubenhagen Kirchenordnung 1581," in vol. 6/2, p. 17; "Grafschaft Oldenburg Kirchenordnung 1573, in vol. 7/2/1, p. 1161: people should not pollute themselves or others with incest; that would bring God's anger, including "fire and sword." Polluting land and people brings misery and destitution. God punishes incest and fornication at all times. The text gives the example of a whole city being wasted for the sin of one person.

[15] "Erfurt Policei Ordnung 1583," in Sehling, *Evang. Kirchenordnungen,* vol. 2/1, p. 372: "because in all ways according to the common rule close affinity and relation is to be avoided in marriage and engagement for discipline (*Zucht,* also modesty) and reputation (*Ehrbarkeit*)," the second and third degrees of consanguinity and affinity in the unequal and equal lines are to be avoided. For an explanation of the method of counting degrees, see later in the chapter; "Mecklenburg Consistorialordnung 1570," in vol. 5, p. 237: "In order to hold more decently and assiduously to [the rules against] intercourse (*Vermischungen*) and cohabitation between the closest consanguines and

tally wanton populace would always find the area at the boundary of a prohibition to be the most provocative, and that it was therefore imperative to move it far enough away so that they would not do any danger to the community at large by polluting the land.

Vying with the image of desire enhanced by prohibition was the constant fear that society's light veneer of culture could all too easily be stripped away and humankind plunged into an animalistic orgy of incest.[16] Parallel to a theme developed in the twentieth century by Lévi-Strauss, the theological message at this time was that culture began with incest prohibitions.[17] Theological texts defined savage (*rauh*) as opposed to civilized people precisely as those without knowledge of incest rules.[18] Such a picture justified the strong hand of the state, which was the only barrier between order and chaos.

affines which are expressly forbidden in divine law, we have included in our land and police ordinance on good grounds and with considerable advice also other degrees, such as between cousins (*brüder und schwesterkinderen*)"; "Kurpfalz, Von der Ehesachen 1556," in vol. 14, p. 224: "and because the first degree of affinity is not held to by the common man willingly, then the second is also forbidden, indeed even the third degree of affinity is also forbidden"; "Kurpfalz Eheordnung 1563," in vol. 14, p. 312: the passage argues that the common herd (*Pöfel*) exist in ignorance and wantonness. If they were allowed to marry their first cousins (*Geschwistrigte Kinder*), then they would also want to marry their siblings (*Geschwistrigte*). Thus it is imperative to forbid second and third degrees of consanguinity (first and second cousins). As for affinity, it is a question of discipline and propriety, and second and third degrees are forbidden there too; "Grubenhagen Kirchenordnung 1581," in vol. 6/2, p. 104: all grades of consanguinity and affinity forbidden by God are to be observed; also forbid up to third degree on the equal line for consanguines and affines, which are forbidden by human convention *propter maiorum reverentiam sanguinis*; "Emden Eheordnung 1596," in vol. 7/1, p. 529: "because in the Lutheran churches in order to avoid among the ignorant all scandal and vice because of this degree"; "Hesse, Reformationsordnung 1572," in vol. 8, p. 406: marriage to close relatives beyond the Mosaic and imperial law is to be avoided for the sake of discipline and propriety.

16 "Wolfenbüttel Kirchenordnung 1569," in Sehling, *Evang. Kirchenordnungen*, vol. 6/1, p. 219: "Since for a considerable time there have been increasing reports that some shameless people, disregarding the fact that they are related by blood or affinity to the degree that they cannot be married according to divine or natural discipline and propriety"; "Merseburg Kirchenordnung 1548," in vol. 2/1, p. 28: "Since in this wicked time when the godless increase enormously; p. 29: "Because many terrible cases happen almost every day, and out of ignorance, the common man touches too closely in the degrees . . . so that incest and blood violation are committed"; "Mecklenburg 1557," in vol. 5, p. 211: "the folk is heedless"; "Kurpfalz Eheordnung 1563," in vol. 14, p. 283: "thus it is found in daily experience that many people without any shame and against all discipline, law, and common decency, are so shameless and heedless that they promise marriage with those people which divine, natural, and civil law and ordinance not only do not allow but earnestly forbid and hold to be horrible and forbidding"; "Hohenlohe Eheordnung 1563," in vol. 15, p. 180: argues that there are those who are breaking all rules and order and undertaking marriages that are horrible and detestable and against natural discipline and propriety; "Emden Eheordnung 1596," in vol. 7/1, p. 528: "because new blood violation, which is a horror in the eyes of the Allmighty, takes place among the folk."

17 Lévi-Strauss, *Elementary Structures*, pp. 12–41.

18 By the end of the eighteenth century, some commentators saw the incest rules and their refinement as having been instrumental in the development of the human race and perfectibility. See e.g., Christoph Friedrich Ammon, *Ueber das moralische Fundament der Eheverbote unter Verwandten*, 3 Abhandlungen (Göttingen, 1798, 99, 1801): "The path of mankind goes from innocence through guilt to education and perfection" (Abh. 2, p. 29).

Still a third rhetorical element in the texts derived from Christian notions about sexuality and the body. Incest rules and the broader extension of marriage prohibitions were always associated with sexual discipline.[19] The law not only ordered social reality but it also subdued the passions.[20] A well-disciplined house might be filled with affection but its chief characteristic was respect, something that could be injured if marriage partners were too familiar with each other already as closely associated kin. But there is also a sense in the legal formulations that near relatives might arouse strong sexual passions and that extensive marriage prohibitions acted as a fundamental disciplining agent by making such people unavailable as sexual and marital partners. Although the general discussion of prohibited degrees gives no indication of which partners might pose the most danger and be the most alluring, the key peril – to judge from the enormous attention it received in the literature in the following century and a half – was almost certainly the sexual attraction of affinal kin such as the wife's sister.

[19] "Mecklenburg Consistorialordnung 1570," in Sehling, *Evang. Kirchenordnungen,* vol. 5, p. 236: "God desires special counsel and wisdom to be recognized by us as he does other virtues such as justice and truth, etc. to be exercised, and commanded and ordained chastity in his Word, so that we will recognize that God is a just, truthful, pure, and chaste God, who is horribly displeased by all fornication and shameful intercourse, and so that we distinguish this true, pure God from all obscene spirits, which drive people to shame and fornication, and on whom one can call with pure and chaste hearts. So that chastity will be recognized and exercised by people, God established the institution of marriage and ordained in His Word that men should not run amok like animals, but always have two people, a man and a woman, whom God has allowed intercourse, live together maritally and keep the one for the other his body pure and chaste, and avoid all intercourse (*Vermischungen*) which God has forbidden in His Word, and from which nature, as God created it, bears a horror and terror"; "Memmingen Kirchenordnung 1569," in vol. 12, p. 264: although God allowed marriage with cousins, in order to bring discipline (*Zucht*), marriage is forbidden up to the third degree in the unequal line (first cousins once removed; the reckoning of degrees is dealt with later in this chapter); "Nördlingen Kirchenordnung 1597," vol. 12, p. 345: "Because in engagement not just that is allowed which is free [according to God's Word] but that which is fitting and wholesome"; "Pfalz-Neuburg, Edikt über Eheordnung 1555," in vol. 13: contains similar wording; "Kurpfalz, Von den Ehesachen 1556," in vol. 14, p. 223: "since the civil magistrates have been commanded to maintain proper discipline among the subjects and to keep fitting order according to divine and natural law, and because the common herd (*Pöfel*) in these time have become so ignorant and wanton, that even siblings want to marry each other if marriage were to be allowed among first cousins, thus the prince despite the fact that marriage between relatives in the second degree on the same line [cousins] is allowed in divine and imperial law forbids such and also the third degree of consanguinity, so that the common man will be kept all the more orderly in obedience to divine, natural law."

[20] An Enlightenment theologian such as J. W. F. Jerusalem, *Beantwortung der Frage ob die Ehe mit der Schwester-Tochter, nach der göttlichen Gesetzen zulassig sey* (Braunschweig, 1754), still argued for incest laws in terms of discipline. They hold desires in check. "There are no laws in the whole world to be found, which for the strictest maintenance of virtue, the consideration of humanity, and protection of the innocent, the stranger, and the needy, which are better instituted and adopted for external peace and to make morally good citizens and to impress upon them the feelings of humanity, justice, order, and modesty, than these" (p. 38). Well into the nineteenth century, conservative Protestant commentators interpreted incest laws in terms of discipline; see, e.g., Heinrich W. J. Thiersch, *Das Verbot der Ehe innerhalb der nahen Verwandtschaft, nach der heiligen Schrift und nach den Grundsätzen der christlichen Kirche* (Nördlingen, 1869).

Blood, pollution, and the wife's sister

Incest prohibitions were always expressed in powerful symbols of blood and pollution, and Protestant scholars, despite their ambivalences, found it difficult to get around the medieval conceptualization of incest as a tainting of blood.[21] Indeed, the German word *Blutschande,* literally a "violation of blood," is scarcely able to avoid such associations. But the heart of the matter did not lie in direct descent or in consanguineal relations as they are understood today. The rule against sexual union of father and daughter or mother and son and all ascendants and descendants was derived by the Protestant theologians and jurists most usually from patriarchal authority – *respectus parentelae.* The issue of blood played an ever more important role in the argument as the discussion moved away from descendants to collateral relatives and in-laws. The problem was to exclude from consideration marriage with the deceased wife's sister or deceased brother's wife and to bring both of these possibilities under the sign of incest or Blutschande.

Since the sixteenth century, at least, incest discussion has always been concentrated on one particular dyad at a time. During the "long" seventeenth century, the crucial pair was the wife's sister and sister's husband. Discussion centered on two biblical texts, Genesis 2:24, which argued that a man and his wife become one flesh, and Leviticus 18:6, which forbade intercourse between a man and the "flesh of his flesh."[22] Opinion was divided over whether the one-flesh idea was to be taken literally, metaphorically, or as a legal fiction, but the notion was never far away that the mixing of "semen" in intercourse made a man and a woman share the same substance and the same blood.[23] Since people

[21] See the article, "Eherecht," in *RPTK,* vol. 5, p. 210.

[22] In the authorized version, Leviticus 18:6 reads: "None of you shall approach to any that is near of kin to him, to uncover their nakedness: I am the Lord." Luther's version: "Niemand sol sich zu seiner nehesten Blutfreundin thun / jre Schambd zu blössen / Denn ich bin der HERR." The words that are translated into "near of kin" or "nehesten Blutsfreundin" were transliterated from the Hebrew as "Sheer Basar" and literally scanned as "flesh of flesh" or "part of flesh" – in Latin, as "caro carnis." The text was discussed in detail by Michaelis, the most influential Old Testament scholar of the eighteenth century, *Abhandlung von der Ehe-Gesetzen Mosis welche die Heyrathen in die nahe Freundschaft untersagen* (Göttingen, 1755), pp. 126–50.

[23] All the fluids in the body were understood to be fungible; see Thomas Laqueur, *Making Sex: Body and Gender from the Greeks to Freud* (Cambridge, Mass., 1990), pp. 35–43; and Barbara Duden, *The Woman Beneath the Skin: A Doctor's Patients in Eighteenth-Century Germany,* trans. Thomas Dunlop (Cambridge, Mass., 1991). See the following texts on "blood": "Wolfenbüttel Kirchenordnung, in Sehling, *Evang. Kirchenordnung,* vol. 6/1, p. 225: "Warning and Instruction. Because man and wife become one flesh through marriage, each one must keep [him or her] self from the other's consanguines"; "Preussen Consistorial Ordnung 1584," in vol. 4, p. 134: "because man and wife become one flesh through marriage, and all blood relatives of the man in whatever degree of blood relationship they are connected to the man, even in the same degree are they related to the wife in affinity"; p. 135: "Item even if a wedding or cohabitation (*Beischlafen*) does not take place, but one partner dies before the wedding, even then from discipline and propriety the [blood] relationship and affinity continue and are diminished neither through death nor any other circumstance, and even less abolished"; "Pommern Kirchenordnung," in vol. 4, p. 367: Argues that is a horror and against divine and natural law to court anyone in "the blood." A man leaves his father and mother and cleaves to his wife and they become one flesh, so that one sees that there is a great difference between parents and wife. He cleaves to his wife and sleeps with

generated by the same parents also shared the same blood, intercourse between a man and his sister-in-law involved the same kind of act as an ascendent having sexual relations with a descendent or a brother with a sister: a man and his wife's sister shared the same blood with his wife.[24] Throughout the seventeenth century a number of celebrated cases demonstrated the obsession with the problem of the wife's sister. In 1595 all of the Jews of Hildesheim were thrown out of the city because one of them had married his sister-in-law. A half century later (1649), a controversy broke out over a duke of Holstein's marriage to his deceased wife's sister, an example of an unhappy marriage that played its way out as a warning well into the eighteenth century.[25] In 1681 a prince of Oettingen first married his wife's sister and then called all of the interested theologians and jurists to a conference on the subject and published the papers.[26] By the early

her, but he honors his parents and has a natural aversion to sleeping with his parents. The text offers examples from Aristotle including the stallion that committed suicide when it discovered that it had covered its dam, p. 367; "Mecklenburg Kirchenordnung 1557, in vol. 5, p. 211: man and wife are one flesh; "Rostock Ehesachen 1581," in vol. 5, p. 293: "And because man and wife become one flesh through marriage, and affinity grows out of carnel cohabitation, it is ignorance to argue that the marriage prohibition in affinity has its origins only in papal law and is not the same prohibition in consanguinity and affinity"; "Hohenlohe Eheordnung 1572," in vol. 15, p. 180: argues that affinity grows out of consanguinity and is to be reckoned for both man and wife according to the same degree as consanguinity. A man has to keep himself away from his wife's consanguines to the exact same degree that he has to keep away from his own.

24 Just this point was still hotly debated in the mid eighteenth century in two anonymous tracts: *Bedenken über die Frage ob die Ehe mit des Bruders Witwe erlaubt sey?* (Frankfurt and Leipzig, 1758), bound together with, *Bedenken über die Frage Ob die Ehe mit des Bruders Wittwe erlaubt sey? Samt derselben umständler Widerlegung.* The first found the blood tie to be a fiction (p. 57). The second argued that the first degree of affinity is not *conceptible sine Idea consanguinitatis* (p. 89). Only dissolute desires lead to marriage with the WZ and BW. In fact, God forbade them because what was involved was an *expletio libidinis furiosae.* He explained the Levirate (the rule that a man had to marry his childless deceased brother's wife to engender progeny in his brother's name) in terms of a crucifixion of the flesh and on that account a domestic good. He argued that the concept of *respectus parentelae* was an innovation and that Leviticus 18 and 20 were only concerned with blood. "If consanguinity is the *solum & unicum fundamentum* on which all *prohibitiones hujus generis* rest, as cannot be doubted, so the prohibition remains after the death of anyone who was the *vinculum* which tied me so closely with a *tertio* or *tertia* that she had to be called my *caro carnis.*" The author called for rigorous use of Mosaic law and noted that if a few dozen people were executed for adultery, it would scare the rest into behaving (no doubt). As for the rules of blood, disobeying them puts us back into a state of pure nature. He departed, however, from the notion of a man and wife becoming one blood through intercourse. He lay stress on the Leviticus 18:6 principle of a tie built on flesh of flesh, not on the physical sharing of blood. In the nineteenth century, a conservative Lutheran theologian still found no essential distinction between consanguinity and affinity – the grounds for both being the unity of the flesh; Thiersch, *Verbot der Ehe,* p. 27.

25 A defense was written by Christoph Joachim Buchholtz, *Pro matrimonio principis cum defunctae uxoris sorore contracto: Responsum juris collegii JCTorum in academia Rintelensi* (Rinteln, 1651). He argued that there was no real blood tie between brother- and sister-in-law, only a *consanguinitatis simulachrum,* p. 109.

26 *Hochangelegene und bisshero vielfältig bestrittene Gewissens-Frage/ Ob Jemand seines verstorbenen Weibes Schwester/ sonder Ubertrettung Göttlicher und Natürlicher Gesetze/ in wiederholter Ehe zu heuratten berechtigt? Durch auff dem in der Fürstlichen Residenz zu Oettingen den 10. October. Anno 1681. gehaltenen Colloquio Ergangene Wechsel-Schrifften/ Responsa und hochvernünftige Judicia; Nach höchstes Fleisses überlegten beyderseitigen Rationibus, und hierüber gefassten Grund-Schlüssen Erörtert:*

eighteenth century, a theologian obtained a dispensation for such a marriage, which prompted a scurrilous exchange of books and the worry that such an example would open the floodgates to the common man.[27] In Württemberg, 75 percent of the cases of incest that came under official investigation involved "in-laws" of one kind or another.[28] The weight of the term "Blutschande" together with resistance to innovation point toward a fundamental unease about this key relationship, which no doubt was caused by considerations of the dynamics of rural and urban households and the problem of constant realignment of close social relationships due to early death and remarriage. Only in the course of the eighteenth century was this form of marriage made possible.

An impediment to alliance

One problem with a symbolics of blood and pollution was how to calculate the necessary distance beyond which the sharing of vital substance was no longer an issue. In the early Middle Ages, the prohibition extended "seven degrees" to sixth cousins related by blood or sixth cousins of a deceased spouse. An appropriate analogy was found in the Creation, which took six days to complete. Narrowing the prohibitions in 1215 to four degrees necessitated a new analogy, this time based on the four humors. With each degree, one humor was lost, until the blood was completely diluted. Such extensive prohibitions prompted a brisk trade in dispensations, and this was one of Luther's chief objections to the whole system. Osiander, one of the architects of a modified canon law system, at first also objected to the medieval church solution as a corrupt device for papal income.[29] With this in mind, the Protestant states, when formulating their codes,

und als ein Curiöses und ungemeines Zweiffel-Werck/ zu eines jeden gnugsamen Unterricht Truck aussgefertigt (Frankfurt and Leipzig, 1682).

27 L. Friedrich Ernst Kettner, *Grundliche Untersuchung der hochangelegenen und bissher vielfältig bestrittenen Gewissensfrage: Ob jemand seines verstorbenen Weibes leibliche Schwester nach Geist- und Weltlichen Rechten heyrathen darff?* (Quedlinburg, 1707). This edition contains various addenda and documents on the entire controversy and references to the different disputes from the Hildesheim case onwards. Kettner held strongly to the notion of a man and wife being one flesh and the wife's sister being "flesh of flesh." It was not a juridical fiction and derived from the fact that the husband and wife had mixed their flesh in physical intercourse – *per commixtionem carnis* (pp. 62–4). That the issue remained tied to the symbolics of blood can be seen from the fact that Kettner's opponent defended marriage with the WZ because affinity was not established *per sanguinem* (Beilage I).

28 Investigations into cases of incest are found in HSAS, Bestand A209. For the period between 1561 and 1778, I located 91 cases. Accepting their conflation of in-law and step-relations as equally affinal, I arrived at the figure 75.3 percent.

29 Andreas Osiander d. ä, *Gesamtausgabe,* ed. Gerhard Müller, with Gottfrid Seebass, 8 vols. (Gütersloh, 1975–90). His early opinion, in agreement with Luther, can be found in "Der Nurnberg Ratschlag (1524), vol. 1, pp. 319–86, here p. 376: "The relatives which God himself forbade must remain forbidden. Similarly, what he allowed, that must remain free." See also, "Gutachten über die Zeremonien" (1526), vol. 2, pp. 249–89, esp. 267–8, 280; "Visitacion der pfarrern afm Land" (1528), vol. 3, pp. 147–64, here 160. In the "Consilium in causa Hunerkops, qui duas sorores duxerat" (1528), in vol. 3, pp. 290–4, he expressly defended marriage with the deceased wife's sister: "God did not forbid marriage according to degrees or ranks . . . but strictly the persons

indicated from the outset that dispensations would be unavailable. Some states prohibited marriage between relatives of the "third degree" (second cousins), both consanguineal and affinal, of the same generation, while others relaxed the degree a half notch by allowing one of the partners to come from the next older generation. But they generally excluded dispensations and for the first time took steps to allow the state to check relationships objectively: through the registration of baptisms, marriages, and deaths.

In the seventeenth century, a large literature arose on the advisability of allowing this or that kind of marriage, and various test cases and petitions led to a strengthening of the boundaries at some points and a loosening at others. Most states ended up with a system of dispensations, but until well into the eighteenth century the law prevented or impeded the formation of long-term or repeated alliances of two families by prohibiting marriage between first and second cousins or a second marriage into the "Freundschaft," or kindred, of a deceased spouse. Just such alliances did develop in Neckarhausen in the eighteenth century, and a great deal of the analysis in the ensuing chapters will be devoted to their properties. But state law in the sixteenth and seventeenth centuries prohibited kinship formations of this kind and was especially concerned with preventing the renewal of alliances in the same generation with a person seeking a mate among his or her deceased spouse's consanguineal kin. There are various explanations for this concern. It is possible that state officials wished to inhibit alliances that would challenge their access to each house. Or the law might have been a response to social and cultural assumptions about the circle of kin so necessary to guarantee property interests that endogamous marriage would create undue strain. Or it all might have derived from the magical properties of ancient texts. Most likely all three considerations resonated with each other.

Incest reconfigured

In the eighteenth century, the incest problem shifted focus. In the first place, middle-class commentators rethought the nature of the house/family in terms of their own experience and new principles of social logic and reconfigured the key dyadic relationship in terms of emotion and moral sentiment or rational altruism.[30] In the dynamics of the new nuclear family, the issue was no longer how to align and realign houses through early death and remarriage but how to think about emotional attachment as the fundamental regulator of inner familial relations and the chief instrument for creating new ties between families. About the

immediately as example" (p. 291). See further to this case his letter to Georg Vogler, in vol. 3, pp. 298–301. His complete turnaround and acceptance of the principles of canon law reckoning by degrees is found in his "Von den verbotenen Heiraten" (1537), in vol. 6, pp. 407–33. Osiander's book was crucial for developing Protestant doctrine. He saw consanguineal kin as collectively responsible for protection and discipline of women. The objection to marriage with affines is that they are our own "flesh and blood."

30 E.g., Ammon, *Moralische Fundament.* The most influential writer was the Old Testament scholar, Michaelis. See *Abhandlung,* pp. 108, 146.

same time as the great student of Mosaic law, Michaelis, shifted the grounds of incest away from a discipline of the flesh and a symbolics of blood to moral reason or moral sentiment, almost every thinker came to identify the central incestual pair as the brother and sister.[31] During that period, Protestant states effectively narrowed down many of the old prohibitions that had prevented intergenerational alliances between families – on the one hand because the objections to such alliances atrophied in the face of an increasingly powerful and bureaucratic state and new theoretical foundations for the family were worked out, and on the other hand because there were new and powerful popular demands for an end to such restrictions. How the state established the conditions for familial alliances can be seen in the law of marriage prohibitions as it developed in Württemberg into the nineteenth century.[32]

Calculating the degrees

While the various Lutheran territories developed similar laws about marriage in the sixteenth century and departed from canon law in similar ways, over time they diverged a good deal. Until the end of the eighteenth century, Württemberg took a rather conservative position, which set it off from more progressive states such as Saxony and Prussia. Part of the task of this chapter is to specify the stages in the development of the Württemberg legal codes so that we can be specific about what was permissible for the Neckarhausen population at any particular time. Any discussion of the rules of marriage prohibition will seem rather arcane, but the degree of effort expended by theoreticians and administrators of our period warrants close attention to their detail.[33]

In the "Marriage and Marriage Court Ordinances of 1687" (*Ehe Ordnung und*

[31] See the excellent article by Michael Titzmann, "Literarische Strukturen und kulturelles Wissen: Das Beispiel inzestuöser Situationen in der Erzählliteratur der Goethezeit und ihre Funktionen im Denksystem der Epoche," in Jörg Schönert, with Konstantin Imm and Joachim Linder, ed., *Erzählte Kriminalität. Zur Typologie und Funktion von narrativen Darstellungen in Strafrechtspflege, Publizistik und Literatur zwischen 1770 und 1920,* Studien und Texte zur Sozialgeschichte der Literatur, vol. 27 (Tübingen, 1991), pp. 229–181. A theologian such as Carl Ludwig Nitzsch distinguished between a "pure" love between brother and sister and the inevitable instrumental love between husband and wife (pp. 66–8, 96–7, 110); *Neuer Versuch über die Ungültigkeit des mosaischen Gesetzes und den Rechtsgrund der Eheverbote in einem Gutachten über die Ehe mit des Bruders Wittwe* (Wittenberg and Zerbst, 1800). He took Michaelis to task for analyzing the matter in terms of rational ordering of the house, and looked for an explanation based on the inner necessity of feelings (pp. 61–5). See also David Warren Sabean, "Fanny and Felix Mendelssohn-Bartholdy and the Question of Incest," *Musical Quarterly* 77 (1993): 709–17.

[32] Sources for the Württemberg laws, ordinances, edicts, and mandates are found in August Ludwig Reyscher, ed., *Vollständige, historisch und kritisch bearbeitete Sammlung der württembergischen Gesetze,* 19 vols. (Stuttgart and Tübingen, 1828–51).

[33] For a review of the rules, see Goody, *Development of the Family and Marriage,* pp. 134–46; Jean-Louis Flandrin, *Families in Former Times: Kinship, Household and Sexuality,* trans. Richard Southern (Cambridge, 1979), pp. 15–30. See also Georges Duby, *The Knight, the Lady, and the Priest: The Making of Modern Marriage in Medieval France,* trans. Barbara Bray (New York, 1983). For Michael Mitterauer's objections to Goody, see "Christianity and Endogamy," *Continuity and Change* 6 (1991): 295–333.

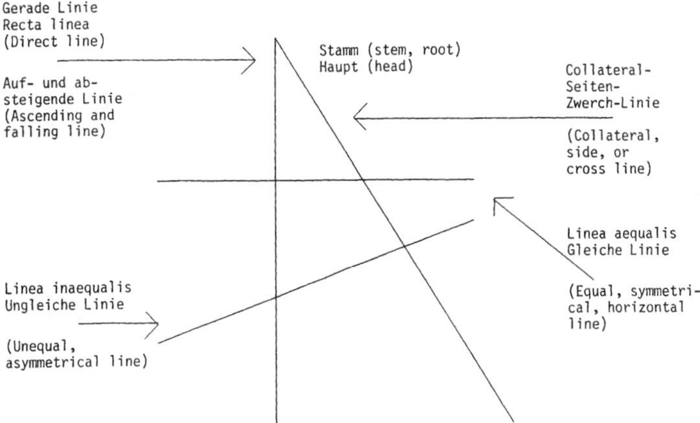

Figure 3.1

Ehegerichtsordnung), the text outlined how kinship between two people was to be reckoned for purposes of incest prohibition.[34] The rules were based on the Germanic law of reckoning adopted progressively by the church in the period after the sixth century and definitively in the eleventh.[35] Essentially the calculus distinguished between a vertical and a horizontal plane on which lines (*Linien, Lini, lineae*) were conceptualized, a perpendicular one to describe descent and ascent, a vertical one meeting the first at an angle to depict collateral relations, and a third and fourth used to figure degrees of relationship crossing these two (Figure 3.1).

Three rules were to be followed in reckoning degrees of relationship between two people. First, there are as many degrees on the vertical axis as there are people, not counting the person at the bottom or top, the point at which the calculation starts – or, from the bottom up, the number of generators, and from the top down, the number of generated. The second rule has to do with the collateral or side line when the two people concerned are on an equal, horizontal axis or line. There are as many degrees of relationship as people in either line away from the common or head "stem." The third rule applies to the collateral line when the two people concerned are on an unequal, asymmetrical axis. In this case, the degrees are reckoned in relation to the person farthest away from the head.

To explain all this, the ordinance offered a diagram (Figure 3.2). In the ascending and falling line, between great grandfather (*Aber-Aehni*) Johannes and the great granddaughter (*Aber-Enkel*) Margaretha, there are five persons and four degrees, so that they are related in the fourth degree in the direct line. Friederich

[34] Reyscher, vol. 6, pp. 85 ff., 30 April 1687. The rules were to follow canon rather than civil law. The reckoning of parricide and incest were the same.

[35] "Consanguinity," *New Cath. Encycl.*, vol. 4, p. 194; Goody, *Family and Marriage*, p. 136.

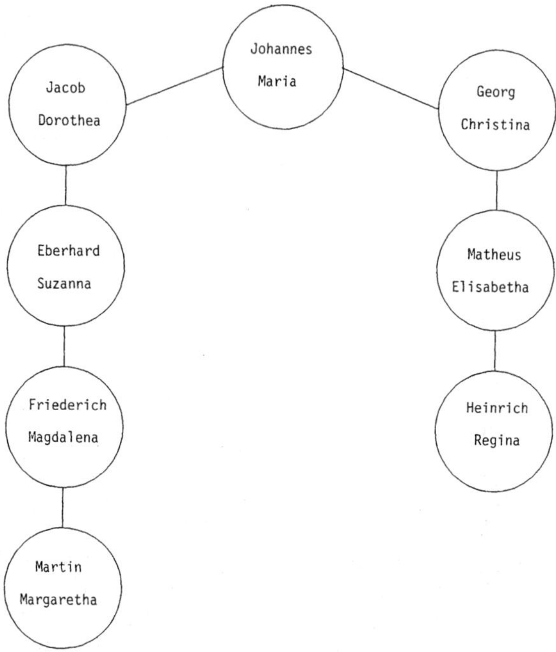

Figure 3.2

and Regina are related in the third degree of consanguinity (*Blutsverwandtschaft*) in the equal collateral line, because each is three degrees from the common root (*Stamm*), Johannes.

The description makes it clear that a *Stamm* is not a line but a person or a point, more a root than a stem. Friederich and Regina are on the same "line" or plane – in a generational sense – and equidistant from the root. One does not reckon the degrees by proceeding from one person to another, in this instance by counting six people (e.g., FFFSSD). Rather, one first determines a generational axis and counts back to a common ancestor. As Jack Goody points out, the Germanic mode of reckoning was based on the "unity of the sibling group," and despite the development of other ideas it continued to represent that notion. It is contained, for example, in the Württemberg description of first cousins as *Geschwisterkinder* (siblings' children) and second cousins as *Kindskinder* (children of [siblings'] children).[36]

[36] Goody, *Family and Marriage,* p. 136. See the discussion in A. R. Radcliffe-Brown, *Structure and Function in Primitive Society: Essays and Addresses* (London, 1952), pp. 64–71. See also the narrative of testimony in a criminal investigation in the Württemberg village of Zell u. Aichelberg from the 1740s in David Warren Sabean, *Power in the Blood,* pp. 133–4, 167–70. Gérard Delille, *Famille et propriété dans le royaume de Naples (xve–xixe siècle)*. Bibliothèque des écoles françaises d'athènes et de rome, 259 (Rome, 1985), pp. 290–2, discusses similar semantics for rural Naples.

The laws of consanguinity also embody the notion of shared substance. If half of Johannes is in Jacob, half also is in Georg, and Eberhard has a fourth, and so on. Friederich and Regina each share an eighth of the substances of Johannes and Maria. In Württemberg legal reckoning, as in canon law, the substance shared by each of these people is blood. It comes to be shared by descendants through the equal commingling of their ancestors in intercourse. But it is not just descendants and ascendants who are related to each other in this way, as already pointed out, but affines as well.[37] If a fiancé(e) dies, the survivor may not marry a close relation of the deceased until everyone is sure that there has been no mingling of blood (*commixtio sanguinis*).[38] This means, for example, that marital or sexual partners have the same degree of relation to blood relatives of either of them. A man's wife is in the first degree of affinity with his father (her father-in-law, *Schwäher*) and the latter's second wife.

As shown in Figure 3.2, the third rule applies to the collateral line whereby the individuals are offset generationally (on an unequal line or plane). Martin is related to Regina in the fourth degree of consanguinity, since he is the furthest away from the head stem (*Hauptstamm*), Johannes.

Here is not the place to offer a history of canon and Protestant Church law on the subject of marriage prohibitions, but some knowledge of Mosaic law is necessary to understand the twists and turns of Württemberg practice.[39] In Leviticus 18 and 20, a series of specific relatives are described as not marriageable – or, more true to the text, not available as sexual partners – with consequent punishments for violations (Figure 3.3).[40]

Neither text mentions ego's daughter. This may have been an oversight or simply taken as given. In any event, in the Leviticus accounts, the emphasis was on lineal ascendants and descendants and their wives, and death was the punishment for sleeping with the mother or father's wife, with the wife's mother, and with the son's wife. The punishment was progressively reduced for other offenses: banishment for sleeping with a sister, and barrenness for sleeping with the brother's wife, the father's sister, and apparently the mother's sister. As one proceeds to the side (B/Z) and down the line (SD, DD, WD, WDD, WSD), the crime diminishes in intensity. The prohibition against the WM, WZ, and WD was put into the context of polygyny and that against the BW was abrogated in case of the latter's death, since the surviving brother was supposed to marry the widow to raise seed in the name of the deceased (the levirate). Altogether, the total set of prohibitions extended to full and half siblings, parents and stepparents, uncles and aunts, children and grandchildren, daughters-in-law, and wife's

[37] "Affinity," *New Cath. Encycl.*, vol. 1, p. 168; Goody, *Family and Marriage*, p. 142.

[38] An example of the kind of trouble people could get themselves into is found in one case among many in the Württemberg archives: HSAS, A209, Bü 35 (17th century). A shepherd spent the night in bed with two sisters. After having intercourse with his own lover, he continued to do so with her sister, who was pregnant by his brother. This case of double incest led to his exile.

[39] Good discussion can be found in Goody, *Family and Marriage*; *New Cath. Encylc.*, s.v. "Affinity" and "Consanguinity"; Flandrin, *Families in Former Times*; and Duby, *The Knight, the Lady and the Priest*.

[40] To simplify matters, I will describe the issues from the point of view of a male *ego*.

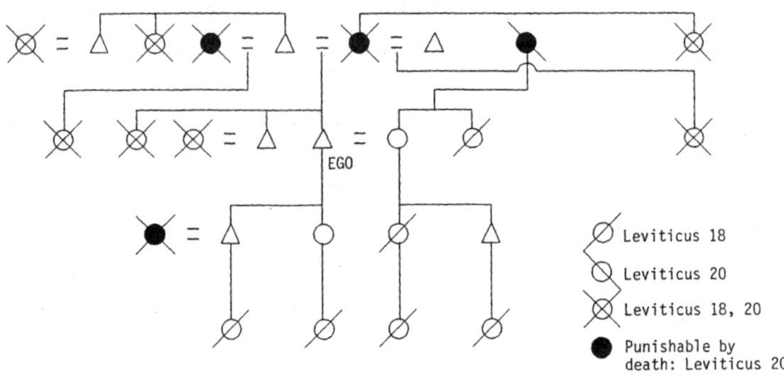

Figure 3.3

mother, sisters, daughters, and grandchildren. In this reckoning, there was no prohibition against the MBW to match the FBW; none against stepsiblings of parents; none against nieces, outside the context of polygyny; none against WM, WZ, or WD; and none at all against WMZ, WFZ, WMBW, WBW, and so on. There was absolutely no prohibition against first or second cousins.

As noted earlier, by the eleventh century the medieval church had systematized and widened the prohibited degrees to include sixth cousins and added affines up to the sixth cousins of the deceased wife. The Fourth Lateran Council (1215) reduced the extension of consanguines to the fourth degree (third cousins) and affines to the fourth collateral degree as well (third cousins of the deceased wife).[41] Despite the fact that Luther had retreated to Mosaic law, when the Protestant state of Württemberg promulgated its first marriage ordinance (*Eheordnung*) in 1534, it railed against "bestial, insolent, and shameless" people who against natural honor (*natürliche Erberkeit*) married relatives of the second and third degree of consanguinity (*Sippschaft*) or affinity (*Magschaft*).[42] According to the text, this had been going on for a long time and was getting worse, causing considerable scandal (*Argernis*). In the second marriage ordinance of 1553, the language was stepped up a notch: such marriages were against divine and natural honor and detestable (*greulich*) and loathsome (*abscheulich*) in the eyes of God.[43] The rule was clearly stated in the second ordinance: no people related in the second or third degree of consanguinity or affinity, such as children of siblings (*Geschwistrigte Kinder*) and grandchildren of siblings (*Kindskinder*), or the deceased spouse's blood relatives of the second degree in the unequal line (WFZ, etc.) could marry

[41] *New Cath. Encycl.*, s.v. "Affinity," p. 169, and "Consanguinity," p. 194; see also Goody, *Family and Marriage*, 144 ff.

[42] Reyscher, "1. Eheordnung," in vol. 4, pp. 66–9.

[43] Reyscher, "2. Eheordnung," in vol. 4, pp. 85–92.

or have sexual relations.[44] This law is, of course, more extensive than that laid down by Moses. The main extension was to collateral lines, but a second marriage to a near relative of the wife was also prohibited. There was no problem with two sets of siblings marrying each other just as there were no such prohibitions under the Mosaic restrictions. As canon law put the matter, "Affinity does not beget affinity."[45]

In the Württemberg criminal code, sexual relations between parents and children and between siblings were all equal in severity, whereas in Leviticus the emphasis is on the direct line.[46] In Württemberg, as in canon law, step-relations and in-law relations were equally affinal and seen as less serious than full-blood relations, while Leviticus considered the stepmother/stepson and father-in-law/daughter-in-law equal in severity to the M/S relation. Furthermore, in Leviticus 20, there is no mention of the stepfather/stepdaughter relation. In the next outer ring of relations in Württemberg law dealing with people related in the first and second degree of consanguinity (BD, ZD, FZ, MZ), again symmetricality was substituted for the asymmetry of the Leviticus prohibition, which fails to mention the BD and ZD. In Württemberg, one proceeded to count systematically one step at a time, making similar degrees similar in nature. It is a completely balanced system, totally cognatic, and built on the notion of shared blood and an understanding that each parent contributed an equal portion to the offspring. The less blood shared by individuals, the less serious the offense, a principle foreign to Mosaic law.[47]

Dispensations

Even though a wide range of marriages had been forbidden since the early Middle Ages, until a serviceable set of parish registers was in place (begun in the 1560s but not usually consistent in most parishes until around 1600) and a well-regulated clerical bureaucracy was trained, it was quite impossible to forbid marriages among extended consanguineal kin to an unwilling population.[48] Once the parish clergy had clear oversight and were willing to enforce the law, then dispensations offered a way for villagers to prolong or reshape their own practices.

[44] One could also not marry an adopted child, godchild, or a child under one's guardianship. Nor could a person marry his or her own son or daughter to his or her charge. These two rules are more conservative than most of the other Protestant church ordinances.

[45] *New Cath. Encycl.*, vol. 1, s.v. "Affinity," p. 169.

[46] In 1586, a mandate dealt with the penalties for violating the marriage prohibitions, Reyscher, vol. 4, pp. 443–50. Although a distinction was made between people related in the ascending and descending line, such as F/D, M/S, grandfather/granddaughter, grandmother/grandson, and those in the first degree of consanguinity (*Blutsfreundschaft*) in the side line (B/Z) whether full or half-siblings, both kinds of acts constituted incest (*Blutschande*) and merited execution. First-degree affinity (*Schwägerschaft*) (MH/WD, FW/HS, HF/SW, WM/DH, B/BW, H/WZ) was punishable by the pillory, whipping, and exile.

[47] According to the 1586 mandate, second-degree affines and consanguines who slept with each other were to get 4 weeks in jail, and third-degree relatives on the equal or unequal line 14 days.

[48] Really, not until the 1630s or 1640s could second cousins be reckoned from the registers.

There are no continuous central records to find out how many dispensations were granted in Württemberg (although they were supposed to be written into the marriage registers), but more important, none tell us how many were sought for and turned down. In various ordinances and law code revisions, reference was made from time to time to popular pressure for dispensations. This discussion will pay close attention to the periods of such demand, but of equal concern is the extent to which villagers internalized clerically imposed laws or observed their own cultural values, which may or may not have agreed with the law. By the time the sixteenth-century codes were being formulated, there had been six hundred years or so of judicial/clerical practice. Yet little is known about the extent to which peasants observed canon law, whether the sanctions were severe for violations, or whether local clergy cared at all. One certainly must not assume that because the church told the rural population that they were not to marry their second cousins, that the latter were aching to do so, even if the promulgators of the Württemberg law codes in the late sixteenth century depicted peasants as violating natural law in an orgy of incest. As parish registers indicate, by 1740 not only were the prohibitions followed, but few dispensations were sought (or obtained), and an even wider circle of kin (see Cohort I) was avoided. Legal practice in Württemberg appears to have followed popular interests and values as much as it led them. I can find no complaints on the part of the clergy about widespread violations of marriage prohibitions such as one finds about fornication and adultery.

By 1628 the lawgivers were ready to contemplate dispensations, bringing up the issue of a surviving spouse marrying a relative of the deceased, specifically someone related in the second degree of affinity on the equal plane or line (first cousins).[49] But not until 1687 were there extensive revisions of the dispensable degrees. The revised *Marriage and Marriage Court Ordinances* (3. Eheordnung und Ehegerichtsordnung) were far more detailed than before, as they now went into the specifics of the calculus of relatedness and took up the issue of dispensation.[50] The law acknowledged that Württemberg prohibitions went far beyond Leviticus but argued that the 16 persons mentioned in that text were only examples and that one should include everyone of like degree. There could be no dispensations for people in the direct line (linea recta) ad infinitum, that is, no direct ascendants and descendants – F/D, grandfather/granddaughter, and so on. This prohibition extended to the second degree of consanguinity or affinity on an unequal line (ungleich Linie): uncles and aunts (FZ, MZ, etc.), nephews and nieces (BD, ZD), and spouse's aunts and uncles, nephews and nieces. There

[49] Reyscher, vol. 5, pp. 397–8. The law stated that the duke was no more ready to grant dispensations in this case than for other degrees, leaving the reader unclear about whether petitions for release from legal restrictions had in fact been entertained even though with some reluctance before this date. Reference was made to the practice of people forcing the issue by getting pregnant. Local officials were to advise couples against such marriages but could send along petitions by widows or widowers with a good reputation, especially if they had minor children to raise.

[50] Reyscher, vol. 6, pp. 85–90.

could be no dispensation in the second degree of consanguinity on the same plane (linea aequalis) – first cousins – without almost unavoidable need (fast unvermeidliche Not). Dispensations were not to be given lightly for second-degree affinity on the equal plane (first cousins of a deceased spouse) or for second-degree consanguinity and affinity on an unequal plane (first cousins once removed). As an example of need, the code offered a poor widow with minor children (literally orphans – Waisen) who could not otherwise marry. Dispensations were allowed for those who were related in the third degree on the same line (second cousins) and who petitioned and appeared in the chancellery office – at significant expense and humiliation.

The law reiterated that relationships between affines were to be reckoned by the same system of degrees as for consanguinity. Specifically allowable without dispensations were marriages between a wife's mother and her husband's father, a stepson of a woman and her daughter from another marriage, two brothers and two sisters, a father and son and a mother and daughter, and two brothers, one with a mother and the other with her daughter. In none of these cases were the two contracting parties subject to shared blood such as a man would have with his deceased wife's sister.

The situation around 1700

At the beginning of the period covered in this book, then, marriage was prohibited between two people related through blood all the way through second cousins, a prohibition less extensive than that maintained by the Council of Trent for Catholic territories – through third cousins – but more extensive than many Lutheran territories, which soon would strip down to the Mosaic examples.[51] The prohibition was valid also for a widow or widower for blood relations of the deceased spouse up to second cousins as well. Such prohibitions made the redoubling of a marriage alliance in adjacent (first cousins) and alternate (second cousins) generations illegal as long as the prohibition was observed but did allow an alliance to be restruck after the lapse of three generations. Furthermore, considered from the point of view of a single generation, an alliance could not be maintained at the death of a spouse by making another marriage to a close relative of the deceased. Yet by the 1680s a system of dispensation was developed, lasting for over a century, which allowed second cousins without too much trouble, although a fee was charged. The difficulty arose, at least in theory, with each step closer in relationship up to first cousins, beyond which an absolute prohibition existed. The duke's "abhorrence" of marriages between cousins was mitigated by his need for cash. In any event, by the late seventeenth century it appears that the zealousness of officials and their ability to reckon kinship with

[51] According to Leopold von Ranke, Frederick the Great abolished all prohibitions not expressly in the Mosaic list as part of his population policy; *Zwölf Bücher zur Preussischen Geschichte,* 2d. ed., vols. 3 and 4, Book 7, Chapter 2, in *Sämmtliche Werke,* 54 vols. 3d. ed. (Leipzig, 1867–1900), p. 285.

the aid of 100-year runs of parish registers made a clear definition of the degrees necessary as well as a system of dispensations advisable. Above all, for present purposes it should be clear that there was no prohibition for second cousins once removed, third cousins, sibling exchange, and the like. Yet in Neckarhausen, at least, until the 1740s, no such marriages took place (see Cohort I).[52] There does not seem to have been pressure from villagers to open up marriage to cousins or to close affines during that period. In fact, they observed a much *larger* circle of prohibitions than the law made necessary. Many kinds of alliances were made between families, but they were of very peculiar kinds. Despite the relatively extended avoidance of kin, the law did allow considerably more flexibility than was taken advantage of during the first 60 years after its promulgation. After that came first a trickle and then a flood of cousin marriages.

The politics of incest

At the end of the eighteenth century, a significant reform in the system of marriage prohibitions was discussed, and the number of dispensable relationships multiplied.[53] Various church and state agencies were anxious, among other things, to bring Württemberg into conformity with other German Protestant states. The question in the first instance was whether the Leviticus prohibitions extended to persons of the same degree. The matter had been brought up in 1784 by a man seeking to marry the sister of his deceased wife and by another who wanted to marry the widow of his brother's son. The Tübingen theological faculty argued that such marriages ought to be allowed, but the more conservative Consistory (ruling body of the church) was not inclined to do so. The Marriage Court itself voted to drop the matter then but was pressured into bringing it up again 12 years later, in 1796. Just how serious such marriages were taken can be seen from a case in 1730 in which the court physician in Urach had been allowed to marry his deceased wife's sister's daughter in return for 300 florins (the cost of a more than modest house in Neckarhausen or about 15 head of cattle). In 1754, a man had secretly married his stepbrother's son's widow outside the territory and had to pay a 100-ducat fine to return to live in Württemberg.

Apparently the 1780s saw a considerable rise in the numbers of dispensations sought (about 120 years after the system had been put in place). Some conservatives were afraid that a change in the law would cause positive religion to lose its grip on the population.[54] The general consensus derived from reading Mi-

[52] Françoise Héretier, *L'exercise de la parenté* (Paris, 1981), pp. 97–106, has examined systems of alliance where extended exogamy rules can be thought of as encouraging marriage between third cousins. This was not the case for Neckarhausen.

[53] Reyscher, vol. 6, pp. 715–68.

[54] In the various debates, most of the anthropological positions of a later date were adumbrated. Some argued that there was a natural horror of marrying close relatives. Others saw in the prohibitions a political program whereby society would be knit together by forcing people to marry at a distance. A few were concerned that in-breeding would create degenerate offspring. Still others saw the issue to be good order in the house – free sexuality would bring moral breakdown at home. There

chaelis was that the different political constitutions of ancient Israel and eighteenth-century Württemberg required different rules. However, the practical problem had to do with changing a law that had heretofore been regarded as the foundation of morality. The lawgivers feared that if a change was made, then all revelation would be considered invalid. If one broke the bond of positive religion, all hell would literally break loose.

The debate was framed in the context of biblical hermeneutics, on the one hand, and the principles of social and political order, on the other. The issues had to do with the relationship of the rules of incest to correct order in the house, care for orphans, and administration of property. By the 1790s, most commentators had accepted Michaelis's position that the prohibitions in Leviticus were rooted in the need to prevent corruption and sexual crimes in the extended Hebrew household. By this principle, the trimmed-down Württemberg household simply needed a law against sexual relations between siblings or between members of the direct line. For those for whom the central issue was caring for children, the wife's sister was in fact recommended as the best substitute for the deceased wife. But some argued that marriage with the brother's wife did not have the same arguments in its favor. Many people hesitated to allow an uncle who administered a niece's property to entertain any hope of marrying her to himself or to his son. Such reasoning had characterized the sixteenth-century debates when the state first formulated its legal principles. Inheritance, property holding, patriarchal values, and the socializing of children to familial obligations in the absence of state bureaucratic organization had encouraged such extended exogamy rules. By the late eighteenth century, so much was expected from officials, it was argued, that there was little danger that an uncle *could* misuse an orphan and that there was no longer a compelling reason to restrict his freedom.

The hermeneutic issue revolved around the specific persons mentioned in Leviticus and the *ratio* behind the list. If the grounds for excluding particular spouses such as the FBW derived from the peculiar conditions of Israel after the Exodus, then it was necessary to ask after their relevance for eighteenth-century Württemberg. Advice was sought from the Württemberg consistory, as well as those in several other Protestant states, from the Tübingen theological faculty, the Marriage Court, and the Privy Council. The list of discussable cases was composed of instances not mentioned in Mosaic law but not yet dispensable in Württemberg: deceased WZ, ZD, BD, WZD, WBD, BSW, ZSW, MBW, WFZ, WMZ.

By 1797 the Württemberg Estates (*Landschaft*) were pressing for long overdue reform. Extending prohibitions from persons to degrees was untenable; in fact, the idea was based on a significant error. Above all, it made no sense to declare certain marriages punishable and then allow exceptions. There were no current "political" or constitutional grounds for continuing any extensions beyond the

was nothing new in any of these arguments; see Goody, *Family and Marriage*, 56–9, and the discussion earlier in this chapter on the sixteenth-century notions.

Mosaic proscriptions, including the BW. To maintain a list based on an illusion, to forbid and then make exceptions, left people at the mercy of officials and demonstrated the arbitrariness of the state. The whole system seemed an attempt by the duke to collect fees, which in fact had risen considerably in the previous years. When the reform finally came on 16 September 1797, the ducal government kept the schema of prohibitions but widened the number of allowable dispensations (Table 3.1) and regularized the system of fees, making a handy profit from what had become an everyday practice.[55]

As Table 3.1 shows, from time to time there is a lack of symmetry between prohibitions expressed from the points of view of males and females. The distinctions express a set of principles that emphasize male authority and agnatic kinship reckoning. Similar agnatic features turn up in the marriage system in Neckarhausen throughout the eighteenth century, which did not derive from the assumptions of bureaucrats and theologians. Yet the coincidence suggests some interaction between social practice and ideological formulations. In the prohibitions under I.A.2.b and c (for a man, his FZ and MZ, and for a woman, her BS and ZS) and the dispensable cases II.A.1 and 2 (for a man, his BD and ZD, and for a woman her FB and MB), for example, the difference has to do with generational superiority. The man could not marry a woman generationally superior to him, but he could take a wife who was generationally inferior. The principle of the FZ and MZ is warranted in Leviticus, but it was not extended to women, and they were not forbidden to marry uncles.[56]

One of the most debated issues involving the Leviticus restrictions was the differentiation of the maternal and paternal uncles. In the end, the proscription of the FBW for a male ego was maintained, while the MBW became dispensable. The correlative FZH was not seen as a problem for a woman. What distinguishes the absolutely prohibited aunts-by-marriage from those for whom a dispensation could be obtained was whether two brothers existed in the senior generation. The prohibitions reveal assumptions about agnatic descent groups: a man from generation II is forbidden to take his paternal uncle's widow as a wife. No other uncle/aunt combination was excluded. The principle of the "unity of the sibling group" that appears throughout this book emphasized an agnatic core, symbolized in the law code, past the late eighteenth century.

The problem of marrying someone who had fornicated with a sibling demonstrates a blind spot. The framers of the law were fully conscious of the situation of two sisters having a liaison with one man, but they did not mention the parallel situation of two brothers linked to one woman.[57] Here, as elsewhere, there seems

[55] In 1808 the table of fees was revised. For a dispensation of first-degree affinity (WZ) and second-degree consanguinity on an unequal plane (e.g., MBW), it cost 28 fl. Third-degree consanguinity (second cousins) and third-degree affinity (second cousins of wife) cost 8 and 6 fl, respectively.

[56] A slightly different logic is found in I.B.1.e and f (for a man, his xSD and xDD, and for a woman, her FxF and MxF) where the prohibition for a man is expressed as a downward extension and for a woman as an upward one.

[57] Their lack of interest reverses the way the issue had traditionally been seen, with the BW more

to have been a tacit premise about brothers forming a core social element, which caused theologians, administrators, and lawyers to worry about some combinations and not about others. Built into the schematic overview therefore are assumptions about gender and power – senior and junior, old and young – and about agnatic structures based on relations between brothers. These assumptions will be explored in my discussion of the networks established by marriage. In the meantime, one must keep in mind that some of the assumptions about gender and social relations cut right through the social hierarchies.

* * *

Exogamy – marriage outside the group – and endogamy – marriage inside the group – depend on the way a particular group is modeled. In today's scheme of things, a person is related in similar ways to the kin of both parents, and the genetic substance is understood to be transmitted equally through both sexes. To that extent, the current scheme is in complete agreement with canon law's reckoning by degrees, wherein blood was understood to be shared equally by men and women. Where the schemes differ is in the notion of sharing genetic substance or blood with people one is connected to through marriage. Reckoning relationships cognatically (that is, equally through agnatic and uterine ties), as pointed out in Chapter 1, creates particular problems for group formation. Each individual – or, better, each sibling group – has a unique set of relatives, which is shared with no one else. Kinship is said to be ego-focused. By contrast, emphasizing one set of relatives – either agnatic or uterine – allows recruitment to a structured group, which, depending on the needs, desires, and traditions of a society, can take on various tasks, from managing property to carrying out rituals. When a cognatic system is coupled with extended exogamy rules, it not only prevents the formation of groups based on familial recruitment, but it also continually fractionalizes the ties of any one house with all the others. Such a system makes it difficult to develop and maintain coherent political structures based on continuing, transgenerational kinship structures in competition with state and ecclesiastical institutions. Thus it is in the interest of states with weak administrative systems to prohibit marriage strategies that can lead to the integration of kindreds or clans.

From the point of view of village society as well, durable and expansive, well-coordinated groups based on lineage recruitment could distort communal social and political dynamics. But there were other reasons for creating extensive exogamy rules, extended to Freundschaften already linked by previous marriages. With high mortality rates and frequent remarriage, any particular house was

strictly hedged in with taboos than the WZ. Two brothers having intercourse with the same woman brought the commingling of their semen in one "vessel." See Kettner, *Gründliche Untersuchung*, p. 69. For an Enlightenment theologian such as Ammon, the WZ was no problem, but he found "inner grounds" to object to marriage with the BW; *Moralische Fundament*, Abh. 3, p. 13. I think the point for him involved the overwhelming moral, social, and emotional closeness of brothers, an objection that did not hold, as far as he was concerned, for sisters.

Table 3.1. *Forbidden and dispensable relations, 1797.*

	Man	Woman
I.	Indispensable cases	
A.	Consanguinity	
1.	Direct line	
	NEVER	
	a. M	a. S
	b. Grandmother	b. Grandson (*Enkel*)
	1. FM	1. SS
	2. MM	2. DS
	c. D	c. F
	d. Granddaughter (*Enkelin*)	d. Grandfather
	1. SD	1. FF
	2. DD	2. MF
2.	Side line	
	a. Z, xZ	a. B, xB
	b. FZ	b. BS
	c. MZ	c. ZS
B.	Affinity (*Schwägerschaft*)	
	NEVER	
1.	Direct line	
	a. FW	a. HS
	b. SW	b. HF
	c. WM	c. DH
	d. WD	d. MH
	e. xSD	e. FxF
	f. xDD	f. MxF
2.	Side line	
	a. FBW	a. HBS (judicial decree 1810)
	b. WZ (W divorced and living)	b. ZH (when Z divorced and living)
	c. Z of living sexual partner (*vitiatae*)	c. Sexual partner (*correum scort.*) of living Z

II.	Dispensable	
	ONLY SIDE LINE	
	Decree of 1798	
A.	Consanguinity	
1.	ZD	1. MB
2.	BD	2.FB
B.	Affinity	
1.	WZ	1. ZH
2.	WZD	2. MZH
3.	WBD	3. FZH
4.	BW	4. HB
5.	BSW	5. HFB
6.	ZSW	6. HMB
7.	MBW	7. HZS
8.	WFZ	8.BDH
9.	WMZ	9. ZDH
	Ordinance of the Marriage Court (1687)	
A.	Consanguinity	
1.	Siblings' children	1. Siblings' children
	a. FBD	a. FBS
	b. MBD	b. FZS
	c. FZD	c. MBS
	d. MZD	d. MZS
2.	All other relatives up to the third degree on the same axis (*gleicher Linie*) inclusive	
B.	Affinity	
	All the rest up to the third degree on the same axis inclusive	

Note: This table is based on the law of 23 March 1798 and was put together in a report of the Marriage Court in 1814. Various issues and problems that arose from time to time modified practice. In 1809 the petition of a man who wanted to marry a woman who had fornicated with his brother while they were both single was turned down for it was concluded that such petitions would never be accepted. In 1810 a similar judgment was passed on a petition to marry the sister of a divorced wife. In 1826 it was discovered that a woman had been married for 10 years to the brother of the man she had first had sexual relations with. Another case in 1829 involved a request for a subsequent dispensation where a man had married the sister of a women he had slept with. It was ruled (in 1833) that the superintendent bishop (*Oberbischof*) could dispense such cases. In many instances between 1797 and 1826, requests for marriage with the widow of the FB were denied. After that no one was turned down except in unusual circumstances.

Source: August Ludwig Reyscher, ed., *Vollständige, historisch und kritisch bearbeitete Sammlung der württembergischen Gesetze*, vol. 6 (Stuttgart and Tübingen, 1828–51), pp. 764–5.

constantly brought into realignment with other families. The rights of the children or those of residual, collateral heirs – frequently also minors – and of both married women and widows necessitated complex ties of godparentage, guardianship, and gender tutelage, which continually called on the services of near kin. In particular, the death of one spouse made necessary the appointment of a guardian to represent the property interests of the line with respect to the children and the collateral heirs. Marriage back into the same kindred or back into one's own consanguineal group confused and distorted interested and disinterested roles and obligations.[58] Of course, what was culturally established as a norm did not always fit the interests of particular individuals. Overall, however, at least in Neckarhausen, there was little desire to change the dynamics of alliance formation before the 1740s. And the same considerations produced a widespread conservatism in the population, to which lawgivers in the sixteenth century responded.

The medieval system – reconfigured and remobilized during the sixteenth century – was modeled on sexual temperance, patriarchal authority, and discipline. It fit extraordinarily well into the conceptualization of the "house" worked out in Lutheran theology and juridical science, which provided the dominant social model of familial relations well into the eighteenth century. It emphasized the house as an effective and efficient property-holding unit with clear tax responsibilities and well-regulated procedures for succession. The developing absolutist government created a cultural strategy to individualize each household politically, while relying on a network of services and controls offered by surrounding kin. In the mid eighteenth century, Prussian Chancellor Ludewig, a keen observer of the exogamy rules, understood that their old meaning had atrophied in the face of a well-articulated bureaucratic state, which effectively monopolized all the physical force of a society.[59] Durable alliances were no longer a threat to state authority. Contrary to expectation, it is precisely within an ideology of emotion and sentiment and a rhetoric of love, developed during the course of the eighteenth century, that tightly coordinated, long-standing familial alliances could develop. After, not before, the state lost interest in extensive exogamy rules, both rural and urban populations clamored for the right to marry cousins and sisters-in-law. "Love" came to form and reform more perfect unions, ensured the efficient reproduction of class, and provided a mask for the interested continuation of familial alliances over many generations. These are all themes that will be developed in the following chapters and brought together in Chapters 22 and 23.

Marriage alliance was only one part of a system of linkages between individuals, families, and households. During the period of extended marriage prohibitions, precluding alliances between families over more than one generation, it was quite

[58] Segalen, *Fifteen Generations,* p. 127, speaks of "patrimonial competitiveness" as an inhibition to marriage.

[59] Michaelis, *Abhandlung,* pp. 138–41.

possible to develop persisting relations through godparentage. Alliances between groups could be formed out of production routines, property management and exchange, debt, ritual kinship, crisis parenting, and gender tutelage. Different strata combined these elements in different ways, and their relative weight and patterned structures shifted kaleidoscopically over time. Even though marriage was the most crucial means for connecting and disconnecting, for linking and dividing, the set of ties has to be looked at as a whole before one can hope to understand the interrelationships of what might be called the "political economy of kinship." This is the task that will be undertaken in the remainder of the book.

COHORT I (1700–1709)

4

Introduction to kinship during the early decades of the eighteenth century

Around 1700 Neckarhausen was a small village of about 340 people.[1] Although it had recuperated from the disastrous collapse suffered during the Thirty Years' War, when its population fell from 520 to 80, the prewar levels would not be reached again until the 1780s. Almost all of the 80 households in 1700 had some land, and wealth distribution, which can be described by a smoothly ascending Lorenz curve, was not much different from the 1860s after the population had tripled. Yet there was significant economic differentiation, and the poorest 50 percent owned at most 18 percent of the real estate. Even at this early date, about a third of the adult males engaged in handicraft production or trade for at least part of the time or for part of their lives. There were a few innkeepers and bakers and a number of masons, carpenters, and smiths catering to local needs. The most numerous of artisans were the weavers, and there were periods in the lives of many agricultural producers when they wove linen cloth to tide themselves over difficult years. At the lower end of the hierarchy of wealth, the village had an assortment of farm laborers; village, field, and forest patrolmen; and herders.

Artisans were well represented in the village power structure at this period. Later, by the end of the century, they would be squeezed out of village office-holding, but during the first decade of the century, they held about half the positions on the *Gericht* (court) and *Rat* (council). Two of the four *Bürgermeister* (chief financial officers) who held office during the first decade of the eighteenth century were artisans. Although the village was dominated by land and agricultural production, there was plenty of scope for direct political participation of handicraft producers. Still, in general, only the wealthiest artisans attained office, and their families had as much land as full-fledged *Bauern* (peasant farmers),

[1] This section summarizes my findings in *Property, Production, and Family in Neckarhausen 1700–1870* (Cambridge, 1990).

which implies that they themselves spent much of their time in agriculture. Overall, artisans, though poorer than Bauern, were not relegated to a distinctly underclass position. The average handicraftsman had about 75 percent as much property as the average Bauer. In 1710, 36 Bauern held 55 percent of the wealth of the village, and 22 artisans held 29 percent.

Relations between householders were sorted out in part according to their access to plow and traction equipment. Larger property holders and older men plowed, harrowed, and carted for poorer households and younger men. Only the largest landholders consistently had full inventories of farm equipment – wagons, carts, plows, and harrows – and the distribution of horses was closely correlated with the amount of land. The complex gear necessary for outfitting a plowhorse usually was found only among very substantial farm proprietors. A good deal of the social dynamics of the village was determined by access to farming equipment. Smallholders had to purchase the services of a farmer with a plow team for cash or in exchange for labor, and larger farmers had to job for poorer villagers in order to amortize the costs of owning and maintaining equipment and animals. Agricultural production necessitated a series of cooperative agreements between people of differential wealth. And when we examine the relationships closely, we find not only that fathers and sons worked out deals among themselves but also that extended affinal kin (in-laws and in-laws of in-laws) plowed and labored for one another. It is clear that the wider circle of kin coordinated their productive activities in a way that linked together wealthy and poor and old and young. Even the tie between brothers-in-law could take on the flavor of a patron–client relationship, since they were frequently from quite different wealth strata, and as a rule agricultural equipment descended to sons and not to daughters and their husbands. It should be stressed that farming tools were closely associated with males, and that the only women who were likely to have them in their hands for a while were widows.

Access to property was more than anything else the result of inheritance. Although there was indeed a land market, it was a modest affair compared to later on in the nineteenth century, and a large percentage of what was sold went to nuclear family members. In fact, sales to people outside the immediate family probably accounted for no more than 10 percent of all property transfers, including sale, exchange, gift, and inheritance. For the most part, marriage and heirship determined most of the distribution of resources in the village. In contrast to later when the market came to play a considerable role, this system can be described as inheritance driven. But even though the land market was not very lively, its nature does indicate a few salient features of social relations. For one thing, no women on their own bought any property during the first decade of the eighteenth century. On the whole, buyers were younger than sellers, but both parties to such transactions tended to be in their 40s. A large percentage of what was sold went to people who were kin, but apart from nuclear family members very few sales went to relatives connected by blood – uncles and nephews, first and second cousins – which distinguishes this period sharply from the

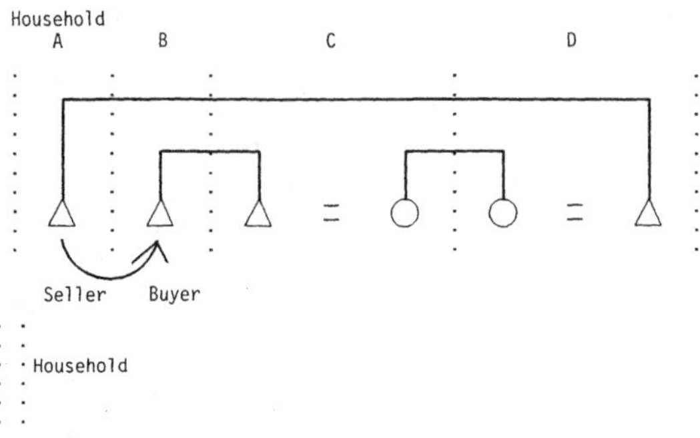

Figure 4.1

second half of the eighteenth century. About 18 percent of sales were from parents to children, and almost all the rest were between members of the same generation. Especially important were sales between people related along affinal chains. A typical example of such a sale was between a buyer and his sister-in-law's brother-in-law's brother (BWZHB). I will sort out this form in detail in the ensuing chapters, but I want to introduce it here in order to emphasize the importance of households being interlocked through siblingship and marriage and sometimes, although not in this example, through godparentage (Figure 4.1).

The men in such a situation were usually asymmetrically ordered to one another in terms of wealth and power, which put land transactions into a context of patronage and clientage, but there was another possibility, which necessitated finding a mediator between parties to a transaction. In those cases (40 percent) where buyers and sellers were not related, they frequently (55 percent) had a godparent in common. It appears that for the small amount of land that escaped familial hands, some form of go-between was necessary, and godparents often fulfilled this role. Yet they seldom directly profited from their own connection to their godkin. There are practically no examples out of the 230 transactions during the first decade of the eighteenth century of godparents buying property from or selling it directly to their clients. It must be emphasized that the property market was relatively small and that accumulation did not, for the most part, take place through purchase of land from unrelated village members. Taking on the position of godparent was not directly linked to a strategy of accumulation through the purchase of land on the market. Position in the village was established through inheritance and marriage, and perpetuation of an estate had a great deal to do with profits from office and exploitation of communal property and the labor of dependant villagers. Godparents used their own resources of wealth, office, and age to build up clienteles, enhancing their own prosperity through successful mediation among their clients.

Marriage alliance at the beginning of the eighteenth century also did not function as an institution of accumulation. Wealthy villagers, rather than searching out their fellows as marriage partners, tended to marry people poorer than themselves. In fact, the wealthiest villagers most frequently married quite destitute spouses. This pattern of asymmetrical marriage had several results. For younger partners, marrying for the first time, ties became correspondingly greater with the family that provided the larger endowment. With first marriages, it was just as common for the wife to be the wealthier spouse as for the husband, and only the more frequent tendency of men to remarry allowed the balance to be tipped in their favor over time. But still, wealthy widowers married relatively poor single women and widows. Inequality of spouses also meant that brothers-in-law were often from different wealth strata of the village or were attached quite unequally to the power structure. Since siblings were always treated equally in this partible inheritance system, unequal marriage created asymmetry among in-laws. As a result, affinal relations were often constructed in terms of patronage. One brother-in-law had a full complement of agricultural equipment, or was a member of the magistrates, or could offer his dependents the opportunity to work. Village social and political dynamics tended to depend far more on vertical linkages than on horizontal stratification. Then, as later, there was no language of stratification that was not filtered through family and kinship. Indeed, the officials' language of "class" sorted people into "good" and "bad" householders, which, however much the categories in reality encoded socioeconomic differences, still offered dynamic discriminations across the hierarchy of wealth.[2]

The flow of property was regulated through family and kin. Whatever the particular balance of wealth between marriage partners, both of them were right-bearing persons. But given the distribution of wealth and power among family members and the village at large, husbands and wives were connected differentially to kin, neighbors, and church and state officials. In the earlier volume on Neckarhausen, I tried to sort out some of the internal dynamics of the family. The primary concern here is how family alliances provided mechanisms for managing and reproducing local hierarchies. Villagers maintained a very strong sense of lineal values, and property rights focused on two essential points: any marriage involved the mobilization of property for supporting the household and for reproducing it by passing on resources to the next generation, but there was also the wider alliance between larger, interested groups, which villagers thought of as "lines."

No matter how long couples lived together, no spouse ever considered giving to the survivor final ownership in any property that he or she had inherited or even in the portion that had accrued through their common effort. Property was meant to be managed and passed along to the children, but failing proper issue, the rights of residual heirs were continually respected. In fact, children never inherited together from their parents collectively but always received lineal property – their *Väterliches* and *Mütterliches,* which emphasizes the fact that the sub-

[2] See the analysis of the language in another village in David Warren Sabean, *Power in the Blood* (Cambridge, 1984), chap. 5.

stance of the marital estate was always temporarily joined and was literally understood as an alliance. To let the property go to a spouse or to the poor would have violated a villager's conception of marriage as alliance and would have broken the tension between kingroups mediated by property.

Among other things, marriage was a property alliance between two people representing separate "lines," and each line provided a backup group to support each spouse and to represent his or her own interests; at the same time, each spouse acted as the representative of that group. Close kin were continually brought into household matters of property management as guardians and *Kriegsvögte* (gender tutors), and where suitable candidates of such positions were not available, they were filled by magistrates or members of the village patriciate.

As noted in Chapter 1, a guardian was established for children whenever either marriage partner died. For all five cohorts, I have chosen in principle a sample of 20 guardians (or *Pfleger*) in order to assess the degree to which kin were chosen for the position and to examine the kind of kin thought to be strongly enough committed to the interests of the children to carry out the task with sufficient care.[3] For this cohort, I was only able to locate 11 Pfleger, 7 of whom were related to the children under their guard. Six of the relatives were uncles, consisting of 3 FB, 1 FZH, 1 M1HB,[4] and 1 MB. The other was an extended in-law of the mother: MHBWHB.

Consider, now, some of the details. In 1704 Andreas Rieth died. His brother became Pfleger. When Johann Ludwig Baltz's widow died in 1708, the Schultheiss became Pfleger together with Baltz's brother from Oberensingen. Jerg Hess and his wife died in the 1690s. In 1710 his sister's husband (ZH) and a member of the Gericht were co-Pfleger for the estate. In 1705 Hans Heinrich Schober and his wife moved from Neckarhausen, leaving behind property and some children. In 1710 the wife's step-sister's husband acted as Pfleger. Heinrich Geiger died in 1710. The guardian for the children of his first marriage were the first wife's first husband's brother and an unrelated Bauer. Andreas Grauer died in 1699. In 1709 his children's Pfleger was related to the widow's second husband – HB1WHB (Figure 4.2). This latter relation looks strange, but it involves a series of marriages and some possible replacement of social roles by the inmarrying spouse, if it assumed the Pfleger was chosen because he was a relative. The Pfleger was the children's stepfather's sister-in-law's current husband's brother.

Choice of a Pfleger had to do with the particular dynamics of the development of a household and the specific moment in the family cycle. The desire to hedge in a surviving spouse who had young children led usually to appointing a relative of the deceased spouse. But the interests of grown children on the verge of marriage might just as easily be represented by a relative of the surviving spouse, especially if senior relatives of the deceased spouse had themselves by that time

[3] See the discussion of the sample and the tables in the Appendix.
[4] Mother's first husband's brother.

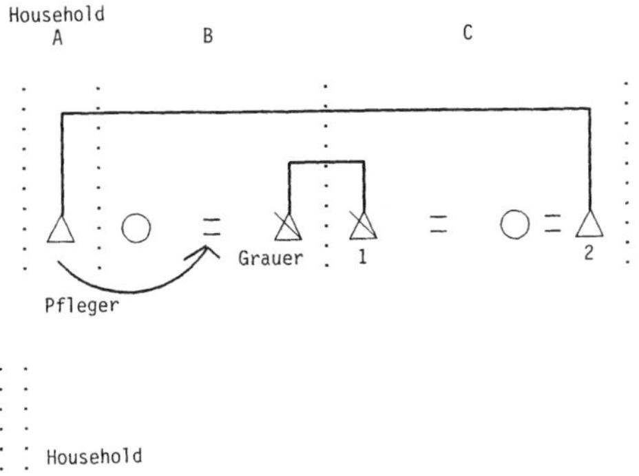

Figure 4.2

Table 4.1. *Occupations of guardians (1700–1709).*

Occupation	Number	Occupation	Number
Schultheiss	1	Not given	2
Bürgermeister	3	Cooper	1
Richter	1	Smith	1
Bauer	2		

passed on. In this instance, the guardian was the brother of the "substitute" for Grauer's brother, the man who succeeded him as head of his household.

Insofar as Pfleger were related, they were most often the closest relatives of the deceased partner, either a brother or a ZH. When both parents were dead, it was usual to have two Pfleger, apparently to represent the interests of the two families contributing to the property mass of the children under guardianship. In general, all of these Pfleger, relatives and nonrelatives, were chosen from among the best-situated families in the village (Table 4.1). One was Schultheiss and four others served on the village Gericht (three being Bürgermeister). Two others were Bauern and two had no given occupation but were apparently also from among those with considerable land. Finally, the two artisans were a cooper and a smith, occupations from among the more substantial artisanal trades in the village.

One important fact stands out: none of these guardians, whether related to their Pflegekinder or not, were godparents to them. There is no indication that godparentage played any role in managing a crisis situation for orphans. As will shortly become clear, godparents were not associated with the "lines," nor were they chosen from among kin with residual rights to the property of a deceased spouse. Godparents during this period were never blood relatives of their god-

Table 4.2. *Occupations of Kriegsvögte (1700–1709).*

Occupation	Number
Schultheiss	1
Bürgermeister	1
Gericht	3
Bauer	1
Not given	2

children, which contrasts strikingly with guardians. On the other hand, the same hierarchical tendency present among godparents was there – the Pfleger was chosen from among the propertied and officeholding groups in the village.

The other set of "outsiders" who were intimately brought into the concerns of a particular household were the Kriegsvögte, the men who accompanied married women to court to advise them concerning their rights and to provide for a third-party confirmation of their free consent. Again, in principle I looked for a sample of 20 but was able to find only 8 for the cohort 1700–09. Of these, 5 were found to be related, 3 to the woman involved and 2 to the husband: B–1, xB–1, MZH–1; HFB–1, HB–1. The sample is small but there are no surprises in terms of the types of relations established: brothers and uncles. One of the women whose Kriegsvogt was related to her husband was a widow. Of the three not traceable, two were not from Neckarhausen and may well have been relatives that cannot be traced through the family reconstitution of a single village. Further, in no case was the Kriegsvogt found to be a godparent of the woman, even for those few from different generations: guardianship, Kriegsvogtschaft, and godparentage called on different people and different kinds of relationships. As for the occupations of the Kriegsvögte, they were clearly from the landed proprietors and magistrates (Table 4.2).

* * *

I once asked an older farm woman in Neckarhausen why some families failed to succeed (*durchkommen*). She told me two quite different stories, both of which had to do with alcoholism. First, she blamed the wife, who, whenever she failed to accomplish all of the chores and get a proper meal on the table on time, drove her husband to the tavern, where he soon took up drinking, which in turn began a long, slow road to decline for the whole family. Later in the conversation my informant blamed drunkenness on heredity. Whenever you find a drunk, she said, you will find someone in the family's past who was also a drunk – it could be an uncle, a grandfather, or a great-uncle. In these two stories, my informant laid out the basic coordinates of family dynamics – alliance and descent – and she also indicated how difficult it is to fit the two together in a single system of meaning. Indeed, concentration on the one or the other has led to the warring schools among anthropologists discussed in Chapter 1.

In Neckarhausen at the beginning of the eighteenth century, descent sorted out the economic and social hierarchy. An individual householder could accumulate property slowly over time, but most of the bits and pieces that became available came through close familial connections. There was a closely knit group of people surrounding any household, which was concerned about its management of property. In the first instance, they were interested parties in the devolution of property. A woman brought her brother or uncle along to court to aid her in her deliberations with her husband about selling or mortgaging or trading her or even *his* property. In analyzing such a situation, attention shifts from descent to alliance and back again, and it is clear that the one shapes the other in a continuing dialectic. The two lines represented by the particular alliance of a single couple were given concrete form at a sale, mortgage application, retirement contract, or estate inventory by the presence of a Kriegsvogt. And in a similar fashion, a guardian representing the allied line was present at any such transaction once one partner to the alliance was deceased.

The nature of the selection of guardians and Kriegsvögte changed during the course of the eighteenth century. That, in turn, had to do with the opening up of the land market, alterations in the conduct of village politics, and changes in the form of marriage alliance. At the beginning of the eighteenth century, rich and poor continually wove webs of connection by marrying each other. Later in the century that practice would cease, but for both periods the important question is how exchanges and alliances ordered the interplay among the different social strata. Marriage was not the only institution to structure and give form to relationships. Ritual kinship also acted as a dynamic distribution mechanism. Yet godparents were not for all seasons. The position of a godparent was characterized by important elements of disinterestedness. Godparents never entered into the management of or gained personal profit from family property. They were never Kriegsvögte or guardians, and they seldom if ever bought from or sold property to their clients. Just because they were disinterested parties in all the things that attached a person to family, they could operate in a wider sphere of mediation. They could bring together their clients in order to buy, sell, or trade land with one another. And they could connect the village's Bürger with its patrician officeholders. The next four chapters explore the forms of exchange and reciprocity among kin and between kin and nonkin in an inheritance-driven property system, criss-crossed by clusters of patrons and clients constructed through marriage alliance and ritual kinship.

5

Kinship as a factor in marriage strategy

At the beginning of the eighteenth century, there were two basic coordinates for alliance formation between households and within and across generations. Inheritance, as already mentioned, distributed individuals onto a clearly marked-out social terrain and prescribed everyone's place in the village hierarchy.[1] Initially, the position of any individual in the village wealth hierarchy was the outcome of birth into a particular family. Devolution established the framework in which marital strategies were worked out, and in contrast to later in the century when the market played a central role in the distribution of village resources, family and kin dynamics were largely circumscribed by inheritance.[2]

The second coordinate of alliance formation was set by exogamy rules and practices (Chapter 3). Because such a large circle of consanguineal kin were not marriageable, alliances struck in a particular generation between householders could not be replicated easily in the following generations. For example, if two "houses" established close relations with each other through the exchange of spouses, the obvious way to reproduce the connection in the next generation was to have the children (now cousins) marry each other. Or the families could wait another generation to arrange marriages between the grandchildren (second cousins). But these sorts of strategies were closed to Württemberg villagers at the beginning of the eighteenth century, either as a result of direct prohibition from the state or because they were unwilling (or practically unable) to take recourse in the possibility of dispensations. Alliance reproduction was also impeded by the prohibition of marrying a close relative of a deceased spouse, which meant that reinforcing or replicating an alliance later on during the same generation

[1] See David Warren Sabean, *Property, Production, and Family in Neckarhausen 1700–1870* (Cambridge, 1990), pp. 363, 373–4.
[2] Sabean, *Property*, p. 413.

through marriage into the same group was also not possible. In a similar way, the lack of marriages connecting sibling groups together more than once in a generation closed off another possibility of redoubling an alliance.

The question here is what kind of alliance system could be constructed when marriage prohibitions (either by law or custom) were so extensive and access to resources so determined by inheritance. While marriage alliance was only part of a larger set of exchanges among individuals, families, houses, and groups of various kinds, it was structurally consequential because it set up permanent relationships between people and for several generations established categories of people who could or could not form new or reform old alliances. It may be objected that any small community contains mostly people who are related in one way or another and that no one could easily avoid relatives in such a situation whenever they transacted business or sought out a spouse. Yet a simple calculation shows that with first marriages 80 to 90 percent of the households even with extensive exogamy rules are not related to an individual in prohibited degrees.[3] If one adds the six or so communities surrounding any village to the marriage pool, the size of the population that is considered to be closely related is reduced to a very small proportion.[4] It simply is not true that members of small communities are always so interrelated that they cannot avoid relatives. Nevertheless many marriages in Neckarhausen at the beginning of the eighteenth century combined elements of affinity and consanguinity in specific ways to reinforce ties that people already had with one another.[5] It is, of course, possible that marriage partners did not have wider strategical considerations in mind, but the very fact of recurring patterns will suggest that choosing a spouse was far from random. In order, however, to establish this and to provide convincing evidence, I have chosen an inductive approach throughout the argument, which accepts at the outset the null hypothesis that there may have been no particular intent to marriages with kin.

In this chapter, then, I am concerned with establishing certain patterns of marriage alliance, which in turn derive from recurring strategies for connecting houses. I have already shown that at the beginning of the eighteenth century,

[3] How many households are in principle open to a person looking for a marriage partner? If one reckons that each parent and grandparent has two siblings and takes the prohibitions against marriage with consanguineal relatives out to second cousins, then in a village of about 350 people (the population of Neckarhausen around 1700), about 80 percent of the households are "nonrelated." Each successive marriage cuts off another 20 percent, the relatives of the deceased wife. In a village of 500, about 84 percent of the households are open for a first marriage, and in a village of 1,000 (Neckarhausen in 1870), about 92 percent.

[4] On the size of the territory of rural marriage, see David Sabean, "Household Formation and Geographical Mobility: A Family Register Study for a Württemberg Village 1760–1900," *Annales de démographie historique* (1970): 275–94; and Carola Lipp, in Wolfgang Kaschuba and Carola Lipp, *Dörfliches Ueberleben: Zur Geschichte materieller und sozialer Reproduktion ländlicher Gesellschaft im 19. und frühen 20. Jahrhundert,* Untersuchungen des Ludwig-Uhland Instituts der Universität Tübingen (Tübingen, 1982), pp. 478–505.

[5] Compare the parallel analysis by Gérard Delille, *Famille et propriété dans le royaume de Naples (xve–xixe siècle)*. Bibliothèque des écoles françaises d'athénes et de Rome, 259 (Rome and Paris, 1985), pp. 227–93.

marriage united people with unequal amounts of wealth.[6] There was no careful matching of field with field and barn with barn to pair up people from the same social stratum. In fact, the wealthiest individuals were most likely to marry partners with no property at all – a common instance being the union of a wealthy widower with an indigent widow. This fact suggests that marriages were more or less random as far as wealth is concerned and that however hierarchies were reproduced, they were not the outcome of endogamous marriage strategies. There were, of course, some couples whose marriage portions were roughly equivalent, but an examination of the marriages of any set of siblings demonstrates that there was no consistent strategy for all the children of a family.[7]

Exogamy rules seem to suggest that marriage between people related to each other was also in some way "random." This can be seen from the exponential way the pool of relatives as potential marriage partners increases for each generation. Assuming that each household produces two children in each generation, a person looking for a first cousin would have four families to choose from, but eight families when looking for a second cousin and sixteen when looking for a third cousin. The more distant or vague the connection, the less determined the choice. Considerable narrowing down of the field could take place by reckoning relationships stemming from the two genders differentially. Suppose, for example, that there was a series of lineages in the village determined by descent from male ancestors and that it was forbidden to marry back into one's own lineage. A man looking for a first cousin, then, could not marry his father's brother's daughter, but he could choose the daughter of his father's sister. In order to understand the exigencies behind marriage choice, one would have to investigate the rules for reckoning kinship. Were there groups in the village recruited by some principle of descent, or did people think of a field of relatives branching out equally on both sides of themselves through both paternal and maternal (agnatic and uterine) connections? Anthropologists have suggested that Europeans have a characteristically ego-focused system of reckoning relatives, which precludes the formation of groups through descent. The culture does not distinguish in practice between different kinds of "uncles" (father's brother or mother's brother) or "cousins" according to some principle setting mother's relatives off from father's relatives. Although this argument is not completely correct – most German dialects distinguish, for example, between the mother's brother and father's brother – it is true that ego-focused reckoning was characteristic of Württemberg rural society as it was in most parts of Europe. The marriage prohibitions and inheritance customs treated all relatives on both sides of a person's genealogy equally. And cousins were all grouped together under the term "siblings' children" (*Geschwisterkinder*; second cousins were *Kindskinder*) with no differentiation of the sibling group by gender.

The paradox considered in this chapter is that despite extensive marriage pro-

[6] Sabean, *Property*, pp. 225–38.
[7] Sabean, *Property*, pp. 234–6.

hibitions, no tendency to class endogamy, a complete and thoroughgoing practice of partible inheritance with sisters inheriting equal amounts of land as brothers, and an ego-focused system for reckoning kin, the pattern of marriage alliances here crystallizes out agnatic relations. In other words, the strategies of alliance combined elements of consanguinity and affinity in a way that emphasized connections between men. In all of this, cousins played a special role for each other but above all, cousins connected to each other patrilaterally (or agnatically) – that is, those reckoned through fathers but not through mothers.

A system of inheritance ought to have an effect on the practical utilization of various kin and might well establish regular exchanges that would encourage certain kinds of marriage alliance. In an area where impartible inheritance is the rule, children can be sharply differentiated in terms of their access to resources and their future life chances.[8] In a situation where one son inherits the farm and one daughter marries into a family of equal standing, the children of the home farm are faced with a clearly differentiated group of kin. The father's brothers, having inherited little property, are not in a position to aid their nephews and do not produce children that are of interest to the heir either as political allies, social companions, or marriage partners. But the relationships to the mother's brother can be quite different, since he himself is the heir to a farm of equal standing. He can offer work for his disinherited nephews, and he and his brother-in-law are equal actors in village and regional social, ritual, and political life. The farms allied together in one generation might well reproduce the alliance a generation or two later, as soon as the prohibitions have lost their force or a dispensation can be arranged.[9] Such alliances would as a matter of course be modeled on "cross" cousins – the mother's brother's daughter (MBD) or father's sister's daughter (FZD) – but not "parallel" cousins – father's brother's daughter (FBD) or mother's sister's daughter (MZD) – because of the initial differentiation of fortunes of the original sibling group. Although an impartible inheritance system ought to privilege certain kinds of relatives, there does not seem to be any reason why a partible system should, especially where daughters and sons inherit the same kinds of property and the same amounts. Yet there is an agnatic twist to marriage arrangements in Neckarhausen. Much of this chapter will be devoted to demonstrating this unexpected phenomenon and exploring its ramifications.

Because relations among siblings seem so elemental for the construction of social relations, it is necessary to pay close attention to the way the children from one family coordinated their interests and marked their status with regard to one another. I have already mentioned Radcliffe-Brown's notion of the "unity of the

[8] A good example is provided by Sigrid Khera, "An Austrian Peasant Village Under Rural Industrialization," *Behavior Science Notes* 7 (1972): 29–36. For the most recent German example, see Jürgen Schlumbohm, *Lebensläufe, Familien, Höfe: Die Bauern und Heuerleute des osnabrückischen Kirchspiels Belm in protoindustrieller Zeit, 1650–1860,* Veröffentlichungen des Max-Planck-Institut für Geschichte, vol. 110 (Göttingen, 1994), pp. 46–58.

[9] Just such a system is described by Elisabeth Claverie and Pierre Lamaison, *L'impossible mariage: Violence et parenté en Gévaudan xviie, xviiie, et xixe siécles* (Paris, 1982), discussed at length in Chapter 20.

sibling group" as the fundamental principle by which various relatives are categorized and classified in a wide range of kinship systems.[10] He recognized that other considerations such as gender or seniority also help to sort out the social arrangements with which various terminological systems are coordinated. But more than any other factor, "the strong social ties that unite brothers and sisters of the same elementary family" can be used "to build up a complex orderly arrangement of social relations amongst kin."[11] In many ways, the common term for "cousin" that appears so frequently in the texts – *Geschwisterkind* – demonstrates this idea quite well.[12] Cousins are those people who are descended from siblings and whose relationships are derived from the coordinate activity of the older generation.

Marriage alliances involve different social and political considerations depending on when they occur in the cycle of a generation. The first marriages of a group of siblings might well reflect strategical interests of the senior generation. That is, a new marriage might reproduce alliances constructed out of political, marital, ritual, or friendship considerations already in place. As time goes on, the marriage strategies of younger siblings or the remarriage of older siblings could take into consideration the political and social dynamics of the older members of the younger generation rather than work within networks constructed by parents who no longer determine how decisions are to be made. The generations remain connected by the initial considerations of the political and social situation and by the durable structural framework put in place by marriage, but the younger generation comes to devise its own strategy, and later marriages can have more to do with alliances developed by older siblings than with those of parents and grandparents. The marriage patterns typical for the early eighteenth century consist of unions that derive both from the social relations of the senior sibling group (fathers and uncles) and from those in turn of the junior sibling group (brothers and sisters).

A method for analyzing kinship patterns

The role that kinship played in marriage strategy can be assessed by tracing out all of the genealogies of the partners in the 67 marriages in my sample.[13] For present purposes, "kinship" is used to denote relatives by blood (consanguines) as well as those by marriage (affines). In the anthropological literature, the problem of kinship and marriage was first investigated in terms of the descriptive categories informants said they used to determine whom to marry or avoid mar-

[10] A. R. Radcliffe-Brown, *Structure and Function in Primitive Society* (London, 1952), pp. 66–7. A European historian who has used the concept is Martine Segalen, " 'Avoir sa part': Sibling Relations in Partible Inheritance Brittany," in Hans Medick and David Warren Sabean, eds., *Interest and Emotion: Essays on the Study of Family and Kinship* (Cambridge, 1984), pp. 129–44.

[11] Radcliffe-Brown, *Structure,* p. 67.

[12] Delille, *Famille et propriété,* p. 292, discusses a similar Neapolitan way of reckoning.

[13] The nature of the sample is discussed in the appendix. I have given a complete set of tables there for each cohort. In this chapter I reproduce tables so that the reader can follow the argument step by step.

Table 5.1. *Distribution of marriages in sample by decade (kin-related).*

Sequence	1660s	'70s	'80s	'90s	1700s	'10s	'20s	'30s	Total
H/W 1	1	3(1)	6(1)	7(1)	11(2)	8(3)	1	0	38(8)
H2+/W1	0	0	2	2	2	1	7(5)	2(1)	16(6)
W2+/H1	0	0	1	2	2(1)	2	2	0	9(1)
H/W2+	0	0	0	2(1)	0	1(1)	1	1	5(2)
Total	1(0)	3(1)	9(1)	13(2)	15(3)	12(4)	11(5)	3(1)	67(17)

Note: H = Husband; W = Wife; 1 = first marriage; 2+ = second and subsequent marriages.

rying. When it became clear that some of the systems that emerged from ethnologists' descriptions were demographically impossible, a dynamic tension was set up between ideology and practice. Here the description starts at the other end, so to speak, with the genealogical link or lack of one between spouses. In the first instance, we do not know how a villager categorized a person whom we can determine to be a particular kind of relative. The tension between perception and practice is therefore missing, at least until we can find working conceptualizations of the villagers in our sources, which give clues to their self-conscious system of classification. We have to proceed through a series of exercises to tease out regularities of behavior or structural characteristics from a tangled mass of data. Perception, ideology, and culture are not necessarily derivative from structure, but the only way to arrive at some understanding of how they are all related is to start where we can best get a foothold.

Table 5.1 presents the distribution of our sample by decade, together with an indication of the number of kin-related marriages.[14] From this table, it appears that kinship was not a negligible factor in choosing a marriage partner (one in four instances), although the level of significance is not immediately clear. It must be stressed that several gaps in the record make genealogical investigation especially difficult for this period. In addition, for those people who married outside the village, tracing any previous tie with a spouse is usually impossible, although hints are given when surnames match or a man chose a wife from the same village as a close relative did. Nonetheless, in just over one-fourth of all marriages some kinship connection can be established. It may be that families followed strategies of making one such marriage, or that second marriages were by preference contracted with kin, or that particular occupational, wealth, or age groups preferred to reinforce established links. As I have already said, however, I would dispute the idea that the figures may have come about by chance and that because a village was a relatively small unit, kin were simply hard to avoid.

The kind of kin chosen as marriage partners did not vary for this cohort over

[14] Note that the sample for each cohort begins with a group of marriages chosen from within a selected decade (here 1700–1709) but is expanded by taking all the marriages of siblings and all remarriages. Therefore the sample as a whole spills out beyond the boundaries of the decade under consideration.

time, but the evidence here does suggest a few things about the frequency. Through the first decade of the 1700s, kin-related marriages were relatively infrequent (17.1 percent) compared with later ones, while the two decades after 1710 display a definite increase (38.5 percent). On the other hand, such marriages were more associated with second unions than with first ones. Out of 47 marriages in which the husband was being married for the first time, 9 were kin-related (19.1 percent), whereas in second marriages the figure is 8 out of 21 (38.1 percent). There were many second marriages in the sample in the 1720s. Taken together, the evidence suggests that kin-related marriages were especially frequent for men remarrying and that the trend over time is due to the fact that the sample includes more of them with each decade. The practice of marrying relatives appears to have been more a part of the developing political and social relations of a particular generation – with the possibility of remarriage being an important tactical resource – than a strategy that linked two generations together.

The first point to note about the structure of kin-linked marriages in our sample is that all the sibling groups there contracted at least one of them.[15] There is no correlation between the tendency to marry kin and a man's father's or father-in-law's occupation, wealth, or position in the village hierarchy, and it does not seem necessary to belabor the point with statistics. There is no correlation either with his own mobility or future position and no suggestion that the age of the spouses had any relevance.[16] Furthermore, the occupational structure of the families concerned seems also to have played no role – since all contracted at least one kin-linked marriage. Even the two that made three such marriages display no particular pattern – the father of one was a well-off smith and Richter, whose four sons split into two Bauern and two smiths, one of the Bauern becoming Bürgermeister. The other family's father was a modest weaver. His son was a cooper who made two kin-related marriages, and the latter's half-sister married a related carpenter.

Of greater interest than absolute number, however, is the pattern of kinship relations. Since this is a complex subject, it is important to proceed step by step

15 Frequency of kin-related marriage by sibling group

Number kin-related	Frequency
0	0
1	7
2	2
3	2

16 Age at first marriage

	Men	Women
Mean	25.5	24.0
Median	24.0	23.0
Mode	23.0	21.0

Age at first marriage for kin-related marriages

	Men	Women
Number	8	13
Mean	23.6	24.2
Median	23.0	25.0

to grasp the issues and the regularities underlying the structure of kin-related marriages. That means equal attention must be given to relatives who were avoided as to those who were preferred. The first step is to draw up a list of the kinship paths between husbands and wives who were related in some way. I am proceeding systematically here in order to make the method and data clear. For subsequent cohorts, I leave such lists and their related tables in the Appendix. Although at first glance the list may seem rather bewildering, its components are actually simple forms that upon comparison are structurally similar. The 17 kin-related marriages, counting from a male *ego*,[17] were as follows:

1. BWBD
2. BWBSWZ
3. FSWBWZ (xBWBWZ)
4. BWBWHBW
5. BWBWBWZ
6. BWFBD
7. BWFBSWZ
8. BWFZHD
9. BWFZHD
10. ZHBD
11. ZHBWBD
12. ZHZHBWD
13. FBDHZ
14. FBDHFD
15. FBWZHW
16. MHBD (xFBD)
17. WFDHZHZ (WxZHZHZ)

Structural regularities

Nine of these marriages (1–9) are traced through the brother or stepbrother (3), and three through the sister (10–12) or wife's sister (17), which means that fully three-quarters of kin-related marriages involved affinal alliances traced through siblings. A few marriages – such as 13, 14, and 16 – were reckoned directly through cousins (father's brother's daughter: FBD), but "cousin elements" show up in some of the other examples as well: 6 (FBD), 7 (father's brother's son: FBS), 8 and 9 (father's sister's stepdaughter: FZxD) – almost all cases reckoning through fathers and fathers' siblings rather than through mothers and mothers' siblings. In the calculation of the path, the third person is most often a male as well (12 instances), a brother or a father. From the point of view of a male spouse, the affinal network into which he married involved coordinating interest with his brother or with his brother's brother-in-law or father-in-law, with his sister's brother-in-law, or with his uncle (FB). For women, the closest link in the chain was most often male, either the father (7 times) or the brother (4 times). Whereas links through the mother seem to have played little role (1 example), those through a sister were frequent (5 instances). Women were connected to their husbands by and large through siblings or through fathers.

Almost all the relationships here involved connections through marriage, sometimes through a series of marriages. That is, the new unions were with affinal

[17] To simplify the calculations and discussion throughout the book when analyzing marriage choice, I have traced kinship paths from husbands, but throughout the book I consider all of the issues from both male and female points of view. The reader can always read a diagram in either direction.

(by marriage) rather than with consanguineal (by blood) kin. They were mostly in-law relations such as the sister-in-law's brother's daughter (1) or the sister-in-law's first cousin (6) or the first cousin's sister-in-law (13). The only one (16) that might be construed as consanguineal (stepfather's brother's daughter: xFBD) instead of affinal was really mediated through a marriage, in this case that of the mother (mother's husband's brother's daughter: MHBD). In this regard, note that in Württemberg law, what we distinguish as in-law and step-relations were brought under the same rubric of *Schwägerschaft* (affinity).

What kinds of relatives were not chosen by men as marriage partners? To begin with, the set of consanguineal relatives were systematically avoided. No marriages occurred to first or second cousins of any kind, parallel (reckoned through same sex siblings such as father's brother or mother's sister: FBD, MZD, FFBSD, MMZDD . . .), or cross (reckoned through dissimilar sex siblings such as father's sister or mother's brother: FZD, MBD, FFZDD, MMBSD . . .).[18] There simply are no examples of marriage with "first-order" affines – no sororate (with deceased wife's sister), no levirate (with deceased brother's wife), no consanguines of the deceased wife (including first and second cousins: WFBD, WFZD, WMBD, WMZD . . .). Looking a bit further afield, one finds no marriages with the first-order affines of a man's siblings – with his brother's wife's sister or with his sister's husband's sister. Nor does one find similar marriages with the deceased wife's relatives. In this assessment, it is necessary to work negatively, first because the marriages being considered did not occur, and second because this exercise consists of negative inference, of trying to determine the size of the kin-group that was avoided by establishing which marriages did not happen. Many of the marriages that were avoided came under the incest prohibitions, some dispensable and some not. Others were quite legal. In the following list and in Figure 5.1, I have noted the absolute prohibitions (*) and the dispensable (**) possibilities. To judge from the marriages that did not take place, the relatives that were "closed" to a male ego as a spouse included:

FZ*	WM*	BW*
MZ*	WFZ*	BWZ
FBW*	WMZ*	ZHZ
MBW*	WFBW	
BD*	WMBW	
ZD*	WZ*	
FBD**	WBD*	
MZD**	WZD*	
FZD**	WZHZ	
MBD**	WBWZ	
FBSD** . . .	WFBD**	
FFZDD** . . .	WFZD**	
MMZDD** . . .	WMBD**	
MMBSD** . . .	WMZD**	
	WFFBSD** . . .	
	.	
	.	

* Absolute prohibition.
** Dispensable according to the Third Marriage Ordinance of 1687.

[18] I also examined third-cousin possibilities systematically and found none.

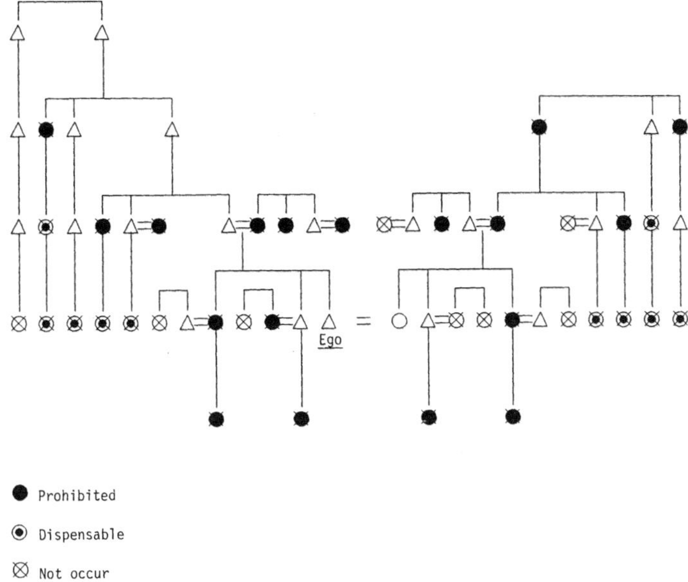

Figure 5.1

One of the striking patterns to notice in many of the kinship paths connecting husbands and wives is the configuration "FB." It goes with FBD (6, 8, and 9 [FZHD], 13, 14, 16 [MHBD]), FBS (7), and FBW (1 percent). Most frequently, it emphasizes connections through a patrilateral (reckoned over the father) parallel (to a same-sex sibling) cousin (FBS/D). What we do not find are connections through the cross cousins (MBS/D, FZS/D) or matrilateral parallel cousins (MZS/D).

Patrilateral parallel cousin/sibling marriages

These regularities will be examined more closely later, but first it is necessary to examine the structure of each marriage in succession to see if there are any formal characteristics common to any of them. To begin with, consider number 6 (Figure 5.2), where a man designated as "ego" married his sister-in-law's (brother's wife's) cousin (father's brother's daughter) (BWFBD). In this instance, the formal relationships depict a clearly symmetrical pattern: two brothers married the daughters of two brothers. From the point of view of wife A, the relationship to B is patrilateral because it is reckoned through her father. It is also parallel because it is traced through her father's brother and not his sister (cross). Since

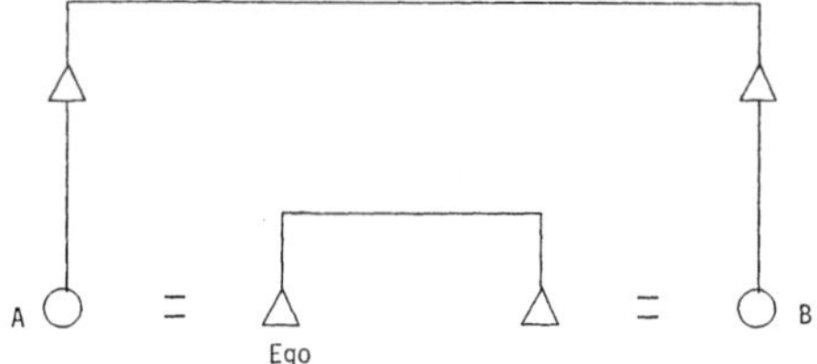

Figure 5.2

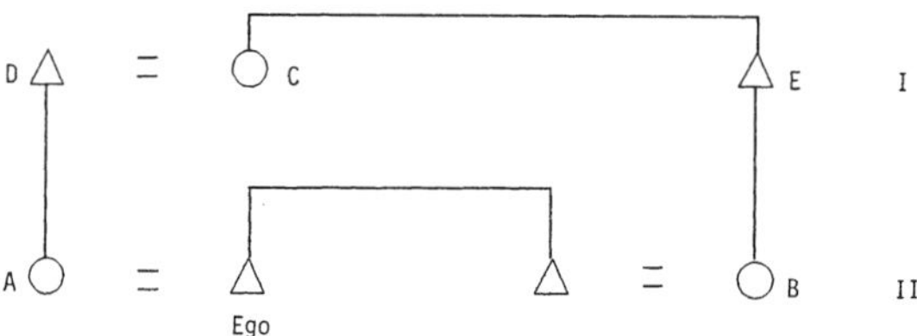

Figure 5.3

B's path to A is the same, the two women are patrilateral parallel cousins. Close attention to this form of reckoning is necessary because cousins related to each other through ascendant males figure prominently in the kin-related marriages in this period.

Similar symmetricality is found in the two marriages 8 and 9 (Figure 5.3). In these cases the daughters of two brothers-in-law married two brothers. The two wives, strictly speaking, were not cousins since A was the daughter not of C but of the latter's "Ehesuccessor" (marital successor). One might call A and B "step-cousins." During this period one almost never finds the children of a brother and sister (cross cousins) marrying two siblings – not in this sample, not in the wider sample discussed in the Appendix (altogether, 195 couples in the two samples), and not in the multigenerational genealogies developed in later chapters, which trace families back to the sixteenth century.[19] Since the parallel male sibling relation in generation I recurs so exclusively that it can be assumed to have structural significance, then it could be that the brothers-in-law D and E in this formation acted like brothers in some fashion after the death of C. Since

[19] Scott Waugh, in *The Lordship of England: Royal Wardships and Marriages in English Society and Politics 1217–1327* (Princeton, 1988), pp. 42–5, finds examples of this form of alliance among the thirteenth-century English aristocracy, but there the senior generation was composed of brother and sister. Delille, *Famille et propriété*, pp. 230–59, finds the same patrilateral parallel form in rural Naples for the same period I am dealing with.

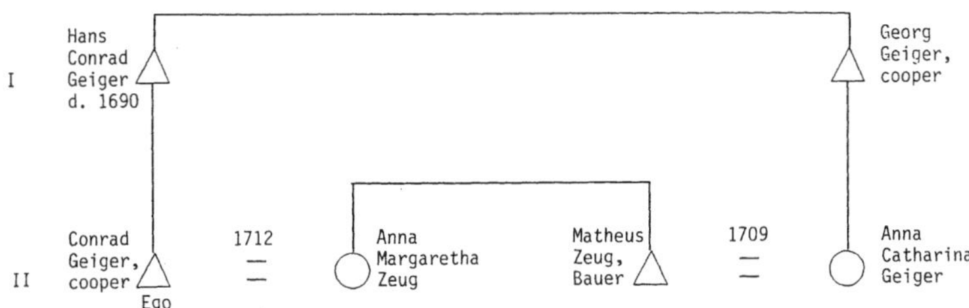

Figure 5.4

in this period there were no instances of cross-cousin/sibling marriages, it could be that the step-relation made this particular formation possible.

Example 13 (FBDHZ) (Figure 5.4) looks rather different from the first 9, since ego connected through an uncle (father's brother) rather than a brother. Although this case introduces some variation, when drawn in a diagram, it displays a shape similar to the first ones examined. This time children of opposite sex of two brothers married two siblings of the opposite sex. But as before male siblings in generation I remain the recurrent structural element. In the overall pattern of this formation, the building blocks appear to be pairs of siblings. At the level of generation II, where marriage exchange was currently taking place, what mattered for siblings was common descent, not sexual pairing. Moving back one generation, the sibling pair was reduced to the figure of two brothers. Apparently, regardless of the way the interests of siblings were coordinated in one generation, a male principle of selection was at work that crystallized out sets of brothers as the generations moved along. How this is to be understood cannot be inferred from this evidence alone, but it does appear that within the larger set of siblings, brothers maintained social relations over time, or fulfilled special functions for each other that enabled their children to enter into a set of coordinated marriages. Tentatively, I would suggest that the marriage of ego in this example connected two agnatic lines, one of which is represented by him and his cousin and the other by the sibling set they married into. In this instance the alliance struck at one generation level (II) (1709) was redoubled a few years later in the same generation (1712). It represents a concentration between two sets of people characterized by agnatic principles. The fact that we find no examples of sibling exchange (i.e., marriage between ego and his ZHZ or BWZ, or two siblings marrying two siblings) argues for a disinclination to redouble exchange for families too close to each other, even though there were no legal objections to such marriages. Cousins marrying siblings apparently widened the distance just enough to make such exchanges desirable.

This particular example warrants a closer look. Conrad Geiger, who married into the Zeug family in 1712, was the son of Hans Conrad Geiger, a weaver, who died five years after his own marriage, when young Conrad was three years old. A year later, the widow married Jerg Meyer from Grossbettlingen. There is no indication in the various postmortem inventories – several are missing – about who acted as guardian for Conrad, but, in view of the information from Chapter 4, the most likely candidate was a brother of the young boy's father. The fact that there is no notice in the burial register of Jerg Meyer's death – or any postmortem inventory for him – suggests that he and the widow Geiger had not made their home in Neckarhausen. She would return for her third marriage in 1713. In any event, young Conrad most likely learned the cooper handicraft from his uncle, Georg, his probable guardian, and perhaps even grew up in his uncle's household. In this particular family, the FB substituted for the F as caretaker of property rights and as instructor in a handicraft. Conrad was most likely attached to Georg's household as closely as it was possible without being a son. Georg Geiger's ward (Pflegesohn) and daughter, then, married the brother and sister Zeug. At the first marriage in 1706, Matheus Zeug brought 108 fl and Anna Catharina Geiger 273 fl – fitting the pattern of asymmetricality found earlier.[20] *In 1712, Anna Margaretha Zeug brought 160 fl worth of property, including nine fields, while Conrad Geiger brought 109 fl worth, together with seven fields.*[21] *In each case, the wife brought the larger portion, with the Geiger family the wealthier partner in one marriage and the poorer in the other. With the second marriage, a balanced reciprocity was established between the two agnatic lines, which raises the possibility that the overall lack of symmetry that each marriage represented was part of a larger exchange system that sometimes approached closure through relatively short circuits but was usually more open ended.*[22]

The Geiger/Zeug marriages provide an example of some of the context that might surround one of the kin-linked marriages we are studying. Probably no such marriage was like any other in terms of its family composition, property relations, power situation, or the nature of its exchanges. We could study many details of each example and would thereby no doubt enrich our understanding of the possibilities, but there is seldom enough material in the records during this period even to begin to describe the meaning of each family's strategical intent. What is present is a series of interlocking marriages at the level of one generation, which suggest that marriage was part of a more complex set of exchanges and agnatic principles of alliance.

According to the temporal and generational aspects of the kin-linked marriages, the patterns that are turning up did not tie generations together in an alternating set of reciprocities – this is not a system in which a marriage exchange in one generation was replicated in another exchange one, two, or three generations later. All the unions were coordinated on a horizontal generational axis in a kind of agglutination process. Although the first opening can sometimes be understood

[20] *Inventuren und Teilungen*, 316 (1.12.1706). See Sabean, *Property*, pp. 225–38.

[21] *Inventuren und Teilungen*, 356 (12.12.1712).

[22] This would involve a play of debt and credit between lines, an essential element in the alliance analyses worked out by Delille, *Famille et propriété*, pp. 217–29; and Claverie and Lamaison, *L'impossible mariage*, pp. 89–110. However, the analysis of all the marriages of this cohort does not suggest such closure but precisely the maintenance of asymmetry.

in the context of the politics of the parent generation, later in the cycle the younger siblings married in the context of the alliances constructed by the older ones. In this study, I count only the marriage that closes the circle, the one that was kin-linked because an earlier marriage set up its possibility. Once the new marriage took place, however, the relationships of the previous marriage were realigned as a result. If one were to abstract time from the system and ask how many spouses were married to partners who were also linked to them by kinship, the number would more than double (the structures discussed later on in this chapter link three or four sibling groups together). Under this calculation, 50–80 percent of the married population would be wedded to a spouse who was also related through affinity during part of their lives.[23] In the example here, the two junior households and Georg Geiger's were connected until 1740, for a period of almost thirty years. If affinal ties are added to the widowed mother of the Zeug children, who died in 1720, then the marriage in 1712 that "closed the circle" brought four households together for a period of time in overlapping affinal relationships. As noted in Chapter 2, the relationships between people whose children were married were politically important and were marked by a special term: *Gegenschweher* (co-parents-in-law).

In the instance being discussed here, Conrad Geiger came to share a mother-in-law with his first cousin. The husband of his first cousin became his brother-in-law, and her sister-in-law, his wife. From Anna Catharina Geiger's perspective, her sister-in-law was now married to her cousin, the young man who probably grew up in the same house with her and who almost certainly worked for her father (Conrad Geiger, although a cooper by trade, had no tools of the craft when he married). Her husband, Matheus Zeug, was integrated into two estates at his marriage, that of his parents (his father died in 1709) and that of his parents-in-law. Since he took no farm tools into his marriage, he was dependent on the older generation for capital equipment to work his own land and that of his wife.[24] *He certainly did not bring any housing or barn space into his marriage either. Whether his wife did is not clear, since a page is missing from their marriage inventory, but given the larger share of his wife's property, he may well have been oriented more toward his father-in-law's economy at first than to his own father's. By the time of his father's death, however, he occupied the building next door, perhaps built in the interim.*[25] *When Conrad Geiger married Zeug's sister, both men became involved in the same two estates. They worked land that came from Zeug's father and mother and had to cooperate with each other directly as far as cultivating their own four contiguous strips was concerned.*[26] *Both men were also oriented toward Georg Geiger's economy in terms of using equipment and in offering labor*

[23] In the analysis of Martine Segalen, *Fifteen Generations of Bretons: Kinship and Society in Lower Brittany 1720–1980,* trans. Z. S. Underwood (Cambridge, 1991), she calls this process "relinking." It is not clear from her discussion whether her figure of 80 percent of all marriages involving "relinking" abstracts time.

[24] For an analysis of this practice, see Sabean, *Property,* pp. 300–311.

[25] *Inventuren und Teilungen,* 344 (16.4.1709).

[26] When a strip was divided among heirs, although each owner planted and harvested his or her own crop, cultivation had to be carried on together for several reasons. Common headlands were nec-

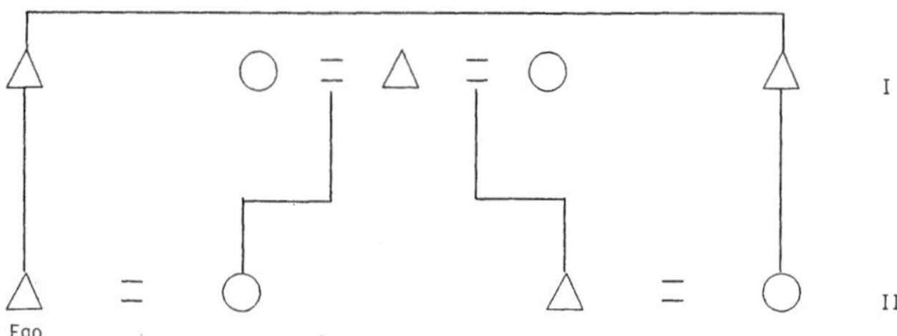

Figure 5.5

to the older man. At Conrad Geiger's death in 1729, Mathes Zeug became the guardian of his 14-year-old nephew.[27]

Example 14 (FBDHFD) (Figure 5.5) is similar, except for having a step-relation (FBDHxZ). Here, as in many other instances, half-brothers or half-sisters appear in the same place as full siblings. Certain ambivalences were built into their relationships, since they only inherited from the common parent and could therefore be sharply differentiated from each other.[28] And, of course, step-siblings brought up in the same household could be subject to psychological differentiation on the part of the parents. People referred to full siblings as *leiblich* (corporal) just as they referred to in-laws connected through siblings as *leiblich* to distinguish those connected through their wives. And there is an example of a man referring to his wife's brother as "my real [*echt*] brother" to distinguish him from her stepbrother.[29] Still, as explained in Chapter 1, godparents connected half-siblings together in a single group, emphasizing their collective unity or the unity of the house they came from.[30] Given the facts of frequent remarriage in this society, children brought up in the same household or sharing a common parent frequently maintained similar political, social, and ritual ties to those that bound full siblings.

Other variations on the schema can be seen in 10 (ZHBD) and 1 (BWBD) (Figure 5.6). Although in these instances the sibling groups were not married to two cousins but to an uncle and niece or aunt and niece, the same sibling for-

essary to turn the plow or harrow at the end of each furrow. Adding a boundary strip in any case would have reduced the amount of available land. Strips that continued to be cultivated as a unit were always listed in the land registers or inventories with their dimensions, the fraction belonging to a particular individual, and their coordinates: "half of a half Morgen 2 and 1/4 Eighths arable strip in such and such a field between so and so and so and so."

27 *Inventuren und Teilungen,* 507 (8.6.1729).

28 For an example, see Sabean, *Property,* p. 198.

29 See David Warren Sabean, "Young Bees in an Empty Hive: Relations between Brothers-in-Law in a South German Village around 1800," in Hans Medick and David Warren Sabean, eds., *Interest and Emotion: Essays on the Study of Family and Kinship* (Cambridge, 1984), pp. 171–86, here p. 183.

30 Cf. the practice of older half-siblings acting as godparents for younger ones discussed by Segalen, *Fifteen Generations,* p. 267.

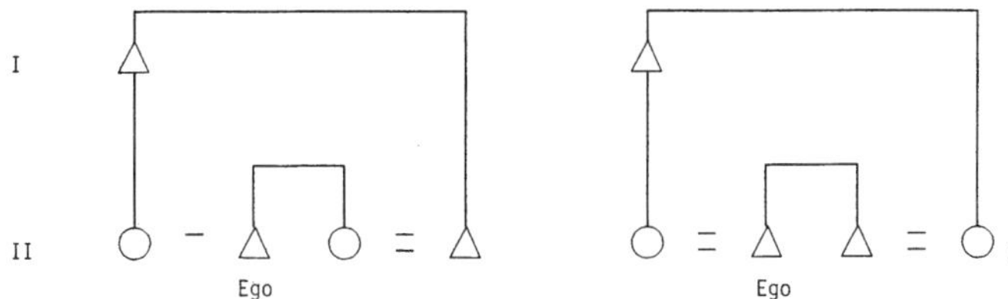

Figure 5.6

mations occur: cross-sex possibilities in generation II and if not parallel male siblings in "generation I," then an apical male in the sense that in the second example the woman "A" stood ambiguously in two generations.[31] Although there are no examples of sibling exchange, where several siblings from one family married several from another – something that frequently occurred in the nineteenth century – these two examples come as close to such exchange as any in this period. It appears that villagers found such intensive, repeated marital alliances as sibling exchange incestuous, or that pastors advised them against such marriages even though they were legal, or that alliances redoubled so intimately were not attractive because although they might bind two houses closer together, they would not maximize links with other households: all of the marriages we have been examining bring around a circle so to speak, linking three, four, or more households together in overlapping affinal relationships.[32] A simple exchange of children would minimize the number of linked households and limit their political and social ties to the community.

Case 15 (FBWZHW) (Figure 5.7) is a variation on the previous one. In this instance, ego was the Ehesuccessor (marital successor) of alter; that is, through a series of deaths and remarriages, he came to take over the household originally founded by his uncle's sister-in-law and her husband. When ego died, his uncle, A, Bürgermeister, became his widow's Kriegsvogt, she being also the latter's "sister-in-law" through marital succession. This example illustrates the principle that a "marital successor" took over the social role of his or her predecessor, not just as husband or wife but as head of a house or his spouse. The Gevatter

[31] Delille, *Famille et propriété,* pp. 244–9, analyzes this kind of marriage in terms of elementary exchange, suggesting that an uncle and niece marrying two siblings works the same as "restricted" exchange (FZD), with the direction of exchange reversed for each generation, while an aunt and niece marrying siblings follows a pattern akin to "generalized" exchange, sending women in the same direction in successive generations. I do not think it is necessary to introduce elementary forms of exchange here. The matter will be discussed at length in Chapter 20, where I will consider Delille's argument.

[32] Outside the two samples of 195 marriages, there was one example from the period: the son of the Schultheiss (chief village administrator) Johann Georg Rieth I (1740–92), named after his father and who served for many years on the Gericht (court) and eventually himself became Schultheiss and married the daughter of a Schultheiss from a neighboring village. His sister married the son. This was certainly a departure from a well-established practice and illustrates how the wealthy and powerful demonstrate their status through anomalous practices.

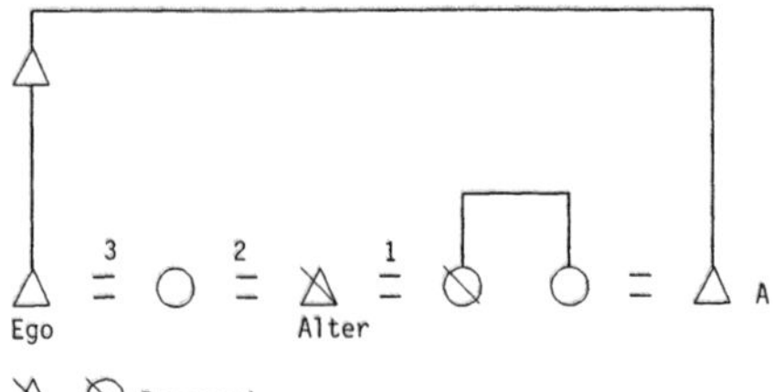

Figure 5.7

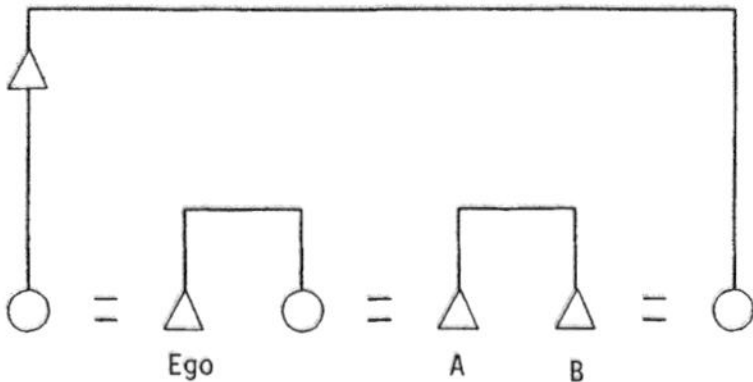

Figure 5.8

(godparent) of the predecessor became the Gevatter of the successor. A man cultivated the same property, becoming part of the network of tool ownership and labor utilization as his wife's former spouse. In this example, alter and ego presided over the same house, and the marriage of ego can be understood to have the same strategic intent of creating overlapping kinship interests and opening up a chain of linkages into the community as the others we have examined.

Number 11 (ZHBWBD) (Figure 5.8) introduces further variations and a structural difference. In this case there are two linked sibling groups further linked with an aunt and niece, although as in case 1 (Figure 5.6), a male stands at the apex. The consanguineal pairs – FZ/BD, B/Z, B/B – involve cross sex and both kinds of parallel sex pairing.

Case 12 (ZHZHBWD) (Figure 5.9) has structural similarities to 11 with a reversed step-relation to that of 8 and 9 (Figure 5.3). Case 7 (Figure 5.10) is similar to this one, except that the senior generation is composed of male siblings in place.

The addition of an extra sibling group in these examples extends the horizontal axis of relations, putting three agnatic groups in relationship to one another. The complex considerations of family members that may have led to such a formation are not apparent from this evidence, so that it is difficult to know, for example, whether the new sets of relations set up among interlocking sets of brothers-in-law was the prime consideration or whether important interests of women were also satisfied by closing the circle on the chain of relatives. The fact that so many of these kin-linked unions were second and third marriages suggests that they

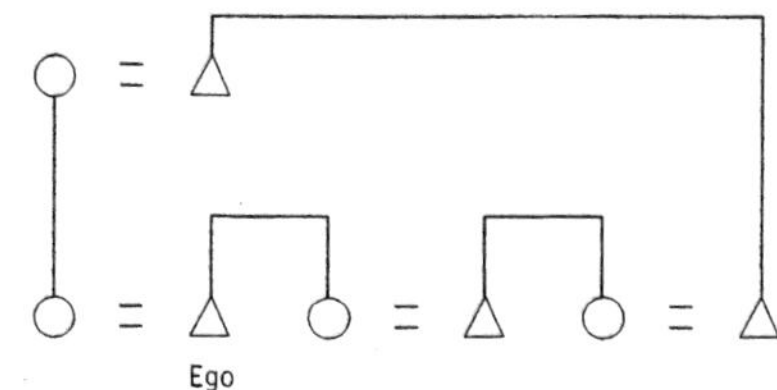

Figure 5.9

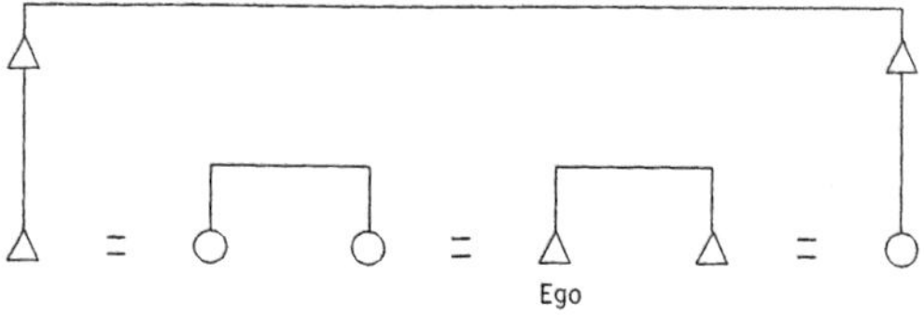

Figure 5.10

grew out of relationships that had been developed by adults of that particular generation over time. Volume I showed that wealth was accumulated in marriage and that a person remarrying was almost always the wealthier partner.[33] With a far greater propensity for men to remarry, an element of hypergamy (marriage of women upward) was introduced. This means that as the final link was closed in these chains, in most instances a wealthy male married a relatively poor female. And it is quite possible to see such marriages as supplying a widower with a housekeeper, or furnishing a widow with secure support, or perhaps both considerations were part of the calculation. In any event, the interlocking sets of people were put together on asymmetrical principles.

Interlocking sibling households

As explained in Volume I, the agnatic bias to cousinship by the mid eighteenth century was rooted in part in the facts of agricultural production and the fissioning of land.[34] The rising population and the process of inheritance by the turn of the century was already leading to the splitting up of strips between landholders who had to cooperate to cultivate them. Given the asymmetricality in marriage relations, the importance of remarriage in the overall structure of kin-relatedness, and the crystallization of pairs of brothers out from sibling groups as the generations turned over, it would seem that the primary force behind the interlocking sets of householders was the chain of relationships between men. Even courtship appears to have taken place within the context of

[33] Sabean, *Property*, pp. 225–33.
[34] Sabean, *Property*, pp. 311–16.

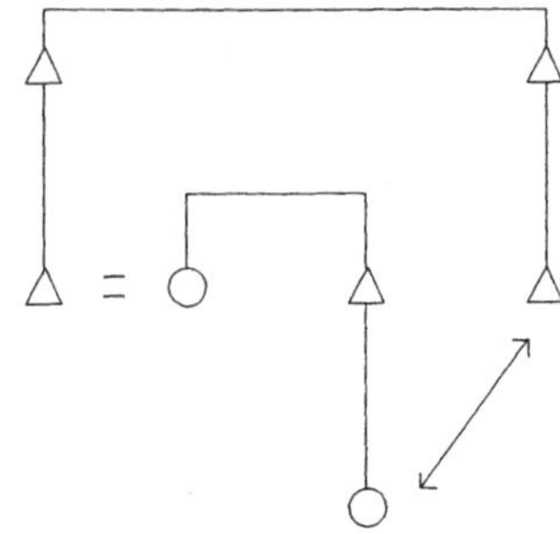

Figure 5.11

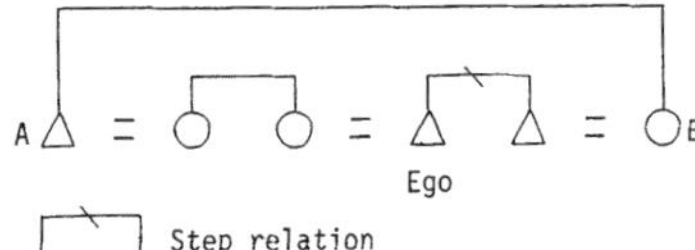

Figure 5.12

male networks. In an early case of contested illegitimacy, for example, a young man from another village began a sexual relationship with a Neckarhausen woman within a few days of his arrival (Figure 5.11).[35] The parents of the woman had observed the correct etiquette: the young man had been brought to Neckarhausen by his cousin who was also brother-in-law to the woman's father, a variation of what is found here:

In these last examples, kinship connections through the BW (cases 1–9) are often structurally similar to those reckoned through the FB (13–15) and through the ZH (10–12). Consider, now, the remaining instances, beginning with 3 (xBWBWZ) (Figure 5.12).

Just as in the last two cases, there are three sets of marriage partners. Instead of being cousins, this time A and B are brother and sister. With the disappearance of the senior connecting generation, such examples as these always involve a horizontal extension to include at least three sibling groups, which like the first structures we have studied avoid sibling exchange. This particular example offers two sets of parallel siblings and one crossed set. The relationships between the males are B, WB/ZH, and WZH; of the females, Z, HZ/BW, HBW. The similarity between this structure and the patrilateral parallel cousin/sibling marriage lies in the fact that it avoids unions between sibling sets, between uncles and nieces, first cousins, and first-order affines while connecting three households

[35] *Kirchenkonvent,* vol. 1, p. 134 (3.5.1744). See the transcript of this case in David Sabean, "Unehelichkeit: Ein Aspekt sozialer Reproduktion kleinbäuerlicher Produzenten. Zu einer Analyse dörflicher Quellen um 1800," in Robert Berdahl et al., eds., *Klassen und Kultur: Sozialanthropologische Perspektiven in der Geschichtsschreibung* (Frankfurt, 1982), pp. 54–76, here pp. 74–6.

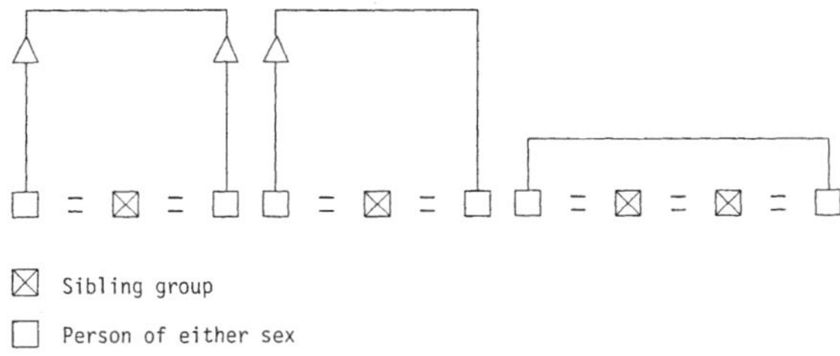

Figure 5.13

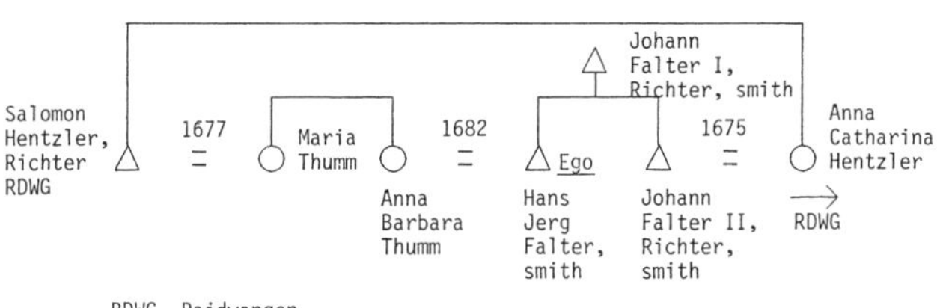

Figure 5.14

together. Any attempt to develop groups as a core of political or economic or social activity involves linkages with other families to maintain cohesion over time. The permutations in this system (or the "structural transformations") appear in Figure 5.13.

As the preceding exercises have established, siblings coordinated their interests in some manner or other and, more strikingly, first cousins did so as well. Cousinship, especially when established through agnatic relations, was a principle of apparent importance at the beginning of the eighteenth century. Although it is impossible to explore all of the structural significance of cousin relations for the period, some of the coordinated activities of *Geschwisterkinder* are already evident and will become clearer still when the changes in their relations over the eighteenth and nineteenth centuries are examined.

It is very difficult to provide details of the larger context of family relations in this early period because of the fragmented nature of the information available on any given network that has been uncovered thus far. When names and occupations are examined in the last case (3, Figure 5.12), for example, it seems that position in the village hierarchy played a role in those relations (Figure 5.14).

In this instance, Hans Jerg Falter, when he married Anna Barbara Thumm in 1682, redoubled a connection established by his brother in 1675. He came to share the same father-in-law with Salomon Hentzler, his brother's brother-in-law. Hans Jerg and his brother were both smiths, as their father had been before them. Only one of them – Hans Jerg first – was able to follow the father on the Gericht at a time, however. The alliances brought the Richter family of Falter in Neckarhausen together

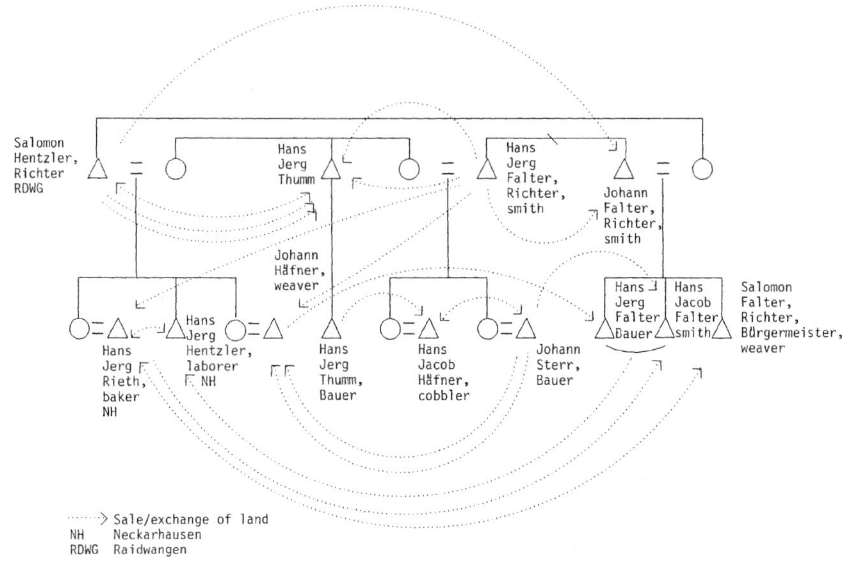

Figure 5.15

with the Richter family of Hentzler in Raidwangen. All three sets of parents called upon the same people as godparents for their children. Both Johann and Hans Jerg Falter had Johann Georg Rieth, Schultheiss in Neckarhausen, and Anna the wife of another Salomon Hentzler, Schultheiss in Raidwangen. Salomon Hentzler and Maria Thumm chose Salomon Hentzler, Schultheiss, and Anna Margaretha, the wife of Schultheiss Johann Georg Rieth. Thus the relationships set up through affinal connections were also within the orbit of ritual kinship. Interactions between the various families over time have not left much trace in the records, but when Hans Jerg Falter died in 1728, leaving minor children from two marriages and a widow, the guardian for one set of children was Salomon Hentzler's son Georg – a resident of Neckarhausen – and the guardian for the other set was Johann Falter II's son, Johann.[36] Another group of sources showing how the marital relations set up in the first generation could involve further exchanges in the next are the records of property sales. Figure 5.15 depicts all the transactions among these people and their children from 1680 to 1724.

In generation I, the various brothers-in-law sold land and buildings to, or exchanged them with, each other – the relationships being B, ZH, and WB. Salomon Hentzler sold off most of the properties that his wife, Maria Thumm from Neckarhausen, had brought into the marriage to his ZH, Johann Falter, in 1685, three years after Johann's brother Hans Jerg married into the Thumm family. Although Hentzler sold the property within his own nuclear family – to his sister and her husband – he did

[36] *Inventuren und Teilungen*, 493 (17.11.1728).

not sell it back into the branch of the family it had come from, that is, to his wife's brother. But both Hans Jerg Falter and Salomon Hentzler did sell to, or trade with, their wives' brother, Hans Jerg Thumm. These transactions fit into the findings from Property, Production, and Family in Neckarhausen, *where I noted that a large percentage of the market in land involved members of the nuclear family. In fact, out of the 19 transactions in this instance, 9 went to brothers and sisters (or their husbands).*[37] *Although Hans Jerg Falter never transacted any property directly with Salomon Hentzler, he did sell to two of Salomon's sons-in-law from Neckarhausen, Hans Jerg Rieth, baker, and Johann Häfner, weaver. They were, of course, also Hans Jerg's WZDHs. One of Hans Jerg's sons-in-law, Johann Sterr, also transacted with Salomon Hentzler's son-in-law, Johann Häfner. All three of Johann Falter's sons dealt with Salomon's Neckarhausen son and sons-in-law. Describing all the relations in both directions involving the second generation, we find: WMZH, WZDH, WB, ZH, WFZS, MBDH, FZDH, WMBS, WZH, WFBS, FBDH, FZS, MBS, WMZDH. This shows clearly how important affinal relatives continued to be, as so many connections were reckoned through wives. If we abstract the affinal connections W and H, however, we find the following relations: B, Z, MZ, ZD, FBS, FBD, FZS, FZD, MBS, MBD, MZD.*

This example shows how an interlocking set of affinal exchanges in generation I continued in generation II but for the most part as first-cousin exchanges. These latter exchanges exhibit no particular agnatic or uterine structures but are distributed cognatically. In many instances, individuals sold off portions of strips that had fallen to them through inheritance to those people who had the other half or another portion. This explains why so many first cousins appear here, although in the larger statistical sample for the whole cohort, cousins were not nearly as prominent as traders in the land market as this example would suggest.[38] First cousins were more likely to continue to cultivate together. It could well have been that most of these cousins were wealthy enough to have their own cultivation equipment and horses, so that they were less likely to want to cooperate with each other. One of the results of asymmetrical marriages was to link together brothers-in-law, the wealthier or older ones plowing and carting for the poorer or younger ones. Not all marriages were asymmetrical, however, and inequality is a relative matter – some sets of brothers-in-law or of cousins were both well off enough to afford production equipment, which they needed to amortize in part by cultivating land belonging to other people. Thus holding parcels in the same strip together might have conflicted with their mutual need to offer services to adjacent landholders. In any event, this case offers another example of the importance of cousins in the early eighteenth century not just as an exogamous group but as a collection of people who continued to display obligation toward one another and traded either services or land.

Case 4 (BWBWHBW) (Figure 5.16) is a variation of case 3 (Figure 5.12). It

[37] Sabean, *Property*, pp. 373–85.
[38] Sabean, *Property*, p. 374.

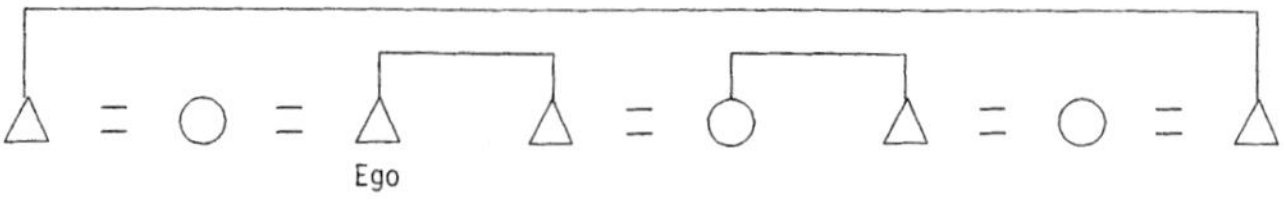

Ego

Figure 5.16

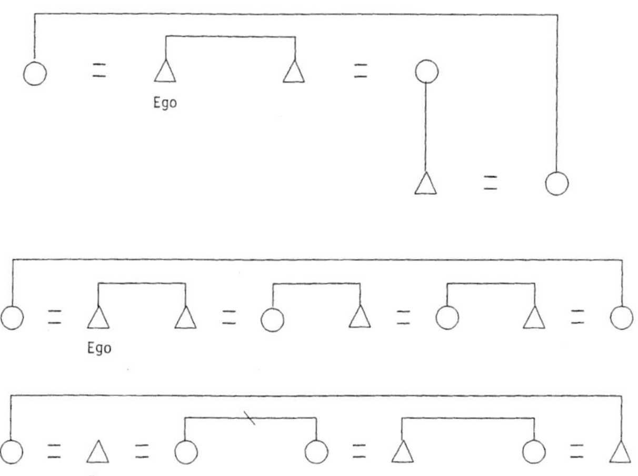

Figure 5.17

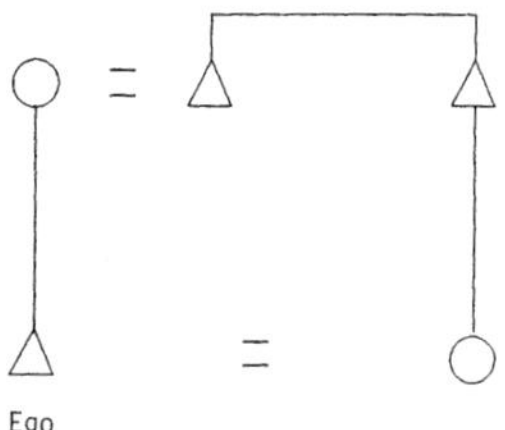

Figure 5.18

involves two sets of parallel and one set of cross siblings, with two instances of marital succession.

Cases 2 (BWBSWZ), 5 (BWBWBWZ), and 17 (WxZHZHZ) (Figure 5.17) illustrate further variations of interlocking sibling sets, either with an added generational twist, an extra sibling group, or a multiple marriage of ego.

The final case, number 16 (MHBD) (Figure 5.18), is somewhat of an anomaly, the closest thing to being a first-cousin marriage as possible. This exceptional example is not particularly late in the period (1715), and only the fact that the relationship was not a full one seems to have allowed it to happen. Since legal thought conflated in-law and step-relations, perhaps this example should be con-

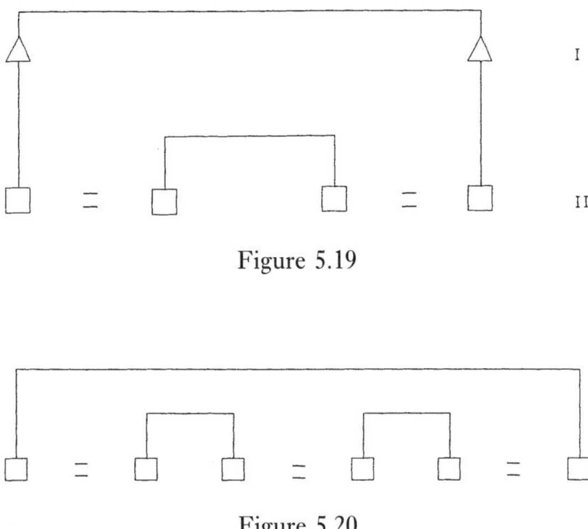

Figure 5.19

Figure 5.20

sidered an affinal relationship. Yet it is still unusual in the way it connects such close relatives.

Variations on a theme

With one exception, all of the examples considered in this chapter conform to a small set of variations. There is first the marriage of siblings with patrilateral first cousins (Figure 5.19). The position of ego, the man making the marriage to close the link, may vary – he can appear in the diagram as son or son-in-law of one of the brothers in generation I or brother, first cousin, or brother-in-law of the other male in generation II. In any of these situations, two males in generation II were already related and the marriage created a closer link by doubling consanguineal ties with affinal ones. One sibling group forged a second link with the children of two brothers. Or in some cases two brothers saw to it that two of their children were brought into a new relationship through marriage into the same sibling group. In most instances, such a marriage "closed a chain" by linking three or more households together.

The other basic form involves the addition of a further marriage in an interlocking set of siblings (Figure 5.20). The man who closes the link in this case already has a relationship to another male in the group as brother or brother-in-law (WB/ZH, BWB/ZHB). The other males are most frequently related as "second-order" brothers-in-law (BWB/ZHB). After the new link is formed, ego is brought into relationship with the third male as a brother-in-law (most frequently WZH/WZH). In essence, the strategy that emerges from this form reinforces an earlier exchange between two sibling groups, by forging a new link with a third sibling group already allied to the original set (Figure 5.21).

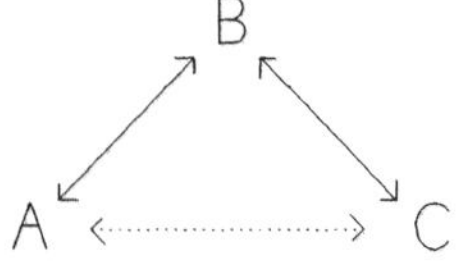

Figure 5.21

Marriage patterns and clientage

As is evident from the politics of *Freundschaften* or kindreds in the period before the construction of a "Vetterles" system (Chapter 2), at that time networks of kin were vertically organized with one or two key members in magisterial positions. To a large extent, close kin acted as patrons and clients for each other and were tied together asymmetrically. This chapter has shown how marriage linked together partners and their kin who were unequal in their political position in the village and in their wealth. Communal politics during the early eighteenth century involved competing "parties" organized around "chains" of people linked together through a combination of descent and marriage. Successful magistrates were described as those who built up a "Freundschaft" or "Partei" over time through successful marital politics, frequently employing strategies associated with remarriage to add important new connections to the old ones. More distant cousins were brought into one's orbit through new ties of affinity. The politics of kinship recognized blood relatives up to nephews and cousins, and the inmarrying spouse (e.g., the cousin's husband) was frequently treated as a full ally. Affinal networks made co-parents-in-law (Gegenschweher) and second-order in-laws such as the sister's husband's brother, the wife's niece's husband, or the marital successor of the wife's brother essential members of an extended Freundschaft.[39]

The marriage strategies described in this chapter play on the same themes. Here the strategies make in-laws out of blood relatives or tie people together in overlapping affinal relationships. Remarriage was an important instrument for building up a personal following or for finding a position within the orbit of someone more powerful. In any event, kinship networks appear kaleidoscopic, constantly shifting and reshifting according to the fortunes of particular individuals and the opportunities for new alliances. The strategic problem was always to maximize both the number of connections and their strength, which led to marriages that closed circles tying three, four, or five households together. Social

[39] The way each chain overlaps with others and the way the chains coalesce into dense networks is not unlike what Segalen understands as a kindred, although she was concerned with networks distributed over a large space; Segalen, *Fifteen Generations,* pp. 114–20. Freeman's analysis, "On the Concept of the Kindred," *Journal of the Royal Anthropological Institute* 91 (1961): 192–220, of how kindreds overlap, of course, pioneered this kind of analysis, but he was concerned with the effects of cross-cousin marriage and the like in a system without unilineal descent groups. Here I am concerned with the use of affinal rather than consanguineal ties.

relationships between allied kin did not end with the death of a spouse but were reconfigured through marital succession, godparentage, guardianship, and gender tutelage.

The interlocking sets of households were not just directed toward politics in the narrow sense. Family interest in caring for indigent widows could well have prompted unions with wealthier widowers. Linking older and richer with younger and poorer houses ensured cooperation in agricultural production. In many cases, men who shared portions of arable parcels found themselves cooperating in the production schedules of several households at once, as brothers-in-law worked the land of their respective parents-in-law together. This aspect will be discussed at greater length in Chapter 6, but it should be clear that marriage constructed cooperative networks of men concerned with growing crops, managing land, administering estates, sharing buildings and equipment, finding work, maintaining respect, defending honor, and participating in the proceeds of local corruption. Each marriage was the result of complex calculation and the availability of a suitable spouse, and although we cannot recover very much of the context of any particular decision, we can understand the shape of the overall strategical situation.

About one aspect of the analysis I am very uneasy. It appears that the networks were constructed by men largely in terms of their own concerns. It may well be that the overall strategic intent of this system was derived from the exigencies of male politics and production routines. This seems to be the inference to be drawn from the crystallization out of male sibling relations as a generation moved along and the special relationship between patrilateral parallel cousins in the structuring of affinal networks. Unfortunately, the sources do not offer much opportunity to speculate on the ways women might have shaped marital strategies, and Pierre Bourdieu warns against taking "official" views too much at face value.[40] But little of my analysis in this chapter comes from self-conscious reflection at all. Even if one posits an overall *strategy* produced in the context of male politics, one still needs to examine the *tactics* of female action.[41] At the level of the household, for example, when the woman was the richer partner or when a younger couple was more in the orbit of the wife's parents' productive enterprise, then she could often be the directive personality, control the purse, or maintain a separate account for her own property.[42] When older, wealthy widows married younger, penurious men, they must have maintained considerable authority in the household. Still for this early period up to around 1740, when various village court protocols become available, little is yet known about gender politics and the contribution of gender to the construction of *Freundschaften* and to village politics as a whole.

[40] Pierre Bourdieu, *Outline of the Theory of Practice,* trans. Richard Nice (Cambridge, 1977), pp. 33–40.

[41] On the distinction between strategy and tactics for social analysis, see Michel de Certeau, *The Practice of Everyday Life,* trans. Steven Rendall (Berkeley, 1988), xvii–xx.

[42] I have dealt with this at length in *Property,* pp. 166–74, 259–85.

Cohort I (1700–1709)

I have suggested that marital politics were closely tied up with constructing political and production networks. But it would be misleading to suggest that village politics drove the system without some idea of how kin networks were put to use in various social contexts. After all, it would be just as easy to imagine that networks of kin constructed for other purposes became implicated in the larger give-and-take of communal government and struggle for the control of village resources. Therefore it is time to look at ways in which the linkages between kin provided the framework for a complex system of exchange.

6

Marriage and kinship practices

Chapter 5 explored the regularities of kin-linked marital unions taken in turn and the implications of recurrent forms for all the individuals linked together in chains that closed back in on themselves. But how are these sets of people, who are asymmetrically connected to one another, interlocked with other such sets? And how did the construction of affinal clusters grow out of the relationships originally established among siblings? These are the subjects of this chapter.

As mentioned earlier, many marriages in Neckarhausen involved strategies aimed at maximizing both the strength of kinship ties and their number. Pursuing both objectives at once led to a typical pattern of reinforcing and redoubling ties between three, four, or five households. But the way new affinal connections could be joined to existing alliances at any "angle," so to speak, suggests that these networks were open ended and flexible enough to react to family crises and shifting political and productive situations. Kinship was not a closed principle, even though it had a systemic quality to it and could act as an organizing mechanism for partisan political groups and village factions of various kinds.

Despite the open-endedness of kinship networks or perhaps because of it, people sought closure from time to time. In the flow of exchange, the institution of marriage and that of godparentage created long-term structures and continuous fault lines, providing regularity, dependability, and concentrated attention. Unlike other forms of alliance, they established permanent switching points and nodal connectors for exchanges of all kinds. Chapter 7 examines godparentage (or, ritual kinship) in considerable detail, but first it is essential to see how affinal chains established by marriage criss-crossed each other, creating dense networks of exchange, and how godparentage among other things intersected to reinforce and extend such alliances. The discussion here opens with two complex genealogies, which might look daunting to the viewer at the outset, but which will be broken down into more manageable units as I develop the argument. The first

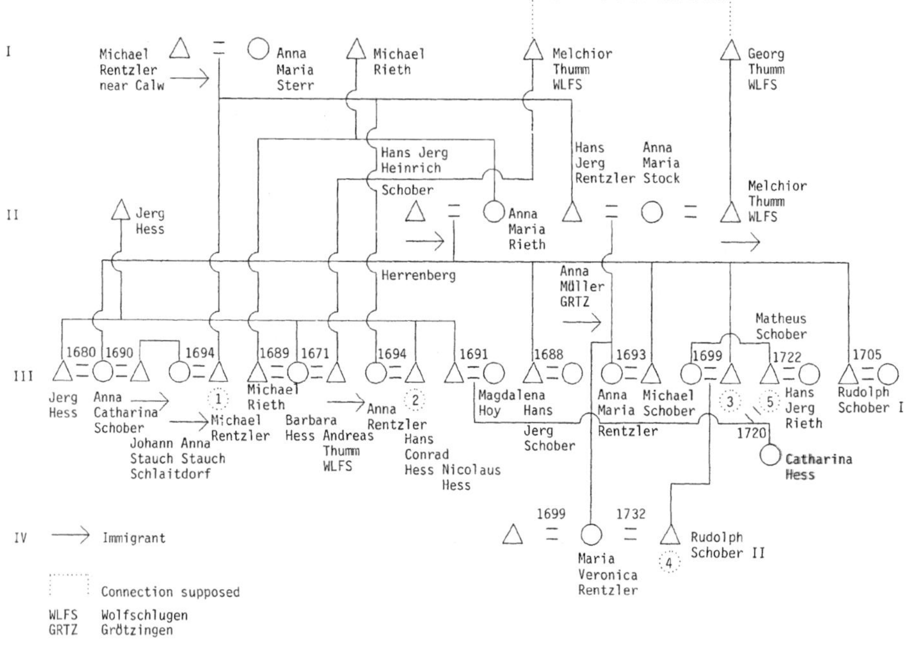

Figure 6.1

example illustrates the interlocking pattern of criss-crossed genealogies; the second adds the complexity of godparentage. Next, the chapter presents some of the ways a structured grid channeled other exchange relationships such as guardianship. It concludes with further comments on the way marriage helped shape the discourse of familial property management and production in the study area.

Intersecting alliances

Intersecting alliances are well represented in the Schober family, among the seven children of Hans Jerg Heinrich Schober and Anna Maria Rieth, married in 1660, twelve years after the conclusion of the Thirty Years' War (Figure 6.1). Hans Jerg Heinrich Schober was the son of Heinrich Schober, resident in Herrenberg, perhaps himself an immigrant from northern Germany (Braunschweig). The younger Schober seems to have married into Neckarhausen with a considerable marriage portion. In 1705, as an old man, he moved again, this time to Hemmingen near Leonberg, where he apparently took over a rather substantial farm. Some of his adult children continued to live in Neckarhausen, and some went with him to Hemmingen and married there. Four sons remained. The oldest, Hans Jerg, became a smith and eventually a member of the Rat. Michael and Rudolph became Bauern – in 1710 all three were in tax quartile III (quartile IV

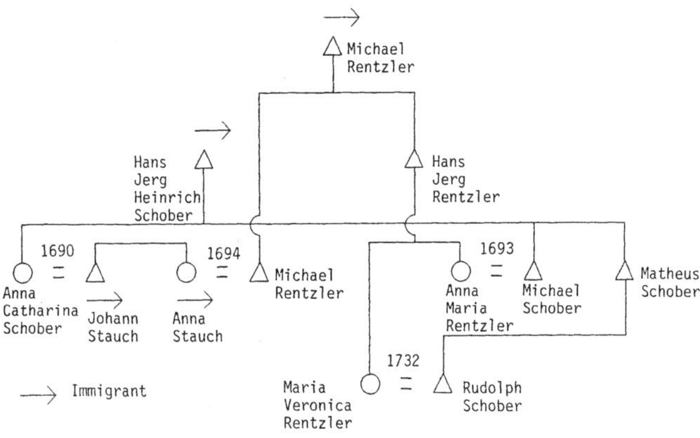

Figure 6.2

being the wealthiest). Matheus, in tax quartile II in 1710, was a day-laborer and forest patrolman. The daughter, Anna Catherina, married a local shepherd and later an immigrant carpenter who in 1710 was in tax quartile III. Two younger sisters married men in Hemmingen where the father had moved.

It is interesting to note that in each generation several of the people in the genealogy emigrated from other villages. Andreas Thumm (III) married in from the nearby village of Wolfschlugen following an earlier marriage by his cousin, Melchior (II). Johannes Stauch (III) married in from Schlaitdorf, as did his sister Anna and perhaps another close relative (Agnes, in 1722). These examples fit well into the pattern of affinal marriages already examined. The immigrants in these cases came as sibling or patrilateral parallel first-cousin pairs. In this cohort, there were no examples of exchange between one kin-group and the same village over several generations. For example, no marriages of the Neckarhausen Schober children took place with Hemmingen residents in the next generation. As in earlier cases, the reinforcement of alliance in this complicated example took place during a single generation. While an early marriage of the following generation could be integrated into an existing affinal network, there was no marriage between consanguines to reproduce the alliance over several generations – as practiced later in the century – and no continuous exchanges with members of particular villages or with a particular family scattered across several villages over many generations. Immigrants into the village integrated themselves by building affinal connections systematically. For example, the children of an immigrant such as Michael Rentzler (#1) made a series of marriages that created a number of close overlapping affinal relationships (Figure 6.2). Michael's son Michael married the sister of the immigrant Johannes Stauch, who was married to a Schober in generation III. One of old Michael's granddaughters married another Schober of generation III, and another granddaughter married a Schober of generation IV (Rudolph).

Particularly interesting is the set of relationships forged by marriage in the larger genealogy (Figures 6.1 and 6.3): Michael Rentzler (#1) married his BDHZHZ,

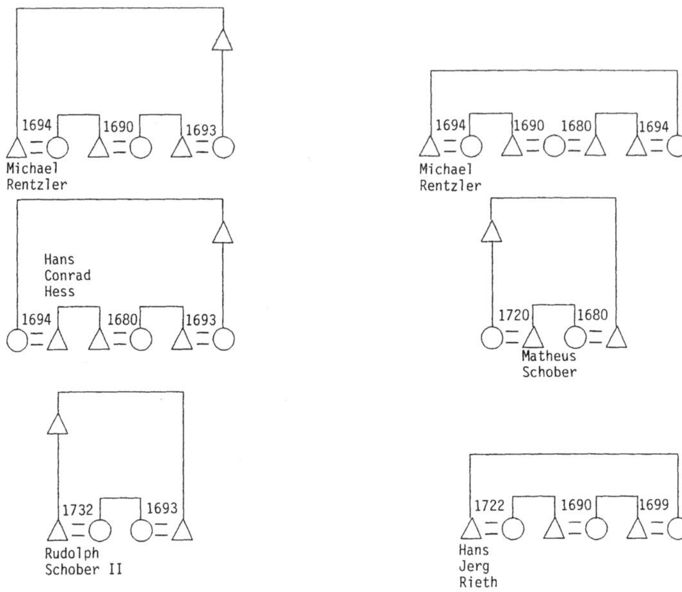

Figure 6.3

who was also his ZHBWHZ. Hans Conrad Hess (#2) married his BWBWFZ. Matheus Schober (#3) married his ZHBD. Rudolph Schober II (#4) married his FBWZ. Hans Jerg Rieth (#5) probably married his ZHZHZ, or perhaps his ZHZHBD.

It appears in this example that the short chains linking two, three, or four households through individual marriages themselves intersect and interlink with one another to create dense networks of exchange that make it possible to speak of "kindreds" (see Chapter 1). Even someone like Hans Jerg Schober (III) (1663–1728), who did not marry a woman connected to himself affinally, was, of course, tied in with the people his siblings married. From 1703 to 1711, for example, he served as godparent for Michael Rentzler and Anna Stauch (his BWFB and ZHZ). His connection to them was not through his own marriage but through those of his siblings. In 1669, he and Nicolaus Hess were guardians for the children of Georg Hess, bringing together a ZHB and BWB in cooperation.[1] In taking account of Hess's marriage, one is led to examine it in the context of the rest of the marriages in its "field." Even if a path could be traced between Hess and his spouse along a series of kinship links, that particular calculus would not "explain" their marriage. In this case, many of the intersecting affinal chains may well have been constructed in part around the fact that Hans Jerg Schober was a member of the magistrates. Affinal unions linking together in-laws with unequal

[1] KB II, 19.2.1699.

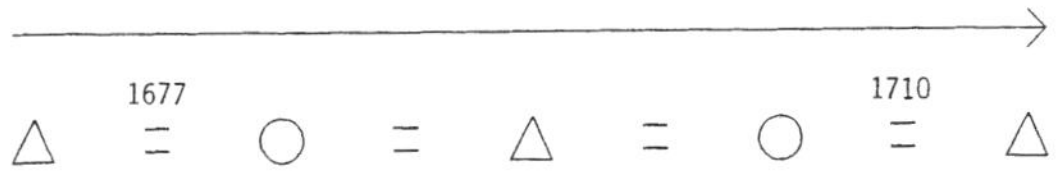

1677 1710

△ = ○ = △ = ○ = △

Figure 6.4

wealth and differential access to power were, among other things, building blocks in the politics of clientage.

The second extensive genealogy examined in detail here (Figure 6.5) is built around the children of Johann Ulrich Haefner and Heinrich Geiger. It adds an interesting dimension because its relationships emerge through four interlocking marriages between 1677 and 1710 (Figure 6.4).

The sibling group in generation II is composed of three Haefners – Hans Jacob, cobbler; Johannes, occupation not given; and Agnes, who married a Bauer in tax quartile III (in 1710, the two sons were in tax quartile II) – and the daughters of Heinrich Geiger from two different marriages. The latter were married to Johann Georg Brodbeck, Bauer and Richter; and Hans Jacob Gemmel, whose occupation was never given in the sources, but who was probably a Bauer. Both of these last marriages came too late to be represented in the tax register of 1710. In this genealogy, there are a number of intersecting affinal chains. *Johannes Sterr (7) married his FZSWZ (the only example I have found involving cross cousins). Salomo Falter (13) married his BWBD. Johann Falter (8) married his BWFBD. Johann Haefner (9) married his MHBD. Friedrich Schober (12) married his BWBWMSW. Conrad Geiger (6) married his FBDHZ. Hans Jacob Gemmel (10) married his BWFZHD. It does not seem necessary to diagram each of these marriages separately, since a quick inspection shows that each either links three sibling groups together or a sibling group with two cousins.*

The other ways in which members of such a genealogical grid were connected can become very complicated. Figure 6.5 shows just the godparent relations connecting people mentioned in the diagram. All five children of the Haefner/Geiger marriages (1, 2, 5, 9, 10) had Johann Georg Schober, a member of the magistrates, as Döte. The full siblings (1, 2, 9) had Barbara, the wife of Schultheiss Michael Hess, and the two half-siblings (5, 10), born after Barbara's death, had Margaretha, wife of Gall Feldmeyer, as godmother (*Dote*). I have not put this set of godparents into the diagram, since they were not part of the genealogical grid. Most godparents were not relatives of their godchildren (as *Döten, Doten*) or of the godchildren's parents (as *Gevatter(inne)n*) (see Chapter 7). In this genealogy, only these particular children had Schober, Hess, and Feldmeyer as godparents, which set them off from the others as a group and underlined their unity as siblings. The various parents in generation II, whose marriages stretched from 1701 to 1737, at the beginning chose godparents (*Gevattern*) from generation I, some of them relatives and some not. As time went on, however, the older members of the second generation often stood as godparents for the younger, the average difference between marriage of the godparents and marriage of the par-

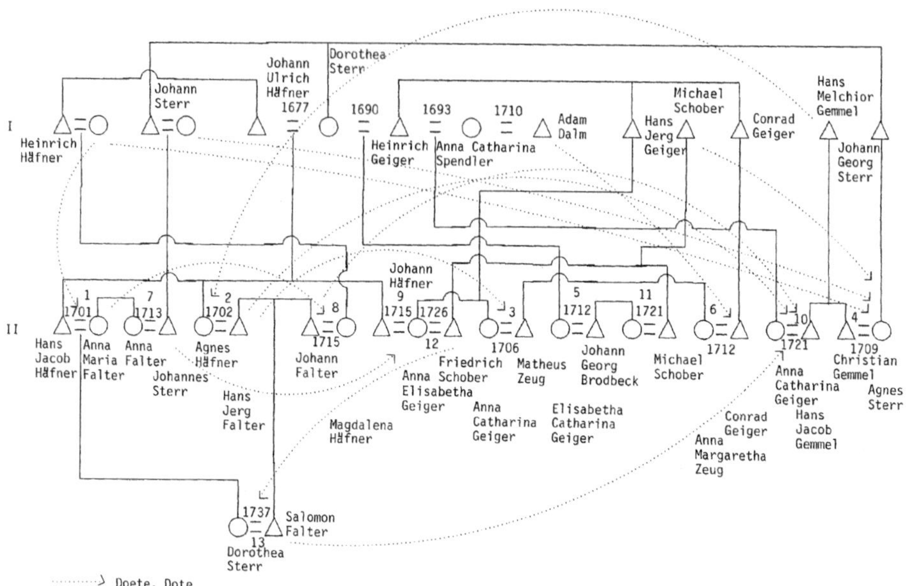

Figure 6.5

ents being about nine years. As the network of marriages was established, later ones not only reinforced kinship links, but they also provided the material for ritual kinship. Godparentage became a flexible instrument for underlining relationships as they developed over the course of a generation or for forging new connections. Because of the durability of the relationship – the godparent fulfilling a social role for a particular child or parent over time and participating successively in the ritual for each new child of a couple or a household – the institution helped structure and shape relations as continuously as marriage did. In this instance, couples 2, 7, 8, 12, and 13 were connected to 3, 8, 9, 10, and 13. Note that the late marriage in the series (13) involved a second one for Bürgermeister Salomon Falter, who had first been married in 1706 and was therefore older than the couple he stood for as godparent. Each of the five Häfner/Geiger children chose a unique set of godparents, which meant that cousins (their children) did not have overlapping Doeten/Doten. On the other hand, uncles and aunts frequently acted as godparents for their nephews and nieces (1, 4, 6, 13), which therefore reinforced cousins in their connections with each other, and cousins acted as Gevatter for each other as well (3, 8, 9).[2] Altogether, the

[2] It was very unusual to find cousins acting as godparents during this period. In the case of the connection between Hans Jerg Falter (2) and Anna Catharina Geiger (3), the calculation involves a step-relation and an affinal connection (WMHBD). See Chapter 5 on this point. Anna Maria Falter (1) was godmother for Magdalena Häfner, her HFBD, or a cousin reckoned through an affinal

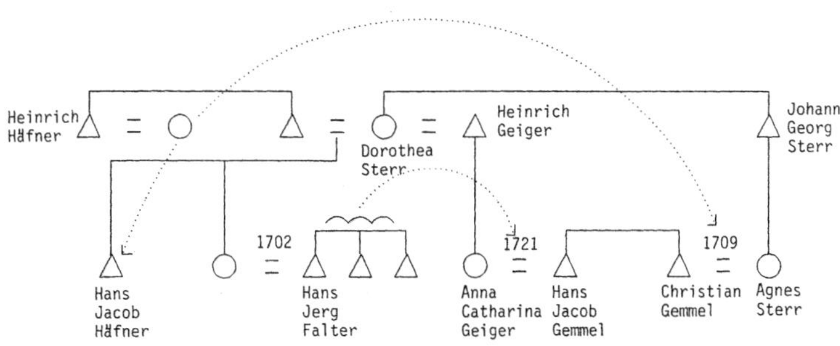

Figure 6.6

interconnections are very tangled, almost bewildering in their complexity. It is apparent, however, that kin relations provided a grid for ritual kinship. In many instances, choosing a marital successor as a godparent emphasized the latter's legitimacy as head of the household into which he married and underlined the continuity of relationship between the two houses (e.g., Anna Catharina Geiger, 10, who chose her father's marital successor, Adam Dalm, or Dorothea Sterr, 13, who chose her uncle's marital successor, Friedrich Schober). If marriage with the affine of an affine brought several "houses" into tighter connection with each other, choosing such a person as godparent could have similar structural meaning. Agnes Sterr (4), for example, chose the wife of Heinrich Häfner as Gevatterin, Häfner being the brother-in-law of her aunt. She also chose her aunt's sister-in-law, the wife of Johann Sterr. In a similar way, Hans Jerg Falter (2) stood as Gevatter for his wife's sister-in-law's sister, Anna Catharina Geiger (3), and Johannes Sterr (7) stood for his wife's brother-in-law's brother, Johann Häfner.

This last point can be explored further by focusing on just one part of the genealogy (Figure 6.6). *When Christian Gemmel married Agnes Sterr in 1709, he married into a network that brought Heinrich Häfner's wife as Dote for his children – his wife's FZHBW. The latter was also Gavatterin for Hans Jacob Häfner, Gemmel's wife's cousin (FZS). Later, after Hans Jacob Gemmel (1721) married his brother's wife's patrilateral first cousin (the classic marriage of the period), he obtained the three Falter brothers successively as Doeten for his children, his WxZH and WxZHB.* Here is a clear example of the way ritual kinship supplemented and reinforced affinal relationships. In these instances, marriage alliance offered a grid for further exchanges, which cobbled together extended affines in more intimate arrangements. Reciprocally, of course, it was possible for godparentage to provide an opening for marriage alliance. That will be explained further in later chapters, but here it should be clear that marriage could grow out of a field of friendship just as much as marriage could structure that field and create "friends."

connection. Finally, Johannes Sterr stood for his FZS, Johann Häfner (9), the only true cousin I have found for this period.

Another way of exploring networks is to examine postmortem inventories for clues about guardianship, Kreigsvogtschaft, wages, and the like. There is no easy way to summarize the findings from this study, but it may be most convenient to consider them from the point of view of successive households. *Records in 1721, 1729, and 1741 indicate that household 1 connected to 4, 5, 6, 7, 9, 11, and 12 in terms of wage labor and guardianship, the relations being B, BWH, BWS, xZ, BWHB, MHBS, WFBS, WZ. In 1729 household 6 was connected to 3, 6, 9, 11, and 12 for wages and guardianship: Z, BWZHZH, FBWSS, WHBS, WZHZH. In 1728 and 1745 house 7 was connected to 1, 2, 4, 6, 9, and 12 for wages, sale of a house, Kriegsvogtschaft, and guardianship: WZ, WBS, WZHB, WZHBWH, FZDH, FZHBS. In 1741 and 1746, 11 was connected to 2, 10, and 13 for wages, rent, and burial costs: WBWFD, BWBWHB, BWHWB. And in 1748, 12 was connected to 13 in guardianship: WHBD.* Although it may be difficult to follow each connection, the overall pattern is clear. The affinal networks set up through marriage were utilized to hire laborers or a farmer with a team of horses, or to locate a Kriegsvogt for a woman or a guardian for children. All of these relationships are configured in Figure 6.7.

This particular set, of course, does not exhaust the ways a person used kin and nonkin. It does illustrate the fact that these networks were open-ended, with certain key points reinforced or particular gateways opened by marriage and ritual kinship. In this period, people did use kin continually for all sorts of things, but kinship was not a closed principle forming circumscribed groups. This strategy of building social and moral ties among relatives is a homology of the strategy of land ownership – many strips scattered all over the landscape to take advantage of differences in microclimates and to avoid tragedies that might follow from too much concentration. Just as each strip would lie near those of different people, necessitating many arrangements for plowing or labor for any one farmer, so the many contexts of village life necessitated relationships that stressed *both* obligation and flexibility.

Sibling solidarity

The point has been made many times that the construction of affinal clusters was based on relationships forged in the first instance among brothers and sisters. A closer inspection of this "solidarity" of the sibling group and its changing relationships over time may help bring to light the formal logic behind many of the strategies of alliance that were available to villagers. If, as already demonstrated, the marriage of patrilateral parallel cousins to siblings consistently shows that relations between two brothers in the senior generation overshadowed those between sisters or between brothers and sisters, then one must ask why this is the case. It may well have been that sibling solidarity changed over the life cycle, and that the dynamics of mutual and divergent interests played a significant role. Since marriage did unite families of differential wealth and political connection, this factor may help to explain why a completely partible inheritance system still

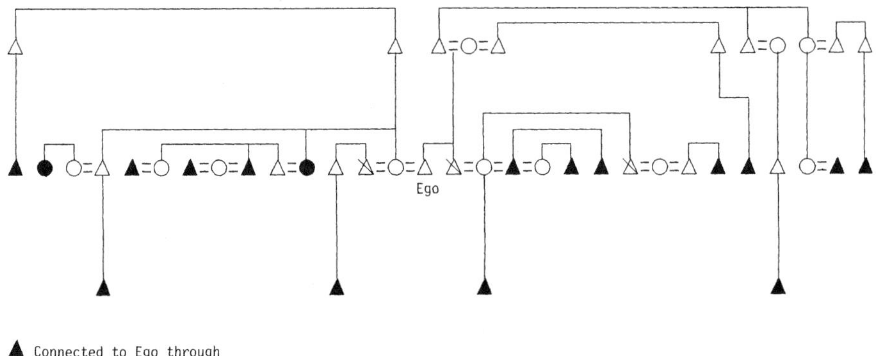

Figure 6.7

privileged male sibling solidarity. The issue of male sibling pairing is particularly important because by the early nineteenth century brother/sister pairing came to dominate the field of kinship – both in Neckarhausen and throughout the propertied classes in Germany, and indeed in Europe (see the discussion for cohorts IV and V and Chapters 22 and 23). In the case of Neckarhausen, explanations may lie in the context of property ownership and management – the gendered, generational, lineal, and affinal allocation of rights and duties – the mutual interest of allied kin in household affairs, cooperation in work, and the distribution of productive equipment.

A great deal of evidence has been offered to show that the B/Z, B/B, Z/Z relationships were fundamental for the choice of spouses in this cohort. Although men in the sample making affinally linked marriages most frequently traced the relationship through a brother (nine times), they also traced lines through sisters (four times). If examined from the point of view of women, the diagrams trace relationships through sisters five times and brothers four times. Thus it seems that although the sibling group as a whole shows evidence of mutuality and coordination of interests at the time of marriage, the relationships between brothers already appear somewhat stronger. Moving up one generation, one finds that almost all links went over the father – this is true from the perspective of either a son or a daughter. From the point of view of a man or a woman marrying related kin in this cohort, their patrilateral parallel connection seems to have been the only significant one. There are almost no cases (apart from the ambiguous xF ones) in which a connection was traced over the mother – not through the MB or the MZ – nor is there frequent tracing over the FZ in this cohort. The patrilateral parallel reckoning shows that the marriage arrangements in generation II were coordinated between the children of brothers from generation I. There is no suggestion that such marriages were arranged for the children of parallel female siblings or cross siblings. This fact makes it all the more likely that a

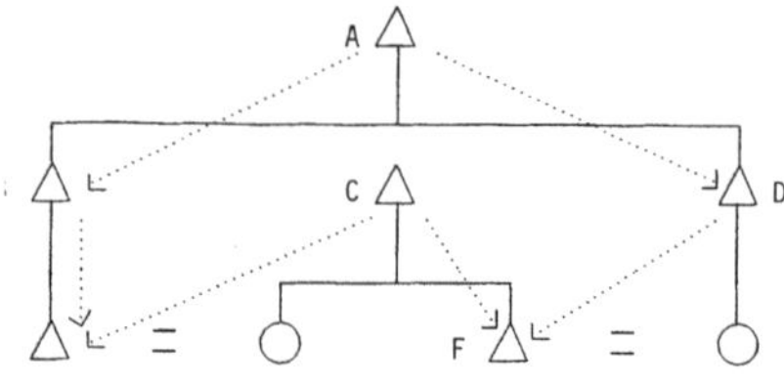

Figure 6.8

special solidarity developed between brothers within the sibling group, as reflected in the interlocking marriages their children constructed in the next generation.

What explains the set of relationships that we find? Some of the results can be elucidated by looking at the rules of inheritance and property management. To reiterate, this was a village that practiced partible inheritance, but with a twist – all children, male and female, inherited equally. That is, property rights fell equally to sons and daughters. No matter what the formal rules of *ownership* were, however, men remained the *administrators* of property.[3] In a sense, then, property devolved upon the son and the son-in-law. In fact, all the sales in the estate inventories and property sale registers (*Kaufbücher*) between fathers and daughters were described as ones between fathers-in-law and sons-in-law: daughters were never themselves mentioned. Likewise, exchanges of property between cross siblings considered such transactions to be between brothers-in-law. In the simple structural case examined here, property devolution can be easily traced (Figure 6.8). The property mass of A was divided between his two sons, B and D. They in turn passed it on to their sons and sons-in-law, E and F, to E as owner and manager and to F, at least, as manager.

Property devolution from a man to his daughter and son-in-law raises a number of ambiguities. In a postmortem or premortem estate inventory, inherited property fell in full ownership to a daughter, and such property would be listed in detail in her marriage inventory.[4] Later, at her own estate inventory at death or retirement, all the family property – hers and her husband's – would be listed without regard to origin. Her estate would at that time be composed of the value of the property she brought to the marriage and a portion of the property acquired or lost by the couple in the interim. Her husband would inherit a portion of her estate and manage the whole of it until he gave some up for the children, retired, or died. It is never clear in the final reckoning whether her estate included the particular pieces of land she brought to the marriage or whether it involved only a claim proportional to her marriage portion on the whole property of husband and wife. At the beginning of the eighteenth century, the latter appears to

[3] See David Warren Sabean, *Property, Production, and Family in Neckarhausen* (Cambridge, 1990), pp. 211–18.

[4] See Sabean, *Property*, chaps. 9 and 10.

have been the case. Thus although she was co-owner of the marital estate, she was no longer owner of specific strips of land, nor, for that matter, was her husband. In theory at least, his position as manager gave him certain rights over the whole property, yet in practice some women ordered their husbands about with respect to their own inherited property.[5] However, aside from the issue of legal theory and practical reality in the management of the family estate, there is still the problem of property devolution outside of inheritance – where a parent sold or gave property to the children during the course of his or her life. The fact that the form of such transactions was always inscribed as male to male when the father was alive (or female to male when a widow sold part of the estate) raises the question of effective ownership and management. When a man sold an arable strip or meadow to his son-in-law, it became the joint property of the couple. But why not then either record the sale as one to the daughter or to both marriage partners at once? If it simply made no difference, why was it such a consistent practice? Perhaps the sale was recorded to the son-in-law because of his authority as head of the household. Or perhaps the transaction simply expressed the assumption that land was primarily an object of male exploitation. In any event, the written record overlay rights that accrued to people regardless of gender with a discourse about property that contained its circulation in a sphere of male exchange.

To work the land it was necessary to mobilize tools and labor distributed unequally among the interested parties to a series of plots.[6] In the model being discussed here, E and F have to coordinate their activities to exploit the property devolving from A. There is also a residual mutual interest in ownership, since if F's wife should die without an heir, part of the property F is administering could fall to E. Furthermore, in this simplified version of inheritance, the property of C is divided among E and F, which gives the two brothers-in-law, E and F, a property mix made up of the same elements. Structurally, one result of a marriage between first cousins and a sibling group is to concentrate property: to create overlapping responsibilities, mutual claims, common borders, and similarity of interest. The son-in-law can be a male successor for a man, and brothers-in-law have the same kind of obligations with regard to production in relation to one another as brothers do. Although the mutuality may be strong, potential conflict is always part of the equation. The link between brothers-in-law must have been a major point of fission (and ipso facto between B/Z) since their children seldom constructed overlapping kin-related marriages.

The problem of "property concentration" must be understood in a special sense, especially since this is often given as an explanation for marriage endogamy. In those places where endogamous patrilateral parallel-cousin marriages are frequent, such as the Middle East, the object of such alliances appears to be to keep property inside the control of an agnatic group, although the simple-minded

[5] Sabean, *Property*, chaps. 4, 6, and 11.

[6] See Sabean, *Property*, chaps. 10 and 11.

understanding of the issue has been effectively challenged by Ladislav Holy.[7] In Neckarhausen, however, no matter what structures we can demonstrate by looking closely at kin-linked marriages, only a very small fraction of land in any one generation could have been rescued by some sort of collectivity defined by agnatic relations. Everything points toward property fissioning in each generation. Probably no son ever held in his hands the same set of arable parcels his father had held. If reassembly of family property were the issue, then one would expect a more or less immediate interest in cousin marriages after the 1680s when they became possible, rather than the 60- to 100-year delay that in fact occurred. Furthermore, if accumulation of family wealth was a goal or if peasants wanted to collect properties previously split off from the property mass, then a strategy involving the children of brothers and sisters or sisters would have done just as well as that involving only the children of brothers in the context of partible inheritance and cognatic kin reckoning. Chapter 5 has already presented an example in which land sales among cousins involved cross cousins and parallel cousins of both kinds. The rules of partible inheritance and the practice of splitting up arable plots among more than one owner ipso facto cast every kind of cousin into contact with one another and could not have privileged agnatic relations in themselves.[8] Furthermore, the goal of protecting the patrimony could be solved in various ways, one of them being a policy of exogamy, accumulating property through aggressive marriage strategies. Any discussion of property devolution and endogamy/exogamy without a careful analysis of the kinds of property available and the ecology of production leaves the important issues hanging in the heir.

If there was an agnatic core in the system of kinship relations in Neckarhausen around 1700, it certainly did not have anything to do with male lineages or the formation of any kind of descent groups. And although the system of exchanges may appear to have been random, since any one individual could turn in many different directions and through a series of short networks involving males and females multiply the number of collaborators beyond the boundaries of any recognizable group, we are still left with coordinate pairs that emerge as structurally significant: B/B, B/B-in-law, agnatic cousins. Property concentrates by creating a discourse of mutual responsibility and common purpose, of cooperative endeavor and intimate exchange, not because it is held in common or because residual claims are of overriding importance, but because it calls on a wider set of people to manage, protect, and exploit it. It forces responsibilities, duties, and obligations on people who end up coordinating some of their activities precisely because marriage and descent create channels along which goods and services flow. Obligation is something that has to be continually constructed, but not every kind of exchange carries the same weight – the choice of a spouse is of

[7] On property concentration, see Jack Goody, *The Development of the Family and Marriage in Europe* (Cambridge, 1983), pp. 43–6; Ladislav Holy, *Kinship, Honour and Solidarity: Cousin Marriage in the Middle East* (Manchester, 1989), chap. 1.

[8] On the details of inheritance, see Sabean, *Property,* chap. 10.

greater structural importance than the sale of a strip of land. Just because of its structural importance in a wider system of exchange, marriage could sometimes be entered into so quickly and so casually. Choice often had a logic to it. To grasp the flow of social life, one must recognize that its course is not random. One must, in other words, analyze the breaks, cuts, dams, conduits, and channels.

From the point of view of property management and cooperation in production, there would seem to be no difference between brothers and brothers-in-law, and, as noted earlier, uncles and nephews and first cousins (or their spouses) frequently were intimately associated in a similar manner. In addition to such associations, the way exogamy rules worked also suggests certain similarities among the B, WB, and FBS. Since there were no cases of siblings marrying into the same sibling group (e.g., a brother and sister marrying a brother and sister), there was at least a practice if not a rule against this sort of marriage, and furthermore there was legally no sororate or levirate – marrying a deceased wife's sister or brother's wife (all this contrasts sharply with practices in the nineteenth century). We also find no marriages with first cousins (although dispensable). Thus the B, the FBS, and the WB were all in sibling groups from which ego could not take a wife (in the case of the WB, a second wife). The easiest way to concentrate wealth would have been to make a B or a FBS into a brother-in-law, but such a strategy was not accessible. What this cohort did develop was a practice of linking siblings or first cousins in marriage through either a third sibling set or a second generational level. Of course, other considerations lay behind these practices. Since marriage structured many different kinds of exchanges, any union would have been subject to calculations peculiar to itself. A daughter as the single heir in a family, for example, would have pursued a different strategy of alliance from that of an immigrant widower. Since marriage policies of the period linked people together asymmetrically, there were many different ways affinal kin could act as patrons and clients to one another. But ownership of property and its exploitation provided a core around which more encompassing exchanges where constructed.

What explains the tighter solidarity of brothers as opposed to brothers and sisters (or brothers-in-law) in a situation where all children inherited equally, throwing brothers-in-law together as mutual heirs of each other and as administrators of property from the same inheritance fund? Coordination through brothers-in-law in terms of production could be as important as coordination through brothers. Brothers-in-law were probably as intimately tied up together exploiting the parents' land and caring for the old people when the time came as brothers were. Since property came equally from the father and the mother and daughters inherited equally with sons, there would appear to be no reason why brothers-in-law would be involved in greater tension over inheritance than brothers would.

The fact that equal rights in property pass to brothers and sisters provides a solidarity of interest. But we must not understand the devolution of rights in a simple manner. For part of the life cycle, children in Neckarhausen were united in laboring for their parents and later for caring for them. They were dependent on the tool-kit of their elders and eventually shared it or parceled it out among themselves.[9] And their land rights were often composed of contiguous strips of larger parcels, just as their apartments and storage spaces were divisions of larger houses and barns. The B/B relationship combined administration and management with property ownership. But although the B/B-in-law relationship was also one of administration, their rights were mediated through the wife/sister, with ownership and administration effectively split between two people. In the end, brothers both held and administered property devolved from their parents in their own right. Although they too would have been pulled in different directions when they married, there could still be many areas in which they cooperated without special tension. Brothers-in-law, on the other hand, carried out all those important tasks, which involved both mutual obligation and divergent interest. The wife's brother or a close substitute appeared with her in court to protect her interests whenever her husband carried out a business transaction affecting the substance of the household's property. At the death of a woman, her brother or a close relative represented her property interests for her children until they attained adulthood at marriage. In this situation, brothers-in-law had a relationship that was potentially full of tension. It represented all the expectations and disappointments of an alliance knit together by a particular couple. For certain purposes, especially when the wife's brother was absent or too young, an uncle or a cousin could take on this ambivalent social role. Over the long term, the relations between brothers often tended to solidarity while those between brothers-in-law became a point of fission. When the next generation grew up, the relation between brothers became the basis for marriage alliance while that between brothers-in-law did not.

Property concentrates because it focuses attention, not because it creates a single, unified group sharing ownership of an estate. I have stressed the mutual links tying a brother and brother-in-law together, plowing and harrowing a plot that they split or working the land of their parents (-in-law). But brothers-in-law were by no means equal in their access to equipment or in their overall wealth or political connections. Farming equipment was closely associated with males. In fact, in estate inventories, handicraft tools and horse, plow, harrow, and the like (*Bauerngeschirr*) were separated out from all the other inventory as special male property. At the marriage of the junior generation, such property was firmly held in the hands of the father, who sold his labor services (e.g., plowing or carting with a horse) to the son or son-in-law.[10] Farm equipment devolved most readily on sons if there were any, and quite frequently on them all equally. As a generation moved on, sons took over the production gear and became the cultivators of plots held jointly with their brothers-in-law. Cooperation in production never meant equality and was always set up as a patron (man

[9] See Sabean, *Property*, chap. 10.
[10] Sabean, *Property*, pp. 301–11.

with equipment) and client (man with labor) relationship. The interlocking chains of brothers-in-law were composed of men with unequal access to land, labor, tools, and power. In those situations where cousins were closely associated, it was unlikely that they would have been equally wealthy, because each household divided wealth among a different number of children and the partners in each generation's marriage alliances had quite different amounts of wealth and political connections.

* * *

Exogamy presents an interesting problem in this period because it combined different levels of political, social, and productive meaning. The coupling of unequal partners continually put constraints on endogamy within strata and certain forms of horizontal solidarity. That did not mean that hierarchy was less important nor that rule and power were not distributed differentially. It did mean that family obligation made the poor exploitable in ways specific to its manner of distributing resources, but that it also forced village politics into a form of clientage. Affinal kin were linked in short, asymmetrical chains, which for any sibling group criss-crossed, some closing back in on themselves through marriage, some through ritual kinship, and others through clientage as the various clusters linked the powerless in the village with its power elite. Kinship was constructed not given, was flexible but not amorphous, and broke the flow of exchange into meaningful transactions without being all-encompassing. We must not think of it as a partial area of human action, a compartment separated off from production, community, rule, neighborhood, or religious ritual. It cut and channeled exchange, formed and deformed action, attributed meaning, and focused discourse. In all of this, marriage strategy was geared simultaneously to the problems of binding and separating. Linking two households together too closely was clearly disadvantageous when it was necessary to set up networks along which one could negotiate. Some members of a family always chose to marry not too far away, recognizing that with distance obligation declined. Here, one generation flowed into the next as the first children in a series made marriages and created relations built on their parents' resources and alliances. As the new generation moved along, younger siblings gradually created ties that grew out of their older siblings' connections. There was no system of alliance of the kind that caused families or lineages to exchange marriage partners over many generations. Such a system did develop in the eighteenth century, however, and it is the subject of later chapters.

7

Ritual kinship

Ritual kinship can have both a social and a spiritual meaning, but it is very difficult to distinguish one from the other in practice. In Zell unter Aichelberg in the 1730s, for example, Hans Jerg Bauer was out drinking with Hans Jerg Drohmann, the godparent of his children, when the latter suborned him to murder.[1] Such a tale, combining as it does spiritual kinship, carousing, and threats of violence, indicates that an account of godparentage has to include the complexities of social context and the ambiguities and shifting perspectives that everyday life presents to people. In his testimony, Bauer expressed shock that his spiritual patron would compromise their relationship. He said, "Godfather, you hold my children at the baptismal font and should warn me against such things." A good point, perhaps, but irony had never characterized Bauer's relationship to his patron and drinking companion before. At least after thinking about it for a long time, Bauer considered that a godfather ought to offer moral advice and example and not lead his dependent astray. A case like this one offers a rare glimpse into some of the values and expectations surrounding the institution of spiritual or ritual kinship and introduces a few of its ambivalences and contradictions. Even the fact that it was not unusual to use the address "godfather" in everyday life is something one can only occasionally document. In this particular story, the interaction of the two men over many years provides a many-layered profile of a patron/client relationship, with the wealthy landowner offering the poorer man carting services, employment, and liquor, and, according to the secular authorities, an example of good domestic management. For this chapter, the material does not offer the rich textures available from such narrative sources, and the discussion is largely restricted to inferences that can be drawn

[1] The case is discussed in David Warren Sabean, *Power in the Blood: Popular Culture and Village Discourse in Early Modern Germany* (Cambridge, 1984), chap. 5.

from the syntax of the genealogical grammar. But the objective is to arrive at an ever richer understanding of the structures that both underlay and developed from social practice by filling in the map of family connections one path and one contour at a time.

Following procedures that are familiar to the reader by now, this chapter takes a selection of godparents and godchildren from the family reconstitution. As explained in the Appendix, the sample for this period covers baptisms extending from the 1680s to the 1760s, with about 85 percent centered on the four decades from 1700 to 1739. Altogether, it includes godparents associated with 164 children from 40 families. The results of the analysis shed still further light on the basic question, did villagers use relatives – in this instance, as godparents – and if so, which ones?

As already pointed out, ritual kinship could channel the flow of social exchanges in specific ways and offer considerable continuity to them. It could reinforce relationships already established through affinity, or it could be used to select out a smaller set from a larger group of relatives to give special emphasis to. But the selection of godparents could also supplement marriage and affinity by building on new possibilities outside the range of established ties. Continuity and permanence were provided by the fact that a godparent usually stood for all the children of a couple and upon his or her illness or death was frequently succeeded by a close relative. Godparents also often remained in place as one spouse succeeded another in a household, so that the Gevatter(in) chosen by an original couple could still be called on even after both partners had been replaced by death and remarriage.

Ritual kinship and clientage

By the mid nineteenth century, the overwhelming majority of godparents (80 percent) was chosen from among close relatives of a couple, which contrasts very sharply with the early eighteenth century when less than 20 percent of them were related to their clients either as blood relatives or as affines. For the most part, rather than fitting into a set of relationships already established by marriage, ritual kinship in this earlier period set up another cluster of connections bringing nonrelatives into intimate and continuous contact with one another. Ritual kinship opened up poorer and less well-placed families to the village power structure and was also used to integrate village patricians into the regional hierarchy.

Ritual kinship changed radically over the study period, not only in terms of the propensity to offer the role to close kin, but also in the way it connected different strata in the village. By the beginning of the nineteenth century, parents and godparents were essentially from the same age cohort. But around 1700, godparents were older than fathers by six years or more and mothers by ten years or more. As already mentioned, the first children in a generation chose established householders from among their parents' generation, while younger siblings often

Table 7.1. *Cohort I: Parents' and godparents' tax quartiles.*

Parents' quartile	Number	Godparents' tax quartile							
		I[a]	II	III	IV	Pastor	(Richter/ Rat)	(Schultheiss)	Nonvillage
I[a]	19	0	0	4	8	4	(5)	(1)	3
II	10	0	0	1	7	1	(2)	(2)	1
III	28	0	1	7	15	3	(12)	(5)	2
IV	31	0	2	6	13	0	(6)	(4)	10

Note: Figures in parentheses included under wealth figures.
[a]In ascending order.

looked for senior members of their own generation, occasionally from within the affinal network, but most often not.

Ritual kinship also altered the way it articulated with the wealth and occupational hierarchies of the village. This clientage system of the early decades of the eighteenth century is documented in Tables 7.1 and 7.2.

All wealth classes found their godparents most prominently from among the wealthy. But the poorest families in the village took their godparents exclusively from the wealthiest (quartiles III and IV), including the pastor and his wife. Although poorer villagers frequently chose members of the magistracy as godparents, they developed ties not just with officeholders but with the wealthy in general. By contrast, the wealthiest villagers spread their choices around more than the other villagers, even though they did not use the pastor at all.[2] Those in quartile IV found a substantial number of their godparents outside the village, and they also turned toward villagers in quartiles II and III rather frequently.

That the wealthy looked for almost a third of their godparents outside the village set them off from all the other strata in the village. Sometimes they maintained close connections with magistrates in Raidwangen, the hamlet across the river that made up part of the larger Neckarhausen parish, but they more frequently turned toward patrons in the regional capital of Nürtingen. In fact, many villagers for several decades after the Thirty Years' War sought out powerful protectors there, including the widowed duchess. But by the end of the century, only a few wealthy villagers still maintained such close contacts. Johann Georg Rieth, the Schultheiss in Neckarhausen from 1640 to 1694, chose the Bürgermeister and a Richter in Nürtingen for his Gevattern, and his wife chose the wife of the city sexton. For a long while, as the practice declined for the majority of villagers, the village patriciate continued to maintain urban contacts. Rieth's son, Johann Georg, who served for a considerable time as Richter and eventually became Schultheiss, cultivated more local notables such as the Schultheiss and his wife from Raidwangen and the Neckarhausen pastor (unlike

[2] See the analysis of godparent relations for another village in Sabean, *Power in the Blood,* chap. 5. The pastor in the particular case was allied with the village poor.

most other magistrates in the village), but he also called upon one of the Nürtingen patricians, someone who received the honorific title "Herr." That the village patriciate also frequently turned to people poorer than themselves suggests that it was quite possible for a patron to have his client as Gevatter, to honor someone in this way in the network of friends. By the end of the seventeenth century, this was a practice among the nobility of southwest Germany, although they accomplished it by multiplying the number of godparents to as many as 10 people. Some of the Gevatter would be princes superior to themselves, some would be neighboring nobles, and some would be their own court officers and local notables.[3] While villagers could occasionally add a godparent or so beyond the customary 2, they could not develop as complex a strategy as nobles or city patricians. Still, taking the class of village patricians as a whole, they displayed parallel traits of turning toward social superiors, equals, and inferiors for godparents.

Those who were most dependent on local elites by the early eighteenth century were villagers in quartile III. These were the less substantial Bauern and small craftsmen, who needed to supplement their incomes by services rendered to larger agriculturalists or by work for the community. At that time, wealthier artisans were well represented among the magistrates, and they could organize poorer and younger artisans as a work force or subcontract parts of larger undertakings to them.

Occupation played a considerable role in the selection of godparents (Table 7.2). Those Neckarhausen residents for whom no occupation was ever recorded in any of the records I have consulted (included are people noted simply as Richter, or Bürgermeister, or Schultheiss) were almost certainly independent agricultural producers. The occupation "Bauer" was frequently taken for granted and often only recorded for agriculturalists who were on the margin of self-sufficiency, whose status was in question, and who might have been considered day-laborers rather than subsistent cultivators. Together, the Bauern, shepherds, and those whose occupations are not given (NGs) make up the class of independent agriculturalists. They found their godparents largely from their own class or from other wealthy landholders, such as innkeepers, and the pastor played little role for them. Indeed, they were rather more inclined to find godparents from among artisans than the artisans themselves were. Of course, all artisans – and all villagers – had some land to cultivate, and many artisans had enough to put them among the wealthiest villagers.[4] In general, Bauern found their godparents among other agricultural producers. Artisans clearly constructed networks for themselves that largely ignored their own occupational group and attached themselves to the class of more substantial landholders and to the village elite – the pastor and Schultheiss, for example.

[3] See the baptism register for the village of Pfedelbach in the former territory of Hohenlohe.

[4] See David Warren Sabean, *Property, Production, and Family in Neckarhausen, 1700–1870* (Cambridge, 1990), p. 460.

Table 7.2. *Cohort I: Parents' and godparents' occupations.*

		Godparents' occupations						
Parents' occupation	Number	Bauer/ Shep[a]	NG[b]	Bauer/ Weaver	Publican[c]	Artisan	Pastor	(Schult-heiss)
Bauer/Shep[a]	33	8	12	0	4	8	1	(3)
NG[b]	11	2	4	0	2	1	2	(2)
Bauer/Weaver	6	0	2	0	0	2	2	(0)
Publican[c]	—	—	—	—	—	—	—	—
Artisan	32	6	17	0	0	5	4	(7)

Note: Figures in parentheses also counted under relevant occupation.
[a]Shepherd.
[b]Not given, but Neckarhausen resident.
[c]Innkeeper, butcher, baker.

Taking all of the evidence together, the choice of godparents during the early decades of the eighteenth century for the most part involved families making connections with people they were not closely related to. Poorer householders attached themselves to patrons who were in position to mediate for them in different ways. Some were attached to households that could offer them agricultural work, while others became inserted into political networks that made village jobs available to them – cowherding, ditchdigging, repairs to the Rathaus roof, and so forth. And some attached themselves to the pastor as an alternative source of power to protect themselves against the harsh system of village favoritism and repression. But the relationships could also be more diffuse and involve all kinds of day-to-day recognition of respect, hope, honor, and prestige. In an earlier analysis, I found that a large percentage of property exchanged by nonrelatives was apparently negotiated between landholders who had a godparent in common, which suggests that ritual patrons acted as go-betweens for their clients in a great many ways.[5] Developing multipurpose networks in a similar manner, village patricians frequently sought for patrons outside the village, especially in the regional capital. Exactly how these many-stranded relationships were used in practice cannot be examined without documentation of a different kind, but they do indicate structural similarities to those created by marriage alliance. Both marriage and ritual kinship developed networks connecting the poor with the rich, clients with patrons, village Bürger with village magistrates. In most cases ritual kinship acted as a system for constructing ties between people that was complementary to that of marriage alliance. But for some people godparentage could support relationships already available in the network of affines.

Kin as godparents

Altogether, 22 of 106 godparents could be traced as kin. They were distributed rather equally according to the wealth and occupation of the parents and over the whole period covered by the sample. Although the majority of godparents do not seem to have been related to the parents, still there was a modest percentage who were (ca. 20 percent). No doubt with some of the records filled in, a few more would turn up, but given the fact that so often the pastor, Schultheiss, schoolmaster, or member of the court or council were chosen (44 times when not kin related), there are not many more links to be established. To put the issue slightly differently, once we subtract the village patriciate and the nontraceable inhabitants in other villages from the list of godparents, the evidence suggests still only a two in five chance that relatives would be chosen as godparents. The nature of such choices, however, reveals more about the principles involved in the construction of kin networks. The patterns point to structural elements similar to those involving kin-related marriages during the period but

[5] See Sabean, *Property*, pp. 379–83.

also suggest alternatives to the fraternal and agnatic foundations for constructing networks.

For each baptism, in principle both spouses chose a godparent, but not one that was sex-linked, in the fashion of godmothers for wives and godfathers for husbands. The list of related godparents is as follows:

Related to husband	*Related to wife*
1. BWZH(2)	10. ZHFB(1)
2. BWH(3)	11. ZHBW(1)
3. BWHB(1)	12. ZHZHW(1)
4. BWM(1)	13. ZHZHD(1)
5. FBW(1)	14. FZH(3)
6. FBWZH(1)	15. FZSW(1)
7. FBDH(3)	
8. WHB [1W1HB](1)	
9. MMZSD(1)	
Godfathers 11	Godfathers 4
Godmothers 3	Godmothers 4
Total 14	Total 8

The first thing to be noticed here is the complete lack of close relatives for godparents. There were no brothers or sisters, uncles (FB, MB) or aunts (FZ, MZ), mothers or fathers, grandmothers or grandfathers, and no first cousins. In all 22 cases, only one was related to a parent by blood, and that one was a second cousin (MMZSD). We cannot take for granted that people kept extensive genealogical information in their heads, nor that they calculated equally on both sides (through the father and through the mother). It could therefore be argued that this last relationship was ignored because it was so "distant." Yet, if kinship were not a factor taken into consideration when choosing godparents, then the almost complete avoidance of second cousins would have been impossible. Villagers were clearly quite consciously foregoing consanguineal kin out to and including first and second cousins. This avoidance parallels the avoidance of consanguineal kin as marriage partners, and discussed later, when people began to marry cousins, they also began to choose them as godparents. Also in this period, just as the closest affinal relations were not available for marriage, so they were not seen as relevant for the choice of godparents: not the sister's husband or the brother's wife. Everything points toward a strategy of reaching outside the close set of kin to create new lines of attachment. People constructed ritual kin ties with others older and more established than themselves, those with wealth or power. But some ties were developed with affinal kin at some remove, usually chosen because of the patron/client implications in the relationship.

One pattern stands out on first inspection, one that contributes to our understanding of sibling solidarity. Husbands tracing horizontally along one generation usually sought out affinal relatives of their brothers. Wives did the mirror opposite: they found relatives of their sisters. This phenomenon offers the first evidence that the strong bond between brothers was matched by a similar one between sisters. Sororal solidarity was not apparent from my analysis of marriage alliance. The politics of marriage showed every indication of being rooted in the exigencies of male production routines, property holding, and village government. With godparents, there appears to have been more possibility for women to develop and maintain networks of their own, and the consistency of choosing relatives of sisters shows that they could maintain important solidarities among themselves. Yet when reckoning took place across generations, both husbands and wives followed a route through the father (9 of 10 cases). For men, the structural configuration of FB contrasts with that of the FZ for women. As noted in Chapter 6, daughters were much more frequently named for paternal than maternal aunts, which together with this evidence suggests that however strong sororal ties were in a particular generation, they did not translate into the same kind of continuous relationships as those constructed by their brothers, either with their parallel or cross siblings. As a generation matured, relations constructed over fathers gained primacy for marriage choice, ritual kin selection, and naming.

From a detailed examination of the kin-related godparents, it should be possible to determine structural similarities and continuities in choice and through the identifiable claims and obligations to reconstruct the moral universe in which these people were situated. The same relationships clearly did not have the same meaning in different situations. The kind of person one married, or chose as Gevatter, selected as a guardian, or named a child after might be quite different in each case. A person could have made a claim to bestow a name on a child without ever expecting to be asked to stand as godparent. Of course, some paths once trodden set up expectations of greater traffic – a godparent might have every right to name his or her Dötle or to be asked to stand as guardian when necessary. I am trying to reassemble, in the first instance, a kind of social map and explore the territorialization of rights and duties, claims and obligations. I want to know where kin served and in what situations, and what kind of kin were chosen in the different contexts of action. In this chapter, I will take a few steps toward analyzing the logic of choosing kin for a particular purpose. The results can then be compared with the findings in Volume I about property sales. As the discussion proceeds, the spaces occupied by kin in the universe of social relations at any period should become clearer.

Cases 1 (BWZH) and 11 (ZHBW) are a good place to begin since they have parallel structures, although in one instance a man chose a godfather and in the other a woman chose a godmother (Figure 7.1). In both of these instances, ritual kinship acted as a crucial tie to close a circle in which three households were linked to one another. Marriage alliance during this period frequently performed the same function, and in this respect the two institutions could both create flexible, open social ties, which were built at the same time on overlapping ex-

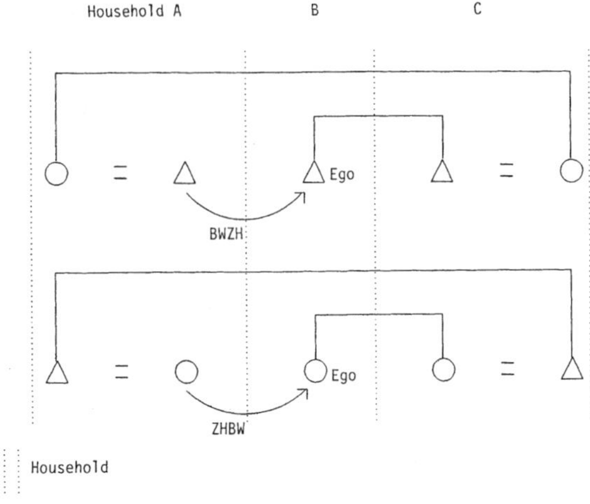

Figure 7.1

pectations of support and obligation. In these cases, godparentage was combined with affinal and sibling ties to create a cluster of mutual interest. Consanguineal ties by themselves were almost without exception not used as building blocks for ritual kinship in this period. Rather, it traversed paths constructed through overlapping marriage alliances. In each instance here, asymmetry in the relationships of people in the chain was of structural importance. There were two cases of men choosing their BWZHs. In one example, a weaver father in tax quartile I found a wealthier weaver godparent (quartile III), who was also a member of the Gericht. In the other example, a Bauer father from quartile III chose an innkeeper from quartile IV. He later called upon his BWM as a godmother – she was married to a Richter in quartile III. In the example of a woman choosing a ZHBW, the wife of a Richter in Raidwangen connected herself to the wife of the hamlet Schultheiss. In each of these instances, the affinal clusters involved relations constructed through siblingship, marriage, and ritual kinship, which connected the patricians with people less well placed than themselves in the village wealth and political hierarchies.

Diagramming each example would not add a great deal of information that has not already been presented in the chapters on marriage. People frequently asked the marital successor of a relative to act as godparent. And there are many examples in which members of one generation sought out members of another. Just to give one example (FBWZH), ego, a cobbler (quartile III), asked a Richter (quartile IV) to be the godfather of his children (Figure 7.2). As in all examples in which a man or a woman traced out a connection over a parent, this one made an agnatic calculation. Men called upon connections to patrilateral parallel relations, while women called upon patrilateral cross ones. Again, two parallel examples should suffice (FBDH and FZSW) (Figure 7.3).

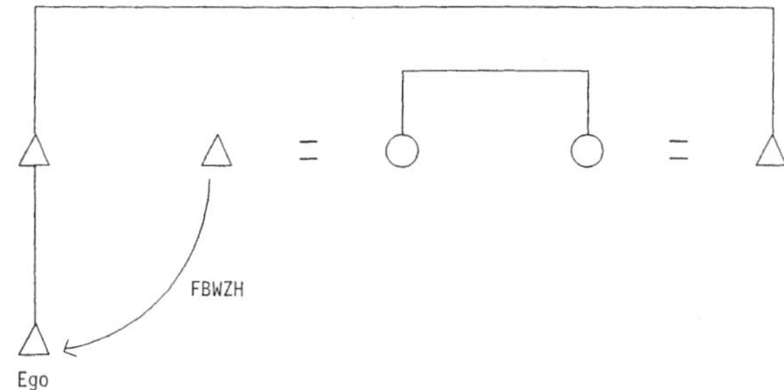

Figure 7.2

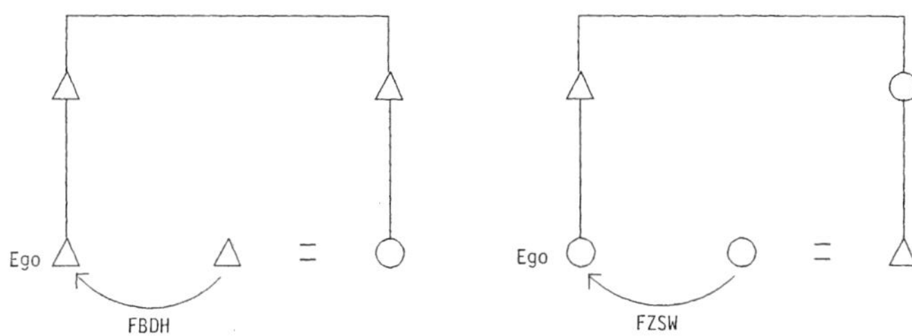

Figure 7.3

There were three instances of men choosing the FBDH. In one case a weaver and grave-digger from quartile I asked a cousin's husband, a Bauer from quartile IV, to be his Gevatter. In another case, a weaver from quartile II made a similar choice. And in the third, a wealthy agricultural producer from quartile IV called upon a Bauer from quartile II who was 11 years younger. This inverse and unusual asymmetry also characterized the female example (FZSW) in which a woman, whose husband was a day-laborer and forest guard from quartile III, found a cousin's wife, whose husband was in quartile II.

Gender and godparents

Sorting out the gender aspects of ritual kinship choice presents some difficulties. It is apparent from those cases where a kinship connection can be established between a parent and godparent that each spouse chose one of the two ritual kin, at least initially. And there is one instance from the 1730s in the church consistory records in which a woman's Gevatter gave her gifts that she considered to be outside the household budget and not under the administration of her husband.[6] The Gevatter, a wealthy merchant in Stuttgart, clearly had a particular relationship with the wife and acted as her patron, in this instance to the irritation of

[6] Kirchenkonvent, vol. 1, p. 1 (11.5.1727).

her husband. The social networks that husbands and wives created for themselves quite often represented their divergent interests and spheres of activity rather than the well-coordinated interests of a house. As I have argued in *Property, Production, and Family in Neckarhausen,* the productive relations of a couple at the beginning of the eighteenth century were structured quite differently from those later on when the agricultural revolution was in full swing. Women were not yet drawn into agriculture in a massive way, and gender spheres of work involved the creation of separate networks for mutual support. In general, male productive networks were centered on agriculture and handicrafts. Although in the absence of court records for this period it is difficult to be precise about gendered space, time, and work patterns, it seems safe to say that women's networks were constructed on the basis of childbirth and childcare, domestic work, gardening, marketing, flax preparation, spinning, and making clothes. Since women were owners of real estate, they were also concerned with developing powerful protectors of their property rights. And there was a village hierarchy of honor and prestige, which called upon their strategical and tactical skills to manage.

Women did not always choose other women as godparents, and the institution should not be seen as providing opportunities of direct bonding between friends. Godparents chosen by women were just as much selected on hierarchical principles of age and wealth as those chosen by men. And the actual person chosen might not be the object of personal connection – one might have sought out the wife of the Schultheiss in order to forge a link more with him than with her. The selection of godparents could emphasize the separate interests and spheres of activity of husbands and wives, but they could also come in the course of time to support certain solidarities. After a spouse died, the survivor might well keep the deceased's Gevatter(in) for the children of the subsequent marriage. And the continuity of a household could be underwritten by the fact that the original godparents, chosen initially to emphasize the separate interests and familial connections of each spouse, could continue to be called upon even after the deaths of both spouses and successive remarriages.

Ritual kinship and continuous alliance

The continuity of godparents has several dimensions. On closer inspection of the data, we find that during the period covered by the first two cohorts – up to the 1740s, at least – certain godparents were continuously associated with particular families over several generations. This practice brings into sharper focus the differences between this period and the subsequent one.

Continuity of godparentage appears to follow three patterns. Before the mid eighteenth century, a powerful man in the village began to act as godfather for the children of a couple and when he became too old or feeble, a son or close relative – sometimes a son-in-law – acted as godfather for the rest of the children of the set. This practice of finding a successor in the godparent's family continued even after the selection of godparents changed its character later in the century. But there is a significant difference between substituting the Schultheiss's son for the father in the earlier period and calling upon a second brother after the first one has emigrated in the later one. Besides this form of continuity, another important practice appears in the later decades of the seventeenth and first three or four decades of the eighteenth century: a practice whereby a person's Döte or Dote acted in the same capacity in the next generation for his or her children. Certain figures in the village during the period maintained their power over a very long time, moving from Rat to Gericht to a position as Bürgermeister or Schultheiss. They were able to act as godparents over more than one generation. Such a person was Johann Georg (Hans Jerg) Rieth, who died in 1694 at the age of 85. He was already Schultheiss in the 1640s and does not seem to have retired until close to his death. His son, also Johann Georg, born in 1664, died at the age of 76 in 1740. When his father died, he was already a member of the Gericht and became Schultheiss in his turn in the 1720s. His son – once again Johann Georg – born in 1715, died in 1761 at the age of 46. He was also Schultheiss and succeeded his father directly upon the latter's death. The first two Johann Georg Rieths were godparents to many people over more than one generation. Partly their longevity helped in their ability to span generations, but by the time the grandson became Schultheiss, villagers had begun to coalesce around their own families more often, and godparents were no longer chosen from nonrelated magistrates. Johann Georg III never was called upon to play the same role as godparent as his father and grandfather had been.

In another pattern of continuity, frequently a godparent in one generation was followed by his or her child or son- or daughter-in-law in the next. That is, a couple would choose a godparent from among the powerful or wealthy in the village, sometimes related in some way but most frequently not, and their children would choose either the same godparent again or a descendant of the godparent. Once patron/client relationships were set up, they tended to be reproduced, but that did not mean that there was no choice. Every family had two Gevatter, one man and one woman, and they were not usually closely related. That fact has implications for gender roles, as I have already noted. Here the point is that each family associated itself with at least two powerful individuals and therefore found itself in overlapping spheres of influence. The history of the relations between two Gevatter and their families would have implications for choice in the next generation. Strategies must have been complex, made up in part from past relationships and the moral expectations set up by earlier patron/client dynamics. Accidents of demography were extremely important. For example, the long-lived Neckarhausen Schultheiss, Salomon Hentzler, or his wife acted frequently as godparents for village inhabitants. But he died childless, making direct succession to his power sphere impossible.

In order to get a sense of the system as it functioned, I examined all of the people on the list of buyers and sellers of land in the decade 1700–1709 to see how many of them or their wives used their own Döte/Dote or his or her

Table 7.3. *Succession to position of Döte/Dote.*

Succeeded by	Döte(22)	Suceeded by	Dote(9)
Self	8	Self	3
W	1	H	
WH	1	HW	
S	2	S	2
D	2	D	
SW	5	SW	2 (1 xSW)
DH	2	DH	1
DHW	1	SWBW	1

descendants as Gevatter(in). The list examined consisted of 41 sets of parents. Of those, 24 demonstrated continuity over two generations (the Döte/Dote or a successor became Gevatter), giving a rate of 58.5 percent (roughly 3 out of 5). Altogether, there were 31 Döte/Gevatter combinations. In the sample, husbands were more likely to have a successor to their own Döte/Dote as Gevatter(in) than wives (ratio 19:12), but not by too much. The succession to the position of Döte/Dote is shown in Table 7.3.

If we look at continuity not from the point of view of a parent but from that of the godparent, men were much more likely to be succeeded by a close relative than women were. In any event, it seems that Doten were usually functioning within the power spheres of their husbands and fathers(-in-law). *For example, Agnes Falter, the wife of Hans, a Richter, was the Dote of Nicolaus Hess. Her son's wife became the Gevatterin. In this instance, the wife of a member of the Gericht was probably called upon because of her husband's position. The two of them were godparents for many families in the later decades of the seventeenth century. I do not think we can analyze their position apart from his place in the village hierarchy. His son became Richter for a time and married a member of the powerful Raidwangen Hentzler family. (Their son Salomon eventually became Bürgermeister). When Hans Jr.'s wife succeeded her mother-in-law, she probably did so as representative of the Falter "house." Succession in this instance was reckoned in the male line, even when wives held the position as godparent. Coalescing around a powerful figure could work rather differently in some cases. The old Schultheiss, Hans Jerg Rieth, sometimes was represented by his daughter Anna Agatha. She was Gevatterin on several occasions even before she was married, a relatively infrequent occurrence in the seventeenth and eighteenth centuries. She represented the Rieth* Hausmacht *when she was relatively young. She also succeeded her father on occasion, becoming Gevatterin, for example, for Catharina Haefner, the wife of Conrad Geiger, whose Döte had been old Hans Jerg Rieth. Anna Agatha's second husband, Friedrich Häussler, also succeeded Hans Jerg's wife, Anna Margaretha, becoming Gevatter for Michael Schober after she had been Dote. Margaretha Rieth herself became Gevatterin for Andreas Rieth, for whom*

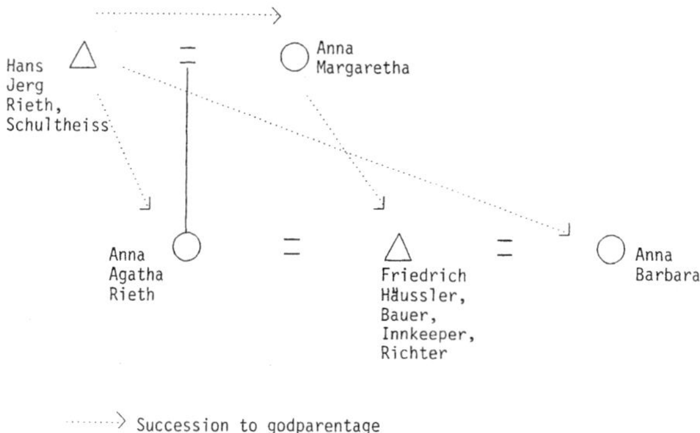

Figure 7.4

her husband had been Döte. Finally, Friedrich Häussler's second wife became Gevatterin for Hans Jerg Schill. Her husband's first wife's father (Hans Jerg Rieth, Sr.) had been both Döte and Gevatter before her. The succession examples illustrated by this family are shown in Figure 7.4.

The practice of familial succession to godparentage appears to have developed in the decades after the Thirty Years' War and lasted until roughly the fourth decade of the eighteenth century. During the Thirty Years' War and in the period of regroupment afterward, godparents frequently came from outside the village. Various Schultheissen from surrounding villages were represented as godparents, but by far the most important source was the market and administrative town of Nürtingen. During the 1630s many Neckarhausen residents had fled to the town, and for a time the parish registers were even kept there. Relationships with the more powerful members of the town remained close. After all, they were an important source of credit. Every indication in the postwar period is that it was a time of brutal social and economic exploitation and gouging taxation. Protection of the most direct kind was necessary. When godparents were chosen from within the village, the choice generally fell on those people best in a position to protect their clients, although it must be assumed that clients sometimes had little choice about being "protected." By the late decades of the seventeenth century there were still godparents chosen from outside the village, especially among the more recent immigrants, but the community gradually closed itself off in this respect from the outside. For many decades the relations between wealthy and poor, powerful and weak, old and young were characterized by loose spheres of influence and overlapping sets of patrons and clients, given concrete form in the choosing of Gevattern and Gevatterinnen. There was a tendency to reproduce the spheres over time, lineal descendants of the Gevattern of one generation becoming the Gevattern of the next. Yet we can only hint at how this worked. The coalition around a powerful individual could dissipate from many causes – the failure to produce a successor, incompetence, the lack of success in the power

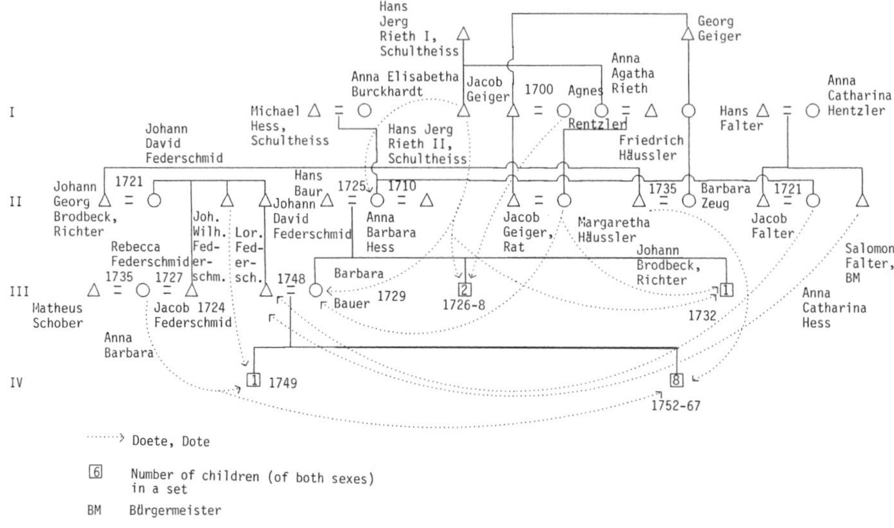

Figure 7.5

struggle. The real successor to his sphere of influence might be a newly emerging figure not closely related to him at all, and we would miss the shift by paying too close attention to lineal descendance. Still there seems to have been a presumption of continuation of a power sphere within a family, represented by the frequency with which sons, daughters, and children-in-law succeeded to the position of parents as ritual kin. This system lasted no longer than the hierarchical structure and social conditions that gave rise to it.

To examine the practice for one family over several generations, I chose two brothers, Michael and Georg Hess, born in 1624 and 1625, respectively, and followed all of their descendants for four generations.[7] To display the whole genealogy through all four generations turned out to be far too complex to follow easily, although I have studied it all in detail. I therefore broke the genealogy into eight segments corresponding to each child from the second generation who married. Even then, it has proved far too tedious to offer each of the segments here. All of them illustrate the same patterns, and so the detailed discussion of one will do.

The discussion focuses on the section of the genealogy pertaining to the second marriage of Michael Hess's (I) daughter, Anna Barbara Hess (II) (Figure 7.5). She married Hans Baur, an immigrant *from the village of Notzingen. All of the children had Hans Jerg Rieth II, Schultheiss, as godfather, the same person who was godfather for Anna Barbara herself. In addition, Barbara Baur's (III) godmother*

[7] Michael Hess eventually became Schultheiss, succeeding Johann Georg Rieth, Sr. He died in 1709 at the age of 85.

was Hans Jerg Rieth's niece, Margaretha Häussler, although Margaretha's position probably stems from the fact of her marriage to Jacob Geiger (II), a member of the Rat. The first two children in generation III had old Jacob Geiger's (I) wife as godmother, while the next two had Jacob Geiger's sons's wife (Margaretha). Here we find a typical example of the inheritance of a position in a male line except it is carried out by women. There is no evidence in any of the material that inheritance of this type passed through women. Two things should be emphasized. First of all, in case after case, a similar inheritance of godparents took place during this period. Second, the inheritance of the position of godparent descended in the male line. As already pointed out, a principle of male descent operated in the system of marriage alliance as well. Here, the patrilineal structure was rooted in political considerations, the constant association of one family as patrons with another as clients. By generation IV the entire structure had fundamentally altered. All the godparents were in some way or other related to Lorenz Federschmid, the father. At that point, there was no longer any continuity with the godparents from the early period. *For the firstborn, Lorenz's uncle (FB) and another uncle's wife (FBW) were godparents. The latter continued to fill the role and was joined by Lorenz's FZHB, Johann Brodbeck, Richter. I do not think that Brodbeck's position was a continuation of the Geiger family patronage – as husband of Jacob Geiger's (I) brother's granddaughter. What argues against that interpretation is the fact that Johann Wilhelm Federschmid (II) had already acted as godfather. He was most certainly replaced after his untimely death in 1751 by someone related to him, in this instance, his ZHB.*

The principles of selection of godparents in the late decades of the seventeenth and first decades of the eighteenth centuries emphasize continuity between generations and the use of the wealthy and powerful as godparents. Various members of the Gericht or Rat or Schultheissen stand out in this regard. By the mid eighteenth century, family connection came to contend with the first principle. There appear, therefore, to have been three stages. First, in the decades after the Thirty Years' War, a handful of powerful villagers were often called upon to act as godparents. But very frequently, godparents were chosen from among well-to-do citizens of Nürtingen, or sometimes from Schultheissen in other villages. The use of outside links was still common in generation I of this genealogy. By generation II, outsiders were far less frequently called upon. The village population regrouped and formed a new system of godparentage. From then on, village patron/client links were primary. They seem open-ended, but perhaps the contenders for power and wealth each created a loose clientele, either standing as godparents themselves or being represented by close relatives – a wife or son or daughter. The old Schultheiss's daughter, Anna Agatha Rieth, as just mentioned, appeared frequently as godparent during the years when her father was still active and her brother was building his position in the village. During this period kin could function as godparents but usually not close kin and always kin well placed in the property or political hierarchy. By midcentury, people began not only to call upon more relatives but also to select much closer relatives as godparents. A typical figure was Johannes Bosch, who appears in this genealogy but not in the segment studied here. He became a powerful and respected member of the Gericht, but in the decades after midcentury he or his wife were usually godparents only for his own grandchildren. In the period from the late seventeenth century into the early decades of the eighteenth, the system of godparentage appears to have been a key institution for the reproduction of hierarchy and power. A man with a clientage constructed on the basis of godkinship could provide a pool for his successor in the power structure to use and to build his own clientage from. The links appear to have been fluid and flexible enough so there is nothing to suggest that a set of clients operated in any way as a closed, tightly coordinated group. Powerful members of the village had a set of people related to them through a loose and often overlapping set of ties quite suitable for developing and maintaining a multilayered set of reciprocities.

8

Naming children

The structure of alliance in Neckarhausen in the early decades of the seventeenth century gave privileged place to affinal kin and to networks of villagers created and maintained for the most part by people on the same generational plane. Most godparents, even though they were older than the parents they were connected with, were still not from a generation above them. They were the active, powerful members of the village. It is true that the oldest siblings often fit themselves into a field of relations constructed by their elders and sometimes chose their godparents from their parents' cohort. But as the new generation developed and modified the configurations of power and wealth, its members chose ritual kin corresponding to those new realities. And younger siblings marrying for the first time and older ones remarrying constructed alliances that linked together existing households and active adults of the village. They did not reproduce older alliances by marrying consanguineal relatives, which would have been a way of inscribing past relationships onto present ones. Traditional alliances were not replicated by new marriages every second or third generation. Although marriage alliance did not provide continuity across generations, sometimes godparentage did, although here again the matter seems to have been tied less to the maintenance of a family tradition than to assembling new power configurations out of the bits and pieces of earlier ones.

The main concern in this chapter is whether the practice of naming children did attach people to the past in some way. It was possible for active members of one generation to use the past to authenticate or authorize relationships in the present. Or they might have developed practices that emphasized the continuity of tradition over time. But it was just as possible for naming to have been a way of forgetting, of obliterating memory of the dead, of underlining current political and social realities without reference to historical ratification.

The cohort identified for the period 1700–1709 consists of 41 families (the

Table 8.1. *Cohort I (naming): Number of times information is missing.*

Relatives of father	Number of times	Relatives of mother	Number of times
FB/FBW	3	MB/W	18
FZ/FZH	3	MZ/H	18
FF	0	MF	3
FM	2	MM	18
FFB/W	25	MFB/W	30
FMB/W	15	MMB/W	30
FFZ/H	25	MFZ/H	30
FMZ/H	15	MMZ/H	30
FFF	19	MFF	28
FFM	26	MFM	30
FMF	5	MMF	19
FMM	14	MMM	31

Note: Total families = 41.

same sample as that for godparents). It presents special difficulties because of the way the selection took place. Because an unusual number of women married into the village, only the names of their parents are known, but not of their siblings or ascendants. This point must be kept in mind during the analysis. Therefore Table 8.1 outlines the number of times information is lacking in the sample.

Naming sons

To begin with sons, 61.4 percent of those in the sample were named after their fathers, paternal uncles, and godfathers (Table 8.2). The practice of naming children after godparents was sometimes ambiguous, since the father and godfather had the same name four times. In fact, if attention were focused on fathers, their numbers would be even more striking (29) and the godfathers correspondingly reduced (6). Naming a son, especially the firstborn, for the father outweighed all other possibilities. Yet, there is no real sign of a rigid rule, not even for the first child, since the firstborn son received the father's name in less than half of the instances here. The general practice and the weight of social expectation had considerable room for variation. Most of the firstborn sons received their names from agnatic kin. By contrast, fewer than half of the second sons found names from the father's side of the family. Overall, the most important source for boys' names after the father was the father's brother. There was some interest in the FF's name but absolutely no indication that lineal ascendants or collaterals (FFB, FFF) provided any names whatsoever. On the other hand, the mother's brother

Table 8.2. *Cohort I: Closest kin match for sons.*

	Birth order							Birth order					
	1	2	3	(3+)	4+	Total		1	2	3	(3+)	4+	Total
GODF	3[a]	5[b]	1	(2)	1	10							
F	14	5	2	(6)	4	25							
FB	9	4	5	(7)	2	20	MB	1	5	2	(2)		8
FZH	1		1	(2)	1	3	MZH	1					1
FF	3	2	1	(1)		6	MF	1	2				3
FFB							MFB						
FFZH	1					1	MFZH						
FFF							MFF						
FMB							MMB		1				1
FMZH							MMZH						
FMF							MMF						
No match	1	2	4	(7)	3	10	Total	35	26	16	(27)	11	88

[a]+3 overlap with father.
[b]+1 overlap with father.

played a prominent role, appearing here 8 times altogether, even though the names of the MB were not known in 44 percent of the cases. Assuming the same distribution in the unknown cases, the number would be on the order of 10 or 11. It could well be, furthermore, that sons were named for the MB rather than for such people as the FZH or FF. We do have the names of MF for all but three of the families studied, but the FF seems to been a more important source for names.

The significant conclusion to begin with is that names were chosen overwhelmingly from the parents' generation. We already know that for the cohort from 1700–1709, there was a tendency, even though godparents were older, to find them from the same generational level. But setting the godparents aside and ignoring the nonmatches, the parents' generation accounted for 83.5 percent of the names given to sons and daughters. Even though information was frequently missing for certain relations, there is ample indication of a lack of interest in names from the paternal and maternal ascendants. For example, the name of the FMF (husband's maternal grandfather) was known in 36 cases. In 5 instances, the F and the FMF had the same name. With the remaining 31, there were 56 chances to name a child after the FMF. In all, there were only 2 sons who perpetuated the latter's name, but they also matched the FB. Put differently, in 54 instances (61.4 percent) the FMF had a name not carried by anyone else in the "name-giving set," and in those instances the name was not perpetuated. If such ascendants provided a field for selecting names, then surely there was adequate opportunity here. All of the evidence points toward shallow genealogical reckoning.[1] Seldom if ever were boys named after a deceased older relative. Names for sons were chosen largely from among the living, active set of male siblings and the brothers of the mother. Insofar as names are concerned, the earlier generations were already largely forgotten. In Neckarhausen, the set of names from ascendants did not provide a field for representing current political and social cleavages.

As already mentioned, godfathers were chosen – largely from nonrelatives – because of social connections among adults. Godparents were older, wealthier, and more established politically. Giving the name of a godparent also comes under the heading of relations among living adults. Even here, though, the godfather played a secondary role, which would be even less if we reversed priorities and matched a name first with the FB or MB. In fact, only in two cases was a son unambiguously called after a godfather, that is, where the F, FB, or MB did not also have the same name. But in these two instances, we do not know the names of the mother's brothers. In general, names tended to reflect relations between close adult kin of the same generation rather than between unrelated people even when they were godparents, although the ambiguity involved in

[1] Martine Segalen, *Fifteen Generations of Bretons: Kinship and Society in Lower Brittany, 1720–1980*, trans. J. A. Underwood (Cambridge, 1991), p. 86, stresses the shallowness of genealogical memory in partible-inheritance South Brittany.

many situations may have left the matter open to interpretation on purpose. From evidence gathered in the nineteenth century (see Chapter 1), it appears that the person a child was named after played a symbolic role when the child reached a certain age, providing him or her with the first suit of adult clothes. If this tradition reached back into this period, then there would have been no ambiguity in the minds of family members at the time of a baptism, even if today's historians cannot always sort the matter out.

Villagers did not use the past as part of the symbolic struggle in the present, at least not through the practices of naming. Indeed, children's names seldom even matched those of the great-grandparents. Out of 87 boys, only 3 had the names of their FFF, and 6 of the FMF. If the missing information with regard to the FFF is kept in mind, then the reproduction of names of the patrilineal great-grandparents among boys may have been on the order of 12 to 13 percent. The fact that these names were used at all, however, was almost always because they were carried by members of the parents' generation. Everything points toward very shallow genealogical reckoning and a quick blotting out of the past. This goes together with the way names were used in everyday life in Neckarhausen. Soon after Alt Hans Bauknecht dies, one of the more junior Hans Bauknechts becomes Alt Hans. There is no distinct way of keeping the names apart. In this way, necronymy (naming after someone deceased) did not occur so much at the naming of a boy at baptism but in the course of his life as one generation succeeded another. Once someone else died, the active, living men succeeded to designations in age ordering, or as active holders of occupations – "Hans Bauknecht, carpenter."

The data examined here furnish overwhelming evidence that children were named in almost every instance after someone specific. I have looked more closely at those cases (10, or 11.4 percent) in which no namesake can be found by this method. In 8 of these, the mother's siblings were not known, and in 1, the father's siblings. As for those who carried the godfather's name, only 2 appear to have been unambiguously named for him. In the only instance in which a child was named after the pastor (who was also the godfather), male relatives also carried the same name. All of the evidence points toward close kin of the parents' generation as the source of most names.

Naming daughters

The analysis of daughters' names presents a few more problems (Table 8.3). For one thing, the number of positions missing is correspondingly greater, especially, for example, the MZ and MM. Among the 41 families studied, 11 included women who married in from other villages (only 2 inmarrying husbands were in the same sample). Since most of the naming of the firstborn daughters can be accounted for, the problem of missing data appears to be serious only from the second child on, for which about a fourth of the girls' names cannot be matched. The firstborn daughter was named about as often for the mother as the firstborn

Table 8.3. *Cohort I: Closest kin match for daughters.*

	1	2	3	(3+)	4+	Total		1	2	3	(3+)	4+	Total
GODM	10[a]	4	3[b]	(6)	3	20							
M	13	2	4	(5)	1	20							
MZ	3	1	1	(2)	1	6	FZ	4	3	2	(2)		9
MBW							FBW	1	2	1	(1)		4
MM	1		1	(1)		2	FM	2	3				5
MFZ							FFZ	1					1
MFBW							FFBW						
MFM							FMM						
MMZ							FMZ						
MMBW							FMBW						
MMM							FMM						
No match	2	7	3	(5)	2	14[c]	Total	37	22	15	(22)	7	81

[a]+2 overlap with mother.
[b]+1 overlap with mother.
[c]Two names created from two adult kin.

son for the father. The mother's sister, however, did not equal the role of the FB among the boys. Even expanding the figure in terms of missing data would only bring the total to 12 or 13. On the other hand, the FZ, and in a secondary way the FBW, seem to have been important. Indeed, apart from the mother herself, the father's relatives outweighed the mother's 2 to 1. Although some of the balance would be rectified if the missing data were filled in, there still seems to have been considerably more reliance on the father's side for girls than on the mother's side for boys. Perhaps this was a result of the break with the family of origin experienced by inmarrying women. Or it could be that since the sample contains so many of them, the data reflect attempts on their part to throw out new lines of attachment, sometimes among the husband's siblings. Perhaps the importance of naming after the godmother is significant here, since most godparents were from the village. Almost a third of the daughters were named after godmothers, who in that cohort were not usually chosen from among close kin.

From this information, there is no way of telling whether mothers had a greater say than fathers in naming daughters. It could be, of course, that husbands were using the names of daughters to emphasize relations with those godparents who had been chosen to their advantage. We have argued that godparents in this period were particularly attached to one of the spouses, but a husband was just as likely to choose the godmother as the godfather. The fact remains that daughters' names were chosen more frequently from the "public" domain than from the private one of the family. They were attached more to the factors that opened out families to the sphere of negotiation, to attachments that were constructed rather than prescribed. Naming them had more to do with the wider political forces than did the naming of sons. Perhaps the naming of boys and girls shows some hint of a solidary perception of the relations of male siblings and a sense of women as negotiable instruments – attaching daughters' names to the male side of the family or opening them out to the wider field of negotiations. Remember, too, that boys were frequently named after the MB. Given the fact that marriage alliance usually established brothers-in-law in an asymmetrical, probably patron/client, relation, naming after the MB could reflect the politics of the alliance. Still, the practice of bestowing names on boys emphasized the solidarity of brothers more than anything else.

Neonymy and necronymy

In this exercise a match has been considered actual only if both the first and second names are the same. In other words, Johann Georg and Johann Wilhelm are considered to be separate names even though they have the common first name of Johann. In fact, Johann was a frequent first name for boys, just as Anna was for girls. In most cases, the second name – Georg, Friedrich, Maria, Margaretha – was the distinguishing one. By proceeding in this way, however, we miss one important possibility. Parents could create a new name out of old parts; for example, Johann Georg and Johann Friedrich could become Georg Friedrich.

By our method of counting matches, this name would not appear in the tables, although it might in some ways represent an even tighter social relationship. If a son's name was created from his father's and uncle's at the same time, he would represent a more specific mediation than if two successive sons were named after the two different adults. In this cohort, however, there were no names constructed for boys in this way. For daughters, there were two instances, one where the mother, Maria, and the godmother, Magdalena, were represented by the daughter, Maria Magdalena, and another where the mother Anna Maria and the godmother Anna Barbara were represented by the daughter Maria Barbara. This practice of creating names increased considerably in the course of the eighteenth century and became a normal practice in the nineteenth, although it was always more important for daughters than for sons. In this instance, the two examples emphasize the importance of the attachment between wives and the Gevatterinnen, whether chosen by themselves or their husbands.

Some mention should also be made of the problem of necronymy, in this instance the naming of children after deceased siblings. The term itself is misleading, since it is not at all apparent whether the repetition of a name involved calling a subsequent child after a deceased one. It could have been – and most probably was – that both were named for the father or the uncle and that repetition arose from the importance of the adult relationship. In some villages in Württemberg, it was considered unlucky to repeat a child's name, but again there seems to have been no invariable rule.[2] It is more likely that such matters were part of a complex village discourse, sometimes used to explain situations after the fact. In any event, reusing children's names in the first decade of the eighteenth century was an infrequent practice – for boys, 8 out of a possible 39 cases; for girls, 2 out of 13. Repetition suggests which relations were considered important to reemphasize, but the figures are too small to say much more, and there are no surprises: 3 Fs, 2 FBs, 1 FF, 2 MBs, 1 M, and 1 GODM.

Some anthropologists have looked at naming practices as a competitive exercise. In such situations, families avoid repeating names already available in the cohort. Strategies are developed to capture symbolic capital by naming a child after a significant ancestor, and finding the right available "space" is a means of simultaneously blocking another family's ability to occupy it. Bernard Vernier has given a particularly brilliant analysis of the symbolics of naming in a society in which names were treated as scarce goods and kin had long memories reaching back many generations.[3] Such long memories, as distinguished from broad memories, seem to be associated with impartible inheritance regions.[4] Martine Segalen

[2] Karl Bohnenberger, ed., *Volksümliche Ueberlieferungen in Württemberg: Glaube – Brauch – Heilkunde* (Stuttgart, 1980; original, 1904ff.), p. 87.

[3] Bernard Vernier, "Putting Kin and Kinship to Good Use: The Circulation of Goods, Labour, and Names on Karpathos (Greece)," in Hans Medick and David Warren Sabean, eds., *Interest and Emotion: Essays on the Study of Family and Kinship* (Cambridge, 1984), pp. 28–76.

[4] For another example of an impartible inheritance region with long genealogical memories, see the work of Claverie and Lamaison discussed in Chapter 20.

emphasizes that in partible inheritance Brittany, people have a widespread knowledge of contemporary kin but a shallow knowledge of kin in the past.[5] Genealogical memory in partible inheritance Neckarhausen, according to naming practices and teknonymy, was short. But there was also little interest in competition for scarce names. Brothers had no problem bestowing names on their sons that were already in use by other brothers. In the wealthy landholding Waldner family, each brother chose names from the patriline for his sons, with several cousins ending up with the same name. There was no competition for the capture of certain key names, nor was there any particular order to naming. Daughters were treated in the same way as sons. Just because one Waldner brother already had a Hans Jerg or Anna Catharina did not stop another from using the same names. Since they were already clearly distinguished through prescriptive rules of descent and affinity, there was no need to mark them with unequivocal names. A comparison with the artisan Bauknecht family shows the same free-flowing duplication of male siblings' names. The safe assumption, on the one hand, that differences were so great that name duplication did not matter, was coupled, on the other, with the stress on the male sibling group as a core set of relationships.

* * *

This chapter has shown that names were exchanged within a relatively restricted group. Sometimes they seemed to carry with them a rather direct, emotional value, associated with the closest relatives and under certain circumstances repeated for several children. Earlier chapters suggested that there were interlocking, often asymmetrical productive and political networks connecting adult brothers and brothers-in-law, which in turn fit into larger networks involving fictive kinship, patronage, and marriage alliances. The building blocks appear to have been coordinate sets of brothers and immediate affinal kin. The whole structure had an agnatic focus even for women, who, whenever they did choose kin for godparents or for spouses, reckoned relationships primarily through their fathers.

During this early period, most of the sons received names from the interacting set of adult men. In the first instance, they came from a group of brothers. In fact, a collection of agnatic cousins was likely to have a more or less overlapping set of names. Supplementing this were names chosen from the father's brothers-in-law, his wife's siblings. It was precisely from this group that his brothers might choose their Gevattern and thereby occasionally a name as well. In any event, names were traded most frequently among a male sibling set, to a lesser extent among affines, and occasionally among affines of affines. It all was part of the construction of ever more loosely ordered foci within which and between which

[5] See Martine Segalen, " 'Avoir sa part': Sibling Relations in Partible Inheritance Brittany," in Medick and Sabean, eds., *Interest and Emotion*, pp. 129–44. See also the discussion of her work in Chapter 20.

various goods and services were exchanged. Some sets of brothers appear to have traded names back and forth so restrictively that they look fairly tightly coordinated as a group, whereas others seem to have fractionalized into several separate associations, more or less close to the kin of some of their wives. This might especially have been the case in those frequent examples where two siblings married two people who were first cousins (patrilateral parallel) to each other.

The names bestowed on daughters may also reflect a system of exchange organized around agnatic kin. A significant number of names came from the siblings of a girl's father. Rather than using the rest to stress the mother's relatives, many came from the godmother. There was for girls, then, a bifocal aspect to naming, since names were taken either from the closest kin, with a greater stress on patrikin than might be expected, or from godmothers, who for the most part were not related to the parents but at least half of whom were chosen by the father and were part of his set of alliances. Here again names were part of solidarity and alliance that were not exclusively but at least tendentially based on male productive and political alliances. A large proportion of the names during this period circulated within the same group that land circulated in, the closest consanguineal and directly allied kin. Godparents could be critical for the transfer of land between unrelated families between which women were also exchanged. In that system, godparents were also a source of names for women, marking out their sphere of influence and underlining their capacity for negotiating among their clients.

COHORT II (1740–1749)

9

Restructuring the system of alliance

During the middle decades of the eighteenth century, kinship changed dramatically. Some people in the village began to marry cousins and to call upon other cousins to be godparents. An alliance system emerged that favored consanguineal relatives over affinal ones, but the connection between the two categories is complicated, and the one was frequently reinforced by the other. When a man or a woman married a cousin, other cousins consequently became in-laws and were then frequently prepared to coordinate their activities in new ways. The innovation lies in the fact that cousin marriages allowed alliances forged in one generation to be replicated in another. Not all sections of the village adopted the new practice at once, and not until the early decades of the nineteenth century was it generalized, although even then the kinds of cousins chosen correlated closely with different social strata. The new system lasted in its essential form until the middle of the nineteenth century, when the systematic alliance of agnatically constructed "lines" gave way to a form of exchange mediated by women.

At this point, it would be tedious and not especially rewarding to go over each indicator of kin interaction to show the precise departures and continuities at every point. A fuller discussion of the intricacies of the system – once it was fully in place and subject to a half century of experience – will be taken up in the section on the third cohort (centered on the 1780s). Each variable studied earlier has been analyzed in the same way for this period as well, but many of the results have been placed in the Appendix. Here the task will be to underscore a few salient features of property transactions, marriage alliance, and ritual coparenthood. In the second chapter of this section, attention will turn to some of the implications of the changes as reflected in the case of Schultheiss Johann Georg Rieth III, the subject of an official inquiry stemming from charges brought by villagers marginalized by new power configurations and forms of kin interaction.

The real-estate market

By the 1740s inheritance still played the major role in the distribution of resources in the village. Nonetheless, the market for real estate had developed in significant ways, even outstripping the 34 percent rise in population, at least in terms of the number of arable plots for sale (which increased by 37 percent). The parcelization process that was such a remarkable feature of Württemberg in the eighteenth and nineteenth centuries was already well under way. For example, an arable plot of average size shrank by 23 percent over the 40-year period, largely because of the practice of partitioning individual strips into separate parcels as parents passed them along to their children. A strip was always divided longitudinally and continued to be cultivated as a whole even though its parts were separately sowed and harvested by different households. In many instances where a brother and sister owned parcels in a larger strip, one brother-in-law plowed and harrowed for the other.[1] For the most part, even as late as midcentury, because of the dominant asymmetrical marriage pattern, one household in such a situation was likely to have more cultivation equipment than the other.

With the turnover of generations, cousins who came to hold contiguous parcels in a single strip were compelled to cultivate them together. In many cases, they coordinated production for years before one of them sold out to the other. But in other instances two cousins who sold property to each other, in fact sold other noncontiguous strips and went on cooperating in the exploitation of the ones that lay next to each other. Whatever the cause, the rise of cousins as buyers and sellers was a remarkable feature of the property market by the 1740s. Despite the fact that the market was opening up and more than 2 times as many people were active in it, even more transactions took place among kin than before, increasing from 64 percent to 82 percent between the two cohorts. Within the even tighter control of real estate transactions by kin, a considerable shift in favor of first and second cousins took place. In the early years of the century, they had accounted for less than 10 percent of all sales and exchanges that passed between relatives. By the 1740s they had increased their position to 40 percent. And at the same time there was an erosion of affinal sales from 30 percent to 20 percent. This shift of focus from people connected through affinal networks to consanguineal kin was mirrored in marital politics and in the selection of ritual kin. Cousins had one important feature as market partners. A sizable majority of sales (2 to 1) took place with cousins reckoned through fathers, in part because agnatic cousins were far more likely to farm contiguous plots than uterine cousins were, the reason being that in the senior generation, brothers much more frequently than brothers-in-law continued to hold plots lying next to each other. I suggested earlier that tensions between brothers-in-law were likely to be greater than those between brothers. And this fact is reflected in the frequency with which brothers-

[1] David Warren Sabean, *Property, Production, and Family in Neckarhausen, 1700–1870* (Cambridge, 1990), pp. 311–13.

in-law sold out their property rights, perhaps to avoid the conflicts that agricultural cooperation entailed. Sales between brothers-in-law were six times as frequent as those between brothers.[2] Thus there was a much greater chance that agnatic cousins would hold contiguous plots, cooperate in cultivation, and end up buying and selling land to each other. Even then a sale did not always operate as a clean break between parties to a transaction. In many cases, plots were sold with payments extending over many years, which gave a certain amount of continuity and long-term structure to the relations between trading partners.

Cousins, then, especially agnatic ones, were increasingly thrown together as the size of arable strips was whittled away and as the market began to play an increasing role in the distribution of resources in the village. But it was not just land that mediated intimate contacts between relatives. Co-ownership in agricultural equipment played an important, if not yet well-understood, role. When Hans Geiger, a well-to-do Bauer, died in 1742, the inventory of his estate indicated he possessed a third share in all the farming implements, while his son possessed two-thirds. At the division of the estate, the son and a nephew inherited equal halves of Geiger's third. As a result, two cousins shared (1/6 and 5/6) a set of farming and traction equipment. Although it is difficult to determine how widespread this kind of co-ownership might have been (or exactly what ownership of different proportions entailed), since over the next 40 years more and more brothers acted as coparceners in equipment (but not in land or other forms of movable property such as cattle and horses), the process of inheritance must have cast uncles and nephews and agnatic cousins together fairly frequently, at least for a period of time.

Land and its exploitation in this partible inheritance village, even though it was individually held and enjoyed, provided many opportunities for the interests of different householders to overlap. In a period when horse traction predominated and horses with all their complex gear were distributed unequally in the population, richer and older folk plowed, harrowed, and carted for poorer and younger ones. Increasingly, overlapping rights in agricultural equipment and contiguous rights in land that had to be cultivated en bloc oriented villagers toward networks pieced together through blood relatives: uncles, and nephews, first cousins, and eventually second cousins. And a fundamental structural element in that system was built on agnatic connections. Producing agricultural goods and regulating the distribution of property made up only a part of the social network of Neckarhausen, however, and other aspects of village relations must be examined before trying to figure out how different parts of the overall system fit together.

Marriage alliance

Although property ownership and management appear to have provided the basis for considerable practical cooperation among consanguineal kin, the first marriage

[2] Sabean, *Property*, p. 385.

Table 9.1. *Cohort II: Kin-related marriages by occupation of husband.*

	Kin-linked	Non–kin-linked	Total	Percent
Bauer	22	29	51	43.1
Artisan	12	20	32	37.5
Magistrate[a]	13	6	19	68.4

Note: The statistics include individuals in a series of marriages only once but count all marriages in assessing whether there was a kin-linked marriage.
[a]Magistrates were included in the above occupational statistics.

alliances forged between cousins seem to have derived less from productive concerns than from political ones. In the 1740s, members of the village magistrates and their children began a policy of closely allying themselves together and in the ensuing decades created an ever tighter set of overlapping marital connections. A few of the central features of the new departures, along with references to appendix tables, will serve to illustrate this trend.

Between Cohort I, centered on the period 1700–1709, and cohort II, centered on the 1740s, the percentage of kin-related marriages rose from about 25 percent to 40 percent (Table A.25). By the second period, there had been a significant rise in such marriages for couples in which both partners were being married for the first time (from 18 percent to 36 percent), so that overall the difference between the rates for first and second marriages became insignificant. In the first cohort, widowers were far more likely to seek out kin for spouses, and they looked for them within the set of extended affines, emphasizing relationships that had been developed by themselves and their siblings. By midcentury, people marrying for the first time were often choosing spouses from within relationships that had been forged by their parents. Their choices were not, therefore, determined by their own experiences as adult heads of households or by the networks of dependency, clientage, or obligation that they themselves had developed, but, rather, by those that grew out of their parents' activities. If anything, men opted less often for kin the second time around (28 percent), perhaps because ties from first marriages were extremely binding. (The practice of keeping godparents chosen by the first spouse for children of the second supports this point.) On the other hand, widows were not willing to trust their fortunes to strangers but chose more often than not (54 percent) to seek a second partner from among close relatives. Or else they became pawns in a game of male ambition and their fortunes part of a political spoils system.

In contrast to the first cohort, there is a strong correlation between officeholding and the propensity to make kin-related marriages (Table 9.1). While there was no correlation between occupation and the inclination to contract such marriages – at most a small tendency in favor of Bauern over artisans (Tables A.26,

A.27, A.41, A.42) – there was a close association with being or becoming a magistrate and marrying a relative. And although the majority of sibling groups (75 percent) made at least one kin-related marriage, a significant proportion did not (6 out of 24) (Table A.40). These families, in sharp contrast to the others, contained no individuals destined for membership among the magistrates.

The information found so far strongly suggests that both Bauern and artisans more frequently chose relatives as marriage partners than they had earlier in the century. On the other hand, the correlation between future position as a magistrate and kin-linked marriage is so strong that the rise must be seen first of all as political in nature. That significant group that made no such marriages was composed of families completely outside the power structure. Although the increased interest in constructing relations with cousins may well have been because of farming, the focus of attention in marriage exchange in the middle decades of the century had to do with restructuring the clientage system and redrawing the lines of political connection.[3] The asymmetrical chains linking affines from different strata gave way to horizontally constructed linkages between families with political influence and families with wealth, which, when exercised within the context of everyday life, redirected the circulation of land and influence and eventually hammered out new contours of class. Family dynamics provided the matrix in which the formation of classes took place, a thesis that will become clearer in the discussion of nineteenth-century Neckarhausen and of class issues in Chapter 22. Dominating the process of regroupment were a coordinated power elite with multiple links to one another and a set of magistrates tied by blood and marriage (Chapter 10). Part of the process involved a refocusing of ritual kinship onto immediate relatives and then the reconstruction of clientages from among close relatives.

Not only did the relative frequency of kin-related marriages increase, but there was also a change in their nature. For the first time, a widespread tendency to marry endogamously – to marry consanguineal kin – developed in the village. This took place without any new departures in law after the revision of the Marriage Ordinance in 1687, which indicated that dispensations for second cousins would be granted quite readily. The law also made it clear that certain unions such as the marriage of sets of siblings to each other had been and continued to be legal without any further ado. Yet early in the eighteenth century, the practice of exogamy had gone beyond the demands of the law. During the 1740s, many villagers abandoned their previous customs and together with others in the Württemberg population pressed the authorities over the next 60 years to open up ever closer relatives to pro forma dispensations. This ultimately led to a revision of the law code in 1797, in which most of the non-Mosaic prohibitions were discarded for anyone willing to pay a fee (see Chapter 3). From the evidence, it should be clear that endogamy was not a "natural" state of intimate village life. Marriage to blood relatives was a practice that developed only in the eighteenth

[3] See the discussion in Sabean, *Property*, chap. 9.

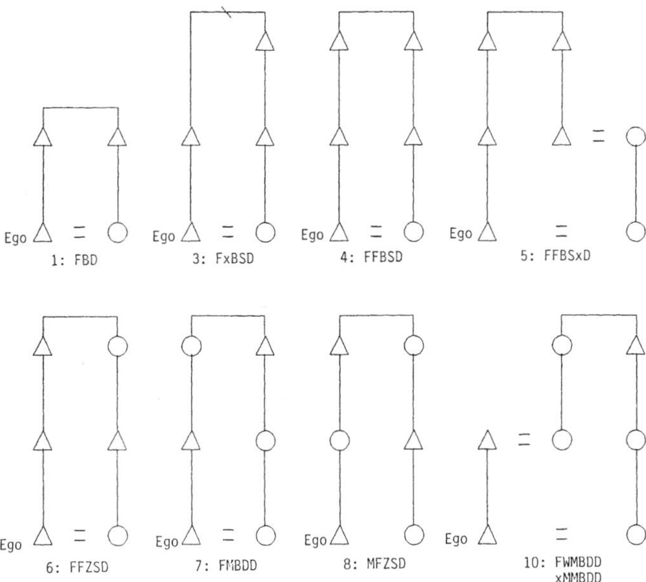

Figure 9.1

century and had its beginnings a good 60 years after legal changes made it possible. And it developed in the context of population expansion, when kin became ever easier to avoid. Interestingly, the rise in consanguineal marriages was a European phenomenon at this time (Chapter 21).

Besides marriage with cousins, there was also a new interest in marriages arranged between two sibling sets. And there also continued to be examples of siblings married to patrilateral parallel cousins, one of the forms frequently encountered earlier in the century. But the practice of linking three sibling sets together in overlapping affinal networks practically disappeared. Overall, the new forms substituted consanguineal for extended affinal networks. By the middle decades of the eighteenth century, about a third of the kin-linked marriages were with consanguineal kin, almost all of them second cousins. The strictly consanguineal marriages from the sample (keeping the numbering from the list in Table A.43) display shapes that are quite different from those found at the beginning of the eighteenth century (Figure 9.1).[4]

All of these examples of first-cousin (case 1), first-cousin-once-removed (case 2), and second-cousin (cases 4, 5, 6, 7, 8, 10) marriages except for one (case 8) were reckoned – from the husband's point of view – through the father, and the

[4] From our point of view, two of these were not strictly consanguineal marriages. The couple conjoined in number 5 received a dispensation for consanguinity (*Verwandtschaft*). See the discussion in Appendix C. In number 10, the dispensation was for *Freundschaft*, exactly as for case 6, which is strictly consanguineal.

majority of wives also made agnatic connections. Already in the early part of the century, whenever consanguineal relationships were involved – as in marriages of first cousins with siblings – such alliances were similarly patrilaterally reckoned. Even though consanguineal marriages did not take place then, kin-linked marriages reveal the importance of siblings in the construction of affinal constellations but demonstrate that sexual pairing within the group of brothers and sisters was important. Least in frequency in constructing chains of kinship was the Z/Z relation. Next was the B/Z relation, which, as far as the junior generation was concerned, was clearly a fundamental building block. Moving back a generation, however, only the B/B relations retained structural meaning. It is hard to resist the conclusion that the construction units of the system were interrelated men who cooperated in agriculture and carried on the political business of the village. As explained in Chapters 4 and 5, affinal connections in one generation could create links in the next one among first cousins, which would be expected to be weakest among matrilateral parallel cousins, stronger among cross cousins, and stronger still among partilateral parallel cousins.

These examples reveal marriages taking place within preexisting relationships for the most part constructed through the activities of people in generation II. In examples 3, 4, and 5, the cousins were the children of two brothers (patrilateral parallel cousins) and in 6, 7, 8, 9, and 10 were children of a brother and sister (cross cousins). The parents (generation II) were still tied together by the bonds that derived from the households they grew up in and that they continued to maintain. But in the next generation (III), such ties were in danger of atrophying as they became more extended. In almost every case the male partner in the third generation sought to reinforce ties growing out of alliances constructed by his father.

Marriage did not, of course, just link two cousins in a new household. Such marriages also made brothers-in-law out of men who were also already related to each other by blood. The father's first cousin's children became the son's spouse and brothers-in-law. Judging from the high percentage of husbands who were or became magistrates who made kin-related marriages, it appears that the direction of movement of women was toward the politically powerful line. The client offered a wife, the patron secured a clientage (3, 5, 6, 7, 10). In cases 3, 5, and 6, father and son were both members of the magistracy and daughters of nonmagistrates married in. In cases 7 and 10, the father of the groom was a magistrate and the father of the bride a Bauer.

Figures 9.2 and 9.3 lay out one example of a union (case 9) that, although not strictly consanguineal, did involve the marriage of a man with his second cousin's widow. Here is a typical series of interlocking marriages involving families of magistrates. Ego, a Bauer, son of a Bauer, married his second cousin's widow, the daughter of a magistrate and step-daughter-in-law of the Bürgermeister. He eventually became a Richter, and three of his sons married daughters of members of the magistracy, at least one making a consanguineal marriage. None of the sons became magistrates themselves. To some degree, the position of ego was

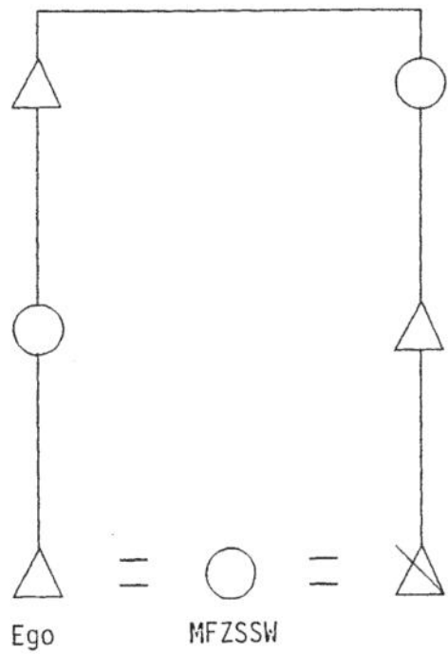

Figure 9.2

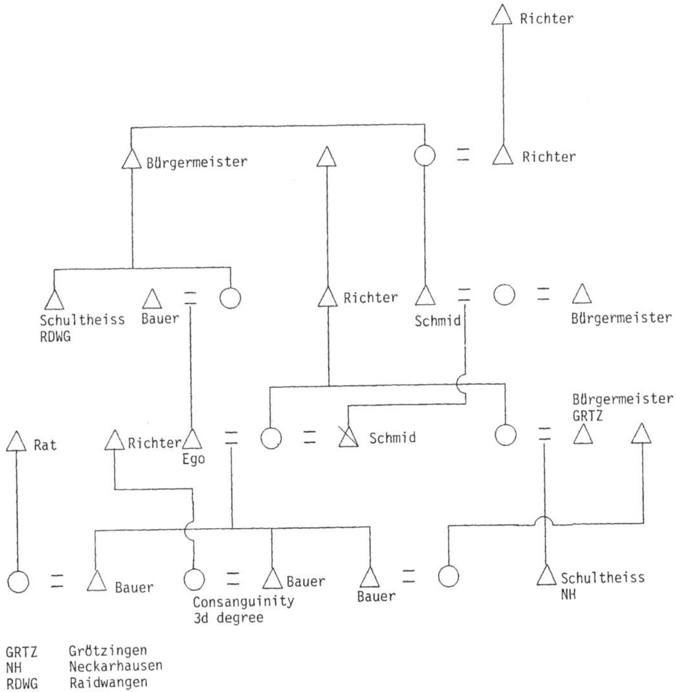

Figure 9.3

unusual because by midcentury, few fathers-in-law were succeeded by sons-in-law on the Gericht (Table A.37). For the most part, both handicraft occupation and position among the magistrates descended from father to son, which supported a sense of lineal continuity and gave structural content to the "lines" analyzed in Cohort III. In this case, ego was one of the relatively rare instances in a cohort where a son-in-law and father-in-law were both magistrates. He did not himself come from a magistrate family and none of his children became magistrates. Nonetheless, after succeeding a second cousin in marriage, he acquired a position on the Rat and later on the Gericht. His marriage was into a family more advantageously situated in the power structure, but he was not able to build a position for his sons out of that connection. The line from grandfather to father to sons offers a typical example of well-to-do Bauern systematically allied with magistrate families. Nevertheless, the marital politics of ego's children show the way active allies among the magistrates reinforced their association through the union of their children. Ego became a co-parent-in-law (Gegenschweher) with three other members of the Gericht and Rat.

Political continuity was closely tied up with consanguineal marriages. Sons from magistrate families, whether Bauern or handicraftsmen, married daughters from related Bauer families, re-creating or developing a political clientele but at the same time connecting power closely to wealth. Well-to-do sons who did not or could not accede to power linked themselves through marriage to magistrate families. Daughters of magistrates did not usually marry men who were or who became magistrates, although there were occasional examples of such marriages. For brothers-in-law to be magistrates together would have created competing centers of power when the point was to develop a support group around a magistrate. When a young man married the daughter of a magistrate, that meant that his chances of becoming one himself were not great. On the other hand, daughters of magistrates could use their connections to create a clientele for their fathers and brothers. Every so often a clever son-in-law of a magistrate could benefit under certain circumstances from the connection and himself aspire to office. But both occupational and political continuity in that cohort tended to go from father to son.

Seeking a bride from within the group of consanguineal relatives meant re-forging an alliance with people whose commitment might have atrophied with distance.[5] The fact of cognatic reckoning itself only exacerbated the problem. Any individual was related equally to people through father and mother, and with the passing of each generation, the number of consanguineal kin grew exponentially. On the one hand, as the distance between people became greater, their commitment to each other declined. And on the other, conflicting loyalties would have arisen in any situation in which a person was related equally to people who were in opposition to each other. A kin-related marriage recentered an alliance and effectively brought many more distant kin into a narrower circle of connection. All the people between the bride and the groom became related to each of them and to one another in more than one way. Such a marriage as

[5] This general issue is discussed by Martine Segalen, *Fifteen Generations of Bretons: Kinship and Society in Lower Brittany 1720–1980,* trans. J. A. Underwood (Cambridge, 1991), pp. 124–8; and Tina Jolas, Yvonne Verdier, and Françoise Zonabend, " 'Parler famille,' " *L'homme* (1970): 5–26. See also Joan F. Mira, "Mariage et famille dans une communauté rurale du pays de Valence (Espagne)," *Etudes rurales* 42 (1971): 105–19.

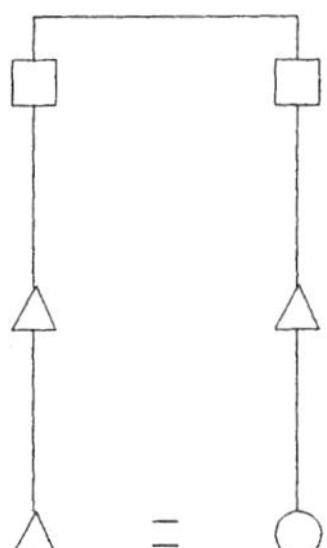

Figure 9.4

practiced in Neckarhausen was also strategic because within its area it tended to erase the field of direct competitors. For a magistrate family to encourage a daughter or sister to marry a young man in a Bauern family meant that no competing magistrate was to be found there. The calculations could be quite complex when political issues were involved, and each alliance involved other crucial matters such as inheritance. However, the findings explain at least in part the agnatic bias within the cognatic system of kin-reckoning. Patrilateral consanguineal marriages seem to have been the strategic anchor in a situation of ever changing group formation, shifting alliances, demographic accident, and varied fortunes.[6]

Let us review the main types of kin marriage we find in this generation. We have already encountered marriage with a second cousin, the dominant form from both the husband's and wife's point of view being a patrilateral second cousin (Figure 9.4). Assuming that parents had considerable influence over the marriages of their children, then most often male first cousins were politicking together. In no case do we find the children of two female first cousins from generation II marrying each other. The cousins themselves were either cross or patrilateral parallel ones, which means that the apical ancestors in generation I were never two sisters. These kinds of marriages were attempts on the part of young husbands to reproduce power relations built up and maintained by their fathers. There was a strong tendency for sons to follow the father's occupation and very little interest in marriage of strategic intent as far as occupation is concerned: a smith the son of a smith did not marry a daughter from a smith family, and no young smith allied himself through marriage to a father-in-law with the same occupation. Among the elite there was a movement of wives from landed families into the politically dominant branch of allied families, which reinforced an agnatic core to the calculation of kinship. Such alliances were only beginning to be extended across more than one generation during the middle decades of the eighteenth century. The political landscape was, of course, newly assessed for each

[6] This appears to have been a general principle for the property-holding classes as a whole throughout the nineteenth century. See the discussion in Chapter 22.

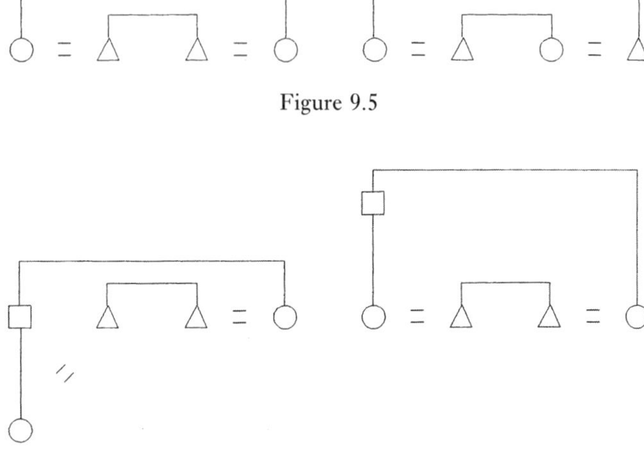

Figure 9.5

Figure 9.6

generation, and fresh decisions were made about strategies for reproducing social and political power. With artisan families finding it increasingly difficult to move upward into the agricultural producing class and with the rise in population, an increased differentiation of social strata was taking place.[7] Consanguineal marriages, hesitant at midcentury, were part of the closing off process. Alliances first struck at the beginning of the century now formed the basis for connecting political position and wealth. The process was driven by political considerations, which in turn eventually laid the foundations for class formation.

Another innovation for this period was the marriage with the BWZ or ZHZ (Figure 9.5). Early in the century sibling exchange was avoided, but by midcentury it became an alternative strategy for families creating closer alliances with each other and reinforcing their social ties through multiple exchanges. But there is also a variation of this type of marriage that can be diagrammed in two ways, one of which is familiar from the analysis of cohort I (Figure 9.6). This form introduces a kind of delayed exchange by offsetting the inmarrying wife one generation, even though it appears to be a political activity of a single generation – at least at the core it involves a single set of siblings. In the most frequent form of these kinds of marriages, the core sibling group was a set of males, and we encounter a movement of women toward the politically dominant group – with at least one brother, or father, being a member of the magistracy.

This generation also contains a form encountered early in the century – the marriage of first cousins to a sibling group (Figure 9.7). As before, the most prevalent form involved the marriage of the children of two brothers. In many cases, this kind of marriage established relationships that were kept alive in a

[7] Sabean, *Property*, pp. 61–6.

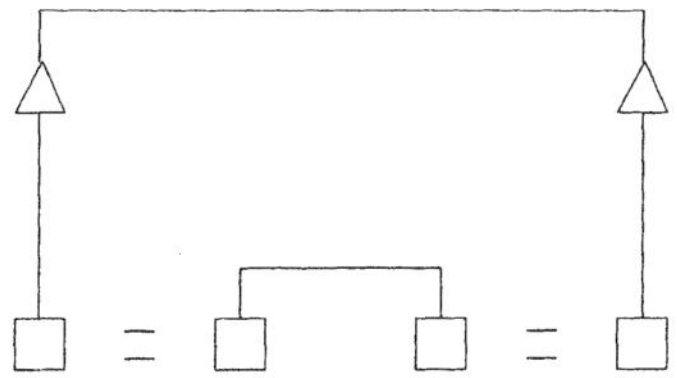

Figure 9.7

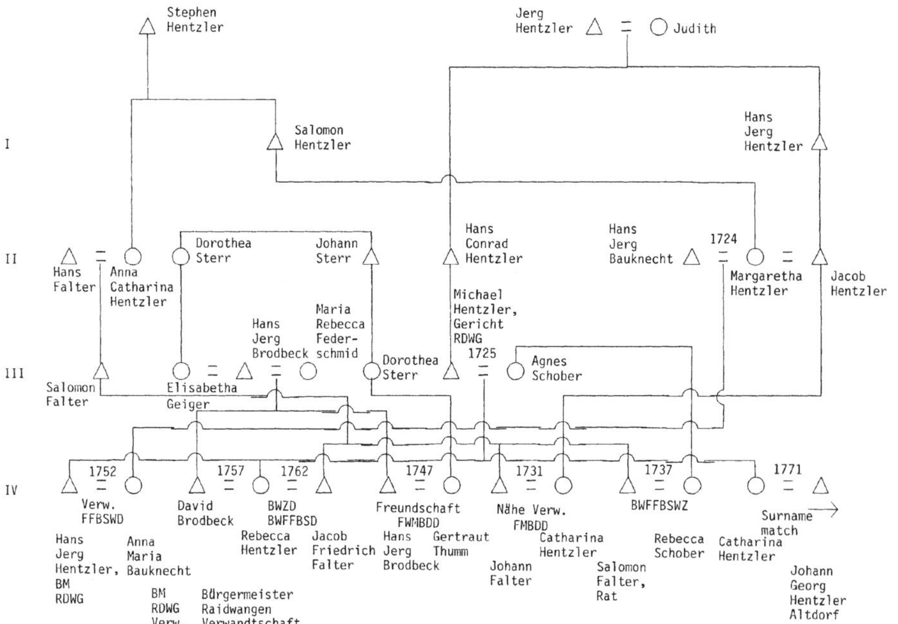

Figure 9.8

later generation by consanguineal links. We no longer find in this generation the linking of three or more sibling sets through a strategic marriage. Perhaps the move toward reinforcing an early marriage by another – as with such marriages as the BWZ or ZHZ – made the wider overlapping linkage superfluous. In any event, it is symptomatic of the movement inward, toward more direct retreading of paths recently taken that the longer, interlinked, asymmetrical chains were no longer of strategic interest.

It would be useful now to look at one sibling group to see how the elements distinguished in this study fit in a coordinated pattern (Figure 9.8; see also Figure 9.11 for a diagram of the selection of ritual parents by the same families). In this instance, we have a number of interlocking families from the villages of Neck-

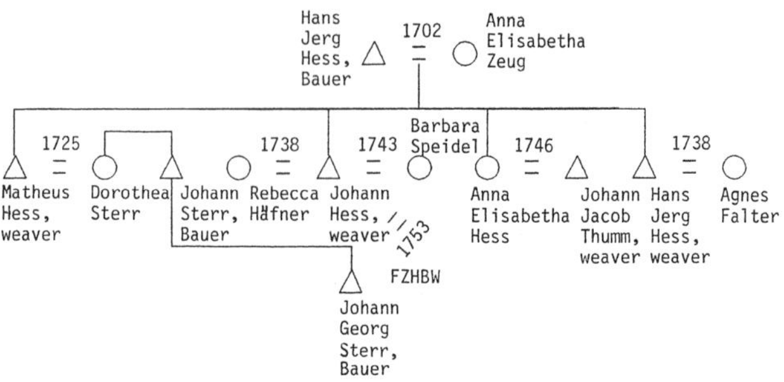

Figure 9.9

arhausen and Raidwangen that together compose the larger Neckarhausen parish. *We are concerned with the marriages of the three children of Michael Hentzler (generation III, married in 1725), a Richter from Raidwangen. The oldest son, Hans Jerg, became Richter in turn and eventually Bürgermeister in Raidwangen. Rebecca married successively in Neckarhausen two sons of two different members of the Gericht. The second daughter, Catharina, moved to the village of Altdorf where she married a Hentzler, the son of a Richter. Although no dispensation was noted in the marriage register, the couple did share the same surname and were probably related. The eldest son obtained a dispensation for "Verwandtschaft" (consanguinity), marrying the daughter of a Bauer in Raidwangen, his FFBSWD (FFBSxD). Note that the step-relation was fully counted in reckoning consanguinity: she was a second cousin, a "Blutsverwandte" of the third degree in the collateral line on the same plane. Rebecca Hentzler's second marriage was to Jacob Friedrich Falter. One of his brothers, Johann, had already allied himself to another branch of the Hentzler family; in fact, his wife and Hans Jerg Hentzler's wife were half-sisters. But Johann himself was a descendant through his paternal grandmother of the Hentzlers: he married his FMBDD (a second cousin) and received a dispensation for "nähe Verwandtschaft." The other brother of Jacob Friedrich Falter, Salomon, had married Rebecca Schober, distantly related to his brother Johann's wife. When Jacob Friedrich married Rebecca Hentzler, he was marrying his BWZD, as well as through his other brother, his BWFFBSD.*

This example shows that some families in the 1740s and 1750s were systematically using various connections to make kin-related marriages. The consanguineal paths here were reckoned in various ways (FFBSxD, xMMBDD, FMBDD), and all marriages of this kind were subject to dispensations for consanguinity. It is also interesting to see a single family such as the Falters systematically tied to various branches of the Hentzler family. Other examples are found in the next three sections of the book.

A similar genealogy laying out the marriages of the four children of Hans Jerg Hess shows practically no such intertwining (Figure 9.9). They were small peasants and weavers, linked to shoemakers, smiths, and coopers – artisans/small

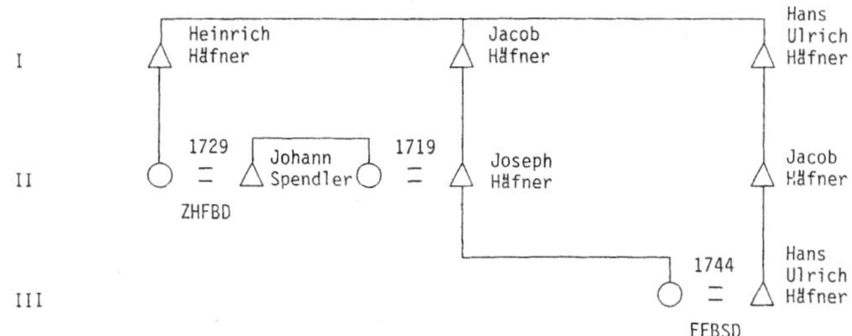

Figure 9.10

agricultural producers. The only kinship marriage to be found was the remarriage of the weaver Johann Hess's widow to the Bauer Johann Georg Sterr, he marrying his FZHBW, an extended affine and by this time a rather old-fashioned choice.

There are many examples of families that practiced one form of kin marriage in Cohort I and another in Cohort II. Alliances established early in the century on affinal principles were reinforced in a later generation through consanguinity. The example here begins with a classic case of patrilateral parallel cousin/sibling marriage (Figure 9.10). *The children of two of the three Häfner brothers of generation I married a brother and sister. Although there is nothing particular about that alliance that prompted the consanguineal marriage (FFBSD) in generation III, we do find the two characteristic marriages of the two periods in the example. Either from choice or necessity, the Häfners avoided a consanguineal alliance early in the century but apparently were closely enough allied to make a marriage 10 years after the opening one to draw themselves closer through the mediation of another family. First cousins apparently coordinated their interests or activities enough to prompt that sort of marriage. Their relationships seem to have predisposed their children by the 1740s to consider a direct alliance without an intervening mediating family.*

This chapter has provided some insight into the eventual dynamics of class formation through the issue of marriage strategy. The shift from asymmetrical affinal alliances to ones based on consanguineal endogamy shows how classes came to interact, were connected to each other, and organized power. The way power worked had a significant influence on class formation and the development of class consciousness, and political considerations prompted the first consanguineal marriages, a form that only two generations later (1780s) became the general practice of the class of independent agricultural producers as a whole. By the mid eighteenth century, village politics came to be dominated by newly formed well-integrated aggressive kindreds, which prompted villagers outside the system to compete by constructing their own kindreds. But as the system developed, kin endogamy and class endogamy reinforced each other in a reciprocal movement.

As demonstrated in my first volume on Neckarhausen, the distribution of resources in the village did not change significantly between 1700 and 1870. The shape of a series of Lorenz curves remained the same even if showing a slow drift toward inequality at first and then back toward greater equality. But such differences were insignificant compared with the overall stability in the shape of the curve. What did happen, of course, with the rise of population and the general unchangeableness of landed resources was that any one group in the society had fewer resources to share. Recovery of wasteland, planting the fallow, and more intensive use of land all added to the overall ability of villagers to produce more, and some individuals could accumulate larger fortunes. Still, the shape of village wealth showed a rising curve of ownership with no radical break between land-rich and land-poor. This framework, however, had to accommodate more people. It led eventually to the pulverization of landholding, the search for by-employments, strata subject to different logics of the market economy, and an ever-increasing differentiation between those with enough land for self-sufficiency and those without. Already in 1739, the pastor acknowledged the growing split between the propertied and property-poor villagers. He wrote in the church consistory records that in the winter spinning bees, both poor and propertied young women mixed together. This was clearly how things used to be in the village, and the pastor found it quite improper.[8] By 1746, the village had etched the social differences in its symbolic use of space: two graveyards were reserved for the Bauern, artisans, and notables on the one side and the lesser folk of the community on the other.[9] Later on, by the turn of the century, the graveyard at the center would be expressly reserved only for the notables and wealthy, while the one at the periphery was for everyone else.[10]

By the end of the eighteenth century, all offices were in the hands of independent Bauern, and village political and social life was dominated by their values. This was not an inevitable conclusion to the social differentiation of the eighteenth century. I have discussed in another book how state and village officials allied in the eighteenth century politically and how the ideology of the "good householder" was used to differentiate among villagers and became the basis for the exercise of *Herrschaft* (domination).[11] Class consciousness was sometimes overt when villagers talked about the relative esteem of individuals according to their wealth but was usually immanent in more opaque idioms of effective householding or active conscience. In any event, the way classes developed and interacted was largely the result of the exercise of Herrschaft, of political, social, and economic domination. In this chapter, we have been looking at the process of creating a political elite through a practice of endogamous marriages. It was not the case that peasants and artisans withdrew among themselves first, and we can find no differences in their overall inclination in this period to contract kin-linked

[8] *Kirchenkonvent,* vol. 1, p. 60 (15.11.1739).
[9] *Kirchenkonvent,* vol. 1, p. 168 (4.11.1746).
[10] LKA, A39, 3060, *Pfarrbericht* (1828).
[11] David Warren Sabean, *Power in the Blood: Popular Culture and Village Discourse in Early Modern Germany* (Cambridge, 1984), chap. 5.

marriages. It was first and foremost the officeholders, whether peasants or craft producers, who restructured their alliances toward their close kin and toward the wealthier, landed members of the community. Kinship and marriage were the matrix both for the exercise of power and the shaping of classes.[12] That does not mean the hierarchical distribution of wealth was not crucial to the dynamics of village social life before the late eighteenth century. It does mean that power was exercised through different channels and to different effect. The creation of cousins was part of a process of redirecting the flow of power and resources and played a fundamental role in the development of an altogether different set of social relations characteristic of the nineteenth-century village.

Ritual kinship

Since there are no tax registers for the cohort of 1740–9, it was not possible to ensure that the selection of a sample was representative as far as the distribution of wealth is concerned, nor could the wealth categories of parents and godparents be correlated. However, it is possible to correlate occupations and to estimate what role wealth played in the choice of ritual kin (Table 9.2).

By midcentury, Bauern tended to find almost all of their godparents from among other landed agriculturalists in contrast to earlier, and given the strong representation of village magistrates, it is clear that they created links among the wealthiest landed villagers. Artisans were also dependent on the same class for a large proportion of their godparents but found a substantial number among the increasingly wealthy innkeepers and other artisans. Thus we find a tendency on the part of the wealthy cultivators to create horizontal links among themselves and to exercise patronage to those below themselves. That both groups tended to establish relations among the village magistracy suggests that godparentage continued to function as a form of political patronage and protection.

As with the land market and marriage alliance system, this period saw a dramatic rise in the number of kin who were asked to stand as godparents. This time, 65.3 percent of the godparents could be traced in some way as kin compared with 19.8 percent in the earlier period (see Table A.3).

The percentage of godparents who were related to the parents of a newborn child rose by more than three times. And the structural change was just as radical: 61.0 percent of the kin-related godparents came from inside the circle from which no godparents were chosen in the first decades of the century – F, M, Z, B, FB, MB, FBD . . . , MZD . . . , FZDD, FBDD . . . , BW, ZH (parents, siblings, uncles, first cousins, first cousins once removed, and siblings' spouses). In the earlier sample, we found only one godparent who was related to a parent consangui-

[12] See the acute remarks by Gérard Delille, *Famille et propriété dans le royaume de Naples (xve–xixe siècle,* Bibliothèque des écoles françaises d'Athènes et de Rome, vol. 259 (Rome, 1985), pp. 365–73. For a parallel analysis for a German regional nobility, see Christophe Duhamelle, "La noblesse d'église: Famille et pouvoir dans la chevalerie immediate rhenane xviie-xviiie siècles," Thèse d'histoire, Université de Paris-1 (28.11.1994), MSS.

Table 9.2. *Cohort II: Parents' and godparents' occupations.*

	Godparents' occupation								
Parents' occupation	Bauer/shepherd	NG[a]	Bauer/weaver	Publican[c]	Artisan	Pastor	Total	Schultheiss[b]	Richter/ Rat
Bauer/Shepherd	28	8	7	1	1	1	46	(6)	(20)
Bauer/Weaver	2	0	0	3	1	0	6	(0)	(4)
Publican[c]	0	0	0	0	0	0	0	0	0
Artisan	15	4	1	5	7	1	32	(6)	(12)

[a]Not given, but Neckarhausen resident.
[b]Also counted under relevant occupations or NG.
[c]Innkeeper, baker, butcher.

neally. By contrast, well over half (57.6 percent) of the kin-related godparents in this sample were blood kin. If the spouses of consanguineal kin are included, the respective percentages are 40.9 and 86.4.

The evidence suggests that the wealthier members of the village were creating closer ties among themselves through the use of godparents. This "drawing inward" was accompanied by an interest in close and sometimes the closest relatives as godparents. Family or kin groups were using a fundamental institution that allowed for the free construction of kinship ties outside of given family relations precisely to redouble some of those preexisting ties. At the same time, village strata were closing off the paths of reciprocal ritual kinship between them. At least the wealthier landholders were less open to choosing godparents from below themselves, even though they may still have been open to acting as patrons for poorer members of the village. It should be emphasized that ties between peasants and notables were stronger than earlier and were in sharp contrast to all the later cohorts. Cohesion developed in the crucible of village politics before it became generalized to wealth and occupational strata as such. Patron/client links became increasingly mediated through family. Someone seeking out a second cousin for godparent was also seeking out a relative with power or prestige in the village. This first took place within the context of social differentiation consequent on population growth, erosion of property holdings, and the development of a class of handicraft producers. Because the children of siblings and childrens' children of siblings often had considerably different access to resources, withdrawal inside the family was not in the first instance synonymous with withdrawal inside class. At the outset, at least, it could have been an attempt to create tighter ties across various strata in an environment of harsher class relations.[13]

By the mid eighteenth century, there was a definite trend to emphasize relationships among people related to each other by blood. People were marrying second cousins and choosing siblings and first and second cousins as godparents. Rather than tracing relationships through affinal lines – that is, making more distantly related in-laws more closely related through marriage or spiritual kinship – people were making in-law and ritual kin-relationships out of existing consanguineal relations. A second cousin became a wife and her siblings became brothers- and sisters-in-law. One of her sisters might stand as godmother for all of the children of the marriage and a first cousin of the husband would become godfather. From the husband's point of view, then, the godmother was his sister-in-law and second cousin all at once. For the wife, the godfather was her husband's cousin and perhaps her own cousin as well.

Looking at how the link between a parent and godparent was composed is a good way to begin to look at the structure of sibling relationships. At midcentury there was a stronger bond between sisters. Not only was the Z/Z relationship statistically overwhelming (nine cases), but perhaps the echo of that relationship was evident in the next generation because of an interest in first cousins for

[13] See the analysis in Sabean, *Power in the Blood,* chap. 5.

women traced through the mother, especially the MZ (four cases). That relationship is balanced by the fact that 87.5 percent of the uncles, aunts, and cousins chosen by men to be godparents were traced through the father. In this situation the B/B or B/Z relation at the generational level of the father was crucial. Even for the wives/mothers, the connection through the father makes up a majority of the cases: 63.6 percent. We have seen indications before of the fact that many relationships grew out of those within the sibling group. There appears to have been a bonding between parallel siblings, B/B and Z/Z, and yet with time as the generations progress only the B/B and the B/Z relationships were translated into enduring political structures. Both men and women succeeded to relationships forged by their fathers. Political, social, economic, and family relationships often grew from the same nexus. And yet there were differences in behavior between the sexes. Women in this cohort, in sharp contrast to their husbands, did not call upon second cousins for godparents at all but tended to emphasize the closest sibling relationship possible. Their choices were more concentrated, those of their husbands more diffuse, perhaps because of differences in their respective political/domestic spheres. The men were expected to negotiate in the village political arena. Only they attended the village assembly. They had to put together the agricultural equipment. They sold the produce. But when women did use wider family networks, they did not develop ones through other women but used those forged by men. I have puzzled over the Z/Z relationship for this cohort (which disappears again for the next one) but do not have enough detail about women's domestic, productive, or neighbor relations to be able to suggest an explanation for such prominence.

For men, cousin relations fostered in one generation were maintained for one more step and reinforced by opening up lines of ritual kinship because cousin relations were particularly important and useful for men in their processes of work, their overall production functions, or their political negotiations. Given the importance of the village magistracy as godparents, young couples were reduplicating and refashioning the lines of political force already created by their fathers. Such a pattern would begin to break down with the economic and social transformations later in the century. But at midcentury, it grew out of the need to link oneself to powerful village officials in order to mitigate the harshness of growing communal divisions, to reproduce the conditions of wealth holding, and to gain access to village resources. A transition was taking place between two different forms of networks. The new ones were based on horizontal connections between consanguineal kin, and they displayed agnatic characteristics derived from property ownership, processes of production, and political partisanship, whereas the older networks utilized office, affinity, and ritual kinship to construct asymmetrical networks of patrons and clients.

Consider now the manner in which godparentage was coordinated in the sibling group encountered in Figure 9.8 as a whole (Figure 9.11). This example has to do with the marriages of two children of Michael Hentzler, Richter in Raidwangen: Hans Jerg (1727–70), who became Bürgermeister there, and Rebecca,

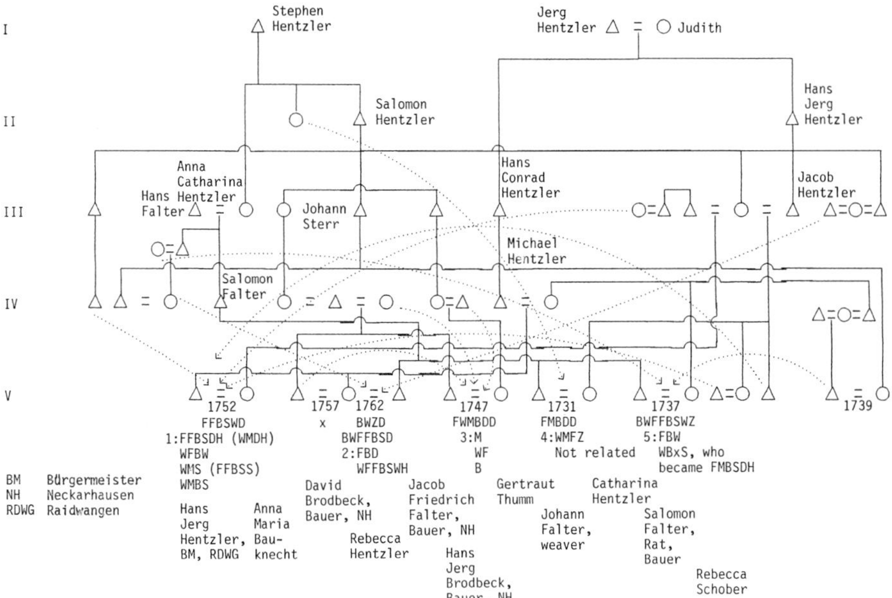

Figure 9.11

who married two different Bauern in Neckarhausen. The genealogy at level V contains three other marriages of siblings of Rebecca's husbands. Each of these marriages involved a kinship link, which demonstrates the importance of second cousins.

To avoid confusion, the links are described step by step.

1. To begin in 1752 with Hans Jerg Hentzler, Bauer, Richter, and Bürgermeister in Raidwangen, and his wife, Anna Maria Bauknecht, also from there: they chose David Hentzler, born in Raidwangen and resident in Altdorf, Bauer, and Anna Maria Bauknecht, wife of Michael, weaver and Richter in Raidwangen, as godparents. David was at the same time the WMS (WxB) and the HFFBSS (second cousin). Anna Maria Bauknecht was the WFBW (aunt). They stood as godparents again in 1756. After that, David was replaced in 1758 by Salomon Holpp, Bauer in Raidwangen, the WMDH (WxZH), who was also the HFFBSDH (second cousin's husband). Salomon died before the next child was born in 1764 and was replaced by Johann Hentzler, schoolmaster in Raidwangen, WMBS (first cousin). All of the godparents were more closely related to the wife than to the husband. Her FBW was godmother for all of the children and, in succession, the godfather was her xB, xZH, and MBS. Only the first two godfathers were second cousins of the husband. One could speculate about relative power spheres between husbands and wives. They might have weighted the ritual kin in her favor given certain power constellations, but he was a member of the Gericht and eventually Bürgermeister. Perhaps things worked the other way around: he was the patron who was building a clientele among his wife's kin by allowing them to be godparents. Or if the wife considered herself to be in a weaker position than her husband, she may have insisted on having many powerful allies. The ambiguity of the godfathers being related to both parents may also have played a role.

2. Jacob Friedrich Falter was a Bauer in Neckarhausen. On his side his FBD (cousin), wife of a Richter in Neckarhausen, stood as godmother for all of the children. For his wife, the Ehesuccessor of her FFBS (first cousin once removed), the latter a Richter in Neckarhausen, was godparent.

3. Hans Jerg Brodbeck, Bauer, was son of a Richter. Beginning in 1748, their first five children had his M and her F, a Bauer in Neckarhausen, as godparents. After her father's death in 1757, Brodbeck's brother became godfather. Here the marriage had a balanced set of godparents until the last child, when his M and B served together.

4. Johannes Falter was a linen weaver and soldier, son of a Bauer and Bürgermeister, who died in 1742 in Austria after 11 years of marriage. I can find no relationship between the parents and the godfather for the children, a Bauer, son of an innkeeper, Michael Häussler. The godmother was Catharina Hentzler's MFZ (great aunt), the wife of a weaver. Here we see a relatively poor branch of two politically powerful families. At least one godparent, who was no longer part of the landed elite, was from the family.

5. Salomon Falter, weaver/Bauer, member of the Rat, son of a Bauer and Bürgermeister, chose his FBW (aunt) in 1738 to stand as godmother. She was by then remarried to Johannes Spendler, Bürgermeister in Neckarhausen. The godfather was the wife's MBxS (first cousin), a weaver, who became a Bauer upon the strategically successful marriage with the daughter of the Schultheiss in Raidwangen. He was also a second cousin of the husband.

The set of marriages here all took place in the middle four decades of the eighteenth century. For the most part, they involved members of the landed elite in the larger parish composed of the village of Neckarhausen and the hamlet of Raidwangen. Three sets of siblings were represented in generation V – the Hentzlers, Brodbecks, and Falters – two of which had members of the magistracy represented. The fathers of each of the sibling groups had been Richtern. As pointed out earlier, each of the five couples had married a cousin or the cousin of a close in-law. Altogether, the group had 13 godparents, only 1 of whom does not seem to have been a relative. Four of the godparents came from the nuclear family (F, M, B, Z), 1 was a first cousin, and 4 were uncles and aunts or nephews. One godparent was a brother-in-law and 1 was the Ehesuccessor of a first cousin once removed. Almost all of the godparents were older than the parents. When a godparent died, he or she was represented by a lineal descendant.

* * *

It is no coincidence that villagers in Württemberg during the 1740s and 1750s began to speak of "Vetterleswirtschaft" and to complain about familial coordination of interest among members of the magistrates. The redeployment of kinship took place in Neckarhausen about the same time that the language of social and political action in other villages of the duchy pointed toward a reconfiguration of power. Cousins really did create alliances with one another that a generation earlier had been quite out of the question. There were many reasons for setting up a regular and systematic system of exchange between households, and the control of real estate and the production of agricultural products certainly played a role, especially in the long run, in the day-to-day cooperation of close relatives. Nonetheless, the fault lines in the system were developed by politically powerful members of the village who sought out consanguines as marriage partners and began to act as godparents for their close kin.

Despite the fact that sisters developed an especially strong association with each other during the middle decades of the century, calling on each other frequently as godparents and naming their children after them (Tables A.11, A.85), agnatic relations were clearly of greater long-term structural interest. For Cohorts III and V, there will be a discussion of the dynamics of marital and ritual kin exchange over several generations, and we will see that such exchange linked agnatic lines together repeatedly for many decades. By 1870, when this study ends, there were families who had continually exchanged marriage partners for at least 150 years. Each generation, however, was faced with a particular political agenda and a field of potential marriage partners. Reproduction of an agnatically structured alliance system grew out of choices that were embedded in practical, everyday cooperation. During the middle decades of the eighteenth century, the dominant concern was rewiring the circuits of political dependency, and that caused magistrates to reinforce relationships by exchanging children in marriage, led "designated" political heirs to build fortune and friends by seeking partners from allied "houses," and encouraged young parents to look for spiritual kin among the politically connected relatives of their fathers.

"Cousin" became the loose designation for "relative" because of its structural centrality. Frequently, "cousinship" and "partisanship" were alternative expressions of the same thing. Parties in a village became organized around familial politics, which over the long run offered support to the wealthy agricultural producers in their domination of the village. Politics in the early decades of the eighteenth century involved the development of "Freundschaften" or kindreds coordinated by one or two magistrates, who utilized networks of affinal kin and acted as patrons to a changing group of dependents. The new politics emerging from the 1740s involved a tight interlocking set of alliances among members of the magistrates, constructing kindreds on new principles. Indeed, there was a reconfiguration of the politics of marriage, ritual kinship, and market exchange, and the villagers behind the change were for the most part those who held office. The troubles of Schultheiss Johann Georg Rieth III analyzed in Chapter 10 show how the new system was implicated in the politics of surplus extraction and the resistance of the village to more efficient and efficacious state mobilization of its resources.

10

Village politics at midcentury

In 1755 the new Nürtingen Vogt, Dreher, came to Neckarhausen at the head of a ducal commission to investigate charges against Schultheiss Johann Georg Rieth.[1] Ten Bürger had accused Rieth of a variety of offenses, including financial manipulation and mistreatment of villagers at the construction of the new Rathaus; failure to take preventative steps against river flooding; corrupt management of tithes, forestland, and sheepfolding; double bookkeeping; dining and drinking at the cost of the village; personal use of village resources (an extra garden plot and portion from the communal orchards); excessive charges, fees, and wages for conducting village business; drunkenness and quarreling; embezzlement of public funds and ducal taxes; accumulating offices; and high-handed and self-interested administration. The plaintiffs also complained that the Gericht and Rat members were all related and made up a single indivisible chain. Vogt Dreher concluded his 443-page report by noting that Schultheiss Rieth had a good reputation (*Praedikat*) and that he was a capable official. He did not consider the complaints to be significant – even though for this or that misdemeanor Rieth had accumulated a substantial fine of 30 Reichsthaler and had to pay half of the investigation costs (85 fl). In any event, the Vogt despaired of finding anyone else of Rieth's *Capacität* to run the village. Since becoming Schultheiss, he had brought considerable order to village affairs and had substantially reduced communal debt. Still, Dreher was concerned about the Schultheiss's public drunkenness – he threw up fairly regularly – and recommended removal from office if he did not learn to control himself. The fact was that all the magistrates were heavy drinkers and that there was nothing particularly unusual in Rieth's behav-

[1] HSAS, A214 Bü 743, "Nürtingen, Neckarhausen. Commissions Acta 1755–9, 1763, 1764. Die Commission über den Schultheissen Johann Georg Rieth zu Neccarhausen, betr."

ior. Summing up, Dreher found Rieth trustworthy and easy to work with, and he could not have wished for a better man in the office.

Only a partial set of the documents relating to this case have survived: soon after the investigation was completed, the protocols of testimony and official correspondence were discarded in the usual fashion. The current file contains a long report (*Relation*) by the commissioner and a summary "extract" composed for the ducal council. The council concurred with Vogt Dreher's assessment of the charges, making minor adjustments of fines for this or that misdemeanor, but undertaking no move to discharge Rieth from office. Various other village officials were fined for their part in illegal activities and condemned to pick up part of the costs of the investigation. In general, the accusations against the Schultheiss were fairly standard for the period and offer a good summary of the temptations and difficulties of holding office. Many issues can be analyzed using this material, but for our purposes the documents offer the possibility of examining the way social networks and power configurations were reordered around midcentury.

One of the standard complaints of the period throughout Württemberg was the coalescence of magistrates into one "chain" of relatives. As usual, what constituted a collusive relationship from the point of view of many of the villagers was frequently dismissed by the investigating officer as not being against the letter of the law (see Chapter 2). Two members of the Neckarhausen Gericht, for example, were co-parents-in-law (*Gegenschweher*). They had arranged for the marriage of their children after working together as Richter for many years. For some of the villagers, such an alliance was evidence of a close coordination of interests, but there was no transgression of the law in the arrangement. Two other Richter were brothers-in-law, but they claimed to have petitioned for a dispensation. In another instance, one of the Bürgermeister was the stepfather of a Richter's son-in-law, which would have made the magistrates step-co-parents-in-law, again a configuration that was not forbidden by law. The stepfather of the same Bürgermeister also served on the Gericht, but in the meantime the Bürgermeister had died and thereby resolved the issue. One member of the Gericht was married to the Schultheiss's niece, and many Richter were related closely to members of the Rat, but none of these relationships were illegal because they involved *diversa collegia*.

Alliances among magistrates

The complaint about family alliances among magistrates was dealt with rather hastily and not taken very seriously by Vogt Dreher. Clearly, the order that the Schultheiss had brought to the village had grown out of the establishment of smoothly running oligarchical control, and Dreher was not about to interfere with that, especially since such oligarchies were solidifying power at the level of Oberamt (county) administration, state administration, the church – at all levels –

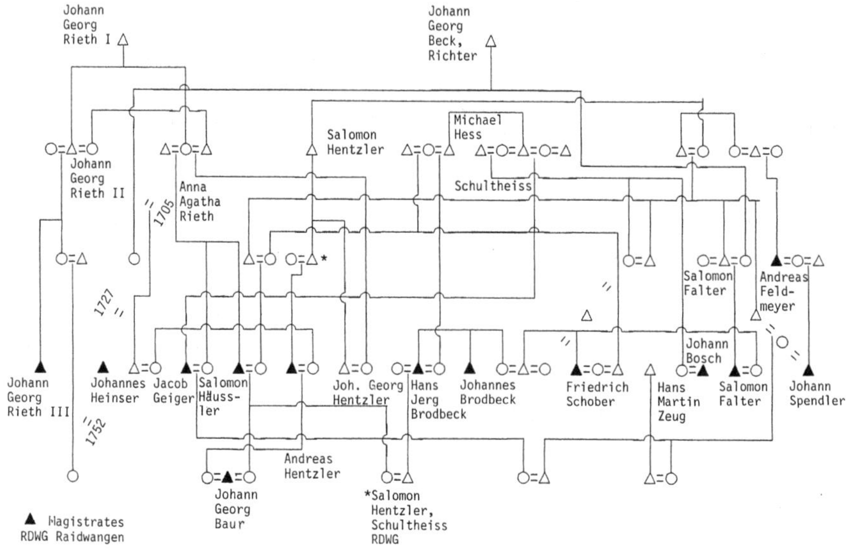

Figure 10.1

and the court at the same time. Since members of the magistrates spearheaded the new practices of consanguineal marriage and their alliances had a great deal to do with the new power configurations, it is necessary to analyze their marital politics at some length. The degree to which they created interlocking marriage alliances can be assessed from the relationships of magistrates at midcentury, shown in Figure 10.1.

A diagram like the one in Figure 10.1 is an abstraction. Many paths between individuals are left out in order to simplify it and present a readily understandable picture of interconnectedness. Johann Georg Rieth III was scion of a long line of village headmen. Both his grandfather and father had married into the regional elite and neither had been remarkably successful in providing the numerous progeny necessary to create multiple alliances within the village. Johann Georg III himself had married the daughter of a Schultheiss from another village. His aunt, Anna Agatha Rieth, the daughter of Johann Georg I, had been a powerful figure at the beginning of the century and had succeeded her father as godparent for many families and in fact was called upon more frequently than anyone else at that time to be Gevatterin. She died relatively young but still provided a foundation for the continuation of the Rieth *Hausmacht.* Two of her daughters married members of the Gericht, Jacob Geiger and Johann Georg Hentzler (who was dismissed from office in 1751), and a son, Salomon Häussler, himself became a Richter, perhaps the most well-connected magistrate in the village. His cousin was Johann Georg Rieth III, and his son-in-law, Johann Georg Baur, succeeded

Rieth as Schultheiss in 1761. In 1755 his sister's husband was a fellow member of the Gericht, and five of his wife's "cousins" were magistrates. Johannes Heinser also represented the Rieth line. He became head of the household founded by Anna Agatha Rieth's marriage in 1686 to Ludwig Baltz, the son of the Schultheiss of Oberensingen. Heinser first took it over in 1727 by marrying Anna Agatha's marital successor and in 1752 renewed the connection to the Rieth line when he married a granddaughter of Johann Georg Rieth II. With these various alliances, Johann Georg Rieth III was well connected with the village patriciate, but he was also closely allied with powerful families in other villages of the district.

The degree of interconnectedness can be seen in Table 10.1. A few magistrates, such as Johannes Bosch and Johann Georg Baur, were connected primarily with their wives' kin. Bosch, who came from outside the village, had married the daughter of Schultheiss Michael Hess. And Baur's father had also been an immigrant. Johann Georg married successively daughters of two different Richter. In fact, he acted as the transition figure between the Rieth and Hentzler lines. First he married the granddaughter of Anna Agatha Rieth, the daughter of Johann Georg Rieth III's cousin, Richter Salomon Häussler. Then (1762) he married the daughter of Andreas Hentzler. Hentzler's father, Salomon, was a wealthy Bauer and long-time Schultheiss in Raidwangen. Both Salomon and his father – another Salomon – were prolific and provided many children who settled in Neckarhausen. Salomon's brother had been on the Neckarhausen Gericht and his son Andreas became a Rat and a prominent Bürgermeister. Andreas's daughter married Baur. His brother Salomon became Rat in 1770 and Richter in 1777 and was Bürgermeister for many years; his son Salomon succeeded Baur in 1768 as Schultheiss, and another son, Christoph, became Rat in 1777 and Richter in 1780.

It is apparent from Table 10.1 how much "cousinship" actually counted in the construction of political alliances. An individual like Salomon Falter had six consanguineal kin among the magistrates, and Salomon Häussler's wife was a "cousin" of five magistrates. It is difficult to underestimate the importance of networks developed on consanguineal principles. Although the Neckarhausen critics of the court apparently did not use the term "Vetterle" during the investigation (even though it is found in various Gerichtsprotokolle during the same decade), the ruling institution was clearly a Vetterlesgericht and the magistrates made up an interlocking chain of relatives. In keeping with the fact that candidates for office in the village were coopted by the Gericht (except for the Schultheiss, who was elected by the adult males as a whole), the power configurations were reproduced in the following generation by the selection of the sons and sons-in-law of the incumbents of 1755 (Table 10.2). And the magistrate families were busy arranging for marriage alliances among themselves. One would expect to find the magistrates further reinforcing links with each other through godparentage.

Table 10.1. *Kinship connections among magistrates in 1755.*

Magistrate	B	F	DH	Uncle/ cousin	Other	WB	WF	WS	Wife's uncle/ cousin	W's other	Co-parent-in-law
J. G. Baur, Rat							x		xxxxx		
J. Bosch, Richter									xxx		
J. G. Brodbeck, Ri.	x				ZHB, ZHZH				xxx		x
J. Brodbeck, Rat	x				ZHB, ZHZH						
S. Falter, Rat				xxxxxx		x				BWB, BWB	
A. Feldmeyer, Rat				xx				x			
J. Geiger, Richter				xxxx		x			xx		
S. Häussler, Richter			x	xx	ZH				xxxxx		x
J. Heinser, Richter				xxx					xx		
A. Hentzler, Rat				xxx							
J. G. Reith, Schult.				xxxx	ZDH						
F. Schober, Richter					ZH, BWB, BWB				xxxx		
J. Spendler, Richter		x		xx					x		x

Note: Steprelations ignored; marital successor counted as substitute for predecessor.

Table 10.2. *Succession to office of incumbents of 1755.*

	Succeeded by				
Magistrate	Marital successor	Son/xSon	Son-in-law	Daughter married magistrate's son	Son/Son/S-in-law married magistrate's daughter
J. G. Baur, Rat		x			
J. Bosch, Richter		xx		x	xx
J. G. Brodbeck, Rich.		x			xx
J. Brodbeck, Rat					x
S. Falter, Rat					x
A. Feldmeyer, Richt.		xx			
J. Geiger, Richter		x	x		
S. Häussler, Richter			xx	xx	
J. Heinser, Richter					
A. Hentzler, Rat		xx	x		x
J. G. Rieth, Schult.	x				
F. Schober, Richter	x				x
J. Spendler, Richter			x		x

Cohort II (1740–1749)

The Rieth family

The study of godparentage at the beginning of the eighteenth century showed that it was customary for two families to be linked over several generations. Above all, Johann Georg Rieth I, his son Johann Georg II, and his daughter Anna Agatha (married to Friedrich Häussler) stood as godparents for successive generations of people who were not related to themselves. That had implications for the way village politics worked. For one thing, it systematically linked families of magistrates to families of nonmagistrates, the village patricians to its poorer folk. The new practice of choosing closely related people, or blood relatives, did away with such ties and marked a significant break in the way social and political ties were constructed.

This new situation can be seen clearly with Johann Georg Rieth III. During the 1740s and 1750s, he and his wife were godparents for eight couples. They linked themselves to their own cousins (first cousins or first cousins once removed) six times and to another family already allied by marriage. In only one case can a previous consanguineal or affinal relation not be traced. In only one of these instances had Rieth's parents been Gevatter for an earlier generation of the line: Johann Georg III was involved in a completely new strategy of patronage. On the one hand, he ignored the long tradition established by earlier generations of Rieths of standing as godparent for particular families and their offspring, and on the other he created multiple links with many of his close allies among the magistrates. He or his wife stood for three of the children of Friedrich Häussler, the husbands of two of which were in the magistrates. The Rieths also linked themselves three times to members of the Falter family, who in turn were already allied to the Rieths through marriage to his cousin Salomon Häussler. This again created multiple connections to powerful members of the Gericht such as Bürgermeister Salomon Falter.

Rieth's strategy was similar to other members of the Gericht and Rat. His cousin Salomon Häussler and his wife were godparents for 10 couples, 3 aunts or uncles, and 7 cousins, including Johann Georg III himself. In 6 of these instances, they acted as Gevattern for other members of the magistrates. Salomon Falter and his wife were godparents during the 1740s and 1750s for 7 couples, 5 of which were nephews, nieces, first cousins, and first cousins once removed. Johann Georg Brodbeck and spouse acted as Gevattern for 6 other couples, a son, a brother, a ZHZ, and 3 cousins. Andreas Hentzler and his wife followed the same pattern, linking themselves to 5 second cousins. The future Schultheiss, Johann Georg Baur, and his wife acted as godparents for 5 of her cousins, with a further connection being untraceable. These 6 magistrates all followed similar patterns, alternatively setting up relations with the consanguineal relations of the husband or the wife, depending on which spouse was better connected, and sometimes dividing their attention between both sets of relatives when both spouses came from powerful families. All of these people stood as godparents for at least some other members of the village magistrates, who in each case were related to one of the marriage partners by blood.

There was one exception to this pattern among the seven magistrates I studied intensively. Jacob Geiger, one of the oldest magistrates still active in 1755, did not usually choose people related to him, as far as I can see – at least not people with blood ties. He and his wife were godparents for 11 couples during the 1740s and 1750s, only four of which were cousins. This case is a reminder that ritual kinship could still be used to construct new relationships, although such a strategy was unusual by this time. Even then, Geiger developed ties with three other members of the magistrates.

The plaintiffs

If the magistrates were bound to each other through multiple ties, the villagers who brought charges or testified against the Schultheiss were connected to one another and to the magistrates in ambiguous ways. The Vogt's report lists 10 men who had instigated the action but does not offer any details about the process of bringing various delicts to the attention of state authorities. In many villages, a number of disgruntled Bürger would band together and either compose a list of complaints or send several of their members to talk to the regional Vogt. Oftentimes such action was regarded as conspiratorial and was either ignored or nipped in the bud. When the Schultheiss and Vogt themselves worked closely together or operated a system of payoffs, it could be very difficult to obtain a hearing or get a line to higher officials in Stuttgart. In any event, there are no leads in Vogt Dreher's report about how the witnesses themselves had gotten together or even if they had. Once an investigation of this kind was launched, the inquisition commissioner usually had each Bürger pass through one by one to answer specific questions and testify about any actions against the prince's *Interesse*. As a result, he could add anyone who witnessed a delict or had their own complaint to the list of people who were bringing charges. Accordingly, although clearly some of the men who accused the Schultheiss of malfeasance had conspired together to do so, others may have been added to the list during the progress of the inquiry and without further evidence cannot be seen as particularly antagonistic to Rieth.

Since tax records are not available for this period, no detailed analysis can be made of the economic status of this group or of the magistrates. It is clear that the magistrates always came from among the wealthier villagers earlier and later in the century, and there is no reason to believe that they were not economically dominant in the village at this period. Indeed, few craftsmen were being taken up into the Rat or Gericht any more, and reference to estate inventories shows that magistrates were all wealthy landowners. Among the vocal

Table 10.3. *Accusers of Johann Georg Rieth III.*

Plaintiff	Occupation	Relatives among magistrates 1755	Relatives among plaintiffs	Godparents inherited from parent to child	Godparents among magistrates[a] 1755	Godparents among plaintiffs
Johannes Bauknecht	Carpenter	0	x	1	1	0
Hans Jerg Ebinger	Bauer, weaver, laborer	x	bxxxx	1	2	0
Jacob Häfner	Weaver	aa	bxx	0	0	0
Caspar Hentzler	Bauer	xxx	xxx	0	3	0
Jerg Hentzler	Bauer	abx	yy	1	1	0
Conrad Hess	Weaver	x	xyy	0	2	0
Jacob Rieth	Tailor	0	xxx	1	1	0
Johannes Rieth	Field guard, Bauer	x	xxxx	1	1	0
Hans Jerg Speidel	Weaver	0	xxxx	0	2	0
Johannes Thumm	Bauer	xx	yyxxx	2	1	0

Note: a = brother, father; b = uncle, nephew; x = first cousin, first cousin once removed (counting relations through spouses and steprelations); y = second cousin (counting as with first cousins).

[a]Including wives of magistrates.

dissidents in the village – those who brought charges against Schultheiss Rieth – were smallholders, day-laborers, and artisans (7 out of 10) (Table 10.3). They expressed their exclusion from power by underlining the familial interconnectedness of the magistrates. And the conflict clearly took on social dimensions as poorer villagers expressed anger and hatred against the newly consolidated village oligarchy.

The political conflicts surrounding Johann Georg Rieth's conduct in office must be understood in the context of the transition during the 1740s and 1750s from a political structure based on patronage and clientage, which connected different social and economic strata in the village through marriage, kinship, and godparentage, to a more stratified structure built around endogamous marriage policies reinforced through ritual kinship. Table 10.3 shows that familial ties among the plaintiffs were much more numerous than those between the plaintiffs and the group of magistrates. On average, each of the "dissidents" had 3.3 "cousins" among the group of conspirators, but only 1.3 "cousins" among the village officeholders. This seems a rather abstract way to express group solidarities, but it points to the possibility that although overlapping kinship ties operated to integrate the patriciate and provide a framework for them to coordinate their interests, familial ties had also begun to provide a basis of opposition. Significantly, none of the men who brought charges against Rieth or any of the other officeholders was himself among the magistrates. And on the whole the kinship ties among the conspirators were dispersed among various magistrates, although four were cousins of Andreas Hentzler, who may have been part of a group in opposition to Schultheiss Rieth. The three Bauer, presumably the wealthiest among the informers, had among them 8 out of the total 13 kin links with the magistrates.

The lines connecting dissidents through ritual kinship show many elements of an earlier structure. None of them, however strong the consanguineal ties, were connected to one another through godparentage. On the contrary, most of them had established ties to richer and more powerful patrons, and all but one of them had an officeholder or his wife as Gevatter(in). Furthermore, although the families of magistrates had broken with the custom of choosing ritual kin from a single patriline over many generations, several of the informers still maintained such continuity. But here again no particular magistrate patriline continued the practice with more than one or two unrelated client families. And the practice would die out completely with that generation. Perhaps village politics spilled over into a wider arena because older ties and loyalties had either been severed or significantly weakened, and new forms of coordination, management of conflict, and domination had not yet been woven into the warp of everyday life. While the widowed mother of Johann Georg Rieth III still acted as Gevatterin for some of her own Doten, her son broke with family custom and sought ties among his cousins and political allies. Although both practices were still visible, they were no longer really viable alternatives.

Political issues at midcentury

The process of social and political differentiation that began to develop during the 1740s helps to clarify several of the issues revealed in Vogt Dreher's investigation. One of the complaints running through the whole document has to do with the fact that Schultheiss Rieth had kept two different sets of books. Such a practice could not have occurred without the collusion of the Bürgermeister responsible for the village accounts. Furthermore, since each set of accounts was presented to the Gericht each year and read aloud, all the Richter had to know about the cooked books as well. According to the procedures established by ducal ordinance, annual accounts were supposed to be read to all the assembled Bürger, but just because of the irregularities, Rieth had begun during the 1740s to keep such information limited to the small group of closely coordinated members of the Gericht. Throughout Dreher's report, there is a sense of strong tension between the magistrates and Gemeinde, and Rieth's practice of restricting information to the small circle of officeholders recognized both his need to maintain secrecy and the growing disparity between the interests of many members of the community and those of its dominant elite. Neither Rieth nor the Bürgermeister could afford to have their bookkeeping practices become common knowledge.

The system of double bookkeeping worked in several ways. For many bills in the construction of the new Rathaus or the repairs to the Neckar river banks, a contractor or craftsman provided an inflated receipt. For example, the mason Köpple did a job for 25 fl, but the Schultheiss and Bürgermeister Schober provided a receipt for 36 fl. The extra 11 fl went into a kitty to be used for charges that never showed up in the books annually audited by the district officials. Money flowed regularly into the Schultheiss's discretionary fund through the frequent sale of wood from the village forest. Every villager had a right to free building wood, and a considerable number of trees were felled each year for that purpose. Part of the return for stumps, branches, and a few extra trunks ended up in the secret accounts. And during the 1740s the Gericht had started to assess villagers a fee for wood, which also helped swell such accounts. Various village resources such as apples and pears from the communal land, instead of being divided among households, were sold off at least in part to provide increased funds at the magistrates' disposal.

The money that was accumulated in this way was used in certain forms of display, which increased the disparity between the rulers and ruled in the village or built friends among regional officials, who in turn supported the practices and policies of the local magistrates. By far the largest expenditures were for meals and drinking by the Schultheiss, Bürgermeister, and members of the Gericht. One of the Richter, Jacob Geiger, owned the most important inn in the village and profited considerably by providing for many of the banquets put on by Rieth and his cronies. Both Vogt Dreher and the pastor remarked on the extraordinary amount of drinking to be found among the magistrates and dated the practice from Rieth's accession to office in 1740. Throughout the year, there were specific occasions when eating and drinking set the magistrates apart as a privileged group – just after Christmas at the annual Ruggericht and in the spring when all the village jobs were parceled out were two of the important ones. At the latter, the available funds were increased through payoffs rendered by each successful applicant. The magistrates wined and dined on the occasion of closing the forest, opening pastures, harvesting, making kindling, and timbering. Whenever the city bailiff (*Stadtknecht*) visited Neckarhausen, instead of the village paying a fee, victuals were gathered for a public meal that the Schultheiss and Bürgermeister shared. Every year at the visitation of the Saltpeter administrator and the customs and excise inspectors, they were shunted off to the inn for a feast so that they would have little time to assess fines. In fact, the customs visitor went from house to house to collect flax, hemp, butter, fruit, and money in exchange for not finding any significant delicts to record. Although not mentioned in the Vogt's report, every real estate sale contained a "Weinkauf," a sum allocated for a drink between the buyer and seller and Schultheiss and a few other officials. By the 1740s, there were 400 such transactions a year. Taken together, the evidence concerning drinking on any kind of official business, which frequently became the occasion for extensive banqueting, suggests an area of high symbolic importance and prestige for village authorities. Their standing was validated whenever an outside official visited the village and took part in the round of status consumption.

Just as important for maintaining their position were the payoffs, bribes, and gratifications rendered by the magistrates to outside officials. The chief gifts had always gone to the Nürtingen Vogt. Rieth claimed that when he became Schultheiss as a 25-year-old, he had tried to cut back on such practices and went for advice to Vogt Wolff, who told him not to worry about it. Vogt Sattler had gotten too greedy and ended up committing suicide once he was targeted for investigation. Even the auditor of the river construction accounts had to be given a gratification. Bürgermeister Schott in Nürtingen, who audited the village accounts for many years, got a significant present for his wedding, and so did the city clerk, Planck, whose good wishes were even more necessary for village officials. Of course, the Schultheiss and Bürgermeister were invited in each instance, another mark of their prestige. Although the secret set of books with all of these expenditures were shown to the Gericht each year, none of these expenses were revealed to the Bürgerschaft. All of what Bourdieu calls "symbolic capital" was in this case underwritten by appropriation from village members hidden in the financial management of communal resources.

Although the two incidents that evoked the most *bitter* complaints from villagers involved the construction of a new Rathaus and the reconstruction of the river bank to control flooding, the prince's administration was most concerned with irregularities in the collection of tithes, which were delivered each year to the ducal government. The construction projects had imposed considerable forced labor (*Frohnen*) on villagers and gave village officials many opportunities to earn daily fees. Bills and receipts were fixed, and payoffs were arranged for officials from outside who were supposed to audit accounts and inspect the workmanship. All of the used equipment and property from the demolition of the old Rathaus disappeared in confused half-public auctions and private sales, none of which were accounted for in any detailed way. While these two large public projects were going on with considerable opportunity for bribes, private enrichment, and coordinated corruption, the Schultheiss was also experimenting with ways to manage the tithe collection and delivery to the greater advantage of the village.

For three years, from 1752 to 1754, Schultheiss Johann Georg Rieth, with the agreement of Vogt Sattler, tried a new system of tithe collection, just after revised procedures had been put in place in 1746. Before any of the changes, whenever spelt, barley, or oats were being harvested, they had to be piled up in sheaves on the fields belonging to each landowner. Under the watchful eye of district and village officials, bonded and sworn officers selected every tenth sheaf to be brought to village storehouses, threshed, and delivered to the duke's barns. Probably because of the costs of such an operation and the many chances for cheating, beginning in 1746, after the harvest was viewed with district officials, the tithe was put up for auction to the highest bidder. The village magistrates and district officials agreed on a price to start off the auction and accepted offers at the rate of 3 Scheffel of threshed grain (5.31 hectoliters) per bid. In this new system, a single villager, bonded by his friends and relatives and supported by a syndicate, purchased the tithe at a price guaranteed to the ducal government. The tithe farmer (*Beständer*) had to hire protection agents, collectors, carters, and threshers, making a profit on the difference between his bid and the amount that was actually collected. Only a wealthy villager could enter into the bidding, and he had to be surrounded by enough family and friends to manage the complex operation and protect his investment.

From the point of view of Schultheiss Rieth and other magistrates, there were two problems with this system. The government had forbidden officeholders to purchase the tithe farm. That would have been all right if matters could have been arranged beforehand, before the official auction in the presence of the Vogt or his delegated agent. Since a protocol of the transaction was kept, with each bidder carefully entered into a register, if the village were to minimize the deliveries to the duke and maximize the profit to some of the villagers, then there could be no deviation from a plan choreographed in advance. The problem was that various villagers refused to collude with Schultheiss Rieth and competed for the bid as they wished. Ever since the tax farm had been introduced, Johann Georg Dorfschmid had placed the top bid, and there were other villagers, such as Richter Salomon Häussler's half-brother, Michael, also willing to step out of line. Rieth brought considerable pressure to bear on Dorfschmid and told him that he would not be able to survive his enemies in the long run. It may be that there was a rival syndicate to the one the Schultheiss was trying to build. Dorfschmid was backed by two Hentzlers, one of them Salomon, the brother of Richter Andreas, who himself later became a Richter and Bürgermeister. The other supporter of Dorfschmid was either Caspar or Johann Georg Hentzler, both of whom were informers against Rieth. Five of the opponents of Rieth were cousins of Andreas Hentzler or chose him as godparent. And Michael Häussler who had refused to follow Rieth's lead and had been abused by him was married to Hentzler's wife's sister. When Rieth died, he was succeeded by Hentzler's son-in-law, and seven years later by his son, Salomon, who after a long term in office was forced to retire for corrupt tithe administration. The contours of opposition suggest that the politics of the tithe farm was organized around two syndicates vying for the spoils.

In 1752 Rieth introduced a variation on the tax farm after arranging matters with Vogt Sattler. In fact, it was this collusion that brought the most serious charges against Sattler and led to his suicide. Schultheiss Rieth called all the villagers together a few days before the auction and explained that the bids would be arranged. But at the auction itself, Dorfschmid broke ranks and drove up the bidding and set the price for the farm. At that point, Rieth changed the whole procedure. He announced that the bidding had set the price but that each villager would be allowed to bring in his own grain, thresh it, and deliver a quantity proportional to the size of his various parcels. With this plan, Dorfschmid had to relinquish his farm, and the job of overseeing the collection fell to Rieth and his cronies among the magistrates. According to Dreher, the expenses shot up to new heights. At each moment of the business, the magistrates gathered to drink. The Schultheiss himself took over the collection, threshing, and storing of all tithe grain on the considerable number of plots belonging to inhabitants of nearby villagers. During the next two years, Dorfschmid was forced out and the magistrates themselves put in 4 or 5 pro forma bids instead of the usual 20 or so, cutting the duke short by at least 8,000 liters of grain. And the profit from the business fell to the magistrates who oversaw the collection, assessed fees, and managed the grain of external landholders. The accounts were read only to members of the Gericht, and according to Dreher, Rieth found an outside accountant willing to be creative. Furthermore, Rieth substituted old grain reserves of the village for newly threshed tithe grain, sending poor-quality goods to the duke and selling off the good-quality stuff cheaply to his friends. Dreher pointed out that if Rieth told the truth about the duke not being shortchanged, then all of the excessive costs had fallen on the villagers themselves. In any event, the experiment was short-lived, and Rieth was commanded in 1755 to return to an orderly tax farm without collusive bidding.

* * *

In assessing Neckarhausen politics at midcentury, it is possible to arrive at Dreher's conclusion that although there were a number of irregularities in Rieth's administration, there were no serious crimes to warrant dismissal from office. His maneuvering in the matter of the tithe might be seen more or less as an attempt to protect the village as a whole from excessive appropriation of their surplus by the state. As far as Dreher was concerned, tighter oligarchical control had meant more orderly financial management and a greatly reduced village debt. The commissioner objected only to the excesses, not to the policy direction as such. There was no problem with a smoothly run tax farm that profited those villagers with enough financial strength to organize and manage it. Dreher himself had not yet been in office long enough to have struck a firm alliance with one of the village factions (he died before the case was concluded), although his predecessor and successors clearly did so.

The investigation into Schultheiss Rieth's conduct in office occurred at a time when the kinship system was being reconstructed. Although the forces behind the considerable changes do not explain all of their implications, it is important to see that the innovations were prompted by the politically leading group in the village. They were the ones who first began to marry endogamously, to choose their second cousins as marriage partners. And as they did so, they made other second cousins their closest in-laws as a result. With the ability of magistrates to distribute office among their cousins and to reproduce their hold on office by coopting each other's sons and sons-in-law, they forced other villagers to rely on cousin networks in turn. Still, the poorer villagers – those who opposed Rieth's oligarchical government – did not yet reinforce consanguineal ties through marriage. Nor did they utilize the possibilities inherent in ritual kinship to underline and emphasize connections that were already in place. It may be that the moral weight given to cousinship was latent – there is evidence from the parallel cousin/sibling marriage form at the beginning of the eighteenth century that patrilateral cousins had a special meaning for each other. However, it is more useful to see "cousinship" as something that was produced in particular historical conditions.

The many strands of overlapping relations to be found among the village patriciate at midcentury certainly made it necessary for other villagers to rely on their own kinship ties. Wealthy villagers without particular access to local political institutions found cousins increasingly useful in their bid to gain access to important resources, and by the 1780s the landholding stratum of the village as a whole adopted the system of overlapping consanguineal ties first developed by officeholders. Kinship dynamics, therefore, lay at the center of eventual class formation. Perhaps it is possible to say that kinship – the particular configurations of marriage alliance and ritual co-parenthood, endogamy, and the politics of cousinhood – was the matrix for the construction of class. Classes are not and were not substantial things with given characteristics and inherent interests but sets of relationships in dynamic tension with each other. And the analysis of kinship is crucial for understanding the processes by which they came into being and were reproduced.

COHORT III (1780–1789)

11

Consanguinity as a principle of alliance

Kinship in Neckarhausen could be constructed around two axes: affinity and consanguinity. But both principles always formed an interlocking system and cannot be seen as simple alternatives. At the beginning of the century, any marriage alliance constructed through affinal links produced in its turn children who were cousins. As demonstrated in preceding chapters, cousins, especially cousins related through fathers, came to be important politically, economically, and socially. It is also apparent that when cousins began to marry each other, they connected their immediate families as in-laws. Despite the fact that ties created from both marriage alliance and blood interconnected and supported one another, however, it is still possible to describe the history of kinship in Neckarhausen during the eighteenth century in terms of a transformation from the affinal to the consanguineal axis. At the beginning of the century, no villagers married anyone connected by blood, but by the end of the century many families had constructed durable alliances through a repetitive pattern of consanguineal unions. Consanguineal marriages, however, were unevenly distributed in the population (see Chapter 12). They spread from the small group of dominant political families to encompass the wealthier village stratum as a whole during a period of increasing social differentiation.

By the 1780s, the population of Neckarhausen had finally recovered from its disastrous decline during the Thirty Years' War. Over the course of the eighteenth century, it rose by almost 70 percent to become a medium-size village of about 520 "souls." Between 1710 and 1790, the occupational composition of the village altered significantly, with the proportion of Bauern among the Bürger falling from about half to a third, while the contingent of artisans rose from a third to two-fifths. By the 1780s, a new group of farm laborers comprising one out of every five adult males had emerged, many of whom found jobs with the village as field patrolmen, mouse catchers, fountain cleaners, tree surgeons, bakehouse or bleaching meadow attendants, and the like. Accompanying these shifts in the numerical strength of different occupational groups were more dramatic alterations in their economic and political positions. In 1710 the average artisan held about 75 percent as much property as the average Bauer, but this proportion significantly dropped to 40 percent by 1790. In turn, the average day-laborer possessed only 20 percent as much as the average Bauer. Not only did artisans suffer a substantial decline in their economic position even as their numbers rose, but they also lost considerable political influence over the century. Around 1700, they had occupied about half of the magistrate positions in the village and had held two of the four Bürgermeister slots, but in 1790 they were reduced to 2 of 23 offices, and none of them had the distinguished careers typical in the early 1700s. For the most part, the magistrate positions were monopolized by a peasant elite; greater social stratification in an enlarged village brought political domination by the landed agricultural producers.

At the beginning of the eighteenth century, the distribution of property was allocated largely by inheritance, and little real estate was sold or traded outside the nuclear family.[1] By the 1780s, the market accounted for almost as much movement of land between people as inheritance (80 percent). There was not just a livelier market for land by the late eighteenth century, but many more people and a larger proportion of the village participated in it, pushing up the price and partitioning plots into ever smaller portions. Altogether, the total sales of arable plots tripled. The price per Morgen (0.32 hectare) rose 350 percent, while the average-size plot was whittled away by 27 percent. In the first decade of the eighteenth century, there had been only 41 buyers, about 12 percent of the average village population during the decade as a whole. By the 1780s, 135 people purchased arable land, just over 26 percent of the decade's average population.

Not only did the market for real estate increase considerably throughout the eighteenth century in terms of the number of transactions, but it also became increasingly formal, and property became less encumbered. Annuities, retirement contracts, and conditional sales, none of which had ever been prominent features of landholding, were rapidly disappearing by the end of the century. Real estate ceased to be bartered, and fewer and fewer sales involved a mixture of buildings, meadows, and arable plots as each item came to be sold piecemeal at its own price. By the 1780s, most land was sold at auction, called out over three successive occasions to ensure the best possible bid. Despite the increase in both formality and frequency of sale, however, there was a considerable rise in the absolute number of arable plots sold to kin, 58 for the decade 1700–1709 and 142 for the decade 1780–9. But there was also a remarkable shift in the kind of kin who bought and sold from each other. Over the three cohorts, the nuclear family accounted for 60 percent, 40 percent, and 25 percent, respectively, of sales

[1] For details on the market, see David Warren Sabean, *Property, Production, and Family in Neckarhausen, 1700–1870* (Cambridge, 1990), chaps. 15 and 16.

to relatives, while the share of cousins rose from 10 percent to 40 percent and then to 50 percent. In the end, the market for real estate was able to integrate a much larger set of kin than inheritance could. Although it may be an exaggeration to contrast a market-driven system of property distribution during the 1780s with an inheritance-driven one at the beginning of the century, there was much more of a balance between the two strategies. What is more, sales to kin placed increasing weight on agnatic relatives. Already at midcentury, sales to agnatic kin outnumbered those to uterine kin by 2 to 1, but during the 1780s, the proportion rose to 3 to 1.

While the market became an instrument for kinship interaction and exchange, it continued to offer a place for ritual kinship activity. In this period, godparents still played an important role in mediating sales between unrelated people – in fact about 60 percent of such sales partners had a godparent in common – but this was a function that flourished during this generation before disappearing altogether during the early decades of the nineteenth century. As marriage became more endogamous, godparentage continued for a generation or two to connect different strata of the village together and provide many instances of mediation, including real estate brokerage.

Marriage during the first half of the eighteenth century brought together spouses with different amounts of wealth.[2] By contrast, after 1760, prospective partners matched marriage portion ever more carefully with marriage portion. The trend only increased after 1830 but even during the 1760s and 1770s about 60 percent of wives brought marriage portions roughly equal to those of their husbands, which was twice as many who did so earlier in the century. After 1760 Neckarhausen entered into a period of "estate" endogamy, reconstructing the material conditions of alliance completely. At the beginning of the eighteenth century, when each household was a connecting point between allied families ordered hierarchically or asymmetrically, disputes between husbands and wives were often about the terms of the alliance.[3] In many instances, the family providing living space or the larger endowment interfered with the economy of the younger couple and made labor or commodity demands resented by the "in-marrying" spouse. Once potential allies eyed each other carefully and launched inquiries into the holdings of spouses recruited from outside the village, marital partners began to reflect on the quantity of property brought by the other spouse and make that an issue in their squabbles. And the new sense of balanced reciprocity set up many more disputes over the dividing line between gender spheres of authority; and prompted also by shifts in the sexual division of labor, expropriation of labor in the household became an issue not between generations, as earlier, but between spouses themselves. In the larger arena of village discourse, social stratification became encoded in a language about family and kinship. Peo-

[2] Sabean, *Property,* chap. 9.
[3] Sabean, *Property,* pp. 163–74, 208–22, 259–99.

ple made the social position of their rivals clear by alluding to their insignificant property or the low esteem of their family.

The last four decades or so of the eighteenth century were also a period in which villagers began to use resources more intensively.[4] The first steps were taken toward the cultivation of root, leguminous, and leafy brassica crops, and crops originally tested in gardens or the summer field began to find their way into the fallow. The community developed intensive pastures on newly cleared land along the Neckar River, planted hundreds of fruit trees, and developed new areas for intensive garden cultivation. By the 1780s flax and hemp appeared in the field rotation, and Neckarhausen began its career as a major producer of high-quality flax. During the last decade of the century there is evidence for the slow introduction of stall feeding. The economic changes together with the rise in population brought about several crucial innovations for the village. The magistrates pinpointed the 1780s and 1790s as the period in which many poor Bürger ceased to be able to manage and fell out of the class of subsistence producers – further evidence for greater social differentiation. It was also the period in which women were slowly being drawn into field agriculture in a major way, as labor for the new hoe crops and as porters for fodder crops carried to the household barns and stalls. Much of the grueling labor in cultivating and preparing flax also fell to women.

To a large degree, the new forms of labor tended to isolate women, while men continued to work in gangs and to politic in the inn.[5] Traditional male work, centered on plowing, harrowing, and carting, remained core activities in the new agriculture, but access to equipment brought new forms of cooperation. During the 1780s, many families passed on farm equipment to all of the sons to hold in common, or occasionally to a son and daughter, which then essentially made brothers-in-law co-parceners in plows, harrows, carts, and wagons. Shared rights often led to shared labor but in any event necessitated coordination in use and cooperation in repairs. Work routines encouraged ever greater solidarity among fathers and sons and brothers, just as village and class politics did. To judge from land sales, marriage, and godparentage, the importance of agnatic kin peaked toward the end of the eighteenth century. Families descending through the male line constructed enduring alliances over long periods of time by the systematic exchange of children and godparents. Along those same paths flowed land and services of various kinds. There is frequent evidence of solidarity among agnatic kin – uncles/nephews, first and second cousins – but also of repeated exchange among two allied patrilines. In terms of cousinship, such alliances can be expressed most simply by cross cousins when two generations are in play, or by patrilateral cross second cousins when three generations are in play (Figure 11.1).

Chapter 1 introduced some of the basic forms encountered in elementary struc-

[4] Sabean, *Property*, pp. 21–2, 52–60.
[5] Sabean, *Property*, chaps. 5, 12.

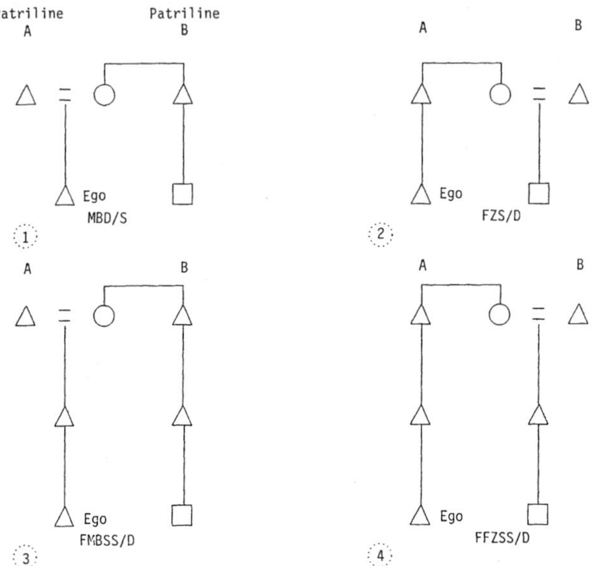

Figure 11.1

tures of kinship: restricted exchange (FZD) and generalized exchange (MBD). Whereas the categories established by Lévi-Strauss are concerned with marriage, the patterns discussed here encompass all kinds of exchange: a man might marry a female cross cousin (MBD/FZD) but also sell land to her brother or choose him as his Gevatter (MBS/FZS). As the chapters on this cohort show, such configurations occur in many different contexts where exchanges took place across generations. Where two patrilines are connected over two generations without the immediate return of a spouse of the same sex, the exchange can best be expressed as a uterine connection, as in example (1): MBD, MBS. When association between the two lines continued for another generation, the most frequent case was for a uterine structure to continue as an agnatic one, as in example (3): relationships constructed by "ego" in example (1) tended to be taken over by sons – "ego" in example (3). Examples (2) and (4) can be reciprocal expressions of (1) and (3). When ego in example (1) exchanges land with a male cousin, for example, the arrangement for the cousin takes the form of (2). But the path to an allied patriline is closer for ego in (1) than for ego in (2), which helps explain why interest in the MB kin tends to show up more frequently than in the FZ kin. Despite the structural regularities that emerge in the next chapters, various permutations of first and second cousins, as well as other forms of alliance between patrilines, continued to occur. Villagers constructed interlocking sets of reciprocities out of bits and pieces of elementary logic, finding a variety of ways to maintain continuous reciprocity between families, sometimes over many generations. The important point to keep in mind is that the agnatic structure to many forms of exchange expresses simultaneously or alternatively solidarity among agnatic kin (growing out of the solidarity among brothers) and/or the enduring alliance between two patrilines (growing out of the exigencies of affinal reciprocity).

The selection of guardians and Kriegsvögte during the 1780s suggests ways in which the territory of kinship was remapped, maintaining some of its older contours while drawing in new paths and byways. Both institutions point toward a special weight given to agnatic kin within a generally flexible practice that maintained connections through various routes over agnatic and uterine relatives. At the beginning of the century, some functions such as guardianship had been narrowly restricted to the closest nuclear kin whenever possible, but by the 1780s they became open to more extended consanguineal kin – to cousins. Other functions, such as godparentage and marriage, had escaped the bounds of blood relationships altogether, but now narrowed down to encompass the field of second and even first cousins. In this generation, some women found Kriegsvögte within a range extending out to cousins, while others still maintained the older practice of finding wealthier or more powerful outsiders – in this generation often ritual kin – to protect their interests.

Although people continued to choose guardians for their children from close relatives during the decade 1780–9, as with all the other indicators of this period, the innovation was to extend the range of effective choice to cousins. Out of the sample of 20 Pfleger, 17 were related to their Pflegekinder. Nine of the guardians were uncles (and one was a father himself) of the children: 1 F, 4 FBs, 3 MBs, 1 MZH, 1 MBWH. In most of these cases, the alliance between two families was directly underlined: whenever one spouse died, the children were appointed a guardian. Apart from the unusual instance of the father performing this role (which happened now and then throughout the late eighteenth and early nineteenth centuries), in every instance balanced reciprocity was set up.[6] In four cases, after a man died, his widow administered the rights of the children with his brother, while in five instances the father had to work with his deceased wife's brother, brother's marital successor, or sister's husband. There were four first cousins of the children or their parents in the sample (1 FBS, 1 MZHZS, 1 FMBS, 1 MFBS), one second cousin of the father (FMFBSS), and two uncles of the mother (MMB, MMZH). Frequently a Pfleger appointed when one parent died remained as the sole guardian upon decease of the second. In other words, it was almost unheard of for a set of siblings to have two guardians. At the same time, there were often separate guardians for the children of separate "beds." When Michael Schach died in 1791, for example, the MZH represented a son

[6] Occasionally a father was appointed Pfleger for his own children, a phenomenon for which I have found no comment in the sources and which I really do not understand. Certainly the institution of guardianship created a culture of expectations, which some fathers relied on, expressing deep disappointment when a guardian was not as active on behalf of his children as he expected.

Table 11.1. *Cohort III: Occupations of guardians.*

Occupation	Number	Occupation	Number
Richter	1	Cooper	1
Bauer	12	Baker	1
Shepherd	1	Weaver	2
Wheelwright	1	Cobbler	1

from his first marriage, a MZHZH represented a daughter from his second marriage, and a MBS the two children of his third marriage.

In this period, there was a significant decline in the number of magistrates who served as Pfleger (Table 11.1). By and large, the criterion for choosing guardians was kinship, and although Bauern held the majority of positions, other occupations were well represented. Solvency and adulthood seem to have been all that was necessary. The patronage element so strong in the early part of the century had disappeared.

As had been the case earlier in the century, guardians were seldom chosen from among godparents, and it was unusual for a man to act as one where his wife was godmother. Godparentage was seldom called upon as crisis parentage. In one case a mother's brother was appointed Pfleger even though his wife had been godparent for the last child, but that child had died at birth. Old Johannes Bosch, a powerful Richter and one-time Bürgermeister, became Pfleger for the children of his brother's daughter in 1786 even though his wife had been her godmother and he was godfather for her children. That is the only clear case of godparentage being reinforced with Pflegschaft, but the father in this instance was a cantankerous personality, who eventually tried to block his sons-in-law from receiving the maternal inheritance, and Bosch may have been selected by the mother precisely because of their close association and his powerful position on the Gericht.

Kriegsvogtschaft was an institution for protecting a woman's rights and attesting to her decision with regard to business conducted before a court. Out of the sample of 20 Kriegsvögte, 12 were traceable as relatives, six related to the woman directly and six related through her husband: 1 B, 2 FBs, 1 MZDH, 1 H1WF, 1 HBWF, 1 HZHZH, 1 HMBWZH, 1 HFFBDDH, 1 HMMZDDH. When women chose their own consanguineal kin, the latter were usually very close relatives – a brother, uncle, or cousin. For the most part, only when women were not from Neckarhausen or were widowed (four cases) did they choose relatives of their husbands, and even then did not look for Kriegsvögte within the nuclear families. In general, Kriegsvögte still came from wealthier, propertied, and politically well-connected families (Table 11.2). The Kriegsvogt was always there to protect the interests of a wife and was potentially in tension with the

Table 11.2. *Cohort III: Occupations of Kriegsvögte.*

Occupation	Number
Richter	7
Schoolmaster	1
Bauer	2
Smith	1
Weaver	2
Day-laborer	1

husband. The first requirement, of course, was that he should be able to read, which may explain the high participation of magistrates. But there was often a strong overlap between godparents and Kriegsvögte. In fact, many of the Kriegsvögte who were not related to a woman were connected to her through ritual kinship. Although the institution of Kriegsvogtschaft demonstrates on the one hand a selection process tracing through males (brother, father, husband) and a readiness to select cousins, there still seems to have been a propensity to find aid and support among people connected less through family than through patronage.

The evidence for the overlapping of godparents and Kriegsvögte is strong and contrasts sharply with the usual distinction between guardians and godparents. *For example, Johannes Moos's wife's Kriegsvogt, Georg Heinrich Dorfschmid, Richter, her MZDH, was Döte for all her children. Johannes Brodbeck, Richter, FZS of Martin Grauer's widow, was also her Kriegsvogt and Gevatter. Wilhelm Hentzler acted as Kriegsvogt for his sister, while his wife was her Gevatterin. Wilhelm Rentzler was FB, Kriegsvogt, and Gevatter for David Bauknecht's wife. The Kriegsvogt for Maria Catharina, Ludwig Zeug's second wife, was old Johannes Bosch, Richter. Bosch was father of Zeug's first wife and godfather for both sets of children. Christina Margaretha, the wife of the future Schultheiss Friedrich Krumm, had Johannes Bosch as Kriegsvogt in 1787; Bosch's wife was Dote both for her and her children.*

* * *

The central concern of the study of this cohort is the maturing of the alliance system that began to be constructed during the 1740s. By the late decades of the eighteenth century, many families had exchanged children in marriage over two, three, four, and five generations. And such durable alliances would continue well into the nineteenth century. Nonetheless, only some sectors of the village practiced this kind of marriage politics, and as was the case for the wealthier landed villagers, class construction and consanguineal endogamy became part of the same project. During the earlier decades of the nineteenth century, they would draw even closer together, moving from second to first cousins, while the artisan and building worker families would only then begin to look among second cousins for spouses. What began as a political ploy during the 1740s became redeployed step by step as an instrument of class strategy. Chapters 12 to 14 sketch in the structural outlines of the reordered system of kinship: marriage alliance, ritual kinship, and naming.

12

The formation of an alliance system

During the 1740s certain villagers began to marry their consanguineal kin. Within another generation or two, some of their descendants repeated those alliances while other families took up the practice for the first time. By the end of the century, many of Neckarhausen's lines had been allied together for seventy or eighty years and continued to trade marriage partners until they fade from sight at the end of the 1860s. If we confined our view in each case to the particular relationship of a specific couple, we would fail to notice that each marriage was part of a larger strategic situation of patterned exchanges coordinating many households and several generations of people. This chapter examines the shape of just such alliances, which connected families over long periods of time and provided dense networks for political, social, and economic activity. In these alliances, property was inherited equally by all children, including daughters, so that the devolution of real estate gave no structural support for the construction of lineages based on one or the other sex; furthermore, people treated paternal and maternal kin equally for such purposes as reckoning prohibited degrees. Despite these features, lines constructed on agnatic principles – which I have been calling "patrilines" – emerged in the systematic exchange of marriage partners between families over several generations. By the 1780s, however, such a politics of exchange was largely confined to the class of independent landholders and was, in fact, an expression of that class in its self-formation.

The decision to marry, or at least to initiate sexual relations, could sometimes be quite spontaneous, but even then negotiations usually took place in the context of familial knowledge and consent. There were tensions between generations, of course, and the practice of "bundling" gave village youth considerable influence over marriage deliberations.[1] In the years leading up to pairing off, young women

[1] See David Sabean, "Unehelichkeit: Ein Aspekt sozialer Reproduktion kleinbäuerlicher Produzenten:

Table 12.1. *Age at first marriage (1780–9).*

	Men	Women
Number	65	79
Range	18–43	17–52
Mean	26.6	26.4
Median	26	23
Mode	23	20

Table 12.2. *Age at first marriage when kin-related (1780–9).*

	Men	Women
Number	21	26
Range	18–36	17–44
Mean	24.3	23.5
Median	23	20.5
Mode	23	20

slept alone in their own rooms and received male visitors. This institution made most of the marriageable youth acquainted with each other and provided a means for developing and maintaining village knowledge about and control over sexual conduct and courtship. There is evidence, however, that during the last several decades of the eighteenth century, the period crucial for the solidification of alliances among the independent agricultural producers, parents directed the matching up of couples much more strictly than before. This can be seen from the fact that children who married kin were much younger than those who did not.

In contrast to the previous two cohorts, age was a factor among couples marrying for the first time who contracted kin-linked marriages (Tables 12.1 and 12.2). Not only were such couples much younger than the rest of their cohort, but also the average age of marriage for both sexes, taking all first marriages into consideration, was higher than before (mean age at marriage for men in Cohort I was 25.5; in Cohort II, 24.8; in Cohort III, 26.6. For women in Cohort I, it was 24.0; in Cohort II, 23.3; in Cohort III, 26.4).

The disparity between mean and median age in first marriages for women points to a new phenomenon. A significant number of them in this period delayed marriage until their 30s and 40s, a practice that played a role in the growing rate of illegitimacy. The tendency for later marriage for some women developed along with a lower mode, which shows that a significant number of women married around the age of 20. While the push to extremes led to an overall rise in the mean age of first marriage, it brought an end to the older practice of marrying more or less according to a customary age. The age of first marriage for kin-related marriages in this cohort was significantly lower, two to three years on average, than for the group as a whole, both male and female. Any marriage contracted before the legal age of adulthood of 25 had to be carried out with the express permission and aid of parents or guardians. Thus the fact that early

Zu einer Analyse dörflicher Quellen um 1800," in Robert Berdahl et al., eds., *Klassen und Kultur: Sozialanthropologische Perspektiven in der Geschichtsschreibung* (Frankfurt/Main, 1982), pp. 54–76; K. Robert v. Wikman, *Die Einleitung in die Ehe: Eine vergleichend ethno-soziologische Untersuchung über die Vorstufe der Ehe in den Sitten des schwedischen Volkstums* (Aabo, 1937).

Table 12.3. *Cohort III: Occupation of husband in kin-related marriages.*

Occupation	Kin-linked	Non–kin-linked	Number	Percent
Bauer/Shepherd	15	23	38	39.5
Artisan	6	16	22	27.3

marriage age and kin-linked marriages correlated so closely suggests a family rather than an individual marriage strategy. Kin-linked marriages often involved a systematic connection of families over more than one generation. Such a pattern of exchange implies an adult strategy to fulfill obligations, calculate risks, and play for advantage. Offering 18, 19, and 20-year-olds adulthood long before they could achieve it on their own and hiving off bits of property to make them half-independent suggest a policy of coordinating interests among separate but allied families.

Kinship and marriage strategy

Wealth and occupation played a considerable role in determining whether people made kin-related marriages during the decades centered on the 1780s. For this period, the study sample was constructed with reference to tax data, which give a clear distribution from all wealth strata and occupation groups in the village. Overall, slightly less than a third of all marriages were kin-related – 29 percent of all, and 32 percent of first marriages – a figure that is lower than at midcentury, perhaps because it is based on a better distribution according to wealth.[2]

Bauern and children of Bauern made more kin-related marriages in terms of their share of the population than did artisans (Tables 12.3 and 12.4). Magistrate families on the whole had a relatively strong tendency to make kin-related marriages as well, but they were now indistinguishable from landholding families as a whole. Occupation as reflected in the records can be misleading, however. Since there were often several similar names in the village at any one time, people were frequently distinguished from each other by reference to a handicraft or trade. Many "artisans" had sufficient agricultural land to keep them busy in its exploitation. Thus the stronger correlation between kin-linked marriages and wealth (tax quartiles III and IV) indicates a politics of peasant familial alliance (Table

[2] See Table A.25. For Cohort I, 25 percent of marriages were kin-related and for Cohort II, 40 percent. There is a problem for the second period because as the sample was expanded by including siblings of the marriage partners under consideration, duplication appeared. Counting the duplicates twice gives a rate of 40 percent. Counting them once gives one of 33 percent. The larger percentage could also be due to the fact that that cohort spanned the shift from affinally constructed to consanguineally constructed ties and may therefore reflect inflated numbers resulting from the overlap.

Table 12.4. *Cohort III: Occupation of husband's father and wife's father in kin-related marriages.*

Occupation	Kin-linked	Non–kin-linked	Number	Percent
Bauer/Shepherd	48	75	123	39.0
Artisan	12	48	60	20.0
Magistrates[a]	14	22	36	38.9

[a]Included in occupational figures.

Table 12.5. *Cohort III: Kin-related marriages and wealth.*

Tax quartile[a]	Kin-related	Non–kin-related	Number	Percent
I	2	15	17	11.8
II	4	9	13	30.8
III	9	10	19	47.4
IV	2	3	5	40.0

[a]In ascending order.

12.5). The wealthier half of the village made well over twice as many such marriages as the poorer half.

During the eighteenth century, endogamous marriages began among the political elite of the village, and only subsequently spread to the wealthier, landholding, independent agricultural producers as a whole. This group began to close itself off from others in the village by renewing exchanges among themselves and forging social and political alliances. They dominated the village in a new fashion, not by marrying their poorer clients, but by maintaining a close network of alliances among themselves, by monopolizing all of the offices of the village, and by developing a new discourse of class in which respect, deference, and honor were distributed to people according to wealth, family connection, occupation, and their willingness and ability to protect resources aggressively.[3] Class and all the practices of class relations were formed within the dynamics of family, and their shape was determined by the way family connections provided a matrix for the exercise of power. Kinship endogamy nurtured class endogamy. What began as a strategy of officeholders, within a generation or two was extended to include the larger stratum of landed peasants. By the early nineteenth century, handicraft producers and artisanal workers in the building trades would in turn adopt a similar strategy for constructing regional networks in an era of occasional work and volatile labor markets.

[3] The dynamics of class discourse can be seen in Chapter 16 and also in Sabean, *Property, Production, and Family in Neckarhausen, 1700–1870* (Cambridge, 1990), pp. 22–4, 238–46, 324–7, 422–7.

The construction of alliance

One can look at any marriage in two ways: from the viewpoint of the couple itself and from that of the wider set of alliances entered into by a household, sibling group, or lineage. Tracing out the lines of kinship between spouses (Tables A.55 and A.56) for this period demonstrates the central importance of cousin marriages during the late decades of the eighteenth century. There were a few first-cousin marriages (FBD, FZD, MBD), with no particular bias in a patrilateral or matrilateral direction, parallel or cross, except perhaps for the significant absence of the MZD. There were also a few first-cousin-once-removed marriages: FFBD, FBDD, MFBD. The striking feature, however, is the large number of second-cousin marriages – those involving third-degree consanguinity. Altogether the various cousin marriages made up about half of the total of kin-related marriages.

Now and then, marriage took place with a relative of a deceased wife (WZ, WMFBDD, W's first cousin). However, such unions were not a prominent feature of the system. Not until the legal renovation of 1796 would it in fact become possible to obtain a dispensation to marry a wife's sister. In fact, such marriages were central to the arguments of theologians about loosening the prohibited degrees: the experts thought that children left by a deceased mother should have one of her close relatives to raise them, and they considered marriage with the wife's sister or cousin to be a chief reason for entering into a kin-related marriage. Even though other relatives of the wife were dispensable before 1796, only in the nineteenth century would they be sought after frequently for marriage partners. For villagers, the primary concern was not nurturing children but maintaining and developing alliances. There was not yet any particular interest in redoubling an alliance by making a second marriage with the same family in the same generation. After all, many of the ties that were created by marriage were not broken at the death of a spouse. Children of a household established obligations with allied families, who provided names, guardians, and Kriegsvögte.

When cousin marriages first developed during the 1740s, there was no tradition either in the village as a whole or in particular family histories for such a practice. Thus it was possible to see how a particular sibling group coordinated their marriages during that period but not yet to understand how families could constitute alliances over time. The first example here brings back into focus a typical case from the early part of the century – marriage between extended affinal relatives. The task now is to show how it fits into a new context of intergenerational exchange. In the discussion of the first cohort, I showed that marriage between affinal kin linked members of a single generation together but did not and could not replicate exchanges entered into by the parents' or grandparents' generation by repeating the same principles. The present example begins with just such a network, one that involves the sibling group of Hentzlers, children of Hans Conrad, Bauer, from the parish hamlet of Raidwangen.

Figure 12.1 displays Holpps, Bauknechts, and a number of Hentzlers from

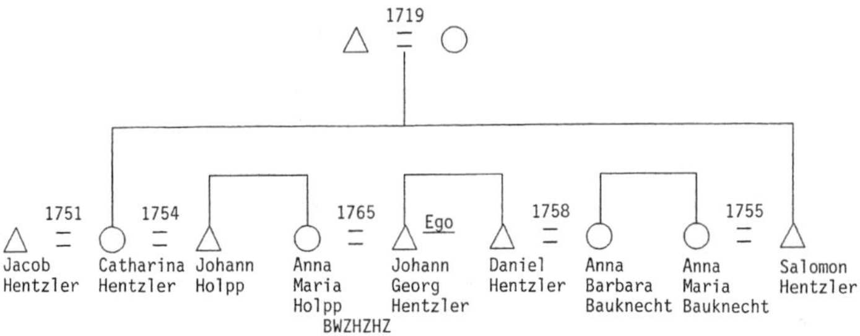

Figure 12.1

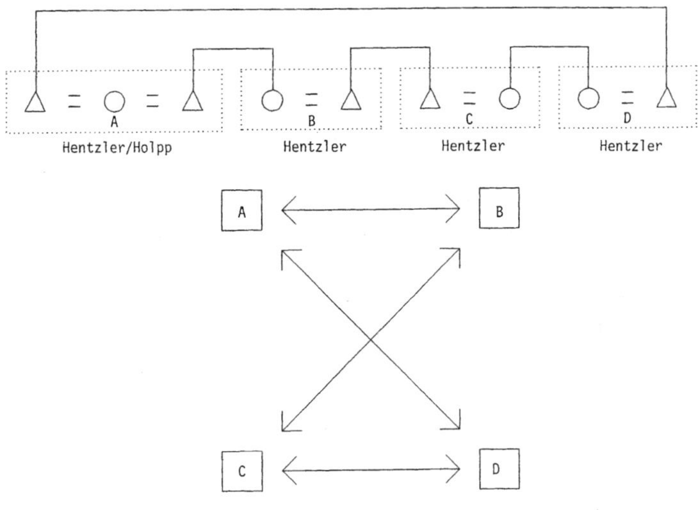

Figure 12.2

different lines intermarried during one generation. Over a 10-year period, a set of overlapping links between four sets of siblings were established. As the analysis proceeds and reveals more and more about the systematic alliances constructed by these families over time, it is important to remember that exchanges developed by particular lines established coordinated households and multiple linkages between families on a single generational plane. This diagram can be schematized to show more clearly how the multiple links between households were structured (Figure 12.2).

In this example the two Bauknecht sisters (households C and D) married Hentzlers who were distantly related as FFFFBSSSS, but more closely as FWBS/FZHS (xMBS/FZxS). It is an example of the frequent practice of two cousins marrying two sisters, although by this time such cousins were no longer necessarily agnatically related. Similarly, for the two households A and B where

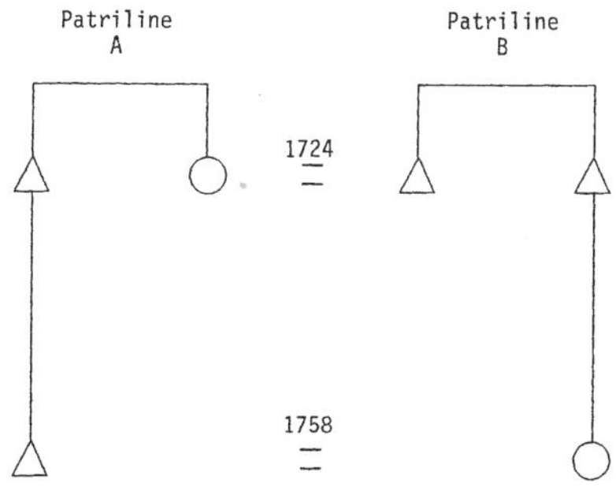

Figure 12.3

the Holpp siblings married two Hentzlers, it is again a case of first cousins marrying siblings. All these forms have already been mentioned in reference to the beginning of the eighteenth century, although no examples of such tightly overlapping interrelationships could be found then. The real departure in practice – already in evidence by midcentury – was that lines that intermarried in one generation did so again. This can be shown in one small section of Figure 12.2, the marriage of Daniel Hentzler to Anna Barbara Bauknecht in 1758 (C), with the aid of a simplified version of an enlarged genealogy going back one and forward two generations (Figure 12.4). As can be seen, an earlier alliance had been made in 1724 between the two lines, so that in 1758 Daniel Hentzler married his FZHBD (Figure 12.3). In such a case, although the two neogami were not consanguineally related, it nonetheless offers another form by which two lines could enter into exchange and repeat it a generation later. The example Gérard Delille discusses to illustrate this form is that of an aunt and nephew marrying an uncle and niece.[4] Because patriline A offers a woman to patriline B in one generation and receives a woman back in the following one, Delille argues, this form is equivalent to a marriage pattern fulfilling the exigencies of restricted exchange, a variation on marriage with the FZD. It is certainly true that elementary forms of restricted and generalized exchange can be expressed in a variety of ways, and many of them appear in the following analysis. The important point is that consanguineal marriages – between first and second cousins and the like – are only an indicator of a more encompassing practice of alliance between patrilines. The alliance system was oriented toward balancing the intensity of reciprocal exchange (utilizing the logic of elementary forms) and proliferating contacts by entering into relations with nonrelated or distantly related kindreds.

I have simplified the subsequent genealogy of the next two generations, showing further marriages with Bauknechts (Figure 12.4). Although the two children of Daniel Hentzler and Anna Barbara Bauknecht (generation II) did not marry Bauknechts

[4] Gérard Delille, *Famille et propriété dans le royaume de Naples (xv*^{e}*–xix*^{e} *siècle),* Bibliothèque des écoles françaises d'Athènes et de Rome, vol. 259 (Rome, 1985), pp. 246–9.

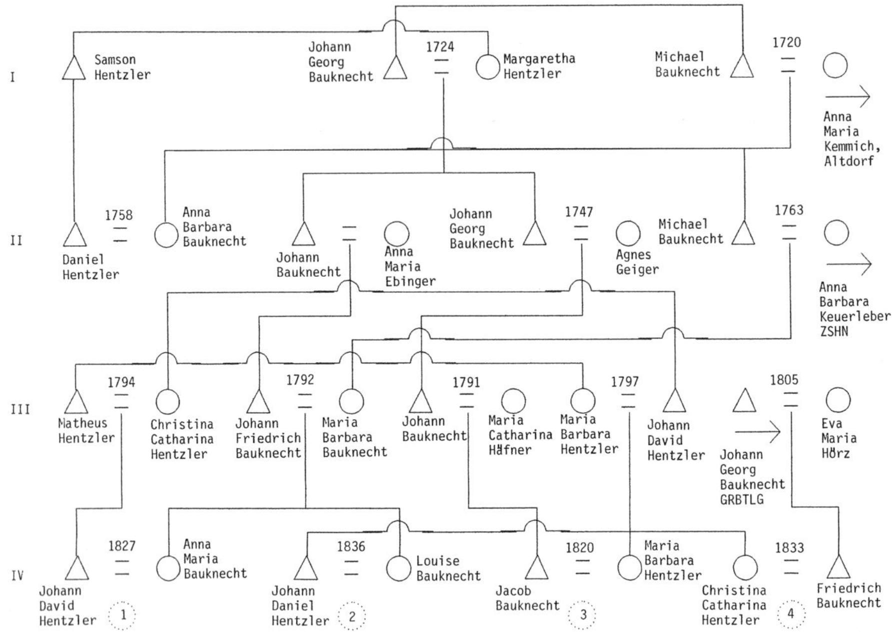

Figure 12.4

(they in fact married siblings from another line of the Hentzler family), four of their grandchildren did. Johann David Hentzler (1, Figure 12.4) married his FMBDD or to look at it another way, he married his FMFBSSD or his FFFZSSD (Figure 12.5).

Thinking of marriage between the two young people as a path traced through the consanguineal kin obscures the essential point that the two patrilines were involved in a series of exchanges that were set up by the marriage in 1724, a time when such repeated exchanges were a completely new phenomenon. That the two lines entered into a series of marriages over the period 1724 to at least 1827–36 argues for an attempt on the part of the various families to maintain and to renew their alliances. From one point of view, the descendants of affinal kin frequently sought to make affinal kin out of each other, and from another, consanguineal kin provided a field within which new affines were constructed. Cousins and wives, cousins and brothers-in-law overlapped and interconnected.

Johann Daniel Hentzler (2, Figure 12.4) married Louise Bauknecht in 1836 (Figure 12.6). Through his father, Johann David, he descended from another line of the Hentzler family, from Hans and Ursula married in the 1560s or 1570s. Johann Daniel married his MMBDD. If this marriage is considered in terms of the particular description of the path in the field of consanguineal kin, then it is difficult to see how it

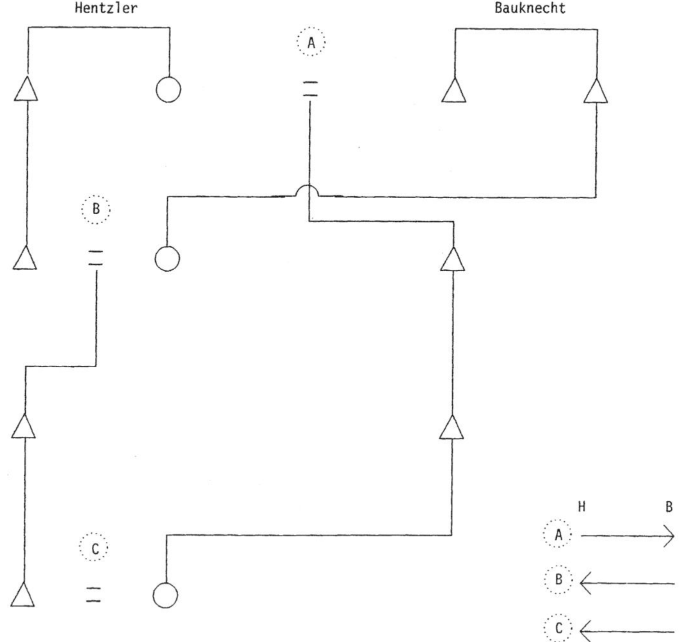

Figure 12.5

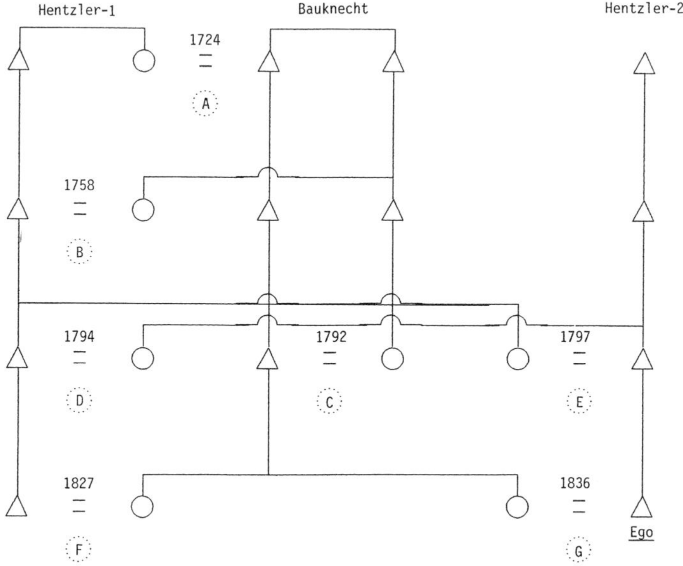

Figure 12.6

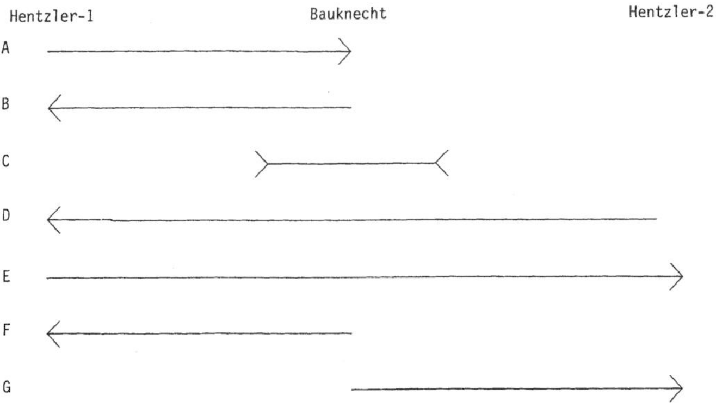

Figure 12.7

could be modeled in terms of exchange between two patrilines. After all, it proceeds upward through women (MM) and downward through women (DD). Yet the larger picture shows a series of exchanges through patrilines, rather more complicated but nonetheless repeated and regular. In this instance, there were three lines in play. In generation III (C) the Bauknechts (1792) made a patrilateral parallel second-cousin marriage (FFBSD). The two Hentzler lines also exchanged daughters (D and E), setting up an exchange relation (among many others) after maintaining a separate existence for six generations. In any event, Hentzler-1 and Bauknecht had already exchanged daughters twice (A and B). In the generation after the two Hentzler lines exchanged daughters, the Bauknechts provided wives to both lines (F and G) (Figure 12.7).

In 1820 Jacob Bauknecht married Maria Barbara Hentzler, his FFFBDDD (3, Figure 12.4). This marriage can be analyzed in the same terms as the previous one, as part of the system of alliances between the Bauknecht patriline and Hentzler-2. It can also be seen as the marriage of siblings (Johann Daniel and Maria Barbara Hentzler) to second cousins (Jacob and Louise Bauknecht: FFBSD), concluded in 1836 by the marriage of Johann Daniel and Louise.

The final Hentzler/Bauknecht alliance (4, Figure 12.4) is interesting even though the relationship cannot be traced. Friedrich Bauknecht's father immigrated from Gross-bettlingen. How or if he was related to the patriline we have been discussing is not known, but it seems significant that the second generation in the village was making marriage alliances of the same kind as the other Bauknecht family.

As mentioned earlier, second cousin marriages were frequent in the later decades of the eighteenth century and continued to be so into the nineteenth. In fact, alliances struck between families issued into renewed alliances in the next or following generation. When each specific relation is examined by itself, tracing can take place through relatives on both sides (the combinations encountered so far are MFZDD, MFBDD, MMBSD, MMBDD, FMBDD, FFBSD). Yet on closer inspection, one finds a series of exchanges between patrilines, which means

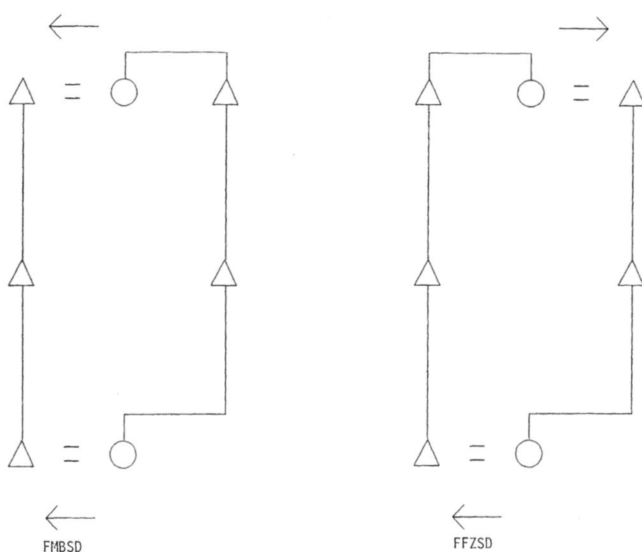

Figure 12.8

that the closest path was perhaps not always the relevant one for concluding an alliance. On the other hand, there may be a different point of view from which to consider any particular alliance. Perhaps men were constructing a system on the basis of their desires and needs, which resulted in the pattern of patriline exchange found here. Yet women may have been crucial for negotiating any particular marriage, working their own networks and constructing relations in their own interest. That could account for the several direct cognatic or uterine paths that are detected in an overarching agnatic structure.[5]

The second-cousin paths do point up the important principle that exchange in the later decades of the eighteenth century most frequently involved alternate generations. A relationship such as FMBSD or FFZSD expresses such an alliance between two lines in the simplest terms. In the case of the FMBSD (generalized exchange), the alliance works by one line providing wives for another in each alternate generation, whereas the FFZSD lines exchange wives back and forth (restricted exchange) (Figure 12.8).[6] The question is, did the system as a whole tend to follow a pattern of restricted exchange, or did it pursue more open, generalized exchange? Perhaps alliances between particular families favored one strategy over another, some preferring a tight alliance between two families, ex-

[5] The point is similar to one made by Pierre Bourdieu, *Outline of a Theory of Practice,* trans. Richard Nice (Cambridge, 1977), pp. 30ff., and elaborated by Ladislav Holy, *Kinship, Honour and Solidarity: Cousin Marriage in the Middle East* (Manchester, 1989), which distinguishes between "official" or "public" (male) and "inofficial" or "private" (female) explanations for particular alliances. In my material, no glosses on conduct are to be found in the sources.

[6] In the diagram, lines descend only from males in order to make the patrilines visually clear.

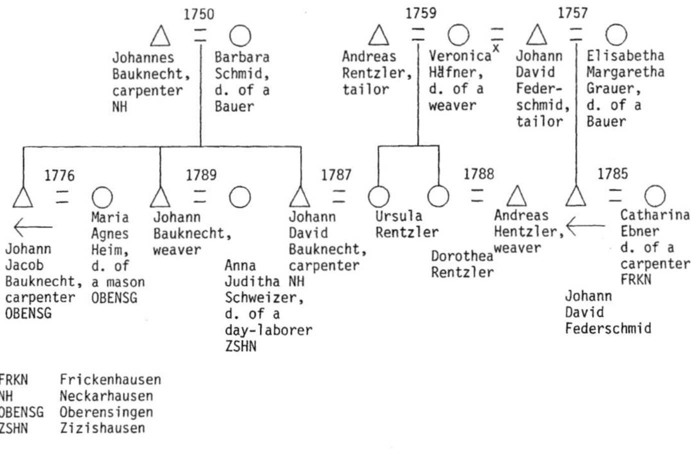

Figure 12.9

changing marriage partners directly back and forth, whereas others formed a larger kindred, linking three, four, or five patrilines together. The importance of Levi-Strauss's distinctions lie in the way families circulate property among themselves and set up the terms of long-lasting symmetrical or asymmetrical exchange. Figures 12.5 and 12.7 do not yet answer the question but point more or less to mixed strategies. I will come back to the issue with more evidence in hand.

An artisan genealogy

Before looking further at a particular case of cousin marriage, it would be well to examine a typical artisan family in which endogamy did not occur. I have chosen to look at the children of Andreas Rentzler, tailor, and along with them the offspring of Johannes Bauknecht, carpenter (Figure 12.9). *This example consists of two small artisan families that were allied with the marriage in 1787 of Johann David Bauknecht and Ursula Rentzler. Johann David was a carpenter, as were his father and elder brother Johann Jacob, who married into Oberensingen. Another brother was a weaver who married a woman from Zisishausen. Ursula Rentzler's father and stepfather were tailors. Her sister married a weaver, and a brother emigrated after marrying the daughter of a carpenter from Frickenhausen. None of the marriages of this group of small artisans were consanguineal. There were no patrilines that had maintained an alliance over several generations.*

Second-cousin marriages

Some of the principles of the system of alliances should be clear by now. In order to show the typicality of our findings, I explore the genealogy associated with the second-cousin marriage of Johann David Hentzler (IX), who married

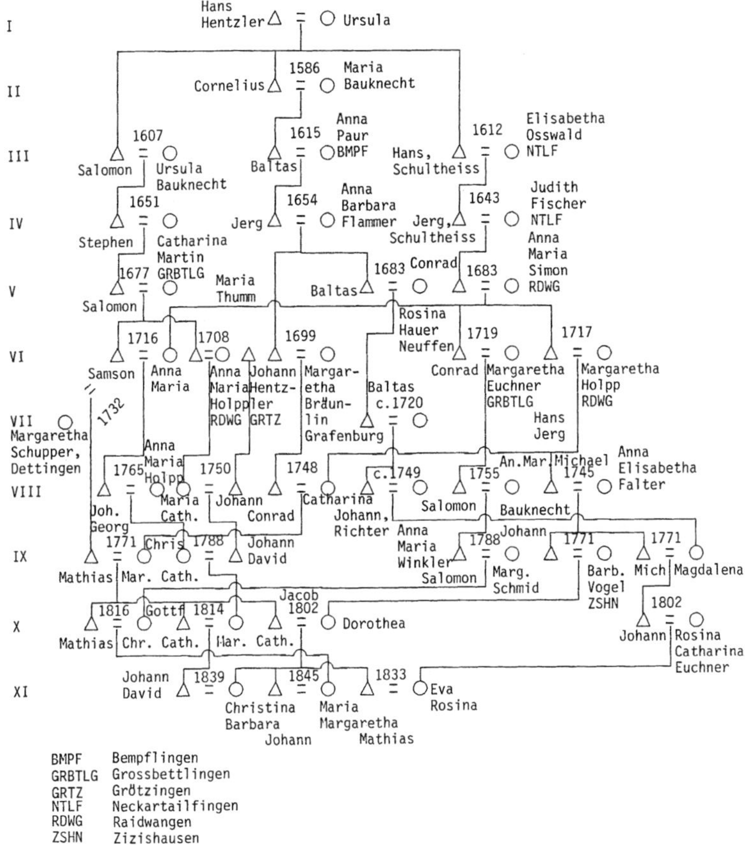

Figure 12.10

his MFBSD in 1788 (Figure 12.10). I have drawn the lines of the Hentzler family preceding this marriage and then looked at the two subsequent generations to see if and in what way the exchanges suggested by that marriage were continued.

It will make our task easier to proceed step by step through the diagram.

1. This deals with three main branches of the Raidwangen family of Hans Hentzler and Ursula (I), sons born in the 1560s and 1570s: Salomon (III), Cornelius (II), and Hans (III).

2. Up through generation V there was no intermarriage between the lines, and wives frequently came from outside the village – between 6 and 8 out of 11. No one in generation V married anyone related up to third cousin of any kind, and the fact that no Hentzler married another Hentzler at all argues for complete lineal exogamy.

3. The period when kin were not sought out for marriage lasted from the 1560s to the early eighteenth century, more than 150 years.

4. Generation VI saw the first marriage between the three lines. Line 3 (that of Hans) provided a wife for line 1 (that of Salomon): Conrad's daughter, Anna Maria, married Samson (1716).

5. Generation VIII saw further examples. Line 3 provided a wife for line 2: the daughter of Hans Jerg Hentzler (VI), Catharina, for Conrad Hentzler (FFFFBSSSD). The daughter of the Raidwangen Schultheiss Salomon, Maria Catharina (line 1) married in Neckarhausen the son of an immigrant Hentzler from Grötzingen. In generation IX, line 2 provided a wife: (Maria Catharina, daughter of Conrad (VIII) for Mathias Hentzler (line 1), his FFFFBSSSSD. Thus during the period, roughly 1720 to the 1770s, marriages established alliances between lines that had maintained independent identities over the seventeenth century. Despite the fact that the surnames were the same, the long period of exogamy made marriages between various Hentzlers in the first half of the eighteenth century conform to the alliance pattern that existed for other families. Note also the marriage in generation VIII of a Hentzler (Johann) from Grötzingen with the daughter of Salomon, the Raidwangen Schultheiss.

6. Beginning in generation IX, the rhythm of exchange quickened and the cycles shortened. Johann David, while descended from the Grötzingen immigrant (Johann, VI), was related to his wife through his mother: his MFBSD (second cousin). Michael Hentzler of line 3 married a woman of line 2, a generation after a woman had gone the other way. That did not make them close relatives if one focuses on the path between them; he married his FFFFFBSSSSSD, or FZHFBSSD. His father's sister had been married to a grandson of Baltas Hentzler, and he married another grandson's daughter. Generation VIII and IX, from ca. 1750 to the 1780s, demonstrated shorter circuits of exchange.

7. In generations X and XI, the first 40 years of the nineteenth century, the circuits of exchange became shorter still and more frequent. Mathias Hentzler (X) from line 1 married the daughter of Salomon (IX) from line 3, his FFWBSSD: line 3 had provided his grandfather with a wife, and him with a wife. Gottfried (X) married a woman from the Grötzingen line, his FxBDD – the Grötzingen line had received a wife from and in the next generation provided a wife for line 1. Jacob (X), also from line 1, received a wife from line 3, just as his brother Mathias, his MMBSD. Johann David (XI) married his FBD (i.e., within line 1). Johann (XI) married his FBD, also within line 1. Mathias married his MFBSD (and his FMMSSSD), that is, just as line 3 had provided a wife for his father, it also did for him.

8. Overall, the exchanges between the three lines were not symmetrical. From generation VI to XI, line 1 received six wives from the other two and made two internal first cousin marriages (FBD). It never provided wives for lines 2 or 3 and only traded with the Grötzinger Hentzlers. Particularly strong was the connection with line 3, where the alliance was maintained by steady traffic in one direction. One finds many examples of this phenomenon, where, in a long-term alliance between two families, one of them systematically provided wives for the other in a pattern of generalized exchange.

Patrilines or matrilines?

It is possible, of course, that modeling in terms of patrilines is a fiction. One could perhaps draw any diagram and show that some line or other exchanged with another one. To test whether this is so, I have taken the last generation represented on the previous diagram and drawn the matrilines – back through the MMM . . . – to see what results I would get (Figure 12.11). The diagram here shows clearly that there are no matrilines between which marriage partners were exchanged. Part of the reason seems to be their comparative length, since at some point or other the apical person migrated into the village. However, between the point at which a matriline can be traced back and the starting point of the reckoning, there is no systematic, recurrent cross-generational exchange at all.

Hentzlers and Bauknechts

These examples have shown repeated exchanges between various branches of the Hentzler family and between Bauknechts and Hentzlers. Although they were particularly prominent members of the village, their pattern of alliance did not differ from other landholding agricultural producers. A more systematic examination brings together some of the elements discovered thus far. For this exercise, I examined the patrilines of what we have been calling Hentzler-1 and 3 and one of the branches of the Bauknecht family. To start with, I looked at all the male descendants of four Bauknecht first cousins who married between 1720 and 1735. The line of Hentzler-1 involved two sets of siblings who were first cousins, marrying between 1734 and 1771. Finally, for Hentzler-3, I selected two second cousins who married in 1745 and 1755, respectively. I followed these people, their parents, and all of their descendants through to marriages contracted up to 1820 (and adding data from the marriages of the children of the last generation). That is, I examined 53 marriages of the Bauknecht line, 72 of Hentzler-1, and 19 of Henztler-3.

To keep the analysis simple, I concentrated on alliances between Bauknecht and Hentzler-1 and between Hentzler-1 and Hentzler-3. In the Hentzler case, 8 of the marriages that the Hentzler-3 patriline made were with Hentzler-1, and in most cases (6), Hentzler-3 families provided wives for the other patriline. Some alliances were characterized by movement in one direction, and as the nineteenth-century cohorts will show, there were several instances in which one line provided wives for another over several generations, expressing a logic of generalized exchange. Other alliances involved many marriages in one direction for a concentrated period with a reversed flow in a later period, one or two generations later. In this instance, between 1792 and 1816, the line of Hentzler-3 provided four wives for Hentzler-1. A generation later (1828–36), half of the four marriages between them reversed direction. To analyze such a structure for restricted exchange, it will not do to test for the frequency of FZD marriages but will be

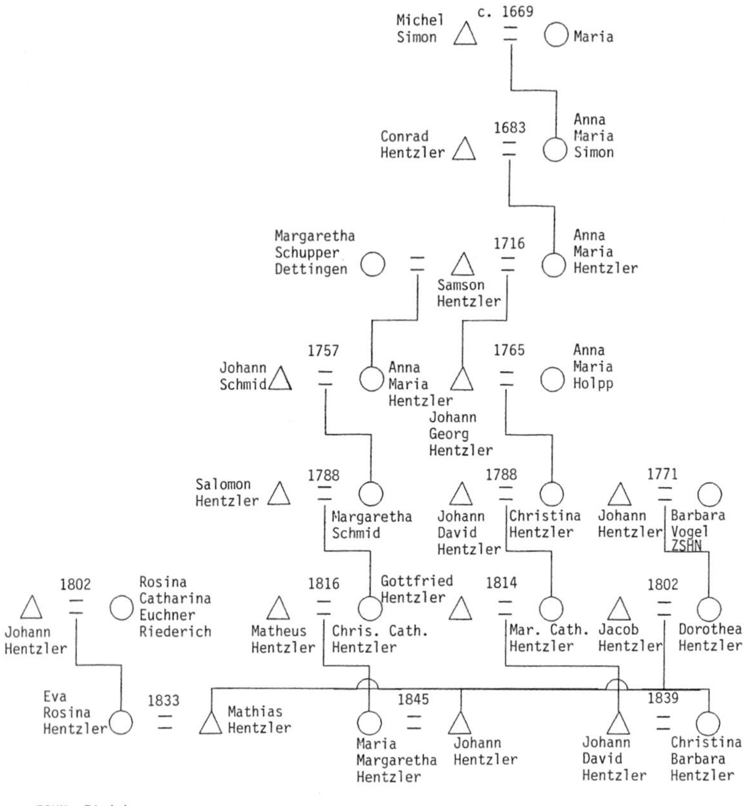

Figure 12.11

necessary to establish the overall intergenerational pattern. This latter pattern does appear to offer an instance in which here two families developed particularly intense relations. It suggests that for social, economic, or political purposes, two families could coordinate a policy of restrictive integration over a generation or two.

It is possible to model the relations between two lines in terms of debt relations, although how one member of a line would feel the debt/credit obligations of another member – say a second cousin or great uncle – remains obscure. It is most likely that the practices developed through intense kin interaction, socializing family members to orient their desires in certain directions.[7] In any event, the marriage exchange can create or maintain alliances that may involve all kinds of other transactions. From Hentzler-3 to Hentzler-1 over a very long period (the first marriage connecting them was in 1716), there was a positive flow of

[7] On desire and debt, see Margaret Trawick, *Notes on Love in a Tamil Family* (Berkeley, 1990), pp. 117–86.

wives, putting Hentzler-1 in a negative position. It would be possible to search systematically all of the records from Neckarhausen for all connections between all members of the two lines, but such an analysis would be too tedious to carry out here. However, some important trends can be detected in godparentage, the other systematic form of alliance. Over the entire period, 13 Hentzler-3 families asked at least one person from Hentzler-1 families to act as godparent for their children. In terms of debt/credit relationships, the flow was reversed: Hentzler-1 families provided Gevattern and Hentzler-3 families provided wives. In fact, the connection was first forged through ritual kinship. By the time the two lines contracted several marriages together (between 1792 and 1816), they had been linked through multiple strands of godparentage for four decades, and if one goes back to a marriage in the 1720s, for seven. Earlier in the discussion of Cohort II, I suggested that the exchange of wives was toward the more powerful patrilines. Throughout much of the eighteenth century, godparentage continued to express asymmetrical power relations as well, with the more powerful families offering godparents to their clients. In this instance, the pattern worked reciprocally. The less powerful Hentzler-3 families provided wives for the more powerful Hentzler-1 line and in turn received godparents from them. Although the links between the two lines were particularly intimate, their alliances, of course, did not inhibit either line from making others. A patriline with numerous members such as Hentzler-1 was able to maintain multiple alliances. Moreover, alliances between any particular line (A) and two others (B and C) were frequently paralleled by further alliances between the associated lines (B and C). Sometimes one branch of a line began a series of exchanges with a new family and in that process differentiated itself from other members of its own line. After a time, if that branch or its allied line did not marry back to the root, they ceased to share any characteristics outside of a surname.

As noted in Chapters 1 and 9, the Gevatter relation involved continuity in several different ways. It was the practice all the way from 1700 to 1870 for a set of godparents to stand for all of the children of a couple. Various occurrences might interrupt a sequence, of course, but it was also frequently the custom to find a close relative of the godparent to succeed or substitute for him or her. This aspect of duration must be taken into consideration in the alliances between families. A Doete/Gevatter maintained in principle a life-long relationship with a godchild and the latter's parent, but the practice of a godparent standing for all of the children over a period of 10 to 15 years continually repeated the exchange and reinforced the relationship. Similarly, a marriage established a continuing relationship between relatives of the spouses. In the Hentzler-3/Hentzler-1 situation, the two sets of people had been linked over long, overlapping periods through ritual kinship. During the period when they first intermarried a great deal (1792–1816), they also created many links through godparentage. In another respect, there had also been continuity in godparent relations in the village: recall that during the first half of the eighteenth century, generations of a family were systematically linked to the same godparents or their descendants. In many cases, a father, son, and grandson or their wives acted as Gevattern for several generations of the same family. That kind of continuity broke down by midcentury as people began to choose kin as godparents, but it appears to have issued into another kind of persistence. Various patrilines maintained relations over time through marriage and godparentage. It was not necessary for the descendants of one family to choose the successors of their parents' Gevattern for their own. Rather, the larger patriline provided a field from which godparents could be found. In some cases, a marriage exchange became the basis for ritual kin exchanges, while in others the Gevatter relation preceded marriage exchanges. Both appear to have been part of an interlocking system of obligation and solidarity. The maintenance of such relations provided a grid, so to speak, within which complex choices were made. Constraints were part of the bargain, but since the strands linking any one individual with others were multiplex, there was also considerable flexibility.

Between 1724 and 1849, the Bauknecht line examined here made a quarter (14) of their 53 marriages with Hentzler line 1 (almost a third of the 72 marriages made by Hentzler-1 were with the 2 lines Bauknecht and Hentzler-3). In their case, there appears to have been a reversal of direction every generation (restricted exchange). In the 1720s the Bauknechts received two wives from Hentzler-1 and in the 1750s sent two back while taking one. Between 1780 and 1791, they took 4 wives, but between 1820 and 36 offered 3 and received only 1. By midcentury, although I have not followed many descendants that far, the only marriage found involves the Bauknechts as wife-receivers, which suggests that the flow was reversed once again in that generation.

While the positive and negative flows reversed themselves each generation, there seems to have been no reciprocal flow of ritual kinship. In the 1720s Hentzler-1 sent wives and stood as godparents for the Bauknechts. In the 1750s and 1760s, when they received 2 wives and gave 1, they stood as godparents four times and received godparents once. During the 1780s and 1790s, again Hentzler-1 both offered wives (4) and godparents (5) for a decade and then for two decades (1793–1817) were the recipients of godparents (10). In the 1820s, they received 2 wives and gave 1, were godparents for two families and received godparents for four. By the 1830s, they were again godparents, and in the next decade provided a wife. Over the whole period there was no neat system of exchange whereby one generation offered wives and received godparents. Although the flow of ritual kin did tend to alternate (in the 1750s and 1760s toward the Bauknechts, in the 1770s toward the Hentzlers-1, in the 1780s toward the Bauknechts, in the 1790s through 1810s toward Hentzlers-1 again, in the 1820s in both directions, and in the 1830s toward the Bauknechts again), such periods did not coincide systematically either directly or reciprocally with the flow of wives (1720s toward B, 1750s toward H1, 1780s toward B, 1820s and 1830s toward H1, 1840s toward B). It appears that these two dominant, land-holding, politically active families were over the long period fairly evenly matched but that in any one generation one or the other line provided the central focal point for political

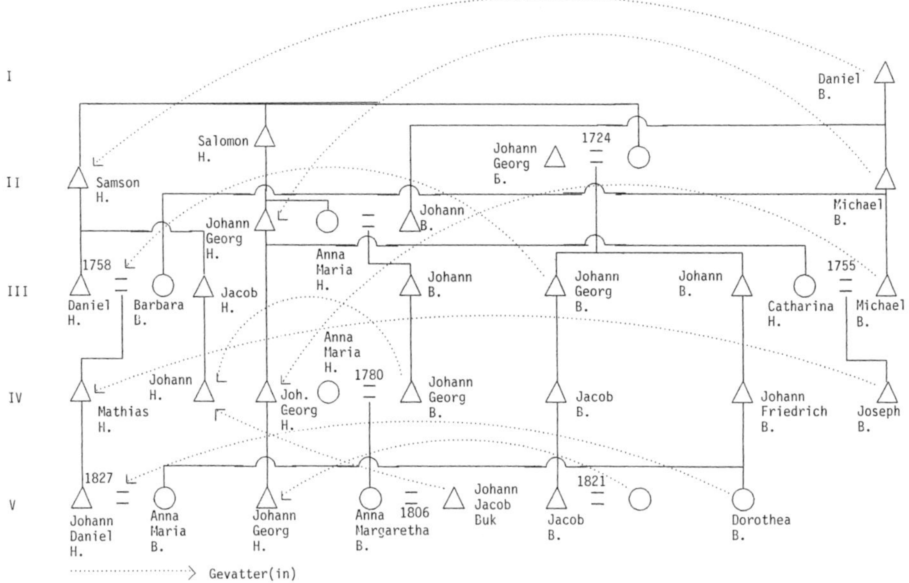

Figure 12.12

organization of kindred activity. The systematic trading of spouses back and forth and the very large number of marriages between the two lines emphasized attempts at tight integration, but neither line was able to dominate the other over the long run. How familial politics worked will be analyzed in more detail in Chapter 16.

Any attempt to diagram a large portion of these exchanges proves confusing since there are so many interrelated strands. The important point to understand is that godparents frequently came from a branch of the related patriline that was not the closest affinal link. Figure 12.12 shows a highly simplified version of one set of exchanges.

In this diagram, the Bauknechts provided godparents nine times for marriages contracted between 1734 and 1827. The Hentzlers provided 5 wives up through generation IV, and the Bauknechts, 1 in generation V. Michael B (II) was a Gevatter for his BWBS, Johann Georg H (III). Michael B's son (III), in turn, was Gevatter for Johann Georg H's son, Johann Georg (IV) – FBWBSS – but he had also married Johann Georg H's daughter and was thus at the same time Gevatter for his WB. Johann Georg B (III) was Gevatter for his MBS, Daniel H, who in turn was married to Johann Georg B's FBD. In the next generation, Joseph B (IV), Johann Georg B's FBSS, was Gevatter for Daniel H's son, Mathias, his FZS. In the final gener-

ation, Jacob B's wife was Gevatterin for Johann Georg H. Although the two patrilines were in constant connection, the closest path between them was HFFMBSSS, and thus offers an example in which people did not choose the closest relatives from an allied patriline.

* * *

The analysis in this chapter has revealed a series of families that allied with each other in multiple ways by the late eighteenth century. Various members of a patriline over a concentrated period would marry members of another patriline, overlaying consanguineal ties with affinal ones or creating multiple affinal ties that would serve as a basis for consanguineal relations as one generation succeeded another. A man's brother-in-law was, of course, his children's uncle. Their respective offspring were cousins. But it is important to understand that a map of potential relations is not equivalent to a social system. The latter is created by claims and dependencies, association, support, exploitation, obligation, service, and domination. Potential relations were put into practice by godparentage, guardianship, and marriage in a systematic way, creating continuing interaction and durable relations. Because such links were so important to people, they could provide the basis for intense conflict and controversy. The practice of kinship described for Cohort IV shows just how often solidarity could be countered by meanness, hatred, and envy. All of these matters were no more random, however, than any other part of social experience.

The families that created multiple, overlapping ties were ones that owned land and controlled agricultural production in the village. In an increasingly populous village at the dawn of a new agricultural era, competition for resources became intense. Landed families arranged to keep property among themselves by developing an endogamous marriage system. During this period, such a practice differentiated them sharply from the handicraft producers and the growing number of people seeking by-employments and engaged in agricultural wage labor. It did so in two ways: the Bauern withdrew, so to speak, to themselves, and in doing so they created a different form of family alliance. A great deal of class practice was carried out through the intensive, multilayered activities of allied kin. But families also allocated scarce resources and created internal boundaries within themselves. By the end of the century, wealthy families with a large progeny frequently had to divide up their property in such a way that children no longer had viable farms. Furthermore, the last generation to come of age at the end of the century held onto property longer than ever before, making it harder for their children to accumulate. Here is where the new market in land played a significant role. The most able children capitalized on kin connections and put together independent farms and in turn continued to build on alliances inherited from their parents and grandparents. Those without the necessary character, skill, or luck fell into the class of poor and out of the pool of potential allies. Family provided chances, but it was up to the individual members to capitalize on them.

This new system of linking patrilines together arose around the mid eighteenth century. During the long seventeenth century, consanguineal kin carefully avoided each other as marriage partners, going to lengths not demanded or expected by the laws of incest prohibition. The implications of the new alliances formed early in the eighteenth century were worked out in a context in which cousin relations were being constructed – on the basis of land partition from inheritance, agricultural cooperation, and above all from political coordination. Quite often, ties of ritual kinship preceded a renewed alliance by marriage. In many instances, one strand linking families was not enough, and several grappling hooks were cast out in a period of concentrated action. Cousinship became an important principle in redistributing wealth both in terms of the property market and in terms of the control of marriages. Many families sought to marry off their children at the end of their teens or in their early 20s to secure and maintain an alliance. Alliances, however, were just that. They provided a basis for claims and obligations, but they did not predetermine action. How the structural aspects of the social system worked out in practice has to be investigated in the biographies of individual villagers or in the detailed protocols of official investigations, an exercise taken up in Chapter 16.

13

Ritual kinship and alternative alliance

All along I have been arguing that both marriage and ritual kinship offer forms of exchange that establish durable relationships between individuals, houses, and families. Each form of alliance in Neckarhausen set up channels along which exchanges of various kinds could flow. There were, of course, other relationships (such as guardianship) that also set up long-term connections between people, but the field from which guardians, Kriegsvögte, and the like were chosen was usually already marked out by marriage alliance or by the prior selection of godparents. Not long after any couple married, they chose two Gevatter(inne)n who in principle stood by them in the church every two years or so for up to two decades and who would be associated as Doten/Döten with the children of the house as long as they lived. Whatever the particular nature of this persisting relationship, the continuing connection itself is evidence of a continually reinforced bond between several households and their kin and friends.

What godparentage was in itself is not easy to specify. It always had a protean aspect. Even people who were not especially pious chose (or had to choose) godparents for their children, which underlines the fact that its spiritual meaning was never stable, or at least not always straightforward.[1] Some anthropologists have tried to find a universal desideratum in the institution, whereby godparents are thought to represent society at large while parents pull in the direction of the family.[2] Family and parents in this solution to the problem anchor children in the specific, traditional, and private, while godparents offer a counterpole, opening their charges up to the larger community. Symbolically, at least, the

[1] Karl Marx and Friedrich Engels were godparents for Liebknecht.

[2] Julian Pitt-Rivers, "Ritual Kinship in the Mediterranean: Spain and the Balkans," in J. G. Peristiany, ed., *Mediterranean Family Structures* (Cambridge, 1976), pp. 317–34.

godparent did take part in a ritual that bestowed a social identity on a newborn infant and in a sense guaranteed the legitimacy or familial status of the child to the larger community – the child's name was not spoken until baptism so as not to make it susceptible to evil attack.[3] Yet neither the community nor the family could be stable entities, and as godparents in Neckarhausen were drawn from an ever smaller circle of kin, it is difficult to think of the polarity between parents and ritual kin as constant in any way. But it is also unlikely that godparents played the same role for each family at any one time. For some people, the institution reinforced bonds of friendship, whereas for others it established patronage relationships. And the man who chose his brother set up rather different possibilities from the man who chose his father's first cousin. From time to time, the records indicate strong emotions centered on ritual kinship, but taken together, all such occurrences do not add up to a single meaning. I think of godparentage as being similar to one of those rivers in Los Angeles that has been channeled into a concrete bed. Much of the year nothing courses through it, but during a storm, it can handle considerable amounts of water. Ritual kinship always has something potential about it, but most crucially it keeps open a permanent line of communication. Now and then, odd things can be tracked along it, but there can also be moments of intense activity. Other forms of communication can run parallel to it just as roads run along a river – marked out by the contours of the landscape – but not necessarily interacting with each other directly. Moreover, just as it is hard to give a definition to a Los Angeles river – and witticisms often run to images derived from sewerage – so is it hard to figure out just what valence to give ritual kinship. What are we to make of the Württemberg saying that if you want to make someone your enemy, first make him your godparent?[4]

Even if it becomes almost impossible to give an account of very many of the ways godparentage could be used in practice, the kinds of people it hooked up can be examined. Significantly, although ritual kinship was slowly reordered in the same direction as marriage, connecting particular kinds of people in new ways, it always moved somewhat in the rear guard. It continued to tie households together along older lines while new relationships were being forged – through marriage and, for some sectors of the population, through the deployment of godparentage itself. The example of Schultheiss Johann Georg Rieth III and his mother at midcentury is instructive. She had maintained relationships with families that had been tied to the Rieths over many generations, while he failed to renew those connections and turned toward his politically well-placed cousins. Over many years, therefore, the family maintained two parallel but opposite strategies of godparentage.

[3] Karl Bohnenberger, ed., *Volkstümliche Ueberlieferungen in Württemberg: Glaube – Brauch – Heilkunde* (Stuttgart, 1980; original 1904ff.), p. 87.
[4] "Gevatter," in Hermann Fischer, *Schwäbisches Lexikon*, 6 vols. (Tübingen, 1904–36).

Cohort III (1780–1789)

Although the social significance of godparentage was changing in the later decades of the eighteenth century, the two faces of the institution – one oriented toward class and familial endogamy and the other toward integrating different groups in the village – were not simply represented by different generations no longer in synch with each other. Ritual kinship continued over several generations to mediate between older and younger people, landed and land-poor, politically powerful and weak, while the politics of marriage more rapidly cut off older circuits of exchange. Yet the ambivalences between the two ways of connecting people were already apparent, and godparentage soon followed the lead of marital politics. By the early nineteenth century, the age differences between parents and godparents would disappear, all godparents would be chosen from very close consanguineal relatives, and they would come from the same class as the parents. The system of choosing godparents prolonged the transition from a kinship system based on clientage to one based on endogamy and eased for a time the more brutal politics of marriage alliance. The different elements of kinship each moved at their own pace and had separate histories but reflected back on one another, presenting at each moment a continually renegotiated social logic.

This chapter turns to the particular relationships that ritual kinship established, with the way people were connected to, or divided from, one another. Whenever individuals were chosen as godparents, others were not chosen – choice bound and cut at the same time. The question here is how the connections between classes were redrawn, what role ritual kinship played in the developing cohesion within class, and what kinds of already existing kin were selected for special emphasis by a redoubling of the relationship with godparentage. As Chapter 12 has shown, the landed population in the village used ritual kinship in coordination with marriage to construct interlocking, durable alliances. This chapter opens by examining single strands of relationship, but the objective will be to see how larger encompassing groups were brought together. Although a second cousin chosen as a godparent could not become a guardian, his or her brother could. To understand any particular tie, one must see how they all fit together.

Once again, it will be seen that cousinship became extremely important for the construction of alliance toward the end of the eighteenth century. Although alliances involved systematic exchanges between patrilines (Chapter 12), women may well have become players in cousin politics. From a larger point of view, a particular marriage might have looked like an exchange in a series of agnatically structured exchanges, but a closer, more direct path constructed over women could also sometimes be discerned. Indeed, the following pages show that women began to play cousin politics in the choice of godparents as well, which strengthens the indication that they were actively entering into the construction of family alliances. And since the system of godparentage has already been examined among independent peasants, the extended analysis in this chapter will focus on an artisan family.

Table 13.1. *Cohort III: Parents' and godparents' tax quartiles.*

	Godparents' tax quartile							
Parents' tax quartile	I	II	III	IV	Nonvillagers	Not given	Total	(Magistrates[a])
I	0	0	2	1	1	9	13	(1)
II	0	1	6	12	4	7	30	(6)
III	1	3	3	13	1	4	25	(12)
IV	0	1	6	6	2	0	15	(4)

[a]Schultheiss, Gericht, Rat: included in wealth figures.

Table 13.2. *Cohort III: Traceable kin by tax group.*

Tax group	N Traceable Kin	Total	%
I	10	13	77.0
II	22	30	73.3
III	23	25	92.0
IV	12	15	80.0
Not given	5	8	62.5

Selection of godparents

For the cohort from 1780 to 1789, it is again possible to use data from the tax register to correlate parents' and godparents' standings in the wealth hierarchy (Table 13.1). By this time also, occupations were given with greater regularity in the various sources.

Toward the end of the century, Bauern tended to find their godparents almost exclusively within their own ranks (Table 13.2). This included those Bauern who also were partly occupied with weaving, who were also among the more substantial members of the village. That they chose no artisans at all as Gevattern meant that the class of landholders were solidifying their relationships by finding ritual kin entirely from their own ranks. When wealthy Bauern from tax quartile IV found godparents from quartile III, it was still from among the landed agriculturalists and not the wealthy artisans that they did so. By the end of the eighteenth century, the Bauern had created tight, overlapping ties among themselves. On the other hand, artisans overwhelmingly sought their godparents not from among their own peers but from among the Bauern, those people who increasingly occupied all the important offices in the village and who of course provided the customers for smiths, tailors, coopers, carpenters, and other craftsmen.

Table 13.3. *Cohort III: Parents' and godparents' occupation.*

	Godparents' occupation				
Parents' occupation	Bauer/Shepherd	Bauer-weaver	Publican	Artisan	Day-laborer
Bauer/Shepherd	31	4	1	0	0
Bauer-weaver	5	0	0	0	0
Publican	—	—	—	—	—
Artisan	22	2	1	5	0
Day-laborer	2	0	0	2	1

Most of the individuals in tax quartile I who also largely chose godparents from among kin were in fact designated in the register as "Bauern" (Tables 13.1 and 13.3). Either they were just starting out by the time they appeared in the tax register and were not yet in full control of their inheritances, or they rented enough land outside their own tax liability to receive the designation "Bauer" and not "day-laborer." Still, they sought their godparents for the most part from among the wealthier villagers.[5]

As at midcentury, the people in tax quartile III were strongly dependent on those wealthier than themselves for godparents (Table 13.1). But they were particularly dependent on the village magistrates, far more so than any other group. Smaller agriculturalists and the more substantial handicraftsmen still tended to seek out the patronage of wealthier, politically powerful relatives. Those lower down the scale simply tied themselves to the more wealthy and do not seem to have made up part of the clientage of the village administrative and political elite.

For the first cohort, I described a circle of consanguinity in which no godparents were chosen. By midcentury, 61.0 percent were chosen from within it, but by the 1780s only 38.4 percent (Table A.14). However, if the spouses of the godparents are included, the figures are 40.9 percent, 86.4 percent, and 79.5 percent, respectively. Within the tendency to narrow the range of choices, there was an ever greater propensity to look for second cousins for Gevattern. In the first cohort, there had been only 1. By the second, there were 5 second cousins, making up 8.5 percent of kin-linked godparents. In this cohort, there were 15 second cousins or spouses (20.5 percent). All cousins and their spouses made up 56.2 percent of kin-linked parents, a significant rise from midcentury (32.2 percent). The process of familialization of the institution involved the systematic inclusion of consanguineal kin descended from common ancestors, together with their spouses.

As mentioned earlier, there was a gradual lowering of the age differential between godparents and spouses over the century. But it was not until after the

[5] In this case, the large number of godparents in the "Not Given" category were dead before the tax register of 1785 was composed. Evidence from estate inventories indicates that they were among the wealthier Bauern.

beginning of the nineteenth century that the differences disappeared altogether. In the later decades of the eighteenth century, godparents were still 5.88 and 7.20 years older on average than the fathers and mothers they represented. This is a reflection of the general trend away from very much older, nonrelated officials and landholders, although the differences in age were still not inconsiderable, and godparents continued frequently to connect generations together. In this cohort, the pastor dropped away altogether and the schoolmaster and Schultheiss were barely represented. Members of the Gericht and Rat remained prominent, only to drop out abruptly in their turn after the beginning of the century.

One immediately apparent change is the radical shift in this cohort away from sisters as Gevatterinnen for the wives. But women were clearly tending more and more to find godparents from among their own kin. By this generation, they utilized uncles and aunts, siblings, close in-laws, and first and second cousins, without any special preference or weight given to a particular relation. Women narrowed down their choice, avoiding nonkin for the most part, but maintained an open flexibility, searching for close but often not immediate relatives to tie themselves to socially. A large majority of godparents on the wife's side were traced through the father, brother, or first husband (72.2 percent). And quite a large number (52.7 percent) were from the senior generation, which emphasized relations between generations, something that would disappear at the beginning of the next century.

The meaning of innovations in the choice of godparents does not lie on the surface, and there is no unambiguous correlation to be found. The first two cohorts reveal a special relationship between sisters, indicated by several different aspects of marriage and godparent choice. But women used no sisters at the beginning of the century as Gevatterinnen, only to choose them for almost a third of their kin-linked godparents by midcentury. The use or nonuse of siblings for ritual kinship does not say much about their relationships directly. It may well have been that the practices of godparentage were changing while the particular constellations between brothers and sisters remained constant. The contrasts of behavior between men and women capture some of the differences. In the first cohort, wives frequently traced through their sisters to find a godparent while husbands traced through their brothers. Two generations later, when people shifted to finding a majority of their godparents from among kin, the close, direct bond between sisters was demonstrated in their frequent selection as Gevatterinnen. By the late decades of the eighteenth century, the practice of using kin for godparents was solidified, but women then chose to use that institution to maintain and develop relations with rather extended agnatic kin. This does not necessarily reflect on the tenor of relations between sisters but does argue that women became active participants in maintaining social networks that had been constructed on agnatic principles. I have already pointed out that gender spheres of work and social reproduction in the first six or seven decades of the eighteenth century sharply divided men and women from each other. Suffice it to say here that sisters were part of a mutual support system, which probably altered under the pressure of changing productive relations. The move away from sisters to agnatic kin as godparents took place within a trend toward choosing ever more kin as godparents. If one assumes that roughly half of the godparents in each cohort were chosen by women, then the percentage that were linked to them through kinship were, respectively, 15.1, 59.2, and 80.0. Thus the lack of sisters late in the century is even more striking. The systematic alliances between patrilines developed for the wealthier villagers were clearly maintained, fostered, and sometimes created by women. They systematically searched among their fathers' kin and first cousins for people to associate with their families over the entire course of child-bearing and beyond.

In the first book on Neckarhausen, I argued that women's work began to change during the last three decades of the eighteenth century as hoe crops and stall feeding slowly began to be introduced into the agricultural round. Over the long run the entire relationship of women to agricultural production was reconfigured. I suggested that their new productive roles gave them a space from which to entertain novel notions about the balance of exchange within the household. Be that as it may, about the time that women were drawn into field production, flax preparation, and stall feeding, they began to make their pressure felt in familial politics, at least those aspects that involved the construction and maintenance of long-term alliances. It was not until after the turn of the century that women created a critical discourse about the "house" and began frequently to sue for separation or divorce. Exactly how to sort out the interconnections between productive and reproductive labor is not immediately apparent, but women did begin to insert themselves in familial politics and reconfigure their place both in the house and in the construction and maintenance of alliance. The close association of sisters early in the century points toward a social formation quite different from the one emerging at the turn of the century. Although, not too much evidence is available on the crucial issues of work and culture for the early period, it is clear that once kinship was redeployed and subject to other strategical considerations, women found a new space in which to maneuver.

The husbands in this cohort also emphasized relationships traced through their fathers, and they too had a substantial number of godparents from the generational level above themselves. For both husbands and wives, cousinship emerged as centrally important during this period. Two conclusions seem inescapable. First, the rising importance of second cousins as godparents coincided with similar shifts for marriage. The whole force of the movement in the second half of the eighteenth century was toward the inclusion of second cousins as marriageable partners and both first and second cousins as ritual kin. Even families that did not marry close relatives did utilize siblings, in-laws, and cousins for godparents, a phenomenon explored in this chapter's extended example. The second conclusion reinforces my earlier finding that as one proceeds outward from the closest to more extended relationships, tracing through the male line becomes more important: for first cousins, relatives of the mother predominated, whereas for second cousins, relatives of the father did so. The forms of the second-cousin relationships are depicted in Figure 13.1.

The use of second cousins or first cousins once removed could well have been a matter of young parents continuing ties constructed by their own parents, particularly those of the fathers. Out of the set of close ties constructed by a man, his son or daughter selected one to emphasize by asking a particular individual to play the godparent role. In several cases, of course, women found Gevatter(inne)n by tracing over a network through their mothers (19, 21, 22), but they more frequently worked connections through their fathers (12–18). Basically, these examples reflect two types of networks, one in which a godparent was located in the same patriline and one in which he or she came from an allied patriline. Examples 3, 4, 7, 8, 16, and 17 readily illustrate how the godparent was selected from a patriline allied by marriage. But how some of the examples involve allied agnatic groups may not be apparent at first glance, so need to be refigured, to permit clearer analysis. Case 10 (Figure 13.2) provides a useful starting point. In this instance, lines A and B became allied in generation I. In generation III, ego chose a Gevatter from the allied patriline, the husband of his second cousin. Case 15 is similar in structure, while case 18 reverses the way the alliance is set up (Figure 13.3). This time, lines A and B also became allied in generation I. Ego in generation III, line A, chose a godparent from generation II, line B, wife of her first cousin once removed. Examples 6, 12, 18, 20, 21, and 22 have to do with interacting allied patrilines in analogous ways.

Another main feature of this generation, the connection forged in this generation between a parent and godparent was not broken with the death of one of the parties. When a surviving parent remarried, the godparents for the next set of children were frequently the same as for the first set. The relatives of the first wife or husband often continued to function as godparents. This means that from the point of view of a particular house, alliances constructed in this fashion were long-term alliances and continued to function even when the linking spouse died. In the same way, when a godparent died, someone closely related to him or her became a substitute. This reinforces the point that alliance occurred not only between individuals, in a single-stranded and personal way, but also involved a larger group of people coordinating their activities and interests.

A good case in point can be seen in Figure 13.4. Notice that with Catharina Beck's first marriage her godmother (Gevatterin) was the Ehesuccessor of her aunt (FZHW). The other godparent was her husband's uncle (HMB). When she remarried after Schober's death, the same two people remained godparents. Ebinger had no Gevatter related to himself, and although one godparent was a relative of his new wife, the other was related to her original husband. As in a continuing household, the same social links constructed through godparentage continued to be in play. When Johannes Brodbeck dropped out as Gevatter, he was replaced by his brother. After Catharina Beck's death, Johann Georg Ebinger married a woman from another village. This time the godparents from the second marriage were kept once more. At that point, none

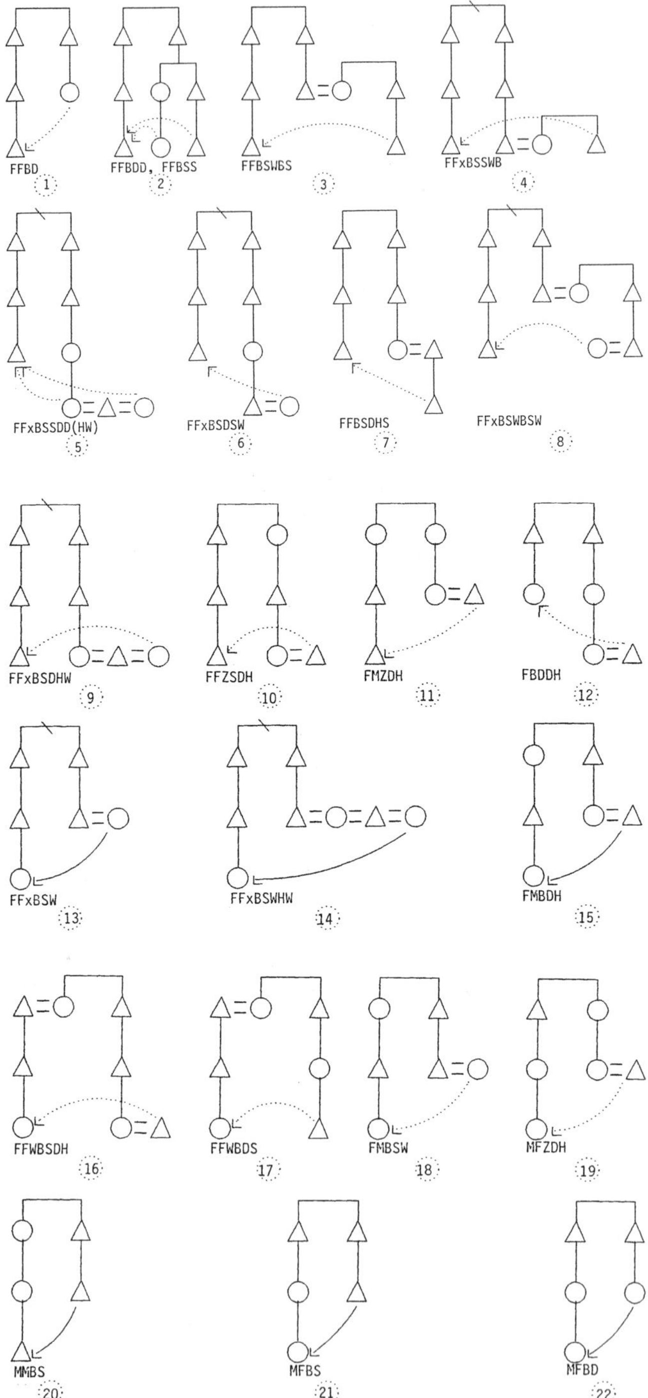
FFBD
1
FFBDD, FFBSS
2
FFBSWBS
3
FFxBSSWB
4
FFxBSSDD(HW)
5
FFxBSDSW
6
FFBSDHS
7
FFxBSWBSW
8
FFxBSDHW
9
FFZSDH
10
FMZDH
11
FBDDH
12
FFxBSW
13
FFxBSWHW
14
FMBDH
15
FFWBSDH
16
FFWBDS
17
FMBSW
18
MFZDH
19
MMBS
20
MFBS
21
MFBD
22

Figure 13.1

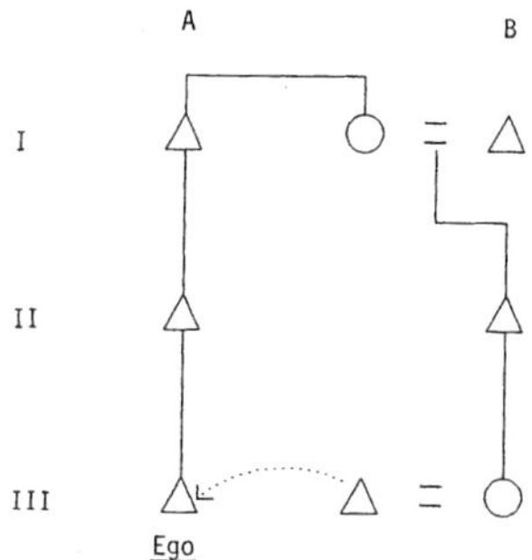

Figure 13.2

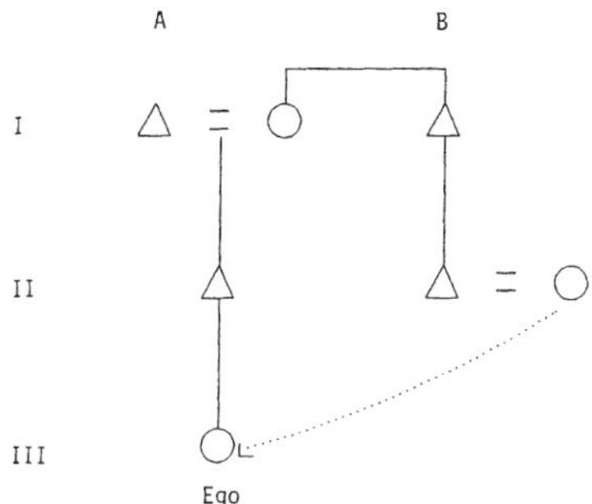

Figure 13.3

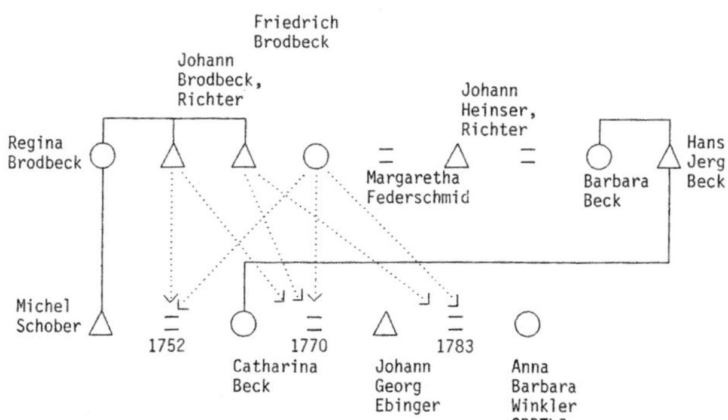

Figure 13.4

of them were blood relatives of either of the marriage partners. The household with its changing personnel had maintained a continuing alliance with members of the original cast – over a period of at least 34 years, until the last child was born in 1786.

Artisans and ritual kinship

Durable alliances, as explained in Chapter 12, were established between various branches of the Hentzler family and the Hentzlers and Bauknechts. These were families who over the last fifty years of the eighteenth century maintained themselves as independent agricultural producers. Many individual members of the families held one magisterial position or another. The long-term alliances utilized both marriage and godparentage in exchanges that linked successive generations as an older member of one patriline stood for a younger member of the other. By the late eighteenth century, godparents and parents tended most often to be on the same generational plane. The same generation that provided marriage partners also provided godparents. In any event, although there was no favored path between the agnatic lineages (one finds BWBS, FBWBSS, WB, MBS, FBD, FBSS, and FZS), a regular and consistent utilization of kinship ties created a grid that was in turn reproduced by marriage and godparentage. Artisan families, by contrast, did not yet create systematic alliances through marriage, and only at the turn of the century would they start to marry second cousins. Yet they did use godparentage to develop and maintain ties with various families allied to them through marriage. However, such connections were not as straightforward as the ones for Bauern families, and they do not look as neat in a diagram. Artisans looked for older, more powerful relatives, the kinds of people who could offer work opportunities, surety, village jobs, and political protection.

An example can be found in the Falter family, a group of solid artisans active in village life in the late eighteenth century (Figure 13.5). For easier comprehension, the members of the Falter line under consideration have been identified with black for the line descending and ascending from Johann Georg and with stripes for the line descending from his half-brother Hans. *For some couples (1, 9, 10), siblings or siblings' spouses acted as godparents, but for the most part parents traced through their FF's relatives, sometimes through his half-brother and sometimes through his other marriage. The example focuses on couple 2, Johann Falter, smith, and Anna Maria Schober, daughter of a smith (Figure 13.6). In this case, all the godparents were from Johann's relatives. The godfather was Friedrich Geiger, who was Johann's second cousin's brother-in-law: FFxBSSWB (1). The first godmother was also a descendant from the Hans Falter branch of the family: Anna Catharina Häussler (2). She married and left the village shortly after 1760 and was replaced by Anna Maria Bosch, wife of Johann Georg Häfner (3). In this case the substitute remained inside the chief branch but switched from subbranch C to B. Johann Falter attached himself through godparentage to wealthier, politically dominant households. Friedrich Geiger, the Gevatter, was a Bauer and Richter. Anna Catharina Häussler was the daughter of Salomon, Richter. One of her sisters was married to Johann Georg*

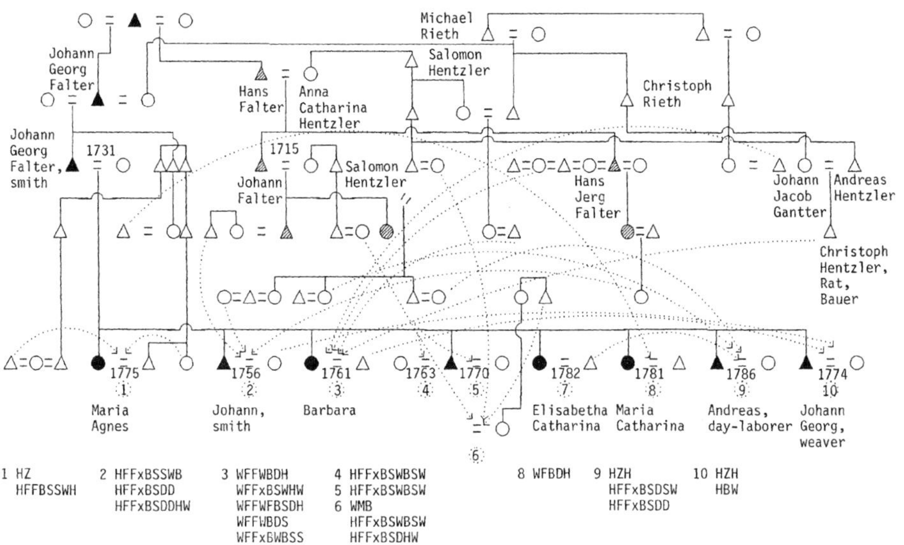

Figure 13.5

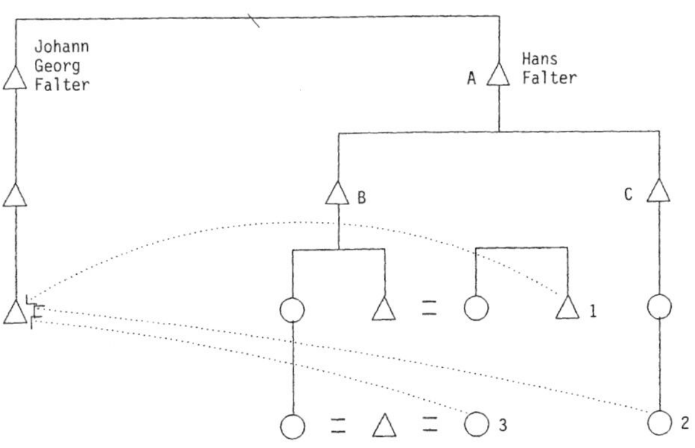

Figure 13.6

Baur, Schultheiss, and another to Johannes Brodbeck, who became Bürgermeister. Johann Georg Häfner, Bauer, had married the daughter of Bürgermeister Salomon Hentzler. His second wife, Anna Maria Bosch, was the daughter of a long-time member of the Gericht, Johannes Bosch. Johann Falter's interest in finding more powerful relatives as godparents is clear, but the strategic considerations of his familial politics seem less straightforward. None of the relatives he chose were particularly close, and it is only their logical structure that suggests that consistent principles guided the selection. Essentially, young Johann Falter chose three godparents who were all

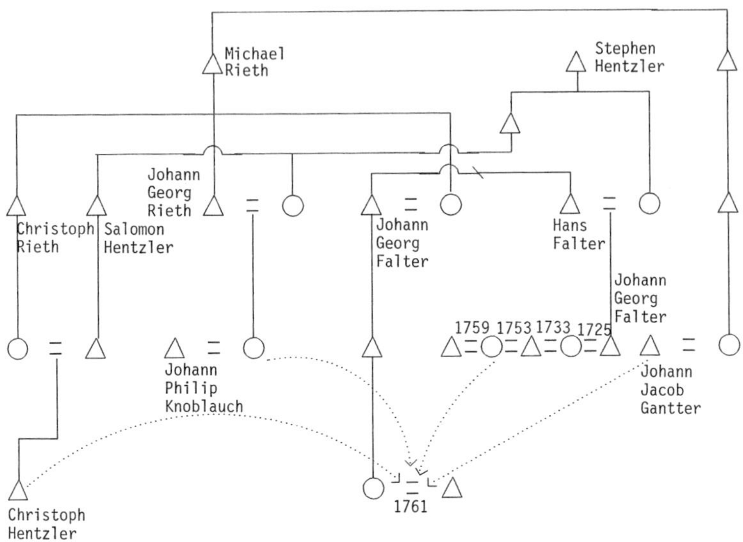

Figure 13.7

from patrilines allied to the Hans Falter branch of his own patriline. The fact that several of his siblings also found godparents allied to Hans Falter's descendants demonstrates that the grandchildren of Johann Georg and Hans still coordinated their activity and supported one another. The Hans Falter branch of the family was wealthier and better connected to the village patriciate and therefore provided many possibilities for the selection of patrons.

In this case, all of the godparents were chosen from Falter relatives. In fact, a large majority (19 from 24) of all of the Falter godparents came from their relatives, to the exclusion of the relatives of their spouses. The Falters were an aggressive, quarrelsome family during the second half of the eighteenth century, and they built their position through alliances based on godparentage with more powerful relatives. This example shows how cousinship developed during this period as a flexible instrument for creating alliances, fostered alternatively through marriage policy or through ritual kinship. An artisan family such as the Falters used ties almost exclusively built on ritual kinship, while Bauern families redoubled consanguineal connections through marriage and godparentage.

The selection of godparents for Barbara Falter, wife of Johann Klein, day-laborer, who immigrated to the village from Köngen, involves another systematic selection of godparents from allied patrilines (3) (Figure 13.7). The first godparents were Johann Philip Knoblauch, Richter, also a village immigrant and Christina Margaretha Hermann (WFFWBDH and WFFxBSWHW). Barbara's grandfather had married a daughter of Michael Rieth, and Knoblauch married one of Rieth's granddaughters. The Rieth patriline provided several godparents for Barbara, but there was also another family in play. A branch of the Hentzler family was allied to both the Hans Falter and the Rieth family, with the result that Knoblauch represented both families – his wife descended from Michael Rieth and Stephen Hentzler. Margaretha Hermann was marital successor of the wife of Hans Jerg Falter, Bauer, scion of the Hans Falter branch. Both of these godparents stood for children from 1762 to 1765. In 1768 the schoolmaster Johann Jacob Gantter was added. He was related through his wife to Barbara Falter – the women were third cousins through the Rieth connection. Knoblauch died in 1769; Gantter had probably been added only as a proxy in 1768, during the latter's illness, and therefore did not appear as Gevatter again. Instead, Christoph Hentzler, Rat and Bauer, was substituted for Knoblauch and was related to Barbara Falter in the same double way Knoblauch was, as a great-grandson of both Stephen Hentzler and Michael Rieth. The choice of Christoph Hentzler for Knoblauch is a good lesson in social succession. Hentzler took the place of his cousin (FFZDH), although also fulfilling a role in the Rieth succession, inherited through his mother (succeeding his MFBDH). Taking all of the selections together, Barbara Falter found members of the village particiate from families that were allied to her in similar ways.

Gall Falter (4), smith, married Anna Maria Schäfer, daughter of a weaver, from Altdorf. The godfather was a Bauer, Jacob Walther, from there. After his wife's death, he married a woman from Bempflingen (5), and Jacob Walther still acted as godfather. The godmother for both marriages was Christina Margaretha, the wife of Matthias Häfner, Richter and Bürgermeister, Falter's FFxBSWBSW. These two were godparents for 11 children, from 1764 to 1779. In 1781 Falter married Anna Maria Zeug (6) (Figure 13.8). The WMB, Anton Häfner, Bauer, became godfather but Christina Margaretha Häfner continued to be godmother for the first child of the new marriage. After that Catharina, the wife of Salomon Hentzler, Bürgermeister, became godmother, again someone associated with the Hans Falter line. She remained godparent even after Anna Maria married Philip Jacob Schaich, an immigrant from Kohlberg. Gall Falter, like his brother Johann, chose godparents from patrilines allied to the Hans Falter branch of the family, selecting individuals who were solid members of the village patriciate.

The last example is Andreas Falter, day-laborer, who married Anna Catharina Schober, daughter of a weaver, in 1786 (9) (Figure 13.9). Michael Hausmann from Nürtingen, his brother-in-law (ZH), was godfather for all of the children (1786–96). The first godmother was Anna Maria, wife of Ludwig Friedrich Hentzler, a baker and son of Bürgermeister Salomon Hentzler (FFxBSDSW). The Ludwig Friedrich Hentzlers seem to have left the village shortly after 1789. In 1791 Maria Magdalena, the wife of Andreas Hentzler, Bauer, Ludwig Friedrich Hentzler's sister, became godmother, substitution by a sister-in-law (HZ). Andreas Falter made choices similar to those of two of his brothers. Ludwig Friedrich Hentzler and his sister were stepchildren of Gall Falter's Gevatterin. Thus the three brothers along with two of the sisters eventually found patrons in the family of Bürgermeister Salomon Hentzler, grandnephew to Hans Falter (Figure 13.10): his wife, daughter, daughter-in-law, daughter's marital successor, nephew, and cousin's husband.

The Falter family's strategy contrasted sharply with that of landowners and substantial peasants. They were smiths, weavers, and day-laborers, married to

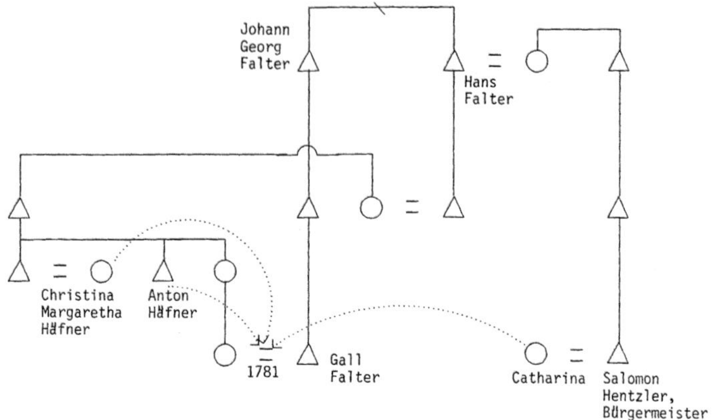

Figure 13.8

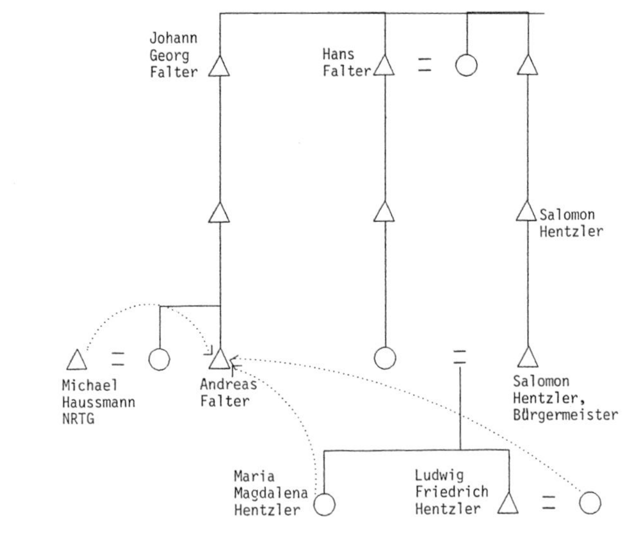

Figure 13.9

weavers, tailors, and day-laborers. Most of the godparents of the Falters were chosen from among Bauern and either members of the magistracy or their wives or children. In general, they emphasized those relatives who were richer and more powerful than themselves. This family did not enter into marriage alliances that involved exchanges over several generations as many Bauern did. Instead of emphasizing two parts of a set of alliances in a balanced way by choosing godparents related to both parents, most of the Falter children found their godparents among one set of relatives. The brothers – Johann, Gall, Andreas, and

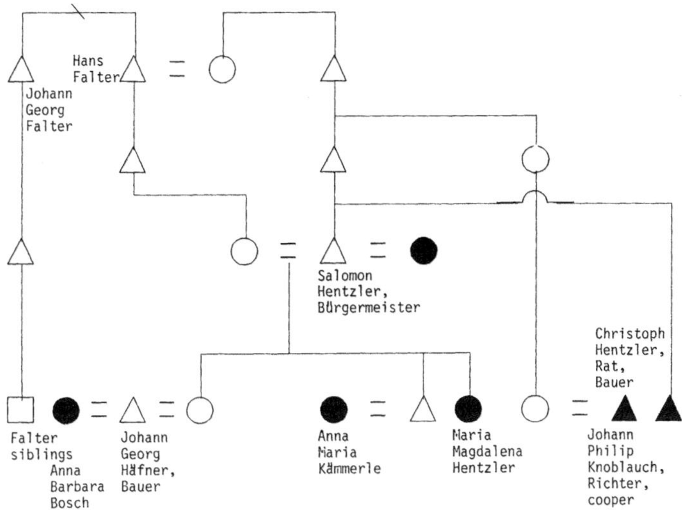

Figure 13.10

Johann Georg – found most of their godparents among older, wealthier cousins, although some of the older siblings acted as godparents for the younger. One of the sisters, Barbara (3), who married an immigrant, followed the same strategy. Another sister, Maria Agnes (1), shows how another artisan family acted in the same way as the Falters. She married a tailor, Johann Waldner, and their godparents came uniquely from his side.

* * *

There were four fora for village politics in the late eighteenth century: the formal administrative and deliberative organs, the "street," the church consistory, and familial alliance. Although women were for the most part excluded from direct participation in "public" institutions such as the court and council, when they acted as decision-making bodies, they were active in all the other instances of communal allocation of resources. Women had always been central players in the dispensing of reputation – what I am calling the "street" here – in the round of gossip, and in maintaining the right of villagers to know about activities that would affect the living conditions of the village as a whole. "Symbolic capital" (Bourdieu) could be built up or dissipated according to an individual's or family's fortunes in communal discourse (Rede). I have dealt with this issue elsewhere and refer to the lucid discussion on the subject by Regina Schulte.[6] This is also

[6] David Warren Sabean, *Power in the Blood: Popular Culture and Village Discourse in Early Modern Germany* (Cambridge, 1984), pp. 147–9, 153–4, 165–73, 239. Regina Schulte, *The Village Court: Arson, Infanticide, and Poaching in the Court Records of Upper Bavaria, 1848–1910*, trans. Barrie Selman (Cambridge, 1994), pp. 111–5.

not the place to discuss the church consistory at any length. On that court sat the Schultheiss as an ex officio member and two village elders, but the pastor chaired the proceedings and kept the record. A close analysis of many texts shows that a collaboration between the pastor and women was frequent, and the consistory became a central institution for women to counter male authority or give gossip an effective voice. This chapter has drawn attention to the new activity of women in the construction of alliance at the end of the eighteenth century. The politics of alliance, of course, was closely tied up with Vetterleswirtschaft and was the private side of public institutions. But the late eighteenth century was a transition period between a politics of kinship constructed around the social and political and productive practices of men and maintained largely through their activities, on one hand, and a kinship politics that emerged in the nineteenth century woven together largely if not completely by women, on the other.

Although women were active in cousin politics and in the construction of family alliances, it is difficult to assess the effectiveness and significance of their activities. Certainly their voice in such matters only grew throughout the nineteenth century. It is important to see, however, that the agnatic principle fundamental to the shape of alliances toward the end of the eighteenth century was not a simple extension of patriarchy, and even later when women came to be the major players in arranging marriages, a patrilineal husk to such social formations remained.

In any event, cousins came to be at the center of political life during the second half of the nineteenth century, and different classes articulated with cousinship in different ways. The internal cohesion of wealthy landholders as a class was produced within an endogamous marriage practice. People chose to marry cousins at the same time that they insisted on finding a spouse of equal wealth. For landholders, consanguinity, affinity, and ritual kinship created an overlapping and dense network of connection. One could say with Flandrin that "class" became a mask for family interest and activity, but it is more correct to say that class practices grew out of the everyday practices of familial exchange.[7]

At the same time as cohesion within class was being produced out of the intense activity of familial intercourse, the lines of connection between classes were being redrawn. Wealthy and poor no longer made up a single connubium, and ritual kinship worked differently for families of Bauern than it did for families of artisans. The artisan Falter family chosen as an example utilized connection to certain families in a systematic way and called upon a series of related magistrates to act as godparents. Its members built connections to the village patriciate in a coordinated manner but concentrated their focus on a particular set of interrelated magistrates and their children. Ritual kinship could be a flexible instrument for familial politics and could be used in practice in different ways

[7] Jean-Louis Flandrin, *Families in Former Times: Kinship, Household and Sexuality*, trans. Richard Southern (Cambridge, 1979), p. 2.

by people of different station, yet choice of a godparent, like the choice of a spouse, was for "life." Both institutions structured other kinds of exchanges and set up channels for the circulation of property, services, and various goods such as names.

14

Naming and patrilineal alliance

Names can be considered from several perspectives. Lévi-Strauss has discussed them in terms of the possibilities they offer for classifying either or both the name giver and the name receiver.[1] This chapter demonstrates that naming children during the late eighteenth century was an exercise that frequently marked out the patrilineal group to which a newborn child belonged, although the purpose was probably to underline the connections of the parents to particular people more than to position the child in a patrilineage. Each newborn was furnished with a surname from the patriline and a single or double Christian name (Johannes, Johann Georg), which offered the possibility of establishing specific ties between parents and particular people. Just as in the early part of the century, names were never used systematically to honor or recall individuals from previous generations.

At the birth of each child the parents had a chance to draw attention to a particular relationship. The field of meaningful relationships, as noted earlier, was always already marked out by the exchange of marriage partners and godparents. Although it was possible to strike out in a new direction or even to ignore relations out of lukewarmness or spite, names were usually in fact exchanged within preestablished networks. Chapters 12 and 13 have shown that Bauern families and others with considerable amounts of property established alliances over several generations that created overlapping ties of consanguinity, affinity, and ritual kinship. The system of exchange outlined and reinforced a sense of attachment to agnatically constructed lines. Artisan families also set up alliances with other families, even though they did not exchange marriage part-

[1] See Chapter 1, and David Warren Sabean, "Exchanging Names in Neckarhausen around 1700," in Peter Karsten and John Modell, eds., *Theory, Method, and Practice in Social and Cultural History* (New York, 1992), pp. 199–230.

ners systematically with any particular patrilines. Their politics of godparentage underscored their own agnatic ties and constructed alliances by redoubling affinal relationships with godparentage. The task in this chapter is to explore the ways the names bestowed on a set of children entered into the dynamics of kinship alliance and fit within a series of patterned uniformities. One would expect that both peasants and artisans would have been concerned with emphasizing patrilineal relationships and that they would circulate names between allied patrilines in accordance with the way such alliances were constructed.

For this cohort, there is far less information missing than for Cohort I (Table A.87). In general, the deficit is only serious for the parents' uncles and aunts (FMB, FMZ, MMB, MMZ) and the maternal grandmother (MMM), but parents rarely had to go that far to find a name to bestow on a child.

Naming sons

In the naming of boys, the constellation F-GODF-FB remained dominant as before and even accounted for a greater percentage of names (70.3 percent compared with 63.2 and 61.4 percent, respectively, for the midcentury and early-century cohorts) (Tables A.87–A.89). In general, the solidification of this triad was due to a marked new interest in the FB. There was no special priority for F, FB, or GODF for the first two children, but the FB gained ground for subsequent boys. The MB continued to supply some names but became far outdistanced by the FB (by 4 to 1). Here the missing data may have led to an underestimate of the MB, but even if the number is inflated to account for the missing data, the result is only 9, a third as many matches as for the FB. There were three instances in which a name was composed from two adults – the FB and GODF, FB and perhaps MZH, and F and GODF, most of them taken from the dominant triad. The data on necronymy show the same kind of emphasis as the rest of the indicators. Boys' names were repeated in 18 out of a possible 40 cases: 3 Fs, 7 FBs, 4 GODFs, 2 MBs, and 2 No Matches. A large percentage of the name givers (ignoring GODF and "No Match") were of the same generation as the parents: 83.9 percent, compared with 79.8 percent (at midcentury) and 83.5 percent (at the beginning).

Fewer than 10 percent of the names given to sons during this period cannot be matched with close relatives of the parents, but the missing data would no doubt account for most of them. Since the overwhelming majority of names came from the generation of the parents, it is clear that at the end of the century, as at the beginning, the exchange of names had to do with the active adults in the village and that deceased members of a lineage were not used to validate relations among the current generation. Immediately apparent from Table A.88 is the considerable use of names from the father's line. Apart from names that do not match anyone in the kin group, they account for 3 out of every 5. The continued use of the father and his brothers as a major pool for names established a strong identity among male siblings. And the less strong but nonetheless clear interest in the father's sister for naming daughters (Table A.89) demonstrates a coordination among siblings as a whole. Most of the rest of the names established connections with allied patrilines. In the first instance, boys' names were chosen from the directly allied line, from the MB and MF. The rest of the names taken from allied lines were mediated through godparentage. As already mentioned, both husbands and wives chose godparents mainly from their agnatic kin and from patrilines directly allied to them. Thus naming after a godparent could involve an exchange between allied patrilines.

Naming daughters

Bestowing names on girls contrasts somewhat with naming boys (Table A.89). This time 13 names were composed from those of two adults, which leaves all of the names accounted for. The mother and godmother dominated the field, but the MZ for daughters in no way matched the strength of the FB for sons. In fact, there was a relatively low interest in symbolically emphasizing sister solidarity through the naming of girls, in strong contrast to the Father/Brother/Son connection. Even the FZ was more prominent than the MZ, although given the fact of missing information, the number in the MZ column could be inflated by one or two points. The special set of links between the wife/mother and her uncles and aunts indicate that women seemed to be finding support from close but not immediate kin and that that was a significant change from earlier in the century (Chapter 13). Changes in production and the woman's role in production probably contributed to the new approach to the formation of networks. The multistranded bonds that sisters constructed through godparentage at midcentury disappeared late in the century and were not reconstructed in the process of naming their children. All the evidence points toward a gradual development of isolated work routines for women during the long transition to intensive agriculture. Although sisters most probably remained crucial for each other in many ways, their productive isolation may have forced them to create ties with older kin and neighbors. In any event, women of that period found it important to emphasize wider kin both for selecting godparents and subsequently naming after godparents. The composition of names fits nicely into earlier findings in this volume, notably the GODM/M combination (Table 14.1). In addition, the necronymy data show no special stress on the MZ (12 occurrences out of 33 possibilities): 5 Ms, 4 GODMs, 1 MM, and 2 No Matches.

In this period naming daughters drew attention to the patrilineal alliance system. After mothers, a couple showed the most interest in naming their daughters for godmothers or combining the names of the mother and godmother to create a new one. Once more, assuming that half of the godmothers were chosen by fathers, then naming after them emphasized the husband's patriline or lines allied to his agnatic kin. The godmothers chosen by wives also came either from their agnatic kin or patrilines associated with them. Using godmothers as namesakes underlined the sets of patrilines in alliance with each other. And daughters fre-

Table 14.1. *Cohort III: Combining names for daughters.*

M+	Number	GODM+	Number	FZ+	Number	MZ+	Number
FZ	1	MM	1	FZ	1	MZ	1
GODM	5	FM	1				
MM	1	—	2				

quently received names from their father's line. Bestowing names on both sexes emphasized the two allied patrilines represented by a particular household and other lines directly associated with agnatic kin. Their circulation followed paths already established by marital and ritual kin alliances.

The artisan family of Falter encountered in Chapter 13 illustrates the naming strategies of a very modest artisan family (tax quartile II). They were closely tied to extended agnatic kin through godparentage: second cousins and their wives playing a central role. For the most part, the godparents were wealthier, and many of them had positions as magistrates. Children were overwhelmingly named after agnatic kin, either the father's relatives or the godparents who were also kin (20 of 23 godparents were). When one of the daughters married an immigrant, her relatives dominated. When she married out or married a resident, then his predominated. Altogether there were 22 sons in this family: 15 were named after the father or his agnatic kin, 4 after the mother's agnatic kin, 2 after her uterine kin (one was not matched). There were 19 daughters, 11 of which were named after the mother or her sister. Fully 8 received names from the father's kin. Altogether, this family demonstrates a central core of agnatically structured relationships. Names underlined the set of brothers and the families allied with their patriline.

A second example comes from a wealthy set of landholding Bauknecht siblings (tax quartiles III and IV). Here the sons of a group of Bauern all had overlapping names provided by the adult male siblings. The sense of identity among the Bauknechts was very strong, as illustrated by the story of their vigorous defense of property in volume I.[2] They all lived next door to each other in the Brückengasse in the center of the village, close to the river. They were prepared to pour out of their houses, father and son, to do battle against officials or anyone else threatening their interests. According to court testimony, they determined the politics of the village assembly for a whole generation. In this group, there was a balanced reciprocity in the selection of godparents. Whether the wives chose the godfather or godmother, they chose agnatic kin, and the husbands chose uterine kin. In naming, however, only one of the 16 boys was called after the fathers' uterine kin (one was unmatchable). Ten came from the F or his agnatic kin and four from the mothers' agnatic kin. There were only 8 daughters, but 3

[2] David Warren Sabean, *Property, Production, and Family in Neckarhausen, 1700–1890* (Cambridge, 1990), pp. 324–9. See also Chapter 16 in this volume.

names came from the mothers' agnatic and 1 from the fathers' agnatic kin (one was unmatchable). The other four were named after the M or MZ.

The nature of the alliances this family of independent agricultural producers entered into was quite different from the alliances of the artisan Falter family. The Bauknechts (see Chapter 12) were involved in systematic marriage alliances over time. The godparents they and their wives chose emphasized the balanced alliances between families of equal station and were far less distant than the godparents the Falters found among their extended agnatic kin. For the Bauknechts, naming after godparents (8 out of 24) was at the same time reinforcing close relatives such as the MB, FB, father's first cousin, or wife's uncle. Whatever the nature of the alliances composed through marriage and godparentage, the names emphasized agnatic relations and marked out a core of patrikin who exchanged names just as they exchanged marriage partners and land. The alliances of the Bauern were tighter, more balanced, more easily coordinated but based on a strong sense of patrilineal identity and exchange with agnatic kin.

COHORT IV (1820–1829)

15

Kinship at the beginning of the nineteenth century

Many people who commented on Württemberg – and indeed on Germany as a whole – during the first several decades of the nineteenth century drew attention to increasing pauperization and a widening split between those with enough resources to maintain independence and those involved in a desperate search for occasional sources of income.[1] By 1828 the Neckarhausen pastor was expressing concern about the poor in the village outnumbering the propertied, and other observers were beginning to speak longingly of an earlier prosperity, visible still in the last generation. Until the 1820s, the older stratification system maintained its fundamental characteristics under the stress of an expanding population. Wealthy peasants extended political domination, and a growing underclass of farm laborers, village servants, and impoverished artisans found new niches for themselves in a "makeshift economy." Although the village population rose from 516 to 738, or 43 percent, between the 1780s and 1820s, the proportion of independent agricultural producers – Bauern – declined from 36 percent to 24 percent, from well over a third to just under a quarter. By the end of the eighteenth century, the average artisan held only 40 percent as much property as the average Bauer, which amounted to a considerable decline throughout the century from an earlier figure of 75 percent. Individuals from the burgeoning group of farm laborers owned only 20 percent as much real estate as a typical Bauer. Not until after 1820 or so did a significant shift in the economic organization of the village take place, with a rapid rise in the number of construction workers, who circulated around the region looking for work. But this development had been prepared for by the growth of a wage-dependent, pauperized group of laborers and semiemployed craftsmen.

[1] For the following, see David Warren Sabean, *Property, Production, and Family in Neckarhausen, 1700–1870* (Cambridge, 1990), Introduction and chap. 1.

It was also during this period that the village made the transition to the intensive form of agrarian production associated with the agricultural revolution.[2] In Neckarhausen, the innovations consisted of stall feeding, intensive meadow cultivation, hoed fodder crops, and the field rotation of flax and hemp. Both inside and outside the village, the period was marked by infrastructural changes as well – drainage, road construction, river channeling and river bank reconstruction, public building, and barn and shed construction. One of the effects of the economic changes was to alter the sexual division of labor and thereby to reorder gender relations. As far as women were concerned, the agricultural revolution meant massive new inputs into farm work – constant, arduous hoeing of the new crops, intensive cultivation and preparation of flax, and care of animals, including individual transportation of green fodder on foot from distant fields. Many of the village men were drawn out of the community for seasonal agricultural labor and colportage, and eventually for construction jobs. The conditions of labor – women rooted in the village, carrying on individual, isolated tasks, supported intermittently by neighbors, and men traveling in pairs, working in gangs, and cultivating villagewide and regional networks in the tavern – brought gender-specific expectations about time, expenditure, and management into conflict.

Agricultural innovation called for considerable new capital inputs, which came at a time of inflationary growth in agricultural and land prices with frequent fluctuations and periods of collapse. The continental blockade and Napoleonic wars, with their boom and bust conditions, were punctuated by a famine in 1816/17. During the first decades of the nineteenth century, many villagers were driven into debt and watched their farms sold piecemeal at auction. For a decade or so after 1810, there was a good deal of unrest in the village, with disturbances and even some violence directed at debt collectors.

The terms of marriage alliance were questioned during this period, especially by women who demanded a greater share in marketing, bristled at their husbands' drinking habits, refused to return after ill treatment, or sued successfully for divorce when their property was threatened.[3] Networks developed by women to carry on agricultural or household chores, frequently in the absence of their husbands, became important. Neighbor women and close female relatives were all that a woman could depend on in certain kinds of crisis situations, since men would never carry fodder on their heads in huge kerchiefs like women, were usually not available for hoeing even if they would do it, and excluded themselves from cooking, cleaning, and care of small children. But women frequently also relied on men as guardians, Kriegsvögte, and godparents and inevitably drew other men into conflicts with their spouses: neighbors, parents, and siblings. The central decades for the analysis in this period lie right in the middle of the great wave of divorce (1805–40) and the rise of a female discourse about alienated labor.

[2] Sabean, *Property*, chap. 5.
[3] Sabean, *Property*, chaps. 4, 6.

Much of the ecological basis for the male networks already examined in this volume continued to exist throughout this period. For example, postmortem inventories point toward the practice of brothers and brothers-in-law owning part shares in heavy agricultural equipment such as wagons and plows.[4] Within the overarching structure of male linkages, however, relations increasingly centered on women or on cross-sexed pairs such as brothers and sisters.[5] The entry of women into the land market during this period speaks for greater self-reliance, and women emancipated by the deaths of their husbands frequently chose to remain unmarried at the head of their households. Between 1810 and 1830 some women bought the land and buildings of their bankrupted husbands, but that was a strategy of married couples. Increasing numbers of single women held on to the property, and many widows were among the most affluent members of the village during the central decades of the nineteenth century. Often, they insisted that heavy agricultural equipment fall to them instead of being immediately divided among the male heirs. Although they may not have plowed or taken a wagon to market, they were able to allocate and manage the use of such resources, and I have argued that the control of agricultural tools even more than the control of land underlay the authority of those who had them.[6]

Children grew up inside a set of relationships constructed by their parents, and their marriage choices can only be understood as reflections on those relationships. Choosing a marriage partner was a complex business involving personal predilection, class position, occupation, parental guidance, age, wealth, and the existing set of alliances. I have shown that alliances during the last decades of the eighteenth century frequently united two patrilines through recurrent exchanges. And I have argued that the agnatic nature of networks was shaped by the context of male productive routines and political activities. Perhaps the situation can best be described as a grid of male linkages inside of which both men and women constructed their activities. Pairing off among the youth of the village was done with public knowledge, continual comment, long-term adjustments, and personal desires, which themselves had been shaped inside the dynamics of class and family. The young woman who invited one of the local youths into her bed did so after several years of visitation by his whole cohort.[7] Yet it was not unusual for the cousin who impregnated his lover to deny it, as many another male would have done at the time, only to end up at the altar. Choice was the result of social practice, of course, and the context of parental and communal values provided the conditions for its exercise. Young women frequently elected to act in such a way as to maintain or develop relationships constructed by their parents on agnatic principles. Wives and mothers were im-

[4] Sabean, *Property,* chap. 11.

[5] Sabean, *Property,* chap. 16.

[6] Sabean, *Property,* chaps. 11, 12.

[7] See David Sabean, "Unehelichkeit: Ein Aspekt sozialer Reproduktion kleinbäuerlicher Produzenten. Zu einer Analyse dörflicher Quellen um 1800," in Robert Berdahl et al., eds., *Klassen und Kultur: Sozialanthropologische Perspektiven in der Geschichtsschreibung* (Frankfurt, 1982), pp. 54–76.

portant for marriage negotiations that fostered the development of the political alliances of their menfolk. Women could be independent and creative actors in this situation, and the alliance of agnatically defined groups must not be interpreted in itself as a fundamental pillar of patriarchy. There was a period, especially during the 1780s, when young men used violence in the sorting out of endogamous alliances, but the experience of a generation brought considerable resistance, and their wives replied to violence by insisting on separation and divorce for ill treatment.[8]

If the conditions for encouraging agnatic ties and patrilineal alliances continued into the nineteenth century, providing an overarching framework for marital negotiations, it is also true that women were capable of developing networks that cut across those constructed on male principles of activity. In analyzing kinship and marriage, property transactions, godparentage, and the like during this period, one would therefore expect to find indications that such activities and institutions frequently grew out of relationships developed by women. If young people were choosing spouses in a complex web of parental and peer pressure and personal inclination, then some of the relationships developed and maintained by their parents, in this period at least, would be those forged by their mothers, frequently with other women.

The sale of land

By the 1820s, the land market had become a central mechanism for the distribution of resources in the village (see Table A.108).[9] Almost as much real estate was bought and sold as was passed on through inheritance. The size of parcels was whittled away even more between the 1780s and 1820s, so that the average size plot was about three-fifths as large as at the beginning of the eighteenth century. Not only did many more people purchase land (by cohort: 41, 102, 135, 232) but they also made up a larger proportion (by cohort: 12.1, 22.4, 26.2, 31.4) of the ever-increasing population. Much land became available because of economic disarray, bankruptcy, and forced sales. The land hunger of a swollen population encountered a new supply provided by indebtedness. With the rapid swings in prices in an overall inflationary trend, the situation became highly volatile.

Despite the larger trade in land, nonrelatives made no deeper inroads into the market.[10] The nuclear family and cousins bought more than half of all the parcels of real estate offered for sale during the 1820s. With the restructuring of ritual kinship, godparents no longer mediated between buyers and sellers. In general, consanguineal relatives managed to increase their control over the flow of property, partly because of the more tightly organized system of alliance.

[8] Sabean, *Property*, pp. 124–9.
[9] Sabean, *Property*, chap. 15.
[10] Sabean, *Property*, chap. 16.

Cousins played just as large a role in the purchase of real estate in the 1820s as in the 1780s. However, the agnatic bias for networks between buyers and sellers declined considerably. In calculating the first step of a genealogical path to a cousin, the ratio in favor of men had dropped from 9:3 to 5:3 (by the 1860s, the ratio would tip in favor of women). At the same time, parallel sex bonding – either FB or MZ – at the apex of each genealogical path (e.g., FB in FBD or MZ in FMZSS) predominated. Both of these phenomena indicate the possibility of social relations constructed by or through women. Any particular path traced between two people was not something created de novo for each particular occasion. The recurrent patterns occur because they were embedded in regular relationships subject to similar constraints and offering the same opportunities for creative activity. If women appear to have become more central in directing social activities or if relationships among themselves more often became the basis for creating new ties, the foundation for their activity appears to lie in new productive, political, and class relationships.

Ritual kin

By the early nineteenth century, almost nine-tenths of godparents were relatives of the parents they stood for, and there was no longer any difference in age between them (Table A.4). Villagers for the first time did not look for ritual kin among those who were more established than themselves but found them among their mates, friends, siblings, and cousins.

The material from Tables A.3, A.14, and A.15–A.17 shows a striking break with the late eighteenth century. People in the more modest wealth categories now sought contacts among themselves or outside the village altogether, breaking ties with wealthier villagers and developing horizontal links with their own class. Even day-laborers were not particularly tied to wealthy villagers anymore. The latter, now dominated by landed agriculturalists, continued overwhelmingly to create ties among themselves, and for the first time, only they found their godparents among village magistrates. The wealthiest Bauern found godparents largely from their own occupation, but when they did find artisans for partners, they looked for those who were as propertied as themselves and who usually exercised a craft for only part of the life cycle. In every way that can be seen, godparentage was completely disengaged from a system of clientage. Links tended to become more horizontal, emphasizing people of the same age and same social standing.

This fundamental alteration in ritual kinship is one indication that class structure in the village had solidified, and that paths between the classes, at least those of this type, had been closed down. With the withdrawal of the protection of the wealthy, artisans and farm laborers now found it more useful to emphasize ties of immediate social advantage in production or in crisis situations. In step with the decline of patronage, there was a growth in the village institutions of aid. The unexpected death of a horse or cow was now partly compensated for by the

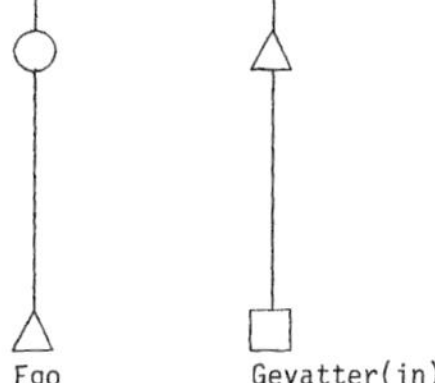

Figure 15.1

village treasury. And the very substantially increased village poor relief fund became a basic support for destitute orphans. Village stores – seed and grain – became regulated enough so that in an emergency situation at least some food and seed were available to those who needed them. In such a situation, personal connection with the village elite did not have as much advantage as before, and the latter were so busy solidifying their political domination of the village in intraclass competition that they had no incentive to cultivate the largely disenfranchised. As the numbers of poor grew, they were cast on each other for self-help or on the village in certain moments of crisis. These changes accompanied a consequent restructuring of the institutions of godparentage.

In this generation, the high percentage of godparents identifiable as kin remained and even grew a few points – from 80.2 percent to 87.1 percent. In Cohort III, 9.6 percent of the godparents were immediate kin of the parents (F, M, B, Z). In this one, they made up a far more substantial amount: 29.4 percent. Adding the BW and ZH, the comparable figures are 19.2 percent and 43.2 percent, respectively, which demonstrate a considerable narrowing of the field from which godparents were chosen. First cousins went from 17.8 percent to 25.0 percent of the total. If all the nuclear family members, uncles and aunts, nephews and nieces, first cousins and first cousins once removed – and all of their spouses – are taken into account, the comparable figures are 68.5 percent and 81.8 percent, respectively. This, too, demonstrates a concentration of the field of godparents.

Cousins, especially first cousins, became crucial for godparent relationships during the early decades of the nineteenth century. The modal cousin-Gevatter was the MBD or MBS, and the modal second-cousin-Gevatter was connected through the FMB. That is, when first cousins were chosen as godparents, the young parents most frequently chose a matrilateral cross cousin (Figure 15.1).

This construction was most frequently used by men, who, in any event far more than women, went outside the immediate family into the wider group of kin. Such a reaching out for a cross cousin emphasizes the alliance of the patrilines, or follows from the relationships of a brother and sister, or reconstructs the relationships of two brothers-in-law, ego's father with his cousin's father. Exactly which consideration was most important cannot be derived from this evidence alone, and the discussions between structuralists who focus on affinal

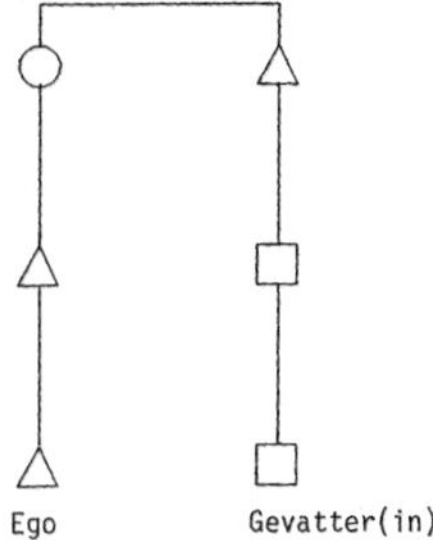

Figure 15.2

ties and functionalists who stress filiation do not help very much without further evidence. In any event, should the newly constructed connection between ego and his cousin continue to develop, then the next generation, reaching out for a second cousin, would trace the path through the FMB: FMBSS/D, FMBDS/D (Figure 15.2).

In both of these network situations, relationships cultivated by men with women appear to have been crucial. When choosing godparents, men were more likely to build on extended consanguineal principles than women were. The latter were wont to use the closest kin or occasionally no kin at all – probably neighbors – a tendency that emphasizes patterns based on different political principles or on different ecologies of labor.

Guardians and Kriegsvögte

Although kinship was just as important for Pflegschaft as in the 1780s and 1740s, a more flexible set of relatives was used. In general the history of Pflegschaft in Neckarhausen demonstrates a clearer stress on relatives, with an extension to cousins. At the beginning, people used either the closest consanguineal kin or nonrelated powerful villagers. Patronage as such played a smaller role over time, while the range of relevant kin was extended. In the overwhelming majority of the cases in the 1820s (17 out of 20), relatives were used as Pfleger, but there was no favored kind. There were close consanguineal kin, laterally extended affinal kin, and extended consanguineal kin.

One case is instructive: when Johannes Bauknecht's wife died in 1821, their three children got separate Pfleger. All the Pfleger were second cousins to the deceased woman, and all traced through her FF, but through three different siblings: FFZSS, FFBDS, FFBDS. This suggests that her father had had an active relation with three first cousins, all nephews and nieces of his father. She then continued the network in the next generation. If only one of these connections had been found, one might have seen it as chance or an exception. But three, all built on the same principle, were chosen for the same purpose at the same time. This example supplements the findings for that generation about women's reluctance to build on second-cousin networks for choosing ritual kin: whatever motivated the selection in each instance did not derive from a lack of cultivation of first- and second-cousin networks in general.

As before, there was little overlap between guardians and godparents. Despite the fact that both godparents and guardians were chosen on the same general principles, no Pfleger who was related was also godparent to the child he was Pfleger for. In only one of the three instances in which the guardians were unrelated to the children did the godfather assume responsibilities as Pfleger. The conclusion is hard to avoid that godparents were systematically avoided as guardians for children – except where parents chose unrelated godparents, and even then in rare instances – despite the fact that both were now chosen from the same generation and the same set of kin.

The final cohort for Kriegsvogtschaft demonstrates the familialization of the office. As already mentioned, during the eighteenth century close kin were frequently called upon as Kriegsvögte, but a substantial number of them were not related to the wife at all, and this was not just a case of wives who had married in from the outside. Indeed, women frequently chose their Kriegsvögte from the Gericht or from among more prosperous landholders. This recognized in part at least the necessity of having people who could read exercising that function. Perhaps the reason why women sometimes chose cousins to support them before the court was to find relatives with the proper hierarchical position who at the same time could read.

In the 1820s, 80 percent of the Kriegsvögte were traceable as kin, most of them kin of the woman – fathers, brothers, uncles, brothers-in-law, or first cousins. No Kriegsvögte came from the husband's nuclear family, but when his relatives were called upon, more distant cousins were chosen. Of the four women marrying in from the outside of the village, three preferred to find a Kriegsvogt not related to the husband in any way.

As was the case earlier, the majority of Kriegsvögte were proprietors and magistrates. The contours of Kriegsvogtschaft are less clear than other indicators of kinship relations. No particular relationship appears with special frequency, say, the FB or the B. Even if the wife's side of the family was strongly represented for the function, outsiders had frequently been found right through the eighteenth century. The hierarchical element stresses the fact that power was felt to be crucial in the protection of women's rights, and wives were fairly flexible in selecting their representatives. Perhaps it was not a particularly good idea to choose someone from the circle of kin who was a potential competitor for the same inheritance. A wife, after all, was balancing a number of commitments. She wanted her rights protected vis-à-vis her husband, but would not necessarily have them best protected by competing siblings. Therefore the net was cast to include cousins and nonrelated powerful members of the community. The selection once made was often reinforced through the Gevatter relationship. For example, Johann Georg Kühfuss's wife used her own Dote and Gevatter, her FZH, as her Kriegsvogt.

Table 15.1. *Cohort IV: Kin ties of underwriters.*

Kin	Number
B	5
ZH	2
WB	1
WZH	1
HZH	1
FB	2
MB	3
FZH	4
BS	1
FBS	1
FZS	2
No relation established	5

Pledging

As far back as records for Neckarhausen are available, they show the institution of pledging (*Bürgschaft*) or underwriting. People who undertook construction work, especially outside the village, or who took on a farm, collected excise taxes, or herded cows, often needed someone else or even a consortium to post a bond for their performance or to guarantee liability. Nonetheless, the spottiness of the records during the eighteenth century suggests that pledging was rather irregular and often done by oral agreement. The mounting debt after 1800 caused creditors to insist more regularly on having debts underwritten (and written), and the increasing mobility of construction workers after 1820 made performance bonds more and more necessary. Still, information about pledges seems to appear only when they were called in or when there was a controversy of some kind. The mounting evidence in the records suggests that bonds were more often required after 1800, but the large number of foreclosures also make the practice more visible. Perhaps there is less of a paper trail from the eighteenth century because people failed far less often. In any event, by the 1820s, a sufficient number of pledges are present to provide some idea of how kin were utilized to underwrite each other's credit.

The data from the cohort 1820–9 is made up of 20 people whose transactions were underwritten by someone else. In several cases there were multiple guarantors, giving 28 links altogether. Since some at least of the multiple guarantors were linked by kinship, there are only 2 cases out of the 20 in which no kinship link at all could be established. The distribution of the 28 individual guarantors is shown in Table 15.1.

The immediate relationships of brother and brother-in-law were balanced by uncles, nephews, and cousins. Part of the reason for the strong showing of uncles has to do with the fact that several of these cases involved minors buying land, which necessitated someone from the older generation as guarantor.

In the case of former bankrupts, it was necessary at that time to have three pledges. When young Friedrich Krumm purchased land from his father's estate, he had as guarantors two of his cousins (FZS) and Johannes Kühfuss, for whom I can find no kinship link. Young Johannes Häfner likewise had three underwriters. Two of them were FB, but for the third, Ludwig Hiller, I can establish no link. Wilhelm Rentzler had two men go surety for him; one was his ZH, while for the other no link can be established. Thus in these cases there was always some kinship principle involved. Each of these examples appears similar – one or two close relatives and one nonrelative. I am not sure whether the pattern had some significance, but it could be that the village court required a "noninterested" party in certain circumstances.

Wider kinship links do not show up at all in the case of underwriting loans and guaranteeing performances. Either the closest kinship links were used – brothers, fathers, uncles, brothers-in-law – or very occasionally first cousins. Failing close kin, one had to go outside the kinship group altogether to find a friend, business associate, or patron, perhaps at a price. Villagers did not disturb the more extended kin links by putting undue weight on them. Nor did villagers risk their property for kin outside a highly restricted range. Very close kin were thrown upon each other for the crucial function of providing trust. Without it, even trivial loans were often hard to come by. Dealing with strangers outside the village meant carrying a piece of paper with the signature of a guarantor and the signature of the Schultheiss assuring that the underwriter was solvent and trustworthy. It is difficult to exaggerate the innumerable ways in which Bürgschaft was intertwined in daily life. With its increased importance in the nineteenth century, it brought new content to the circle of close relations. One man ripped down the sign over his brother's pub and made a public scene over the latter's business dealings. He henceforth refused to go surety for him.[11] Underwriters became interested parties in the management capacities and diligence of their fellows and frequently scrutinized their behavior. It was not at all unusual for a woman to claim the right to interfere in her husband's economy when she pledged her property to guarantee his performance.

There is some suggestion that a ritual kinship link in the absence of other kinship ties could be built on for purposes of guaranteeing trust. But that relationship appears to have been rather residual. In fact, there are more cases in which the *Gevattersohn* stood as guarantee for the Gevattermann. In general, people used a multiplicity of ties for various purposes. Becoming a Gevatter did not imply a particular obligation to support a man and his family in crisis situations: not as guardian for orphans nor as guarantor for solvency or performance.

[11] *Schultheissenamt*, vol. 2, f. 24 (5.4.1843); f. 46 (9.4.1844). See the case in *Property*, p. 297.

The godparent relationship was not one that could take a great deal of material weight. Indeed, if it created obligation, it was more likely to flow toward the Gevatter rather than away from him. On the other hand, the relationship could be utilized in the situation of Kriegsvogtschaft, which was a purely representative role – of spokesman – and carried no material burden. Perhaps too heavy a material interest would have put the spiritual link with the children or indeed with the parents in danger. The very fact that godparentage did not normally develop an economic function helps us to see how it differentiated various roles. After all, Bürge were chosen from the same field as were godparents. Thus the fact of not utilizing the same specific link in two ways throws light on both. The closest kin links could obligate people for real material risk, such as underwriting. From a slightly larger field (first and even second cousins) a range of relationships could be developed. Occasionally one could find Bürge there, but far more frequently godparents, guardians, Kriegsvögte, political allies, and marriage partners.

Occupation and marriage strategy

During the early decades of the nineteenth century, occupations changed considerably, as indicated by the various designations in village records. Bauern were often also day-laborers. In fact, several people labeled "Tagelöhner" most of their lives were in tax quartile III, not the poorest members of the village. They had some land, apparently not enough to be self-sufficient, but had to supplement their living by farm work. Many Bauern or day-laborers were weavers either seasonally, during periods of economic difficulty, or over the course of the life cycle. The agricultural round seemed to go especially well with weaving, and that combination remained prominent during the first several decades of the nineteenth century. Of course, one of the important commercial crops in Neckarhausen was raw flax, which easily combined with its preparation, spinning, and weaving into cloth. In any event, the combination weaver-day-laborer-Bauer was frequently to be found during this period. The fact that the population increase had not been accompanied by a change in the overall pattern of land distribution meant that many more people had enough land to maintain more than a marginal existence if they could supplement their output with wage-labor and the production of cloth.

Another group that made up an ever more significant part of the village was that of village servants: the village (*Dorfschütz*), vineyard (*Weingartschütz*), field (*Feldschütz*), and forest patrolmen (*Waldschütz*), and night watchmen. Eventually the village hired a tree surgeon, bullkeeper, stock inspector, mouse and mole catcher, street cleaner, fountain cleaner (three of them by the 1830s), ditch-digger for the highway, communal oven and cloth-bleaching meadow attendants, and several handymen for communal property maintenance – smiths, wheelwrights, mechanics, and carpenters. At any one time there could be 20 to 30 such positions being filled by villagers, mostly smallholders, farm laborers, or small artisans, who sometimes earned a large part of their living from village work and sometimes supplemented it with what they earned elsewhere. The amount of work available in such positions as field patrolman varied greatly by season, the job being most crucial when the crops neared harvest.

Another group that began to emerge in the village was composed of the various pub-owners. Some had full-fledged inns with accommodations, cooked food, and beer, wine, and alcohol. Others simply had the right to serve wine or beer. The number of coopers (who often developed into innkeepers), butchers (who sold cooked meat and eventually beverages), and bakers was also growing. As a group, people associated with the food trades came to be among the most prosperous members of the village.

As before, the peasants produced a large share of artisans, while the artisans reproduced themselves. By the 1740s, it had become difficult for artisan families to accumulate enough capital to set sons up as independent landed proprietors. In fact, there were two different life cycle patterns of handicraft producers – which I discussed in Volume I.[12] Some farm families had their sons trained in a handicraft that they never exercised or carried on only until the older generation retired or died. In a similar fashion, some propertied artisans passed on both skills and land so that their sons were able eventually to establish self-sufficiency as landed proprietors. But the majority of artisans in this generation never became independent agricultural producers, although all of them had some land and shared in the communal parcels apportioned to all married Bürger. At the bottom of the scale, the day-laborers/village servants either produced artisans or reproduced themselves. By the 1820s, the village population had more than doubled from the starting point of this study (340 to 738), and with that increase the contours of class became more clearly outlined. Deterioration of status between each generation was a continuous process, while upward mobility was much more difficult to achieve. One of the significant changes by the early nineteenth century was the small percentage of artisan fathers whose daughters married Bauern. Throughout the eighteenth century, about half of the artisan fathers-in-law had Bauern sons-in-law. By now this was reduced to one in five. In general, the fact that wealth had come to be so carefully balanced at marriage meant that fewer and fewer children from handicraft families could expect alliances with landed proprietors. Bauern families in turn married among themselves even though many of their children practiced a craft for a decade or so after they married. Also recall that the parents of this generation had gotten land earlier than any other previous one and then held onto it much longer, with the result that their children remained dependent for a longer period, married late, and acceded to a full inheritance only 15 to 20 years later.[13]

During this period, the average age of marriage rose, and a much larger percentage of men and women did not marry until the age of 29 or older (Table

[12] Sabean, *Property*, pp. 316–20.

[13] Sabean, *Property*, pp. 256–8.

A.24). During the decade 1700–09, 11.6 percent of the men and 9.6 percent of the women who married for the first time did so over the age of 29. For the 1820s, the comparable figures are 26.0 percent and 33.3 percent. The mean age of first marriage for men and women had risen steadily since the 1740s by three and four years, respectively, to 27.8 and 27.2. By this time, people who made kin-linked marriages were no longer minors. In sharp contrast to the 1780s, when many families were developing and extending familial alliances for the first time, now they were one to two years older on average than the rest of their cohort rather than younger. The generalization of consanguineal endogamy to all sectors of the population took place with the cooperation of adult children almost 30 years old. Everything points to coordinated family politics, except perhaps for those children who were so thoroughly involved in the mobile labor market that they escaped all ties with the village.

Kinship and marriage strategy

For the cohort centered in the 1820s, the percentage of kin-linked marriages was slightly lower than for the 1780s (25 percent compared with 29 percent: Table A.25). However, many families had begun to maintain long-term alliances with families in other villages, a phenomenon that cannot be reflected in the statistics. Furthermore, many alliances between patrilines were maintained by exchanges that were either not structurally endogamous or would not be captured by our strict criteria. Even then, only 1 out of 10 families (sibling groups), as compared with 2 out of 10 during the 1780s, failed to contract at least one marriage between cousins or close in-laws.

The cohort centered on the 1820s captures an important transition in the alliance system. In the marrying generation itself, artisans were by this time just as likely as Bauern to make kin-linked marriages. By contrast, artisan parents were less inclined to arrange kin-related marriages for their children than their Bauern, publican, or farm laborer counterparts. This discrepancy comes from the fact that there were two groups of artisans, those descended from traditional handicraft families and those from larger property owners and independent agricultural producers. Since the latter group continued the practices of their parents and grandparents, they swell the statistics and mask the fact that artisan families were just beginning to construct alliances, calling on second cousins while Bauern were already interested in first cousins and other forms of renewed exchange with shorter circuits between generations. Furthermore, those artisans who were moving into the more mobile trades such as masons and carpenters were likely to construct alliances with families scattered across many villages – which keeps such exchanges out of our statistics.

In the overall trend, the propensity to marry consanguineal kin began during the 1730s and 1740s first with families closely connected to the village political elite. By the 1770s and 1780s, the class of independent agricultural producers as a whole created a series of overlapping and recurring alliances among themselves.

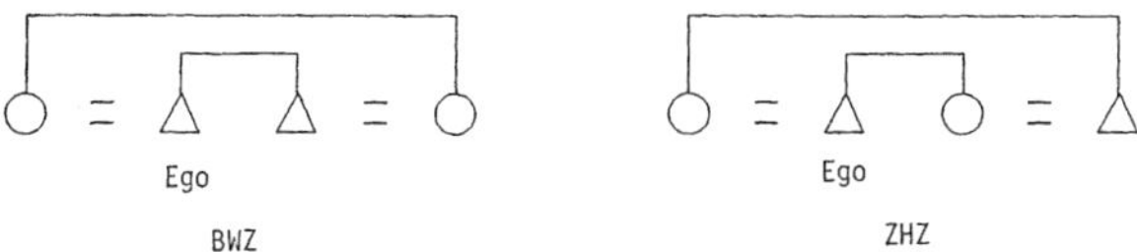

Figure 15.3

Their children, of whatever occupation, continued the practice, while the poorest artisan families generally lagged behind into the early decades of the nineteenth century. By midcentury, at least, the propensity to marry kin was shared by all occupational groups, with the exception of the emerging group of factory workers, but with farm laborers very much in the lead. Everything points to the period of 1800 to 1830 as a time when the endogamous alliance system became generalized, although many of the poorer families were just taking the first steps in that direction. Endogamy began to escape its original projects of political domination and class cohesion. Although marriages endogamous to a family and to the village might best serve the purposes of the dominant stratum of Bauern, those poorer handicraftsmen whose jobs in the building trades, road construction, and the like took them continually on the road began to construct regional alliances, the exact dating of which is difficult because the method of family reconstitution can rarely capture events outside of the confines of the village.

Cousin marriages continued to be structurally predominant in the first several decades of the nineteenth century. However, first-cousin marriages were no longer exceptional, and all the evidence suggests shorter circuits of exchange (WZ, ZHZ, first cousins). The rise of the first-cousin marriage can be seen in the context of the development of other first-cousin arrangements in village life – godparentage, land sales, and so on. Still, it should be emphasized that connections with second cousins and beyond remained crucial to social relationships. Furthermore, the systematic alliance between patrilines frequently created social bonds between people who were not exactly cousins to each other at all. The circuitous route of genealogical calculation is not the most apt instrument to capture the massive way that family members were implicated in each other's marital connections.

A few examples from the two lists in Tables A.68 and A.69 call for some comment. This period contains numerous examples of what can be called sibling exchange (see Figure 15.3). Formally, such a marriage arrangement is captured in the formula, ZHZ, and that seems to have been the most usual form of sibling sets marrying each other. In the other situation (BWZ), the symmetry of two families exchanging children of the same sex is lost, and movement, so to speak, is in one direction.

In my earlier analysis of cousin marriages, I pointed out that marriage was part of a larger exchange system through which alliances of greater or lesser duration could be set up and within which a great variety of transactions could take place. I also showed that the alliances could not best be thought of in terms of a particular recurrent preferred marriage type such as FZD or FFZSD. Rather, members of two patrilines frequently made several marriages over a short space of time that called for another spurt of exchanges a generation or two down the line. In fact, even when each generation was marked by such exchanges, any one marriage was most likely to be at least as extended as a second cousin, which formally, at least, describes alternate generation exchange. The particular path in the genealogy for individual couples did not turn out to be the best description of the alliance system. Furthermore, any particular period of intense intermarriage between two lines was most likely to be marked by exchanging women in one direction, although there were always exceptions. The next set of exchanges a generation later sometimes reversed the flow and sometimes did not. In classic terms, there does not seem to have been any dominant manner of linking one patriline with another, either by constantly offering wives and receiving them in turn from a third line (generalized exchange) or by setting up a debt/credit balance, sending women in one direction in one generation and reversing the flow in a later one (restricted exchange). The particular balance was not important, and in any event any one line had recurring exchange relations with several other lines at once, some appearing to involve unidirectional movement and others reversing the relationship every other generation, and others displaying no particular form at all. It is, of course, extremely difficult to quantify such complex relations and compare whole patterns of alliance, but it does seem that the multiple exchanges were seldom likely to be formless. At any one time, two allied lines usually sent women in one direction. In general, the direction of exchange had to do with the overall practice of hypergamy. Many families, despite treating all children equally in the long run, endowed daughters with more land and movables at marriage than they did sons.[14] With a policy of matching portions more or less equally, the resulting tendency was for women to marry upward. The wealthier or more politically powerful line received women – increasingly valuable in themselves as agricultural workers – and a dividend in property. Some lines retained a structural asymmetry over many generations while others alternated their fortunes. At any moment the clustering of exchanges in one direction reflected the overall balance in the alliance.

In the case of sibling exchange (BWZ, ZHZ), the innovation involves an alliance set up in one generation and renewed in that same generation. This is no longer the realm of patrilines, and it makes little analytical sense to speak of a "minimal segment," the smallest unit of such a line. In any case, the point of a recurring alliance was not to link "patrilines" together in some peasant reification project. It was rather to strengthen and redouble social ties that would have atrophied if not recast. Many marriages, of course, followed quite different strategies, striking out boldly to create new relations, which alternatively died with the particular actors or became the basis for later calculations. With sibling

[14] Sabean, *Property*, pp. 233–6. See the discussion in Chapters 1 and 22.

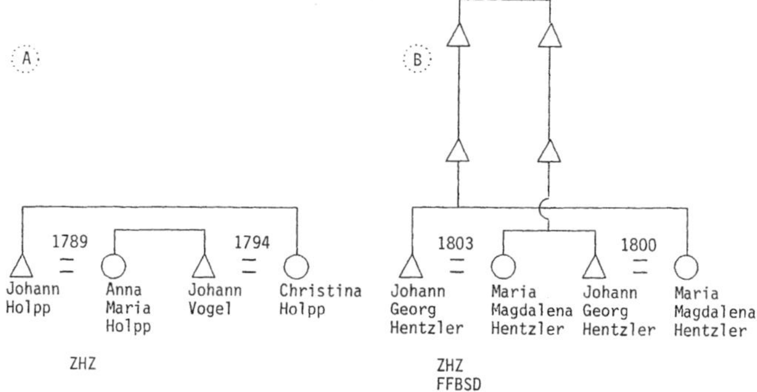

Figure 15.4

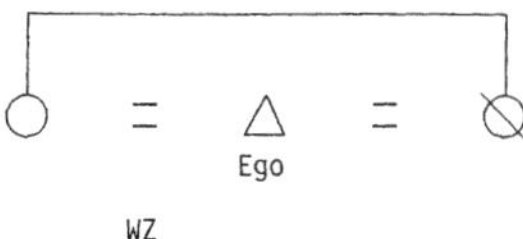

Figure 15.5

exchange, an alliance was redoubled as soon as possible, and it concentrated relations, not dragging in so many interallied households as a marriage between second cousins would do. Furthermore, since in most examples women were exchanged in both directions, such arrangements offered closure more quickly than longer, multigenerational circuits of exchange. On the other hand, a sibling exchange could have been part of a larger project that overlapped with longer-term alliances. In example A (Figure 15.4), the exchange involving Johannes Holpp and Anna Maria Vogel in 1789 was reversed five years later by their siblings. As far as I can see, there were no prior or subsequent exchanges between the two families. Perhaps the lack of such an alliance led them to this close arrangement. On the other hand, in example B, not only did the two couples marry patrilateral parallel cousins, but the one couple also renewed an alliance made three years earlier by their siblings. This is an example of how an alliance could be reinforced with multiple ties to create a far more intimate set of relations between families than was possible in the eighteenth century.

Another form of alliance renewed within one generation was marriage with the WZ (sororate) or wife's close relatives (Figure 15.5). Although not in the sample, there is also at least one example of a man who married his deceased brother's wife (levirate). However, marriage with the WZ was far more usual than with the BW, although both became dispensable in 1789. Both forms offer examples of the renewal of an alliance in the same generation. Perhaps such a practice would have come about earlier had there been no prohibitions, but marriage with

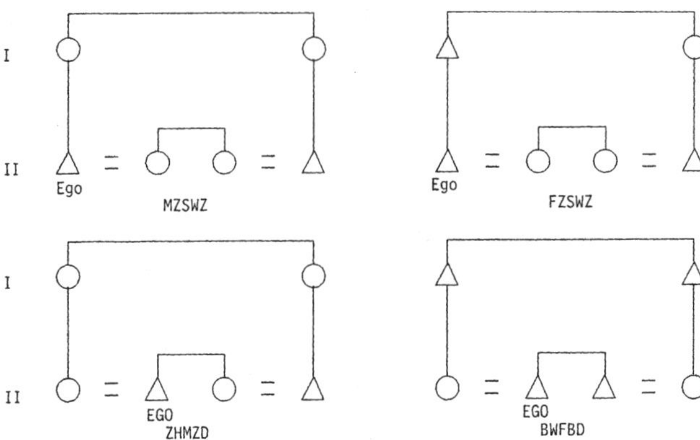

Figure 15.6

the ZHZ or BWZ had been unrestricted all along and yet no one had sought to contract such unions. In both instances, single generation alliances were clearly a departure for the period.

In several examples of WZ marriage, the second wife had lived unwed for many years, marrying her ZH when he was in his late 50s or 60s. I suspect that she had in fact been providing labor for her sister and brother-in-law for years and probably had lived in the same house with them. Such marriages reveal the possibility that many of the women who delayed marriage until their late 30s or 40s or who never married at all had similar arrangements. The new involvement of women in agricultural labor gave them a useful economic place in agricultural households. Not all marriages with the WZ, however, involved such configurations, and the death of a young wife could prompt a renewed alliance with her family for other reasons. It is difficult to see behind such marriages in alliance terms, since the widower remained bound to his wife's family through inheritance and property rights anyway. When an older couple worked out a mutual arrangement, the husband's chief concern might well have been for a housekeeper, and old age was not a time for constructing new alliances. For a young couple to tread the same path meant narrowing down and concentrating relationships. Insofar as labor mobilization in intensified agriculture had become central to the alliance system, perhaps the sororate was a very effective way to provide the spouses, especially the husband, with reliable labor. There is also a suggestion in these marriages (WZ) and other forms of alliance involving single-generation connections (ZHZ) of networks which were constructed through women. We will continue to explore this possibility as the argument develops.

Another form of marriage alliance encountered in this period is the "classic" marriage of two first cousins with two siblings (Figure 15.6). This form, as pointed out earlier, is also one in which the alliances were both made on one generational plane. The great innovation in the early decades of the nineteenth century is the fact that the first cousins were no longer just patrilateral parallel. In Figure 15.6, generation I displays sisters or cross siblings for the first time. Even in the one case here in which two cousins were involved in social relations constructed by two brothers, they themselves were both women. These examples provide hard evidence of networks being constructed through women. It could have been the case that such relations were forged by women seeking support from each other under new labor conditions. Volume I provided evidence of a restructuring of relations between husbands and wives. With women demanding greater information from their husbands and greater say in economic transactions, they may well have been hammering out new forms of support for themselves.[15] I argued earlier that exchange between patrilines was based on male networks that in turn were embedded in village politics and the exigencies of male production routines. None of these factors were eroded during the nineteenth century, and alliances constructed and reconstructed on the basis of social relationships between brothers and brothers-in-law will continue to be seen. On the other hand, one must not imagine that women had not been active mediators in the marriage market. Certainly they were usually present at prenuptial negotiations, and widows did play a strong role overseeing the marriages of their children. Patrilineal alliances and agnatic principles of network construction did not necessarily mean that women were not crucial to negotiations, communication, and management. There may well have been ample scope for them to further their own interests. During the 1780s, young men were particularly violent in their attempts to oversee the marriage market, but although the politics of the wealthier and more aggressive sons coincided with the class endogamous project of their elders, there were still considerable tensions with the older generation, and village and regional officials clamped down hard on them. The apparent domination of men in controlling the marriage market, whether patriarchs or their sons, waxed and waned over time. Over the course of the eighteenth century, there was a good deal of fluctuation in the balance of power between the sexes in household arrangements and presumably in the construction and maintenance of alliances. Despite this caveat, without further evidence the details of women's activities in kinship politics will have to remain unclarified. The alternative hypothesis is also possible, namely, that the agnatic cast to kinship in the eighteenth century derived from men being more central for kinship matters. By the mid nineteenth century, women had become the more active figures throughout the property-holding classes in Germany (Chapter 23), with consequent shifts in the structures of reciprocity.

When networks constructed more systematically through women do begin to appear, there should also be signs of change in political arrangements or in production. With the growth in village population and construction of class and endogamous institutions, large numbers of men were no longer active in village politics. Many of them were more concerned with maintaining regional networks

[15] Sabean, *Property*, chaps. 3, 4.

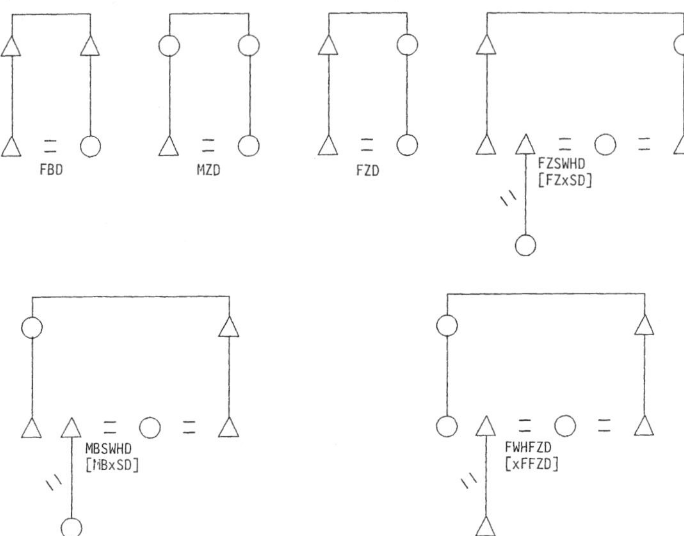

Figure 15.7

useful for locating casual employment opportunities than with developing ties to some local magistrate or other. In such a situation, for local connections at least, there was more scope for the development of alliances growing out of relationships between sisters and sisters-in-law: quite frequently, men circulated around the region engaged in seasonal and occasional labor, while their wives remained rooted in the village, tending the crops, raising the calves, and preparing the flax. Since female labor had become so central to agriculture and linen production, there was also a new ecological basis for their cooperation. Furthermore, the period of time spent in other villages as maids provided a basis for creating social ties beyond the boundaries of Neckarhausen.

Besides the many new forms of renewed single-generation alliance, one also finds the marriage of first cousins, which involved adjacent generation exchange, also a form that had few precedents in the eighteenth century (Figure 15.7). Although the samples provided no instance of MBD marriages, there are many examples from the period. No kind of first cousin was avoided. Especially important to note is the MZD marriage that could not involve a renewed alliance between two patrilines. Newlyweds in such a situation were clearly operating within the ambiance of two sisters.

First-cousin marriages are also very narrowly focused. Like marriage with the WZ or BW, such a union is intended to build the most intimate ties with close relatives. In one of the FBD instances in the sample, the man was also marrying his BW. In such instances, the couples appear to be eschewing the construction of broader alliances, the kind that lead outward, creating multiple connections

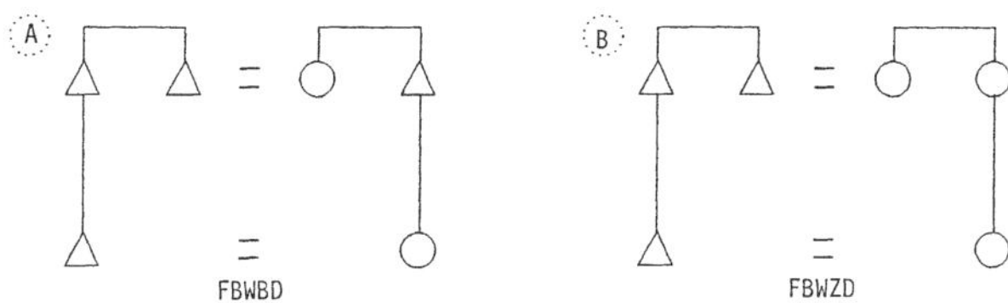

Figure 15.8

with overlapping second cousins and affines. Instead, such unions seem to arise out of the most intimate relations and rest on the powerful interests and emotions generated by cousinship. Fragmentation of the intravillage connubium that had once dominated the village led to quite different strategies: on the one hand, a new propensity to marry outside village society altogether and, on the other, a tendency to marry the closest possible relatives. Different strata and occupational groups followed different patterns, but even families occupying similar niches could adopt different policies. Some families continued to maintain long-term alliances while occasionally turning in on themselves to marry within the line. Other families neglected patrilineal alliances altogether, at times turning completely outward, and at others inward as possible. All of these new strategies avoided the construction of open, village-based networks, connecting different strata together.

There is one more form to comment on (Figure 15.8, example A), which earlier was a recurring feature of patrilineal alliance. Now, however, as shown in example B, the relationship of two sisters appears to have been crucial for the second-generation marriage. Although alliances between patrilines continue to turn up right through the 1860s, there are more and more examples of networks constructed through women that cut across, so to speak, the overarching system of alliances. It is also clear that once consanguineal marriages had been in place for 50, 60, and 70 years, any couple could be related to each other in multiple ways. If one assumes that many agnatically constructed networks had political meaning, were part of the village public system of *Parteien,* and were rooted in male social dynamics, that would not preclude women from working toward alliances that satisfied more than one desideratum.

I have suggested that alliances were by no means restricted to the village. Unfortunately, the method of family reconstitution is a poor instrument for exploring intervillage or regionally based marriage exchanges. Yet there are many hints in the information available that suggest many families married systematically with members of another village, or with a particular family in another village, or, more interestingly, with one family scattered over several villages. This phenomenon continually shows up for a few families with the surname Keuerleber. But it can be demonstrated for many other patrilines in Neckarhausen (Figure 15.9).

Whenever I have constructed a genealogy for a Neckarhausen family, I have

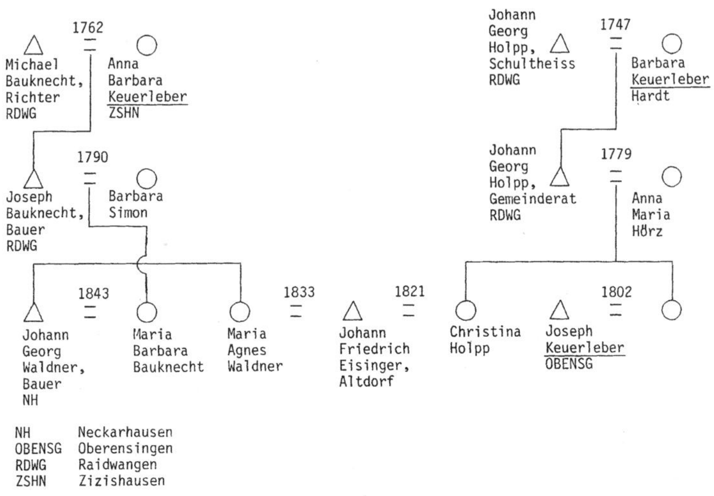

Figure 15.9

noticed that certain surnames – such as, in this case, Keuerleber – recur. This particular name did not turn up in the Neckarhausen records very often. Its appearance illustrates how a genealogy drawn at random is likely to contain an uncommon surname sprinkled about in it. Even more remarkable is the fact that the three times Keuerleber occurs here, each of the individuals involved was from a different village. And yet it seems highly unlikely that their appearance happened by chance, given the fact that the name was so uncommon in the village genealogies. It occurs exactly 10 times in approximately 2,500 marriage records as groom or bride or as the maiden name of a mother of one of them, roughly 10 in 10,000 chances of occurrence. In this instance, in generation I, Johann Georg Holpp and Michael Bauknecht married Keuerleber women from Zizishausen and Hardt. Two generations later a Holpp granddaughter married a Keuerleber in return and both the Ehesuccessor of a Holpp granddaughter, and a Bauknecht granddaughter became allied with a "mediating" family, the Waldners. If the Keuerleber descent had any relevance for this latter arrangement, then it suggests that networks constructed through women had crucial importance. At this point, however, one can only speculate about such linkages. What seems more certain is the Holpp/Keuerleber alliance involved the Keuerleber family from two different villages.

Another example of recurring alliance between villages is taken from one of the sibling groups in our sample, the children of Michael Franz, born in Frickenhausen and a Bauer in Raidwangen (Figure 15.10). He first married the daughter of the shepherd in Raidwangen and subsequently married a Hörz from Grossbettlingen. An analysis of the frequency of kin-linked marriages (Table

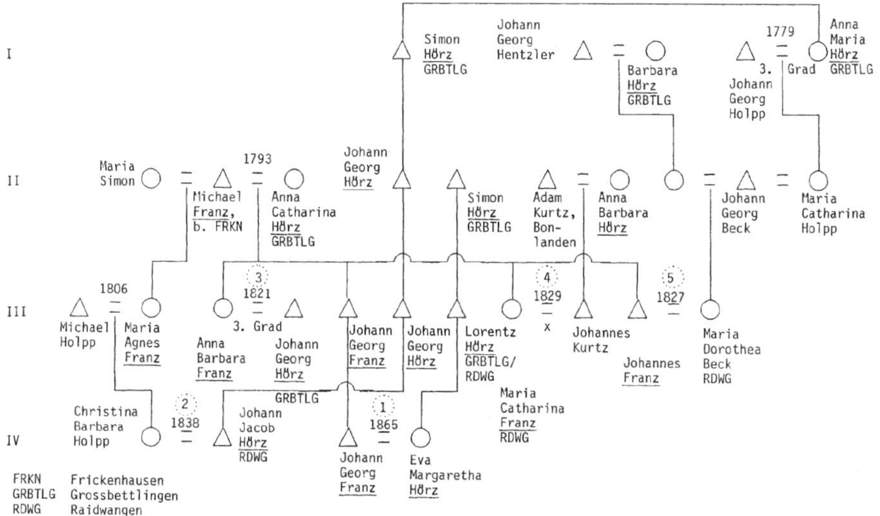

Figure 15.10

A.68) shows only one instance, a "3. Grad" (second-cousin) example among their five children. However, an examination of the genealogy demonstrates that the Hörz family from Grossbettlingen recurs repeatedly. In the generation after the one under consideration, the connection continued. Michael Franz married a Hörz (II) from Grossbettlingen. His daughter, Anna Barbara, made a second-cousin marriage to a Hörz from Grossbettlingen, which suggests that since alternate generations are in play, his father or mother had allied to the Hörz's before him. Another daughter married a man whose mother was a Hörz. Finally, his son married Maria Dorothea Beck, whose maternal grandmother was a Hörz from Grossbettlingen. The latter's Ehepredecessor's mother was also a Hörz from Grossbettlingen. Her brother had married a Hörz also from Grossbettlingen. In generation IV Michael Franz's granddaughter, Christina Barbara Holpp, married into the same line. His grandson, Johann Georg Franz, made a further alliance as late as the 1860s. Thus the Franz alliance with the Hörz Grossbettlingen family lasted at least from 1793 to 1865 and included six marriages with people descended from the Hörz family. Many of these marriages involved continual exchange between the lines (Figure 15.11). In most cases, second cousins (twice, explicitly "3. Grad") or further define the nature of the exchange, stressing alternate generations on the model of FMBSD (1) OR FFZDD (2) OR FFBDD (3), MFBDD (4) (no longer uniting two surname lines), MFZDD (5) (also not uniting two surname lines). The fact that the crucial connection in several cases was made through the mother or through the maternal grandmother points again

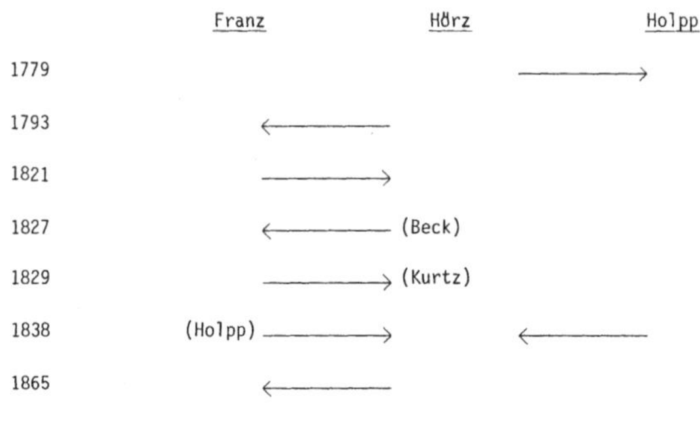

Figure 15.11

to the possibility of constructing marriage alliances through networks maintained by women. Even so, a patrilineal framework lies at the center of this genealogy, but its very existence was dependent on connections through uterine offspring.

The frequency of kin-linked marriages in each cohort is, however, rather deceptive. In the last few pages, I have shown that many marriages with outsiders involved relatives that are only remarked in our tabulations if a dispensation was obtained and duly noted in the marriage register. Even marriages within the village would end up in the non-kin-linked column if the path between neogami did not fit the restricted criteria. The marriage of Johann Häfner to Christina Geiger in 1826 was considered as part of our original sample and was found not to be endogamous. Nonetheless, it is in fact the last (at least up to 1870) in a century-and-a-half series of exchanges between the two families, the first marriage occurring in 1661 when Conrad Geiger moved into the village from Grossbettlingen (Figure 15.12). *Ignoring the mutual marriage of a Häfner and a Geiger to the same woman in generation III, the exchange between the two families was regular and reciprocal (Figure 15.13). At the beginning of the chain, the Häfner family provided a wife for the immigrating Conrad Geiger from Grossbettlingen (II). Two generations later, the Geigers in turn provided a wife for the Häfner family (IV). An exchange in the other direction duly took place further down the line two generations later (VI). The final exchange was separated by only one generation. The overall pattern of exchange – alternate generations (second cousins, FFZSD, etc.) during the eighteenth century and adjacent generations in the nineteenth – fits the modal case. Although the exchange was systematic and repeated, the exchanging parties each time were not usually directly descended from the previous couple involved in the exchange. This means that the genealogical connection between the marital partners themselves was ever more attenuated. For example, the relationship in generation IV in 1715 was FFBDSD or FWHBD, whereas in generation VI it was FFFMFBSSSD or FFFBWHSSSD, and in generation VII, FFFFFBDSSSSD or FFBDHBD. The methods followed here would scarcely pick up relationships such as these later ones. Nonetheless, they can be seen to have been part of a regularly recurring pattern of exchange.*

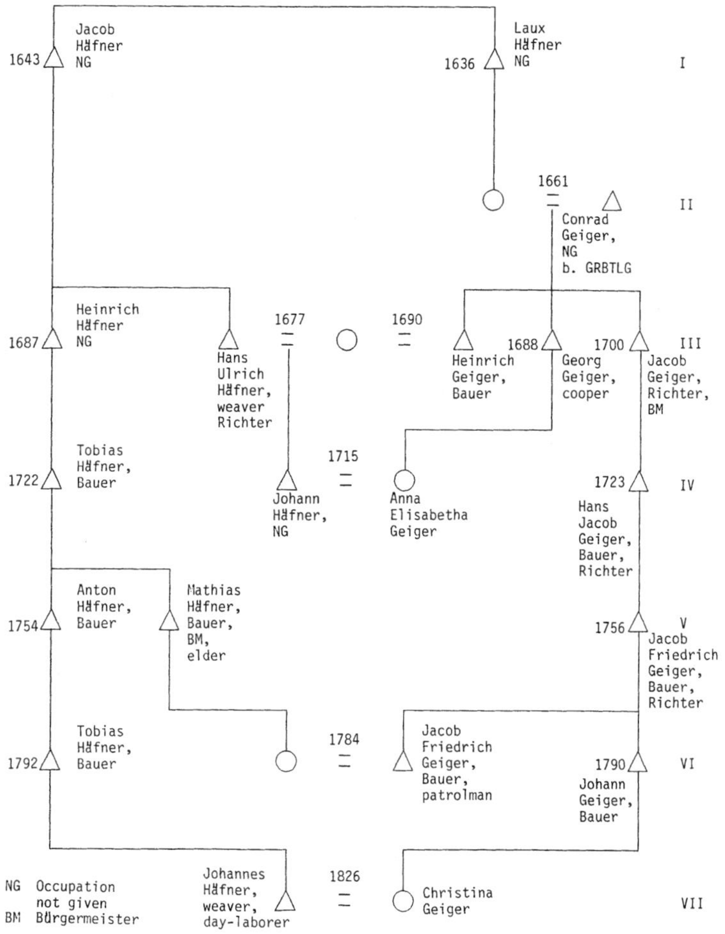

Jacob
Häfner
1643
NG
Laux
Häfner
1636
NG
I
1661
II
Conrad
Geiger,
NG
b. GRBTLG
Heinrich
Häfner
1687
NG
Hans
Ulrich
Häfner,
weaver
Richter
1677
1690
Heinrich
Geiger,
Bauer
1688
Georg
Geiger,
cooper
1700
Jacob
Geiger,
Richter,
BM
III
Tobias
Häfner,
1722
Bauer
1715
Johann
Häfner,
NG
Anna
Elisabetha
Geiger
1723
Hans
Jacob
Geiger,
Bauer,
Richter
IV
Anton
Häfner,
1754
Bauer
Mathias
Häfner,
Bauer,
BM,
elder
1756
Jacob
Friedrich
Geiger,
Bauer,
Richter
V
Tobias
Häfner,
1792
Bauer
1784
Jacob
Friedrich
Geiger,
Bauer,
patrolman
1790
Johann
Geiger,
Bauer
VI
NG Occupation
not given
BM Bürgermeister
Johannes
Häfner,
weaver,
day-laborer
1826
Christina
Geiger
VII

Figure 15.12

Häfner
Geiger
1661
1715
1784
1826

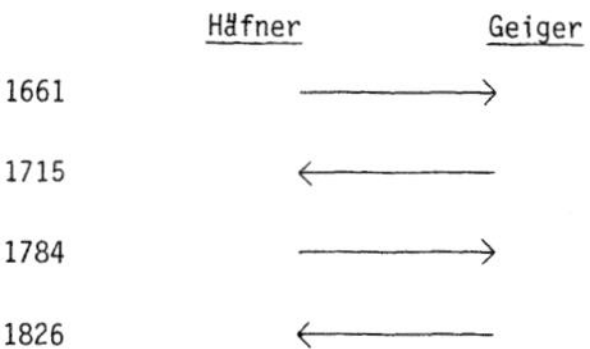

Figure 15.13

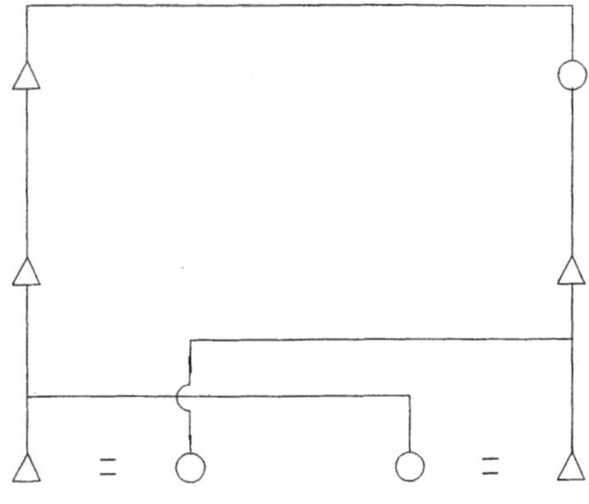

Figure 15.14

When all of the marriages of all the children in this genealogy throughout Neckarhausen history are examined, the FFZSD/FMBSD emerges as the modal pattern in this family (Figure 15.14). In formal terms, the reckoning of relation, from the point of view of the husband, is up the male line, across to a cross-sexed sibling and then down the male line, in the fashion: FFZSD, FFFZSSD, or in the reversed direction, FMBSD, FFMBSSD. Such a description provides a neat summary of alliance between two patrilines with reciprocal movement of exchange at the two connecting points.

In this alliance, the exchanging lines during the eighteenth century were composed largely of families of landed proprietors (although a weaver and cooper appear), who were either members of the magistracy or had close relatives on the Gericht. The actual marrying couples were not themselves magistrates. By the time of the initial case in the nineteenth century, neither parent was in the formal power structure, and the marrying groom was only a marginal landholder. Overall, this genealogy also fits quite neatly the paradigm of kin-linked marriages early in the eighteenth century connecting Gericht families, whether artisans or Bauern, marriages between Bauern later in the century, and finally in the nineteenth century marriages generalized to artisans and marginal landholders as well.

The Häfner genealogy is, of course, by no means unique. I have carried out the same exercise for many other families, with similar results. Each family history has its own variations, but the overall pattern has already been established. Many more examples could be found to demonstrate the family trees described here are not unusual. To take but one example, consider the pattern in Figure 15.15, which also places marriage into a larger set of exchanges. *One of the marriages from the original sample involves a continuous alliance between the Brodbeck and Petermann patrilines. I have simplified the genealogy to show just their alliance, although it is similar in some respects to the genealogy of the Häfners, and even includes an instance in which a daughter successively married two brothers, in 1831 and 1852. The Brodbeck family was founded in 1621 in Neckarhausen when Michael Brodbeck*

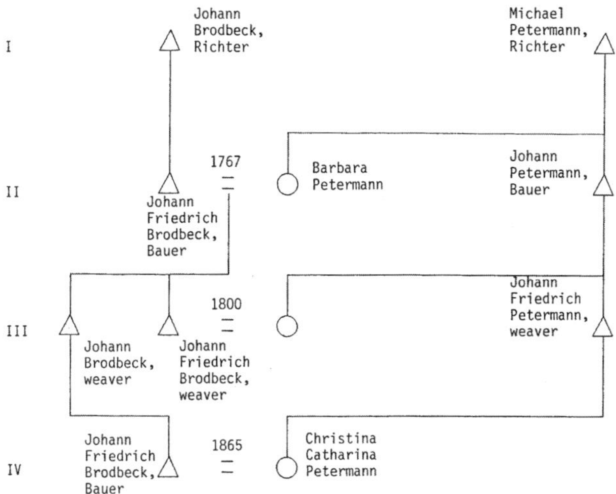

Figure 15.15

immigrated from Aich. The Petermann family descended from Jerg, who married into the village in 1620 from Neckartailfingen. The first marriage between the two families took place in 1767.

Following a first alliance in 1767, a renewed alliance occurs in each adjacent generation thereafter, always with women moving in the same direction. In generation III, the relationship is MBD and in the subsequent one, FBWBD and FMBSD. As pointed out earlier, this latter chain expresses alternate generation exchange just as the FFZSD does. Both imply the renewed alliance of two lines. However, FFZSD is equivalent to balanced exchange with the direction reversed every other generation (restricted exchange), while FMBSD describes movement in the same direction (generalized exchange).

In order to understand how this alliance fits into another set of exchanges, I examined the family reconstitution for godparent (Gevatter) connections from the beginning of their first marriage to 1833, and I also combed the various court protocols and postmortem inventories for clues about debt, plowing services, guardianship, and Kriegsvogtschaft for the period 1800–29. Since one diagram with all the information would be too confusing, I have mapped the information on two separate ones (Figures 15.16, 15.17).

During this period, Barbara Kraut (IV), the daughter of Catharina Petermann, acted as godparent for Johann Friedrich Brodbeck and Maria Catharina Petermann, her MZS and MBD (Figure 15.16). As first cousin to both of the spouses, she, in a sense, mediated their alliance. In this manner, the relationship between all three people exemplifies the central Gestalt of cousinship so important to the period. Brodbeck had married a first cousin (MBD) and had another first cousin (MZD) as Gevatterin. For his wife, the same Gevatterin was related as FZD. Barbara Kraut was also

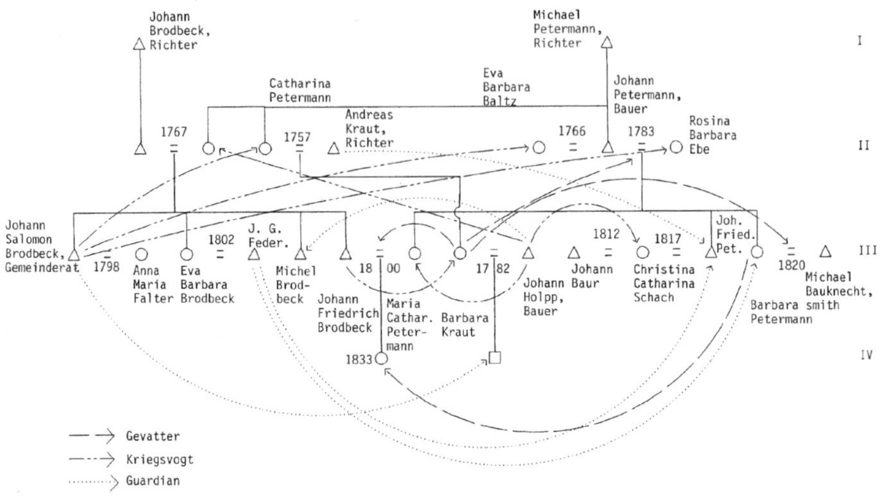

Figure 15.16

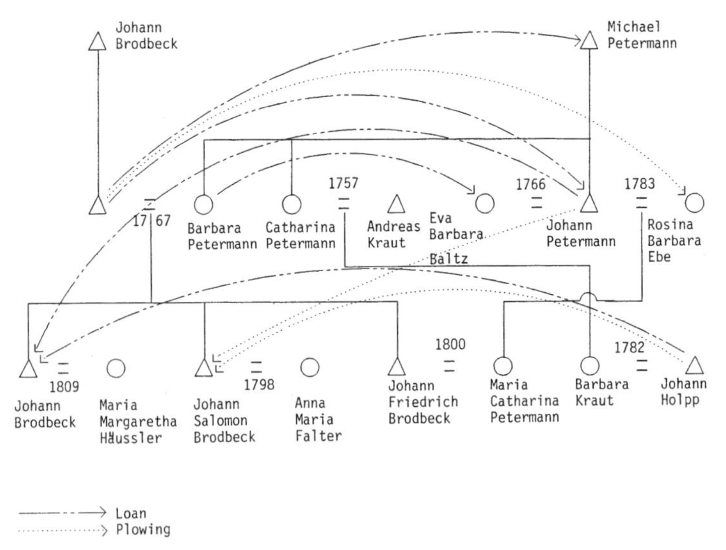

Figure 15.17

Gevatterin for her MB and the latter's daughter, Barbara Petermann. In fact, for both Petermann sisters she was Dote and Gevatterin. During the first decade of the nineteenth century, Johann Salomo Brodbeck acted as Kriegsvogt for an elderly Petermann aunt (MZ) and two wives of a Petermann uncle (MBW). He became a Gemeinderat and was therefore particularly useful as Kriegsvogt and as guardian –

ultimately for Kraut's grandchildren (IV). Andreas Kraut himself had been guardian for Johann Friedrich Petermann (III), his nephew (WBS), and his son-in-law, Johann Holpp (III), was in turn a guardian for Michel Brodbeck (III) (WMZS). Johann Georg Federschmid (III), married to a Brodbeck, acted as guardian for two Petermann children, his WMBS and WMBD. Johann Holpp, Andreas Kraut's son-in-law, was also an important figure as Kriegsvogt, serving for a Petermann wife, Christina Catharina Schach (WMBSW), and two Petermann women married to Brodbecks, his wife's MZ and MBD (MZSW). In all of these relationships, first cousins, uncles, aunts, nieces, and nephews criss-crossed between the two lines, creating multiple links of protection, advice, and service. In many instances, a mutual relative, not descended from either line, played a mediating role between them both.

Of course, not all of the debt and plowing relationships that existed between these people are found here (Figure 15.17). The records capture only a few of them by chance. Johann Friedrich Brodbeck (II) plowed land for his brother-in-law's widow, Rosina Barbara Ebe. His brother-in-law, Johann Petermann (II), had earlier plowed land for his son Johann Salomo (III). The latter had also received plowing services from a MZDH, Johann Holpp (III). In two generations, Brodbecks and Petermanns, their offspring and sons-in-law, worked each other's land. They also lent each other money or sold each other strips of land. Michael Petermann (I) was in debt to his son-in-law, Johann Friedrich Brodbeck (II), as was his son Johann (II). In turn Johann lent money to Brodbeck's son, Johann (III). Brodbeck's wife lent money to his brother-in-law's wife (her BW), and finally a Petermann son-in-law, Johann Holpp (III), lent money to a Brodbeck of his generation, his WMZS. From the point of view of the two third-generation Brodbecks, Johann and Johann Salomo, they borrowed money from and payed for plowing to a maternal uncle and a maternal aunt's son-in-law. This example vividly illustrates how affinal and consanguineal relationships overlapped and reinforced each other.

* * *

This chapter has shown a village in a highly charged social atmosphere consolidating and extending the system of marriage alliances developed in the fourth, fifth, and sixth decades of the eighteenth century. The village's population was swollen, its agriculture was experiencing extensive capitalization and intensification, class differentiation was increasing and the pains of harsh economic cycles and subsistence crises were sharply felt, regional mobility was increasing and the village economy was being integrated into wider markets, property holdings were becoming decimated and subject to rapid turnover, and pauperization was becoming commonplace and was affecting the pattern of social relations. Marriage exchange, however, was part of a more encompassing set of exchanges that patterned the activities of everyday life, shaped political life, and provided the stuff of village discourse.

The village relied on two fundamental institutions to create long-term relationships between people: marriage and godparentage. At the beginning of the eighteenth century, both led to the creation of new linkages with "strangers." Godparentage was the institution that at that time allowed for the greatest continuity from generation to generation, since patrilines of godparents were continuously associated with certain patrilines over time. The two families, Gevatter and parents, remained "strangers" to each other in that they were not related through blood.

In the course of the eighteenth century, godparents gradually ceased to mediate age groups, relate wealth strata, or link unrelated families. Marriage became the institution for continuing old alliances or creating new ones. And godparentage largely became a function of prior decisions about marriage, which not only created ties between families but also provided breaks, rifts, and fault lines in the social landscape. Choice of a spouse was, of course, limiting – whatever paths were opened up forced others to close down. There were countless cousins around, and to choose one necessarily meant to reject all the others. If one wished to keep a particular relationship open anyway, it to be worked all the harder.

The moment of decision about marriage was also one about class. The long social-sexual apprenticeship of village youth with their age cohort gangs, bundling customs, and street brawls taught each child about class realities in direct, practical ways. Reputations were built, histories of families reviewed, and the marriage market continually scanned in a round of gossip at the Spinnstuben, in the bedrooms of unmarried women, on the resting benches at the top of the hill, or at the village pump. In such continuous comment, the network of cousins/affines was always a field for mobilizing political support, public reputation, class hegemony, and popular resistance.

Any particular marriage opened up channels, so to speak, along which other things could flow. Some of the more regular goods and services that moved along these channels between affines and cousins were names, pledges, godparents, guardians, and Kriegsvögte. But a host of other exchanges took place as well, exchanges that are less easy to document in any systematic way but that came to characterize close relatives, such as lending ready cash and helping in agricultural production. During this period the field of consanguineal kin came to be more regularly defined and continually utilized as some relationships, such as guardianship, moved outward from the nuclear family and others, such as godparentage, moved inward from nonrelatives. First and second cousins eventually provided a field for the construction of affinal kin.

During the early decades of the nineteenth century, alliances between patrilines continued be reinforced. In many instances, individuals who were not particularly closely related in terms of categories of direct consanguineal paths continued alliances that had begun 60 or 80 years earlier and had been renewed several times in between. The villagers focused more on "families" and "lines" than they did on particular kinds of relatives. That is, they were not looking for, say, a FFZSD to marry but were predisposed in many instances to marry into a family that already had multiple ties with their own.

Even as they maintained and constructed such patrilineal alliances, many people followed a strategy of concentrating and narrowing down relations. Some families exchanged children directly as siblings married siblings, and some renewed alliances in the next generation, choosing the closest consanguineal relatives as affines. There was also a frequent practice of remaining with the same alliance by marrying the deceased spouse's closest relatives. In all of these situations, the closest overlap of affines and consanguines seems to have been counteracting the strong pressures leading to conflict: divorce, sibling rivalry, subsistence competition, and political backstabbing. This period, it will be remembered, was one of intense marital conflict and it also brought new tensions between siblings and brothers-in-law. During the period after the Napoleonic Wars, subsistence crises set family against family in a battle to prevent starvation. This was preceded and followed by enormous inflation in land values, new levels of indebtedness, forced sales, and bankruptcies – a situation in which family members expressed anger when the property of relatives escaped their grasp or saw their own misfortune lead to the enhancement of the fortune of close kin as cousins and brothers-in-law bought them out.

Every family practiced a different strategy of marriage. In many cases during this period, women played key roles in mediating alliances. Widows, for example, retained all the strands of family authority and were reluctant to diminish their power by marrying again. But even where a father was present, the alliance system could be manipulated by women who contributed heavily to family production for the market. Criss-crossing the system of patrilines were a series of networks constructed on the basis of sister/sister or sister/brother bonding. Different marriage strategies were based not just on gender considerations, however. Kinship could coordinate village production groups or political alliances, or regionally based artisanal crafts, especially in the construction industry. A cobbler or a weaver might think differently about the social qualities of a spouse from a mason or a road pavior. A child from a family in which several siblings were lined up to reestablish old alliances might strike out in a new direction, or one squeezed out of a good village marriage by successful machinations of his or her rivals might look outside the village inside or outside the wider kinship network for a spouse.

In the end, no single strategy and no single set of values produced a system of preferred marriages. That does not mean that unions were in any way random or that strategy was a matter of pure manipulation divorced from mediations of production, class, sentiment, and politics. Kinship, the set of exchanges, the system of alliances, help, service, conflict, enmity, hatred, and partisanship were all part of a wider discourse that in turn was based on things that people argued about, reflected upon, expressed rights to, or things that obligated them or subjected them to rules in some way. "Things" that can be resolved in this manner into social relations are given the name "property," and in the end kinship and class are fundamentally arguments about holding, transmitting, redistributing, managing, and accruing it. There is no single direction in which an argument about property has to go and no single way in which kinship interconnects with or constructs class relations. In Neckarhausen, social processes cannot be fully understood without a thoroughgoing analysis of kinship, but kinship remains without content outside of the social processes themselves. It has no universal meaning, is not something that was replaced in the process of modernization, and should not be viewed as quintessentially integrative, local, archaic, or disinterested.

16

Kinship and practice at the turn of the century

The use of kin in a society never emanates from a single strategy, applied by all individuals. Although many generalizations about structure can be drawn from statistical correlations, it is impossible to describe a kinship system adequately without examining the logics of different occupational, wealth, political, gender, and age groups or taking into account the diversity of practices, whose creativity *and* reiteration continually shape, support, and reconfigure relationships between individuals and classes. This long chapter presents 13 biographies of village men who interacted with one another during the last two decades of the eighteenth century and first two decades of the nineteenth. Each of them, to use Pierre Bourdieu's image, was dealt a different hand and each maneuvered within the rules of the game with quite different resources, skill, and intensity. The biographies are based on scattered references in the sources, but the breaks, surprises, and inconsistencies would still be there if the record were fuller. The point of the exercise is to explore the range of kinship practices by steadily shifting the point of view and to link them to different strategies of class, family, and political culture.

Each biography interacts, so to speak, with the others, and reflects back on the singularity of a particular life but also adds to an unfolding story, whose focus, despite abrupt shifts in temporality and perspective, follows a line of social and political development. For the most part, that story tracks the male political culture of Neckarhausen up into the 1820s. The growing independence of women in the politics of kinship is missing in this account because biographies of women are difficult to construct from the records. In public documents, women occupied a different political space from men – they were not to be found in the taverns, at the assembly, or in the work gangs in the woods or along the river channel where many of the incidents that provide the basis of our accounts took place. It is quite possible to chronicle domestic histories – as I did in Chapter 11 of

Property, Production, and Family – where women's characters and intentions are in full display. But at least through the 1820s, parallel biographies of the kind that follow could not be reconstructed from the texts. The discussion of kinship and the politics of gender will resume in the investigation of Cohort V.[1]

The stories in this chapter are a reminder that kinship is constructed, not simply given, and that the context in which kinship operates continually changes. From the vantage point of particular lives, aspects of character refuse to go away. Each person decides to some extent how to live his or her life, and exhibits different degrees of loyalty, shrewdness, diligence, steadiness, trust, and temper in the give and take of everyday life. Character contributes greatly to what a person can do with the kinship resources at hand and to the kinds of strategies he or she adopts and the goals he or she sets. The stories, however, make up a larger story, and similar characters and similar strategies may have quite different consequences in different contexts. Some of the shifts and changes, despite their parallels in the wider world of the early nineteenth century, seem immanent to local society. This appears, for example, to be the case with class endogamy and the production of class within the dynamics of marriage and the construction of kinship relations in myriad everyday exchanges. But over time, class itself becomes a resource in village political life, and careers can be made by falling back on class support where kinship networks prove too brittle. Of course, not all aspects of the social and political context of a village history come from within. In the larger story that emerges in this account of local life, the state intervened to reconfigure administrative and legal institutions and redraw the lines of power by professionalizing clerical procedures, the management of village resources, and the exercise of police powers. How to elucidate these issues and how to show the interaction of structure and practice calls for different narrative strategies on the part of the historian, and for different skills on the part of the reader. The tune of this chapter derives from the way a series of different tones resonate with one another, or – to vary the metaphor – the way its landscape emerges in the montage effect of a series of snapshots taken from many slightly different angles and superimposed on one another.

The whiner

Johannes Heinser, Bauer (1756–1812)

One evening in 1801, Johannes Heinser sat in the tavern with a cousin while Schultheiss Friedrich Krumm occupied a back room with several village magistrates. The Rat and Gericht had just met, as they did each year, to fill vacancies

[1] The sources for this chapter are found in two commission investigations (HSAS, A213, Bü7030; A214, Bü746; D 80, Bü63) and in the village *Gerichts- und Gemeinderatsprotocolle, Kirchenkonvents-protocolle, Vogtruggerichtsprotocolle, Kaufbücher, Schultheissenamtsprotocolle, Inventuren- und Teilungen, Gemeindepflegerechnungen, Oberamtsprotocolle in causis fori mixti* (1801–12), STAL, F190, Band 9, and *in causis civilibus* (1812–43), F190, Band 10–11, 257–74.

among themselves and to appoint or reappoint village officers, from patrolman to mouse catcher. Heinser was complaining about the officials (*raisoniert über die Herren*), and one witness found him "drunk as a pig."

Heinser was clearly upset about how village business had been conducted that day, but he also deeply resented the arbitrary and corrupt management of village affairs. For one thing, Schultheiss Krumm had gathered many of the most lucrative executive positions in his own hands, including administration of the forest and sheepfold, and Heinser was particularly exercised about favoritism in the allocation of building wood and the distribution of kindling. Furthermore, he said, the Schultheiss and Bürgermeister stole wood for themselves and connived with others to do the same. More than anything else, however, Heinser was upset about the high-handed way the Schultheiss circumvented the principles of equality. Once a year, village men labored in the local forest to make up a load of kindling for each household, to be distributed by lot. But the two chief magistrates arrogated the right not only to first choice but also to an extra supply before the rest of the cartloads were allocated. And as sheepfold master, the Schultheiss had added an extra 60 sheep of his own to the herd, way out of proportion to anyone else.

The issue of fairness became a burning one in the several decades leading up to Friedrich Krumm's election to office. Magistrates, however rooted in the village, were rulers, whose authority came directly from the prince, and the Schultheiss had a good deal of power to command respect or to order people to act or desist from action according to his own judgment and interest. A villager was out of order – *rebellisch* – when he publicly complained (*raisoniert*) about official decisions and actions. Krumm's successor (his brother-in-law) brought a villager before the district court for *raisonieren* in the Nürtingen tavern.[2] The Schultheiss and Bürgermeister fined a villager in 1807 because he often *raisoniert* over them.[3] And in a fierce altercation in 1820, one villager took a stick after another who had accused him of complaining (*raisonieren*) about official decisions.[4] Complaining was a normal activity for many villagers, of course, but the Schultheiss always had the option of considering his honor or the honor of his office insulted and could fine or jail the offender. Just because magistrates had significant power to repress dissension, villagers were very concerned about evenhandedness and an equal administration of the rules. The kind of complaint Heinser loudly declaimed in the tavern led the next year to a village cabal against Schultheiss Krumm and not only his dismissal from office but also a month-long prison sentence at hard labor.

The exercise of power and the problems of self-serving administration were not the only issues between Heinser and Krumm. The Schultheiss had inherited one of the largest fortunes in the village and had married a woman with an

[2] *Oberamtsgericht*, STAL, F190, vol. 11 (14.9.1815).
[3] *Gericht*, vol. 6, f. 213 (6.6.1807).
[4] *Oberamtsgericht*, STAL, F190II, vol. 258 (14.6.1820).

extraordinary inheritance to match his own. He was also well connected through inheritance and marriage to other wealthy Bauern and to his fellow magistrates. He had come up through the Rat and Gericht and had served as Bürgermeister for several years before being elected to the office of Schultheiss. In 1800 he was the fifth richest householder in the village, while Heinser was fiftieth (out of 167). Such differences in wealth were usually expressed in a language of reputation. In another village during the mid eighteenth century, wealthy and poor villagers confronted each other as "good" and "bad" householders.[5] Here in Neckarhausen, a Krumm supporter called Heinser a man of poor reputation (*einen schlecht prädicierten Bürger*) as a way of ranking him in the village hierarchy.

The incident at the tavern on the evening after the officers had been reappointed involved a confirmed sentiment of equal rules for everyone. There had always been a curfew in Neckarhausen, and over the years it had been more or less enforced depending on the zeal of the watchmen and the complaints of neighbors and pietists. A few weeks earlier, the Schultheiss had assembled the villagers, insisted that the curfew be respected, and threatened violators with a fine – or even a few days in the lockup. Yet on the evening in question he himself drank wine with several magistrates way past closing time until well into the morning hours. Witnesses contradicted each other over exactly what happened, whether Heinser was drunk, and exactly how late the officials stayed in the tavern, but the story makes no sense if indeed Krumm had not violated the rule he insisted on enforcing. Heinser parodied Krumm's exercise of privilege by sending in the night watchman to tell the magistrates to leave at the "order of Johannes Heinser" himself. During the investigation into Krumm's conduct of office the next year, Heinser suggested that Krumm's drinking tabs were frequently taken care of by falsified receipts. In all likelihood, his public, half-drunken intervention had made it difficult for the Schultheiss to hide the substantial tab of 30 fl (one and a half times the price of a cow) for the drinking party in the village accounts. In fact, the Bürgermeister who would have had to connive with Krumm egged the officials on to retaliate.

Out for revenge, Krumm went straight to Heinser's house, where he tormented him for a while with a hay fork. Along with the night watchman, the forest patrolman Michael Feldmaier, and a host of hangers-on, including the Bürgermeister, he marched Heinser off to jail with kicks and blows. A few hours after his incarceration, Heinser broke out of the jailhouse and ran home, where Krumm and the others sought him out again. There in his house, he pulled his knife and lunged for the Schultheiss only to cut patrolman Michael Feldmaier severely in the wrist.

Later in the same year that Heinser tried his jest, he, along with several men from another, nearby village, sent a letter to the duke. They complained that Schultheiss Krumm had so badly conducted his responsibilities as administrator

[5] David Warren Sabean, *Power in the Blood: Popular Culture and Village Discourse in Early Modern Germany* (Cambridge, 1984), chap. 5.

of the estate of their cousin (*Vetter*), the drunkard and wastrel Johannes Rieth, that what had been one of the most substantial patrimonies in Neckarhausen of 8,290 fl had been reduced in a few years to 2,607 fl. They accused Krumm of acting arbitrarily, producing no accounts, drinking along with Rieth and his comrades, and paying bar tabs out of the estate. A few months later, they wrote again that at Christmastime Krumm, Rieth, and a group of friends in a tavern in Nürtingen got so drunk that they had to be driven home in a cart. The letters led to a thorough investigation, with Krumm held responsible for all the new debts he paid for since taking over as administrator. He himself accused the informers of acting from malice (*Gehässigkeit*): they had often been punished for their wicked behavior. Such antagonism existed between Heinser and Krumm that neither could speak of the other's motives in any other terms than arrogance and hate.

Johannes Heinser was the son of a Richter and in 1784 had married Maria Dorothea Falter, the stepgranddaughter of another Richter. The two of them had a kind of first-cousin-once-removed union – his father and her grandfather had been married to sisters. Heinser's marriage conforms to the pattern of alliance between closely associated magistrate households. The senior generation was represented by two brothers-in-law, whose position ought to have been taken over by Johannes. Although his own father had died a few years before his marriage, his wife's stepgrandfather continued in office for another six years, retiring just at the right time (1790) for the 34-year-old Heinser to take his place. However, it was during the 1780s and 1790s that two powerful networks of allied families, one dominated by Friedrich Krumm with his Geiger and Bosch allies and the other by the Hentzler family, consolidated their power and controlled entry to the council and court. Neither Heinser nor his wife were closely related to either of these families. That did not mean that they were not connected to powerful men in the village. Heinser's wife's brother joined the Rat during 1801, the year Heinser had his run-in with Krumm. By 1804 the brother-in-law was Richter, and he eventually obtained a seat on the church consistory. Almost certainly, during the early 1790s the future prospects of the brothers-in-law was thought to be the other way around. Heinser had become godfather for his wife's brother and, being 11 years older and godfather, probably expected to act as a patron or as the central figure in a new power configuration. Heinser had been raised in a Richter household where village issues had continually been under review, but just when his brother-in-law pushed ahead, his only forum had already become the tavern and his political comment considered "complaining." Michael Feldmaier's testimony in the 1802 investigation of Schultheiss Krumm characterized Heinser as a "wicked" (*ruchloser*) man, a gloss on the attitudes and actions of someone whose promise had never been fulfilled.

It was already apparent during the early 1790s that Heinser was not in a position to make much use of inherited capital. Except for his brother-in-law, no one called upon him or his wife to act as godparent, save two families who needed an extra person for twins or a young woman who bore an illegitimate child. This contrasts decidedly with Friedrich Krumm and his wife, who were godparents for 7 families, or even more with the central figure in the Hentzler clan and his wife, who stood for 27. He also never moved out of the class of small producers. At their marriage, he and his wife put together a farmholding much less than half of what his father had. This, of course, was typical of the intergenerational dynamics in Neckarhausen, which left children with enough property to keep them rooted in the village but not enough to make them independent of their parents' enterprises. Throughout his married life, Heinser sold just as much land as he bought, and at his death in 1812 at the age of 56, he had exactly the same number of arable strips as he started with. The only difference was that they were now laden with mortgage debt. Together, Heinser and his wife lost over 1,100 fl during the course of their marriage. Just as he had failed to get himself elected to office and was largely ignored as a godparent, he was not successful at accumulating property and presumably was not much of a farmer. Buying land required either ready cash from profitable farming or credit, and he does not appear to have had or desired to have had access to the mortgage market for the purchase of new property. That kind of financing by and large came from sources outside the village, from commercial and rentier capital in cities and towns. But any application for a loan went through the local village mortgage bureau on whose board sat the Schultheiss and members of the Gericht. Some of the tension between Heinser and various officials certainly played around issues of honor, consideration, and credit. And since no one in the village was willing to underwrite any of his loans by offering a mortgage bond, he could only raise money secured on land and buildings he already owned.

Some of Heinser's property transactions involved buying and selling strips of land between close relatives – a brother, step-father-in-law, or cousin. But most of the bits and pieces he traded back and forth did not involve close or extended family members at all. In no respect does Heinser seem to have cultivated a network of kin. He was only a Kriegsvogt twice, once for his brother-in-law's wife – for the same couple for which he stood as godparent. After 1794, there is no trace of him acting in this position of trust again. Perhaps his attitude toward family is best illustrated by an action he took the year before he married. Gall Feldmaier sold Heinser's mother a meadow, after which, as frequently was the case, it was offered at public auction to ensure a fair market price. Heinser proceeded to outbid his mother and purchase the piece of land. Nineteen years later, Schultheiss Krumm called Heinser a man hated by God and the world, a person who had treated his mother in an inexcusable manner. A year later, his mother turned over two gardens and a vineyard to Johannes's children in return for the "care" she had received from Heinser and his wife. To skip a generation like that was unusual and occurred most often when a parent mistrusted or was in conflict with a child: recourse consisted in investing ownership in the grandchildren. That she passed on property at all was probably due to pressure on Heinser's part, but her response was to deny him ownership, if not usufructory rights, in the land.

Johannes Heinser had been heir to a magistrate and wealthy Bauer and had made the kind of marriage that was expected of magistrate and Bauer families. But he did not evoke the kind of trust, esteem, and loyalty that would have allowed him to capitalize on the resources he started with. For most of his life, he was well situated in the third quartile of tax payers, but he slowly burdened his property with debt. He was not able to cultivate a network of kin or friends through godparentage, Kriegsvogtschaft, or loan guarantees, yet kinship was an idiom ready to hand for some of his purposes. He organized a network of cousins and evoked the connection of cousinship in order to intervene in Krumm's administration of Rieth's estate. The very choice of his mother as godparent for his children showed a disinclination to build relations within a larger kinship network with his own age cohort. His wife followed a similar strategy, using her stepgrandfather during the early years of marriage both as Gevatter and as Kriegsvogt. Without a wide and varied social network, husbandly skill, or reputation, Heinser seems to have dissipated his patrimony, all the time presuming to speak as a social equal among more successful men. He appears to have been the kind of irritating fellow that a rich village headman would treat with contempt and slap around a little.

The enforcer

Michael Feldmaier, day-laborer, Bauer, field patrolman, forest patrolman, tree surgeon, mole and mouse catcher, beggar warden (1764–1830)

Michael Feldmaier held a variety of village offices over his lifetime. In 1795 at the age of 30, he was appointed temporary watchman for the harvest fields (*Güterschütz*) and at the same time took on the jobs of tree surgeon and mole and mouse catcher. Two years later, he became the field patrolman, one of the three police officers, dealing respectively with the village, fields, and forest (Dorf-, Feld-, and Waldschütz). Such positions usually fell to men with enough property to ensure liability for damages but with insufficient income to support themselves independently. For most of his life, Michael Feldmaier, was in the second quartile tax bracket and in 1800 was ranked 96 out of 167 taxpayers. Village officers usually had good connections to the magistrates and were dependent on their goodwill in order to continue in the job. Family tradition sometimes played a role – both Feldmaier's father and grandfather had been village patrol officers before him, and during the first 15 years of the nineteenth century, his brother and two cousins alternated with him in one or the other constabulary positions. When appointments and reappointments were made each year in April, it helped to have particular supporters on the Gericht. Young Michael had a Richter uncle (MZH), and his sister married the Richter Gall Feldmaier in 1806. In 1801, he was probably dependent on the unrelated Schultheiss Krumm for his job as forest patrolman, which explains his zeal in helping to capture Johannes Heinser, after the insolent parody of Krumm's conduct of office, and knocking the drunken man continually with his nightstick on the way to the jailhouse. It could well be that Heinser was so irritated that the stab at Feldmaier's wrist had really been meant for him rather than Krumm or that Heinser did not care which one of them he hit.

During his first year as field patrolman, Feldmaier accused Richter Christoph Hentzler of stealing a sack of grain in the Nürtingen mill. Failing to provide proof, Feldmaier received a fine, which led him to abuse the officials and denounce the judgment. That in turn brought a 24-hour jail sentence, whereupon he accused a fellow Bürger, Mathes Sterr, of receiving stolen grain and being in cahoots with Hentzler. By the end of his first annual appointment, Feldmaier was not renewed – again bringing him to reproach the magistrates publicly and incur a fine. Although the political cleavages that ruptured the village several years later were not yet completely fixed by this date, his opponent, Christoph Hentzler, was a powerful member of the Gericht, one of the richest men in the village, and not someone to trifle with. Christoph's brother had been Schultheiss until 1788 and was still a political force in the village. One of his cousins was the richest man in the community and a fellow Richter. The Schultheiss at the time probably leaned toward the Hentzler faction – he was Christoph's sister's stepson and married to Christoph's wife's sister – but whether he did or not, Feldmaier had made an unwise choice when he spread rumors about the Richter, at least for the short term. A few years later, these men were on opposite sides in the controversy surrounding Schultheiss Krumm. Feldmaier was his supporter, whereas Christoph Hentzler and Mathes Sterr were his active critics.

A year after Michael Feldmaier went empty-handed, Friedrich Krumm succeeded the recently ousted Schultheiss. With the balance of power among the magistrates shifted in Feldmaier's favor, he received his old position as field patrolman back. Two years later he became forest patrolman, just after Krumm assumed the office of Waldmeister (forest administrator), the crucial position for any partisan exploitation of the woods. There were more complaints about Krumm's handling of the forest resources than about any other matter; moreover, Krumm's successor, his brother-in-law Conrad Hiller, seems to have maintained the corrupt practices in the forest, keeping the experienced and loyal Feldmaier on until 1809. A few years before he lost his office, Feldmaier was attacked for arbitrary and illegal disposal of wood by Christoph Hentzler's son, young Salomon, who accused the patrolman of paying tavern bills by selling timber in neighboring villages. Perhaps Feldmaier's activities got too hot for Schultheiss Hiller to handle, especially since his own tenure of office was marked by a noticeable rise in public drinking among the magistrates and illegal maneuvers to pay for it, but it may well have been the case that Feldmaier was no longer capable of handling such a physically demanding job. In 1810, he was demoted to mole and mouse catcher, the position that he held for the next ten years with a few terms interspersed as field patrolman, perhaps as his health allowed it. During the early 1820s, he managed a five-year stint as field patrolman again, followed by a few years as beggar warden, keeping track of traveling indigents and dispensing public alms.

In 1812, when he was 47, Michael Feldmaier spent an evening in the tavern together with his second cousin, the village patrolman, amusing themselves teasing several of the young unmarried men about the current lack of manliness among the youth. Each side talked about the right young lads of their generations, but Feldmaier stopped the conversation by calling all the young fellows "bedpissers." Andreas Falter, who had defended his own cohort, grew silent, followed the married men outside, and stabbed Feldmaier in the chest with a severe blow from a broken knife, enough to cause considerable bleeding and immediate concern but ultimately no permanent injury. Feldmaier had turned away Falter's challenge to fight because he was too old to do so. His wretched back led him constantly to get up to walk around the room. The judge rejected Falter's story about Feldmaier knocking him down, sure that the latter was not "man enough" to do such a thing. This short vignette about manhood and verbal challenge, married and unmarried status, and male honor and aggression is too schematic to do more than suggest certain themes. But it testifies to a fellow old in his mid-40s, whose reputation was based on having "once been a man." Feldmaier held one village post or the other throughout his life to supplement the small earnings from his farm. He was vigorous enough in his 30s to have been a player in village affairs and to have won respect in the physical defense of honor. But he was never able to build upon his small stake to expand his holdings. By the 1820s, he had a reputation as a heavy schnapps drinker, something that was probably already the case 10 or so years earlier.

Like many of his generation, Feldmaier and his siblings called upon close relatives for support, but they were also dependent on the patronage of wealthier, more powerful, and often unrelated villagers. The godparents for his children were the wife's brother-in-law (ZH) and his aunt (FZ). He and one of his brothers married sisters, and he stood as godparent for the other couple. One of his cousins, Gall Feldmaier, Richter and long-term Bürgermeister, acted as Kriegsvogt for Michael's wife (Maria Agnes Schach). I can find no record of Feldmaier himself fulfilling the role of Kriegsvogt. His wife's brother became guardian for the Feldmaier children. In the early years after his marriage (1792), Michael was executor for an estate and guardian of the children of an unrelated family.

Feldmaier was an active buyer and seller of land throughout his life, even though he never managed to accumulate much for any period of time. He was involved altogether in 68 transactions (plus 6 as Pfleger). Examining his genealogy cursorily, I found 38 out of 68 (55 percent) sales to have been sales between kin – nuclear family members, brothers-in-law, first and second cousins. At his marriage in 1792, he and his wife combined 6 arable plots and 3 other strips of agricultural land. For a brief period between 1795 and 1798, he bought up 7 more parcels. Then up until 1810, he sold as many parcels (14) as he bought (14). Like many other landholders in Neckarhausen during the two decades after 1810, he went bankrupt. Much of his property was sold at auction by a court-appointed executor – 12 parcels of land altogether. But surprisingly, his wife bought almost all of them and acquired 2 remaining parcels through redemption.

The strategy of a wife purchasing property, frequently all of the property, from a bankrupt husband developed for the most part after 1800 and lasted for several decades. It arose in the context of a crisis in credit in the state of Württemberg, which led to two great revisions in mortgage law (*Pfandgesetz*) in 1825 and 1828.[6] Most indebtedness, or at least the kind that led to insolvency, involved an overextension of mortgage credit in a situation of high volatility of land prices and a boom and bust situation in agriculture. Despite the fact that husbands were the administrative heads of communal property, no man could burden his spouse's property with debt without her express permission before a court and in the presence of her Kriegsvogt. Nor could her property be pledged or sold for his debts without her express agreement. In the eighteenth century, however, most women most of the time threw their lot in with that of their husbands. They allowed their property to be mortgaged and paid off their husbands' debts with their own land. A wastrel or drunkard might prompt a suit by a wife to declare him incompetent (*Mundtod*) and to have all his affairs put under an administrator, but honorable debts of a hard-working man were understood to be the concern of both partners.

During the economic dislocation associated with the agricultural revolution, population rise, pauperism, protoindustrialization, the war economy of the Napoleonic period, the continental blockade, the boom and collapse of agricultural and land prices, and the poor harvests and famine of the postwar period, many farmers fell into debt and insolvency. It is not easy to gather statistics from the available sources, but certainly rich and poor suffered alike, and many of the wealthiest members of the village crashed during this period. Various strategies were worked out to cushion the effects, but one of the most effective – over the short run at least – was to protect the wife's property from the husband's creditors. Before the court, she simply refused to accept liability for his debts. Many women then used their own resources to recover the lands of their husbands. Foreclosure for some people could turn out to be a way of reducing the amount of debt. In a phase when land fell in value, a landholder not able to cover his loans would have all demands settled when the state forced a sale of his property. Creditors, of course, only received a percentage according to the ratio of debt to income from the sale. The wife's property could then be used as collateral to float a new loan and recover the husband's real estate. It would take a great deal of careful calculation to prove – something that goes too far afield at the moment – but it could well be the case that villagers for the most part did not bid aggressively against a woman trying to buy back her husband's land and buildings. That would mean that they effectively colluded against outside creditors

[6] David Warren Sabean, "Soziale und kulturelle Aspekte der Geschlechtsvormundschaft im 18. und 19. Jahrhundert," in Ute Gerhard, ed., *Handbuch für die Rechtsgeschichte der Frau* (Beck Verlag: München, forthcoming [1997]).

who stood to lose in a less than competitive bidding situation. The fact that for 10 out of 12 parcels, Feldmaier's wife put in the high bid suggests that no one felt secure enough to interfere. At this point, Feldmaier had a brother-in-law and an uncle, who in turn had two cousins, on the Gericht. He had been a long-time associate of Friedrich Krumm, whose brother-in-law was now the overseeing Schultheiss. The executor of the estate was the husband of a second cousin, Salomon Brodbeck, the newest man to join the Gericht. It appears that the political structure of cousinship protected Feldmaier and his wife from the immediate effects of the economic crisis. Twelve parcels, including the house and barn, were sold from Michael's estate to his wife in 1814, about three-quarters of their collective property. But their strategy only staved off disaster, for during the next two years she sold four parcels and he sold three. In 1817, they sold nine and bought four fields, after which they had to be contented until Michael's death in 1830 with one arable strip in each of the three fields, one vineyard, and two gardens.

The year 1814 was one of great tension in the village over the economic troubles. Several years earlier, Feldmaier had reported young Salomon Hentzler for spreading the rumor that Schultheiss Hiller had a list of 40 villagers about to face foreclosure. Hentzler was fined and himself forced into bankruptcy within a year. In 1814 there was a minor riot in the village when the marshal (*Presser*) came to attach the goods of one of the Bürger. Unexpectedly, wealthy and powerful villagers were forced into bankruptcy, including men like Bürgermeister Johannes Falter, who had frequently managed the affairs of minor children. And the occasion of his failure revealed an instance of collusion between him and Feldmaier. Shortly after Falter's bankruptcy, one of his wards, Jacob Friedrich Schach, returned from abroad and sued him for cheating his estate of 150 fl. Almost 20 years earlier, Falter had wanted to buy two fields from the Schach estate on credit but was barred by law from being in debt to his own wardship. In order to purchase the land, he set up a dummy sale through his nephew Michael Feldmaier, who was hardly in a position to refuse, since he needed friends on the court in order to get one of the village jobs. Feldmaier later protested that he had acted out of kinship considerations, for on the one hand Falter was his uncle (MZH) and on the other Schach was his brother-in-law (WB). Although Schach, as a sibling of his wife, was his "good friend" (*Freund*), Falter's appeal to *Freundschaft* was difficult to deny. It never occurred to Feldmaier that anyone with so much property and so few children could end up in foreclosure. In 1814 he could no longer cover the debt to his brother-in-law because he himself was insolvent (although at that time the family property was intact through the sale to his wife). Each year as Falter had paid off the interest and perhaps some of the principal, Feldmaier had signed an acknowledgment of further indebtedness in the wardship accounts. All of this must have been an open secret when Falter began to work land that used to belong to his ward and had been auctioned to his nephew.

Bankruptcy continued to have consequences for a person after foreclosure and public auction. Once forced into receivership, a Bürger could no longer hold a position of trust, such as a wardship, or handle public monies, a considerable loss of honor and reputation. The year after his failure, Feldmaier had to suffer public humiliation at the hands of Schultheiss Hiller, who scolded the insolvent (*Gantmann*) for collecting sheepfold fees in the course of his duties as field patrolman. Feldmaier's angry outburst, which brought him four days in jail, revealed the weaknesses and frustrations built into a career based on loyalty and service to men more powerful and independent than himself.

Michael Feldmaier was one of a group of interrelated men who kept peace in the village. They were required to report all delicts to the authorities, a matter that was especially important for the forest patrolman. Each year, he might well present a list of more than a hundred people who had committed some form of crime in the woods. Such a job required considerable evenhandedness – a patrolman was much like a referee who has to keep a game going, making judgment calls, ignoring some fouls while censuring others – and Feldmaier did not always escape the charge of favoritism and corruption. Above all, a peace officer was part of the support group of the dominant political faction among the magistrates. It certainly helped to have relatives among the village officials, but the older forms of patronage through marriage and godparentage did not bind farm-laborers/village job holders so tightly to richer, more powerful men any more. Various contenders for political power built factions through loyalty and services, offering jobs, loan guarantees, and mediation in financial and property transactions. Michael Feldmaier was an enforcer, who expected to be rewarded for his loyalty. His reputation as a "real man" waned with his physical deterioration, and he ended up dulling the pain of memory and a bad back with lashings of hard liquor.

The patsy

Mathes Sterr, Bauer, day-laborer, trader (1766–1830)

Just before the turn of the century, Mathes Sterr took over the ducal farm in Jüstingen. The exact dating is unclear from the record, but it probably happened around 1798 when Sterr sold 13 parcels of land in Neckarhausen, in all likelihood to raise capital to buy out the previous farmers, who included the current Schultheiss of Neckarhausen, Johann Georg Baur, the previous Schultheiss, Salomon Hentzler, and two other Bürger, the Friedrich Geigers, father and son. Old Geiger was a member of the Gericht and uncle to the current Bürgermeister, soon-to-be Schultheiss, Friedrich Krumm. The consortium, which had not made a success of the farm, was dissolved when Sterr paid off or assumed 7,000 fl worth of debts. This was a sizable fortune that can be measured against those of various witnesses to conflicts in 1802. The field patrolman, Michael Feldmaier, had a holding worth 200 fl. Gall Feldmaier, a member of the Rat and later Bürgermeister, was worth 800 fl. Young Salomon Hentzler, nephew of the old

Schultheiss and a substantial Bauer, had property worth 2,500 fl. Only Friedrich Krumm by that time stood out with a considerable fortune of 7,000 fl.

Mathes Sterr by no means had the financial strength to take over the Jüstingen farm by himself. In 1795 he was in the third quartile of taxpayers in Neckarhausen, a Bauer well above subsistence but not in the same league with the kind of men who held positions among the magistrates. At his marriage in 1784, he and his wife combined 12 arable strips and 10 other parcels of agricultural land, a very large property for newlyweds. His father even provided him with all the agricultural equipment, a sore spot for his older brother (by 13 years), who blamed Schultheiss Hentzler for helping with the deal that sent the father into retirement and left Mathes with the gear. Each brother had a separate apartment in the same house – with the retired father living with Mathes. The older son became dependent on the younger for the tools to cultivate his own land, which perhaps underlay the considerable tension between the two brothers and their wives, who all traded insults and accusations of thievery over the years. During the next decade or so after his marriage, Mathes prospered, buying 20 new parcels of land while selling only 9. In 1798, however, he sold off the 13 properties, probably, as I have suggested, in order to take over the Jüstingen farm. In the same year, Friedrich Krumm, the administrator of the wastrel son of the last Rieth Schultheiss, Johannes, set up a temporary deal whereby Sterr was to take over Rieth's considerable estate as Pfleger or guardian and farm it back to Krumm himself. In any case, Sterr was busy outside the village with the ducal farm, where the key to his financial calculation was substantial backing by various villagers in Neckarhausen. As far as I can make out, the chief farmers had been the Geigers, financed by Schultheiss Baur and old Schultheiss Hentzler. In order to bail themselves out and make a fresh start, they bankrolled Sterr – with Schultheiss Hentzler and Bürgermeister Krumm providing surety (*Bürgschaft*) for the whole venture.

Sterr had married at the uncommonly young age of 18, and must have shown considerable promise, since he was marrying into the politically dominant family at the time. Occasionally a young couple forced the hand of parents by getting pregnant, but this was not the case for young Mathes Sterr and his wife, Christina Hentzler. Her father had died at the age of 32 in 1769, and her mother died two years before the wedding. She was clearly the object of concern for her uncles, and one of them, Schultheiss Hentzler, came up with the cash to pay for a dispensation to declare Mathes of age. The kinship connections of Christina Hentzler and her husband are depicted in Figure 16.1.

At the time of Mathes Sterr's marriage, Christina's uncle, Salomon, was Schultheiss, and another uncle, Christoph, was a Richter. Christoph was her guardian and later Kriegsvogt, and he and Salomon's wife Catharina were godparents for the Sterr children. Their uncle, another Salomon, was a member of the Gericht and for many years Bürgermeister. A few years after Sterr's marriage, this Salomon was succeeded on the Gericht by his son Johann Wilhelm Hentzler. The Hentzlers were also closely allied with the Johann Georg Baurs, father and

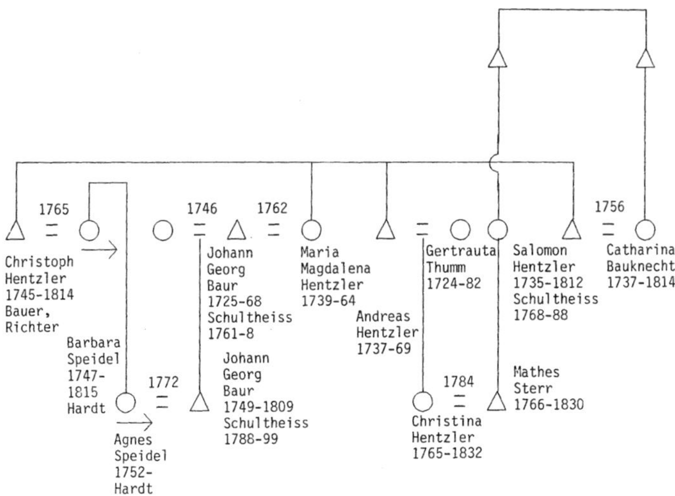

Figure 16.1

son, who bracketed Salomon Hentzler's term as Schultheiss. The father married Christoph's and Salomon's sister just after he took office in the early 1760s. His son and Christoph Hentzler married sisters from the village of Hardt. All of these close connections suggest that young Johann Georg Baur was the Hentzler house candidate for Schultheiss when Salomon was forced to resign for manipulating the tithes on wine in 1788. Baur was in turn ousted by state authorities, although the details are not part of the record. His successor in 1799, Friedrich Krumm, was apparently not part of the Hentzler alliance system but received the backing of old Salomon at the time of his appointment.

There are indications in the late 1790s that Krumm cooperated closely with the Hentzler family and its allies. In 1795 Mathes Sterr carted grain and fodder for Bürgermeister Krumm and Schultheiss Baur, who were operating a business together to supply troops engaged in the Napoleonic wars. And Salomon Hentzler and Baur had financed the undertaking at Jüstingen for Krumm's uncle and cousin, the Geigers. When Mathes Sterr took over the farm, the financial support came from Salomon Hentzler and Friedrich Krumm, representatives from both family syndicates.

Sterr quickly went broke over the Jüstingen farm. By 1800, he was in receivership, and after the sale of all of his real estate, he was the only person in the tax record to have no property at all, the poorest man out of 167 taxpayers. By 1801, he was one of the two chief organizers, along with Christoph Hentzler's son, young Salomon Hentzler, of the attempt to drive Friedrich Krumm from office. He subscribed to the original complaint, went the rounds to many Bürger to gather evidence and signatures, and traveled to Neufen to find a lawyer to draw up the particulars in proper form. The core of the group that Mathes coordinated included two uncles, a brother, and two cousins of his wife, all Hentzlers.

The failure of the Jüstingen farm venture had significant consequences for Krumm and Salomon Hentzler. They had posted a very high bond and stood to lose an estimated 1,800 fl. According to Sterr, Krumm enticed him to give false testimony about Hentzler and to absolve Krumm of liability in the business. A key figure in the negotiations between Krumm and Sterr was the Richter Gall Feldmaier, Sterr's first cousin (FZS). The two of them, Feldmaier and Sterr, were referred to as *Geschwistrigkind* (children of siblings), and it was understood by all sides that such cousinship gave them mutual responsibility and loyalty to each other. But in this case, cousinship had been the basis for both continuous ties and tension with each other over time.

Gall Feldmaier was 16 years older than Sterr. His mother, a sister to Mathes's father, had kept house for the old man for many years and thus had actually taken part in raising young Sterr, who was five years old when she moved in. Gall had acted as guardian for Sterr and his sister and had represented Mathes in the 1785 dispute about the inheritance of agricultural equipment. The relations between Sterr and Feldmaier were not always smooth, however. When Gall claimed 6 fl from Mathes in 1690, the latter called him a "bitch's cunt" (*Hundsfoz*). Still that appears to have been an aberration in their association, and Feldmaier remained close to the Sterr family and succeeded Christoph Hentzler as Christina Sterr's Kriegsvogt, continuing in that capacity well past the events of 1801–2.

Once Sterr was completely broke, he was dependent upon other men for work and credit, and there was some discussion about the possibility of getting one of the village public jobs. That may have prompted him to go through Gall Feldmaier to offer to testify that Salomon Hentzler had promised to pay the whole debt from underwriting the Jüstingen farm venture. At least Krumm testified that the offer had come from Sterr himself and had been rejected. Mathes Sterr, on the other hand, alleged that Krumm had sent Gall Feldmaier with an offer of help in return for his perjured testimony. During the time when all this was under discussion, Krumm apparently put Sterr under considerable pressure and treated him in ways unbefitting his honor. He yelled insults ("Cannalie" – malicious person) out the window at Sterr's wife. At one point, another Bürger was in a dispute with Sterr over an issue having to do with tithes. Krumm had said in front of several men that the Bürger should have beaten Sterr to death, the joke being that the other man was old and physically incapable of doing anything of the kind. Sterr called upon the carpenter Adam Falter as a witness to the event, but Krumm impeached Falter on grounds that he was one of the signers of the complaint and therefore partisan.

According to Sterr, when Krumm put pressure on him to swear the false oath against Salomon Hentzler, he did not want to do so, since Hentzler was his

"Vetter" (wife's uncle, in fact, although Sterr and Hentzler's wife were also first cousins once removed). Gall Feldmaier, however, left him no peace and offered him a village job, enough grain to feed his family for a while, and some money. Feldmaier arranged for the two parties to meet at an inn in a neighboring village where Sterr agreed to the bargain. During the negotiations, Gall Feldmaier as "Geschwistrigkind" held him by the hand. Although Sterr got some of what was promised, the whole deal fell through once Krumm and Hentzler worked out an agreement between themselves. Nonetheless, when Sterr noised it about that Krumm had enticed him to perjury, Krumm called him before the court to prove it. Sterr ran away, chased by the Schultheiss and, among others, the forest patrolman, Michael Feldmaier. After waving a knife around and threatening to slit a few throats, he was captured and jailed. Sterr came away with his honor compromised, subject to public scorn by Schultheiss Krumm, who described him as a "liederlicher Geselle" (lewd fellow), the slanderous term that led to more libel suits in the village than any other.

Perhaps Sterr felt betrayed. In any event, he became one of the most active enemies of Krumm and one of the leaders of the group who petitioned for an investigation into his conduct of office. Despite the fact that young Salomon Hentzler and he (cousins by marriage) were the ostensible leaders, the investigating authorities discerned old Salomon Hentzler and his brother, Richter Christoph, as the real leaders in the cabal. Sterr's disappointment and the ties of kinship put him solidly in the Hentzler camp. He had to consider that the two men were his wife's uncles, that Christoph and Salomon's wife were godparents for his children, that Christoph served as guardian and Kriegsvogt for his wife, and that Salomon had underwritten his farm in the first place. Or it could have been that he was doubly tricked by Krumm. A half year after the events in the Oberensingen inn, Sterr's wife learned at Jüstingen that after all the debts had been settled, there had in fact been a surplus of 470 fl, which had been sent along through the authorities, presumably to the village. An incensed Sterr burst into the village court while it was in session, angrily asked where his money was, and offered to return all the insults Krumm had heaped on him and his wife.

The records do not clear up this last issue, but there were consequences for all the principles in the attack on Krumm. The Schultheiss himself was dismissed, had to serve four weeks in prison, and pay a large fine. Sterr spent eight weeks in the local jail for his unruly behavior and was condemned to pay part of the costs of the investigation.

Sterr's fortunes fluctuated considerably in the next years, often bolstered by support from his relatives. Between 1809 and 1812, he purchased 21 parcels of land while selling only 1. That put him back into the third quartile of landholders, a very substantial recovery from his earlier disaster. From the estate of Christoph Hentzler, he acquired a house and barn and several arable fields. From two estates administered by Gall Feldmaier, he purchased 4 parcels of land. Quite surprisingly, he also acquired four parcels from Friedrich Krumm. Perhaps business was business, or people could put aside hatreds more easily than we would suppose. Still the most effective help came from his Hentzler allies. Already in 1806, young Salomon Hentzler had gotten his cousin Andreas to lend him 100 fl for a common venture with Mathes Sterr, "who had no credit anywhere anymore."

By 1812, Sterr was in trouble again. One of his protectors, the old Schultheiss Hentzler, had died, and young Salomon found out at the estate division how much Sterr had cost the family. Salomon's reaction was so angry that Sterr had to take him to court for expressions of the most intense hatred (*Feindlichkeit*) he had ever seen. Salomon swore at him on the street and at night cut down his fruit trees out of revenge. Whether because of a collapse in his credit backing as a result of unskilled farming or because of the fluctuations in the price of agricultural produce, Sterr began to sell off his property – 7 parcels during 1813–14. By 1815 much of his land was sold at forced auction – 11 parcels – but as so often was the case at this time, a large portion of them (8 parcels) was purchased by his wife. She in turn had to sell 4 of them right away in the same year. In 1815 and 1820, Sterr was back in the lowest quartile of taxpayers. During the 1820s, the couple managed slowly to put together a small holding with 9 more parcels, edging themselves up into the second quartile. What began as a brilliant career run by an enterprising farmer ended in relative poverty and loss of reputation. By the time his son, Young Mathes, wanted to marry in 1822, the latter had no property nor any expectation to any. He was a completely wage-dependent, unskilled worker who "worked everywhere wherever he could."

The life of Mathes Sterr is a good lesson in the use of kinship. He started out with considerable capital – a good-sized farm and solid connections to those with political power and credit. But there were ambivalent attitudes toward him. Perhaps he was too young when he first married to have been called upon as godparent, but by the time he emerged as a substantial landholder, no one bothered to honor him or his wife for the position. They were the kind of people who did not build but only used the connections they were given, or perhaps it is better to say that they were used by them. Sterr seems to have been the instrument for a number of people to get themselves out of a bad investment, and he quickly lost all his property as a result. He was manipulated by kin on both sides to further their political ends – Krumm against Salomon Hentzler and the Hentzlers against Krumm. Sterr was never able to develop new connections of his own. He was never godparent, Kriegsvogt, or guardian, fulfilling the kinds of roles that would build up personal loyalty or create new "capital" to be passed on to the next generation. In similar fashion, every time he built up his estate, it dissipated either through mismanagement or false economic calculation. He was a man without credit or character, relying on the credit of his family and friends, who used his simplicity or loyalty for their own aggrandizement.

Cohort IV (1820–1829)

The go-between

Gall Feldmaier, Bauer, Richter, Bürgermeister (1750–1834)

Most of the discussion about peasant marriage puts the issues in terms of reproduction, the production of progeny – heirs – and the construction and continuous devolution of a patrimony. The rules of inheritance and the demographic fortunes of a family present certain problems for each household to solve, but the goal of a successful farm manager and politically active adult male is understood to be both the procreation of children and a suitable settlement of productive resources on each of them. However, someone like Gall Feldmaier introduces several complications in this picture of peasant strategies. To begin with, in 1775 at the age of 27 Feldmaier married a widow with 5 children 14 years his senior and past child bearing. Not only that, but he chose widows twice more, producing unexpectedly a single child from his third wife when she was 43 and thought to have been no longer fertile. His wives were 41, 43, and 41, respectively, at marriage (he was 27, 54, and 56). Everything points toward Feldmaier as a remarkably successful political operator. He built a dense network of allies out of a bundle of kinship ties. He began with little property of his own but maintained himself in the top quarter of taxpayers for more than 30 years by becoming the manager of property belonging to his wives and their minor children. He became an active and successful member of the Gericht and held office as a Bürgermeister for many years. Still, even as a politician he seems primarily to have been a mediator or a seconder of initiatives of others with independent wealth and more assured connections to family members with wealth and power of their own. Gall Feldmaier was the reliable manager of his wives' property and a man who could be trusted by different factions in the village. He never built a property of his own to manage and pass on to his heir, and perhaps it was the anomaly of his position that made him suitable as a go-between in so many situations. He could be seen to be disinterested precisely because he was not competing to transmit a patrimony of his own. In the end, however, he was not able to maintain the balance between factions, and he finally threw his lot in too intimately with the corrupt administration of Schultheiss Hiller. His crooked books finally cost him a considerable loss of land and dismissal from office.

How did Feldmaier use his meager resources to build a substantial position in the village? Much earlier, his father had been a Richter in the village, but the old man died when Gall was only 7, apparently not leaving a great deal of property for the boy to inherit. Within a short time, his mother married into the nearby village of Oberboihingen, where he spent his youth with every expectation of assuming Bürgerrecht there. At the death of his stepfather, however, his mother returned to Neckarhausen to become the housekeeper for her brother, Johann Georg Sterr, the father of 5-year-old Mathes. Gall soon followed her to become a farm servant. By the time he was 27 and still propertyless, he had few expectations of being able to make a match among any of the wealthier women

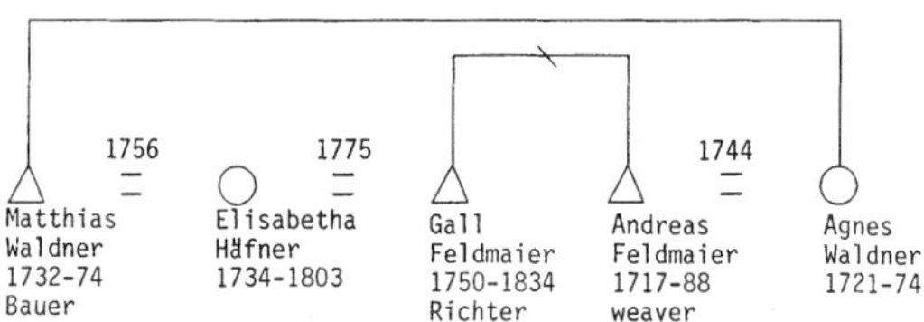

Figure 16.2

of his own age. Already couples had been balancing their marriage portions fairly closely for several decades. His only chance was to find a propertied widow looking for a reliable manager, someone willing to give him an edge through familial connections. In this case, his much older half-brother provided the crucial link. The newly widowed Elisabetha Häfner was the latter's sister-in-law (Figure 16.2).

Over the years, Feldmaier developed a network based on providing important services to people. He or a wife were godparents to 12 couples, he was guardian or estate administrator for at least 18 people, and he was Kriegsvogt for no less than 20 women. As guardian or executor, he oversaw the sale of more than 80 pieces of real estate. Even before he married, he was asked to act as guardian for the 40-year-old daughter of his future wife's sister. Perhaps his responsible work there made him a suitable marriage prospect. Soon after his marriage, he became the guardian of Uncle Sterr's children, including Mathes, with whom he maintained close relations for 40 years. He was the guardian for several of his various wives' brothers and their children, and for his own brother's children and grandchildren. During the period 1808–11, he was called upon to act as executor for seven estates of people unrelated to himself, at least not closely. Most of the instances involved the failure of one of the magistrates or their sons – young Salomon Hentzler, the son of Christoph, for example, or Friedrich Krumm himself. Apparently state authorities insisted on the appointment of a familial outsider, a nonpartisan, in the case of a forced sale. After all, the auction had to satisfy the creditors in Stuttgart or Esslingen, who stood to lose in any kind of rigged bidding. From inside the village, from among those in power, an executor had to be responsible to familial interest. Just his neutrality and independent position was guarantee that he could negotiate the complex goals of family interest. He had to see that a fragmented estate was distributed among the kin-group. Knowledge of the politics of estate execution prompted state officials to dismiss Feldmaier as Friedrich Krumm's executor almost as soon as he was appointed in favor of a completely independent outsider from Nürtingen. In the case of Feldmaier himself in 1813, when much of his property was sold at forced auction, the overseeing, independent, unrelated Bürgermeister Salomon Brodbeck saw to it that all but a few pieces fell to his wife at what were in all probability rigged prices.

Most of Gall Feldmaier's god-kin can be shown to have been close relatives.

In several cases, he was concerned with maintaining close relationships with the children he raised with his first wife and with her relatives – WHB, WFBDSD, WxFS, WSS. His wife was godparent for her niece (BD) and cousins (FBDS). Feldmaier also cultivated connections with his own close relatives, a niece (xBD) and cousins (MBD, FxBSS). He worked his kinship network more widely in his numerous duties as Kriegsvogt. He aided his own niece (XBD), and the wives of nephews (xBSW), grandnephews (xBSSW), and cousins (two different MBSW, FxBSW). Moreover he was very active for his first wife's relatives – her nieces (ZD, BD), wives of nephews (four different BSW), and women connected by marriage (BDHM). He also aided women connected to his second wife (HZ, HZSW, HZSD). I have been led to believe both by the logic of the institution and by the result of my statistical analysis that a Kriegsvogt usually but not always was chosen from a relative of a woman in order to balance the authority and interest of her husband, especially in the early years of marriage before the spouses might have reached an accommodation or learned to trust each other. However, in over half of the cases in which I can trace the genealogies, Feldmaier was a closer relative of the husband than of the wife. This suggests again that he built his network as a mediator, as someone who could be seen to be fair from both sides. All of his activities taken together indicate, on the one hand, that he constructed a dense network of kin, and, on the other, that he helped other powerful figures maintain their own familial integrity.

When his first wife died in 1804, Feldmaier came away with practically no property. Her estate was worth 2,175 fl, but there were five adult sons to divide it all. Feldmaier had little claim because most of the property had been assigned to the children at the death of their father and only held in usufruct by their mother. Still four of the sons had received marriage portions that if returned for a recalculation – as was the custom – would have given the estate a surplus for Feldmaier to inherit. All he took with him was his own marriage portion of about 350 fl and a debt of 300 fl related to a bond he had posted for someone who had gone bankrupt. Feldmaier seems to have taken seriously the responsibilities of training his wife's children and setting them up, but he himself did not profit from his labors. Indeed, in the nine years before his wife's death, he sold nine parcels of land and turned over the house and barn to his stepsons.

Soon Feldmaier was married to another widow with minor children. She was a Häfner originally from the village of Zizishausen, perhaps a relative of his first wife. She died unexpectedly within two years, but presumably he continued to raise the two young girls who were 10 and 8 at the time. One of them in fact later married the son of one of the boys he had raised by his first wife. In the series of exchanges that grew out of Feldmaier's alliances, he and the children frequently used the step-relations involved in his marriages to continue alliances over time.

Feldmaier's second wife brought a substantial holding of 4,000 fl in real estate and another 700 fl in movables. In this unusual matchup, he contributed only two arable plots worth 300 fl. But he was Bürgermeister, and effectively promoting marital alliances among his circle of friends and relatives. At this wife's death, he came away with a slightly higher stake than before, altogether about 925 fl. But even then he presented the children with 20 fl and saw to it that the married children from his first wife (of three marriages) got all the cultivation equipment. Both of these gestures were unusual. Among thousands of inventories, such gifts occurred with great infrequency. Villagers calculated closely and gave away very little. Major family quarrels could be caused by sums that small or smaller. As for cultivation gear, the most frequent strategy was to provide children with property but to keep the tools. This meant either that the children would have to hire the father to do their plowing and carting or that he could use the gear to negotiate their cooperation and compliance.

Feldmaier's third wife, again a widow, was in fact his father's stepbrother's son's daughter, a first cousin once removed. She, again, had minor children (three), ranging in age from 11 to 3. One of them would eventually marry Gall's cousin's son. Gall had been Kriegsvogt for the cousin's wife and Pfleger for their children. The marriage (after his death in 1835) then was between his stepdaughter and his ward. The new couple, Gall Feldmaier and Anna Catharina Feldmaier, the widow of Johannes Dorfschmid, each brought about the same amount of property to the marriage. They combined nine arable plots and seven other parcels of agricultural land. The death of his second wife together with his new marriage dropped him from the seventh richest taxpayer in the village to fifty-fourth, from quartile IV to quartile III. From then until his loss of office and the forced sale of his land in 1813–14, he remained well above subsistence, a respected householder and farmer and village Bürgermeister. Feldmaier had always been a careful administrator but not very adventuresome. In none of his marriages did the couple produce much of a profit over the course of the union, and he did not speculate a great deal in land. He only ever purchased 14 plots of land, none after 1809.

The alliances that grew out of Feldmaier's ties were not for the most part endogamous, not an interweaving of patrilines whose continuity derived from the devolution of patrimony (Figure 16.3). Feldmaier married three of his stepchildren to the children of other magistrates. Anton Waldner, the son of his first wife, married the daughter of Schultheiss Johann Georg Baur in 1793. In 1811 the daughter of his second wife, Anna Elisabetha Speidel, married a son of the Richter Johann Wilhelm Hentzler.[7] And finally relations between Feldmaier and Schultheiss Krumm were continued after Feldmaier's death when his stepdaughter Anna Thumm married Krumm's son (1835). There were also marriages arranged between his various stepchildren and between them and his other kin. Maria Thumm, daughter of his second wife, married the son of the son of his

[7] There had already been an earlier exchange involving these families. A sister-in-law of Elisabeth Speidel was married to another Hentzler son.

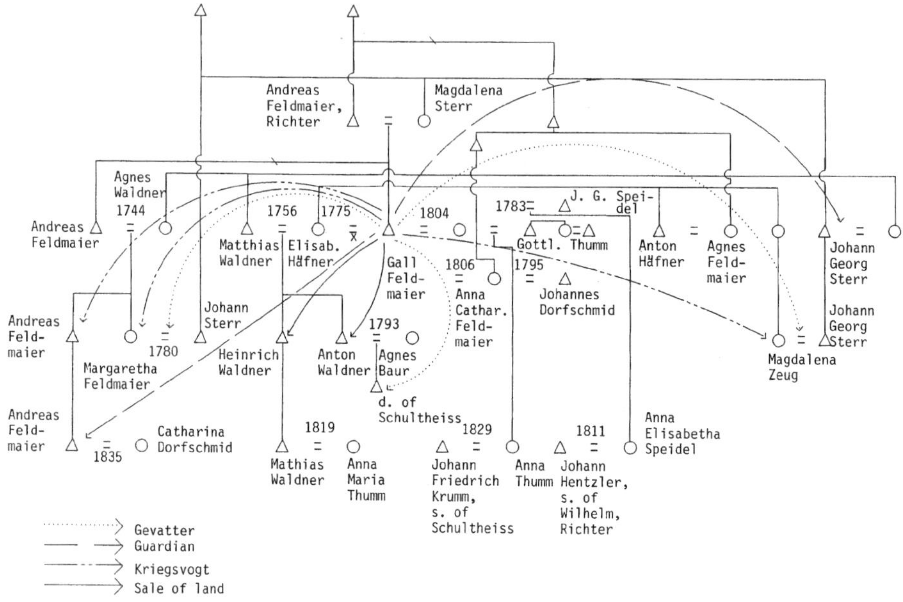

Figure 16.3

first wife. And Catharina Dorfschmid from his third wife married his brother's grandson. His first wife's sister's daughter, Magdalena Zeug, also married her first husband's sister's son Johann Georg Sterr (1779). These series of alliances were maintained and given continuity in part by a regular use of spiritual parentage, ersatz parentage, and management of property. It was not a continuous line of property devolution but constant exchange that gave structure to the system.

Gall Feldmaier's role in the negotiations between his cousin and earlier ward Mathes Sterr and Schultheiss Krumm seems typical of a mediator – later neither side would agree on who sent Feldmaier to whom. A few years earlier, the tavernkeeper Bross had beat Sterr up for interfering with his collecting the bill from a drunk's pocket. Feldmaier was the witness but gave a testimony that supported both men. He offered to use his new position as a magistrate to help the bankrupt Sterr, and he pleaded with Schultheiss Krumm to consider Sterr's wife and children. When Sterr made the scene in court, accusing Krumm of cheating him, Feldmaier backed the Schultheiss's testimony just part way. Only after Krumm finally came under enormous pressure from his enemies was Feldmaier uncustomarily forced to take sides.

Once Feldmaier was Bürgermeister and working together with Schultheiss Hiller, there was a steady stream of complaints about their administration of the forestland. In 1805 he and Hiller sold a log illegally. Young Salomon Hentzler said he stole wood from the Rathaus in 1807. And several other Bürger complained about (*raisoniert*) corrupt wood deals. In the same year, there were two more complaints about forest delicts. In 1808 not only was he part of a group stealing wood, but he and Hiller were also keeping fines from wood others stole. By 1812 state officials made Feldmaier and the Waldmeister actually sign a statement to the effect that they had read the royal edict about fraud. The next year, he was suspended from office and had to place all of his property as security for losses under his stewardship as Bürgermeister. That led to the forced sale of his estate and dismissal from office. As already noted, most of his property was sold to his wife. In 1815 and 1820, Feldmaier was down to quartile II in the tax list. After his foreclosure, he ceased to be a Pfleger or Kriegsvogt. In the years just before and after his wife died (1823), all the rest of his property ended up at auction, after which the 73-year-old dropped from the tax list.

Each year after his bankruptcy until his death in 1834 at the age of 83, he was auctioned off to the lowest bidder for room and board. For a while, one of his nephews or grandnephews of his first wife took him in by posting the lowest bid. But he finally ended up with his only daughter, the unmarried Barbara Feldmaier, for the last two years of his life. No patrimony had been passed to her: the maintenance or building up of such property had not been part of Gall Feldmaier's strategy. They lived together on the little she could earn and what she received from the village for his subsistence. Soon after she took over his care, she produced her first of five illegitimate children – all by different fathers, three of whom she could not name. Feldmaier's estate inventory records laconically that all the old man left was a few unusable clothes and bedcovers.

The disappointment

Young Salomon Hentzler, Bauer, day-laborer (1774–1861)

Young Salomon Hentzler was one of the best-connected Bauern in the village. He was the son of Christoph Hentzler, a wealthy Bauer and member of the Gericht. His childless uncle, the Schultheiss old Salomon, had raised him and in 1794 even provided some of the endowment when he married at the age of 20. His marriage to the 19-year-old Friederica Regina Geiger was a classic political union, calculated to draw together the two Richter families of Geiger and Hentzler. Friederica Regina's father and grandfather had both been Richter and her mother and grandmother had both been Häusslers, descendants through the female line of the earlier Schultheiss Rieth dynasty. The Häussler family had its share of Richter, and two of the daughters had married magistrates, one of them the successor – Johann Georg Baur – to the last Rieth Schultheiss in 1761. Friederica Regina was a second cousin to the second Johann Georg Baur, successor to Alt Salomon Hentzler, and first cousin to *his* successor, Friedrich Krumm. By birth and marriage, young Salomon was a central figure connected to both sides during the political altercations around Schultheiss Krumm's term

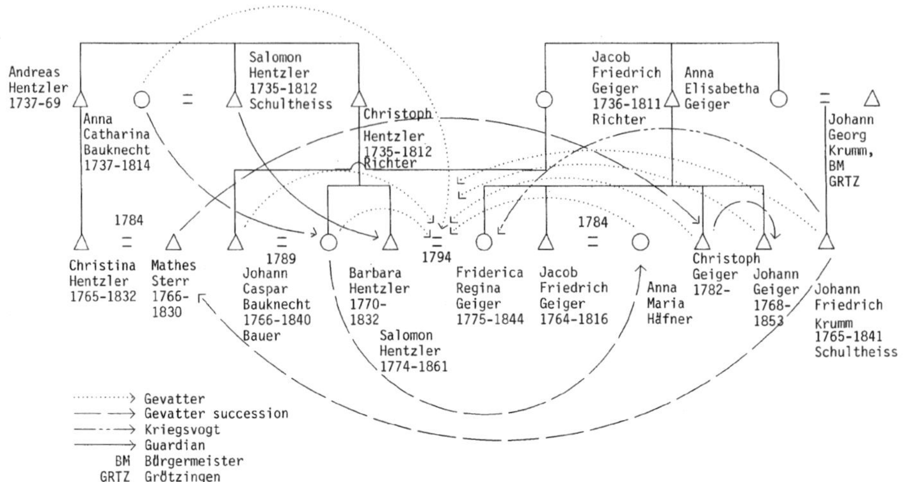

Figure 16.4

of office. The alliance was underscored by ritual kinship. For the children born to Salomon and Friederica Regina from 1769 to 1809, the godparents were Friedrich Krumm and Anna Catharina, the wife of old Salomon Hentzler. Anna Catharina was succeeded by young Salomon's sister, the wife of Caspar Bauknecht. Krumm lasted until 1812 and was followed in 1814 by Mathes Sterr, whose wife was a niece of old Salomon and Christoph Hentzler. In 1816 the godfather was Christoph Geiger, Friederica's brother. For the last child in 1819, another Geiger brother, Johann, and the widow of another recently deceased brother stood as godparents. Some of the switches, for example in 1814, may have reflected emphases in the alliances of the young Salomon Hentzlers, but the remarkable fact is the persistence of both Krumm and a Hentzler from 1796 to 1812 right through the period of the hottest conflicts between the families, with young Salomon taking the lead in organizing the attack on Schultheiss Krumm. Furthermore, Krumm was Kriegsvogt for Friederica Regina at least between 1795 and 1804. Salomon and his wife were called upon to be godparents for only two families, she for her second cousin (FMBSD) and he for his brother. Schematically, the relationships are traced out in Figure 16.4.

Young Salomon Hentzler started off his career as a Bauer quite well. Together he and his wife brought 12 arable plots of land to their new household plus 7 other meadows, gardens, orchards, and flaxlands. His uncle and foster father – called his "Vetter" in the text – the old Schultheiss, added several strips of land to the property of the young couple, but he did so rather tentatively. He noted that young Salomon's behavior had not pleased him recently. He was displaying some unnamed character flaws, and it was not at all clear whether he would settle down to manage his estate (*hausen*) in a proper manner. The uncle warned that improper conduct would lead to having the strips of land taken away. Exactly what the young man had done is not clear from the record at the time.

A few years later, in 1799, Salomon's wife complained before the church consistory that her husband had been drinking too much and acting violently. On the particular occasion, he came home drunk and struck her. He also used horrible language against her parents and swore at them and at her. Worried about the effect of his behavior on her endowment, her parents, the Richter Jacob Friedrich Geiger and his wife, counseled divorce before the property went down. Salomon was quite unmoved by his wife's and her parents' complaint and said that many a woman had been beaten without the need to bruise a quill – that is, write a protocol – over the matter.

How this incident fits into a larger picture is not at all evident from the record. This was the period when the Geigers, father and son, were pulling out of the Jüstingen farm by turning it over to Mathes Sterr. Old Salomon Hentzler, Schultheiss Baur, and Bürgermeister Krumm were all tied up with the deal financially. It could well be that Salomon's anger against his in-laws had to do with the politics of this very large undertaking. Whatever tensions there were at the time of the incident between him and Friederica Regina, property and its exploitation were part of the problem. Although there were indications in the end about Salomon drinking, there are no incidents of him sitting with others in the tavern past closing and no indication of public drunkenness outside of this case before he reached his 50s. And this is the only example of violence toward his wife. From the context, it appears that there was extreme tension between himself and the Geigers that prompted the scene of domestic violence.

Salomon may well have received some property from one side or the other of the alliance in the 10 or so years after he married. In 1795 he was in the third quartile of landholders, but by 1800 he had risen into the fourth quartile and was ranked 29 out of 167 Bürger. Five years later he had moved up to position 10. During this time he bought 8 parcels and sold 7, so his rise must have been linked to inheritance. At the peak of his holdings (1805), young Salomon bought half of the house belonging to his father-in-law, and after considerable dispute divided it in half with his brother-in-law, Johannes Geiger. Salomon and his wife were to keep the older man in their apartment for the rest of his life. In the next years, the position Salomon built or had built for him was rapidly dissipated, but at the height of his fortunes, he was wealthy, aggressive, and willing and able to assert himself against the interests of others – but in a way that did not necessarily lead to an advantage for himself.

One of the direct charges Salomon brought against Schultheiss Krumm was that he had treated him rudely during the auction of the grain tithes. According to the Schultheiss, Hentzler had showed up to the auction in a bare shirt and had stood insolently with crossed arms and bid hastily and without thinking. He had to tell the Richter Christoph Hentzler to have his son show proper respect. Salomon testified that the matter had nothing to do with respect or with the way he was dressed. Rather, there had been a collusive practice ever since Johann Georg Baur had left office. The Schultheiss supported the development of different syndicates and coordinated the bidding through agreements reached beforehand. Each year the tithe farm passed around in turn to a different syndicate. And furthermore the Schultheiss himself took part quite illegally as a silent partner. Since Krumm had been in office as Schultheiss, the duke had allegedly been cheated out of 500 Scheffel (almost 2,500 bushels) of grain, a considerable amount for three years of corruption. The Schultheiss was angry because Hentzler bid in the face of the corrupt practices he had organized and coordinated.

Exactly what was going on between Krumm and Hentzler is not developed further in the record. It is hardly believable that fixing the tithe first began with Krumm. After all, that had been an issue under Johann Georg Rieth III during the 1740s and 1750s. Schultheiss Hentzler himself was forced out of office because of problems with tithes on wine, although it is possible that he had not cooperated in fixed bidding on the grain tithe. His father, after all, had led the attack on Schultheiss Rieth in the 1750s. There had been considerable opposition to Hentzler toward the end, and he said that he had been very strict with people, which caused some unrest. Whether his "strictness" involved an open, noncollusive bidding on the tithes is not clear, but his successor, who was unceremoniously booted out of office by the duke's officials, most probably already was deeply involved in such schemes. The question is whether young Salomon was fronting for others, such as his father or uncle, or whether he had rather naively jumped into a situation he did not really understand. As a very well-to-do Bauer, he may have felt capable of taking over the tithe farm even as inexperienced as he was. He may even have been acting within a context of younger Bürger pushing for a part of the action controlled by their elders. In any event, this experience, among others, prompted Hentzler to organize an attempt to unseat his wife's cousin, Kriegsvogt, and Gevatter from office.

All the meetings of the cabal took place in young Salomon Hentzler's home. For some time before it became clear that there were enough substantial complaints, various villagers had discussed the general way the village was being run. Salomon took it upon himself to get individuals to formulate their specific knowledge or injuries and to write them down in a form they were willing to sign. On one particular day, Hentzler sat at home and had various people brought along, most of them fetched by his cousin's husband, Mathes Sterr. Take the example of one of Salomon's cousins, young Andreas Hentzler, a 37-year-old Bauer worth 500 fl. Several weeks before the document was put together, Christoph Hentzler, Salomon's father, asked him if he knew just how partisan Krumm's administration of the forestland was. Andreas knew all about that, and Krumm had failed to let him have the wood necessary to repair his house. Christoph told him to go along to young Salomon and add his complaint. At the meeting, Salomon read the entire document and everyone signed. But during the investigation, Andreas no longer could rightly say all that was in it because he had such a bad memory. He did know that Krumm was always hateful to him. There had been a dispute about a loan when Krumm was Bürgermeister, from which time Krumm had been his enemy and had done everything to seek revenge, such as fining his boys too heavily for a trivial delict in the woods. And Krumm had even said they should be hanged for pilfering wood. There were other issues such as sheepfold money, but Andreas kept coming back to favoritism in dispensing building wood.

The 50-year-old Adam Falter, carpenter, worth 1,000 fl, had been one of those who had often discussed the disorder in the village "household." He did not like the special privileges the Schultheiss and Bürgermeister took with the annual kindling portions. And he too complained about partisanship in parceling out building wood. For example, Krumm gave lumber to Salomon Brodbeck for a pigsty for free, but when he requested some there was none to be had. The forest was being destroyed by excessive sale of wood, and the two village leaders used the occasion of administering the forest to pay themselves expenses for the day. Krumm also did the sheepfold accounts so tardily that no one could remember what they owed or paid.

Young Salomon Hentzler, of course, capitalized on many personal injuries of particular Bürger. One objection to such behavior was voiced by the volatile Johann Georg Riempp, a 52-year-old Bauer, worth 800 fl, but once a man of more significant wealth. He said Salomon came to his house to persuade him to sign, but he had not really thought there was much wrong in the village. His signature was not meant to attest to all of the complaints. But he had one difficult experience with the Schultheiss. Several years before there had been a muster of the village lads eligible for military service. The local doctor had pronounced two young men healthy for service, but Krumm had arranged for a doctor in Stuttgart to declare them unfit. Because of that, his son came next in line and was forced to serve. His son had always said that if Krumm had not gone to Stuttgart, he would have been able to stay out of the army.

Hentzler wrote up the complaints of Johannes Heinser and Mathes Sterr, who had felt themselves ill treated by Krumm, but he also got inexperienced young Bürger like Johannes Kühfuss to sign the complaint, who had no real charges against Krumm but who thought signing the petition was a neighborly thing to do. One neighbor got him to go along to a second neighbor who took him to Hentzler's house, where everyone was assembled. After Salomon read the memorial, he protested ignorance in the matter. But he was persuaded by the argument that it would not cost him anything. He now denied knowledge about each of the complaints and maintained that he, like most of the Bürger, was satisfied with Krumm.

Young Salomon Hentzler, 28, was the youngest Bürger to sign the accusation and one of the richest – worth 2,500 fl. He was still upset about the way he had been put in place at the tithe auction. He criticized Krumm for plowing past the border of a field, for being partisan with building wood, for drawing up the village budget without consulting the other magistrates, and for selling grain to the village without actually delivering the goods. He had suborned Mathes Sterr to give a false oath in the legal case against his "Vetter," the old Schultheiss Hentzler. And there were other issues such as an army deserter living in the village and improper fines levied for certain crimes. Adam Falter and others falsified bills for work done for the village at Krumm's request. Krumm drank in the tavern at the expense of the village. He took extra days of the sheepfold and had 80 sheep too many in the herd. Finally, the smith Dammel had made a chain the Schultheiss fancied, so he took it and charged it to the village.

Despite the fact that Krumm was dismissed from office and punished, the government fined young Salomon for organizing the unlawful assembly (*verbotene Zusammenrotierung von Bürgern*). During the next few years, Salomon reached the height of his wealth, but he was never able to translate his angry, destructive activities into a positive program or develop a new network of friends in power. Salomon's connections on the court were dismissed or soon died, and Krumm was succeeded by his brother-in-law.

Between 1806 and 1809, Salomon lost 15 properties, almost all of them by forced sale. For part of the time, Gall Feldmaier was established as the executor of his estate. By 1810 he was still in the third quartile of taxpayers and ranked 49 out of 177. Then again between 1814 and 1818 he lost another 10 properties, dropping down to the first quartile. During his slide, he attacked various people, notably Mathes Sterr, whom he accused of costing the family so much money. He apparently cut Sterr's trees out of revenge and revealed that the latter had a "whore" in another town. After 1815 he no longer had a house and in 1818 landed on the public dole. The next year, the Gericht recorded that he and his family had no place to stay and that the village would have to make room in the sheep barn for such indigents. For many years after that, his family moved from apartment to apartment, from private accommodation to the poorhouse and back. For a few years in the 1830s, he became the village tree surgeon, but mostly he comes into the records after the age of 60 for drunkenness and swearing. One man traveling through the village on his way to Ulm was surprised to be called "sow ass" by an old, broken man. Salomon lasted to the age of 87, living in the care of various villagers, who finally refused to keep him because of his drunkenness and filth. At the time of his death (1861), he was living in the care and support of his 61-year-old, unmarried daughter. Already in 1844, at the death of his wife, the inventory recorded that he possessed only the most essential personal things. His two daughters had to pay for the mother's casket and burial. At his death, he still had nothing, and the two daughters once again came up with the funeral expenses out of their meager earnings.

Prototype I

Johann Wilhelm Hentzler, Bauer, Richter, Gemeinderat, Bürgermeister, forest administrator, church consistory elder, orphan court juror (1752–1829)

During the investigation into Friedrich Krumm's conduct of office in 1801 and 1802, the principal role of Johann Wilhelm Hentzler was one of absence; at least at key moments in the record his name was not there. His cousins, the Richter Christoph and the old Schultheiss Hentzler at first hid behind more active Bürger such as Mathes Sterr and the young Salomon Hentzler, Christoph's son. But in the end they signed various petitions and were spoken about by Krumm's faction as the real force behind all the unrest in the village. Neither Wilhelm Hentzler nor any of his children played any role in organizing the cabal or in proposing any of the complaints that led to Krumm's punishment and dismissal from office. If Wilhelm Hentzler was not a public player in this particular Hentzler family political maneuver, he was not at the same time a Krumm supporter. When the Schultheiss marshaled witnesses from the Gericht to defend himself against the charge that he allowed a deserter to live quietly in the village, Wilhelm was not among them. And there had been a charge about the Schultheiss not assessing a particular woman a high enough fine for pilfering from someone else's field. Again, Wilhelm Hentzler, although a member of the Gericht, did not testify either way. After charges and countercharges had been issued and the investigating commissioner had heard evidence on each point, a number of magistrates from both the Gericht and Rat spoke as supporters of Krumm in the name of both institutions and the "better part of the Bürgerschaft" against the rebels. Once again Wilhelm was missing from the list. The commissioner himself did not see Hentzler as neutral in a formal sense, since he was connected through kinship to the Richter Christoph. When it came time to take up each point of accusation with the magistrates as a whole, Christoph – by then the oldest Richter – and Friedrich Krumm were excluded as parties to the complaint. Richter Jacob Bosch, Krumm's father-in-law, and Wilhelm Hentzler, Christoph's "co-parent-in-law" (*Gegenschweher*), were also dismissed as relatives too close to be trusted to provide neutrality and non-partisan testimony. It is also possible that it was regarded as illegitimate to force such close relatives to provide testimony against each other.

Wilhelm himself was never accused of being an accomplice of Krumm in any way regarding false receipts, rigged bidding of tithes, or corrupt administration of the forest. And he never seems to have been around when particular events developed in the tavern – he was a tavernkeeper, but his establishment did not attract the rowdy element, and he was staid enough eventually to become a church consistory elder. He was not a drinking companion of the Schultheiss. Yet he was not a negligible figure in village politics and administration. For a while after 1795, he served as Bürgermeister and much later he would become

Waldmeister for five years. He would be one of the several magistrates to continue in office in 1819 when the village constitution was revised by the state, turning the Gericht, which had filled its members by cooptation, into the Gemeinderat, whose members were elected by the village at large. During his term of office he was the village representative on the commission to renovate the mortgage records, and he accumulated a number of offices, including that of elder in the church consistory (*Conventsrichter*) and estate and orphan-court-juror (*Teil- und Waisenrichter*).

The records reveal the kind of man who was chosen to fulfill responsible offices throughout his adult life. However he used his connections and influence, he did not do so in an openly partisan manner. At one point, he was chosen to be the volatile Johann Georg Riempp's property administrator and guardian of the children after a history of considerable provocation on the part of Riempp, which points toward an expectation of calm, consistent, business-like dealing.[8] He seems to have acquired the job because of the kinship connection to Riempp's wife on the one hand, and his position as a magistrate on the other. Kinship, power, and good sense seem to have provided him with the right set of tools for the job. When the issue of Friedrich Krumm blew up, his low profile as far as the record is concerned bespeaks a man whose kinship ties had boosted him into a position of authority but whose temperament caused him to operate with balance and evenhandedness. It could be objected that the Hentzler party simply left him out of their complaints since he was one of theirs, but there were enough charges and countercharges to fix him in the record if he had been an active participant in Krumm's shady practices or ran the tavern where most of the deals were worked out.

Hentzler was also active in building a network of cooperation through godparentage, Kriegsvogtschaft, and guardianship. He was especially busy as an estate executor or administrator during the difficult time of the first two decades of the nineteenth century. He and his wife were called upon as godparents for seven families. For the most part, the relationships involved did not extend too far into the wider kinship network: WZ, B, Z, S, FBSD, FBSDH. Over his lifetime, he acted as Kriegsvogt for at least 10 women, many of them fairly close relatives: MBW, Z, BW, FBSSW, FBSW, DHM, FBSD, FFZD. Almost all of the connections through godparentage and Kriegsvogtschaft involved the agnatic network of Hentzlers. He had a few connections with families that were not directly related, but most of his network was developed among his paternal relatives. This did not mean that his activities were restricted to close kin. For the seven estates for which he was assigned to administer foreclosures between 1809 and 1815, only one belonged to the circle of Hentzler kin, that of his first cousin

8 For more details, see David Warren Sabean, "Young Bees in an Empty Hive: Relations between Brothers-in-Law in a South German Village around 1800," in Hans Medick and David Warren Sabean, eds., *Interest and Emotion: Essays on the Study of Family and Kinship* (Cambridge, 1984), pp. 171–86.

once removed, Gottlieb Hentzler. As *Güterpfleger* administering a forced sale, it was not usual to call upon someone too closely connected to the family. The job called for competence, responsibility, and neutrality, and Wilhelm Hentzler and Gall Feldmaier were among the most frequently utilized magistrates for the occasion. Still, when examining the total set of responsible positions Wilhelm was involved in, it is remarkable how frequently he can be seen to act as a central figure coordinating Hentzler family interests.

In many ways, Wilhelm Hentzler fits the stereotype of the Württemberg Bauer. In this partible inheritance system where the real estate collected together by one household was dispersed among the children and where an active market in land played a significant role in the distribution of property, new households were supposed to be anchored in the village with a modest stake of land and expected to accumulate an additional holding through hard work and careful use of resources over time. In turn, such families were to reproduce the structure when they set up the next generation with start capital and habits of diligence and good husbandry. The wisdom of the system was captured by the proverb advising against putting a young bee colony in a full hive. A small inheritance was supposed to drive a family toward a goal of accumulation – but not so as to build an ever richer patrimony in each generation. Rather the object was *durchzukommen* – to succeed – which meant to come through life debt-free, with each child properly established and the parents' honor intact. Not many biographies in this set fit the model very well, but Wilhelm Hentzler seems to have done it according to the book. At the time of their marriage, he and his wife began with a good but by no means wealthy holding of 14 parcels of land. From that point until 1801 he slowly purchased 25 more parcels, selling only 9. Combining these with pieces from inheritance, he emerged as the wealthiest man in the village. From 1790 through 1815, he was always in the top quartile of taxpayers. His failure to purchase new land for the first 10 years of the nineteenth century and his slow drop from first to sixth to eighth place in the wealth hierarchy over the decade coincided with the marriages of most of his numerous children. As befitting the model, he set each of them up with an endowment similar to his own. Once they were established, he bought a few more parcels, but by 1818 when his wife died and he had reached the age of 66, he decided to let a substantial amount of the estate go to the children. He kept a small set of holdings and all of the debt, most of which had come about through underwriting people who had been foreclosed on, including one of his own sons. In the year following his retirement, he sold seven parcels, including three-quarters of the house and barn to his children. Still, for 1820 and 1825, he was listed in the third quartile of taxpayers. By the time of his death at 76 in 1829, he held a quarter house, a field, a garden, and a vineyard, enough to keep an old man busy and independent.

Land and real estate did not comprise the total patrimony Wilhelm Hentzler received or passed on. His father had been a member of the Gericht and long-term Bürgermeister before him. He entered the Rat the same year his father died. One cousin was Schultheiss and another sat on the Gericht at the time he

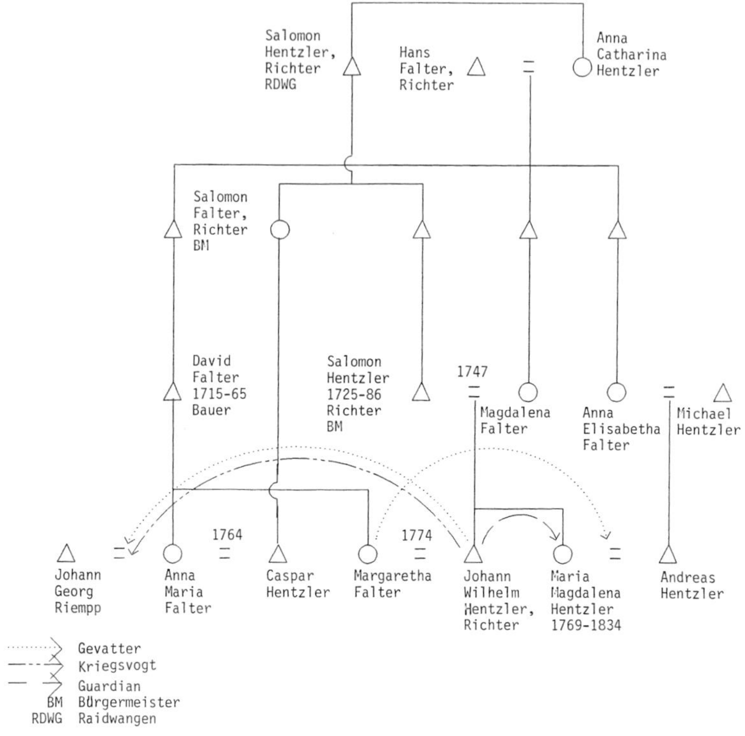

Figure 16.5

was coopted to office. All of these connections were important for him, but he also made a strategically favorable marriage that utilized elements of the alliance system his parents and their parents had constructed. He in turn was instrumental in helping his children construct their unions out of alliances he had worked at holding together. Especially notable is the consuming interest in the Hentzler network, which operated not only within the village of Neckarhausen but with continual connections to Raidwangen from where the family had come in the first place and where they provided Richter and Schultheissen throughout the eighteenth and into the nineteenth century.

There are many ways of abstracting parts of the genealogical connections that Wilhelm was involved in. I will examine only two before I look in turn at the alliances constructed for his children. First, there was a constant, many-generation exchange between the magistrate Falter and Hentzler families (Figure 16.5).

The alliance between the two families pictured here lasted from the late seventeenth century well into the nineteenth. The first exchange was followed two generations later at midcentury by another and then one generation later by three

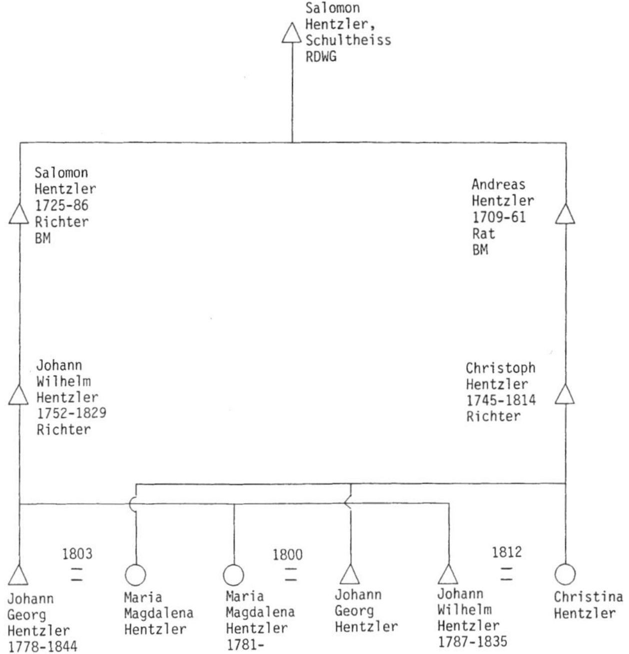

Figure 16.6

more. Although marriage provided an overall framework, the possibilities that were established were put – in the example here – into play by Wilhelm Hentzler as successful farmer and magistrate through godparentage, Kriegsvogtschaft, and guardianship over many decades. He acted as a central figure not only for the management and administration of his own holdings but helped coordinate credit and the exploitation of land by his close allies.

Wilhelm Hentzler had seven children, most of whom made marriages with consanguineal kin. Hentzler himself had married his MFBSD. His son Jacob in 1798 married his MMBD. Anna Catharina in 1804 married her FFFZSD, a second cousin once removed. The two children who did not marry kin made politically strategic marriages: a son, Johannes, married Bürgermeister Gall Feldmaier's stepdaughter, and Maria Barbara married the son of the Richter, Johannes Baur. But most fascinating was the strategy of connecting the families of the two first cousins and Richter, Christoph and Wilhelm Hentzler, not once but three times. In fact, the marriages produced two couples with exactly the same names – Johann Georg and Maria Magdalena Hentzler (Figure 16.6).

Besides the tight overlapping marriage alliances produced in this way, Wilhelm acted as godparent for his daughter Maria Magdalena and her husband Johann Georg and also for some of the children of his cousin Christoph who were not connected by marriage. He was also Kriegsvogt for Christoph's wife. Following all of the relationships among the children of the two cousins over their lifetimes demonstrates a continual exchange of goods and services, as well as tensions and conflicts. But one incident in the formation of alliance is particularly instructive. In 1809 Christina Hentzler, the daughter of Christoph, was brought before the Gericht (on which her uncle served) because she was pregnant. She gave as the father of the child her second cousin, young Johann Wilhelm Hentzler II, who promptly denied it. He did admit that he had visited her in her room but offered another young man as the chief suspect. Young Wilhelm wanted to have nothing at all to do with her and he certainly did not want to marry her. In her testimony, she insisted that she had no relations with anyone else and reported that he had wanted her to take an abortifacient because of the shame of having to go before the officials – his father included. The lad he blamed it all on alleged that he had only visited Christina once, and young Wilhelm himself had been present. Several weeks later, Wilhelm returned and admitted that his conscience convinced him that he was not free from her (*weil er sich in seinem Gewissen überzeugt fühle, da er nicht rein von der selben seye*).

Alliance formation must not be seen as something that takes place outside of practical everyday concerns. In this instance, the only two young men who had made their way to Christina's room and even come into question as the father of the child were sons of members of the Gericht. The brother of young Wilhelm's rival eventually married one of Wilhelm's sisters. There was then an expectation of the kinds of suitors that were suitable. Wilhelm and Christina established their relation inside the dynamics of property considerations, the reputation and social position of families, and the history of exchanges of allied families. The two prior marriages of their siblings and the relationships between their parents provided the context of their courtship. Nevertheless, despite all the previous history of familial interaction, their personal drama also played out in the context of male aggressivity, sexual culture, and reluctance to settle down. Young Wilhelm was not looking to get married or to renew the exchanges of an alliance forged by his father when he fooled around with his cousin. The consequences, however, were to do just that.

The obsessive

Christoph Hentzler, Bauer, Rat, Richter (1745–1814)

During the investigation into Friedrich Krumm's conduct of office, the Schultheiss and several of the magistrates, including Gall Feldmaier, insisted that the investigating officer take down their statement about the machinations behind the unfair and partisan attack. According to them, the whole affair could be laid at the door of the old Schultheiss, Salomon Hentzler, and his brother, Richter Christoph, both of whom had poor reputations (*schlechten Credit*) in the village and were despised (*verachtet*) by every good and well-behaved Bürger. The two men had coordinated their relatives in order to drive a wedge between the magistrates and the common villagers. They were behind everything and ought to be revealed as the chief culprits of all the recent unrest and rebellion. Although they were astute enough not to lead the cabal publicly, anyone could see that they called upon others to carry out their evil and immoral plans. Despite attempts to appear high-minded, they were motivated only by the basest impulses of hatred and envy.

It was true that the two older men stayed behind the scene as long as they could. It was Christoph's son Salomon who ran around to assemble complaints, to arrange a meeting, to compose a petition, and to encourage various people to sign. One of the most active collaborators of young Salomon was old Salomon's and Christoph's niece's husband, Mathes Sterr. Their nephew Andreas, and Christoph's son, Andreas, were present at the meetings and signed the petition. But the trouble for the malcontents was that the Oberamtmann in Nürtingen who received the document put the matter into the hands of Scribent Gök, one of the scribes in the county clerk's office, who conducted a desultory investigation under the assumption that the petitioners were merely troublemakers. This prompted the two Hentzler brothers to put themselves at the head of the conspiracy and address a petition directly to the duke, asking for a nonpartisan investigation of the issues by a commissioner from outside the district.

Gök had demonstrated, according to the petition to the duke, the greatest possible partisanship. As soon as he arrived, he said: "This time they would have to put us in our place. We are *Kreuzsacrament*[9] and not worth enough for anyone to put so much work into." Gök proceeded to operate arbitrarily and in a high-handed manner and would not listen to the complaints. Accordingly, the Hentzlers became afraid that the petitioners would be considered rebels and agitators, so they stepped to the fore as current and former magistrates to lend seriousness to the complaints. They asked for a new commission set up by the duke himself to allow neutral handling of the situation. The Oberamtmann Storr had filed a report with the duke based on Gök's investigation, summarizing each of the 30 original complaints, evidence, and testimony. Storr dismissed each one as groundless, not proven, not demonstrated by unbiased testimony, contradicted, testified by someone of questionable reputation, subject to misunderstanding, false, trivial, inadmissible, or settled. He concluded that the real problem was Christoph and Salomon Hentzler. Old Salomon had resigned as Schultheiss in 1788 but had been allowed to keep his place of honor in the church. Because the two men had incited unrest in the village, they ought both to be punished, Salomon to lose his place of honor and Christoph his position on the court. After receiving both documents, the ducal officials decided to send in a new commissioner and appointed Vogt Zeller from Denkendorf to carry out a thorough investigation.

[9] An untranslatable curse, meaning "Holy Cross Sacrament." The word "Sacrament" was the most used curse in Württemberg and prompted the verb form "sacramentieren": to sacrament, or to swear.

Vogt Zeller went through the original 30 complaints point by point, as well as 7 new ones brought up by the plaintiffs. He questioned each witness, allowed Krumm a rebuttal, and after excluding the chief parties and their closest relatives went through each complaint one by one with the magistrates. At the conclusion, the Schultheiss and both Bürgermeister brought complaints about the old Schultheiss and his brother, the oldest Richter. Christoph was accused of stealing a sack of grain from a wagon going to the imperial troops, grapes in the vineyard, and limbs from the woods. He answered to the first point that the matter had already been handled by the Oberamt and that Michael Feldmaier had been fined for false testimony. There had been another occasion, he said, but he was laying a trap for the carter, whom he suspected of thievery. As for the stolen grapes, the evidence was only hearsay. He did steal tree limbs with his son-in-law, but that was a matter for the local court, not a commission. After all the charges and countercharges were protocoled and supporting documents added to the file, Zeller submitted his report. By this time he simply labeled the case as one of charges by the two Hentzlers against Krumm and both Bürgermeister and countercharges against the Hentzlers. After ducal officials considered the reports, various fines and punishments were given out, and the costs of the investigation were divided up according to the weight given to each individual's culpability. Since many delicts come to light for the first time during the investigation, both sides had to contribute, with Krumm assessed the highest amount of 30 fl. Young Salomon Hentzler, his brother Andreas, and the former Schultheiss Hentzler each had to pay 15 fl. Christoph Hentzler came away with costs of only 10 fl, but he was dismissed from office. Two months later (December 1803), he petitioned the duke for reinstatement, pointing out that he had served 6 years on the Rat and 20 on the Gericht. All his mistakes had been trivial, and he had always worked for the good of the village, which stood to lose a useful man. His family was being injured because he had lost his position in such an innocent manner. His petition was denied out of hand a few days later.

Christoph Hentzler had not been one of those magistrates who created a large, expansive network among villagers. In contrast to Gall Feldmaier, only once was he called upon to administrate an estate under foreclosure, and that was for another Hentzler, his first cousin. Usually when he served as guardian or Kriegsvogt, he did so for his close relatives – he was Pfleger for his nephew and niece (BS/D), Kriegsvogt for the niece (BD), a cousin's wife (FBSW), his daughter, another cousin's wife (FBSW), this time the spouse of Wilhelm Hentzler, his cousin and co-parent-in-law. As godparent, he stood for two cousins (FFBS), a niece (BD), and a son, as well as for one of the Falter women closely allied to the Hentzler line. But in general, in almost every case, his activities as guardian, Kriegsvogt, or godparent were devoted to agnatic kin, except for the rare exception, another Hentzler. This intense concentration on the Hentzler family also played out in the marriages of his children. The three marriages of his sons and daughters with the children of his agnatic first cousin, Wilhelm, demonstrate a rare concentration on one family but also a rare instance of lineal endogamy.

Most consanguineal marriages in Neckarhausen were with an allied line, the Hentzlers with the Falters, Häfners with Geigers, Petermanns with Brodbecks. Such an alliance is always signaled by the existence of a cross-sibling part of the path between the two neogami – *MB*D, *FZ*S, F*MB*SD, F*FZ*SD. Such a path involves the exchange of children between two allied lines who have exchanged once before. In this case, the three sons were marrying back into the same agnatic line – the apical ancestors in the path (F*FB*SD) were male siblings from the same line, not exchanging partners. Altogether, Christoph had 10 children. Besides the three married to Wilhelm Hentzler's children, there was one other lineally endogamous marriage by one of his daughters – from the point of view of the son-in-law, a FFBSSD. This marriage developed relationships already well-worked by Christoph. He had stood as godfather for two of the sons of his great-uncle Samson – his daughter married the son of a third. In this respect as in all the others, Christoph concentrated on a group of agnatic relatives. The other children's marriages were more open, but some of them show traces of intense activity around a particular center. Two of his daughters married the same man 20 years apart (1794, 1816), and another daughter married a son from the allied Bauknecht family, Johann Caspar Bauknecht (his FMBSSD). Bauknecht was the cousin of Friederica Regina Geiger, who married young Salomon. Altogether five of Christoph's children married children of magistrates. The eldest son married a woman from outside the village, and the youngest daughter married and left the village 14 years after Christoph died.

Marriage is subject to complicated negotiations between parents and children, as well as between the prospective partners themselves. From a vantage point well outside the everyday life of these people, it is difficult to find an explanation for the particular configurations of lineal endogamy in this family, but the peculiarity of so many marriages of that type stands out. All his life Christoph worked a relatively restricted network, putting most of his energies into his agnatic kin, concentrating on particular points in a larger set. This concentration, if not to say obsession, looks the same whether one examines Kriegsvogschaft and guardianship, godparentage, or marriage alliance. A sister married old Johann Georg Baur, the Schultheiss succeeded by his brother Salomon. Her stepson, the successor in turn to Salomon, and Christoph married sisters. When Krumm accused the two Hentzlers of coordinating their relatives in fomenting the rebellion, he knew what he was talking about. Apart from Christoph and old Salomon Hentzler, there were 11 signatories of the complaint, 9 of whom were related to Christoph: 2 sons, 3 nephews (BS, BDH, ZxS), 2 brothers-in-law of his children (SWZH, DHB), a brother-in-law of a cousin (FBSWZH), and a cousin who also married his wife's sister (FBDS/WZH).

Krumm and his allies suggested that the Hentzler party were in bad repute and for the most part failed farmers. They were probably alluding to the spectacular failure of Mathes Sterr, who had overreached himself with the Jüstingen farm. The relative ineptness of young Salomon Hentzler was suspected but not yet proven. And Johannes Heinser had never developed his early promise. However, Christoph had been enormously successful as a farmer, and the slow erosion of his holdings after 1800 was due to the fact that he was endowing a large number of children (between 1789 and 1803, seven of them) – handsomely. In 1800 two of his sons and one son-in-law were in tax quartile IV, while one son-in-law was high in quartile III. In keeping with his single-minded concentration on close family relations, he was unusual in his policy of accumulation. His father died in 1761, leaving an estate worth about 4,000 fl (for him and his wife), 2,495 fl of which had been acquired during his marriage. That kind of accumulation was remarkable although not unusual for much of the eighteenth century and contrasts sharply with the first several decades of the nineteenth century. Over the next two years, his widow added another 800 fl worth of land. What they passed on was debt-free. When Christoph married in 1765, he brought 14 parcels of land and his wife brought 500 fl in cash. He seems to have been cut from his parents' mold. In any event, he was extraordinarily unusual in the fact that he only ever bought land and never sold any except for a single arable plot in the year before he died. Between 1764 and 1803, he steadily acquired land, solidly integrating each piece into his farm before he went after another – altogether 32 parcels. He began to endow his children in 1789, concluding eight endowments by the time of his death in 1814 at the age of 69. Most of his children within a few years of marriage were to be found along with him among the top quarter of taxpayers in the village, although he reached his peak holdings in 1790 at the age of 45. At that point he was as wealthy as his cousin Wilhelm and almost twice as wealthy as Friedrich Krumm. By 1795 with four children endowed, he was equal with the rising Krumm and worth about 75 percent of what his cousin was now worth. In 1800, he was ranked 13 of 167 and by 1810, 19 of 177. The erosion of his property was strictly related to the demographic cycle of his family. At his inventory in 1814, the clerk noted that his debts exceeded his assets largely because he had given out so many portions. He and his wife had managed their affairs so well that none of the creditors sought to force a foreclosure, so the officials left it to the widow to begin to settle her debts after the harvest. By the winter, the year she herself died, she sold off all her remaining property to her children – 14 parcels. Like the cousin, Wilhelm Hentzler, Christoph and his wife fit the Württemberg peasant model: steady acquisition of a holding through saving and hard work, the endowment of children – in this case an unusual number of them – and a decline into old age with a sufficient holding to ensure independence. In Christoph's case, only two plots of what he had inherited and acquired ended up in hands outside the family – everything else went to the children. He did not in the end "come through" debt-free, but he and his wife ensured that all the property stayed in the line.

How did he manage his success? Early on in 1793, one of his cousins blamed him for always being in a quarrel with someone. There is evidence for some of this in the record – a boundary dispute here, an uncollected debt there, but nothing unusual. Perhaps a good example of what his cousin was talking about occurred in 1808 when he was 63. He and his children were engaged in a boundary dispute with each other that got out of hand. Village officials had been unable to mediate in the conflict, and the parties appealed to the Oberamt to settle the matter legally. He had trained the children in close dealing and hard-headed negotiation, and they had learned their lessons well. A few years later he and young Salomon had to take their dispute about who had paid how much in the other's name in various transactions to the court. Neither would recognize the other's claims. Perhaps it was the readiness to enter into contention even with his children that made him a good husbandman. His concentration on a narrow range of kin bespeaks a restricted sense of interest. This explains his readiness to go after Friedrich Krumm, especially after Krumm and his brother had squabbled over the debts from the Jüstingen venture. Perhaps Christoph was also angry over the suborning of his kinsman (BDH) by Krumm. All Christoph could fall back on was a narrow circle of kin – they were at once his greatest resource and his greatest limitation.

The big man

Old Salomon Hentzler, Bauer, Schultheiss (1735–1812)

In 1809 Johannes Bosch, the son-in-law of Schultheiss Hiller, came to the 73-year-old Salomon Hentzler for marital advice. Bosch had not lived in Neckarhausen for a long time. Friederica Regina Hiller had gotten to know him as a young soldier who cut quite an attractive figure. Their courtship was marred by a string of lurid details about his past, which slowly came to light, and by her father's stiff opposition to the marriage. Perhaps he thought about the possibility of a secure position in the village as the Schultheiss's son-in-law or of a significant settlement on his bride, giving him the chance to begin serious life as a farmer. Later he said that Friederica Regina had pushed him into marriage and that he had gone through with the wedding only reluctantly. Afterward, he discovered that Hiller intended to keep him on a short leash and that the expected marriage portion had so many strings attached to it that his freedom of movement was greatly restricted. He began almost right away to quarrel with his new wife and then with her family.

Johannes Bosch had lived outside the village for a decade, and by the time he came to talk with Hentzler had only been back for two years. He had not impressed anyone with his diligence and cultivation skills, partly because he did not have enough land to farm and no one in the kinship network of the Hillers seemed to want to call on him for wage labor in the fields. Without a great deal of capital, he tried to put together employment as pubkeeper, which does not appear to have been very successful. Nonetheless, from time to time enough men gathered together and loosened their tongues from the wine for Bosch to get an earful about the past of the village he had not experienced. It was no accident, then, that Bosch went to Hentzler ostensibly for advice about his marriage but really in order to tell tales about misappropriation of funds and cheating on ducal revenues. He opened his remarks to Hentzler with a litany about his marital problems, and the former Schultheiss with all the wisdom of his years counseled patience – at least that is how he reported the matter. But then Bosch said he wanted to take advantage of the occasion of their talk to tell Hentzler about the illegal activities of his father-in-law, the Schultheiss, both of the Bürgermeister, and the Waldmeister. For one thing, there had been far more tithe wine left over from the year before than anyone was aware of, and these men seemed determined to drink it all. Everytime there was any kind of meeting of the officials on village business, the wine flowed freely. Bosch wanted to know if it was legal for the magistrates to drink at the expense of the village.

Alignments in village affairs seem to have shifted from time to time, or perhaps they were never hard and fast simply because of complicated intertwining of interests and everyday practices. Words like "enemy" and "deadly enemy" were frequently to be found in village discourse, and "hatred" and "envy" were motives that people easily ascribed to action. When Schultheiss Hentzler himself left office under a cloud, he had referred to "envy" and "revenge" as the motives of those anxious to see him go. And Schultheiss Krumm had ascribed motives of "hate" and "envy" to Hentzler and his brother during their organized attempt to drive him from office. There is no question that hatred could characterize relations between people for a long time or that there were great fault lines between families in the village that determined politics for a generation or more. The problem in a village like Neckarhausen was that the very nature of production created ever new alignments in a kaleidoscopic pattern. Calling a neighbor to book at one boundary could bring revenge by the same neighbor or his brother or brother-in-law at another. Knowledge about past delicts could be used strategically when under attack. Deadly enemies in one sphere could be forced to cooperate in another. This does not mean that such a village ecology forced integration on people in the long run. After all, hatred generated in a particular conflict could inhibit coordination in many others. It is important to understand that what mediated between people pulled them together and split them apart at the same time, and the more necessary reliance on others was, the more potential there was for disappointment. It is surprising how quickly bitter feelings could be erased or the closest friendships lead to "irrevocable" hatreds.

In another place and for an earlier time, I have argued that peasant relations were frequently situational, that memory did not act as an instrument of long-term habit.[10] At least that is the way that villagers in the sixteenth century expressed it. They suggested that no memory traces would continue to affect relations once conflicts were formally resolved. Or neighborly and friendship feelings would be thrown into confusion once certain rights were under adjudication. Their point was that feelings and attitudes flowed out of the context of particular situations. A realignment in social relations – at least in the way they talked about the matter – brought reconciliation, not vice versa. I do not want

[10] Sabean, *Power,* chap. 1.

to suggest that this aspect of sixteenth-century peasant culture persisted without any change, especially after many generations of pietist preaching, but my expectation of irrevocable cleavages in the village continually is disappointed just as my expectation that closely integrated relatives will continue to look out for each other's interests. Perhaps in many situations, the principle of my enemy's enemy being my friend was the operative one. Johannes Bosch had it wrong too. He thought if he went to Salomon Hentzler, he could stir up matters and get even with his father-in-law. After all, six years earlier Hentzler had driven Friedrich Krumm from office. And now one of Krumm's closest supporters and brother-in-law was Schultheiss Hiller. Bosch banked on the continuity of feelings to bring his father-in-law into discredit.

Sons-in-law make very poor anthropologists, and Bosch was no exception. He thought he could feed into Hentzler's continuing resentment but instead gave the old man a chance to do a good turn for the Schultheiss with no cost to himself. Or there may have been subtler motives, a kind of *Schadenfreude* in bearing tales of fooling around with the wine tithes – for after all Krumm had used Hentzler's history of wine revenue corruption in his counterattack. Whatever the motive, Hentzler immediately took Bosch's accusations to Hiller, who called a meeting of the Gericht to deal with his son-in-law's charges. Bosch had to take everything back and admit he was after revenge because of the conflict with his wife and had no knowledge of anything illegal that Hiller had done.

Surprising shifts in social alignment characterized much of Salomon Hentzler's life. He had in fact led the charge against Krumm and backed the furious activity of his nephew, namesake, and ward, young Salomon, in organizing the cabal against the Schultheiss. Yet throughout the incident, from 1796 to 1809, the two Gevattern for Salomon, Jr., were Friedrich Krumm, on the one hand, and Anna Catharina, the wife of old Salomon, on the other. In 1811 the two Hentzlers, uncle and nephew, sold their very substantial house, which they shared by halves, to Krumm, and when old Salomon died in 1812, Krumm came up with the ready cash for his funeral. Similar shifts and turns marked Salomon's relations with Bürgermeister Holpp, who was deeply in cahoots with Krumm in his corrupt use of the village forest and who was instrumental in fixing many of the false receipts. Holpp was part of the group who led the attack against the Hentzlers on behalf of the "better part of the community." During the investigation, Holpp and Hentzler were confronted with each other over the charge that Hentzler had earlier stolen grain belonging to the state. When Hentzler called Holpp a "godforsaken man," the latter said that if he ever said such a thing again, he would tell things about him that would make his bones under the earth shame themselves, which stunned Hentzler into silence. The upshot of the investigation for Holpp was a substantial share in the court costs (20 fl), dismissal from office, and 14 days at hard labor. In 1805 Holpp and Hentzler were trading insults, Hentzler calling Holpp a "thief" and Holpp calling Hentzler an "arch scoundrel" (*Blitzspitzbuben*). Only Holpp's maid had been able to restrain him from jumping on his rival. In front of the court, Hentzler innocently wanted to know why

Holpp was so antagonistic (*Feind*). A few years later, Salomon was at odds with schoolmaster Hiller, the son of the Schultheiss. In this instance one of the few witnesses to back Hentzler's version of the incident was Holpp, who went so far as to tell Schultheiss Hiller to keep his mouth shut. Such a shift in alliance had happened much earlier in Hentzler's career. After he was forced out of office, Johann Georg Baur succeeded him. Baur's father had been married to Salomon's sister, and Baur and Christoph Hentzler were married to sisters. With such connections, Baur was certainly the Hentzler family candidate for office. But within two years, they were at loggerheads. Christoph Hentzler had purchased a house from Friedrich Hentzler, baker, and for some reason the payments had to go through the Schultheiss. Salomon, who owed Christoph some money, was expected to go along to Baur with the cash in hand. Courtesy dictated that Hentzler make the payment inside Baur's house, but Salomon refused to enter and remained outside by the fountain. Why Hentzler was angry is not clear, but the attempt to conclude business in the street was certainly an insult. According to the protocol, he also used "Du" words for Baur, which can only mean such expressions as "Du Spitzbube" (you scoundrel) and the like. After a while Hentzler left, but was summoned again by Baur. This time he ostentatiously drove by, which prompted Baur to jump out of his house and grab Salomon to force him to enter the house. Later, up by Christoph's field, Baur encountered Christoph's sons Andreas and Salomon, who called, "Du liederlicher Geselle, du Höllreck, du Lumpp." Baur, who wrote the protocol himself, allowed as how he had also let his mouth "go for a walk" (*spazieren*). In the end, he claimed "satisfaction" not for old Salomon's actions but for those of his nephews.

Apparently after Baur was thrown out of office – the reason is not to be found in the available texts – Krumm had the support of the Hentzlers. How the relationship went sour cannot be said exactly. Christoph's obsession with his own family interests may have played a role. Certainly his newly married and well-to-do young sons were throwing their weight around the village. Salomon Hentzler and Krumm got into a vicious court battle over the debts arising from security and probably investment in Mathes Sterr's farm in Jüstingen. Salomon and Christoph were certainly incensed at Krumm's attempt to suborn their niece's husband at a time when the coordination of kin was crucial for the Hentzler *Hausmacht*. Even after Hentzler and Krumm resolved their differences, there may have been new issues, but Salomon did not voice any complaints directly and did not sign the original petition. Only when Scribent Gök's investigation threatened to turn the Hentzler faction into rebels did he and his brother as long-time Schultheiss (and therefore ducal servant) and Richter enter the scene openly in a petition to the duke. Krumm and his associates immediately turned on the two men as their chief target, their aim being to destroy their official positions in the village hierarchy.

Schultheiss Hentzler had resigned from office in 1788 with the condition that he would keep his position of honor in the church next to the Schultheiss – this, of course, meant that all during his conflicts with Baur and Krumm, the two men stood side by side in front of the pastor each Sunday morning. He also maintained "personal freedom," which exempted him from such duties as road and bridge gang work and participation in the ducal hunt. Krumm's faction demanded the loss of Hentzler's rank and privileges. In the end, he did lose his privileges and was condemned to pay 15 fl in court fees.

Hentzler had become Schultheiss at the age of 33 and held office for 20 years. According to him, since he did not have any children, he was strict with the villagers, which caused resentment leading to a false accusation and pressure from the local pastor and the district Vogt to resign. The crime had to do with the ducal tithe on wine. Salomon had been the celler master for eight years, during which time it had been the custom for many villagers to give him a gallon or so when he measured out the ducal tithe. Altogether, he might receive about 20 gallons of wine in this fashion. The problem was that he poured the duke's wine and his own together into the same barrel and at the end of the day poured his off to take it home. That is when those filled with "envy and revenge" reported him for stealing the lord's wine. Witnesses were, of course, divided, but the pressure was enough for him to plead ill health and resign. The whole story was dug up by Krumm and his faction to suggest that there had been a cover-up and that Hentzler should have been dismissed from office and punished more severely. That he came away with his honor intact gave him considerable social and political power even though he was no longer in office. It is remarkable how at each occasion when accusations and counteraccusations began to be thrown at each other, villagers were able to call upon knowledge of old and hidden delicts. One of Hentzler's attackers in 1802, the Bürgermeister Johannes Holpp, related that many years earlier he had been Hentzler's servant and had carried ducal grain to Hentzler's storeroom for him. Thirty years before, the ousted Schultheiss Baur had been Hentzler's servant, and he had stolen wood for Hentzler.

Old Salomon Hentzler was in a peculiar position in Neckarhausen. He was a well-connected man of considerable power. But his wife and he produced no children, not even stillbirths or infants who survived for a time. It must have been clear to them after a decade or so that they would not be able to have any direct heirs. Perhaps his strictness had to do with the fact that he had no alliances to make, but in any event the lack of direct heirs certainly determined a good deal about where he put his energies. Curiously enough he seldom acted as Kriegsvogt, not even in the period between his marriage in 1756 and becoming Schultheiss in 1768 – although perhaps because he married so young (21), he would not have been sought after for the job, at least for the first several years. He also was very seldom asked to be guardian. Again, he was the oldest son in the family and had become Schultheiss at a young age, which probably gave him little opportunity to do so. He was the Pfleger of his disabled brother Friedrich, whose property he managed to sell to other members of the family, notably his brother Christoph. He and his wife began with a nice property of 26 parcels and a half house. Up until he became Schultheiss in 1768, he bought 14 more and for another decade picked up a few more pieces. By that time, since it was clear that he would have no heirs, he began to slough off land – 21 parcels between 1778 and 1789. By the end of the century, everything he sold went to his brother Christoph and Christoph's children. He and his wife (especially his wife), in sharp contrast to other services they could have offered, stood for more couples as Gevattern than anyone else of their generation – 22 altogether. Between them, they concentrated on three clusters of Petermanns, Häusslers, and Hentzlers, accounting for 16 couples. At least 18 of the godkin were closely related to Salomon and his wife, almost all nephews and nieces and first cousins. As time went on, they stood for the children of the first cousins. There was a special concentration on his brother Christoph's family – for Christoph himself and for his sons Andreas and Salomon and son-in-law Caspar Bauknecht. Catharina was the godmother for Salomon's niece, Christina, married to Mathes Sterr. Furthermore, she stood as godmother for Barbara Kraut, her cousin's daughter, who married Johannes Holpp, Salomon's young servant and later Bürgermeister and opponent during the Krumm affair.

Did Salomon mean to imply that since he had no children all the villagers were his children? Halfway through his term of office, he started rapidly to disaccumulate – many of the plots he sold to his old servant Johannes Holpp. His energies became focused on managing village affairs. He certainly paid attention to family concerns, but during the early years, he and his wife put most of their energies as godparents into a plethora of her cousins. It was only after he resigned from office that he began to focus on the Hentzlers – mostly his nieces and nephews. As the village chief magistrate, he certainly was not uninvolved in defrauding the duke or in stealing the odd log from the forest. But he still must have run a fairly tight ship, which led to his being replaced by a younger generation much more ready to use office to line their pockets and to provide abundant perks. At the age of 53 Salomon was largely left with nothing to do. He was used to running his farm with the best hired help, and there was little for a capable man like him to do but to expand his activities in the family – most notably the large one of his brother Christoph. Perhaps his entry into the fray against Krumm was conditioned by his bossy temperament and the aggressive activities of his newly come-of-age nephews.

The politician of class

Friedrich Krumm, Bauer, Rat, Richter, Bürgermeister, Schultheiss, forest administrator (1765–1841)

While he was still Bürgermeister in 1798, Friedrich Krumm was made administrator of the *asotisch* and *incorrible* Johannes Rieth, only child of Johann Georg Rieth III, the last Schultheiss Rieth, who died in 1761. Young Rieth had married a woman from Neckartailfingen, the daughter of a Richter, in 1773. Shortly thereafter he began a drinking and carousing career that lasted until his death in 1805. After repeated jail sentences and warnings from his wife and her relatives, his mistreatment of her and the children led to a separation. A charge of adultery concluded the marriage with a divorce and property separation in 1785. By that time, Rieth had driven an estate worth (according to one misinformed observer with great exaggeration) 40,000 fl down to 1,036 fl. During the next 10 years or so, he was involved in two more accusations of illegitimately fathering children. He broke out of jail in Nürtingen once and led his pals in a parade across the bridge to a tavern. Another time, they broke down the wall of the Neckarhausen lockup to get him to come for a drink. Rieth never drank alone and he never let anyone else pay. In 1797 his mother left him 5,764 fl, increasing his estate to 8,290 fl. Within a year, because of the danger to his property and the threat to the inheritance of his children, he was declared incompetent (*Mundtod*) and put under an administrator, who was ordered to sell all the real estate, pay off the debts, and allow Rieth only to live off the annual interest.

Krumm soon became Schultheiss and was immediately taken up in succession with occupying French troops and quartered imperial soldiers. He gave the accounts over to his brother-in-law, Conrad Hiller, the schoolmaster, although he himself remained responsible for the Pflegschaft. Krumm was no match for the wily Rieth, who despite regular announcements that no one was to serve him wine on credit continued to run up unbelievable bills at the taverns. How he managed to do so behind Krumm's back had a great deal to do with how cash circulated in the village economy. In general, people did not maintain cash hoards but moved liquid funds quickly into paying off debts, investing in property, or lending to someone else. Quite frequently villager A, when he or she came into funds, would pay off C for a debt owed to B. Usually this was done at B's request, but C might obtain a court order or just convince A to pay him or her for what B owed. The politics of debt payment could be complicated and involve different strategies and calculations. In Rieth's case, when buyers purchased his property at auction, they did not pay immediately but were "referred" (*verwiesen*) to Rieth's creditors – according to form, by his administrator Krumm. But Rieth was a forceful personality, ever ready to break up a bar if refused a drink, and capable of persuading a buyer to pay up by settling a debt at this or that tavern. In this way, new debts were taken care of and the credit for his drinking kept coming. His "cousin" Johannes Heinser, however, accused Krumm of colluding in the behavior, paying off new debts, and drinking along at Rieth's expense. The upshot of the investigation, concluded in 1802, was to make Krumm liable for every new debt that was incurred after Rieth's declaration of incompetency.

The fall from 8,290 fl to 2,600 fl overstates what Krumm had to pay because Rieth and his creditors had concealed a few thousand gulden worth of debts at his inventory. Still Krumm stood to lose several thousand as a result of the investigation, which he considered prompted by malice and envy. It came at a time when he had just had heavy claims on his estate from the bond he had placed along with Salomon Hentzler to underwrite Mathes Sterr's Jüstingen farm. And it also coincided with the ducal investigation into his conduct of office brought about by his godson young Salomon Hentzler and Mathes Sterr, supported by the likes of Johannes Heinser, old Salomon Hentzler, and the Richter Christoph Hentzler, and buttressed by resentments of volatile characters like Johann Georg Riempp.

The accusations against Krumm that led to the commission investigation in 1802 essentially involved favoritism and misappropriation. He was supposed to have allowed deserters to live safely in the village, assessed light fines, treated disputants in verbal and real injury cases in a partisan manner, distributed kindling and lumber unequally, interfered with the draft, acted arbitrarily in his own interests, and treated magistrates and Bürger high-handedly and arrogantly. There were accusations of false billing, appropriation of goods belonging to the village, inflation of expense accounts, stealing, keeping false accounts for sheepfolding and sales of wood, putting extra sheep in the village herd, personal use of village funds, cheating the excise tax accounts, fixing the tithe auction, and enticing a Bürger to perjury. Ultimately the consequences were severe for Krumm, even though many of the charges were dropped or found to be unsubstantiated. He ended up at the conclusion of the investigation in October, 1803, with a number of fines, orders to render compensation, a large bill of 30 fl for investigation costs, four weeks at hard labor, and dismissal from office. His associate Bürgermeister, Johann Holpp, whose help was necessary for all the falsified records and receipts, was punished almost as severely. Curiously enough, young Salomon Hentzler was fined 10 Reichstaler for instigating the cabal against Krumm in the first place, which makes clear that the authorities, while not able to overlook Krumm's crimes, still saw the attack as a sort of rebellion. Christoph Hentzler, who hardly appears formally in any of the investigation, lost his seat on the Gericht and old Salomon lost his privileges.

Friedrich Krumm was not born in Neckarhausen, and he only received citizenship (*Bürgerrecht*) in the village just before he got married (1787). Nonetheless, both he and his sister, whose father had been a wealthy miller and Bürgermeister in Grötzingen, a contiguous community, were raised as orphans by relatives in Neckarhausen (see Figure 16.7). Another brother or cousin eventually became Schultheiss in Grötzingen. Krumm's mother was Anna Elisabetha, daughter of Johann Jacob Geiger, Richter. Her sister, Agnes, married Johann Georg Bauknecht, who raised Friedrich's sister. A brother, Jacob Friedrich Geiger, Richter, became Krumm's guardian and brought him up. Friedrich eventually courted the daughter of another Richter, Jacob Bosch, whose half-brother had married the widow of Johann Georg Rieth III, Schultheiss and father of the infamous Johannes. Friedrich's sister, Elisabetha, eventually married the young schoolmaster, Conrad Hiller, who was to succeed Friedrich as Schultheiss.

By the time Friedrich was in his late teens, he was a rival of his young Bauknecht cousins. During the mid-1780s as their generation came of age, there was a significant change in courtship practices. Up until then, the old bundling customs were under tight control, and it was unusual for a young man to contest the testimony of a woman who reported him as father of her child. But during

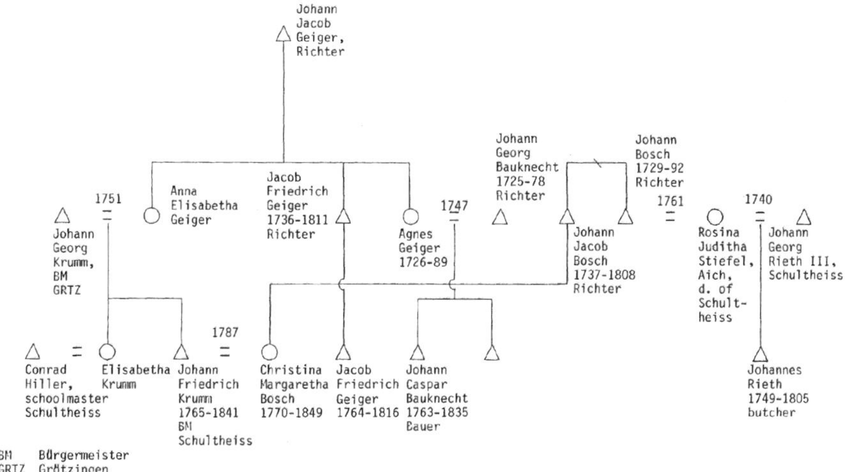

Figure 16.7

the 1780s, rival groups of young men squared off against each other, waited around the street to start fights, raided the rooms of young women to find their enemies, and challenged the statements of a woman by listing all the other men who had visited her. Some of the battles had to do with competition for specific women, others with attempts on the part of wealthier young men to exclude poorer ones from access to women of their standing, and still others with those who took it upon themselves to police the morals of the village. During this period, the women over whom they fought frequently received the epithet "Hur." Michael Feldmaier, for example, had hung around outside the door of one woman and beat her lover with a club to teach him a lesson. Things had gotten so violent that the Vogt issued an order to forbid the young men to be on the street after 8 p.m. They had been running around causing trouble with the excuse that they were out to catch unmarried fellows hanging around girls. The lover of one young woman, in an effort to deny culpability, named Jacob Bauknecht, Krumm's cousin, a visitor to her room. He maintained that he had only come along to see if his "enemy" was there to beat him up and in turn suggested another cousin, Friderich Geiger, as a possibility. He also went around spreading the rumor that Krumm visited "the whore" as well. Geiger and Krumm grew up in the same household together, supported each other closely, and were on the lookout for Bauknecht to get even. The two encountered Jacob Bauknecht and his brother, Johann Caspar, and began a fight that did serious injury to Jacob. Geiger later said he beat him so badly out of hatred because he had mentioned him before the consistory in the pregnancy case. Geiger's father also eventually joined the battle and slapped around his sister Agnes, the Bauknecht's mother. There were stiff fines for all of them, with Krumm designated the chief aggressor for kicking Jacob once he was on the ground. Four years later, after he was married, Krumm complained that he had been poorly represented by his guardian, old Friedrich Geiger, who would have done better by him if his own son had not been involved.

During this time, Friedrich courted the extraordinarily young (14) Christina Margaretha Bosch, daughter of the Richter, Jacob, who moved into her parents' room to protect her reputation. Three years later, she married Krumm at the unusual age of 17. Such young marriages during that period seem to have been tied up with family politics, for partners who were close kin married on average a full two years younger than others. It was precisely during the 1780s when two aspects of the same politics were in play: youth groups enforced class endogamy on the street and in the bedrooms and parents gave permission to their minor children (under 25) to hive off parts of the estate and found new households. Marrying close kin was tied up with a new "class" endogamy. Strategies of matching wealth and strategies of renewing familial alliances were sometimes alternatives and sometimes parts of the same thing. In the case of Friedrich Krumm, there had been exchanges between Bosch and Geiger families before and both were linked to the old Schultheiss Rieth *Hausmacht* either directly – Krumm's wife Christina Margaretha's uncle was married to Johann Georg Rieth III's widow – or indirectly – Friedrich Geiger and his father were both married to Häusslers, descendants of Johann Georg Rieth I's daughter.

The young couple put together two of the largest marriage portions the village had ever seen. In 1808, when Krumm's wife's father died, she received another substantial sum, including a house and 23 parcels of land, all worth more than 3,000 fl. Between his marriage in 1787 and his dismissal from office in 1803, he added 10 fields to his substantial holdings, so that by 1800 he was the fifth richest Bürger, behind Wilhelm Hentzler, who was in first place. By 1805, he had surpassed Hentzler and in 1810 was the richest man in the village, with twice as large a holding as Hentzler, fallen by then to eighth place. From 1790 to 1820, Krumm remained in the fourth quartile of taxpayers. But that did not happen without severe blows to his fortune.

During the late 1790s, Krumm's uncle and former guardian and his cousin, the two Friedrich Geigers, got involved with the ducal farm in Jüstingen, with investments by Krumm and Schultheiss Baur among others. They bailed themselves out by underwriting Mathes Sterr in his bid to take over the farm, which quickly led to failure and considerable costs for Krumm and old Schultheiss Hentzler. Shortly thereafter Krumm was faced with paying several thousand gulden as a result of his poor handling of Johannes Rieth's estate. And within a year, he was cashiered from what had been a lucrative office and once again faced with stiff fines and the necessity to make restitution. During this time, he did not cease to go surety for various people, but his greatest financial disaster was once more pledging his fortune for his cousin Geiger, who took over the Jüstingen farm again. In 1811 Krumm was forced into foreclosure for the first time.

Gall Feldmaier was appointed administrator of the forced sale of all his land and movables, but when the property was offered for sale, there were no takers. Feldmaier testified that the villagers were afraid of Krumm's brother-in-law, the current Schultheiss, and the other powerful relatives. As a result, the Oberamt officials stepped in to arrange for an outsider as administrator. In this crisis, Christina Margaretha Krumm pledged her property for her husband's debts, and his nephew, schoolmaster Hiller, and cousin, Jacob Krumm, Bürgermeister in Grötzingen, offered to post a bond. In that year, the Krumms lost 14 parcels of land plus their very large house and barn to their debtors. It was then that his godson, young Salomon Hentzler and old Salomon Hentzler sold their house and barn to him.

The Jüstingen farm failure of Krumm's cousin had led to a suit in 1809 with a certain Rommel, who had taken it over – the same year that Krumm defended himself against obscure and quickly hushed up charges of running a counterfeit ring with the smith, Mathes Dammel. Rommel was accused of massive cheating on the sale of produce and equipment. Eventually, in 1824, the suit was won by Geiger (by that time dead) and Krumm. In the meantime, another demand for 1,055 fl in 1813 led to a second foreclosure for Krumm. Schultheiss Hiller had to be reminded by the authorities three times to sell Krumm's properties, but he protested once again that no one would bid on them. An outside administrator sold 1,100 fl of unmortgaged properties, which apparently all remained in Krumm's hands by the ruse of pledging them to the buyers without actually turning over ownership.

The tensions of the forced sales and outstanding suit finally led to a split between Krumm and his brother-in-law, Conrad Hiller. Krumm went to the Oberamt to report many fraudulent practices of the Schultheiss. He accused Hiller of cheating the village out of as much as 5,000 fl. Apparently there were severe irregularities in the mortgage registers, and the two Bürgermeister were part of the fraud. It was largely this accusation that led to the ouster in 1816 of Hiller and both Bürgermeister and the appointment of Salomon Brodbeck as temporary Schultheiss (*Amtsverweser*) for the next four years. In any event, in 1816, 26 parcels of land belonging to Krumm as well as his house and barn were subject to forced auction. His wife bought the buildings and 17 of the plots. In 1817 his wife traded the house worth 1,900 fl for one worth 800 fl. By 1822, once again there was a forced sale but not until the authorities again appointed an outside administrator after no one would bid for the properties. This time the lands that had been mortgaged in 1813 fell to the gavel, and the Krumms lost 19 parcels. By 1825, Krumm had fallen to quartile II of taxpayers, and during the next five years passed on much of what was left to his children as they got married. His creditors, including Conrad Hiller, forced him to sell his house in 1827 to his son. After that Krumm held on with only a remnant of his patrimony. In 1837, at the celebration of his fiftieth wedding anniversary, the Gemeinderat provided a sack of flour for the celebration because of his destitution. When he died in 1841 at the age of 75, the inventory remarked that except for a few movables he had nothing of value.

Friedrich Krumm had been at the center of a family alliance, which fell apart when it failed to succeed in their farm venture. Their resources had outgrown the village, but they invested in agriculture during a period of crisis and heavy capital investment costs. Although Krumm was never directly involved with production or management, he put his considerable fortune at risk for his uncle and cousin. His activities as Kriegsvogt and godparent were also invested heavily in the Geiger family, as well as in the children of his brother-in-law, Conrad Hiller. He saw himself as representative of the better part of the village, and his short term of office was characterized by a heated discourse on social difference. As a youth he had been aggressive in the practical politics of endogamous alliance formation, and as a powerful magistrate had used a language designed to sort out not so much families against one another as different strata coordinated through a constantly renegotiated set of familial alliances. The preservation of his own estate from destruction was prolonged by powerful support from relatives who continually scared off potential buyers. By the early 1820s, the man who had lost a fortune underwriting his relatives could find no one willing to underwrite him. But family connection still played a role even as investment shifted to the next generation. Krumm's godson, the new schoolmaster Hiller, and the latter's brother Ludwig underwrote young Friedrich Krumm's buy-out of his father's remaining estate, forced on to the market by the creditors, prominent among whom was their own father.

Prototype II

Adam Falter, carpenter (1749–1818)

It is a truism in anthropology that the wealthy and powerful have more relatives than others. That is to say, more people recognize or seek to recognize their kinship connection because it is to their advantage to do so. Likewise those with power express that power through the larger networks they develop and the number of dependents they have. Someone like Bürgermeister Gall Feldmaier or Schultheiss Salomon Hentzler developed very large clienteles out of their in-laws, nieces, nephews, and cousins through godparentage, Kriegsvogtschaft, surety, and guardianship. Marriages among their kin appear to have been choreographed, and genealogies display recurrent patterns of exchange. For the carpenter Adam Falter, the density of kinship looks impoverished largely because he had so few contexts in which to display his interest and concern. In that sense, kinship appears to have been a steady feedback system. The more chances people had to display their relationships, the more foundation they provided for reproducing them in some fashion or other. Falter was only once godparent – for the illegitimate child of his first cousin once removed (FZSD). He never was called upon to be a Kriegsvogt or guardian.

The sources provide a striking contrast in kinship practice in the case of Adam Falter and Gall Feldmaier. Feldmaier and his wife were godparents for 12 couples, and he was guardian for 18 people and Kriegsvogt for 20. But in part the contrast is between formal, documentable practices and those of a less formal nature. The very fact that Falter was called upon as a ritual parent in a crisis situation for a cousin suggests a background of informal practice that relatively seldom made its way into texts.

Although Falter practiced his craft as carpenter throughout his life, he also developed a fairly substantial agricultural holding. By 1800 he was well within the top quartile of landholders, ranking 28 out of 167. Originally, each of the two young spouses in 1775 brought one arable strip in each of the three fields. He contributed a meadow, and his wife, two vineyards. Most of their property transactions during the first 10 years or so involved an exchange of parcels with a cousin, uncle, or sibling in order to gain the most advantage from a particular location. After 1786, for 10 years, Falter purchased about one new field each year. Then for another 10 years, at the peak of his wealth, he sold a few more pieces (13) than he bought (10). By 1810 he had fallen to quartile III, but during the bad years when so many other villagers were going broke, he slowly added pieces for a net gain of 7 parcels, boosting himself back into quartile IV, where he remained until his death at 70 in 1818. Falter appears to have made a steady profit from his work as a builder, which he sank regularly into land purchases. Throughout his life, he developed and maintained a considerable estate, mixing farming and carpentry in a mutually supporting way. He must have been a man of solid reputation even if he was not inserted into a dense network of kin and did not marry or arrange marriages for his children in such a way as to maintain or develop a systematic alliance with any particular families. He probably had more to do with other carpenters and masons than he did with his own kin, many of whom were weavers or craftsmen of some kind. Some of these professional associations only began to work themselves out into renewed familial alliances in Adam's grandchildren's generation. Adam's son-in-law was Salomon Brodbeck, who became temporary Schultheiss after Conrad Hiller was dismissed from office. In some ways, Brodbeck represented the middle ranks of the village, many of whom were not yet part of tight kin alliances or were only just building them. When it came time to elect a permanent Schultheiss in 1821, the "establishment" saw to it that he was not kept on, although his power base was sufficient to accumulate important offices as a Gemeinderat.

The 54-year-old Adam Falter was not at all an organizer of the group who brought charges against Friedrich Krumm, but he was a vociferous and respected critic and an early signer of the document. He specifically testified that he was outside the network of kin that put together the document. There was no one in particular who had contacted him or put special pressure upon him to sign. He recounted how he had talked with his fellows about the lack of order in the way the village was being managed. He spoke as an expert carpenter about the depletion of the forest, and most of his criticism had to do with the use of the woods. He was exercised about the annual apportionment of kindling, especially about the advantages that were taken by the chief magistrates and some of the village officers. More important for him was the way building wood was made available to various Bürger. Indeed Salomon Brodbeck (his son-in-law) had received wood from the Schultheiss for a pigsty gratis but when Falter applied for the same, it was denied him. The different way father-in-law and son-in-law were handled suggests that they were parts of completely different networks with different connections to the community officials. In concluding his testimony, Falter argued that on the one hand the Bürger did not receive enough wood for building and maintaining their houses, while on the other the woods were being depleted by mismanagement and a propensity to make a profit by selling too much. This looks like a contradiction, but his point had to do with even-handed treatment. People with financial strength could bid on logs that were offered for sale by auction, and the practice of the magistrates was clearly to overcut the woods in favor of the wealthier landholders and full-time Bauern. What was needed was a plan of giving each Bürger a certain amount of sawed wood each year. Such a policy fit in with the ideology of communal exploitation of village commonland. The village fruit crop or willow wands, for example, were divided up evenly to all the villagers, who presumably then sold or gave what they did not need to other villagers.

Adam Falter had his say once the petition had been sent along to the Oberamtmann and Scribent Gök had carried out his investigation. That seemed to satisfy him, and he had no inclination to support the Hentzler faction in their quest to unseat the Schultheiss. Falter was not in any one of the particular family networks nor solidly part of any particular political faction. He therefore withdrew from the group of plaintiffs and no longer continued to press charges against Krumm. He had been a witness against Krumm in favor of Mathes Sterr, who had complained about the partiality of the Schultheiss' treatment of his complaint against Georg Friedrich Häussler. His testimony had been discounted as a fellow plaintiff, but once he withdrew, it was once again accepted as nonpartisan.

Falter may have been a critic of the way the village was managed, but he always was part of the payoff and bribe system involved in village business. Perhaps that is why he changed his mind about the investigation – too close a look at the details would have implicated him. In fact, one of the results of the commissioner's report was a fine for inflating a bill at the request of Schultheiss Krumm. Falter, along with two other carpenters, had been engaged by the village to carry out repairs to the bridge over the Neckar leading to Raidwangen. As usual for such work, the three men were allowed to eat and drink at the tavern at the expense of the community. Krumm got them and the tavernkeeper to sign a greatly inflated expense account, which allowed him to siphon off enough funds to pay for his own or the magistrate's tabs. During the investigation, Falter and many of the other construction workers were implicated in other false receipts and bills.

Johann Adam Falter was part of the village public. He was not very well connected to the establishment but was hard-working, resourceful, thrifty, and respected. He certainly was not against cooperating with those who gave him a job, yet he was quite capable of acting independently. He was not the kind of person who pushed either principle or resentment to a final conclusion. He was not the kind of person either who went surety for someone else, but on the other hand he was integrated enough and trusted enough to be able to borrow small amounts of money from many people. Unlike those villagers who failed after 1810, he did not have much of his land mortgaged to outside creditors. Yet he did carry a hefty debt, even if well within his means (against 1960 fl property, he had 775 fl debt). In a rather unusual way most of what he owed was to people inside the village in small amounts of 10–40 fl. He certainly was not a speculator but built his estate piece by piece and kept it on a solid foundation. And he was not willing to part easily with what he had put together. At the death of his first wife in 1795, one of his sons-in-law, Johann Georg Ebinger, contested the estate division. He claimed that the marriage portion of his wife had come from both parents, while Falter maintained it was to be considered an advance on the maternal inheritance – the dispute having to do with grandparental inheritances that had fallen to Falter's wife during the course of their marriage. Falter won the dispute, which the two men refused to settle by compromise, saying that he was not the kind of man who would just give part of his substance away. Several years later (1808), Ebinger complained to the court that he had bought a meadow from Falter, who then had the transaction entered into the records as part of the maternal inheritance. The discovery of the deception led to a fine for Falter. He not only was not the kind of person who would give something away but he also represents a stereotypical peasant cunning.

The new professional

Conrad Hiller, schoolmaster, poor relief administrator, sheepfold administrator, forest administrator, Schultheiss (1758–1842)

In 1815 Conrad Hiller, one-time schoolmaster in Neckarhausen and current Schultheiss, was under investigation for fraud and illegal conduct of office. The man who instigated the investigation was his predecessor and brother-in-law, Friedrich Krumm. Within a few short months, Hiller was dismissed from office. The next year, he passed on almost all of his property to his numerous children, reserving only the livestock and grain stores for himself. After this retirement, he lived for another 24 years, spending much of his time defending himself against complaints about actions he took while in office.

Conrad Hiller may well have been chosen for office because of his professional capabilities. He had never served as a magistrate, but perhaps tenure as schoolmaster precluded holding a position as a Rat or Richter. In some villages, the schoolmaster acted as clerk of the court, keeping the protocols of the Gericht, but that was in his capacity as a skilled writer and did not give him any authority beyond his office as teacher. When Hiller acceded to the Schultheiss position, he gave up his job as schoolmaster and passed it on to his son. Although he was Krumm's brother-in-law and can be seen as a successor to the Geiger-Krumm-Bosch familial alliance system, there are indications that he was elected precisely because he was above faction. He was not already part of the magistrate squabbles, and as schoolmaster had cultivated a bearing as learned and competent. He had accumulated a large farm holding and had numerous children coming up to marriage age – two sons would become schoolmasters and a daughter would marry one.

Hiller had a very orderly mind and was a master at writing bureaucratic prose, heavily laced with Latin phrases. He had ample time to demonstrate his competence in the 25 years he served as schoolmaster and the 20 years he kept the accounts of the poor relief fund. His competence can be clearly seen by comparing the protocols he wrote to those of his two predecessors. He knew how to parse a sentence, to distance himself from the action, and to maintain a pithy, logical style. In terms of learning, skill, and temperament, Hiller should have been an excellent Schultheiss. There were moves on the part of the central bureaucracy to professionalize village government right from the beginning of the century. Over time, fewer criminal matters were handled in the village court. Rather than the Gericht deciding this or that misdemeanor, allowing for an appeal to the Oberamt, it was restricted to writing up an incident to be presented to the district court. By the late 1830s, the Schultheiss office itself took over this function, assessing minor fines directly and writing up presentments for the court in Nürtingen. Clerks from Nürtingen had always recorded inventories and kept many of the accounts, either as the receipts were brought to them by village officials or on periodic visits to the village. By the 1820s, an accountant responsible for all the mortgage, sales, and land registers came to live in the village. In the 1860s, the Bürger simply voted their accountant, a man with no roots in the village, into office as Schultheiss. Conrad Hiller was the first in a line of professionals, a man trained in letters, acquainted with Latin, and familiar with pietist positions on the Second Coming – a departure from the peasant Schultheissen, who were never trained for the position and whose primary task had been to exercise ducal authority in situ.

With all of his skills, Hiller simply failed to keep orderly accounts, continued the corrupt practices of his predecessors, and used his office to line his pockets. During the 10 years after he retired, he had to defend himself against a series of complaints. Some of the charges against Hiller seem to have been based on resentment. He had exercised his office very much to his own advantage, and with the new regime, villagers were out for revenge. Back in 1809, Hiller's son-in-law, Johannes Bosch, had been accused of chopping up fruit trees belonging to people he wanted to get even with, one of the chief targets being Conrad Hiller himself. Since Bosch had been acquitted, there was no one to assess for damages, so Schultheiss Hiller and the other magistrates paid for them out of village funds.

By 1820 people were saying that the trees had grown back and that Hiller and the others ought to have to pay back most of the money.

More unsettling, given Hiller's competence as an administrator and his familiarity with documentation – way back when Krumm was accused of running Johannes Rieth's property into the ground, Hiller produced several pages of careful accounting for his year or two substituting for Krumm – was his disorderly bookkeeping. In 1820, he was accused of collecting too much sheepfold money from Christoph Hentzler's estate in 1814. In 1821 it was discovered that he had delayed paying excise money due in 1812 until 1814. In 1823 a Bürger pointed out that he had entered a sale of wood improperly as tax receipts. His poor relief accounts from the period before he became Schultheiss presented problems for Gall and Michael Feldmaier. Hiller had also confused accounts that caused considerable litigation in 1823 because the various men or their underwriters had all been bankrupted in the meantime. As sheepfold and forest administrator, he had paid out money that could no longer be traced. In 1813, a group of carpenters who had padded their expense accounts were told by the court to pay the money back, but Hiller managed to set the entire amount under the outstanding taxes of only one of them. In 1823, young Salomon Hentzler accused Hiller and two of his sons of having sworn a false oath with regards to his property transactions – and continued to bring suit all the way to 1836. By 1837, the 79-year-old Hiller himself started to demand back pay as schoolmaster from 1788 to 1802, when his promised raise had not been paid.

Hiller was a feisty character, hard-working, diligent, and thrifty. The son of a teacher from another village, he became schoolmaster at the age of 20 and immediately married one of the wealthiest young women in the village, the orphan of Johann Georg Krumm, Bürgermeister in Grötzingen, and Anna Elisabetha Geiger, daughter of the Neckarhausen Richter. She was brought up by her aunt Agnes, the widow of the Richter Johann Georg Bauknecht and father of Johann Caspar. She brought 1,320 fl worth of credit and 1,370 fl cash to match Conrad's portion of 870 fl. The young schoolmaster supplemented his school salary by cultivating the land of people without traction animals and agricultural gear, and sank all the earnings into land. Immediately after the marriage, he purchased 10 parcels of land and continued to buy up real estate through to the termination of his office as Schultheiss – a net gain of 37 parcels. Not until just before he retired in 1818 was he forced to sell eight strips of land, but that made his estate debt-free to pass on to the children. By 1810 he was the seventh wealthiest man in the village, and he had already endowed two children. In 1814, after the death of his wife, and in 1816, he passed along substantial portions to his children, altogether about 1,200 fl each. All during his years as schoolmaster, he had complained about his pay and had even taken home firewood from the schoolhouse. Schultheiss Hentzler had to warn him about his sarcastic (*spitzhundig*) badmouthing of his job and order him to keep the schoolhouse warm enough. He only got an effective raise shortly before his brother-in-law was cashiered.

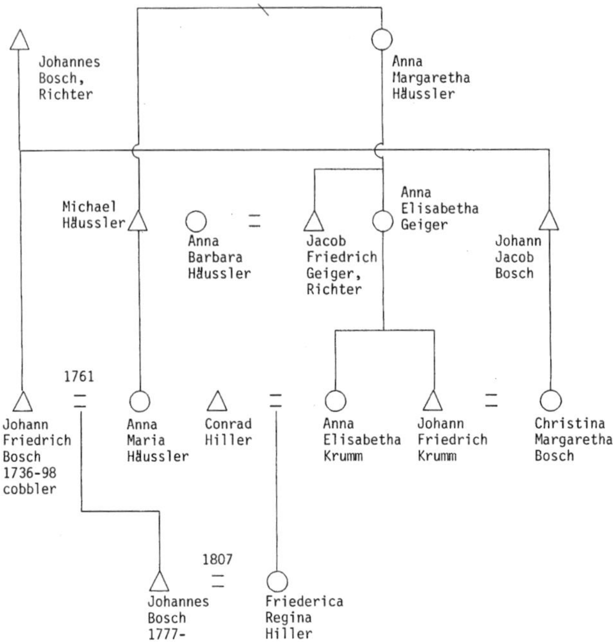

Figure 16.8

Schultheiss Hiller set each of his children up with a solid dowry, but he was very skeptical about the man his daughter Friederica Regina brought home. Johannes Bosch, 30, the son of Friedrich, had spent a term of service in the army and had been discharged with a pension. From the point of view of familial alliance, this was a good match. Young Bosch was a cousin of Friedrich Krumm's wife, and he was also related to Hiller's wife through the female line. His mother was a Häussler, a family intermarried with the Geigers over several generations. The Hillers stood as godparents to three Häussler women, all related to Anna Elisabetha, Hiller's wife: MB(W), MBD, MMBD (see Figure 16.8). But genealogy was not enough, for this was also a period when fortunes were more closely matched at marriage, when alliances were continued not with just any relative but with representatives from branches of the family that had maintained equal status. Johannes's father had been a cobbler and had left him no inheritance. All he really had to bring to the union was his pension and the expectation that he would work the land his wife would receive with her dowry. Unfortunately, he falsified his pension document to make it appear as if he would receive 20 fl per month instead of only 10 fl. Schultheiss Hiller might have been willing to steal a few logs and that sort of thing, but an alteration to a royal document was tantamount, he said, to lèse-majesté. It was also discovered shortly before the marriage that Johannes had financial obligations with regard to two illegitimate children in the residence city of Ludwigsburg. What was already forgotten was the illegitimate child he had fathered in Neckarhausen eight years earlier. Hiller thought the whole affair was a mismatch, but he was not able to dissuade his daughter. All he could do was make a special arrangement for her dowry. He gave her various plots of land only in usufruct (*nutzniesslich*), keeping full ownership and the tax obligations in his own hands. He called together a session of the Gericht and recorded his intention not to let his property pass to a son-in-law, whose capacity as a householder he suspected.

By 1809 Friederica Regina had initiated a divorce with the full support of her father. Bosch had not been able to make much of a go at farming, and apparently was not in demand as a laborer. He tried opening up a bar for a time, but his only success was to run up a large bill on credit for his father-in-law and the other magistrates. Friederica Regina cut that portion out of his ledger once it looked as if they were going to get into trouble for drinking at the cost of the village. That and other things led to constant tangles with his wife, who finally left because of mistreatment. But she was mostly concerned about his debts and the fact that she was not able to live at a level that she had expected. Furthermore, Bosch got into trouble with Friederica's uncle Krumm, who at least once beat him up. He tried to bring his father-in-law to book about drinking at the cost of the village by gossiping to old Salomon Hentzler. He implicated Krumm in a counterfeiting scandal. And he finally went along cutting up fruit trees belonging to his father-in-law and brother-in-law. Before Friederica Regina pushed through her divorce, she managed to complicate matters by getting pregnant by a young baker journeyman in Stuttgart, who was originally from Neckarhausen and visited her there because she was "known to his father's house."

Much of Hiller's term of office was spent trying to protect the village patriciate, including his brother-in-law Krumm, from foreclosure. In 1812 he received a sharp reprimand and fine from higher authorities for not reporting a number of Bürger who had gotten deeply into debt. In the previous year, Gall Feldmaier, who had been appointed to sell some of Krumm's property at auction to settle debts, said that people were afraid to bid for any out of fear of reprisal from his brother-in-law Hiller and other relatives. Two years later, officials sent a notice to Hiller about making a list of Krumm's properties, but he delayed several times. He tried to get away with his lack of action by holding an auction three Sundays in a row with no takers, but the government finally stepped in and appointed an external administrator. During the next year, a marshal came to repossess some property of one of Hiller's wife's Häussler relatives. The Bürgermeister and several others shoved him around until he went to the Schultheiss to enforce compliance. But even in Hiller's presence, one villager choked him and others threatened him with a severe beating. Not until he threatened Hiller with a report to the Oberamt did the Schultheiss offer him protection.

The property situation of Friedrich Krumm began to grow desperate in 1814–15. The lawsuit that was leading to his bankruptcy was not settled until 1824, and during the long, drawn-out affair both he and Hiller were unsuccessful in finding someone to post bond for him. Why the two of them eventually had a falling out is not spelled out in the records. It appears that Hiller finally buckled under pressure to sell Krumm's property. Oberamt officials interpreted Krumm's accusations of fraud and self-interested administration as a maneuver to put off foreclosure.

There were more forces behind Hiller's dismissal than Krumm's desperate attempts to stave off disaster by betraying his brother-in-law. Hiller ran the village at a particular moment of crisis when many patrician families were in danger of failing. Masses of property came on to the market all at once, a sudden bonanza for the land-hungry small producers. Attempts to manage the flow of property, to intimidate potential bidders so as to channel the parcels to wives and other family members at favorable prices must have produced considerable resentment in the village. A key instrument in his management of propertied interests was a fraudulent manipulation of the mortgage records. At the same time, Hiller coordinated a period of excessive drinking at village expense and a riotous exploitation of the woods. In the end, the *village* was "punished" by having its Schultheiss taken away altogether. Hiller's successor was only an "office administrator" (*Amtsverweser*) – one would use the term "regent" in another context. Salomon Brodbeck would never have the full respect of the office, partly because of the provisional nature of his appointment (not for life) and partly because he represented the lower end of the village hierarchy – the smallholders, artisans, and emerging group of newly mobile building workers. To reestablish control of village resources, families would have to tighten up their alliances even more, especially in a situation where there was less and less room for village officials to coordinate the control of resources, to falsify records (with the establishment of a resident professional accountant), to manipulate tithes (a new system of 10-year contracts was established in the 1820s), or to raid the woods (30- and 60-year rotation projects were established). The break with past practice was symbolized by a new sobriety among village officials. The new village leaders would be concerned not so much with ruling their fellows and keeping order as with coordinating state projects for correcting the course of the river, drainage, highroad maintenance, redrawing the field boundaries, crop rotation, redemption of feudal dues and tithes, health regulations, and the like. Hiller presided over one of the last administrations of heavy drinking and shameless, undisguised self-interest.

The voice of property

Johann Caspar Bauknecht, Bauer, member of Bürgerausschuss (1766–1840)

In 1819 the constitution in Neckarhausen, as in all Württemberg villages, was revised, essentially restructuring the old six-member Gericht (court) and four-member Rat (council), both of which had been filled by cooptation, by creating a new eight-member Gemeinderat (village council) and nine-member Bürgerausschuss (citizen's committee). Richter who previously held lifetime tenure could remain on the Gemeinderat if they wished, but vacancies were filled by election by all the enfranchised Bürger first for a limited term. A second election brought life tenure for a candidate. The Bürgerausschuss was elected from among all the Bürger for two-year terms. There was not a great deal of difference in the social composition of the two institutions. The average age of the Gemeinderat members was a few years greater than that of members of the Bürgerausschuss, but the overwhelming majority of both groups was composed of men in their 30s and 40s. The average tax bill for members of both corporations was exactly the same, and with two exceptions from each of them, all were in tax quartile IV – the remaining four being solidly within III. Bauern held the majority of votes in both cases. The Gemeinderat had two tavernkeepers who were also Bauern, a wealthy cooper, and a tailor. The Bürgerausschuss was slightly more diverse, with a cobbler, a baker, a wheelwright, and a weaver who later inherited his father's prosperous tavern.

One of the men elected to the new Bürgerausschuss was the wealthy Bauer and son-in-law of Christoph Hentzler, Johann Caspar Bauknecht, 53. Caspar was a cousin of Friedrich Krumm, one of the young men who had been active in the sexual politics of the 1780s, when the youths battled it out in the street over the issue of matching up couples from the same wealth strata. He and his brother had gotten into a pitched battle with Krumm and another cousin because of rumor-mongering about which young women they had been visiting. Young Caspar appears to have been not just part of the group competing for marriage partners but also a member of a crusade to control the morality of his generation. His mother's strong pietism may have preordained his activities in that direction. In 1784, at the age of 18, he and several other boys were caught pulling up rosemary in the Bürgermeister's garden, a symbolic act suggesting sexual improprieties in the household. A hearing was held to determine if there was any evidence against the daughter.

Caspar did not come into the records of the various courts after his marriage very often. He never sat in a tavern past closing or got into a drunken brawl with anyone. He was never accused of stealing, scolding, slandering, or pilfering. He was not active in any of the politics of the Hentzler, Bauer, Krumm, or Hiller administrations. He also did not play much of a role in family politics. He was only once called upon to be a godparent – a case of twins for his sister-in-law when an extra pair of godparents were required. And his wife succeeded her aunt as godmother for her brother for several years. He was called upon to administer the estate of his wife's uncle when old Salomon Hentzler, the earlier administrator, died, but someone else soon took it over. He was once a Kriegsvogt for a sister-in-law. Altogether he does not seem to have been very active in the politics of alliance. But he was the kind of cautious and diligent Bauer who came through the period of agricultural dislocation of the first three decades of the nineteenth century successfully and set up each of his three children with a very large endowment.

Caspar's father had been a Bauer and Richter and his wife was the daughter of a Richter. Their marriage in 1789 was a classic example of alliance of wealthy Bauer/magistrate families, a second cousin once removed (FMBSSD). In 1828 their eldest son married Rebecca Falter, daughter of a member of the Gemeinderat and from the same Falter patriline that had provided his mother's great uncle and cousin with wives. Caspar was tied through marriage to the Hentzler faction and through descent to the Geiger-Bosch-Krumm familial constellation. He and his wife had godparents from both sides, the wife of old Salomon Hentzler and Conrad Hiller, schoolmaster and later Schultheiss. Although Caspar never played a prominent role in any of the political conflicts between these families, he was certainly well connected with the politically active members of the powerful family syndicates.

From his marriage to his "retirement" in 1832, Caspar Bauknecht remained in the top quartile of taxpayers. Most of his property came from inheritance – at his marriage and at the death of his wife's father in 1814. Before he married, he bought five parcels of land, but he waited a decade before he purchased another plot. Even then, he only bought a piece every three or four years, picking up just seven parcels altogether. For the most part, he and his wife husbanded their patrimony, never went very far into debt, never ventured much onto the land market, and seldom underwrote anyone else's ventures either. The picture that emerges from the sources is that of a man whose attention was centered on his household and agriculture. His accession to the Bürgerausschuss in 1819 and constant reelection through the 1820s speaks of the respect with which he was regarded by his fellow Bürger.

Bauknecht may not have mixed it up at the high political level of village affairs, but he was the kind of villager whose opinion counted. He and his two brothers lived in adjacent houses down by the river below the Rathaus not far from the bridge to Raidwangen. One of the brothers and another who died years earlier had each contracted second-cousin marriages to daughters of magistrates as Caspar had done, and were solidly linked to the village patriciate. The three brothers in 1820 all paid about the same amount of tax, which put them among the very richest landholders in the village. Caspar seems to have been the leader of the three, outspoken, and, according to testimony, the leading voice on the Bürgerausschuss. He was a strong conservative voice in the name of property, order, and hierarchy, and he had nothing but contempt for Salomon Brodbeck, the temporary administrator of the Schultheiss office, who succeeded Caspar's Gevatter and cousin's husband, Conrad Hiller – Hiller's wife had been brought up in the same household as Caspar.

The issues that divided Brodbeck and Bauknecht do not lie on the surface of the records. In 1820 there was a huge blowup and battle along the Neckar river bank between Brodbeck and the Bürgermeister Deuschle and several of their supporters, on the one hand, and the Bauknechts and their relatives – people with close ties to the recently ousted Schultheiss Hiller – on the other.[11] Caspar had taken the lead as a member of the Bürgerausschuss at the village assembly to attack Brodbeck's competence regarding the maintenance of the Neckar river bank. The Bauern who had gardens along the river were anxious about flood damage, and they had little confidence in Brodbeck's leadership. Behind the vociferousness of their critique, however, was probably a division that began to run more clearly through village politics. The Bauknechts by heritage and alliance represented the propertied interests in the village. Brodbeck, by contrast, was much less well connected. His father-in-law was the carpenter Adam Falter. Although the younger man eventually put together a substantial holding, equaling Caspar at the beginning of the 1820s and moving well past him by the end, he was by no means so closely tied to the politics of the patricians as Hiller was. All through his term of office, there was considerable opposition to him, which grew so strong that the Oberamtmann had to announce expressly in the village that he would listen to no further complaints and that he would back whatever Brodbeck did.

The immediate cause of conflict – the river bank construction – had led Brodbeck to announce in the village assembly that they needed a donkey. Caspar suggested that they had enough of them in the village, the target of his barb being Brodbeck and Bürgermeister Deuschle. That jest had been only the latest cause for hard feelings among the two men. Several days later Brodbeck and Deuschle brought along the wheelwright Lötterle and his stepson, Salomon Vogler, to carry out some of the work that needed to be done. Lötterle and Vogler were closely related to Brodbeck's wife – her uncle's marital successor and her cousin (MBS). In order to place some supports, Lötterle stood in one of the gardens belonging to a Bauknecht. Johannes Winkler, a son-in-law of Conrad Hiller, happened to come along at the time and raised a hue and cry, which caused the Bauknechts to come pouring out of their houses to do battle. The three brothers, along with two of their sons, and Winkler's brother-in-law, Mathes Braun, jumped Lötterle and chased Vogler along the bank and threw him into a ditch.

Amidst all the shouting that went on, a great deal about attitudes and political splits comes to light. Jacob Bauknecht threatened Lötterle and Vogler contemptuously as men of insignificant fortune, which reflects some of the tensions between the landholders and the middle-rank artisans. In fact, Lötterle himself was on the Bürgerausschuss and had received a larger block of votes than Caspar Bauknecht, who had split the Bauern vote with two other men. The tensions between the Bauknechts and Lötterle grew out of social competition in the village, which came to be expressed in terms of class rather than family. And yet the discourse in the event continued to conflate the two modes of thought. In the

[11] See the discussion of the affair in David Warren Sabean, *Property, Production, and Family in Neckarhausen, 1700–1870* (Cambridge, 1990), pp. 324–7.

hot exchange, Bürgermeister Deuschle played his own social card by holding up to Mathes Braun the fact that he was in tax arrears – and so was his father. That remark brought Deuschle a stiff fine – it was just the kind of attack on honor that the law did not allow.

Caspar Bauknecht taunted Brodbeck and Deuschle about his now famous joke about the donkeys. The Bauknechts argued that Brodbeck had no interest in protecting their property but had only undertaken the repairs to the bank in order to pay himself a day's wages. They were not concerned enough about the matter to take proper advice and to carry out the work competently. And they had chosen for the work precisely the people who represented the other political direction in the village. The specific issue at the moment was a concrete one about garden plots, but the larger, more encompassing one was about property and its protection and about the support of inherited patrimony. Gone were the days when patricians had a Schultheiss who could intimidate buyers at an auction and who appointed trustworthy administrators to coordinate the sale of foreclosed estates to ensure that the property would fall to family members at collusive prices. Caspar Bauknecht was a dominant voice in the Bürgerauschuss in the aggressive defense of property just at a time when economic conditions led to an even greater flood of property onto the market – a flow harder to manage without a more cohesive set of familial alliances in the face of officials no longer chosen through cooptation and tight oligarchical control. That did not mean that elections at large did not return wealthy landholders for the most part, but it did mean that accession to office was no longer rooted in the familial politics and alliances of the institutions themselves. Families had to organize the village at large if they were to coordinate their interests in the absence of an oligarchical Vetterlesgericht.

The Wizard of Innovation

Johann Salomon Brodbeck, day-laborer, Bauer, Rat, Bürgermeister, temporary Schultheiss, Gemeinderat, orphan court juror, church consistory elder, poor relief administrator, tax assessor, boundary supervisor, sheepfold administrator (1772–1847)

Salomon Brodbeck developed a career in Neckarhausen because of sheer competence. Neither by inheritance nor by marriage was he closely tied into the village power structure. His father was a well-off Bauer and his father-in-law a carpenter, but neither held office. At his marriage, at the age of 26 in 1798, Brodbeck was described as a day-laborer, and by 1800 was only in the second quartile of taxpayers. Already in 1803, however, he was coopted for a place on the Rat. Two years later, he was chosen to administer the estate of old Jacob Friedrich Geiger, Richter, the uncle of Friedrich Krumm and Gegenschweher of Christoph Hentzler. The foreclosure on his estate must have been a spectacular affair. This was the first of a long string of major failures of village patricians, throwing large amounts of property onto the market. Some of Geiger's financial troubles had developed from the Jüstingen farm investment, which eventually plagued his son and led to the ruin of his nephew Krumm. When an estate was put under an administrator, the business was usually handled in a routine manner and no special remarks were set into the official texts. But in this case, Brodbeck's particular capacities were discussed, and it was pointed out that he was extraordinarily skilled at writing. By that the Schultheiss meant to convey that he was well organized, was experienced at keeping acounts, and could be trusted to document the process of breaking up the estate and settling the demands of creditors carefully and responsibly. But the remark was gratuitous unless there were other reasons to find his appointment questionable. At 33, Brodbeck was most probably much younger for the job than creditors and regional officials would have expected. Although he was on the Rat, he had little experience so far, and certainly was not of the standing of someone like the 55-year-old Gall Feldmaier. In all likelihood, the powerful members of the village, most of them closely tied up with Geiger through family or business connections, were looking for a bright young man to pull their irons out of the fire. And he did not disappoint them. He either invented, imported, or implemented the practice of selling an estate at auction to the wife of an insolvent debtor. It is possible that the Geiger family and Schultheiss Hiller let Brodbeck run the auction while quietly intimidating potential bidders. But it is most likely that Brodbeck coordinated the whole production and that his competence in the matter was signaled by Schultheiss Hiller's remark about his capacity as a scribe.

The rest of Brodbeck's career worked out in tension between activity for his own familial alliances, which were carefully cultivated but which largely involved people outside the orbit of magistrate families, and competent work as an official. When the village household became totally confused and disordered under Gall Feldmaier's direction as Bürgermeister in 1813, Salomon was chosen under pressure from the Oberamt officials to succeed him – at the same time that he presided over the foreclosure of Feldmaier's estate. The Oberamtmann was putting pressure on Neckarhausen not only to bring its accounting procedures into order and cut down on the graft but also to speed up the introduction of a number of agricultural innovations. The fashionable program for that generation involved year-round stall feeding of livestock and a more intensive development of meadowland. The shift from pasture lots to stalls involved considerable capital investment, a large-scale exploitation of the woods for extending barns and constructing cribs, and careful coordination of feeding schedules and management of village commonland. District officials thought that the combination of the learned Hiller and innovative Brodbeck would offer just the direction that the village needed to solve its crisis. But it was not long before Hiller was driven from office and was replaced as temporary Schultheiss by Brodbeck. In fact, Brodbeck was imposed on the village from above, precisely in an attempt to break up the old power configuration, abrogating the village right to elect its own headman. The Oberamtmann also appointed Wilhelm Deuschle as Bürgermeister, a young man with a career almost exactly parallel to Brodbeck's. Within a short time, old Schultheiss Hiller and two of the previous Bürgermeister, together with a delegation from the community, brought a complaint against the two men, but the officials from the Oberamt expressed their full support, refused to let them resign, and announced that they would entertain no further complaints.

By 1819 a reorganization of the village institutions was under way. The magistrates and representatives of the community put pressure on the Oberamt to reestablish a Schultheiss, but that was put off for future action. The new Bürgerausschuss, under the leadership of Caspar Bauknecht, immediately brought up an old matter of a log stolen by Schultheiss Hiller in 1814. They wanted to know if the theft should not really have been charged to Salomon Brodbeck, who was Bürgermeister at the time. Bauknecht and his friends kept up a running attack on Brodbeck and Deuschle, undermining their authority with steady criticism from within their own official position and with sarcastic remarks at village assemblies. It was during this period that the Bauknecht family, seconded by in-laws of the Hillers, attacked Brodbeck, Deuschle, and their relatives at the river bank.

In 1820 the election for Schultheiss deprived Brodbeck of his positions as chief magistrate and clerk of the court – the keeper of the minutes of the Gemeinderat. But he fell back to his appointment as Gemeinderat, where by 1825 he had accumulated a large number of offices: orphan court juror, church consistory elder, administrator of poor relief, livestock inspector, meat and bread inspector, tax valuator, and boundary supervisor. He held all of these positions until his death at 75 in 1847. He also held the position as sheepfold administrator for several years, an office that caused him some trouble and earned him a reputation for running an office in his own interest.

In 1825 he had a run-in with his wife's stepmother, who, interestingly enough, is referred to as his Gegenschwieger in the text. That term was usually reserved for the mother of a man or woman's daughter- or son-in-law – a co-(or corresponding)parent-in-law. Here the term operates on the conflation of step and affinal relations. What made them Gegenschwieger/Gegenschweher was the fact that each was married to a part of a "stem" – in this case a father and daughter. In the altercation, Christina Bross made a point of his self-interested handling of the sheepfold accounts, calling him a *Pförchbescheisser* (a sheepfold cheater). But she also revealed a side to Brodbeck's reputation that bears commenting on. She attributed his position to witchcraft. He was a man whose powers were understood to be ambiguous and hereditary at that. Christina brought an old issue of his father's sister having been suspected of killing a horse through her powers as a witch. Her charge may or may not have been taken seriously – it came after he had called her a "Hurloch" – but it points to a way of understanding Brodbeck's place in the village hierarchy. He had not been boosted into position by a network of men in power who were all related to him. Nor was his position over the long run one of support for one or the other of the competing

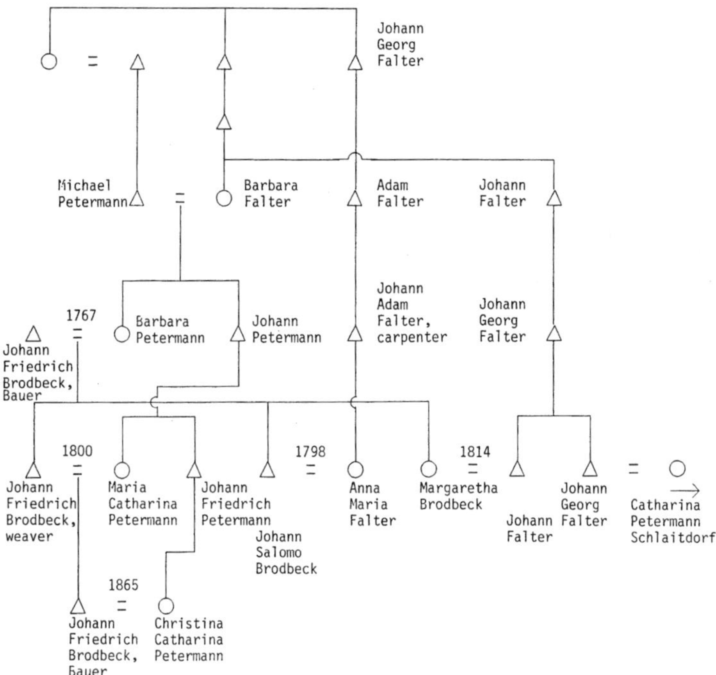

Figure 16.9

family syndicates who had managed village affairs. Since he was not rooted in "old corruption," there was something inexplicable or magical about the way he had attained power and accumulated offices in the village.

It would be incorrect to say that Brodbeck was outside the Vetterleswirtschaft of the village. Although he was not tied to the familial alliances of the village patricians, he did cultivate his own family connections, and his kin were involved in an alliance system that spanned several generations. The Brodbecks were closely allied with the Petermanns, and both exchanged frequently with a branch of the Falter family. Although there were several other such alliances, and the next generation drew on connections with other allied patrilines for marriage partners, this abstraction shows sufficiently how some of the exchanges continued over many generations (Figure 16.9).

Salomon's father had married a Petermann in 1767. This was followed by his brother's marriage to his MBD in 1800. In turn, his nephew in 1865 married another Petermann: also a MBD. Salomon himself married a Falter. His maternal grandfather had done so before him and his sister did so as well. Her brother-in-law, Johann Georg Falter, married a Petermann from Schlaitdorf, presumably closely related to the Petermanns in Neckarhausen. If Salomon's kin constructed alliances like those of the magistrate Bauer families of Geiger, Bosch, and Hentzler, they were connected largely with carpenters, weavers, tailors, smiths, and modest Bauern. Salomon was very active in knitting them all together. He and his wives were godparents for seven other couples – brothers, sisters, uncles, and cousins, and a sister's sister-in-law (ZHZ). He acted as Kriegsvogt for 18 women, almost all of them related to himself or one of his three wives – especially prominent were Brodbecks, Petermanns, and Falters. For many years, he was the Pfleger of his sister's destitute orphans. Between 1805 and 1829, he was called upon to administer 11 bankrupt estates.

When Salomon first gained a place on the magistrates as a young man in 1803, he was probably regarded as a useful fellow by the village patricians. And he was soon called upon by them to manage foreclosures for some of their families. He himself was not among the wealthier villagers and only slowly rose from taxpayer position 94 in 1800 to 78 in 1805 to 67 in 1810 (from quartile II to III). Not until 1820 and a very slow accumulation of property did he move up to quartile IV. Bits and pieces of inheritance played a role, and until the early 1820s, he added a new parcel of land by purchase about every year and a half. Even though he endowed several of his children, he kept a considerable estate until he died at 75 in 1847, passing on a large house and barn and 33 parcels of agricultural land. His wealth did not really begin to accumulate until the 1820s. In the previous decade, he made himself useful liquidating estates of the likes of old Jacob Friedrich Geiger and Gall Feldmaier. But after 1820, he handled only estates of people related to himself in some way. He contrasts sharply with Gall Feldmaier, whose position was not unlike his own. Both men were married three times. Both were active and powerful men in the village. The two of them were called upon to administer more foreclosures than anyone else. But Brodbeck did not tie his fortune to servicing the wealthy members of the village for very long, and he was greatly concerned with building his own patrimony. He maintained a strong center of activity in familial concerns completely outside the power structure. He was not called upon to be godparent for any magistrate families, and he chose a mason from another village as his Gevatter and a single woman from Nürtingen as Gevatterin. As temporary Schultheiss from 1816 to 1820, he caused considerable consternation among the closely allied dominant families of the village. The first thing they did when they were provided a platform in the newly constituted Bürgerauschuss was to attempt to tarnish his reputation with theft. He was the kind of person they wanted as a tool for their own interests, not as a ruler. He was too rooted by background and connection in handicraft production, building trades, and smallholding to maintain easy relations with the patriciate. If in the end, Gall Feldmaier had no familial network to fall back on, Brodbeck now shored up his political position by the solidarity of the class of smallholders. It was not until he was in his 70s (a few years before he died) that one of his daughters married a Hentzler – the grandson of the straight-laced patriarch and fellow consistory elder, Johann Wilhelm.

Johann Salomon Brodbeck was a transition figure between two village constitutions. He came to prominence in a system in which magistrates filled their ranks by cooptation, and he finished out his years in one in which accession to office came by election at large. He himself never had to stand for election, since his Richter position gave him tenure on the new Gemeinderat at the outset. He was an early example of a new man come to power, whose position was rooted more in factional politics determined by class than by family, although he himself had a firm base in familial alliances of handicraftsmen. The context of politics after the 1820s would shift once again with the rise of a mobile workforce centered in the building trades and a shift in the sexual division of labor associated with intensification and capitalization of agriculture. Brodbeck was not a reflection of that new world. He represented the burgeoning group of smallholders and artisans who had been squeezed out of power during the eighteenth century and excluded from a villagewide connubium through endogamous marriage politics and redrawn foci of ritual kinship. In a village rapidly growing in numbers, these two groups began to cultivate their own social ties and self-consciousness through a systematic cultivation of kin. In this situation, kinship once again acted as a breeding place for class.

COHORT V (1860–1869)

17

Kinship in the mid-nineteenth-century village: An introduction

By the 1830s the structural changes associated with the agricultural revolution were well in place. Stall feeding had clearly triumphed and the village had reorganized and intensified its pasture and meadowland.[1] The fallow field was largely planted to fodder crops, and the production of potatoes had risen considerably. Root and fodder crops involved long hours of careful hoeing, carried out for the most part by women. They continually harvested green fodder crops and grass throughout the summer and carried them in hay kerchiefs on their heads from the fields to the stalls in the village. The 1830s were years of intensive flax cultivation, preparation, and spinning – all tasks in which women were predominant. During the previous two decades a new emphasis had been placed on having sufficient firewood for washing day, another aspect in the revision and reorganization of women's work during the period. An ideal of cleanliness and housewifery had developed in the village precisely at the time when women were being drawn into agriculture in a massive way.

I have suggested in Volume I that the intensified production routines were part of the explanation for the wave of conflict between husbands and wives that characterized the first four decades of the century.[2] By the 1830s, the new division of labor had triumphed, and within a decade or so some accommodation between husbands and wives had taken place. By the early 1840s, separations and demands for divorce had declined considerably so that in 1848 the pastor could report that the morality of the village measured in terms of marital conflict was on the mend. In 1862 the next pastor observed that such open hostility between spouses was quite infrequent.

[1] David Warren Sabean, *Property, Production, and Family in Neckarhausen, 1700–1870* (Cambridge, 1990), chaps. 1 and 5.

[2] Sabean, *Property,* chap. 4.

A number of other changes in the social, economic, and legal context of family life redrew the lines of responsibility and power in the family. Already by the late eighteenth century, marriage portions of husbands and wives had become carefully balanced. It was no longer frequent to find women with either much more or much less property than their husbands. During the period of exceptional marital conflict (ca. 1800–1840), a key point in the wives' attack had had to do with safeguarding the substance of their property, although partly because the argument was so effective, women may have learned to frame their needs in its terms. By 1828 the law had made them administratively competent, which, despite all its ambivalence in meaning and effect, did, formally at least, ratify their independent voice in the direction of the family economy.[3] Part of what was at issue was the disappearance of institutions such as Kriegsvogtschaft, which in practice had meant the insertion of a male relative of the wife at every decision affecting her property rights. After 1828 a wife represented herself. Women also became important pledges, guaranteeing the performance of their husbands as village officials, horse traders, and skilled construction workers. Putting their own property at risk gave women a formal right to comment on and judge the character of their husbands' work routines, and they took many an occasion to do so before the pastor, the Schultheiss, and the village court.

Many men of the village were increasingly involved in movement around the larger region searching for jobs.[4] One of the important structural changes as far as occupation was concerned was the increase in all kinds of workers involved in road, railroad, canal, and building construction – masons, stone masons, carpenters, joiners, plasterers, and paviors, as well as unskilled laborers digging ditches, hauling rock, and spreading sand and gravel. If during the first several decades of the century, men circulated around the territory looking for work while periodically returning to the village, some began by the 1840s to leave more permanently. Many, of course, left their wives in the village to cultivate the gardens and plots of hemp and flax and the few strips of grain and turnips, while they took on piece work during the construction season elsewhere. But during the fifth, sixth, and seventh decades, the village balance of permanent residents tipped in favor of women until there were 100 adult women for every 85 men, which in demographic terms is a significant skewing of the sexes. Widowed women ever more frequently failed to marry again and kept family property in their hands well into old age.[5] After 1800, young women pregnant outside of wedlock increasingly testified either that they had no interest in marrying the father of their child or that they would not do so until they both could bring enough property together to found a household, and in sharp contrast to the eighteenth century, many young women began to have more than one illegitimate child.[6] An ever larger percentage of women by midcentury married above the

[3] Sabean, *Property,* pp. 212–3.
[4] Sabean, *Property,* pp. 49–50, 64–5, 319–20.
[5] Sabean, *Property,* chaps. 5 and 6.
[6] Neckarhausen, Skortationsbuch, vol. 1 (1822–69).

age of 30, but there was also a more significant number of women who never married at all. In what might be called the "feminization" of the village, women often became the central figures in agricultural decision making. They also showed considerable resourcefulness in developing part- or full-time activities in colporting everything from pins to yeast. Perhaps one of the reasons for the lessening of tension between spouses lay in the fact that absent men could not start a fight. But more likely, after a generation or two of de facto women's control of the purse strings in many instances and the solidification of their alliance with village authorities, a new customary division of responsibilities had become routinized. Volume I documented the rise of a pattern of self-exploitation, which commentators on women late in the century saw as characteristic of peasant producers. It took a generation or two for women to become accustomed to the unrelenting pace of work and to refashion a pietist worldview to give meaning to their lives.

In the new situation, one would expect to find many networks of information and patronage established by women. They would often have to find someone to do the plowing and harrowing and would themselves be available for arduous agricultural labor for other families. The trend from the 1830s on was toward heavier capitalization of agricultural production. Since more households had some equipment available, horizontal reciprocity was more possible.[7] There was no longer a monopoly of wagons, plows, and traction animals by the larger landholders. In this situation, resident women had equipment to trade in return for plowing services and the like. Widows made sure that all of the tools passed into their hands rather than to male heirs. They also controlled storage areas, stalls, and houses, so that many resources of all kinds were available for them to dispense. The younger generation of sons, daughters, and sons-in-law were dependent on them for the use of agricultural equipment for many years, which gave them considerable authority within several (semi-) dependent households. They had become active in the property market as well. We have also seen that although children all eventually *inherited* equally, the endowment of daughters was much greater than that for sons, which meant that women were anchored in the village and as a group, even during the early years of marriage, "controlled" more resources than their husbands.[8] As women grew older, they became experienced in wielding authority, managing farm and trading enterprises, pursuing the interests of themselves and their families, and negotiating effectively within their kindreds.

There are many indications that women were more assertive in the nineteenth century. Their use of the various terms for "house" and "family" and the emphasis in their everyday language on the contractual aspects of marriage and on

[7] Sabean, *Property*, chap. 12.
[8] Sabean, *Property*, chap. 9.

reciprocity are but two examples.[9] Male terms of abuse in marital conflict, such as "Hur," symbolized women as actively in competition with themselves. Once the century wore on, women came to swear and call on the devil or lightning, entering an area previously reserved to men, in this way developing a language of practice that implicitly challenged male hierarchy.

The structural patterns of kinship use also show that networks centered on women became more important by the mid nineteenth century. As noted in Volume I, in the 1860s about four out of five people who sold real estate made more than 50 percent of their sales to kin.[10] Although nuclear kin played an ever greater role, so too did cousins. This time, however, the cousin networks were more likely to be traced over mothers than fathers, in contrast to earlier in the century and in the eighteenth century. If one examines the apex of a cousin network – the MB in a MBS or a FMBSS – one finds that sisters and cross siblings dominated, to the practical exclusion of brothers. As far as the nuclear family was concerned, sales to daughters (sons-in-law) and sisters (brothers-in-law) outweighed those to sons and brothers almost 5 to 1. In every instance, women came to inhabit key structural roles in land sale networks. As will be shown for godparents, the cross-sibling connection prevailed. Men chose their sisters, and women, their brothers. Furthermore, in the naming of sons, the FB was replaced in importance by the MB or MZH, another indication of a shift in focus away from B/B relations to B/Z ones. Also, Z/Z connections are more often displayed than B/B – for example, use of the ZH by women for a godparent outweighed the BW 5 to 1.

At the beginning of the eighteenth century, marriage alliances involved asymmetrical linkages connecting those with power to those without it and those with wealth and property to those less well endowed. That structure gave way to an alliance system systematically linking patrilines, which tended to create horizontal linkages of people with similar amounts of wealth and power. Agnatically structured networks were utilized to coordinate access to resources and services and to refashion the relation of village strata to each other. An overarching patrilineal pattern of exchange is still discernible by the fourth decade of the nineteenth century, but with several generations of systematic linkages many marriages now reflect matrilineal exchange. However, a closer look at the two generations of participants in the marriage market – the parents and the marrying generation – shows interconnections that suggest "matrifocal" networks – overlapping sets of exchanges wherein a senior woman is a key relative to both neogami. The fact that women came to be more centrally placed ecologically in agricultural production appears to have supported an informal power structure that mediated between people looking for marriage partners.

[9] Sabean, *Property*, chaps. 3 and 4.
[10] Sabean, *Property*, chap. 16.

Table 17.1. *Population and wealth indices.*

Index	Bauer	Artisan	Worker
Population			
1710	100	58.3	—
1790	100	78.0	—
1870	100	144.9	40.8
Total wealth			
1710	100	53.5	—
1790	100	30.7	—
1870	100	58.7	9.3
Average wealth/individual			
1710	100	74.1	—
1790	100	39.4	—
1870	100	40.3	22.9

Occupation and social differentiation

After the 1820s, Neckarhausen experienced increasing social differentiation.[11] The average population for the decade 1860–9 was 25 percent higher than for the period 1820–9 (it rose from 738 to 924). As a result of increasing population and the changing economic conditions, there was a greater diversity of occupation – many more artisans with more different crafts were represented and the village had a substantial new group of factory workers who worked in the nearby town of Nürtingen. One way of looking at the changes in structure is to measure the two other major groups in the village against the independent agricultural producers. To this end, Table 17.1 treats the Bauer population, its total share of village wealth (i.e., taxes paid), and the average share of wealth of each individual as indices against which the share of other occupations is measured.

During the course of the nineteenth century, the factory workers and craft producers, many of whom were involved in the building trades, weaving, dyeing, and shoemaking, came to outnumber the independent agricultural producers by 2 to 1. By the 1860s, the number of families whose income was based primarily on factory labor composed a new and rather substantial group in the village. There are hints from time to time in the sources that men with artisan and agricultural occupations also worked at least occasionally in the new factories as stocking knitters or mechanics. A significant number of young, unmarried people also made the trip to Nürtingen each day, contributing their wages to the household or putting a portion aside for marriage. More important to the economy of

[11] Sabean, *Property*, pp. 40–3, 49–51, 61–5.

the village, however, at least through the seventh decade of the century, was the overall rise of handicraftsmen. Although their total share of wealth measured by property taxes rose considerably between 1790 and 1870, the average share for each individual measured against the average share of independent agricultural producers remained about the same, which was about half of what it had been at the beginning of the eighteenth century. The average artisan had two-fifths as much property as the average Bauer, a factor that contributed to the maintenance of village social and political hierarchies.

Occupational continuity between fathers and sons shows a surprising number of Bauern in this generation coming out of artisan families. To a large degree, this is the result of life cycle mechanisms and the new conditions of property holding. The average age of landholders continued to rise during the nineteenth century. In 1790, for example, men over 50 held 35.7 percent of all landed wealth in the village, but in 1870 the figure was 51.8 percent.[12] The average age of sellers of land reached a new high of 52.6, more than 10 years older than at the lowest point of 41.6 in the 1740s. And the age of buyers had risen to 41.8 from a low in the 1780s of 33.4. Access to land came at a much older age after midcentury than ever before. During the previous several decades, the children of many landholders became used to practicing artisanal trades, often into their late 40s or early 50s, before becoming independent agricultural producers. Two patterns of familial control of resources in the village played a role in the way handicrafts fit into the life cycle.[13] Families with considerable resources utilized their wealth and kinship networks to build up the patrimony for their children, many of whom exercised a trade for a decade or two before piecing together enough land to become independent. For many years, they might appear in one of the lowest quartiles of taxpayers; however, their strategic position in a well-coordinated kinship network gave them access to credit and land, the market for which was increasingly managed through familial connection. While on the one hand poor artisans reproduced themselves, on the other the craftsmen and laborers descended from the wealthy were frequently able to use their kinship "capital" to construct a considerable estate piece by piece. In all of this, women came to play a key role. Their activities in coordinating kin, managing land, and dispensing reputation were crucial for accumulating resources, reproducing hierarchies, and circulating goods.

[12] Sabean, *Property,* chaps. 15 and 16.
[13] Sabean, *Property,* pp. 316–20.

18

Networking with kin around the mid nineteenth century

Thus far, this book has been mapping a series of activities that linked different individuals and families together. Perhaps the term "territorialization" best emphasizes the fact that each set of transactions had its own terrain and lines of communication. At the beginning of the eighteenth century, for example, godparentage, marriage, and guardianship connected people together in quite different ways and followed paths that were constructed for different purposes, at different times, and in different areas. At the same time, the topography of communication was shaped by a few major routes that gave definition to the landscape and provided certain access points or places of departure for various kinds of commerce. At the beginning of the eighteenth century, marriage alliance and ritual kinship offered alternative means for linking networks, but by the mid nineteenth century, selection of godparents by and large followed trails already well marked out by marriage.

As a group, the institutions under consideration in this study were subject to increasing "familialization" and became more interconnected. And clearer definition was given to a group of kin extending out to cousins who could be called upon by individuals and families for a variety of tasks. As Chapter 19 shows, the tendency to marry close consanguineal kin continued to increase at least up through the 1860s, and cousins continued to play an important role as godparents. But there was also a narrowing down and focusing on brothers and sisters and their spouses for godparents, pledges, and guardians. What was new was the careful way both sides of an alliance were balanced and their reciprocities were choreographed through ritual kinship and naming.

Godparents

Many of the structural changes encountered for the early nineteenth century persisted into the decades after midcentury (Tables A.3–A.6). Godparents remained about the same age as parents, and even more of them were kin. Just as at the beginning of the century, Bauern found godparents largely among their own group (Tables A.15–A.16). In fact, wealthy villagers overwhelmingly chose godparents locally and from their own class. Artisans and factory workers were more likely to extend their networks to outside the village and were not so tied to wealthy villagers as they had earlier been. The tendency for classes and occupational groups to withdraw among themselves already evident for the second, third, and fourth decades of the nineteenth century only intensified. Godparentage had become and remained a way of sorting out lines of relationship inside the wider kinship universe, occupational groups, and classes.

In this cohort, the number of godparents traceable as kin to the parents rose to 82.1 percent (Tables A.3, A.17). The percentage of those godparents identified as kin who were from the immediate family (F, M, B, Z) was 44.9 percent, compared with 9.6 percent in the 1780s and 29.4 percent in the 1820s. If one adds the BW and ZH, the figures are: 1780s, 19.2 percent; 1820s, 43.2 percent; and 1860s, 53.6 percent. The trend from the late eighteenth century was toward an increasing contraction of the field from which godparents were chosen. Cross siblings were especially important, sisters for husbands and brothers for wives. When choosing close in-laws, husbands relied on the BW and wives, the ZH. However, in this cohort in-laws played a smaller role altogether – in favor of siblings: in the 1820s the choice of BW/ZH in relation to siblings was 1 to 2; in the 1860s, 1 to 5. In the 1780s, first cousins made up 17.8 percent of the kin-linked godparents; in the 1820s, 25.0 percent; and in the 1860s, 30.4 percent. All of these figures indicate that the circle of consanguineal kin was being drawn more tightly around the marital pair, with a more intensive and systematic use of cousins. As I shall continue to demonstrate, the period witnessed less the "rise of the nuclear family" than the solidification and systematization of kindreds and alliance. Taking together all of the parents, siblings, uncles and aunts, nephews, first cousins, and first cousins once removed, the comparable figures of the three cohorts are: 68.5 percent, 81.8 percent, 92.8 percent. Overall, the composition of the general field did not change from the beginning of the century, but there was a gradual shift to the center of that field. Second cousins also played a role, but as before only for husbands. The circle from which women chose was narrower and focused more directly on immediate kin.

The choice of godparents systematically emphasized brother/sister relations. Men chose considerably more women as Gevatter[inne]n but placed a special emphasis on their sisters. And they were just as likely to find godparents from their uterine as from their agnatic kin. Women followed the opposite strategy, preferring godfathers to godmothers and brothers to all other kinds of relatives, and when brothers were not available, they sought out their sisters' husbands. Cross-sex reciprocity in the selection of ritual kin reflects the construction of networks in which women had come to occupy key positions. But this is just one piece of evidence for a much larger field of activity in which women helped determine the state of play. I will also point out in Chapter 22 that throughout

Table 18.1. *Cohort V: Names for boys constructed from those of two relatives.*

F+	Number	GODF+	Number	FB+	Number	MB+	Number
GODF	2	FB	5	FB	1	FZH	1
FB	1	MB	1	—	2	—	1
MB	3	MZH	1				
—	2						

at least the property-holding classes in Germany and beyond, the brother/sister dyad came to be at the center of familial relations at the turn of the century. In this, Neckarhausen followed a general pattern. If, for Neckarhausen, that constellation was indeed rooted at least in part in the key role women came to play as social mediators, then these will also be the lines of a coordinate shift across much of the social spectrum.

Naming

By the 1860s, choosing names for children was closely connected with the choice of godparents and displayed the same kind of cross-sex reciprocity. Since more godfathers were chosen by mothers than fathers, then using them for naming boys most often emphasized uterine connections, and the greater interest in the mother's brother over the father's brother points in the same direction. In fact, there was little interest in the father's brother at all except where a name was created by joining those of the godfather and father's brother (Table 18.1). This practice of developing new names from combining elements from more than one namesake, which only in this generation became frequent for naming sons, underlined a particular alliance by bringing together both sides in a more intimate way. It is also to be found in several instances in which the father's and mother's brother or godfather's names were combined.

There was no longer a strong patrilineal bias in naming boys, except for the fact that fathers still accounted for many of the sons' names. Uncles (FB, MB) accounted for 24 (31.2 percent) instances, apart from the cases in which they were also GODF. Altogether, there were 34 couples with children in the sample. In 18 instances, the godfather was a sibling or sibling's spouse and 10 times provided a name: MB-13 (7), MZH-2 (1), FB-3 (2). There were 15 godmother/aunts, providing 8 names for daughters: FZ-9 (6), FBW-2, FM-2 (1), MZ-1 (1), MFBW-1.

There was a marked reciprocal structure here, with the MB acting as godfather and providing a name, and the FZ as godmother, also providing a name. All the evidence suggests that naming was used to mark the alliance and, more intimately, the relationship between a brother and sister, with the wife's kin providing a significant percentage of boys' names. Any sibling set would share names from two patrilines, those of the F and FB and those of the MB.

For this period, daughters were named after godmothers even more than after mothers, thereby giving emphasis to agnatic relations. And the father's sister was more prominent than the mother's sister. Composing names for girls from two adult names reached a new height – in all 24 cases (Table 18.2). Since many of the godmothers were chosen from the husband's sisters and husband's brothers' wives, naming for godmothers, especially when combined with other names, emphasized affinal ties. Just as with boys, any sibling set combined names from both sides of the alliance, but the practice of combining names allowed for greater symbolic mediation of the allied lines than naming children alternately from the two sides.

Naming children was an act that marked relations between adults. In general, the emotional content of a name did not allow parents to go very far afield, so that at the beginning of the eighteenth century, when godparents were mostly chosen from people who were not related to the parents by blood ties, they were not a ready source for forenames for sons. Even when close kin ties were represented by names, they were distributed differently over time.

At the beginning of the eighteenth century, naming practices set off a core group of brothers who continually reemphasized relations with one another. Even daughters were more likely to receive names from their father's side of the family than from their mother's. In that period, however, in contrast to sons, they often were called after their godmothers, who usually represented wider political alliances of the family, frequently those of their fathers.

From the mid eighteenth century through to the third or fourth decade of the nineteenth, a central core of agnatically defined relatives who exchanged names becomes solidified. At the beginning, sororal networks were embedded within patrilateral ones, but most women soon abandoned sisters for a wider range of patrikin. Over the whole period of this second stage in naming practices, the exchange of names involved creating various foci of agnatically defined kin who shared names in common.

The third stage emerged by the fifth and sixth decades of the nineteenth century. By then there was an end to a patrilateral bias in naming. A group of brothers and sisters were equally called after patrilateral and matrilateral kin: fathers and uncles, mothers and aunts. This practice was embedded in a recognition of exchange relations between agnatically defined groups, but it also suggests that wives played a greater role in naming their sons and that they more systematically utilized the relationships with their siblings. In a reciprocal manner, husbands cultivated their sisters and saw to it that their daughters were frequently named after their own close kin. In a parallel way, both spouses relied heavily on their first cousins, who in turn acted as sources for names. The act of bestowing a name became in this way a central symbol for alliance construction and maintenance. This new structure recognized a balanced reciprocity in the power of both men and women to mark out spheres of influence. It also under-

Table 18.2. *Cohort V: Names for girls constructed from those of two relatives.*

M+	Number	GODM+	Number	FZ+	Number	MZ+	Number	MM+	Number
MM	2	MZ	3	MZ	1	MZ	1	—	1
GODM	4	FZ	1	—	1	MBW	1		
FZ	2	—	2			—	1		
MZ	1								
—	3								

lined the brother/sister relationship as the emotional core of inner familial and wider kindred experience.

Guardians

For the 1860s, 15 from the sample of 20 Pfleger were relatives, but the field had narrowed to the closest consanguineal kin and uncles. The father himself acted as guardian three times. Other guardians were: FB, three times; MB, three times; MZH, two times; FZH, two times; and F1WB, once. There was one cousin: MMBS. Just as before, there are examples in which a relative of the deceased parent became Pfleger. But for this period the novel practice of choosing a relative of the survivor emerged. Quite surprisingly as well, fathers now frequently acted as guardians of their own children. I am not exactly sure how to explain these changes, but the evidence suggests that the institution had altered somewhat by midcentury. A guardian seems to have become less a protector of lineal property than an aid to the surviving parent. There was no longer any necessity to balance both sides of the alliance in a context in which the alliances had become so much tighter, given the practice of choosing godparents from a narrow field and symbolizing the close reciprocity through a balanced exchange of names. At the same time, village and state institutions developed the capacity to protect property that devolved upon children through a professionalization of the new class of notaries and by the separation of judicial and administrative institutions. Oversight was easier, and guardians became less administrators of their wards' property than spokesmen for them before the courts. One father expressed disappointment that the guardian of his son was not an aggressive enough representative before the authorities.

As found earlier, guardians who were relatives of their wards were seldom their godparents too – in this sample, only once. Since Pfleger were chosen from the same generation and the same kinship field as godparents, the lack of overlap underlines once again that godparent-kin were not usually considered appropriate for the position. It was quite the reverse in the five cases in which the Pfleger were not related to the parents. One was godfather for all of his Pflegekinder. Another was godfather for all those in the marriage born after 1836. Salomon Waldner was Pfleger for Johannes Klein's children, and although he was not the godfather, his brother Johann Georg was Gevatter for both him and Klein. Here there seems to be a curious paradox. Where kinship was the basis for selection of godparents, the same principles but not the same people were used to select guardians. By contrast, wherever godparents were not chosen from the kinship group, the role developed a residual function for crisis situations. Where godparents were used to make new social connections, they could be used again in new situations, a phenomenon that points toward a reconfiguration of the institution around midcentury. But perhaps it was less that godparentage changed its function than that guardianship did. A nonrelative godparent was not a patron but a friend of the household, someone who could easily take over the task of advising godchildren/wards and speak up for them when they sought jobs in Stuttgart, married into a Black Forest village, or sought to emigrate to America.

Pledging

Almost all pledges were immediate relatives: father, brother, and brother-in-law (Table A.106). In a sense they were all in-laws since in most cases a husband and wife usually borrowed money or placed their property at risk together. Any husband underwritten by his brother by implication obtained a guarantee for his wife. By the mid nineteenth century, sibling and in-law relations were criss-crossed with debt and performance guarantees.

As was the case earlier in the century, godparentage and pledging could be closely linked institutions. In all of the examples I have been able to find (four cases), the Gevatter/Bürg relationship was reciprocal. Rather than the godfather acting as patron and continuing in that relationship by guaranteeing the solvency of his client, it was the other way around. Spiritual guarantee was returned by material guarantee. Such reciprocity – which shows that godparentage could be brought into contact with other social functions – underlines the absence of overlap with guardianship. Although the same field of choice existed for guardians, godparents, pledges, and names, and the lines continually criss-crossed, some functions overlapped and reinforced each other, some were reciprocal and worked exchange on different planes, and some were largely incompatible. Within a similar field of selection, various choices set up a system of territorialization in which alliances were struck, supported, and reproduced.

* * *

This study has mapped various networks connecting kin, other kin, and nonkin through property transactions, godparentage, naming, guardianship, Kriegsvogtschaft, and pledging. The results indicate that certain principles of selection moved in parallel ways and that one kind of relationship could frequently throw light on another. It is time now to review each of the structures that has emerged in the preceding chapters and show how their different elements interlocked to form a pattern at each stage in the development of the kinship system.

Ritual kinship was used in the eighteenth century to ally families across generations. At the beginning of the century it linked patrilines that were not already tied by marriage exchange. In general, villagers avoided close kin in favor of extended in-laws or nonkin altogether and chose older, wealthier, and more powerful villagers as patron-godparents.

The asymmetricality established by unequal marriages created short chains of affinal relatives who provided patrons and clients for one another. Brothers and brothers-in-law operated as coordinate groups linked to the wider village polity through godparentage and marriage. This political organization was symbolized through the restriction of male names to the closest consanguineal kin and the opening of female names to nonrelated godmothers. In this period, godparents could be very important in diffuse ways involving influence and moral relations. A large proportion of property transactions, for example, between "strangers," involved people connected through common godparents. On the other hand, godparents were not expected to act as substitute parents in crisis situations. And they did not at that early period become concerned with the internal dynamics of family property relations through Kriegsvogtschaft.

By the mid eighteenth century, the more powerful villagers began to cast horizontal links out to one another, and magistrates began to look among themselves for ritual kin, while continuing to exercise patronage toward the poorer and less powerful members of the village. But the patronage system began to become "familialized" as people radically changed their practices of selecting marriage partners and godparents. Over half of the godparents were now consanguineal kin, but there was still a crucial role to play in mediating between clients. Godparents continued, for example, to bring unrelated parties together in property transactions. Close to 4/5 of all real estate sales between "strangers" involved common godparents. As godparentage became familialized, the doubled figure of the godparent/Kriegsvogt, who just might also have been the FB, appeared. With the shift to overlapping alliances – marriage and ritual kinship, still marked by asymmetricality in terms of power, age, and wealth – godfathers came to be an important source for names. In many ways, godparentage and marriage were alternative means for building alliances. Where there was already kinship as a basis for systematic connection between families, a godparent was never used as a substitute parent. But where godparentage itself was the basis for an alliance (which might later lead to a marriage alliance), it could well become part of crisis management and carry considerable material weight.

By the late eighteenth century, godparentage was systematically extended to second cousins. Gevatter were still older, and magistrates figured prominently, although the pastor, school teacher, and Schultheiss no longer played much of a role. By this time, godparentage was closely tied up with marriage alliances, but not so tightly that it could not continue to bring together unrelated families in property transactions. In many ways, godparentage and marriage still remained alternative ways of constructing alliance. Artisans continued to stress richer, more powerful kin in a much larger, agnatically structured universe. Their ritual kin were not part of a marriage exchange system linking patrilines over time. By contrast, Bauern families did create a balanced, reciprocal system involving cousin marriages and a selection of cousins and close affinal kin as godparents. An agnatic naming pattern highlighted a patrigroup that in turn exchanged marriage partners and godparents. In this structure, guardians were never chosen from among godparents who were at the same time kin. But as before, if ritual kinship was used as an opening for exchange, then guardianship became possible. Women relied heavily on close agnatic kin for their godparents and Kriegsvögte.

In the early nineteenth century, much of the patronage aspect of godparentage had disappeared. Indeed, if anything, the godparent was the recipient of material advantage as the preceding analysis of pledging shows. Everything points toward symmetry and equality. Husbands and wives brought equal marriage portions. They each overwhelmingly chose immediate kin or first cousins as godparents, although men continued to use agnatic second cousins as well. There was no difference in age any more between parents and godparents, and social groups tended to choose ritual kin from their own ranks. Because many spouses selected their godparents on the basis of cross-sibling ties, an overlapping set of tight affinal relationships was created. Bauern preferred siblings, and artisans preferred first cousins, and as before Bauern reduplicated marriage exchange with godparentage while artisans tended to rely more on the latter institution as the foundation of alliance. In this period, both boys and girls were more frequently named for agnatic kin, although exchange relations stressing the MB were beginning to be apparent. Women continued to use agnatic kin as godparents and Kriegsvögte. By this time guardians and godparents were chosen from exactly the same field of kin but never involved the same people.

By the mid nineteenth century, godparent links were even more internal to class. Artisans still sought ritual kin over a wider geographical range and from a wider kinship universe than Bauern. Overall, however, godparents were chosen from an ever narrower field. And they involved systematic reciprocity – the wife chose her brother and the husband his sister. This was reflected in the final destruction of the agnatic structure to naming. Boys were named after the MB/GODF and girls after the FZ/GODM. Balanced reciprocity stressing alliance and networks constructed on uterine as well as agnatic principles marked the practice. Even in this structure, people did not use the same kin as godparents and guardians. Even more than earlier in the century, pledging and godparentage were reciprocal and the latter institution had clearly become a channel of exchange whereby spiritual and material flows moved in opposite directions.

Another way of looking at the shifts in the territorialization of kinship is to focus on cousins. Quite remarkably at the first part of the eighteenth century, they appear to have played an ambiguous role for one another. Although agnatically related cousins entered into a peculiar form of marriage alliance – not with each other but with a third sibling set, demonstrating a readiness to coordinate their activities – they did not choose each other as godparents, guardians, or Kriegsvögte. Moreover, they entered into very few property transactions with one another. From the political evidence described in Chapter 2, it seems that cousins could be counted on for diffuse support inside loosely structured kindred.

By the mid eighteenth century, all this had changed. There had been, for example, an extraordinary growth in the market for land. Sales to kin in fact became more rather than less prominent, and first and second cousins came to take a large chunk (30 percent) of the market as a whole. There was a considerable agnatic bias in the structuring of cousin networks – on the order of 2 to 1. During this period, cousins became – if they had not already been – central in agricultural production for one another. As observed in Volume I, men relied on cousins for plowing, harrowing, and carting services. Parallel to this reliance on cousins came a radical restructuring of godparentage – focused first on nuclear kin but also encompassing first cousins. Whereas there had been no consanguineal kin as godparents at the beginning of the eighteenth century, by midcentury more than 50 percent were related by blood. These cousin networks were overwhelmingly agnatically structured for women as well as men. As a result of the importance of cousins as godparents, they became a source for naming children. During this period, first cousins can be found as guardians and Kriegsvögte, both selected on agnatic principles. Altogether, the rise of first cousins marked the middle decades of the century.

By the late eighteenth century, there was a systematic extension of relations to second cousins with a growing agnatic stress. Cousins made up a whopping 50 percent of kin-related property sales in a greatly expanded market – now reckoned agnatically at 3 to 1 compared with 2 to 1 at midcentury. During this period, second cousins went from less than 10 percent of kin-linked godparents to more than 20 percent (all cousins from 30 to 55 percent). Even for women, a large majority (over 70 percent) of these cousins were reckoned agnatically. During this period, Bauern overlay marriage alliances with godparentage and vice versa, while artisans tended to build alliances on agnatically structured godparentage alone. Both groups maintained an agnatic bias in naming both sons and daughters. During this period, cousins, especially first cousins, figured more prominently as guardians. Women chose their own first cousins or the second cousins of their husbands as Kriegsvögte. This maximum extension of interest to second cousins coincided with a systematic construction of alliances between patrilines. However, the use of cousins varied by class, with artisans going further afield, more likely to stress protective relations and build on regional networks.

Early in the nineteenth century, the cousin networks were maintained, but developed in different directions depending on the circumstances. Cousins remained prominent in the property market but became very much overshadowed by nuclear kin. Although the networks of cousins selling land to each other remained more agnatically biased, they were far less so than in the late eighteenth century. Godparents also were more concentrated on close kin, but first cousins increased their share from 18 to 25 percent. Men were far more apt to seek out second cousins than women were, but both first and second cousins fit neatly into an alliance model, as already noted. With godparents providing many names for children of both sexes, cousins became sources for names, but children were not usually named after them if they did not also happen to become ritual kin. As before, artisans used extended cousin networks to find godparents, building alliances on that institution rather than on marriage. In that period, guardians were just as often found among second cousins as first. Almost half of the kin-related Kriegsvögte were cousins, but this time women stressed uterine networks just as much as agnatic ones. Also during this period, although pledging was centered primarily on nuclear kin, there were also many uncles, nephews, and first cousins who guaranteed their relatives' credit, but there appears to have been no possibility of going beyond first cousins within the kinship network for underwriting risks. In general, during this period, while cousinhood remained central to alliance, there is also evidence of uterine principles playing more of a role and women constructing networks through other women.

By the mid nineteenth century, cousins were still playing about the same role in the real estate market, but this time tracing took place on a uterine basis in a majority of the cases. Even more godparents were chosen from among first cousins (30 percent of kin-related ritual kin), and second cousins continued to be important for husbands. It seems that women were apt to use matrilateral parallel cousins and men to choose second cousins through the patriline. As for names, they clearly no longer were chosen on an agnatic basis but emphasized matrilateral kin as much as patrilateral. Altogether there seems to have been a greater focusing on the kin directly around a particular couple, with those connected to the wife being just as important as those connected to the husband. In our sample, only one cousin acted as guardian, significantly, perhaps, a uterine cousin. There was only one cousin in the sample who underwrote a transaction – a FBS. If cousins retained a great deal of their function and continued to make claims on each other, there does seem to have been a shift away from connections having material advantage such as caring for wards or guaranteeing performance to those involving social and political support and influence, such as godparenting, providing access to property through the market, providing plow and work teams, and coordinating votes.

19

Matrifocal alliance

During the fifth, sixth, and seventh decades of the nineteenth century, many families had been in alliance for well over a century. Despite the convergence in marital strategy between Bauern and artisans, families continued to differ according to the amount of property they had accumulated. Even within the same stratum, however, certain families seemed to be obsessed with forming consanguineal unions. Almost all sibling groups in the sample contracted at least one kin-linked marriage, but some of them made a remarkable number of them – two contracting seven each (Tables A.72, A.73)! During this period, the practice of marrying kin substantially increased in frequency, to reach the highest rate of any period discussed so far (25 percent, 39 percent, 29 percent, 26 percent, and 49 percent, respectively). Consanguineal marriages were not practiced before the 1740s, but then they increased in both absolute and relative terms through and beyond the middle decades of the nineteenth century.[1]

The statistical evidence from the cohort (Tables A.74, A.75) demonstrates that both Bauern and artisans made more kin marriages than ever before. By contrast, most in the new group of factory workers made no such alliances at all. Since this study does not go beyond 1870, nothing is known of their fortunes, but it could be that like the artisans of the eighteenth century, they delayed a generation before conforming to the dominant practice. The best correlation is with wealth: the poorest, including the new group of factory workers, were relatively disinclined to marry kin – although one marriage in five among them still involved endogamous alliances.

The wealthiest families sought out kin for their new alliances, with magistrate families in the lead, followed by Bauern and then by the better-established craft

[1] In Chapter 21, I show that consanguinity reached a high point everywhere in Europe between 1880 and 1920.

producers. The artisanal families of middling rank, especially those associated with the mobile occupations connected with building and construction, either struck out in new directions or developed regionally based alliances not usually recoverable by the methods used in this study. By contrast, the poor families in the village who were dependent on community jobs, such as cleaning the fountains, sweeping the streets, trapping mice, and burying the dead, looked inward for their marriage partners. The new class of factory workers tended to come from the small artisan families, those whose fathers were most subject to the vicissitudes of the economy and who traveled around the region looking for occasional work. They, along with other children who received few resources from their families, did not look so frequently inside the kin network – at least inside the village – for spouses.

Alliance formation and women

I have argued that the development of agnatic cohesion and an alliance system that linked patrilines with each other over many generations developed within an ecology of male work routines and political practices. Certain aspects of men's labor remained the same during the nineteenth century – plowing, ditch-digging, lumbering, for example – but more and more village men spent considerable time jobbing in skilled and unskilled positions outside the village. And the conditions for male political activity changed markedly as well. After the state negotiated 10-year contracts for tithes with the village beginning in the 1820s, one major focus for collusive activity came to an end. With the appointment of a resident accountant in the 1820s, there was less opportunity for corrupt bookkeeping and rigged mortgage registration – all of which had been crucial for a village political culture closely tied to the reproductive problems of a peasant landholding class in crisis. The context of village politics changed in many ways, which are not necessary to rehearse here, but one effect of shifting from a system of cooptation was to reconfigure the composition of the magistrates. Even for the 1830s and 1840s, it no longer would be useful to speak of a "Vetterlesgericht," not because the "Gericht" had become the "Gemeinderat," but because the institution no longer consisted of a set of relatives coopted from among themselves. The politics of kinship shifted from the public to the private sphere. The work of knitting together voting blocks as well as alliances to coordinate the real estate market, work gangs, plow teams, and prayer groups in a less easy to manage political system could no longer be directed from above by a few key magistrates. More coordination among families was necessary, and this was made possible by a considerable increase in the number of endogamous marriages.

The analysis of the alliance system will show that a framework of exchange between patrilines remained in place. But it also becomes possible to find other paths between neogami that work on matrilateral or uterine principles. And within the overarching frame of a particular marriage, an older woman is frequently to be found in a key position – someone who in all likelihood negotiated the union and who did the work of coordinating exchanges and managing the relations between various branches of the family. At least, I will offer this conclusion tentatively here and put it on the agenda for those who have better court records for the period.[2]

That systematic exchange between matrilines did not occur in the eighteenth century has already been established. As the alliance system first took form, exchange relationships developed in a context of agnatic connections, which were in turn rooted in male productive routines and political practices. Whatever role particular women played as go-betweens for setting up marriages, they worked to solidify the network of patrilateral alliances. They also frequently acted as godparents in ways that worked to maintain established patrilateral connections and male political blocs. The ecological foundation for agnatically based alliances, as has also been established, was modified by the steadily increasing inclusion of women in agricultural production, their developing interest in issues of marketing and other traditional male activities, their vocal opposition to male social and political activity centered in the tavern, and their tendency to continue unmarried, to seek divorce, or to remain widowed. During the nineteenth century, many women accumulated significant amounts of property and bought and sold land. By midcentury, the adult population balance had shifted from a female to male ratio of 1:1 to 1:0.85. With all of these changes, one would expect networks constructed by and through women to become increasingly important, and examples have already been cited in which this appears to have been the case.

Pierre Bourdieu has adumbrated the issue in Kabyle society and proposed two explanations for any particular marriage alliance there.[3] On one hand, the official, public, male explanation stresses agnatically based alliances, fitting in some way into an ideology of marriage with the patrilateral parallel cousin. On the other hand, in actuality marriage negotiations in Kabyle are conducted primarily by women, and they set up alliances that satisfy their own purposes. The ethnographer is able to trace another route between marriage partners that is in fact based on uterine principles. In the Neckarhausen situation, no information is present to indicate "official" or "public" ideology of alliance. In that respect, one cannot yet know whether there were conflicting male and female strategies of alliance formation, although if parental influence was involved in marriage choice, the divergent interests evident for many marriages in the village must have worked themselves out in different gender strategies.

During the 1950s a number of anthropologists studied societies in which women assumed considerable independence in the household and maintained

[2] During the 1820s and 1830s, many private law and criminal cases that used to come to the village court were dealt with in Nürtingen. All of the Kreisgericht (county court) records from the town have been destroyed.

[3] Pierre Bourdieu, *Outline of a Theory of Practice*, trans. Richard Nice (Cambridge, 1977), pp. 33–61.

independent property rights. Kinship analysis in many of their studies made use of the notion of "matrifocality."[4] Although conditions in mid nineteenth century rural Württemberg differ in many respects to the Caribbean areas for which the notion was first developed, the factors of a mobile male workforce and continuity in the household provided by women suggest certain parallels. "Matrifocality" points to the centrality of older women as stable factors in maintaining households, carrying on agricultural production, marketing produce in the local cities, organizing expenditures for food and clothing, and developing and managing contacts with other households. I do not want to argue that in Neckarhausen most households were matrifocal in the sense that headship was invested in women. But I want to use the term to suggest that they came to be central figures in the coordination of marriage politics and in providing continuity in household management. From the fact that many men were gone for part of the year, that children continued to remit a portion of their earnings even when working in Switzerland or France, and that women often managed household accounts, it seems likely that many households were for long periods organized and managed by women. In the many instances of widows holding on to land, buildings, and tools, it is also clear that a space for independent economic and social activity was made available to them.

Marriage alliances

In this cohort as well as in the previous one, second-cousin marriages are the most frequently encountered structurally, the modal type. But there were also many first-cousin marriages. Overall, there was a rising frequency of consanguineal marriages from first cousins to first cousins once removed to second cousins, dropping off with second cousins once removed. Beyond that were many marriages of more extended consanguinity, some of which are examined in the following discussion.

Since the various forms have already been treated in great detail in previous chapters and there are no surprises here, a detailed step-by-step analysis of each case seems unnecessary. The two lists of kin-linked marriages in Tables A.78 and A.79 contain many instances of renewed single-generation alliance, such as WZ and ZHZ. Affinal connections of this nature suggest, as pointed out before, that women played key roles in creating and maintaining networks. Men were far more apt to find wives through connections established by their sisters than through those maintained by their brothers.

In the case of first- and second-cousin marriages, the majority of them express classic situations of alliance between patrilines, on the one hand, and relations that grow out of the B/Z bond, just as the single-generation alliance of the ZHZ

[4] See Raymond T. Smith, *The Negro Family in British Guiana: Family Structure and Social Status in the Villages* (London, 1956).

type, on the other. There was no particular, favored kind of cousin marriage; instead, there was a practice of linking patrilines together through multiple marriages, usually with wives at any one time going in one direction. In the following generation, the flow might continue in the same direction or be reversed. In such a structure, a couple was not part of a constantly recurring pattern of replicating the marriage of their parents or their grandparents. If patrilines were systematically linked together, however, certain forms were most likely to recur: FZD, MBD, FMBD, FMBSD, FFZSD. All of these forms express an alliance formed in one generation and reformed in the adjacent or alternate one. Nevertheless, people were not looking for a certain kind of cousin but were making affines out of consanguineal relatives, who connected families together on agnatic principles and who were the offspring from earlier affinal alliances. Some of the actual paths between two spouses seem tortuous, indeed, and only make sense in the context of all of the alliances between their respective families. Taking all of the cases through second cousins, about three-quarters of them (12 of 17) express, formally at least, alliances between patrilines.

Another way of looking at the issue is to consider the manner in which marriage alliances were constructed in practice. Of course, there is little evidence of a direct nature to go on, since there is no testimony in court records about how particular individuals came to marry or how the marriage market was brokered. If one assumes that marriages within established kinship structures were continually discussed and commented upon and were subject to more or less complicated negotiations, then one might try to locate the key players in the round of gossip and the central brokers within family alliances. Taking the set of second-cousin marriages from the sample, one finds female first cousins at a key structural position in four instances and sisters at the apex of another. This suggests that the practical work of alliance building was frequently carried on by women. In none of these five cases did the marriages connect two patrilines. In fact, three of them (MFZDD, MFZDSW, MMZDD) could be construed as matrilineal alliances. It is unlikely that there were different forms of lineal exchange in competition with one another; rather, the ecological base for cooperation had shifted from the mid eighteenth to the mid nineteenth century. If patrilines had developed within certain productive and political exigencies, the nature of social arrangements shifted, and many networks of informal power came to be constructed by women.

Third-cousin marriages

The sample in this period had a substantial number of third-cousin marriages (seven), which, formally at least, involve four generations in alliance. They provide an opportunity to explore the alliance system as it had developed through the fifth, sixth, and seventh decades of the nineteenth century. Two of the marriages have been selected for closer examination of the overall phenomenon.

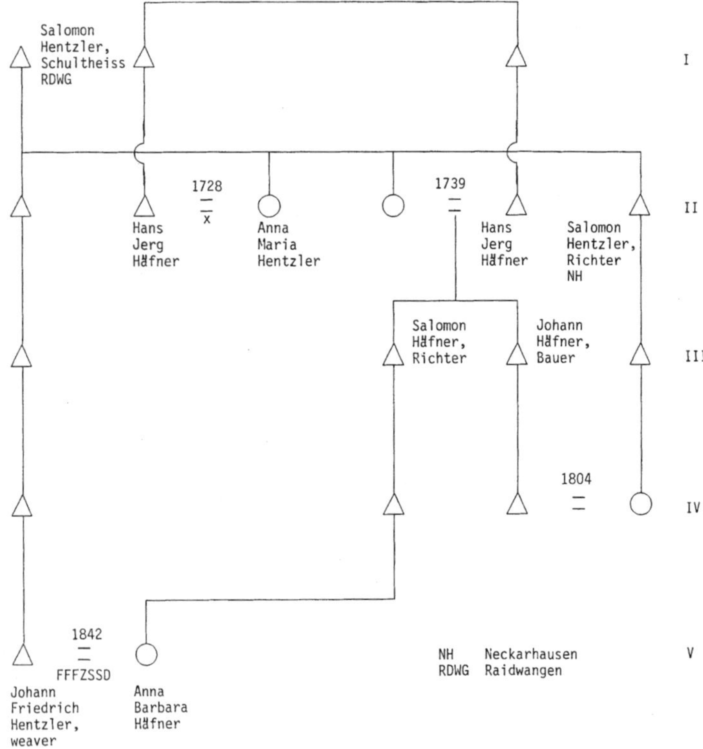

Figure 19.1

Third-cousin marriage (A)

The first case provides insight into the complexity of alliances as they had developed by the mid nineteenth century. At the outset, each case is analyzed in terms of the patrilineal alliances that became so crucial for the eighteenth and early nineteenth centuries. Then each genealogy is examined in as many ways as possible to determine how other paths connect the neogami. To avoid too much complexity, no effort is made to examine other ways that connect people, such as godparentage or guardianship, except to note from time to time this or that link helps explain the findings.

The first patrilineal alliance, case A, arises in the marriage of Johann Friedrich Hentzler, weaver, in 1842 to Anna Barbara Häfner (V) (Figure 19.1). Hentzler was a direct male descendant from Salomon Hentzler, Schultheiss in Raidwangen, married in 1708 (I). Two of Salomon Hentzler's daughters married Häfners, patrilateral parallel first cousins of each other (II). Hans Jerg Häfner and Anna Maria Hentzler had no children. A lineal male descendant of the other Hans Jerg Häfner two generations later (1804) married a lineal descendant of Salomon Hentz-

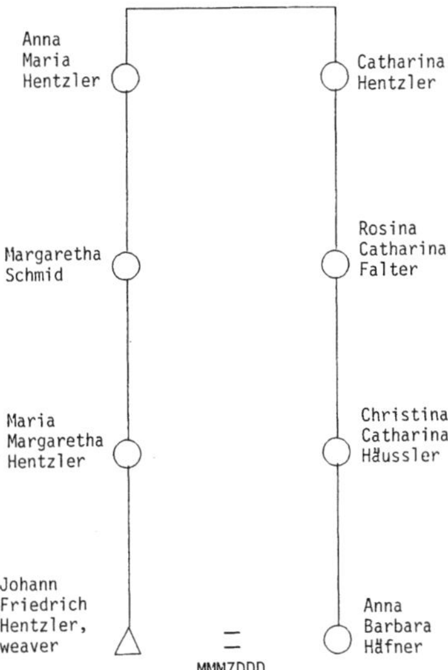

Figure 19.2

ler, making a typical second-cousin marriage, FMBSD (IV). This is a classic example of the Neckarhausen alliance system: around 1740 the construction of an alliance between siblings and first cousins; in the alternate generation a renewed alliance between the issue of one of the couples and the line; in the nineteenth century, a renewal of the alliance in the adjacent generation.

Thus far in the analysis, I have considered this case from the viewpoint of two patrilines. It is also an instance of matrilineal endogamy (Figure 19.2). It might be possible to show interconnections built on matrilineal exchange in generations II and III, but carrying out the genealogical investigation for each instance proves too tedious.

Now consider this marriage from another point of view (Figure 19.3), that is, by looking at the multiple connections of both the Hentzler family and the Häfner family to the Grauers. Before Johann Friedrich Hentzler and Mathias Grauer (III) married sisters in 1842, Grauer's sister had married Hentzler's uncle, and his aunt had married Hentzler's aunt's divorced husband (II). Another aunt of Grauer (Anna Maria (I)) had seen her daughter married to the Häfner sisters' matrilateral parallel first cousin. All of these relationships reflect a network of women: mother/daughter, aunt/nephew, cousins. The importance of the mediating Grauer family for Johann Friedrich Hentzler is demonstrated by the added link of Mathias Grauer (III) as Gevatter. All the evidence together can be used to model this alliance on the classic Neckarhausen principles of interlocking patrilines. At the same time, however, the marriage was matrilineally endogamous. If uterine relationships played any role in negotiating the union, then there must

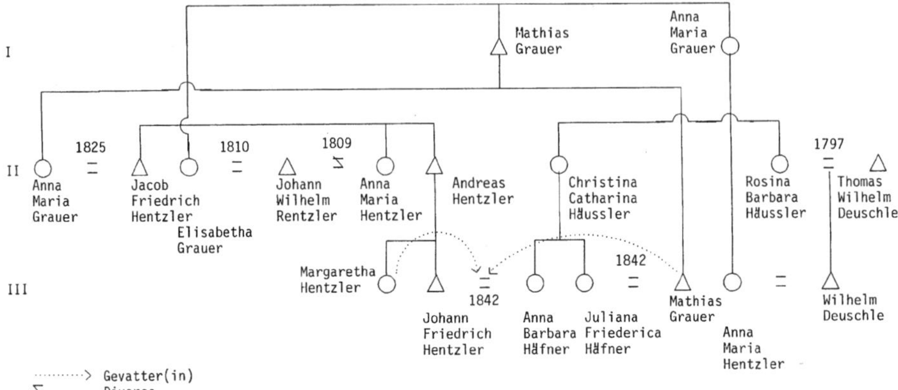

Figure 19.3

have been close relations between Maria Margaretha Hentzler (III) and Christina Catharina Häussler (III) (Figure 19.2), matrilateral parallel second cousins, but the various court protocols have left no traces about these two women for us to analyze. In any event, the final exercise revealed a network of women surrounding the marriage of Johann Friedrich Hentzler and Anna Barbara Häfner, a network that also "mediated" the closely connected couple of Anna Barbara's sister and Mathias Grauer. My hypothesis is that Anna Maria and Elisabetha Grauer and Christina Catharina and Rosina Barbara Häussler played key roles in maintaining the set of alliances.

Third-cousin marriage (B)

The next example, MFFBSDD (1843), is a clear case of adjacent generation exchange involving two patrilines (V) (Figure 19.4). In this example, the son of Johannes Kühfuss, who immigrated from Bempflingen in 1769, married the daughter of Michael Hentzler in 1798 (IV). Their son married the daughter of a second cousin of the mother (V). Two branches of the Salomon Hentzler patriline provided wives for the Kühfussen, father and son. In the following generation (VI), another Kühfuss married a Hentzler woman reckoned either to the Salomon Hentzler patriline or that of his brother Samson. A few observations on this genealogy are helpful here. First of all, the marriage in 1843 between Kühfuss and Hentzler brought together two families that had been closely allied to a third, Lieb, from Reicheneck. I have had to fill in part of the genealogy, since it involves individuals born outside of Neckarhausen. That family was well-placed, holding a large farm in tenancy (Hofbauer) (Figure 19.5). Hofbauern or Hofmeyern composed a small but wealthy class of farmers who held the occasional large tenancies scattered throughout the territory. They were often quite mobile, moving from tenancy to tenancy, very unlike the rest of the rooted peas-

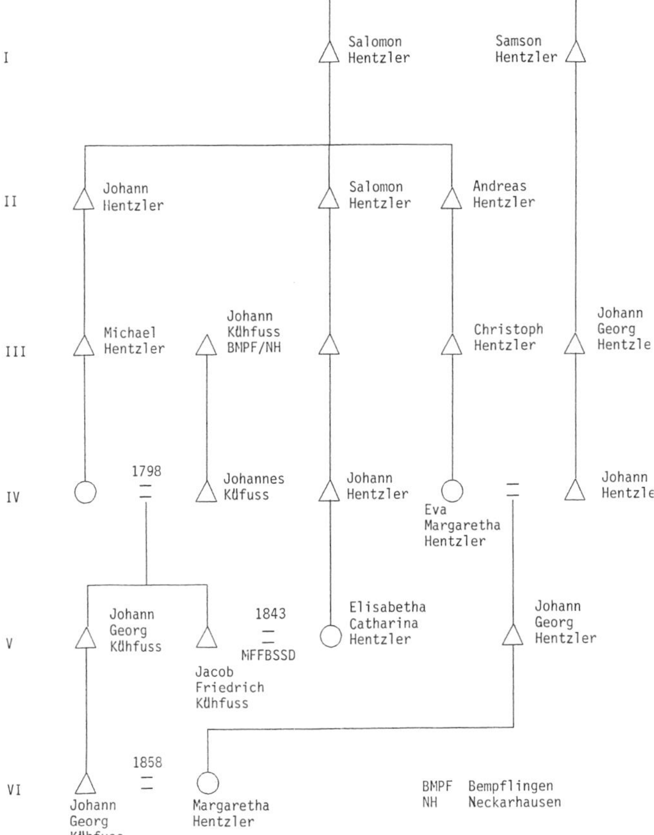

Figure 19.4

antry. In this case, Martin Lieb was Hofbauer in Raidwangen, but he left the village before he died. His daughter married into a Neckarhausen family. A generation later another Lieb from a Hofbauer family, this time from Reicheneck, married into the village, probably a niece of Juliana. About the same time, Anna Maria Wacker, also from Reicheneck, whose father was a Hofmeyer, married into the village and had as her Gevatter the schoolmaster from Reicheneck, probably Christina Barbara Lieb's brother. These individuals offer the only examples of the occurrence of the name "Lieb" in the entire history of the parish registers. It therefore seems no coincidence that their descendants married. In this instance, the marriage in 1843 would have been based on social relations between second cousins in generation III, kept together by immigrating women.

The spouses were linked in many other ways. A year after they married, two of their cousins married (Figure 19.6). In this case, Maria Friederica Waldner

Cohort V (1860–1869)

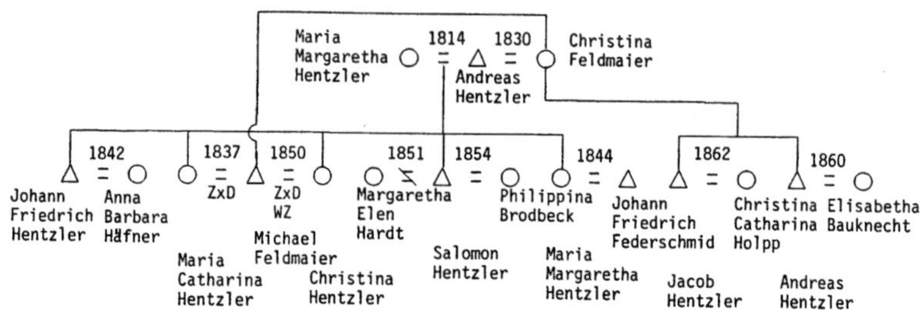

Figure 19.5

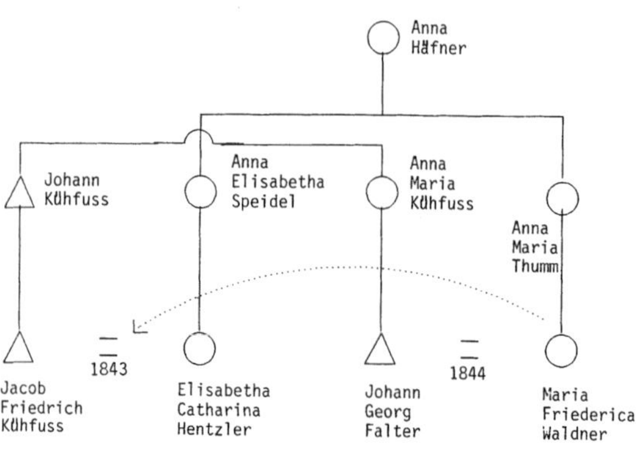

Figure 19.6

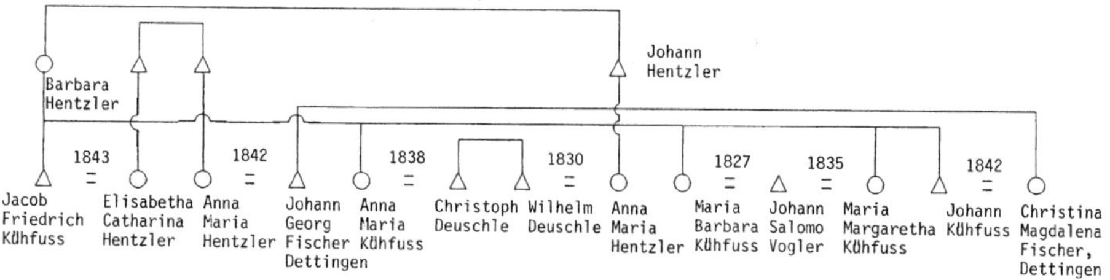

Figure 19.7

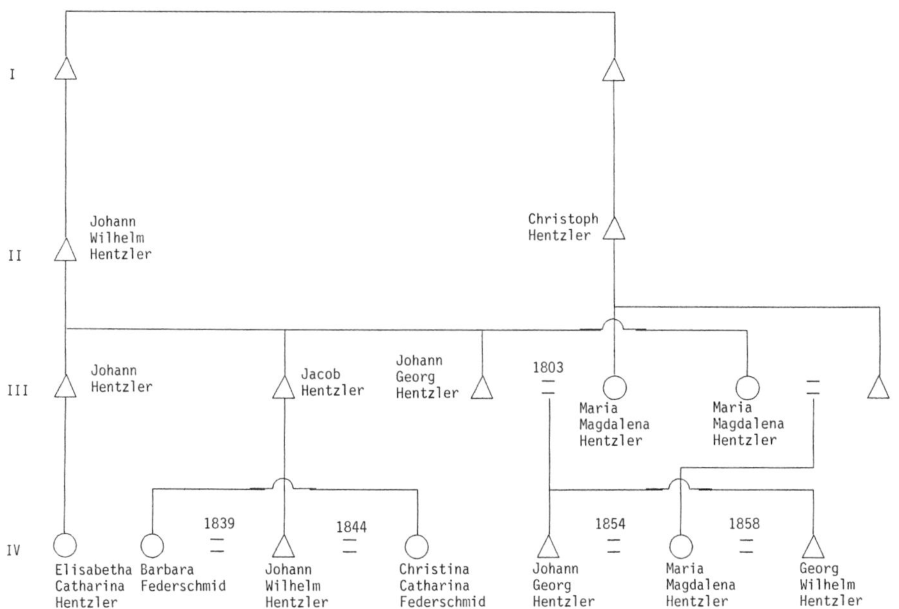

Figure 19.8

was a matrilateral parallel first cousin of Elisabetha Catharina Hentzler, and Johann Georg Falter was a cross-cousin of Jacob Friedrich Kühfuss. Again, linkages among women seem to have been important.

Although consideration of the wider kin networks in any detail is too baroque even for my tastes, it would be useful to glance at some typical formations on each side of this particular genealogy (Figures 19.7 and 19.8). The two Deuschle brothers married two cross cousins (Figure 19.7). Johann Salomo Vogler married two Kühfuss daughters. And two Kühfuss brothers and two Fischer siblings from Dettingen were married to two sisters who were patrilateral parallel cousins to each other. Now recall the marriages between the children of Johann Wilhelm and Christoph Hentzler (II), first cousins to each other, described in Chapter 16

(Figure 19.8). Three of the siblings from each family married each other. In generation IV, a daughter of one of the endogamous marriages married two sons of another one of them – the strictest example of patrilineal endogamy in village history. Another fourth generation son married two sisters.

Finally, look at the marriage between Johann Georg Kühfuss and Margaretha Hentzler (Figure 19.9), generation VI in Figure 19.4. This is the final exchange between the two families, although from the original point of view the couple were fourth and fifth cousins to each other. But on closer inspection, one again finds uterine networks that were perhaps socially more important. The first part of the diagram (A) shows that the couple were "second cousins," related matrilineally. The stepgrandmothers to each of the newlyweds were sisters and were alive at the time of the marriage. The second part of the diagram (B) indicates that they were second cousins by another route involving uterine reckoning as well.

A Bauer family

Another way of looking at the issues is to examine sibling groups as a whole to see how they coordinated their activities or made similar choices. The first family to look at involves the children of the Bauer, Johann Georg Ebinger, who married Rosina Barbara Deuschle, daughter of a cooper and Gemeindepfleger, in 1830. They had three sons, all of whom also became Bauern. The marriages of two of the brothers are rather straightforward (Figure 19.10).

Johann Georg Ebinger (III) married his MMBDD and Heinrich Ebinger married his MMZDD. Thus both of them were involved with matrilaterally defined kin. Their father, Johann Georg (II) died in 1839, long before either of them married, but their mother, Rosina Barbara Deuschle, was still alive. She saw one son marry her matrilateral cross cousin's daughter, and another, her matrilateral parallel cousin's daughter. This is a very good example of a network constructed through women and provides strong evidence for matrifocality. *The marriages involving the second son, Wilhelm Salomon Ebinger, are a little more complex. His wife, Margaretha Bauer, had been married before. In fact, she had been involved in a cousin/sibling marriage with Friedrich Bauknecht (Figure 19.11).*

In this case, Bauknecht's first cousin (a cross cousin, MBD) married Johann Wilhelm Baur in 1852. Five years later, Bauknecht married his cousin's husband's sister. Seven years after that (1864), the latter's brother and a sibling of Bauknecht's cousin also married each other. In the meantime, however, Friedrich Bauknecht had died, and his widow remarried, this time to a first cousin (matrilateral parallel) of a sister-in-law's sister-in-law (Figure 19.12). Subsequently, the father of the allied Falter family acted as godfather for Ebinger's brother, Heinrich. From the point of view of Rosina Barbara Deuschle, again, one finds her son marrying into a family closely allied to her niece (ZD). There is, however, another route that appears to work better in alliance terms (Figure 19.13).

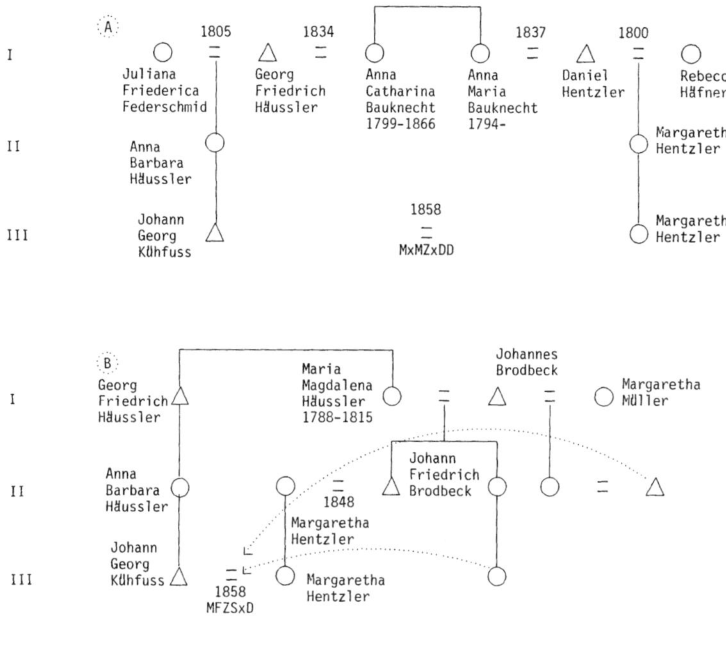

Figure 19.9

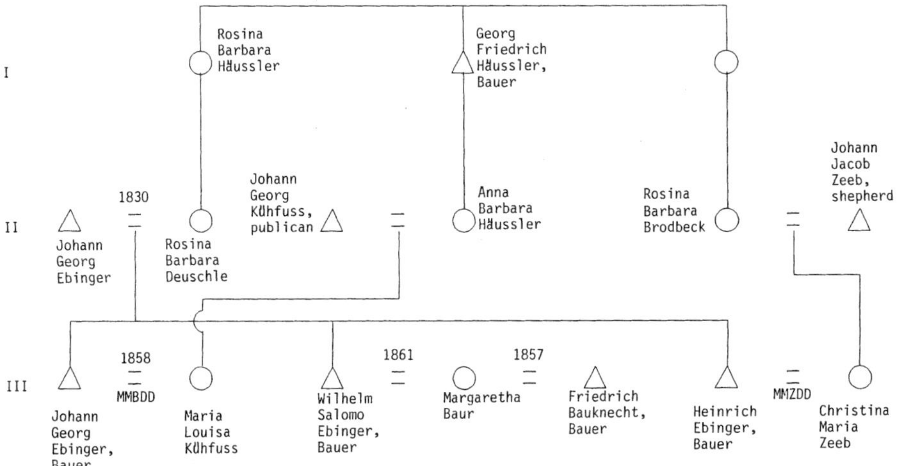

Figure 19.10

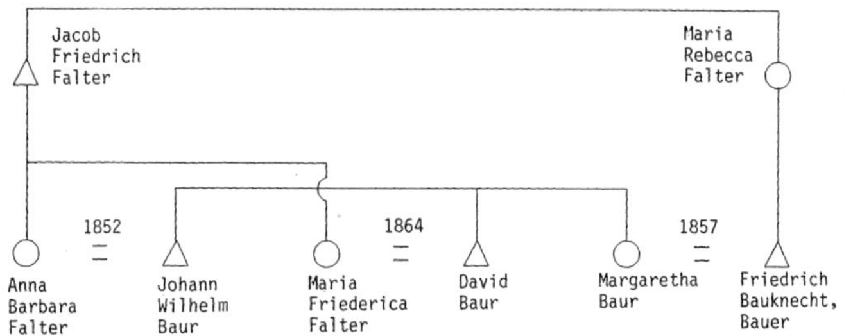

Figure 19.11

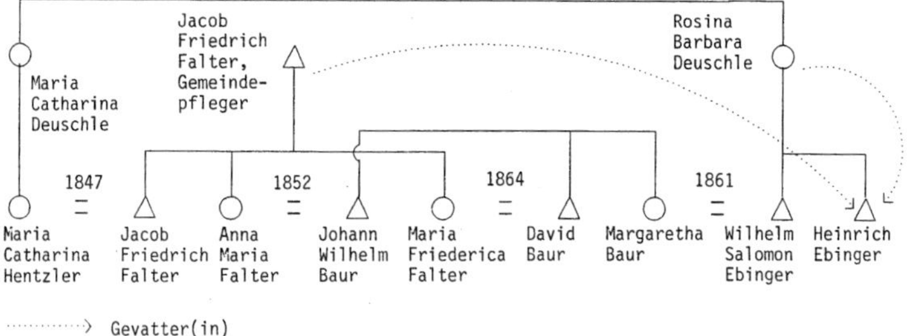

Figure 19.12

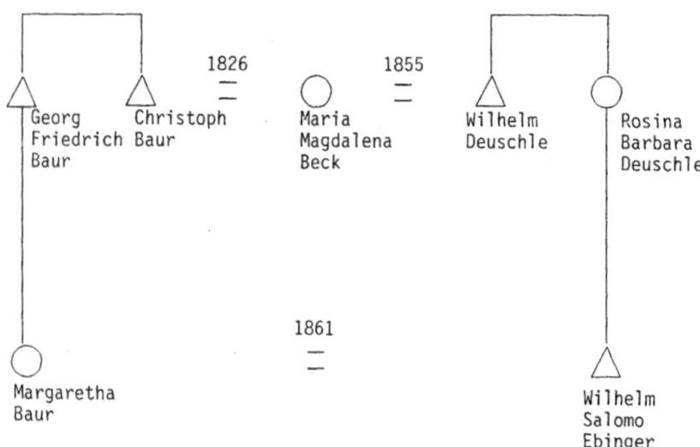

Figure 19.13

In this case, both Rosina Barbara Deuschle and her sister-in-law, Maria Magdalena Beck, who "mediated" between the two families, were alive at the time of the marriage in 1861. Even in this instance, some of the central positions in the network were occupied by women. Rosina Barbara Deuschle was in a key position to arrange for her son to marry her sister-in-law's niece.

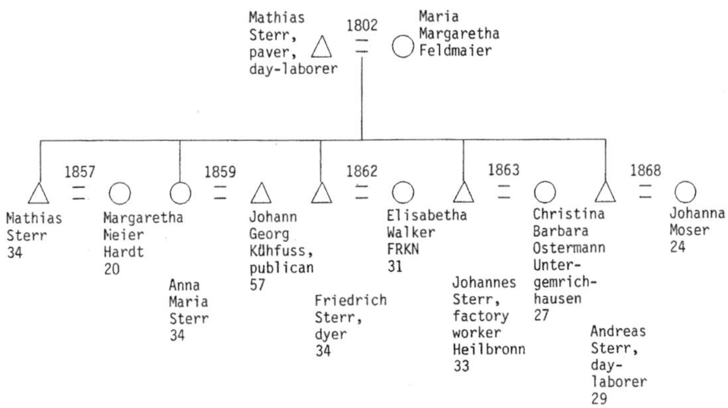

Figure 19.14

An artisan/laborer family

The second example of a set of siblings is offered by the children of Mathias Sterr, a pavior (*Pflästerer*), who spent the last years of his life as a day-laborer (Figure 19.14). The Sterrs were an old Neckarhausen family. The grandfather had been a Bauer and trader (*Händler*) and was descended from Bauern. The four brothers represented here were artisans, factory workers, and laborers – none of them among the wealthy members of the village. Three of the brothers married women from outside the village, apparently unrelated to them – at least there are no surnames from their parents that had ever occurred in Neckarhausen. One of the sons moved to north Württemberg and married a woman from near Heilbronn where he lived and worked. Most of the brothers and sisters married when they were well into their 30s. Anna Maria (34) married the very much older widower Johann Georg Kühfuss (57) in 1859. Although he came from a wealthier family of Bauern, shepherds, and innkeepers, few of his seven siblings made endogamous marriages, and two of his brothers emigrated to America. Most of the children of that generation had become or married weavers, dyers, paviors, masons, workers, or laborers. The family as a whole, just like the Sterrs, displayed mobility and showed little tendency toward endogamy. Only one Kühfuss, significantly a shepherd, continued an old alliance with the Hentzler family. The youngest Sterr, Andreas, was a laborer by occupation and at the time of his marriage was in the military. He married a Neckarhausen woman, Johanna Moser, daughter of a shepherd, who had emigrated from Dörnach. Almost all of the siblings of her mother had married out of the village, and several had left.

Taken altogether, the Sterrs represent a particular pattern of worker, small-artisan, farm-laborer families. By the 1860s, they displayed several generations of mobility, and they frequently married people from outside the village. In turn, they were allied to families who were not very inclined to endogamy and who

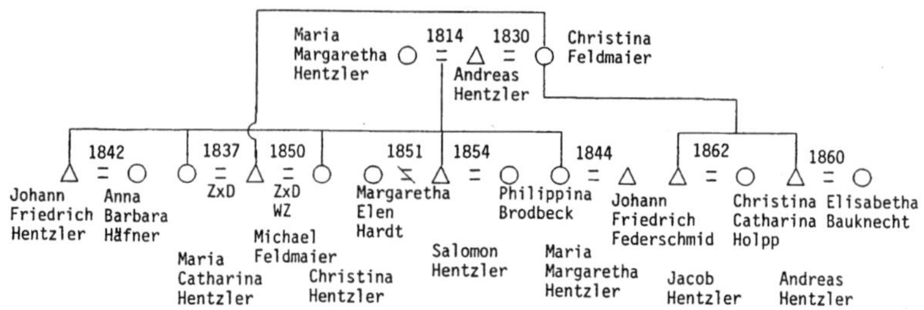

Figure 19.15

were not so concerned with constructing overlapping networks of kin through strategies of recurrent marriage alliance. For those families, there are no repeated unusual names in the family genealogies that would indicate wider regional alliances. This does not mean that family connections were disregarded altogether. At least three of the siblings used first cousins as godparents for their children, and relatives from outside the village were frequently represented as well.

A Bauer/craftsman family

The third example of a sibling group comes from the seven children of Andreas Hentzler and his two wives, Maria Margaretha Hentzler and Christina Feldmaier (Figure 19.15). *One striking feature of this genealogy is the fact that seven years after Andreas's second marriage, the brother – Michael Feldmaier – of his new wife married his eldest daughter. When that daughter died, Michael then married her younger sister, Christina (1850). Andreas's oldest son, Johann Friedrich Hentzler, married a Häfner who was descended in a patriline from a family that was allied with both branches of the Hentzler family from which he descended. This particular marriage has been analyzed in detail in case A (Figures 19.1, 19.2, 19.3).*

Salomo Hentzler first married an apparently unrelated woman from Hardt, but was soon divorced. He then married Philippina Brodbeck (Figure 19.16). This marriage did not involve prior kinship between the neogami; however, his half brother Andreas later married the sister of his brother-in-law's wife. His brother-in-law, Johannes Brodbeck, had married his first cousin's widow. Andreas Hentzler's wife's sister had married a first cousin (FZD) (path not shown), and one of her brothers married a "Verwandte" from another village. Finally, Maria Margaretha Hentzler married a first cousin of the two Brodbecks (Figure 19.17).

Taken together, these marriages reveal a substantial number of Bauern and craftsmen in this genealogy. Gemeinderäte were frequently represented in the senior generation. There was a continual interweaving of marriage alliances. One finds a father and two daughters marrying siblings, B/Z exchange, the levirate,

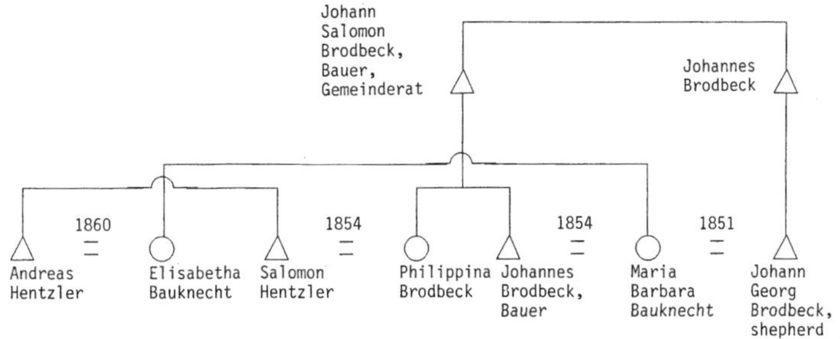

Figure 19.16

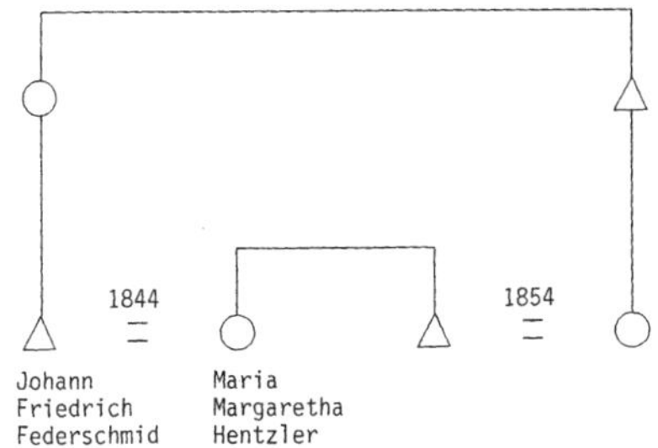

Figure 19.17

the sororate, a woman marrying two cousins, and first-, second-, and third-cousin marriage. There are criss-crossing alliances between the Hentzlers, Bauknechts, and Brodbecks. Any analysis of particular marriages demonstrates continuities between generations or within the generation, and the networks that were established frequently reveal women in key positions of mediation.

* * *

This chapter has dealt with a period that brought together again many already interwoven strands of family alliance. Families from the wealthier, landed stratum continued to exchange children between patrilines, which also continued to provide a focus for associations of ritual kinship and more practical, everyday matters as well. Some of the families at the lower end of the social scale did not foster a systematic multigenerational set of marriage alliances, although they certainly used kin in multiple ways and worked to foster regionally based relationships useful for people whose occupations frequently took them on the road.

The system of kinship alliances did shift in several crucial ways, however. For one thing, the range of matters dealt with in a more narrowly defined kinship universe increased. The choice of godparents was narrowed for the most part to a circle encompassed by first cousins. Other aspects such as land sales and guardianship moved outward from the nuclear family to and beyond first cousins.

Within this more circumscribed focus, marriage choice involved many strands of overlapping relationships. A particular couple might be defined just as easily through matrilines as patrilines, the patrilines showing a regular, systematic exchange pattern over many generations. Although the matrilineal link did not have the same depth, it may well have been the operational one. What the twofold link (patrilineal and matrilineal) did do was open up a degree of ambiguity and the possibility of reckoning alliances in multiple ways.

The importance of networks constructed by women for this generation needs to be emphasized. It is, of course, very difficult to calculate a balance of power or to abstract out from many-stranded relationships certain sets that were more crucial than others or particularly dominant. Both men and women were social actors, with ties to many different people, sometimes in tension with each other, sometimes in coordination, and sometimes just in different spheres. A particular marriage involved many contingencies, and when it came time to find a spouse, the chance contact of a father or the particular friendship of a mother might have been the means for making a choice. Nonetheless, all the evidence points toward the structural importance of networks constructed by or through women. Often, the crucial pair on which the system of relations came to be constructed was the brother and sister. Whereas the system of patriline alliances proceeded from the B/B bond in the eighteenth century, the B/Z pair kept the possibility of maintaining old family alliances in the mid nineteenth century but also – coupled with the narrowing down and concentration of the system (first cousin, B/Z exchange, sororate, levirate) – encouraged the construction of alliances through personal networks involving women. In this situation, cousins remained structurally central to the system, but it appears that the grand alliances had lost their functional importance in organizing the political system of the village and dispensing patronage. In the context of small peasant agriculture and unskilled and craft labor, overlapping, interlocking practical reciprocities produced coordinating kindreds that were useful for organizing agricultural production, trading tools, providing channels of information and contacts for employment, and coordinating blocks of voters. Women came in many instances to provide a village anchor for all of these activities and therefore became coordination points for both men and women. The system had to remain open and flexible to meet productive, political, and social exigencies and at the same time had to be tight enough to create obligation and fulfill expectation. Marriage strategy was central to the system. More than ever, people made in-laws out of cousins, creating coordinate sets of relatives with multiple anchors in the village, useful for workers exporting their skills to the surrounding region.

CONCLUSION

20

Neckarhausen in European comparative perspective

> To put flesh on the genealogical bones it is necessary to understand the hierarchies of the group, the organisation of production, modes of agricultural operation, the nature of production, and the organisation of local markets.
>
> – Martine Segalen, *Fifteen Generations*

In the final four chapters, I want to take up the challenge of comparative analysis and offer evidence to show how much the course of history in Neckarhausen followed its own path and how my findings about kinship there open up issues and connections for the course of European history as a whole. The section opens with the discussion in this chapter of the range of bahavior in European rural societies. In Chapter 21, it then moves on to the question of whether the rise of consanguineal marriage in Neckarhausen was part of a more general pattern in Germany and Europe. These two chapters lead inescapably to the question of the relationship between kinship and class (Chapter 22) – which has already been raised here and there in the account of Neckarhausen. Chapter 23 brings the discussion to a close with some observations about the interconnections between kinship and gender in the nineteenth century.

In each of the chapters on the family history of Neckarhausen, I have established reciprocal relations between kinship and social forces. I have found that kinship comprises a territory, where "rules" and practices cannot simply be resolved into material interests or be derived from economic concerns alone. It was not a superstructural feature of productive relations lying at the foundation of society. That is why an analysis of kinship reveals certain formal features and general principles, which are familiar to anyone versed in comparative social analysis. The fact that kinship has its own space does not, however, absolve us from tracing the links between its dynamics and productive enterprise, group formation, political networking, property management and distribution, social stratification, and market exchange. It is the very autonomy of kinship in any social system as a set of values and obligations or as a space in which unresolved tensions of debt and credit attain free play that allows kinship to function as a support for the social order and to reproduce its inequalities.[1] Any particular connection made between kinship and any

[1] The theoretical analysis of this point is found throughout the writings of Pierre Bourdieu.

other "domain," however, carries weight in the long run only after the analysis is subjected to the discipline of rigorous comparison.[2]

Since social facts are always conditioned by their positions inside a set of specific relations, comparative method has to proceed by discussing the structural features of each society it wants to set in relief in some detail. In this chapter, I will take up a number of issues by comparing the social context of kinship construction in several communities with the complex development in Neckarhausen. This will allow me to explore the formal features of Neckarhausen kinship as well as the recurrent patterns of familial exchange across Europe. In particular, I will examine the construction of lines and lineages, the fashioning of inter- and intragenerational reciprocities, and the circulation of patrimonies and endowments. More abstractly put, the questions to be examined are how do form and structure articulate with interest and choice; how do certain formal characteristics of kinship coordinate with strategies based on class, hierarchy, power, and feeling; how does inheritance (partible, impartible) provide a context in which different logical features of kinship play themselves out; and how do kin utilize the specific ecologies of resource, region, and market to manifest honor, fulfill need, pursue interest, and obey moral imperative? The comparative method, by using each society as a foil against which to measure the other, makes it possible to grasp the singular features of each.

I have chosen three regions for comparison with Neckarhausen: rural Naples, southern Brittany, and the Gévaudan in southeastern France.[3] Each of them has been the object of seminal research on kinship and on the complex interplay of productive, market, political, and social forces. These studies are all primarily concerned with rural society, and this comparison, restricted at first to agricultural regions, produces a range of conceptual and theoretical tools that will be applied to aspects of European social organization beyond the village in Chapters 21 to 23. Finally, I will look carefully at the problem of transition from "classic" to "modern" Europe: the break in social organization – in particular, kinship organization – and the complex set of shifts in family relations from mercantile to capitalist society. A central aspect of that set of shifts is the refocusing of relationships from vertical to horizontal – from clan to class, descent to alliance, and patrimony to investment.

Rural Naples

In his book on family and property in the Kingdom of Naples, Gérard Delille deals with marriage alliances among the nobility and rural folk from the fifteenth

[2] See the remarks on the concept of "domain" in Chapter 1.

[3] A few other studies could have been used, but the three I have chosen are the richest ones in languages I can read. For work in Italy, see Raul Merzario, "Land, Kinship, and Consanguineous Marriage in Italy from the Seventeenth to the Nineteenth Centuries," *Journal of Family History* 15 (1990): 529–46. One should also consult Andrejs Plakans, *Kinship in the Past: An Anthropology of European Family Life 1500–1900* (Oxford, 1984), for a sobering judgment of what the journey into the tangled thicket of historical kinship analysis implies.

to the nineteenth centuries.[4] This discussion will concentrate on the dynamics of the peasant populations but with a glance from time to time at certain formations common to all classes. Delille discusses two ecologically different areas – called zones 1 and 2 – the first characterized by small peasant production and the second by latifundia worked by wage labor. In zone 1, in the hilly region along the Amalfi coast and the Valley of the Irno, small and medium peasant cultivators produced wine, citrus and other fruit, and textiles. The coastal and interior plains (zone 2) produced cereal crops and livestock on large – frequently ecclesiastical – estates with mobile wage labor.

The two regions supported quite different family and kinship arrangements. In zone 1, during the fifteenth and sixteenth centuries, agnatic lineage quarters developed in the villages. Inheritance was partible, although women normally received only movable property and married out – residence was patrivirilocal (determined by the husband's or husband's father's location). Dwellings were constantly extended and divided, so that children inherited portions of a building – doors, windows, garden plots, rights of passage and usage. In the course of time, such buildings resembled fortress blocks containing separate apartments for different families, all linked by agnatic bonds through the constant fissioning of property from generation to generation. Having reached a certain size, a lineage group would partition, frequently colonizing another part of the territory. Delille gives the example of one large village with more than 670 hearths, divided into 12 administrative districts (*casali*) averaging 55–60 hearths, each district dominated by one or two lineages. Typically, lineages in the region comprised 10 to 20 families, although Delille found one as large as 174.

Three conditions were necessary for the perpetuation of lineages: that only men divided up the houses and land, that dowries were composed of movable wealth, and that the sale of property was subject to considerable restriction. Indeed, almost all of the few sales were internal to the family. In the course of the sixteenth century, after a particular family was forced to sell off land bit by bit, any capable descendant would attempt to reassemble all the pieces. Because the system did not allow for capital accumulation, recuperation of the ancient possessions of a family became socially valorized. Sales were seen as temporary, and contracts often specified the conditions for revocation and return of the land.

In zone 2, no one before Delille had discovered lineage quarters, and observers accustomed to the highly structured lineage forms thought of the region as anarchic and "disordered." Among agricultural laborers, people with the same surname did not gather together in the same place. Delille has found, however, that there was indeed stability to the system but one based on *uxorilocal* (determined by wife's location) marriages. Families arranged to pass real estate on to their daughters, and men commonly married in. The possibility of female lineages has

[4] Gérard Delille, *Famille et propriété dans le royaume de Naples (XVe–XIXe siècle)*, Bibliothèque des écoles françaises d'Athènes et de Rome, 259 (Rome and Paris, 1985).

escaped observation because of the difficulty of studying a population with constant surname changes. A close look at the records, however, shows many blocs of three to four women sharing a common surname. After a generation, all the related women in the same location would end up with different surnames.

The two zones were characterized by opposed but reciprocal logics. In zone 1, land was scarce and children competed with one another for resources. Brothers frequently formed the key cooperative units – sometimes even cultivating land in common. And over time families arranged for the outmigration of men. In zone 2, labor was scarce, and the system was oriented toward attracting male labor. There the cooperating or coordinating male pair was composed of brothers-in-law. The lineage quarters (zone 1) were closed, did not easily accept strangers, and expelled men. But the area of female succession was open, readily accepted outsiders – and women married much younger and had higher rates of fertility. Despite recruitment respectively through agnatic or uterine kin, the kinship system in each instance was essentially cognatic, or, in Delille's terminology, "bilateral." After the demographic troubles of the late seventeenth century, some villages in the lineage quarter region shifted to a system in which property descended to women and residence became uxorilocal. In this situation the logic of choice was determined by the necessity of attracting male labor in an area decimated by plague. Delille concludes from the ease of response to a new situation that the system of descent and kinship alliance was flexible and could favor either male *or* female descendants according to social and economic exigencies.

Delille puts most of his energy into discussing the kinship system for the partible-inheritance, small peasant region of zone 1. There the shift over time from an exogamous to an endogamous marriage alliance system followed a course similar to that in Neckarhausen, although no lineage quarters developed there and the partible inheritance system distributed real estate equally to sons and daughters all the way through the period. Houses were frequently partitioned, but residence was determined by availability, and young couples were just as apt to share space with the wife's parents as with the husband's.

There were essentially two different systems of marriage alliance for Delille's zone 1, one for the late fifteenth to the end of the seventeenth centuries and another developing progressively in the eighteenth century, emerging full-blown in the nineteenth. Just as in Neckarhausen and Germany as a whole until the eighteenth century, the earlier system in rural Naples was characterized by negative rules – one was not allowed to marry within an established and wide range of kin. Because there were no prescriptive rules about who one should marry, anthropologists and historians have usually assumed that there was no structure – and could be no structure to marriage alliance. Whatever regularities one found were ascribed to statistical probabilities. People married for reasons of class, wealth, sentiment, neighborhood, and so forth but did not set up systematic exchange relations with kin or maintain alliances over time – how could they if they were forbidden to marry anyone already linked to them by blood? The importance of Delille's analysis is precisely that it shows reciprocities were indeed possible and that mechanisms of exchange operated not despite, but because of, marriage prohibitions.

Delille poses the problem of kinship alliance for the "classical" period (ca. 1500 to ca. 1720) in terms of Lévi-Strauss's categories discussed in Chapter 1. In his argument for complex societies, wherein the only rule is that one may not marry again anyone related closely to him or herself, Lévi-Strauss concludes that alliances cannot take place among groups across generations and that neither restricted nor generalized forms of exchange are possible. This study has shown, however, that aspects of such elementary forms can be found in Neckarhausen for both the "classical" and "modern" periods.

Delille argues even more strongly that both restricted and generalized forms of exchange were possible in both peasant and noble groups during the sixteenth and seventeenth centuries, precisely the period in which the church was able to impose its rules of marriage prohibition most strictly. Delille found that the open, complex kinship system contained a series of interlocking structures. To begin with, there were numerous cases of sibling exchange, where two brothers married two sisters, or a brother and sister married a brother and sister. Such exchanges consolidated links cast in a single generation but could not be replicated in the next without violating the rules against consanguineal marriage. Another form to be found was the marriage of two siblings with two people who were cousins to each other – most usually patrilateral parallel cousins – a form that crops up in the same period in Neckarhausen. And another variant involved the marriage of two cousins with two people who in turn were cousins to each other. Both of these latter forms also involved relinking on the same generational plane but could not be replicated in the following several generations without violating the rules against consanguinity. In all of these cases, Delille finds principles that suggest the linking of patrilineal lines, which suggests common dynamics in the two very different societies. He also finds many examples of several lines intermarrying in a generalized form, such that lineage A married into lineage B, which in turn was linked to C, and so forth, with the return to A mediated by several steps. With this form, continuity can be developed over time, but it involves several lineages and precludes tighter alliances between two at a time. In fact, however, both nobles and peasants developed forms of exchange that allowed relations between two lineages to persist for more than one generation. The basic forms involved what Delille calls "collaterals" – uncles and aunts and nephews and nieces. The tighter form, involving restricted exchange, characterized the marriage of an aunt and nephew with an uncle and niece (Figure 20.1). In this example, the exchange of marriage partners – since we are dealing with male lineages, of women – in generation 1 from lineage A to B was returned in the following generation by an exchange from B to A (compare Figure 1.1). There is no violation of the rules of consanguinity here, and it provides an example of restricted exchange in a complex (open) system, an example of "structure in a structureless" system. Although reciprocity here can persist over two generations,

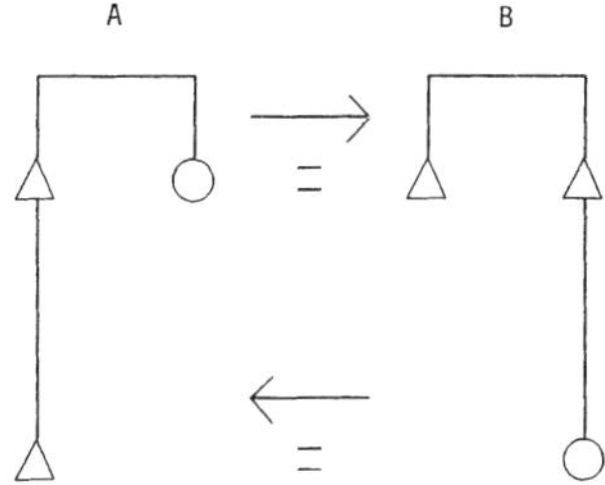

Figure 20.1

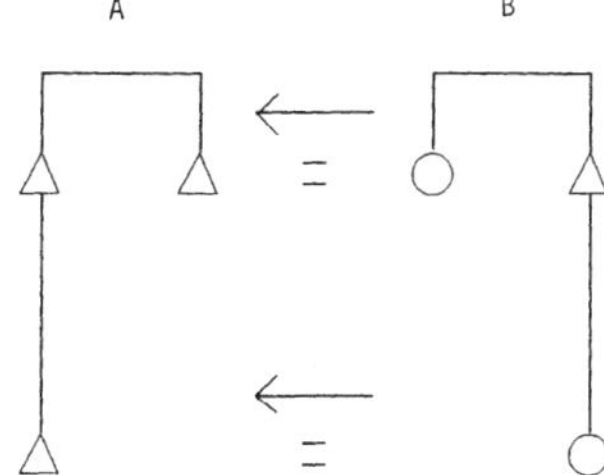

Figure 20.2

it cannot be prolonged to a third without violating the rules of consanguinity. But a second form can do so because as generalized exchange it can integrate an alliance between several lineages (an uncle and nephew marry an aunt and niece, Figure 20.2). In this form, the uncles and aunts were always paternal – thus linking two male lineages together. Since the lineage that received wives did not return them, it forced the wife-giving lineage to seek alliance with a third group. This particular form developed in Neckarhausen only during the "modern" phase of endogamy and intergenerational alliance.

Delille makes two important observations about this material. First, calculations were made on two planes: kinship and material interest. On one hand, the lack of prescriptive rules allowed families to calculate the best possible alliance in terms of the most advantageous possibility for reproducing the group. On the other hand, the use of a kinship idiom created tight bonds of mutual interest and coordinated practice. Second, any one family could follow different strategies during any one of several generations. One child could be involved in a sibling exchange, while another linked up with a lineage that was in turn tied up in the previous generation with a lineage that a generation earlier had entered into an alliance with his or her own lineage. Still another child might strike off in a completely new direction. In order to see how the system of practices worked, one has to examine the whole coordinated set of exchanges. There were, of course, other forms – one that frequently took place was that between a widower and his daughter and a widow and her son. Here again, one encounters restricted exchange and a structure that could not persist beyond the two generations involved.

Each form of exchange was able to take part in tight overlapping structures by the fact that the set of siblings in any one generation could coordinate their marriages so as to maximize the strategic position of the whole lineage, moving out in new directions for some and fulfilling older debts for others. But the system received further integration by the practice of direct consanguineal marriages just past the degrees of prohibition every fifth, sixth, or seventh generation. Delille demonstrates that in this society people normally had memory of ascendants back three to five generations, and that consanguineal marriages took place just at the point where memory began to fade. He argues that the two systems of exchange – those within the degrees of prohibition (sibling exchange, uncle/nephew with aunt/niece, widower/son with widow/daughter) and those beyond the degrees linking two lines of a lineage back again – worked not autonomously but symbiotically. They were alternating principles for the circulation of people and goods within coherent dynamics of exchange.

The society in which these forms of marriage exchange took place was highly articulated. Marriage was calculated in order to defend the order or to improve one's position in the order, but also to maintain clients and to link oneself to powerful patrons. The principles of filiation coupled with various strategies of alliance allowed for the construction of vertically integrated groups of kin who worked, socialized, and carried on politics together. As in Neckarhausen up to about the 1740s, agnatic principles of organization were stressed within a larger structure of cognatic reckoning of kin. In zone 1 in the Kingdom of Naples, only males inherited land and immovable property, which gave greater coherence to the male lineages in terms of residence and the holding of blocks of land, but even in Neckarhausen, where daughters inherited exactly as much and the same kinds of things as sons, agnatic forms of linking – revealed in the coordinate marriages of patrilateral parallel cousins and in naming practices – dominated marriage, the construction of clientages, and village politics. In Naples, the rise of endogamous marriages during the eighteenth century went together with the destruction of lineages at the same time that endogamy ended the older form of clientage and brought about the restructuring of village politics in Neckarhausen.

The system of lineages in rural Naples had expanded and solidified during the sixteenth century and into the first half of the seventeenth century but began to break down during the period of economic and demographic crisis between 1680 and 1730. The size of lineages fell dramatically after the 1656 plague, but by 1730 when the population had recuperated, they had not. By 1798 the old system was simply no longer there, having been replaced by isolated families and groups of no more than two or three hearths. At first, after the shock of losing more than 50 percent of the population, the territory with male lineages reacted by adopting practices of uxorilocality and neolocality (residence not determined by the location of either parent) – anchoring women with property and seeking to attract men. But by 1730 completely new mechanisms of alliance were put into place. The older system of "collateral" marriages and the parallel "coupling" (*bouclage*) of consanguines beyond the prohibited degrees disappeared altogether, to be replaced by ever increasing rates of consanguinity. And that rise was accompanied by the selection of closer and closer blood relatives as marriage partners. Although not statistically frequent, there were even examples of uncles marrying nieces. And the restriction regarding close affines disappeared as well – many men married the sisters of their deceased wives.

Delille puts the change in kinship dynamics into the same context as that found for Neckarhausen. For one thing, the market in land expanded considerably, and the price per unit of land rose to unheard of heights. As far as the possessing classes were concerned, the new endogamy was designed to prevent dispersion of property, but the poorer classes abandoned the older forms of reciprocity for immediate interest as well.

> In short, the phenomenon can be interpreted as the sign of a fracture separating the different social classes ever more deeply. The propertied marry within an ever more narrow circle of kin in order not to disperse and partition their land, while the working classes by contrast always more frequently marry according to immediate situations and interests, excluding all mechanisms of reciprocity over the medium and long term and finally at the cost of all structuring of the system as a whole. (p. 366)

Delille is quite right to see that the new endogamy was closely tied up with class formation and with the abandonment of marriage reciprocities that bound wealthier members of the society together with the poor. I do not think, however, that the new endogamy entailed the abandonment of structure or of long-term reciprocities. Quite the opposite: new forms of systematic exchange developed that abandoned older mechanisms of clientage, lineage, or clan formation, all those ways of integrating groups vertically. Delille also passes over the problem of managing the new land market too quickly and does not analyze the problem of "dispersion." His brief discussion suggests that landholders simply married among themselves and monopolized the holding of land by that simple mechanism. But class endogamy is designed – as seen in the analysis of Neckarhausen – to provide multiple forms of exchange and the broad coordination of a class in its efforts to manage credit, land markets, officeholding, and corruption, all of which could only have been done by real but flexible structures and a well-coordinated system of reciprocities. Delille is wrong to say that the "collateral" system as an exchange between families is in contrast to the endogamous system as a refusal of exchange by remaining within the family. An examination of the marriage politics of sibling groups would show a multiplicity of alliances with different lines, some close, some far, and some striking off in new directions. These are actually two contrasting systems of exchange, one built around clientage and the vertical integration of groups and one built around class and horizontal integration – perhaps no longer of "groups" but of flexibly coordinated strata. Both systems were built on durable, multigenerational exchanges – at least in the Kingdom of Naples. In Neckarhausen, the construction of clientages was far more the work of each particular generation, since the inheritance of both men and women precluded the formation of anything like durable, property-holding male lineages.

There have been several explanations for the rise of endogamy in the eighteenth and nineteenth centuries. The French demographer Sutter argued that as each family expanded in size with increased fertility, it gave families an opportunity to marry kin and also made kin less avoidable.[5] But as Delille points out, his position supposes the persistence and continuity of an endogamy of extremely rigid groups. It also does not account for the movement from distant to close consanguinity. And in many areas where population continued to increase after World War I, endogamy declined – often rapidly. Other scholars, such as Georges Duby, explain the phenomenon by the declining authority of the church, but this argument supposes that before the nineteenth century the church imposed its policy against a natural tendency of people to marry into the family. Delille's explanation is tied to a consideration of class. He quite rightly sees the wealthier rural strata as the group that led the movement. "Now, in the nineteenth century, consanguineal marriages are always in essence a fact of the propertied classes. Simply put, it is the physiognomy of these propertied classes that changes: the nobility in decline, which lived in Naples and in some of the larger cities of the province, gave way little by little to a more diffuse and numerous rural bourgeoisie" (p. 369). The problem posed for the rural "bourgeoisie" had to do with its inability to adopt feudal techniques such as the fideicommiss (entail) for keeping property intact. The bourgeoisie was unwilling to impose primogeniture, nor could it slough off unwanted children to a declining church establishment. And under the influence of Napoleon, the new law of inheritance in 1806 forced the division of family property among all the heirs. This called for mechanisms to paliate the effects of legal changes and maintain over the long term the integrity of the familial patrimony.

Delille's argument concerning nineteenth-century endogamy is brilliant but too narrowly tied to property, or perhaps better said, tied to a too narrow understanding of property. With an eye to the most dramatic forms of consanguinity such as first-cousin marriage, he misses the possibility that artisans and farm laborers might have been constructing wider regional ties on the basis of endogamous marriage – perhaps using second cousins as in Neckarhausen. Furthermore, his reliance on the concept of "patrimony" does not help in examining the strategies of new strata of entrepreneurs, who were not protecting the dispersal of family property but creating new wealth. The problem of endogamy and class formation will be the subject of Chapter 22, but I want to note here that Delille is one of the few scholars to see the connection and importance of the problem. He argues that endogamy first involved marriage within agnatic

[5] Jean Sutter, "Facteurs d'endogamie et de consanguinité," *Population* 23 (1968): 303–24. See the discussion in Chapter 21 in this volume.

lines at the end of the eighteenth and beginning of the nineteenth century to control the dispersal of property inherited for the most part by sons. But further into the nineteenth century, daughters increasingly inherited as well. Under these circumstances, the only way for a family to recover its property was for a son to marry a cross cousin (MBD, FZD). Consanguinity, he argues, was unhooked from the problem of endowing daughters and the circulation of *dots* and refitted to the problem of transmitting patrimonies. Still, Delille admits that his argument does not explain very well the vastly different endogamy rates from region to region.[6] I would argue that we need to think through a wider definition of class and to investigate the very different strategies of different classes – first-cousin marriage being only one solution to configuring the forms of reciprocity. And the notion of patrimony is too narrow to cover such diverse phenomena as noble estates, peasant farms, artisanal and management skills, occupational and merchant networks, entrepreneurial know-how, and commercial investment. Delille is quite right, however, to insist that the mechanisms of kinship and marriage that are seen today are not the product of a linear evolution. The eighteenth and nineteenth centuries witnessed, in his language, a contraction of the system of alliance to the limits of incest after which the system "imploded with an extreme violence." What he does not explore, after providing a foundation for considering the issues, is the problem of class formation and its transformation during the long nineteenth century. He does underscore that even though the dynamics of alliance were more open than in primitive societies, actors still responded both in the mean and long run to determined schemas. Kinship did not dominate the economic as it is said to do in primitive societies, but the two were still quite strictly imbricated with each other.

Gévaudan

Elisabeth Claverie and Pierre Lamaison have studied a kinship system that might be seen as the opposite of what has been found for Neckarhausen. They examined the impartible-inheritance region of Gévaudan in the department of the Lozère in southeastern France. Their book, *L'impossible mariage,* is based on their separate dissertations.[7] In Lamaison's case, the work focused on a family reconstitution extending from the late sixteenth century to about 1872/3, while Claverie studied notarial and judicial records over the same time period but with greater concentration on nineteenth-century materials.[8] There is some difficulty, how-

[6] Unfortunately, Delille has not been able to investigate statistically the relative weight of parallel and cross cousins over time. This means that he cannot say whether his consanguineal marriages are marriages back into male lineages or whether they express repeated exchanges between lineages. The latter can function quite efficiently in terms of restricted and generalized exchange, something he denies is possible with marriage among blood relatives.

[7] Elisabeth Claverie and Pierre Lamaison, *L'impossible mariage: Violence et parenté en Gévaudan XVIIe, XVIIIe, et XIXe siècles* (Paris, 1982).

[8] Lamaison published a separate study, "Les stratégies matrimoniales dans un système complexe de parenté: Ribennes en Gévaudan (1650–1830)," *Annales ESC* 34 (1979): 721–43.

ever, posing the questions I am asking in the framework of their analyses. For one thing, Lamaison takes the story only up to 1830, and there is no clear indication that he examined the demographic data beyond that date.[9] Both authors have also stated that consanguineal marriages were infrequent throughout the seventeenth, eighteenth, and nineteenth centuries. Their evidence up to 1830 is convincing, but they provide no hard data to demonstrate that older marriage patterns persisted beyond that date. Indeed, from the 1926–30 statistics provided by Sutter and Tabah for all of France, the Lozère had rates of consanguineal endogamy (through second cousins) in the top 13 percent of all departments.[10] Oral testimony, Claverie and Lamaison report, suggests that people have always married their cousins, but they argue that the logic of the social system precluded such alliances. However, it does appear that the region did develop considerable endogamy in the course of the nineteenth century. I have no doubt that the sharp rise in consanguinity took place after 1870, but in the absence of statistical analysis I must put aside that part of the story and concentrate on the conceptual issues associated with the classic ancien régime phase.[11]

Like South Bigouden in Brittany and Neckarhausen, Gévaudan had a completely cognatic familial ideology. Kin were reckoned equally through men and women, and there was no succession to property or social position based on patri- or matrilinearity. In contrast to the other two situations, however, inheritance was fundamentally inegalitarian in Gévaudan. Succession to the head of a household – an *ousta* – privileged one child, and excluded all the children who received dowries from any further inheritance. Such a system – called "préciputaire" – characterized many, especially southern, areas in France – and contrasted sharply with the more egalitarian – northern – custom that required all endowments to be returned at the decease or final retirement of parents in order to equalize all of the children.[12] Gévaudan is a classic region of "stem" families, with generation after generation of the same family inheriting a farm complex, but contrary to what one might expect, descent was not particularly agnatic. Up to 1830 at least, in fully more than 40 percent of the cases a daughter succeeded the previous

[9] I first assumed that Lamaison had extrapolated his findings with regard to marriage alliance from the period before 1830 for the rest of the nineteenth century. After consulting with the authors, I found that Lamaison had systematically consulted the civil registers up to 1872–73. At the time that he started his work, the registers after that date were closed.

[10] Lozère was among the 40 percent of departments that had more than 50 percent second cousins among consanguineal marriages. The other 60 percent put stress on closer kin. Jean Sutter and Léon Tabah, "Fréquence et répartition des mariages consanguins en France," *Population* 3, 4 (1948): 607–30.

[11] The authors agreed in a private conversation that by the 1920s their region had very high rates of consanguinity but insist that the change came only after 1870.

[12] The classic work on the subject is Jean Yver, *Egalité entre héritiers et exclusion des enfants dotés: Essai de geographie coutumière* (Paris, 1966). See also Emmanuel Le Roy Ladurie, "Family Structures and Inheritance Customs in Sixteenth-Century France," in Jack Goody, Joan Thirsk, and E. P. Thompson, eds., *Family and Inheritance: Rural Society in Western Europe, 1200–1800* (Cambridge, 1976), pp. 37–70. The custom of equalizing at the death or retirement of the parents was practiced also in Neckarhausen; see David Warren Sabean, *Property, Production, and Family in Neckarhausen* (Cambridge, 1990).

head, and there were many instances of several generations of female heirs even when sons were available. The selection of one particular child to succeed took place at an opportune moment in the family cycle and depended both on the parents' desire to choose the most effective new manager and on a suitable marriage alliance for the household. What gave the entire system stability was the continuation of patrimonies rather than patrilines over many generations.

The Gévaudan was a mixed-stock and grain-growing region with considerable weaving, especially among the poorer households. Farms were scattered over the hilly countryside in small hamlets containing anywhere from 1 to 20 oustas. Kin were also dispersed among the different hamlets, although there was a tendency for a few allied families to dominate any one settlement. Practically no one married beyond a 15-kilometer limit, and the restricted number of patronyms indicates a closed society of about 6,000 interacting people. Nonetheless, consanguineal kin did not marry each other. Up to 1830 at least, only 35 marriages out of 1,900 unions (1.9 percent) involved consanguines up to third cousins. All such marriages involved cadets, and no heir to an ousta ever married a blood relative.

According to the authors, this society had two distinctive features: each ousta displayed a fundamental aggressiveness toward all the others, and each had an active and detailed memory of its history over many generations. All the members of a house, including the servants and unmarried relatives, were continually mobilized to prevent slights to its honor or incursions on its territory. In turn, the members of each ousta probed the strength and resolve of its neighbors in a perpetual display of violation and revenge. The authors speak of "a dialectic of aggressivity, which is inscribed in familial memory and the memory of the village and for which the affront and shame has to be put to right" (p. 261). The society was characterized by frequent violence, and the solidarity of ousta members was ever elicited within practices of continuous brutality. Toward the outside, the ideal was to shame, dishonor, or crush a rival, with no feelings of compassion for families who lost out in the severe competition. Old hatreds and rivalries were inherited and brought continually into play so that a slight to honor in one generation might finally be avenged by the grandchildren. "Kept in memory, never abandoned, hereditary because felt as a weight generation after generation, vengeance with its long delays, its chronic tensions, configured the relations of force ever anew" (p. 22).

Mobilization for aggression or defense frequently required the coordination of kin. Kinship linked houses of different wealth in this highly hierarchical and inegalitarian society, and every powerful ousta developed a large clientele. Debts, agricultural services, and myriad other exchanges created a web of obligation that sorted out families into loose associations. By far the most important good that circulated among oustas was the *dot* (dowry), the property hived off from an estate that accompanied an outmarrying child and excluded him or her from the inheritance. The movement of dots between oustas was deeply embedded in collective memory, and the structured system of exchange required extensive knowledge of how any particular patrimonial line was linked to any other through the circulation of endowments. Each ousta was conceptualized as a property-holding entity extended in space and as a moral and social unit extended in time. And the linkages to other houses conflated space and time. "Between the ousta-household, materialized by a real presence in the countryside, and the ousta-line, historical, memorialized . . . and immaterial, . . . all social experience is given form, discourses and behaviors are sorted out, [and] strategies are perfected" (p. 36). Claverie and Lamaison link the aggressivity and form of alliance together in the idea that each ousta had to be autonomous in order to exchange with the others. Even clients found ways of asserting their honor and the integrity of their property through transgression against their more powerful patrons. Maintaining distance and inculcating respect were necessary for any house to maintain viability on the marriage market and ensure its own continuation from generation to generation. The authors go so far as to suggest that this dialectical game required one family to attack another just to give the latter an opportunity to display its capacity to protect its honor and goods.

Each alliance was determined by the necessity to avoid consanguineal kin, a practice that the authors derive not from church prohibitions but from the necessity to maintain autonomy and coherence of the patrimonial line and the injunction to match partners who were equal. The status of a prospective bride or groom was derived from the standing of the ousta in the hierarchy of houses and the particular place he or she held in the internal hierarchy of the family. There was a strong belief in inheritable traits, and the well-known history of each house was part of the construction of symbolic capital that helped sort out the hierarchy. Everyone was "known and foreknown" – a theft by a grandmother was recalled when a granddaughter came under suspicion for a similar fault. "In the memories of the village, an order of verdicts and judgments is continuously restaged. The history of their alliances, of their mistakes, and of their past victories is rehearsed for each house and its members" (p. 225).

Given the exigencies of alliance – to marry within a restricted territory, to avoid blood relatives, and to marry according to one's rank – the number of available choices at any one time was limited. But within such limitations there were strategic considerations that determined how an ousta would link itself to other families in the region. A house could choose to strengthen ties with another by a series of multiple exchanges, returning a dot in as direct a fashion as possible, or it could enter into a more generalized exchange pattern, letting a dot circulate among related patrimonial lines before having it returned several generations down the line. This latter strategy was crucial for the creation of "clans," of interdependent houses of patrons and clients. Such a series of related houses, the authors conceptualize as "poles" – which tended to form in each parish – a series of patrimonial lines systematically linked through the exchange of endowments.

> At each generation, each ousta seems to have the choice between several directions of alliance: either restricted exchanges, allowing powerful lines to engraft with one or two other houses . . . , or generalized exchanges with several oustas, establishing systems of

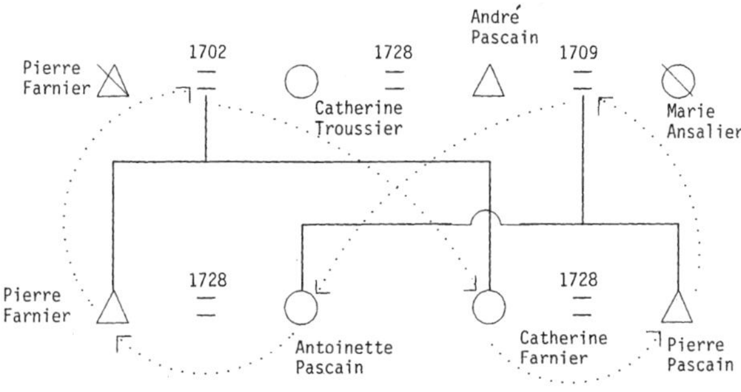

Figure 20.3

clienteles or of 'clans,' on which are sketched new alliances. . . . The network of solidarities is in perpetual transformation and each exchange, facing past or current alliances can in fact be imputed with the coincidence across one single marriage to politics carried on with different houses. (p. 288)

Lamaison and Claverie claim that an open system of clan formation, which was the dominant consideration, seen from the perspective of several generations or all the alliances of a sibling group, precluded consanguineal marriages that would have restricted ties and kept property within patrimonial lines. Rather than circulating it and creating the multiple ties and dependencies, each ousta needed to maintain its validity.

The first kind of strategy – multiple links between two patrimonial lines – could often in fact get around the necessity actually to exchange endowments (Figure 20.3). In the example offered here, three marriages took place on the same day, each with a contract specifying the size of the dot and the conditions of the marital estate of each new union. André Pascain, after working for many years for a cousin and scraping together a supplement to a modest dot, in 1709 married Marie Ansalier, heir to a small property. She died 16 years later, leaving five children. In 1728 Pascain married a widow, and on the same day two of his children married two of the children of his new wife. The closed cycle of dots made it unnecessary actually to exchange property. Pierre Pascain was the heir to one ousta and Pierre Farnier to the other. Pierre Pascain and his new wife resided with his father and his new wife, Pierre's wife's mother. According to their contract, young Catherine brought 200 livres to Pierre, who ceded it to his father in exchange for the heritage. The father in turn endowed his outmarrying daughter with the same sum, giving it to the son-in-law, who ceded it to his mother in exchange for his heritage. Catherine the elder gave it to her daughter, Catherine the younger.

This kind of "closed" circulation, while creating very strong ties between the two households and getting around the problem of breaking up part of the patrimony to endow children, was not designed to multiply relations with other patrimonial lines. It was too restrictive to offer a line that might have chosen such a strategy over several generations of enough mobilizable ties to protect itself in the severe competition it necessarily had to engage in. Just as in Neckarhausen and rural Naples, any successful strategy had to balance the strength of particular ties with their number, and even in the case of this particular family, the marriages of other siblings were designed to open the family up to different alliances. Similarly, no patrimonial line could look to avoid dividing up some of its resources for endowing cadets because over time it would have had no debts to call in, no other lines obligated to return its gift. The exchange of dots and the establishment of alliances were the foundation for a whole system of reciprocities necessary for the continuation of an ousta and the reproduction of a patrimonial line.

The more general form of exchange involved the mediation of one or more lines between the opening of one exchange through an endowment and the return of the dot (Figure 20.4). Lamaison utilizes Lévi-Strauss's term "generalized exchange" to describe the reciprocities of this group, which entered into exchange with the expectation of an eventual return but with the direction of circulation not predetermined. All of the cycles Lamaison studied were built on a combination of three movements among associated lines: the endowment of an out-marrying cadet by a parent/heir, or of a cadet by a parent/cadet, or of a cadet by a sibling/heir. "The cycles are linked, intertwine, and are superimposed at each generation and along the generations."[13] Every house developed a complex politics of reciprocity, seeking both to keep its rank and to enter into the most prestigious alliances. A house had to be linked, on the one hand, to others inside the parish in a dense network of interconnection and, on the other, with oustas outside the parish, using now the strategy of closed, repeated exchange and now that of generalized exchange suited to the creation and maintenance of clans.

An example of how a series of interlocking exchanges can take place is shown in Figure 20.5. Since any house was engaged in a multiple set of strategies, a return could be mapped by multiple routes. What was absolutely necessary to the system was a set of intermediaries. And as Pierre Bourdieu has pointed out, time is essential to the asymmetrical tensions that maintain a social relationship.[14] To return a gift too soon is to reject it. The cycles of reciprocity here maintained debt/credit relations throughout the eighteenth century.

At that period in Neckarhausen history – at the beginning of the eighteenth century – when the reproduction of households was largely determined by inheritance, there were no patrimonial lines such as one finds in the Lozère at the same time. And the system of linkages between houses was not determined by the circulation of endowments. The criss-crossing and interlinking of households drew upon affinal connections matching wealthy with poor and establishing ever-

[13] Lamaison, "Stratégies matrimoniales," p. 737.

[14] Pierre Bourdieu, *Outline of the Theory of Practice*, trans. Richard Nice (Cambridge, 1977), pp. 3–7.

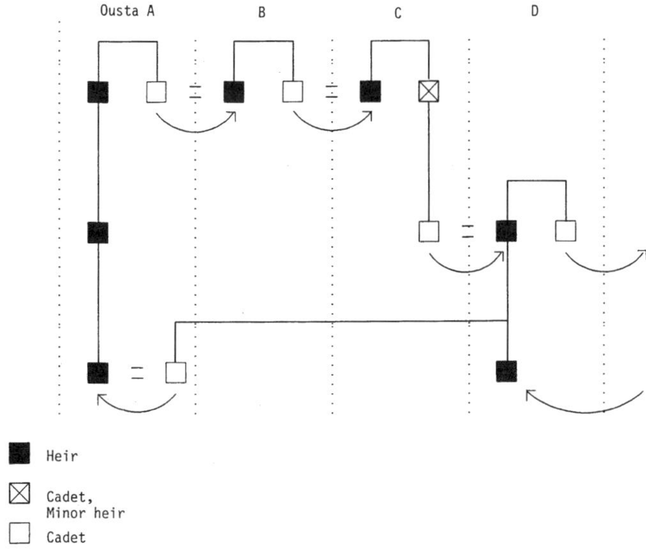

Figure 20.4

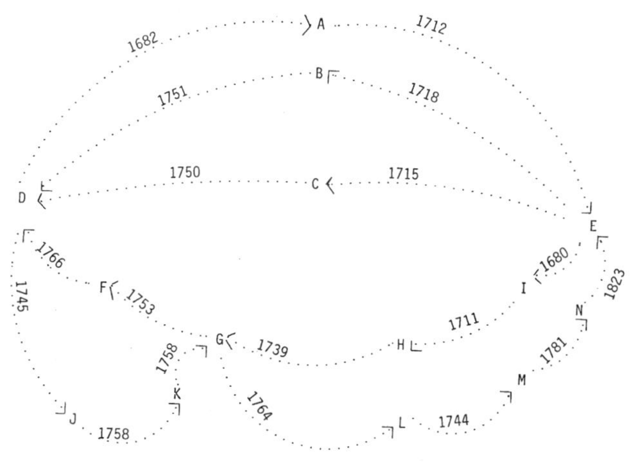

Figure 20.5

changing conglomerations of patrons and clients. The goal was much the same, however, for the two societies: building clanlike groups or kindreds that could be coordinated for protection, labor, tools, capital, and the exploitation of village resources. Yet the terrain in which associations were formed differed considerably. Neckarhausen residents exploited a territory based on three-field agriculture with interlocking strips and in 1700 was already four times larger than the largest hamlet in Gévaudan. There was never a stable patrimony, and cultural forms such as naming were designed to erase memory rather than extend it across several generations. In Gévaudan the ousta cultivated land scattered in parcels interspersed with woodland and had to defend isolated and lonely pastures far away from the homestead. The ousta cultivated memory as much as it did land as a means of marking out its social and material space and creating cohesion in a fearful and intimidating landscape.

Lamaison and Claverie are able to adopt Lévi-Strauss's categories of exchange despite the fact that exchanging groups could not be created through rules of linear descent. Although there were no patrilines, there were patrimonial lines, and these acted as exchanging groups, maintaining cohesion over many generations. But the fact that they did not reproduce alliances through consanguineal ties gives a clue to the situation in Neckarhausen in the period after the Thirty Years' War. In Neckarhausen the hierarchy seems to have been built around certain nodal points: wealthy, aggressive officeholders acted as competing centers building – often overlapping – clienteles around themselves. Agnatic connections gave some stability to the system, with brothers, their sons, and nephews coordinating their production, politics, marriages, and naming practices – all in the absence of stable property units and farms, houses, or lines identifiable over more than one generation.

By the middle of the eighteenth century, Neckarhausen broke with the clientage system of organization and created a structure whereby partners, services, and property over many generations were exchanged between patrilines. The paradox lies in the fact that memory continued to be shallow – naming practices together with teknonomy were designed to quickly blot out the past. Is the fact of consanguineal endogamy tied to the constant division of property in each generation? In Claverie and Lamaison's argument, the avoidance of endogamy was adopted in order not to concentrate property and to maintain the coherence and viability and independence of each house. Was endogamy adopted in Neckarhausen to combat the dispersion of property in a partible inheritance situation put under pressure by population rise, indebtedness, and the development of a land market? Not in any direct way. What took place was more like the construction of syndicates to manage the flow of property and resources rather than a policy of protecting a stable, transmitted estate.

The situation for Gévaudan over the long run is obscured by our inability to follow the process of shifting from the "classic" kinship system to the "modern" one. Early twentieth-century statistics clearly show that consanguineal endogamy strongly characterized the region a hundred years after the discussion of the data by Lamaison stops. His argument for the avoidance of consanguineal marriages derives from three concerns: people wanted to maintain the independence of each house, avoid concentrating property, and ensure that as many cadet members of an ousta as possible could be independently established. Certainly it was not a problem of consanguineal marriages as such but simply a problem of avoiding marriages between two heirs. All other marriages would have had the same dynamics of asymmetry and the circulation of endowments. In no system in Europe where consanguineal marriages were frequent did all marriages involve relatives. There was always more than enough room for opening up new alliances. Part of the explanation for the lack of strong unilineal thinking derives from the fact that farm complexes offered an already linear structure in place. But why then did people avoid kin? The authors concentrate on the circulation of dots and disregard the possibility of chaining through affinal kin. Thinking about systematic connections among affines might have offered forms similar to those discovered by Segalen or those found for Neckarhausen at the beginning of the eighteenth century. In any event, I think they are right to see that the avoidance of consanguineal kin was closely tied to the construction of clans and the politics of clientele formation. The point was to knit together groups defined vertically, supporting hierarchies through integration of wealthy and poor, much as in the systems in early eighteenth-century Neckarhausen and rural Naples. Claverie and Lamaison point to several developments in the nineteenth century that offer clues to a restructuring of social relations. Population pressure and economic reorganization there as well brought about increasing social differentiation. Long before a mass exodus began, families had to exclude more and more cadets from any hope of endowment, and a large class of dependent poor developed. The authors point toward an increasing "individualism" – which is not described in great detail – but suggests behavior loosened from ousta solidarities and increasingly embedded in class culture. It was in the context of class formation that consanguineal endogamy seems to have arisen – the creation of dense transfer points coordinating interests, activities, and values along horizontal rather than vertical tracks.

In the context of a different reproductive system but in a similar reorientation from vertical to horizontal relations, Neckarhausen developed much earlier an alliance system in which related kin continued to exchange with each other over the generations. It did not lead to the concentration of property as such – although this can be thought of in two ways – in terms of piecing together strategically useful pieces of land (e.g., putting back together previously divided fields) or in terms of accumulating wealth. In Neckarhausen marriages were never concerned with reassembling a fractured patrimony through marriage. It was much simpler to buy a pasture from a cousin than to spend the rest of one's life in wedded bliss to attain it. As for concentrating property by marrying a cousin, it was just as easy to attain that goal by marrying out – as many people in fact did. One has to see continuous exchanges between lines as part of a wider system of maintaining social and political hierarchy through the systematic coordination and mobilization of horizontal connections. In the absence of patrimonial lines or clearly demarcated houses with stable traditions in a society, the coordination can take place in various ways. It can associate male siblings together and reproduce their relationships as the generations turn by continuing to offer a basis for cooperation to their successors. Without founding continuing alliances on the memory of agnatic lines, such lines can still be thought of as exchanging with each other over many generations. But there was no reference in the actors' language back to unilineal principles, only the concentrated attention of parents and children on other people connected most intensely through fathers and brothers. Such coordination could just as well take place through the mediation of strategically placed women. The difference is that the patrilineal situation reflects solidarity among brothers, while the "matrifocal" one reflects networks constructed by women on the basis of multiple ties, not particular solidarity with sisters. What is clear is that all of these forms in Neckarhausen and Gévaudan constructed dense overlappings of kin on the basis of constant reciprocities, marriage being only one of the most highly structured switching points.

South Brittany

Martine Segalen has studied the economy and marriage system for the South Breton region of Bigouden, centering her work on the community of Saint-Jean-Trolimon.[15] Like Württemberg, this region was characterized by partible inheritance, the equal division of a family estate to all children, male and female, but there was one crucial difference in the kinds of goods that circulated in the two places. In Bigouden until the end of the nineteenth century, peasants did not own or have inheritable rights to the subsoil. Their property consisted of movables (cash, furniture, livestock) and "reparative rights" (the buildings, crops, and topsoil on the lands they farmed). Leases lasted for nine years, and only in exceptional cases could tenants arrange with a landlord to have a tenancy divided among some of the heirs. In many cases no child succeeded a parent on the farm. There was no attachment to a particular holding in a population that continually moved around the region, abandoning one leasehold and taking on another as the fortunes of the family or its domestic cycle altered. Kin were dispersed over the entire territory: most people married or moved out of the place they were born but sought partners strictly within the confines of South Bigouden. Segalen stresses that the most important good that circulated in this situation was information – knowledge about the property situation of prospective spouses and about available leases. The system of partible inheritance favored no particular child: most of them married and did so on average much younger than in other parts of France. In a situation where there were no active youth groups to provide a counterbalance to the wishes of the older generation, marriages were almost always arranged by the parents.

Over the course of the nineteenth century, partible inheritance, coupled with a significant population rise, altered the conditions of wealth accumulation considerably. During the last half of the eighteenth century, a very wealthy stratum of farmers emerged who accumulated leases and sublet a number of them (to kin). In the first decades of the nineteenth century, population pressure caused

[15] Martine Segalen, *Fifteen Generations of Bretons: Kinship and Society in Lower Brittany 1720–1980*, trans. J. A. Underwood (Cambridge, 1991).

such families to parcel out the leases among heirs, and over the course of the century each generation held fewer resources than the previous ones. Despite increasing impoverishment, however, the distribution of wealth maintained a stable curve – much as in Neckarhausen. Only at the end of the century, when landlords sold their subsoil rights to tenants, did a process of farm partition begin, which had the effect of equalizing the distribution of wealth throughout the society and impoverishing everyone.

For present purposes, I examine the structures of kinship alliance from the late eighteenth to the end of the nineteenth century, the period of growing competition for productive resources. Just as in Neckarhausen, the reckoning of kin was radically cognatic: relatives traced through men and women equally. In the first instance, argues Segalen, this was the result of a partible inheritance system that stressed the equal contribution of both lines, but cognatic accounting was central in Gévaudan (impartible inheritance) and rural Naples (male lineages). Despite the dubious correlation between collateral reckoning of kin and equality between male and female heirs, Segalen is right to stress the fact that the form of partible inheritance was part of a complex set of practices that precluded the establishment of lineages. Couples matched their marriage portions equally, and both sexes received a dowry from their parents. Knowledge of ancestors was very shallow, and judging from present-day evidence, many people could not remember the surname of at least one of their grandparents. Knowledge of great grandparents was almost nonexistent. Evidence from naming practices in Neckarhausen indicates that earlier generations also fell into forgetfulness there. Parents seldom named their children for their own parents and never for their grandparents, and the practice of teknonymics induced quick forgetfulness of the deceased. Although vertical information in Bigouden and in Neckarhausen was scanty, knowledge of horizontally reckoned kin was extensive in both places. Segalen adopts the term "kindred" to designate this shifting group of individuals that was tied to a person through blood or marriage. Any spouse's information about the relatives of his or her partner was just as extensive as that about his or her own.

Segalen introduces the concept of the "kindred" to describe a set of interacting kin who systematically exchange with one another but who lack certain features, classically described by Lévi-Strauss, of societies that enter into repeated patterns of reciprocity. Basically, although there was repeated exchange, there were no groups that exchanged with one another. In contrast to single-son inheritance regions or those territories marked by constant succession of the same family to a farm, here there was no "house," no "symbolic attachment to a place." As a result, there was no spatially constructed center around which family organization could be conceptualized. The strong bilateral reckoning of kin, coupled with the constant dispersal of relatives on new tenures, precluded the development of unilineal descent groups. In Neckarhausen, despite a similar bilateral reckoning, partible inheritance, and equal partitioning of the parental estate, it seemed that indeed a unilineal – in this case, a patrilineal – structure could emerge. Yet I would agree with Segalen that such lines did not constitute exchanging groups.

The patrilineal feature that stands out in the diagrams in this study resulted from a series of horizontal connections arising from everyday exchanges among men through work, property holding, and politics. Between the two societies, the crucial difference had to do with the way farms were constituted. In South Bigouden, leases could not be partitioned, and thus a family was scattered over the region, whereas in Neckarhausen tenancies were constantly divided and the closest kin continually anchored in the village. Yet in nineteenth-century Neckarhausen, different occupational groups developed different spatial distributions of kindred. Peasants remained more rooted in the village than artisans, who relied on kin providing an information network distributed across the region. Segalen describes the kindred in the following way:

> The domestic group was situated within a vast network of consanguine and affinal ties with which there was no patrimonial interaction but via which essential information regarding tenancies and marriages would circulate. A genealogical memory that was brief in relation to previous generations but vast at the level of collaterality and alliance – those are the twin features of family organisation as delineated by the mode of property transmission. In a word the system was distinguished by its horizontality. (P. 86)

In Segalen's analysis the kindred is considered from the point of view of a particular person, an ego, who "locates himself within a kinship system that is invariably concrete and never disembodied from locality and employment" (p. 90). All of the consanguines and affines together with consanguines of affines and affines of consanguines make up the kindred. At one level, such a kindred is not and cannot be a property-holding group. But Segalen refers throughout to a more loosely structured bundle of rights and claims designated as the "patrimony." The kindred, in terms of the network of kin who interact with one another, keep the patrimony intact by ensuring members of equal status access to property by means of homogamous marriage. In the end, she is suggesting that the patrimony of the kindred constitutes a complex but integrated communication system, exchanging knowledge, ritual support, and spouses.

Segalen, borrowing from an earlier study of the village of Minot in Burgundy, adopts the term "relinking" to describe how kindreds maintained stability.[16] In Lévi-Strauss's account of generalized exchange, specific groups based on unilineality exchange wives in one direction and bridewealth in another. The circularity of the system ensures that wife-givers will be rewarded eventually by receiving a suitable wife in return, and the movement of women and property in opposite directions maintains the tensions of asymmetric gift-giving and the necessity to close the circle once again. But here there were no groups, strict bilaterality, and a dowry system that caused wealth to follow the spouse in the same direction. Segalen, however, still wants to hold on to the notion of exchange:

[16] Tina Jolas, Yvonne Verdier, and Françoise Zonabend, " 'Parler famille,' " *L'Homme* 10 (1970): 5–26; "Cousinage, voisinage," in *Echanges et communications, Mélanges offerts à Claude Lévi-Strauss* (Paris, 1970), pp. 169–80.

"What gave that system its structure were those very stable kindreds that counter-balanced the individual mobility of domestic groups. . . . Within themselves, kindreds organised an active policy of exchange" (p. 122). Reciprocity lay in getting back a spouse in such a way that the patrimony did not become detached from the set of lines with which it was associated. "This opening-up process was necessary to avoid falling into the trap of consanguine marriage while still remaining among people one knew" (p. 122). In this way, the system exemplifies Lévi-Strauss's picture of generalized exchange, whose purpose in the end was to ensure marriages among people of the same status. Segalen is not clear here why she thinks of consanguineal marriage as a "trap," and it is important to see that the system of relinking that she discovered in Brittany arose at the same time and developed similar features to those in areas that came to integrate kindreds through consanguineal forms of exchange.

Consanguineal marriages never played much of a role in South Bigouden in contrast to affinal ones. Although toward the end of the nineteenth century, consanguineal marriages to distant cousins did make up an increasing number of marriages among kin, close consanguines were avoided, and the region never attained rates typical even in other parts of the same département. Between 1831 and 1970, Saint-Jean-Trolimon had a 2.7 percent rate of marriage between all up through third cousins, in contrast to nearby Plogoff with 8.9 percent. The special feature in the system examined by Segalen is the relinking through close affinal kin, which attained rates of 80 percent in the second half of the nineteenth century.

Segalen begins her analysis with examples from the eighteenth century of chaining or "cascading" that interwove generations and provided families with the possibility of accumulating wealth through the multiplication of leases held in one hand or ensuring succession to a linked line. Figure 20.6 provides several examples. About these examples Segalen comments: "Without there having been any question of a rule-induced regularity or of conscious behaviour, it is possible to see these chain marriages as a manifestation of the thing that underlies the whole system of kinship and marriage in the region, namely the enormous stability of kindreds and the high level of people's knowledge about their matrimonial and social situations" (pp. 97–8). Because for the most part Segalen was only able to trace genealogies back to the 1720s and 1730s, she is not able to comment on the earlier system of marriage. What should be clear, however, is that she has located a strategy that was closely tied up with the development of increasing social differentiation, the formation of a wealthy stratum of farm tenants, and the monopoly of office by the wealthier tenant farmers. She points out that the wealthier the lines were, the more integrated they were and the fewer links they had with other lines. Poorer lines were linked to a wider number of other lines, but both ends of the spectrum were similarly dispersed throughout the region. As population pressure ate away at the resources of wealthier lines, they too sought to create wider networks of information by integrating more lines in their matrimonial politics. Segalen points out that the small growth in distant

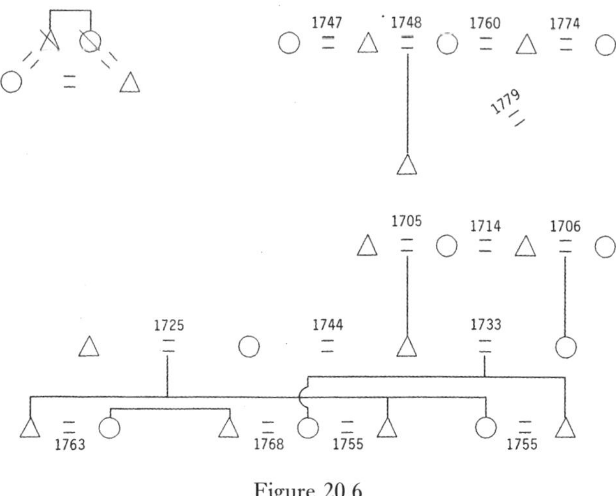

Figure 20.6

consanguineal marriages at the end of the nineteenth century was a by-product of close affinal linking and had nothing to do with reconstituting a farmstead broken up by inheritance but with information circulating about vacant farmsteads. After several generations of affinal marriages, not only were generations confused, but any individual had multiple consanguineal and affinal relations with others.

Segalen develops the thesis that the ties of kinship between very close relatives are "characterised by affectivity and competitiveness" (p. 126). It was therefore necessary to avoid such kin in favor of those where "partimonial competitiveness" was insignificant. "There seems to have been a conscious policy of not marrying relatives where there were interests at stake" (p. 127). In Bigouden, this led to a stress on close affinal kin as marriage partners and, where consanguines came in question, only those who were "no kin at all." She compares her material with a study of nineteenth-century Valencia, where there was also a partible inheritance system and where first cousins, quite unlike those in South Bigouden, shared no affective ties.[17] The high rate of consanguineal endogamy was possible because cousin ties were slack and because such marriages allowed each generation to put divided patrimonies back together. In Bigouden,

> kindreds were not groups of kin sharing a collective feeling of belonging, owning assets in common, and having identical interests to defend. They were nameless groups comprising those individuals who were "no kin" but were nonetheless not total strangers. It

[17] Joan F. Mira, "Mariage et famille dans une communauté rurale du pays de Valence (Espagne)," *Etudes rurales* 42 (1971): 105–19.

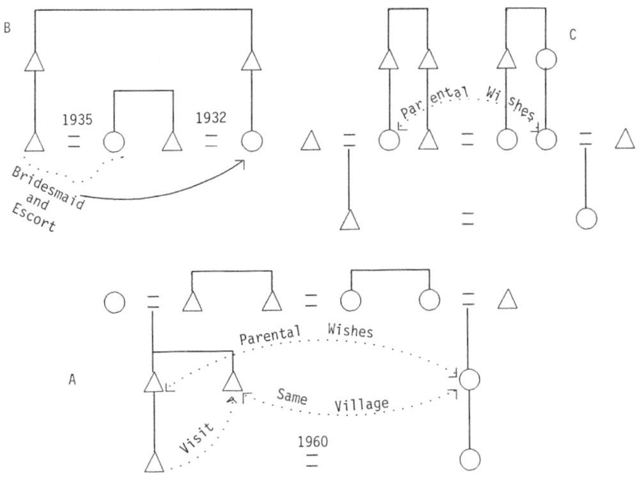

Figure 20.7

was members of his kindred that a person must marry, without any feeling of incest being involved – first because of the coolness of affinal relationships and secondly because the church did not prohibit such unions. A member of one's kindred was preferred as a spouse because his or her own kinship (and therefore also economic and social) situation was already known as a result of a previous marriage. And there could be no relationship of competitiveness with such a person over a shared patrimony. (pp. 127–8)

Relinking was the result of parental wishes. Children had no great opportunity to get to know each other on their own, although certain festivals and the very large weddings provided opportunities for parents to make young people whose marriage was already under consideration acquainted with each other (Figure 20.7). In example A here, the bridegroom visited his uncle frequently in another village where the mother of his future bride also lived. His father and her mother negotiated the marriage that took place in 1960. In example B, the partners who married in 1935 were brought together by their parents as bridesmaid and escort at an earlier wedding in 1932. And the marriage in example C was effected by the mothers – whose cousins were married to each other – of the neogami.

Segalen observes:

Matrimonial exchanges are unintelligible outside their social and economic context. . . . In South Bigouden if a man marries his first cousin or his father's first wife's niece it is not because she is a consanguine or an affine. Either she is in line to succeed to a farm that is about to become free or her dowry, added to the capital already accumulated, will suffice to set the couple up on their own. Here, too, matrimonial regularities are impossible to explain in isolation from the social relationships of production and outside the economic context within which they occur. (p. 146)

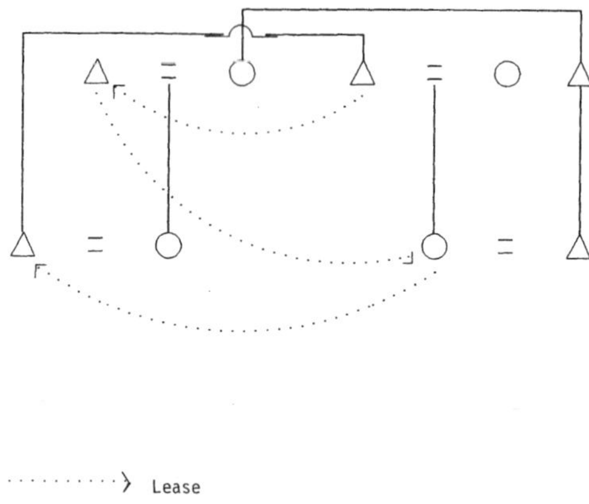

Figure 20.8

This point can be illustrated by the example of how a particular lease circulated within a kindred (Figure 20.8). Segalen points out that guardianship, godparentage, loans, political support, aid in insolvency, and other forms of exchange circulated in the same manner.

Segalen concludes that studies of European peasant societies have drawn contrasts between single-son and partible inheritance regions that are too sharp. She thinks that important continuities run through different rural social formations. In many ways, all peasant societies tend toward egalitarianism, but what links them even more centrally is that they all "develop marriages between affines" (p. 292). This latter point, for her, is the desideratum for future research.

Segalen's study raises a number of issues for the conceptualization of the findings in Neckarhausen. She provides an important analysis of a society with a relatively short memory, where ancestors play little role in the discourse of everyday politics. Yet despite short vertical genealogical reckoning, people were able to develop extensive knowledge of kin scattered over an extended territory. The constant interaction of relatives as guardians, godparents, lenders and borrowers, and so forth provided extensive knowledge for channeling resources to various individuals. Segalen is primarily concerned with strategies for locating marriage partners, for maintaining and developing long-lasting ties. She also underlines the role of mediators, of individuals – usually older, often women – who maintain the necessary knowledge and who constantly discuss the different possibilities of connecting up the circuits. A young man provided with a wife may be quite oblivious to how the particular arrangement came about and years later might not be able to give even a vaguely correct account of how his marriage was arranged. He might think he caught the eye of a bridesmaid at his older brother's wedding, not knowing how much discussion lay behind the pairing of two particular patrimonies.

Different societies in Europe modeled relations among kin in different ways, some of them – both rural and urban – using a map of genealogical ancestors in the give and take of everyday life. Vernier offers a fine example of this for a Greek community at the turn of the twentieth century.[18] In nineteenth-century German middle-class discourse, ancestors offered men a strong sense of genealogical continuity, of a patrilineal grid that gave them orientation and stability in a rapidly changing society.[19] In the early volumes of the *Allgemeine deutsche Biographie,* patrilineal discourse so predominated that mothers and wives of famous men were frequently not mentioned at all. Segalen's analysis calls attention to horizontal networks and to the importance of affinal connections, and this clearly is the missing element in much consideration of the role of kin in European societies. She considers two contrasting territories: consanguineal and affinal. In the former group are to be found rivals for the same patrimony, deep emotional attachments, the closest coordinating kin. Marriage jumped over such "interested" kin to draw back into the familial orbit those people connected by marriage just beyond the space where emotion and competition ruled.

Some of the issues Segalen raises in her analysis of relinking can be studied for Neckarhausen for the period at the beginning of the eighteenth century. There, the intent of relinking through affinal chains was opposite to that of Segalen's late eighteenth- and nineteenth-century example. Affinal marriages dispersed the "patrimony" in Neckarhausen, linking wealthy with poor. In Segalen's example a similar strategy was intended to keep a set of resources (leases) inside a group of allied lines and to match like with like. It does appear that the system of clientage operating inside Neckarhausen in the early period cast close relatives together emotionally and materially on the basis of work by central political and financial figures in the village who constructed "friendships" around themselves. Such a system may well have followed the logic Segalen suggests and practiced extensive incest prohibitions more as a result of social organization than from pious adherence to state–church rule. Indeed, I have argued that the values precipitated in religious ordinances were widely shared among the population. Still, the two affinal systems worked basically in quite different contexts – in South Bigouden it knit together lines of people across an entire district, whereas in Neckarhausen it structured the dynamics of faction formation inside a modest-sized village.

The affinal system that Segalen describes also developed in a quite different phase from the affinal "relinking" system in Neckarhausen. In South Bigouden, it first emerged in a period of population increase and was associated with social differentiation. Those most intent on the practice were accumulating leases and monopolizing property for themselves. In the similar phase of population increase and economic development, Neckarhausen (and rural Naples) abandoned affinal

[18] Bernard Vernier, "Putting Kin and Kinship to Good Use: the Circulation of Goods, Labour, and Names on Karpathos (Greece)," in Hans Medick and David Warren Sabean, eds., *Interest and Emotion: Essays on the Study of Family and Kinship* (Cambridge, 1984), pp. 28–76; "Emigration et déreglement du marché matrimonial," *Actes de la recherche en sciences sociales* 15 (1977): 31–58.

[19] See the discussion in Chapter 22 in this volume.

relinking for a consanguineally driven system. In Neckarhausen, children replicated the marriages of their parents and grandparents more directly. Both forms of "endogamy" – consanguinity in Neckarhausen and relinking in South Bigouden – were developed in the context of social differentiation and class formation (although Segalen never speaks of "classes" but only of social hierarchies). In this period of increasing population, familial dynamics in Neckarhausen were established in the context of an ever-growing land market internal to the village. By contrast, the marriage system in South Bigouden was not concerned with a land market but with succession to leaseholds, which by and large maintained their integrity throughout the nineteenth century. Marriage always linked people across the district in South Bigouden, whereas marriage in Neckarhausen always involved a majority of village-endogamous unions of people who would live out their lives in place. In Neckarhausen, in the phase of building systematic alliances between the same families over time, people began to overlay close consanguineal kin and affines in a tighter system. Marriage partners no longer came from what Segalen considers to be the "cool" side of the line but from the "hot" side – the relatives most interested in the family's economy, those for whom the emotional bonds and competitiveness were most in evidence. By contrast, the desire to extend out further through chains of in-laws – in South Bigouden in the nineteenth century and in Neckarhausen at the beginning of the eighteenth century – had to do with building extended kindred and maximizing the group of clients or the number of contacts offering reliable communication. The extensive exogamy practices coupled with building and operating affinal chains could be modeled in terms of marriage with those kin who were "no kin at all," the two analogous structures being oriented to opposite concerns – homogamy in Bigouden and heterogamy in Neckarhausen.

Although the marriage structure in nineteenth-century Neckarhausen cannot be reduced to the competition for land, the building of affinal relations through class and consanguineal alliances has to be understood in the context of competition for resources in a situation in which landholding was subject in each generation to increasing fissioning. The constant overlapping of the same relationships through underwriting loans, choosing godparents, acting as guardians, putting together plow teams, and selecting marriage partners was an effective way of managing the property interests of a series of allied families. In contrast to South Bigouden, the manner in which resources circulated encouraged a strategy of tighter integration. Nonetheless, Segalen is right to see affinal relations as a key to various European rural societies. The point in Neckarhausen was to make consanguines into affines. Every link in the chain of an alliance set up a new series of exchanges between those brought into the orbit of a household.

The newly mobile workforce in Neckarhausen that developed increasingly from the first decades of the nineteenth century seems to display Segalen's logic of marrying and choosing godparents beyond the closest relatives. And as in South Bigouden the purpose was to develop networks across the region, which served as communication fields for men in building trades looking for short-term and casual employment, who coordinated work teams for road, railroad, and building construction. But even here there was for many families a strong tendency to find consanguineal kin to turn into affines. I would not rule out, however, the possibility that other strategies could also have been at work. Certain forms of affinal marriage are known to have increased in Neckarhausen just as they did in Saint-Jean-Trolimon – sibling exchange, the sororate, the levirate. Perhaps workers also utilized affinal chains in the district when looking for marriage partners – it would be difficult to find them by our method of family reconstitution limited to one village. But the important point is that consanguineal marriages themselves brought a series of in-laws, who played a various roles for one another over the life of a family, into tighter integration.

* * *

One problem with many of the classical anthropological studies of kinship lies in the contrast that Lévi-Strauss draws between societies organized on "elementary" principles and those based on "complex" ones. The formulation is not a completely happy one because "elementary" and "complex" do not overlap with simple and advanced economies. Furthermore, investigations into the practical realities of elementary prescriptive systems suggest their demographic improbability and a problematic relation to reality. Jack Goody and Pierre Bourdieu have each in their own way tried to move the discussion away from structuralist assumptions to a study of practices, without thereby losing the interpretive power to paint cultural areas with broad brush strokes.[20] In my remarks here, however, I want to remain inside European culture, and my aim is to understand the forms of kinship that arose during the late eighteenth century and lasted well through the nineteenth.

The basic point raised by Lévi-Strauss is that formal, structural principles of kinship exist where society is largely organized around kinship. In such societies, the web of social relationships is dominated by the exchange of women, whose properties are largely determined by differential descent. Lévi-Strauss's principle of exchange is modeled upon the notion of the "gift," the circulation of which puts groups into a fundamental tension of always being one another's debtors or creditors.[21] Modern European society is "structureless" in the specific sense that there are no rules of exchange and no prescriptive principles that conjoin people to particular marriage alliances. Nor are there any specially marked out groups with clear boundaries that exchange marriage partners. Debtor and creditor relationships are not embedded in collective memory, because there are no groups

[20] Jack Goody, *Production and Reproduction: A Comparative Study of the Domestic Domain* (Cambridge, 1976); *The Development of the Family and Marriage in Europe* (Cambridge, 1983); and *The Oriental, the Ancient and the Primitive: Systems of Marriage and the Family in Pre-Industrial Societies of Eurasia* (Cambridge, 1990). Pierre Bourdieu, *Outline*; *The Logic of Practice,* trans. Richard Nice (Stanford, 1990).

[21] The theory was worked out by Marcel Mauss, *The Gift: Forms and Functions of Exchange in Archaic Society,* trans. Ian Cunnison (London, 1966).

exchanging marriage partners who maintain and service such memory as part of their strategies of alliance formation. Formal kinship structures, embedded in elementary forms of restricted (FZD) and generalized (MBD) marriage, are opposed by material interest, property considerations, and a money economy.

This study of Neckarhausen and the comparative excursion into three quite different rural territories indicate that there were indeed formal aspects to kinship throughout both the "classical" and the "modern" periods. But in contrast to the social groups discussed by Lévi-Strauss, no society was organized around one particular form of exchange. The system in Europe offers a kind of bricolage, utilizing bits and pieces of exchange principles, adding up in Delille's phrase, to "structure in a structureless system." Through the construction of dense networks of overlapping and parallel lines, utilizing now this and now that strategic principle, families built in the tensions of classical exchange, keeping the flow of alternating current active throughout the system. Segalen's work shows that it is not necessary to have established groups in order to have exchange, and both Delille and Claverie and Lamaison provide examples of stable exchanging partners that do not fit the model of unilineal descent. Segalen also shows that deep memory is not necessary to keep the play of reciprocity alive. In the criss-crossing of active members of any one generation connected to one another through marriage or blood, a dense network of integrated activity itself constitutes a system with more or less well marked out boundaries. In such a network, alliances established by marriage provide some of the most basic channels for the pattern of exchange throughout the society. The different principles of exchange allow families to balance the strength of ties with their number. Only the overall strategy calls for both restricted and generalized gambits, so to speak. In Delille's "classical" model, a number of restricted exchange practices, such as marriage between an aunt and nephew pair and an uncle and niece pair, fit together with generalized exchange forms, and both fit within a larger framework of consanguineal return after four or five generations. In the analysis of Claverie and Lamaison, centered on the circulation of dowries, families could create strong ties through short cycles of circulation or proliferate ties through longer ones, the authors consciously working with Lévi-Strauss's conceptualization of restricted and generalized exchange. Segalen too offers alternate patterns of "cascading" (restricted) and more open strategies of relinking.[22] For Neckarhausen, I have contrasted two quite different periods. In the first I found patterns like those analyzed by Delille – siblings marrying patrilateral first cousins, uncle and niece marrying siblings or aunt and nephew. In the second, there were alternative strategies of restricted (FZD) and generalized (MBD) exchange and even a form designed to create the tightest coordination inside a patrilineage (FBD). Here once again, the alternative perspectives of different strategies were oriented toward consolidation of social ties and the proliferation of new ones. A departure in one generation provided the foundation for renewal in the next.

[22] She expressly denies the possibility of consanguineal return after many generations have passed.

Each of these studies poses the paradoxical question of how kinship (form) and class (interest) can be coupled together. The new forms of endogamy, whether consanguineal (Naples, Neckarhausen, Gévaudan after 1870) or relinkage (South Bigouden), were all clearly related to a shift away from vertically structured clans, lineage quarters, and clienteles to more horizontally structured social relations. Consanguineal and all the other forms of kin-linked marriages in the nineteenth century were closely bound up with homogamy. And in the new situation, obligation, mutual recognition, and cultural stabilities were intertwined with reciprocities constructed through affinal and consanguineal networks. The new forms of kinship utilized elementary principles of exchange to construct flexibly coordinated strata out of a complex web of reciprocities. The system was oriented at one pole toward a practice of homogamy and at the other toward what Segalen sees as a coordinated information system. Repeated exchanges across a landscape participated in the layering of strata, and the intense activity of intercourse with peers shaped the practices that we recognize as class. Integrated groups could also become interconnected with boundary-crossing policies of hypergamy. But just because only daughters could be exchanged upward, the boundaries of class could be all the more sharply policed.

In an effort to locate the recognizable elements of exchange and exchanging groups in Western society, French scholars have fixed their attention on the notion of "patrimony" and on the *dot* as the most regular form of gift-giving they could find. Patrimony, however, as an essential element to the kinship system is of limited value. It is rooted primarily in the dynamics of the classical period, when family property was regarded as something to be preserved and passed on – as a bounded and recognizable estate. In the conditions of the nineteenth-century economy, wealth was too fluid, opportunity too inviting, and the risk of losing everything too much on the surface for people to be concerned with mere protection of a particular estate, succession to a craft, or property rights in public office. Segalen's destabilization of patrimony into a network of rights, claims, obligations, and information serves largely to rid the concept of usefulness altogether. Dowry, as anyone familiar with nineteenth-century society knows, was a chief element in establishing homogamy/hypergamy and setting up the long-term circuits of exchange (see Chapter 22). I doubt, however, whether conceptualizing the circulation of dowries as a way of bringing back structure into the network of family reciprocities is useful. The nineteenth century would increase their value almost exponentially as a factor in determining particular marriages but decrease their value in a culture of shallow memory for maintaining the repeated alliances between patrilines over time. The connection between class and kinship must be sought in the dense network of reciprocities that created homogeneous spheres of cultural recognition and in the implications of strategic bricolage rooted in new endogamic alliance practices.

21

Consanguinity in modern Europe

Although various disciplines have been concerned with kinship in Europe, none has yet considered how the region's diverse aspects of familial reciprocity have connected with one another over time. Some biographers and social historians have discussed the manner in which particular industrialists or groups of workers utilized kin, but few writers have examined the phenomenon systematically, let alone comparatively or conceptually. Of the work that has been done, more has focused on marriage than any other aspect of kinship, no doubt because since the mid nineteenth century biologists and geneticists have been interested in the physical and mental effects of consanguineal marriages on descendants. But their interests have been confined to people who demonstrably share the same "blood" or genetic makeup – those who descend from a common ancestor. For these scientists, other conceptions of incest can get in the way of their investigations. Thus a series of dispensations that failed to distinguish between marriage with a cousin and marriage with the wife's sister would fail to offer the kind of information they need. In many studies of endogamy based on easily accessible records of dispensation, just such problems arise: the rate can be skewed by the fact that an unknown percentage of couples avoided applying for dispensations, or officials might have left gaps in their records; various categories have often been handled indiscriminately (first and second cousins, cousins and sisters-in-law, relatives by blood or marriage and godkin); and reckoning of relationships might be haphazard or fail to follow prescribed rules.[1]

[1] Angelo Serra, "Italian Official Statistics on Consanguineous Marriages," *Acta Genetica* 9 (1959): 244–6, underscores the difficulty of obtaining statistics on consanguinity for the exacting standards of genetic investigation. What he says about genetics is, of course, just as true for the study of kinship. As he puts it, the data in official statistics are based on the "bona fide" of the partners and the "bona voluntas" of the officials, neither of which he puts much faith in. "The *official*

Consanguinity in Neckarhausen

To help fill the gaps just described, this chapter offers a comparative analysis, which begins with the changes in the propensity to marry kin over the eighteenth and nineteenth centuries. The primary areas of interest are Germany and Central Europe, but also to some extent northern, western, and southern Europe. The objective of the Neckarhausen study has been to determine the ways both affinal and consanguineal kin were coordinated and the way alternative kinship systems were configured according to the principles of selecting or avoiding one or the other kind of kin as marriage partners. An important finding of this study is that there is no necessary connection between the rates of marriage of consanguines and affines nor between those of one degree of consanguine or affine and another: the rate of marriage between first cousins does not predict that between third cousins or between brothers-in-law and sisters-in-law, nor does a particular choice of consanguines indicate what kind of or how many affines will be sought out. Table 21.1 summarizes the results of the investigation of the five Neckarhausen cohorts.

Even without wishing or being allowed to marry relatives related by blood, a significant number of people could find partners among families already allied to them through marriage. Early in the eighteenth century consanguineal kin were avoided well beyond those legally prohibited. I found, for example, not only no second-cousin marriages (prohibited but dispensable) but also no third-cousin marriages (not prohibited). In that situation as well, affinal marriages revealed certain patterns, defined at one end by the disinclination to link households already "too closely" allied with one another again, and at the other by recurrent links between groups of households allied through marriage or connected by agnatic descent. Over the period, marriage with affinally connected kin declined, in part at least as such unions were "absorbed" through marriages with consanguines; after several generations of consanguineal marriages, the same individuals could be both blood relatives and in-laws.

Since the emphasis here is on the way social networks were constructed, genetic studies that concentrate on consanguineal ties are of limited value. Many of them extrapolate from first-cousin marriages to general rates of consanguinity, but the legitimacy of that operation is called into question by my results. In Neckarhausen from midcentury to midcentury, the rate of first-cousin marriage more than doubled, but the ratio of first- to second- and third-cousin marriages fluctuated considerably. In the middle of the eighteenth century, villagers were much more interested in second-cousin marriages, and there were no families constructing new alliances with third cousins. The ratio of first-, second-, and third-cousin marriage was 1:5:0. By the late eighteenth century, both first- and

statistics *so far published on consanguineous marriages are absolutely unsuitable for solving problems of population genetics*" (p. 246).

Table 21.1. *Consanguineal and affinal marriages in Neckarhausen.*

Cohort	Number in sample	Kin-related	Percent	Affinal	Percent	Blood	Percent	First cousin	Percent	Second cousin	Percent	Third cousin	Percent
Cohort I, early 18th century	67	17	25.4	17	25.4	0	0.0	0	0.0	0	0.0	0	0.0
Cohort II, mid 18th century	100	39	39.0	31	31.0	8	8.0	1	1.0	5	5.0	0	0.0
Cohort III, late 18th century	101	29	28.7	17	16.8	12	11.9	2	1.9	2	1.9	2	1.9
Cohort IV, early 19th century	122	32	26.2	18	14.8	14	11.5	2	1.6	4	3.3	2	1.6
Cohort V, mid 19th century	83	41	49.4	13	15.7	28	33.7	2	2.4	7	8.4	9	10.8

third-cousin marriages grew in relation to second-cousin ones, with a ratio of 1:1:1. Early in the nineteenth century, it was 1:2:1, and by midcentury, it was 1:4:5. Considering that the number of available marriage partners increases with the widening of the circle of kin from first to second to third cousins, only the last ratio reflects an interest in all kinds of cousins out to and including third cousins, with frequencies increasing – even if in decreasing proportion – with availability. The lesson here is that consanguinity can only be extrapolated from first-cousin data with great care.

Between 1740 and 1870, the overall rates of consanguinity for Neckarhausen rose considerably. For ease of discussion, I have not given the rates for first cousins/second cousins/third cousins once removed. But for all identifiable consanguineal marriages between 1740 and 1870, the rates rose by 400 percent. Altogether about a quarter of the marriages at the beginning of the eighteenth century took place between kin, even if none involved relatives by blood. By 1870 half of them did so, but by then one out of every three marriages reproduced alliances between consanguineal kin. This rise of endogamous marriage was a general phenomenon in Europe during the nineteenth century, and the pace and direction of change in Neckarhausen fits well into the usual pattern. From the data in this study, it seems that a 1 or 2 percent rate of first-cousin marriage (the rate reported in most genetic studies) *can* indicate a far higher rate of kin-linked marriages. In fact, the experience in Neckarhausen during the nineteenth century suggests a cumulative rate 15 to 20 times greater than that for first-cousin marriages alone. Taking just consanguineal marriages, the overall proportion between cohorts II and IV was 6 to 7 times that for first-cousin marriages alone. By cohort V, it was 14 times greater. The point here is not to measure genetic similarities but to gauge the extent of the restructuring of kinship through kin-linked marriages. At the same time, the data produced by geneticists will be used to track a wider phenomenon.

Consanguinity in Central Europe since ca. 1880

Most genetic studies begin at some point late in the nineteenth century or early in the twentieth. Depending on when a particular study was done, comparisons can be carried out over a more or less long period. All of the studies concur in the description of a high point in consanguineal marriages reached between 1880 and 1920, with a regular and sometimes abrupt decline to a point in the 1950s when such marriages became insignificant almost everywhere.

Studies of the marriage of consanguines have generally followed three kinds of methodological procedures: genealogical investigation, tabulation of dispensations, or extrapolation from surname matching (isonymy). All of the approaches can be useful, but each provides certain limitations. Thoroughgoing family reconstitutions familiar to historical demographers offer the most accurate data, and although they are generally limited to one or a small group of parishes, they can be used to check work done by other means. In a study of four parishes in the Pyrenees, Jacqueline Bourgoin and Vu Tien Khang found that rates based on a total family reconstitution were double those established by a study of official dispensations.[2] On the other hand, when standard methods of extrapolation from surname matching were used, rates were too high.[3] During the 1920s, various Central European geneticists carried out studies of selected localities using genealogical techniques. The methods varied a good deal, and the details of the procedures were not always rigorously discussed.[4] Most of the researchers apparently followed the ancestors of a particular cohort back through parish registers or consulted the local *Familienbücher* (registers of families) or *Ortssippenbücher* (village genealogies) or *Stammbäume* (family trees).[5] A few took the trouble to check through the parish registers of all the surrounding villages.

The rates of endogamy from these various studies varied significantly (Table 21.2).[6] All of the authors pointed out that the use of dispensation records intro-

[2] Jacqueline Bourgoin and Vu Tien Khang, "Quelques aspects de l'histoire génétique de quatre villages pyrénéens depuis 1740," *Population* 33 (1978): 633–59.

[3] For various views on the usefulness of isonymy, see John Friedl and Walter S. Ellis, "Inbreeding, Isonymy, and Isolation in a Swiss Community," *Human Biology* 46 (1974): 699–712; and their "Inbreeding as Measured by Isonymy and by Pedigrees in Kippel, Switzerland," *Social Biology* 23 (1976): 158–61. A comparison of the "pedigree" and "isonomy" methods for two Swiss villages and a warning against the "careless application of isonomy" (p. 375) is found in Walter S. Ellis and William T. Starmer, "Inbreeding as Measured by Isonymy, Pedigrees, and Population Size in Törbel, Switzerland," *Human Genetics* 30 (1978): 366–76.

[4] But see Hermann Brenk, "Ueber den Grad der Inzucht in einem innerschweizerischen Gebirgsdorf," *Archiv der Julius Klaus-Stiftung für Vererbungsforschung, Sozialanthropologie und Rassenhygiene* 6 (1931): 1–39, esp. 2–6, 9, 15.

[5] The method of studying ascendants through *Ahnentafeln* (tables of ancestors) was followed by Swiss researchers Egenter, Grob, and Brenk, as well as by Wulz and Kühn (Table 21.2 and footnote). This involved taking all or a selection of current marriages and following them back through their ancestors to a particular point in the seventeenth or eighteenth century. Although such a method gives good results for the observed generation, it is useless for studying rates in earlier generations because of out- and inmigration and marriages that produced no descendants. Only a family reconstitution together with cohort analysis can study consanguinity over time. Many of the authors – above all the Swiss – assume that their isolated villages always were characterized by consanguineal marriages, but this assumption has not been tested, and the results of work by Kühn, Khang, and others puts it in question. Egenter (Table 21.2) offers data that he does not follow up suggesting that village endogamy developed in his isolated Catholic village only after the seventeenth century. Several of the studies give much higher consanguineal rates for purely village endogamous marriages. The rates in Table 21.2 are for the population as a whole and not for the village-endogamous marriages alone.

[6] For Bergkirchen and Amt Dachau, Gustav Wulz, "Ein Beitrag zur Statistik der Verwandtenehen," *Archiv für Rassen- und Gesellschaftsbiologie* 17 (1925–6): 82–95. Note that he started with a sample of 100 marriages for Bergkirchen, so that all the percentages have no numbers after the decimal place. At a crucial passage in his paper, a misprint puts the sample at 200, and many researchers have correspondingly miscalculated his rates. For Hirschau, Wurmlingen, and Unterjesingen, see Adolf Spindler, "Ueber die Häufigkeit der Verwandtenehen in drei württembergischen Dörfern," *Archiv für Rassen- und Gesellschaftsbiologie* 14 (1922–3): 9–12. For Hohenzollern, see Wilhelm Reutlinger, "Ueber die Häufigkeit der Verwandtenehen bei den Juden in Hohenzollern und über Untersuchungen bei Deszendenten aus jüdischen Verwandtenehen," *Archiv für Rassen- und Gesellschaftsbiologie* 14 (1922–3): 301–5. For "Obermatt" [Illgau] in Central Switzerland (Schwyz), see Arnold Egenter, "Ueber den Grad der Inzucht in einer Schwyzer Berggemeinde und die damit zusammenhängende Häufung rezessiver Erbschäden," *Archiv der Julius Klaus-Stiftung für Vererbungsforschung, Sozialanthropologie und Rassenhygiene* 6 (1931): 1–39. For Lungern in the Swiss Kanton of Oberwalden, see Hermann Brenk, "Ueber den Grad der Inzucht in einem innerschweiz-

Table 21.2. *Consanguinity in Central European places, early twentieth century.*

Place	Period	First cousin	Second cousin	Third cousin	All through second cousin	All through third cousin
Bergkirchen (Dachau), Bavaria[a]	1900–1925	2.0	3.0	9.0	7.0	16.0
Amt Dachau (rural)[b]	1848–1922	0.6	0.57	0.08		1.4
Hirschau, Württemberg, Catholic[c]	1890–1922	2.7	11.7	8.1	14.4	26.1
Wurmlingen, Württemberg, Catholic[c]	1890–1922	0.7	7.2	2.9	10.1	15.9
Unterjesingen, Württemberg, Protestant[c]	1890–1922	2.5	4.4	4.4	6.9	11.8
Haigerloch, Hohenz., Jewish[a]	late 19th century	4.9	2.4	3.6		10.9
Haigerloch, Hohenz., Jewish[d]	1900–22	16.2	3.4	2.6		22.2
Obermatt, Switzerland, Catholic[a]	1871–1931	11.5	32.7	11.5	53.8	73.1
Lungern, Switzerland, Catholic[a]	1874–1922	1.9	7.4	14.4	9.6	28.1
Amden, Switzerland, Catholic[a]	ca. 1890–1932	0.7	7.1	10.0	9.9	22.0
Wien (city)[b]	1901	0.68				
Wien (city)[b]	1913–14	0.63	0.26		0.96	
Wien (city)[b]	1929–30	0.44	0.18	0.65		
Wien (territory)[b]	1901	1.2				
Wien (territory)[b]	1913–14	0.99	1.23	2.3		
Wien (territory)[b]	1929–30	0.74	0.98	1.72		
Köln, archdiocese, Catholic[b]	1898–1943	0.37	0.46	1.0		
Village B, Eifel[a]	1910–37	0.00	11.5	1.9	13.4	15.3
Village E, Eifel[a]	1910–37	0.00	4.2	5.6	4.2	9.8

[a]Ahnentafel (genealogy).
[b]Dispensations.
[c]"Durchforscht" (started with all living marriage partners and consulted the church registers).
[d]Oral testimony.

duced particular distortions. Gustav Wulz, for example, consulted dispensations recorded in the village church registers for the entire Bavarian district of Dachau, with 40 rural parishes. For one village (Bergkirchen), he took a sample of 100 couples and followed their ancestors back through the marriage registers in order to establish independently whether the couples were related. He discovered that third cousins, although they required dispensations (this was a Catholic parish) up to 1918, seldom sought one out. Therefore the data for third cousins for the rural district were useless. He estimated that the ratio between first, second, and third cousin marriages was on the order of 1:2:4. Using that ratio, the figures for the whole district ought to have been on the order of 0.6, 1.2, and 2.4, respectively, with the total figure for all blood relations through third cousins around 5.9 percent, which is still only about a third of the rate for the one village he studied in detail – and that village had nothing unusual about it.[7] Herbert Orel, in his study of the Diocese of Wien, which was based on dispensations granted by officials of the archbishop, similarly considered the reporting of third and even second cousins to be faulty. Both he and Wulz believed the statistics for first cousins to be more reliable. Urban areas consistently reported fewer cousin marriages than rural areas. Since the former have never been the object of family reconstitution studies, the results there cannot be checked. Except for early work by George Darwin on London, geneticists have not used isonymy to study urban districts, the one method available to provide an independent check on official reporting and dispensation records. His results suggest considerable undercounting in statistics reported by government and church officials.[8] Certainly it was easier in the cities to hide blood relationships for whatever reason – suspicion of authorities, disinclination to pay a fee, or uneasiness in the face of mounting medical opinion against consanguineal marriages. The simple assumption that urban rates were lower is not warranted by the materials so far at our disposal.

In Table 21.2, several examples stand out. Among the Jewish population of

erischen Gebirgsdorf," *Archiv der Julius Klaus-Stiftung für Vererbungsforschung, Sozialanthropologie und Rassenhygiene* 6 (1931): 1–39. For Amden in St. Gallen, see Walter Grob, "Aszendenzforschungen und Mortalitätsstatistik aus einer st. gallischen Berggemeinde," *Archiv der Julius Klaus-Stiftung für Vererbungsforschung, Sozialanthropologie und Rassenhygiene* 9 (1934): 237–64. For Wien, see Herbert Orel, "Die Verwandtenehen in der Erzdiözese Wien," *Archiv für Rassen- und Gesellschaftsbiologie* 26 (1932): 249–78. For the archdiocese of Köln, see O. Freiherr von Verschuer, "Neue Befunde über die Häufigkeit von Blutsverwandtenehen in Deutschland," *Zeitschrift für Morphologie und Anthropologie* 46 (1954): 293–6. His statistics are based on Friedrich Panse and Josef Krings, "Die Häufigkeit der Blutsverwandten-Ehen der katholischen Bevölkerung in der Erzdioziöse Köln von 1898–1943," *Rheinische Vierteljahrsblätter* 14 (1948): 148–56. For two Eifel villages, see Arthur Kühn, "Inzucht und Auslese in zwei Eifeldörfern, *Archiv für Rassen- und Gesellschaftsbiologie* 31 (1937): 482–505.

7 Hermann Brenk, "Ueber den Grad der Inzucht," compared his findings with those of Wulz and came to similar conclusions. His rates for first and second cousins calculated from genealogies were not too much higher than those based on dispensations. But for third cousins, the genealogies offered rates almost 70 percent higher.

8 George H. Darwin, "Marriages between First Cousins in England and Their Effects," *Journal of the Statistical Society* 38 (1875): 153–84.

Haigerloch in Hohenzollern studied by Wilhelm Reutlinger in the early 1920s, first-cousin marriages were extraordinarily high (16.2 percent) in the two decades after 1900, whereas in the villages in the Eifel examined by Arthur Kühn, there were none at all. Reutlinger's work was used to suggest that consanguineal marriages among Jews was a distinguishing characteristic of their race, but other studies have shown high rates of consanguinity for other population enclaves.[9] Reutlinger based his study on oral testimony, and it may well be that his respondents conflated cousins of all sorts – he did think that his rates for second and third cousins were too low – and his study for the second half of the nineteenth century based on written records produced much lower results.[10] In Neckarhausen, marriage alliances were supplemented with godparentage, and the various exchanges based on land, political alliance, and property administration (guardians, Kriegsvögte) helped create a specific system of intrageneration and proximate generation connection. The ecology of the enclave Jewish population of Hohenzollern based on petty and wholesale commerce rather than land ownership and agricultural production and failing an institution such as godparentage might well have supported an endogamy favoring first cousins. At the other end of the scale were the two agricultural Eifel villages, both with high rates of consanguinity, but with a complete avoidance of first cousins. There the tight system of alliance was built upon marriage exchanges involving second and third cousins. Kühn and Adolf Spindler, who studied three villages in Württemberg, thought the rates they worked out for third cousins were considerably understated. Despite reservations with regard to the data, one can suggest that some populations in Central Europe more or less systematically built alliances through tight overlapping of first- and second- and sometimes third-cousin marriages.

Even allowing for problems with the data, there is no guarantee that populations that put a premium on first cousins were much interested in connections built upon more extended relations. At the same time, other populations might well have avoided the closest relatives, while working connections among a wider set. Yet it is worthwhile asking what a particular rate of first-cousin or second-cousin marriage might indicate. In my last Neckarhausen cohort, I found a ratio of 1:4:5 for first to second to third cousins. Wulz found 1:1.5:4.5 for Bergkirchen. The three villages of Hirschau, Wurmlingen, and Unterjesingen gave the following results: 1:4.3:3; 1:10.2:4.1; 1:1.8:1.8. And the three Swiss villages, Obermatt, Lungern, and Amden suggest, respectively: 1:2.8:1, 1:3.8:7.6, 1:10.1:14.3. All of these villages indicate a preference for second-cousin or third-cousin marriages, but they also show that a first-cousin marriage rate of 1 to 2 percent can be associated with a much more encompassing pattern of kin-linked marriage alli-

[9] E.g., in Sweden just before the mid nineteenth century, the high nobility attained first-cousin marriage rates of 19.7 percent: Carl Henry Alström, "First-Cousin Marriages in Sweden 1750–1844 and a Study of the Population Movement in Some Swedish Subpopulations from the Genetic-Statistical Viewpoint: A Preliminary Report," *Acta Genetica* 8 (1958): 295–369.

[10] The central Swiss village of "Obermatt," with its strict Catholic population and excellent documentation, showed much higher rates of consanguinity.

ances. For Neckarhausen, by the mid nineteenth century a 2.4 percent first-cousin marriage rate went together with a rate of 33.7 percent for all blood relatives out to and including third cousins, and a further 15.7 percent affinal-marriage rate.

Consanguinity in Europe during the twentieth century

Geneticists generally pay little attention to sororate, levirate, sibling exchange, remarriage with the wife's kin, marriages connecting step-relatives, or marriages connecting lines where the partners are not blood relatives. But consanguineal marriages make up only a part of a wider system. Indeed, Martine Segalen and Philippe Richard report that in a region in Brittany only 3.6 percent of the marriages there involved consanguines out to third cousins, whereas a full 80 percent of them involved affinal links.[11] That study along with many others suggest that the rates of consanguineal and affinal marriages almost everywhere in Europe reached a peak in the several decades before World War I. After that, except for an occasional reprise during the 1920s, the rates for consanguineal marriages fell steadily until the 1950s and 1960s, when they became insignificant (Table 21.3).

It is instructive to examine two comparable studies based on diocesan records that are listed in Table 21.3. These studies were done at different times but point to similar trends. One was carried out in Wien (Vienna) by Herbert Orel (1932) and the other in Milan by Angelo Serra and Antonio Soini (1959).[12] Both of these

[11] Martine Segalen and Philippe Richard, "Marrying Kinsmen in Pays Bigouden Sud, Brittany," *Journal of Family History* 11 (1986): 109–30. Their findings are discussed at length in Chapter 20 in this volume.

[12] For Norway, Letten Fegersten Saugstad, "Inbreeding in Norway," *Annals of Human Genetics* (London) 40 (1977): 481–91; and Tobias Gedde-Dahl, Jr., "Population Structure in Norway: Inbreeding, Distance and Kinship," *Hereditas* 27 (1973), pp. 311–32. See also Saugstad, "The Relationship between Inbreeding, Migration and Population Density in Norway," *Annals of Human Genetics* (London) 30 (1977): 331–41; and Saugstad and Ørnulv Ødegård "Predominance of the Extreme Geographical Proximity of the Spouses of Heirs to Independent Farms in a Mountain Valley in Norway between 1600 and 1850," *Annals of Human Genetics* (London) 40 (1977): 419–30. For the rural district of Jara in Spain, see R. Calderon, "Inbreeding, Migration and Age at Marriage in Rural Toledo, Spain," *Journal of Biosocial Science* 15 (1983): 47–57. For Spain, see J. Pinto-Cisternas, G. Zei, and A. Moroni, "Consanguinity in Spain, 1911–1943: General Methodology, Behavior of Demographic Variables, and Regional Differences," *Social Biology* 26 (1979): 55–71. For the Pyrennean Roncal Valley, see Andrew Abelson, "Population Structure in the Western Pyrenees: II. Migration, the Frequency of Consanguineous Marriage and Inbreeding, 1877 to 1915," *Social Biology* 12 (1980): 92–101. For Errazu in the Baztan Valley in the Spanish province of Navarre, see Andrew Abelson, "Population Structure in the Western Pyrenees: Social Class, Migration and the Frequency of Consanguineous Marriage, 1850–1910," *Annals of Human Biology* 5 (1978): 167–78. The data for France – chosen here for selected French departments – are from Jean Sutter and Jean-Michel Goux, "Evolution de la consanguinité en France de 1926 à 1958 avec des données récentes détaillées," *Population* 17 (1962): 683–702. (An excerpt of this article was published in the *Eugenics Quarterly* 11 (1964): 127–40.) See also Jean Sutter and Léon Tabah, "Fréquence et répartition des mariages consanguins en France," *Population* 3, 4 (1948): 607–30; Jean Sutter and Claude Lévy, "Les dispenses civiles au mariage en France depuis 1800," *Population* 14 (1959): 285–303; Jean Sutter, "Fréquence de l'endogamie et ses facteurs au xixe siècle," *Popu-*

studies were based on records of dispensations kept at the level of the archbishopric. Orel divided his data between the city of Wien and the countryside and focused on the periods 1901, 1913–14, and 1929–30. In the city he found the rates of first-cousin marriage fell steadily, from 0.68 to 0.63 to 0.44. In the rural areas, although the rates were higher, the decline followed the same path: 1.2, 0.99, and 0.74. Despite the fact that the rates for second-cousin marriages were underestimated, they too demonstrated the same regular decline. Serra and Soini were able to observe a similar trend in the three provinces of the Milan diocese (Como, Milan, and Varese) at a vantage point 27 years later. Taking the rates for first-cousin marriages for rural Como for three selected periods, 1903–23, 1926–31, 1933–53, they found a regular decline: 4.42, 2.83, and 1.24. Rural Milan and Varese both dropped from similar high points to similar lows: 4.73 to 1.08 and 3.71 to 0.90. The city of Milan, starting with lower rates, also followed the same trend: 1.92, 1.03, and 0.64. The authors point out that the rates at the end of the long period 1933–53 were consistently much lower than at the beginning and therefore concluded that all the remaining genetic "isolates" had broken up in the course of the 1930s and 1940s and that for all practical purposes consanguinity had ceased to be a significant phenomenon throughout the population by the 1950s. Here I do not want to discuss the different levels at any point in time in the two populations nor examine closely the issues of undercounting. Both studies show that the rates of cousin marriage were significantly high around the turn of the century. Even with first-cousin marriage rates of 0.68 and 1.92, the cities of Wien and Milan point toward the systematic exchange of kin in the decades before the First World War. The extraordinarily low rates of second-cousin marriage may well have resulted from the ease with which couples could get away with not reporting their relationships to the authorities.

Overall figures for Norway demonstrate the same fall that can be found in Central and Southern Europe.[13] Rural Norway saw a drop in all consanguineal

lation 23 (1968): 303–24. For Como, Milan, and Varese, see Angelo Serra and Antonio Soini, "La consanguinité d'une population: Rappel de notions et de résultats: Application à trois provinces d'Italie du Nord," *Population* 14 (1959): 47–72. For Wien, see Orel, "Verwandtenehen." For Köln, see Panse and Krings, "Häufigkeit der Blutsverwandten-Ehen," pp. 144–7. For the Eifel villages, see Kühn, "Inzucht." For Belgium, see Fr. Twiesselmann, P. Moreau, and J. François, "Evolution de consanguinité en Belgique de 1918 à 1959," *Population* 17 (1962): 241–66. See also an earlier study for Antwerp and Mechelen, R. Deraemaeker, "Inbreeding in a North Belgium Province," *Acta Genetica* 8 (1958): 128–36.

[13] A genealogical study of a single parish in Western Sweden considered as an isolate by J. A. Böök and C. E. Måwe, "The incidence of Cousin Marriages in a West-Swedish Rural Community," *American Journal of Human Genetics* 7 (1955): 426–9, suggested no essential decline in first-cousin marriages between the period 1905–25 (1.2 percent) and the period 1940–1 (1.3 percent). Carl A. Larson, "The Frequency of First Cousin Marriages in a South Swedish Rural Community," *American Journal of Human Genetics* 8 (1956): 151–3, found in a genealogical study of a South Swedish village a declining rate: 1901–13, 2.4 percent; 1914–26, 1.8 percent; 1927–39, 2.0 percent; 1940–52, 0.0 percent). He points out that the incidence between the two villages is comparable but says: "The rates of cousin marriages obtained by Böök and Måwe in a community they regarded as a geographic isolate, and by me in a community that was not such, were calculated on a small number of positive observations and admit of no far-reaching conclusions as to the general frequency of first cousin marriages in rural Sweden." Böök also studied all the marriages in the

Table 21.3. *Consanguinity in Europe during the twentieth century.*

Place	Period	First cousin	Second cousin	Third cousin	All through second cousin	All through third cousin
Norway (rural)	1870–91				8.13	
Norway (rural)	1942–72				1.00	
Norway (urban)	1870–91				2.62	
Norway (urban)	1942–72				0.43	
Norway	1860–90				6.69	
Norway	1905	1.28			2.74	
Norway	1915	0.36				
Jara (Toledo, Spain)	1900–79					6.70
Jara, 4 hamlets	1900–79					24.25
Spain	1911–14	1.72	2.19		4.58	
Spain	1925–9	1.90	2.61		5.21	
Spain	1940–3	1.49	2.02		3.59	
Roncal Valley, Pyr.	1877–1915	1.67	3.75	8.12		14.36
Roncal Valley (shepherds)						20.48
Roncal Valley (ag/for)						13.76
Roncal Valley (artis/grade)						8.47
Roncal Valley (day-labor)						7.69
Errazu, Baztán Valley	1850–1910					6.47
Errazu (owner occupiers)						16.30
Errazu (tenants)						3.70
Dept. Finistère (Fr)	1926–30				3.82	
Dept. Finistère	1946–50				1.30	
Dept. Finistère	1956–8				0.91	
Dept. Pas de Calais	1926–30				1.98	
Dept. Pas de Calais	1946–50				0.92	
Dept. Pas de Calais	1956–8				0.67	
Dept. Cher	1926–30				1.53	
Dept. Cher	1946–50				0.63	
Dept. Cher	1956–8				0.41	
Dept. Moselle	1926–30				2.60	
Dept. Moselle	1946–50				1.41	
Dept. Moselle	1956–8				1.22	

Dept. Lozère	1926–30				4.49	
Dept. Lozère	1946–50				4.20	
Dept. Lozère	1956–8				2.50	
Dept. Gers	1926–30				1.48	
Dept. Gers	1946–50				0.87	
Dept. Gers	1956–8			0.58		
Dept. Hautes-Alpes	1926–30				5.27	
Dept. Hautes-Alpes	1946–50			2.90		
Dept. Hautes-Alpes	1956–8				1.20	
Como (Italy)	1903–23	4.42	3.38		9.16	
Como	1926–31	2.83	2.80		6.35	
Como	1933–53	1.24	1.75		3.29	
Milan (city)	1903–23	1.92	0.38		2.61	
Milan (city)	1926–31	1.03	0.25		1.43	
Milan (city)	1933–53	0.64	0.24		0.98	
Milan (rural)	1903–23	4.73	2.26		8.15	
Milan (rural)	1933–53	1.08	1.11		2.40	
Varese	1903–23	3.71	2.22		7.02	
Varese	1933–53	0.90	0.90		1.97	
Wien (city)	1901	0.68				
Wien (city)	1913–14	0.63	0.26		0.96	
Wien (city)	1929–30	0.44	0.18	.65		
Wien (territory)	1901	1.20				
Wien (territory)	1913–14	0.99	1.23		2.3	
Wien (territory)	1929–30	0.74	0.98		1.72	
Köln (archdiocese)	1918–22	0.50	0.58		1.19	
Köln	1928–32	0.38	0.34		0.84	
Köln	1938–43	0.14	0.17		0.35	
Village B, Eifel	1820–80	0.00	6.80	1.4	7.10	12.0
Village B, Eifel	1910–37	0.00	11.50	1.9	13.40	15.3
Village E, Eifel	1820–80	0.00	6.60	11.7	6.60	27.6
Village E, Eifel	1910–37	0.00	4.20	5.6	4.20	9.8
Belgium	1918–19	0.98	0.99	2.31		
Belgium	1935–9	0.49	0.79	1.48		
Belgium	1955–9	0.22	0.61	0.97		

marriages up through second cousins, from a high of 8.13 in 1870–91 to a low of 1.00 in 1942–72. For urban Norway, the figures are 2.62 to 0.43. It should be emphasized that the overall rates flatten out differences of class, occupation, and geography, and that the reported incidence is always too low – with an increasing failure to register the more distant relations. Nonetheless, the trend over the twentieth century for all European countries seems to be well established, and by the end of World War II, areas with high rates such as rural Norway ended up with levels comparable to other regions or countries such as Belgium.[14]

In France, Jean Sutter and Jean-Michel Goux have carefully gone over all the data based on Catholic dispensations department by department, for the period 1926 to 1958. In earlier studies, Sutter, along with Léon Tabah and Claude Lévy, examined data from the nineteenth and early twentieth centuries. Table 21.3 presents examples of rates up through second cousins for six selected departments. The authors find the same steady decline throughout the twentieth century, observing that by 1946–50, the "disappearance of endogamy is almost total."[15]

Another significant finding has been reported by Andrew Abelson for two valleys of the Pyrenees. Between 1850 and 1910, rates of consanguineal alliance up through third cousins among farmers who owned their own enterprises in Errazu in the Baztán Valley were drastically different from those for tenants: 16.3 and 3.7, respectively. And in the Roncal Valley, different occupations demonstrated quite different behavior in this regard: sheepherding (20.48), agriculture/

population in three North Swedish parishes at the end of 1946. He argued that the first-cousin rates were directly correlated with the degree of isolation of the parishes: 0.95, 2.85, 6.80. J. A. Böök, "The Frequency of Cousin Marriages in Three North Swedish Parishes," *Hereditas* 34 (1948): 252–5.

[14] Julia Bell, "A Determination of the Consanguinity Rate in the General Hospital Population of England and Wales," *Annals of Genetics* 10 (1940): 370–91, offers figures from Dahlberg for "Prussia" and "Bavaria" for the period 1875 to 1933 (p. 372). The statistics for both states demonstrated a high point of first-cousin marriages during 1875–80 (Prussia) or 1876–80 (Bavaria) – 0.71 and 0.87, respectively. The rates then fell steadily, reaching a low point of 0.20 for both at the end of the period. The rates for any period should be viewed with extreme caution, but the trend is typical for other European areas, some of which started the decline a decade or two later. Dahlberg gives no sources for his statistics, other than to describe them as "official." The critique of such statistics is offered by Orel, Serra, and Sutter discussed earlier in this chapter. See Gunnar Dahlberg, "On Rare Defects in Human Populations with Particular Regard to In-breeding and Isolate Effects," *Proceedings of the Royal Society of Edinburgh* 58 (1937–8): 213–32.

[15] Sutter and Goux, "Evolution," p. 687. There is also a study of a single village, Chateauponsac in the Haute-Vienne, by Emile Crognier, "Consanguinity and Social Change: An Isonymic Study of a French Peasant Population, 1870–1979," *Journal of Biosocial Science* 17 (1985): 267–79. Crognier bases his study on surname matching (isonymy) and reckons mean coefficients of inbreeding for each decennial period of his study. The highest correlations were for the decade 1870–9. The decline from the turn of the century was interrupted by a short postwar restoration. Different occupations attained maximums at different periods: cultivators, 1880–9; craftsmen, 1890–9. In general, however, Crognier, sees the 1930s as the crucial period for changing attitudes toward marriage. By the 1970s, inbreeding was virtually extinguished. His results, together with a longer treatment, are to be found in Emile Crognier, Daniel Bley, and Gilles Boetsch, *Mariage en Limousin. Evolution séculaire et identité d'une population rurale: Le canton de Chateauponsac (1870–1979)* (Paris, 1984).

forestry (13.76), handicraft/trade (8.47), day-labor (7.69). This analysis suggests that the high rates of endogamy found in the decades before World War I were the result of different kinds of strategies and not the random effects of isolation. I will come back to this issue later.

Figures for England are difficult to come by because marriage prohibitions have not been as restrictive as on the continent (there was no prohibition against first cousins after the reforms of Henry VIII, for example), and because there was no provision for dispensations. Nancy Fix Anderson thought that cousin marriage was a common practice for all preindustrial propertied classes and argued that the widespread phenomenon she found for nineteenth-century England was a continuation of older practices, but there is little evidence to suggest that the tendency was widespread before the mid eighteenth century.[16] Ethel Elderton, a Galton research scholar, early in this century brought together what statistics she could find.[17] Several of the studies were based on isonymy – and all of them dealt with various subpopulations. Using isonymy, George Darwin worked out the following proportions of first-cousin marriage for different groups: middle classes, 3.5 percent; peerage, 4.5 percent; landed gentry, 3.75 percent; London Metropolitan area, 1.5 percent; a selection of large towns, 2.0 percent; and a selection of rural districts, 2.4 percent. A study of the Great Ormand Street Hospital found a proportion of 1.3 percent, close to that for the London Metropolitan area. Pearson's study of professional classes produced a figure of 4.7 percent, similar to Darwin's for the middle class as a whole. Another study of doctors also found 4.7 percent. "This proportion refers to the middle classes only, where the percentage of cousin marriages is certainly higher than in the working classes."[18]

The rise of endogamy

Given the fact that most studies of the kind examined in the preceding sections picked a beginning point just before World War I, the rise of endogamy is much less well documented than its gradual – and sometimes precipitous – disappearance.[19] Bourgoin and Khang's detailed study of four Pyrenean villages based on

[16] Nancy Fix Anderson, "Cousin Marriage in Victorian England," *Journal of Family History* 11 (1986): 285–301.

[17] Ethel M. Elderton, *On the Marriage of First Cousins* (London, 1911). See also Darwin, "Marriages between First Cousins in England," esp. pp. 162–3. A shorter version: "Marriages between First Cousins in England and Their Effects," *Fortnightly Review* 18 n.s. (1875): 22–41, esp. 29–30.

[18] Elderton, *Marriage of First Cousins,* p. 23. J. G. Masterson, "Consanguinity in Ireland," *Human Heredity* 20 (1970): 371–82, refers to Cameron's 1883 study of 7576 marriages, of which 0.57 percent were found to have been among first cousins. Julia Bell in 1940, in "A Determination of the Consanguinity Rate," using some cohort figures from rates determined in various hospitals showed that the rates increased by age cohorts, which suggests that consanguinity had declined in England as well from the end of the century (p. 376). It should be noted that she put forth her figures with some hesitation.

[19] Jean Sutter and Claude Lévy, "Les dispenses civiles au mariage en France depuis 1800," *Population* 14 (1959): 285–303, shows that brother-/sister-in-law marriages were not allowed by civil author-

a complete family reconstitution showed that until 1790 there were very few consanguineal marriages. Then the rates rose to a peak between 1890 and 1914, whereupon they fell abruptly.[20] In Kühn's study of two villages in the Eifel, although his methodology was less thorough (tracing through the church registers for ancestors), he also found a rise throughout the nineteenth century.[21] In village B, the rates for the period 1813–37 for marriages up to third cousins was 6 percent, compared with 12 percent for 1820–80. In village E, the respective rates were 11.8 percent and 27.6 percent. Egenter was not particularly concerned with the historical development of his Schwyzer mountain village, but he provided evidence, which he did not develop, showing that villagers married people from other parishes through the seventeenth century, so that in the subsequent period consanguinity rates and village endogamy rates rose together.[22] The study covering the largest area for the early nineteenth century is Carl Henry Alström's analysis of first-cousin marriages in Sweden between 1750 and 1844.[23] Alström noted that Sweden after the Reformation continued to forbid marriages between first cousins and allowed dispensations only beginning in 1680 – about the same time that German Protestant territories began to provide for dispensations.[24] In 1844 the regulation requiring a dispensation to marry a first cousin was abrogated. Following dispensation records up to that point, Alström shows that first-cousin marriages, although first allowed in 1680, were seldom found before 1750 (over that period they had reached a rate of 0.2 percent). But then they rose steadily in frequency to about 1 percent in 1800, to reach a high of 1.5 percent in 1844.[25] After that there was no need to get a dispensation, and therefore no records were kept. However, Alström was able to look at rates among the nobility for whom

ities until after 1832. Dispensations rose steadily to a high point in the 1870s and 1880s. A general decline began in 1819. Similarly, civil dispensations for uncle/niece and aunt/nephew rose steadily from the second decade of the nineteenth century to a high point in the 1870s and 1880s. Again World War I witnessed the beginning of a sharp decline. In 1889–90, such marriages made up 0.053 percent; by 1941–5 the figure was 0.006 percent of the total.

[20] Bourgoin and Khang, "Quelques aspects," figure a coefficient of consanguinity based on the probability of genes being identical and do not give the percentage of each kind of marriage. For a longer treatment, see Jacqueline Vu Tien Khang and André Sevin, *Choix du conjoint et patrimoine génétique: Etude de quatre villages du Pays de Sault de 1740 à nos jours* (Paris, 1977). Jean Sutter, "Facteurs d'endogamie et de consanguinité," *Population* 23 (1968): 303–24, presents dispensation data for one village in the Loir-et-Cher from 1812 to 1955. Between 1812 and 1835, annual consanguinity rates up to second cousins were always between 2 and 3 percent. The rates rose to a peak around 1900. Between 1870 and 1900, they were always above 3.5 percent, with some rates between 5 and 6 percent.

[21] Kühn, "Inzucht," pp. 491–3. Wulz, "Ein Beitrag," for the Amt Dachau, showed rising rates of consanguinity up through third cousins: 1848–72, 1.16; 1873–97, 1.38; 1899–1922, 1.69.

[22] Egenter, "Ueber den Grad der Inzucht," p. 373.

[23] Alström, "First-Cousin Marriages in Sweden," pp. 295–369. For a Norwegian mountain valley, compare Saugstad and Ødegård, "Predominance of Extreme Geographical Proximity." Between 1600 and 1850, the parish was a marriage isolate: only 1.2 percent of marriages of heirs were contracted with residents of another parish. Yet before 1800, there were no first-cousin marriages.

[24] Alström, "First-Cousin Marriages in Sweden," p. 302. See Chapter 3 in this volume for a discussion of dispensations in Germany.

[25] Alström, "First-Cousin Marriages in Sweden," p. 302.

good genealogical records were available.[26] The class as a whole already had a 3.5 percent rate by 1750, which rose beyond 6 percent by the 1820s and held steady to the end of the century. Both the high and low nobility developed extraordinary rates of first-cousin marriage by the mid nineteenth century (19.7 and 15.7 percent, respectively).

Jean-Marie Gouesse has examined the rates of endogamy for Catholic Europe during the early modern period through to the twentieth century on the basis of papal and episcopal records of dispensations.[27] In the late sixteenth century, he notes, the Council of Trent introduced the same rigor that German Protestant states were demonstrating at that time. Until the end of the seventeenth century, dispensations were extraordinarily difficult to come by and were available only on high political grounds. Even though things loosened up during the seventeenth century, Gouesse found only 310 papal dispensations per year under Innocent XI for the period 1683–5 for all of Spain, France, and Italy for all "second-degree" kin, without distinguishing between first cousins by blood or by alliance (marriage with the wife's first cousin). It was only in the eighteenth century that the rate of dispensations began to rise rapidly. For example, between 1756 and 1781–4, the number of dispensations given out per year increased by 626 percent. When Gouesse compares the years 1583–4, 1683–4, and 1783–4, he finds the number of papal dispensations rose from 57 to 621 to 3,156 (1:11:55).[28] Yet all of this was dwarfed by the rise during the nineteenth century. Between the 1760s and 1860s, the rate for France increased elevenfold and, measured against the population, rose 8.5 times. Gouesse argues, as I have for Neckarhausen, that the rise of familial endogamy was pushed from below and broke the resistance of the clergy and church establishment. It was not just a rise in cousin marriages, however. By the 1780s, a few men were allowed to marry their sisters-in-law after the death of their wives – about five per year. By 1880, three marriages out of a hundred involved brothers and sisters-in-law.[29] Gouesse concludes

[26] Alström, "First-Cousin Marriages in Sweden," pp. 334–41.

[27] Jean-Marie Gouesse, "Mariages de proches parents (xvie–xxe siècle): Esquisse d'une conjoncture," *Le Modèle familial européen: Normes, déviances, contrôle du pouvoir.* Actes des séminaires organisés par l'école française de Rome, 90 (Rome, 1986), pp. 31–61.

[28] In an earlier study, Gouesse examined papal registers for France, Spain, and Italy for the eighteenth century and tabulated dispensations for marriage between "close kin": brother-/sister-in-law, uncle/niece, aunt/nephew, first cousins. He found that the rates almost tripled between 1736 and 1786. Dispensations for such marriages appear to have been first possible for the nonaristocratic population during the first decade of the eighteenth century. He suggests that endogamy had a strong urban flavor and was especially frequent among judicial elites. Contrary to his expectations, endogamy was weak in Mediterranean France and among some viniculture regions. "L'endogamie familiale dans l'europe catholique au xviiie: première approche," *Mélanges de l'école française de Rome: Moyen âge: Temps moderne* 89 (1977): 95–116.

[29] Gouesse, "Mariages de proches parents," pp. 49–52. In another article devoted to marriage between brothers- and sisters-in-law in the eighteenth century, "Epouser les deux soeurs," *Annales de Normandie,* numéro special (1982) [Réceuil d'études offert en hommage au doyen Michel de Boüard, vol. 1]: 253–67, Gouesse offers evidence of a rapid rise of papal dispensations for Europe and the colonies during the 1770s and 1780s. The increase was due largely to the spread of such dispensations to "social inferiors."

that "in Europe" endogamy rose at the end of the eighteenth century, reaching a high point between the mid nineteenth century and World War I, and that it fell rapidly from the 1920s onward.[30]

The overall trend in endogamous marriage was strikingly similar, according to the available data, for Catholic and Protestant Germany; Catholic Italy, Spain, France, and Belgium; and Protestant Sweden. Before the eighteenth century, there was no significant endogamy anywhere in continental Europe. None of these studies examine second-cousin marriage before the nineteenth century, but the study of Neckarhausen suggests that people may well have started to marry more extended consanguineal relatives before they got on to first cousins. There, the 1740s proved to be the crucial decade for the change. In Sweden, France, Neckarhausen, and the four villages in the Pyrenees studied by Bourgoin and Kang, cousin marriage and other forms of close kin alliances were well in place by 1800. Their numbers rose to reach a peak most often during the 1880s, although sometimes it was earlier and sometimes later. Whatever relationship one uses to track the rise (uncle/niece, brother-/sister-in-law, first cousins, affines), the overall trend appears to be the same throughout wide areas in Europe. However, different areas, different occupational groups, and different classes created vastly different forms of alliance. Whereas some may have relied on reiterated first-cousin exchanges, others made use of more extended consanguines, and still others integrated kindreds through a highly flexible form of affinal alliance (see Chapter 20). All of these forms appeared in the eighteenth century and became crucially important for social organization in the nineteenth century, only to disappear again in the twentieth – at different rates, but everywhere.

* * *

Many who have studied the decline of consanguinity assume that earlier rates had always been high. If modern communications and mobility brought an end to marrying close kin, then earlier factors of isolation and small village size must have encouraged inbreeding. And many geneticists aware of the massive educational campaign waged by the medical profession toward the end of the nineteenth century thought that consanguinity and the ignorance of its effects went hand in hand in earlier populations. George Darwin described the hilarity with which the idea of counting cousin marriages in the census was greeted in the British Parliament in the 1870s. But it did not take long for a bioevolutionary perspective to come to dominate public opinion.

A number of authors have found that the rate of inbreeding correlates nega-

[30] André Burguière has studied one wine-growing parish in the Parisian Basin for the eighteenth century: "Endogamie et communauté villageoises: Pratique matrimoniale à Romainville," *Annales de démographie historique* (1979): 313–36. His statistics were gathered for the period 1718–87 and deal only with the population that married within the parish. He found that already in the period 1718–40, 61.5 percent of village endogamous marriages were with consanguines up to second cousins. The rate actually declined to 38.5 percent for the period 1765–87. This is the only study I have found that suggests high rates before 1750.

tively with population density. Letten Saugstad presented evidence for this for all of Norway, as Deraemaeker did for Belgium.[31] Angelo Serra and Antonio Soini found that consanguinity correlated negatively with the size of settlement.[32] Several problems remain unresolved, however. Statistical correlations at a high level of aggregation blend out all the differences and countertrends. Deraemaeker himself showed that for some periods certain urban areas had greater rates than rural areas, and that larger cities often had higher rates than smaller towns.[33] He thought that people in cities were much more likely to marry a cousin related through a mother than a father in order not to call attention to similar surnames and tip the authorities off to their relationship. He assumed that people in the city before and after World War I still had a social reason for linking up with relatives but for whatever reason sought to conceal their consanguinity.[34] Since all studies of consanguinity in urban areas except for George Darwin's from 1875 are based on official inquiries or counting of dispensations, the relative rates at any particular time are not too reliable. And there is some counterevidence. Alström found no correlation between consanguinity or physical geographical factors and population density in Sweden and was skeptical about the relationship between consanguinity rates and isolate size.[35] One of the few scholars to disaggregate a population is Abelson, who found in the Pyrenees that there was no specific correlation at all with population density or village size.[36] On the contrary, the rate of first-cousin marriage had to do with occupation and property ownership. On the basis of a comparison with other European data, he concluded that "the frequency of consanguineous marriage is associated with assortative mating by social class."[37] That, of course, was the point made by George Darwin early in the search for an understanding of the levels and dynamics of inbreeding. Doctors – despite their own ideology – married their first cousins far more often than industrial workers did.[38] Observations of this kind suggest that an open and important question for understanding kinship and social organization is the one of class.

Closely tied up with the argument about density is that of mobility. The situation in Norway, Ireland, and the Pyrenees, among others, suggests that greater social and geographical mobility caused rates of consanguinity to decline.[39] Part of the problem with this argument, however, is its fixation on one variable at a time. Note that in Neckarhausen, for example, well-to-do peasants began to

[31] Saugstad, "Relationship between Inbreeding," p. 334; Deraemaeker, "Inbreeding in Belgium," p. 134. See also Twiesselmann, et al., "Evolution," p. 256.
[32] Serra and Soini, "Consanguinité," pp. 64–5.
[33] Deraemaeker, "Inbreeding in Belgium," pp. 128–32.
[34] Deraemaeker, "Inbreeding in Belgium," pp. 133–4.
[35] Alström, "First-Cousin Marriages," pp. 295–8.
[36] Abelson, "Population Structure II," pp. 94–8.
[37] Abelson, "Population Structure," p. 176.
[38] Darwin, "Marriage between First Cousins," pp. 156–63.
[39] Saugstad, "Relationship between Inbreeding," pp. 334, 338; Masterson, "Consanguinity in Ireland," p. 381; Abelson, "Population Structure," pp. 174–5.

marry their second cousins a generation or two before artisans did. At a time when peasants were constructing closer ties through first cousins, sibling exchange, and the like, the class of newly mobile artisans began to construct regional rather than local ties through marriages to second cousins and perhaps more extended kin.[40] Furthermore, the highly mobile agricultural producers of the region studied by Segalen eschewed consanguineal links altogether, in favor of an intricate and integrated system of affinal marriages.[41] The studies by geneticists have blended beyond recognition the different ways different populations have found to organize their social lives through and around kin.

In contrast to many other investigators, Sutter was well aware that close consanguineal marriages had arisen in the modern era. Any idea that small, isolated villages had always practiced inbreeding simply was not true. His problem was to account for its rise. He isolated three factors that together or separately explained why the breaking up of isolates during nineteenth-century industrialization led not to an expected lowering of consanguinity, but paradoxically to a rise: differential fertility, declining mortality, and migration.[42] These were in turn related to the demographic transition, which gave rise to different demographic behavior patterns for different parts of the population. Whereas some families began to limit fertility, others maintained older fertility schedules under conditions of lower mortality and as a result produced much larger families. On the one hand, a certain number of lineages disappeared, and on the other, the remaining ones had many more cousins available, which under conditions of random mate selection caused rates of consanguinity to rise. In other words, the rise in consanguineal marriages was a purely demographic phenomenon, which went into decline once the demographic transition was completed. Many other authors point to smaller sib sizes and the fact that there were fewer cousins to choose from to account for twentieth-century trends.[43] One problem with Sutter's model is that he never tested it empirically, and it was constructed primarily to explain the phenomenon in France – whose demographic transition was quite different from the transition elsewhere in Europe in that its practices of family limitation were well in place more than a century earlier than those in Germany, for example. Delille points out that Sutter's argument supposes the persistence and continuity of an endogamy of extremely rigid groups, but that is not what one observes in southern Italy where Delille studied the phenomenon.[44] The theory also explains poorly, as Delille points out, the passage from far consanguinity to near and all the other forms of kinship marriage that increased everywhere in Europe: sibling exchange, sororate, levirate, affinal alliances, and so on. Further-

40 Abelson himself points to similar conclusions: "Population Struct ıre," pp. 171–5; "Population Structure II," p. 101.

41 Segalen and Richard, "Marrying Kinsmen," pp. 111–15. See Chapter 20 in this volume for an extended discussion of Segalen's findings.

42 Sutter, "Frequence de l'endogamie."

43 Saugstad, "Inbreeding in Norway," p. 488.

44 Gérard Delille, *Famille et propriété dans le royaume de Naples (xve–xixe siècle)*. Bibliothèque des écoles françaises d'Athènes et de Rome, 259 (Rome and Paris, 1985), p. 386.

more, the timing of the decline in consanguinity in different areas in Europe does not correlate closely with the completion of the demographic transition.[45] During the nineteenth century, many highly mobile families, precisely the population that was supposed to leave those remaining no choice but to marry cousins, had high rates of consanguinity.[46] Sutter's model also does not account for affinal marriages such as those Segalen found for Brittany.[47] Nor does it account for the fact that each region in Europe showed greater preference for different kinds of cousins – agnatic or uterine, parallel or cross, first, second, or third.[48] And finally Sutter assumes that there were no changes in social organization that might have contributed to an interest in marriage with close kin as a way to reconfigure the networks of social reciprocity.

In the period around World War I when the decline in the rates of consanguineal marriage took place everywhere in Europe, perhaps the single most important explanation for the trend is the medical profession's widespread panic about degeneration – what Martin Ottenheimer calls its "bioevolutionary perspective."[49] With the dense network of local doctors throughout Europe convinced that every sign of degeneration, from bad teeth to inattention in school, was the result of inbreeding, the news about the effects of such practices was easily propagated. The decline in rates of consanguinity in most parts of Europe probably has had more to do with the penetration of medical opinion than with migration patterns and the opening up of communications. Many of the correlations with density or geography are more likely correlations with the presence of medical practitioners.

Toward the end of the nineteenth century two competing systems of thought had begun to take hold. One sought an understanding of human relationships in social forces, networks, and conditions, whereas the other emphasized the physical. Social scientists in Europe had never given much thought to familial endogamy, although during the latter half of the nineteenth century they became interested in cousin marriages among primitives. Indeed, cousin marriages came to be associated with primitives by several generations of anthropologists married to their own cousins.[50] Social analysis of European societies then began concentrating on the concept of class, and kinship as an integrating factor in class

[45] On this point, see also Delille, *Famille,* p. 368.

[46] I will come back to this in Chapter 22. See Anderson, "Cousin Marriage," p. 285.

[47] See Chapter 20 in this volume.

[48] See Gedde-Dahl, "Population Structure in Norway," p. 216; Deraemaeker, "Inbreeding in Belgium," p. 134; Alström, "First-Cousin Marriages," p. 299.

[49] Martin Ottenheimer, "Lewis Henry Morgan and the Prohibition of Cousin Marriage in the United States," *Journal of Family History* 15 (1990): 325–34.

[50] For a start on this problem, see Ottenheimer, "Lewis Henry Morgan" (Morgan was married to his cousin); and Anderson, "Cousin Marriage," p. 293. Georg Simmel, whose middle-class colleagues and Jewish friends showed high rates of consanguinity (see Chapter 22 in this volume) thought about familial endogamy strictly as a phenomenon of primitive societies: "Die Verwandtenehe," *Aufsätze und Abhandlungen 1894–1900* (Frankfurt, 1992), pp. 9–36. Max Weber, the theoretician of class par excellence, had no time to give to kinship in modern society, despite the fact that he was married to his first cousin.

relations was largely ignored. This needs some explanation and will be discussed further in Chapters 22 and 23, but the rudiments of an argument can be sketched in here. In general, those scientists and political figures concerned with the social tended to analyze social pathologies and problems of political mobilization in class terms. Another group approached human relations from a bioevolutionary perspective and hence conceptualized political mobilization on the basis of race or nation rather than class. Of course, biological and social perspectives were extraordinarily fluid and never worked within air-tight ideological compartments. But it is safe to say that whereas social scientists ignored the question of kinship and class, biological scientists, by attacking cousin marriage, sawed away at one of the root supports of class integration (see Chapters 22 and 23). Despite its lack of empirical evidence, biological opinion against cousin marriages had already lobbied for attention early in the century, but with no great success. Not long after, however, the biological arguments began to have an impact in the United States, as can be seen in the laws prohibiting the marriage of first cousins from midcentury onward.[51] In Europe, where the state intruded far less directly into the private sphere, it was left to a massive campaign at the end of the century to roll back the practice. It could well have been tacitly understood in America far earlier that the way to break down class and ethnic cohesion was to attack one of its main supports, but in Europe the campaign against others carrying on the practice was undertaken by those most guilty of it – at least if George Darwin's rates for doctors can be believed. It also seems to have been the case that certain forms of economic organization made familial alliances less adaptive. If the Rothschilds and Siemens and hundreds of other families developed their enterprises with the intensive use of kin, as argued in Chapter 22, by the end of the century limited liability companies and the rise of a managerial class made the reliance on kin less necessary. It was only then that the biological perspective won the day. These trends are reflected in the paths taken by scientific and scholarly discussion of kinship and class. Analysts seem tacitly to have agreed upon a division of labor, allocating class to sociology and its related disciplines and kinship to anthropology and biology. The important fact that few observers have yet come to terms with, however, is that kinship and class dovetail with each other.

[51] Ottenheimer, "Lewis Henry Morgan."

22

Kinship and class formation

From the preceding chapters it is clear that Neckarhausen and other rural areas experienced a reconfiguration of kinship as an endogamous alliance system, and that this transformation was closely connected with the articulation and systematic integration of classes.[1] If the rise of a new alliance system was a general phenomenon in Europe toward the end of the eighteenth century – as I have argued in Chapter 21 – then that kinship was probably tied up in some fashion with the formation of classes throughout the society. In Delille's view, endogamy in the rural region around Naples was initiated by a rural bourgeoisie whose social relations were determined by fluid forms of wealth. He is quite right to suggest that kinship and class had a great deal to do with each other, but the phenomenon needs to be investigated more as part of an encompassing shift to modernity than as a pathology.

Delille's work is subtle and challenging, one of the most important studies of kinship in a European context. However, he has looked at the relationships back to front. Class differentiation and capitalist social relations, in his schema, produce, or at least are the foundation for, innovative patterns of familial alliance. And although this correlation is compelling, I believe that kinship was not a dependent variable but an active factor in constructing class-based networks and providing essential class experience. Furthermore, it was an innovative and creative response to newly configured relationships between people and institutions, around the circulation of goods and services, and within newly organized polities. The new class constellation arose in the context of an increasing differentiation

[1] See the important new work by David Luebke, "Terms of Loyalty: Factional Politics in a Single German Village (Nöggenschwil, 1725–1745)," in Thomas Robisheaux and Max Reinhard, eds., *Infinite Boundaries: Order, Disorder, and Reorder in Early Modern German Culture* (Sixteenth-Century Studies: forthcoming, 1997). Luebke argues for a Black Forest community that kinship became the organizational element in eighteenth-century politics and faction-building in contrast to earlier.

between public and private spheres of activity. Kinship (private) and class (public) worked reciprocally or dialectically against each other. As both Hegel and his latter-day student Habermas have shown, the kind of personality suited to negotiating in civil society was fashioned in the realm of bourgeois "private" relationships: without the bourgeois family (and its kinship culture), no bourgeoisie.[2]

It is no secret that interest in class as an analytical category has rapidly evaporated over the past several decades.[3] An aggressively self-conscious "classless" political and historical culture has ceased to think about itself in class terms and has projected that view increasingly onto the past. All that is left of class for many historians of the nineteenth century is the impoverished figure of "class identity," which essentially shifts the view from collective to individual experience, although even the individual is not left whole but dissected into a variable set of sexual, class, national, ethnic, and work identities.[4]

The task here is not to rescue class for historical analysis, but since the discussion is all about the role of kinship in class formation, I do need to clarify

[2] G. W. F. Hegel, *Elements of the Philosophy of Right,* trans. H. B. Nisbet, ed. Allan W. Wood (Cambridge, 1991), pp. 199–219; Jürgen Habermas, *The Structural Transformation of the Public Sphere: An Inquiry into a Category of Bourgeois Society,* trans. Thomas Burger (Cambridge, Mass., 1991), pp. 43–56.

[3] Some of the major players in the German discussion are: Ulrich Beck, "Jenseits von Stand und Klasse? Soziale Ungleichheiten, gesellschaftliche Individualisierungsprozesse und die Entstehung neuer sozialer Formationen und Identitäten," in *Soziale Welt,* Sonderband 2: *Soziale Ungleichheiten,* Reinhold Kreckel, ed. (Göttingen, 1983), pp. 35–74; Stefan Hradil, "Die Ungleichheit der 'Sozialer Lage,' " in ibid., pp. 101–18; Stefan Hradil, "System und Akteur: Eine empirische Kritik der soziologischen Kulturtheorie Pierre Bourdieus," in Klaus Eder, ed., *Klassenlage, Lebensstil und kulturelle Praxis: Beiträge zur Auseinandersetzung mit Pierre Bourdieus Klassentheorie* (Frankfurt, 1989), pp. 111–41; Klaus Eder, "Jenseits der nivellierten Mittelstandsgesellschaft. Das Kleinbürgertum als Schlüssel einer Klassenanalyse in fortgeschrittenen Industriegesellschaften," in ibid., pp. 341–92; Reinhard Kreckel, "Klassenbegriff und Ungleichheitsforschung," in *Soziale Welt,* Sonderband 7: *Lebenslage, Lebensläufe, Lebensstile,* ed. Peter A. Berger and Stefan Hradil (Göttingen, 1990), pp. 51–79; Berger and Hradil, "Die Modernisierung sozialer Ungleichheit – und die neuen Konturen ihrer Erforschung," in ibid., pp. 3–24; Manfred Teschner, "Was ist Klassenanalyse? Ueber Klassenverhältnis, Ausbeutung und Macht," in *Leviathan. Zeitschrift für Sozialwissenschaft* (1989): 1–14.

[4] A consequential nominalism is to be found in William M. Reddy, *Money and Liberty in Modern Europe: A Critique of Historical Understanding* (Cambridge, 1987), pp. x, 6–7, 24, 29, 39, 47, 69. See also Stefan Hradil's critique of Bourdieu, "System und Akteur," p. 125. On realist and nominalist approaches to class, see Kreckel, "Klassenbegriff," p. 51. Bourdieu's take on class realism can be found in, "What Makes a Social Class? On the Theoretical and Practical Existence of Groups," *Berkeley Journal of Sociology,* 32 (1987): 1–17, here 1–3, 8, and "The Social Space and the Genesis of Groups," *Theory and Society* 14 (1985): 723–44, here 724–5. Hans-Ulrich Wehler accepts the notion that there was no unified working, business, or propertied class in the nineteenth century, but avoids extreme individualist assumptions: "Vorüberlegungen zur historischen Analyse sozialer Ungleichheit," in *Klassen in der europäischen Sozialgeschichte,* ed. Hans-Ulrich Wehler (Göttingen, 1979), pp. 9–31, here pp. 12–13, 20. Reinhard Kreckel summarizes ways in which issues of gender have moved social analysis to the category of identity and to the problem of personal histories: "Klasse und Geschlecht: Die Geschlechtsindifferenz der soziologischen Ungleichheitsforschung und ihre theoretischen Implikationen," *Leviathan: Zeitschrift für Sozialwissenschaft* (1989): 305–21. For a substantial reworking of the themes, see Kathleen Canning, "Gender and the Politics of Class Formation: Rethinking German Labor History," *American Historical Review,* 97 (1992): 736–68.

what I plan to talk about. To begin with, it does not make much sense to consider class relationships outside the coordinated and managed access to property, even if not all property relationships are class relationships. Kinship and the alliance system of the nineteenth century were crucial for concentrating and distributing capital; providing strategic support over the life of individuals; structuring dynasties and recognizable patrilineal groupings; maintaining access points, entrances, and exits to social milieus through marriage, godparentage, and guardianship; creating cultural and social boundaries by extensive festive, ludic, competitive, and charitative transactions; configuring and reconfiguring possible alliances between subpopulations; developing a training ground for character formation; shaping desire and offering practice in code and symbol recognition ("something in the way she moves"); training rules and practices into bodies; and integrating networks of culturally similar people. It is, of course, easiest to demonstrate how kinship operates for middle- and upper-class groups. My work on Neckarhausen and the studies by Delille, Segalen, and others have now "put flesh onto genealogical bones" for rural property-holding groups through expensive and painstaking work. The difficulty, at this stage of collective knowledge, lies in what to say about wage-dependent social strata. I will come back to the few indications I can find in the literature about workers and laborers but should note that in Neckarhausen, at least, mobile construction workers among other things constructed their own endogamous kinship networks, which suggests that kinship was also a factor in the articulation of working-class culture and in securing wage-labor opportunities and support systems for property-poor and propertyless groups in the society. The rest of this chapter brings together a set of observations about the processes and dynamics of German middle- and upper-class kinship in order to suggest ways of thinking about the relationship of kinship and class for the society as a whole. This exercise moves away from the village and from rural society but is prompted by an interest in setting microstudies in comparative contexts and by the heuristic problems raised by discussions of general historical processes.

Patrilines and exchange

One aspect of the kinship system discovered for Neckarhausen is the systematic development of patrilines. Over time, the lines were able to develop more or less distinct profiles, depending on the larger set of considerations that helped determine alliance, but once produced they persisted in giving structural coherence to the system. In the everyday give and take on the village street, a shared surname was enough for outsiders to associate people with the same moral qualities or political purposes. Middle- and upper-class familial dynamics demonstrate a similar concern with maintaining coherence by cultivating identity with a surname group or a male-defined line. Certain families such as the Rothschilds or Siemens provided symbolic notoriety in this regard – Werner Siemens himself used the sixteenth-century Fuggers and the Rothschilds as his models – but male lineages, at least over the course of time, were constructed with considerably conscious effort by a wide range of junkers, merchants, officials, industrialists, bankers, professionals, pastors, and literati.[5]

During the second half of the nineteenth century, family members devoted more and more time to narcissistic reflection on their own genealogies and newly constructed chronicles.[6] It was then that many families founded archives and formally entrusted them to a particular member, sometimes the same person who produced the family newspaper.[7] Collections of letters and diaries of grandparents or great aunts and uncles were privately published at the end of the nineteenth and beginning of the twentieth century for family members.[8] Most of these documents originated during the Vormärz or in the decades following the midcentury revolutionary period, testimony to a growing interest in maintaining a trail of family tradition but also to founding generations that documented themselves ever more volubly and self-consciously. The publications of old family papers celebrated a lineage and provided a practical exercise in building familial attachment.

Many families – the decade of the 1870s was a crucial one in this regard – went so far as to institutionalize themselves formally as legally registered associations (*eingetragene Vereine*).[9] A typical example was the Delius family from Bielefeld and Bremen, whose members met in Bad Oeynhausen in 1873 to consider establishing just such a foundation.[10] A formal constitution, drawn up in

[5] Even robber bands were recruited in terms of male lineage principles: Ernst Schubert, *Arme Leute, Bettler und Gauner in Franken des 18. Jahrhunderts.* Verein der Gesellschaft für fränkische Geschichte, Reihe 9: Darstellungen, vol. 26 (Neustadt a.d. Aisch, 1983). On Werner Siemens's thoughts on "Dynastie" see, Karl Helfferich, *Georg von Siemens: Ein Lebensbild aus Deutschlands grosser Zeit,* 3 vols., 2d ed. (Berlin, 1923), vol. 1, p. 165; vol. 2, pp. 56–7, 106. On Siemens, see also Jürgen Kocka's splendid article, "Familie, Unternehmer und Kapitalismus: An Beispielen aus der frühen deutschen Industrialisierung," *Zeitschrift für Unternehmergeschichte,* 24 (1979): 99–135, here 123.

[6] Friedrich Zunkel, *Der Rheinisch-Westfälische Unternehmer 1834–1879: Ein Beitrag zur Geschichte des deutschen Bürgertums im 19. Jahrhundert.* Dortmunder Schriften zur Sozialforschung (Köln, 1962) remarks on this for the East Elbian lower nobility, p. 103, and Rhineland entrepreneurial families, p. 106. For another example, see Hildegard von Marchtaler, *Aus Alt–Hamburger Senatorenhäusern: Familienschicksale im 18. und 19. Jahrhundert.* Veröffentlichung des Vereins für Hamburgische Geschichte, 16 (Hamburg, n.d. [1958]), who based her work on family genealogies previously done by the families themselves. Kocka refers to the development and revision of the Siemens family genealogy, "Familie, Unternehmer und Kapitalismus," p. 123.

[7] See D. Barth, "Das Familienblatt – Ein Phänomen der Unterhaltungspresse des 19. Jahrhunderts," in *Archiv für Geschichte des Buchwesens* 15 (1975): 121 ff. See also Kocka, "Familie, Unternehmer und Kapitalismus," p. 123.

[8] Typical examples: Luisa Rebensburg-Reich, ed., *Aus Tanta Carlotas Nachlass: Familienbriefe Sieveking/Cramer aus Hamburg, Basel, Genf u.a.* (Hamburg, 1937) (Carlota Sieveking was born in 1831); Ernst von Harnack, ed., *Johanna Thiersch, geborene Freiin von Liebig. Briefe aus ihren Jugendjahren 1848–1855: Für die Familie zusammengestellt zum Gedächtnis ihres 100. Geburtstages,* mss. ed. (Berlin–Zehlendorf, 1936); Otto Bansa, ed., *Ein Lebensbild in Briefen aus der Biedermeierzeit: Zur Geschichte der Familie Bansa in Frankfurt a. M.* (Frankfurt, 1914).

[9] On this, see Zunkel, *Unternehmer,* pp. 103–6. See also Kocka, "Familie, Unternehmer und Kapitalismus," p. 123. An important study in this regard for a Berlin/Prussian noble family is, Rüdiger von Treskow, "Adel in Preussen: Anpassung und Kontinuität einer Familie 1800–1918," *Geschichte und Gesellschaft* 17 (1991): 344–69, esp. 358, 367–8.

[10] *Deutsches Geschlechterbuch. Genealogisches Handbuch bürgerlicher Familien,* vol. 193, also pub-

1879 and revised in 1923, was registered before the Bielefeld County Court. Like many other such documents, this one proclaimed the purpose of the organization to be "to awaken and strengthen interest in family ties" and to offer support to "needy and worthy members of the Delius family and their spouses," especially to "guarantee their education."[11] The covenant defined the family in terms of all the descendants of Johann Daniel Delius, born in 1707, who carried the name Delius, or whose parents did so. Spouses of regular members (eligible at 18), widows of those who bore the name, and anyone who by virtue of adoption by regular members received the name could become "extraordinary" members of the association. The association provided for formal officers and meetings at biennial family gatherings. Over the following century, family members met at some hotel or other on a regular basis (39 times between 1873 and 1985) and in considerable numbers: at the *Familientag* of 1899, 43 adult Association members were photographed together. All the elements of constructing male lineage consciousness can be found in this example. While daughters were conspicuous as active members, their children, in turn, were expected to become attached to other male lines.[12] Institutionalized meetings cultivated those relationships, which long before the 1870s had been maintained by families like the Deliuses through more informal visits, vacations, and family festivals. Perhaps organizational innovation became necessary to establish familial coherence as relations became ever more extended with each generation. Or perhaps the new tourist infrastructure – railroads and hotels – made it attractive to gather together periodically in a central place. Whatever prompted the spurt of registered foundations from the 1870s onward, two principles of family cohesion were underscored and given special emphasis – recognition through surnames and coordination of educational and other opportunities for children.[13]

lished as *Westfälisches Geschlechterbuch,* vol. 7, prepared by Uta von Delius (Limburg an der Lahn, 1987). Uta v. Delius maintains the considerable documentation in the family archive in Bielefeld – which includes a library of general genealogical publications (p. 7). A family newspaper published every two or three years was founded in 1913. The volume refers to similar Familienverbände or Stiftungen for the Schrader, Meier, and Retberg families (pp. 591–2). This large and complex genealogical work is strictly organized around male lineage principles. Occasional excursions into the genealogies of allied families trace back through male lines in each case.

[11] Von Treskow, "Adel in Preussen," pp. 367–8, relates how the family association founded in 1876 between the old noble line von Tresckow and the much richer "bastard" branch von Treskow broke up in 1893 because members of the younger line did not think themselves liable for supporting their superior but poorer relatives, while the latter wanted the illegitimate origins of the von Treskows formally written into the statutes.

[12] The principle that women and their children became assimilated into the male line they married into was widely recognized by propertied classes. See, e.g., von Treskow, "Adel in Preussen," pp. 351, 357. It is possible that among propertyless workers that female lines composed the stable centers of family networks. See the early work on London dock workers by Michael Young and Peter Willmott, *Family and Kinship in East London* (Harmondsworth, 1962), pp. 31–61. Josef Mooser, *Arbeiterleben in Deutschland 1900–1970* (Frankfurt, 1984), pp. 156–9, provides hints that that may also have frequently been the case in Germany.

[13] Both the Siemens and Delius family associations were concerned with offering support to elderly and poor members of the line who faced losing class status. See Kocka, "Familie, Unternehmer und Kapitalismus," pp. 122–6, and Heinz-Gerhard Haupt, "Männliche und weibliche Berufskar-

Throughout the nineteenth century, while lineages were being constructed by cultivating surname ties transmitted through men, alliances were also constructed with other similar lineages. Such alliances themselves gained meaning and shape from the fact of coherently consituted lines.[14] Despite the necessity of opening up to other families, however, there was always a good deal of marriage back into a line. Continual intercourse among people with the same surname, coupled with narcissistic celebration, provided the grounds for endogamous desire. Reading through the Delius genealogy, one continually stumbles across Delius–Delius marriages. Or to take another example, the Remy family from Bendorf, early entrepreneurs and merchants in mining, iron, and steel, offers an instance of repeated marriage back into the male lineage.[15] The author of a recent genealogical study constructed five kinship diagrams (*Stammtafeln*) in which one out of five (19.5 percent) of the 92 marriages depicted since the founding generation around 1700 involved both partners with the surname Remy. The concern with male lineages, of course, made the necessity of male heirs all the more poignant, and for historians of industrial families working closely to their sources, the word "Stammhalter" (son and heir, literally: lineage preserver) flows easily and unconsciously from their pens.[16]

The strong sense of lineage correlated closely with the systematic cultivation of alliances: two or more families in continual exchange over a generation, and, with repeated marriages between lines, over several generations, in many cases lasting longer than a century. Relationships between individuals opened up whole families and their surrounding relatives and friends to each other. And the particular alliance between partners constituted by marriage never isolated a couple and their children – much of the literature on the "rise" of the nuclear family

rieren im deutschen Bürgertum in der zweiten Hälfte des 19. Jahrhunderts: Zum Verhältnis von Klasse und Geschlecht," *Geschichte und Gesellschaft*, 18 (1992): 143–60, here 158–9.

14 Although both men and women maintained active ties with maternal and paternal relatives and indeed maternal relatives continued to be of strategic importance, there were many observers who glossed the special cultivation of the husband's network as an injunction. See, e.g., Lorenz von Stein, *Die Frau, ihre Bildung und Lebensaufgabe*, 3d ed. (Berlin, 1890), p. 27: "As soon as the wife enters her house, a wall of separation begins slowly but inexorably to be built between her and all of her old relations." But women were important in building and maintaining identification with lineages identified through male transmitted names. At the Delius *Familientag* of 1899, half (22 of 43) of the assembly were women, with married daughters conspicuous by their presence. Indeed, the editor of the genealogy published in 1987 is a woman descendant with the surname. See *Deutsches Geschlechterbuch*, vol. 193.

15 Brigitte Schröder, "Der Weg zur Eisenbahnschiene. Geschichte der Familie Remy und ihre wirtschaftliche und kulturelle Bedeutung," in *Deutsches Familienarchiv. Ein genealogisches Sammelwerk*, vol. 91 (Neustadt an der Aisch, 1986), pp. 3–158.

16 A modern historian such as Hans Spethmann, *Franz Haniel, sein Leben und seine Werke* (Duisburg-Ruhrort, 1956) continually stresses male lines and uses the term "Stammhalter" frequently. I would suggest that most historians have assumed nineteenth-century familial lineage ideology uncritically and without much attention to its social purpose. Clara Heitefuss, the firstborn child to a merchant family in Corbach/Waldeck, was made to realize how much more the male carrier of the surname, or the *Stammhalter*, meant to her relatives: "A little brother was born. The Stammhalter. The joy in him almost outweighed the joy in the first child." She could not bring herself to leave out the qualifying "almost" (*schier*); Clara Heitefuss, *An des Meisters Hand: Lebenserinnerungen* (Schwerin, 1939), p. 16. She was born in 1867. Her father loved to "cultivate ties with relatives" (p. 12).

fails to balance the story with an account of the dynamics of larger groups accessible to each other through the mediation of their particular marriages.

Friendship between kin-groups

It was commonplace for people in the nineteenth century to talk about the way friendships opened up relationships to a whole family or "Haus" and to extend such relationships to a family's larger circle of friends and relatives. At crucial turning points in his autobiography, the Hamburg patrician Emil Lehmann (b. 1823) described the way new acquaintances introduced him to the social life and friendship of their whole families.[17] The phrase "Freundschaft mit unserer ganzen Familie" repeats itself throughout his account.[18] Professor Wiggers from Rostock (b. 1811) preferred entry to those families that limited their commerce with others, valuing depth of experience over extensiveness of connection.[19] And he, like many other people of similar station, sought relations with a family before choosing one of the daughters for a wife.[20] Phrases like "most intimate ties with a family" appear frequently in correspondence and autobiographies.[21] Cleophea Bansa, from a Frankfurt banking family, wrote to her son Gottlieb in Manchester that she found it fine for him to run around with other young men, "but I also feel that intercourse with families is necessary."[22]

Marriage was just as much an opening to a larger family as friendship was. Marion Kaplan makes the point for Jewish middle-class families at the end of the century that for spouses there was a sense of marrying into a *family,* expressed at times as love at first sight between in-laws and bride.[23] Carl Zeiss had developed such close ties with his in-laws that after the death of his first wife, he approached his father-in-law (by that time married to his sister) to find him

[17] Emil Lehmann, *Lebenserinnerungen,* 3 vols. (Kissingen, [1885]–1895), e.g., vol. 1, p. 29.

[18] E.g., Lehmann, *Lebenserinnerungen,* vol. 1, p. 61.

[19] Julius Wiggers, *Aus meinem Leben* (Leipzig, 1901), p. 98.

[20] Wiggers, *Leben,* p. 162. This was the same for the theologian and church administrator Bernhard Rogge (b. 1831), *Aus sieben Jahrzehnten. Erinnerungen aus meinem Leben* (Hannover and Berlin, 1897), p. 189. A similar experience for the classical philologist Reinhold Pauli, *Lebenserinnerungen nach Briefen und Tagebüchern,* ed. Elisabeth Pauli (Halle a. S., 1895). August Kestner, the Hanoverian representative in Rome (b. 1777), cultivated the Beaulieu family and was disappointed that class differences (*Stand*) kept him from marrying the daughter Julie, Hermann Kestner-Köchlin, ed., *Briefwechsel zwischen August Kestner und seiner Schwester Charlotte* (Strassburg, 1904), p. 59: "Even less can I ever again hope to attach myself to such a family as the Beaulieus, where Julie has in part gone over into my being."

[21] E.g., Rogge, *Sieben Jahrzehnten,* p. 189: "Innigste Bande mit der Familie"; Gottfried von Leinsberg, *Das Paradies meiner Kindheit 1825–1840* (Lübeck, 1909), p. 49: "eine der intimsten Freundinnen unseres Hauses"; Charlotte Kestner, *Briefwechsel,* p. 128: "All of those who are called Kestner have one more time in him won a friend for life, for if I would even want to find him partisan for us in the long period when he lived with us, I can better take measure of his friendship from the lively and heartfelt feeling that he fostered for other far distant friends."

[22] Bansa, *Lebensbild in Briefen,* p. 149.

[23] Marion A. Kaplan, *The Making of the Jewish Middle Class: Women, Family, and Identity in Imperial Germany* (New York, 1991), pp. 87, 90.

another bride within the "Verwandtschaft."[24] Cleophea Bansa, after her son had criticized three cousins for accepting arranged marriages and marrying too young as well, described how successful marriage presumes a melting together of two families:

What you remark about matters of the heart, I wholeheartedly approve of. You should act just like your father, who let himself be bound to a relationship by no one and nothing except the voice of his heart, which promised him [someone of] the same cultivation [*Bilding*] and perspectives, together with suitably respectable external circumstances – which is absolutely necessary for continual contentment in the fusion of two families that ought to constitute *one*. Although everyone calls the three young men in question too young, still very favorable circumstances and their mutual families bless them.[25]

She went on to say that all the families were connected to the same firm and that the daughters were raised to make their husbands happy in quiet domesticity. This passage documents how at least one middle-class woman at midcentury fit together such diverse elements as upbringing and love, cultivation, style, and success, nuclear family and larger kin, domesticity and business into an intricate mosaic of intense intercourse between whole families.

Creating opportunities for social and affective relations was only part of the range of possibilities for middle-class marriage. Marriage frequently forged business connections with a newly or repeatedly allied family.[26] In her study of the Remy lineage, Brigitte Schröder details how each alliance brought continual trading and investment opportunities in its train. Three families made so many marriages together around 1800 that they became a powerful economic group: "In this period, the families Remy, Hoffmann, and Freudenberg formed a syndicate in the iron industry around the middle Rhine, a considerable empire, which certainly has not yet been fully totalled up."[27] A few other examples should suffice to make the point. When a Hamburg Schubach daughter married an Amsinck son in the late eighteenth century, that opened ties for the Schubachs to all the most important Dutch families in Hamburg.[28] Or in a similar fashion, when Moritz Warburg married Charlotte Oppenheim in 1864, that forged links for the Warburgs with the leading Frankfurt banking houses.[29] A chronicle of the Haniel family analyzes the way marriage ties opened up connections to allied families

[24] Horst Alexander Willam, *Carl Zeiss 1816–1886*, Beiheft 6, *Tradition: Zeitschrift für Firmengeschichte und Unternehmerbiographie* (Munich, 1967), pp. 73–4. Zeiss's son married his father-in-law's granddaughter, whose father – Zeiss's brother-in-law – was Zeiss's closest friend.

[25] Bansa, *Lebensbild in Briefen*, p. 161.

[26] See the discussion by Gunilla-Friederike Budde, *Auf dem Weg ins Bürgerleben: Kindheit und Erziehung in deutschen und englischen Bürgerfamilien 1840–1914* (Göttingen, 1914), pp. 26–61. There is also a fine account of Jewish family alliance by W. E. Mosse, *The German Jewish Economic Elite 1820–1935: A Socio-Cultural Profile* (Oxford, 1989), pp. 161–85.

[27] Schröder, "Weg zur Eisenbahnschiene," p. 53.

[28] Manfred Pohl, *Hamburger Bankengeschichte* (Mainz, 1986), p. 39.

[29] E. Rosenbaum and A. J. Sherman, *M. M. Warburg & Co. 1798–1938: Merchant Bankers of Hamburg* (New York, 1979), p. 46.

throughout the eighteenth and nineteenth centuries.[30] Socially, culturally, and economically, friendship and marriage provided bonds not just between individuals but between houses, families, lineages, dynasties, circles, and networks.

One must not always think of kinship as something that integrates, however much it presumes a discourse of "amity."[31] Two families brought together by marriage might well have little inclination or opportunity to develop intimate relationships with each other. Gabriele Reuter (b. 1859), whose mother's closest relatives were predominantly estate owners in the Prussian Province of Sachsen but whose merchant father stemmed from a parsonage in Mecklenburg, described how different the two sides of the family were, the former mobile and tied to state business, the latter rooted and provincial. She also pointed out that every particular family passed through a cycle of integration and fission. A great part of her early childhood had revolved around the social life of her maternal uncle's estate at Althaldensleben, and close observation of their intercourse led her to the conclusion that "in the development of any family there are days when it appears to have reached its apogee, all its vigor gathered as if at one focal point and proclaiming itself shining and happy to the world."[32] This description was, of course, preface to a chronicle of a cooling of relations between different parts of the family. Cleophea Bansa in Frankfurt four decades earlier had described a similar breaking up of one network while implicitly recognizing that in the process new ones were being formed: "In the family everything is turning out differently from earlier. Each family in the family lives now more for itself and its adults and small children and gathers a group of friends which suits its atmosphere."[33] The son of Doris Focke, who edited her correspondence, explained why relations had cooled with his mother's side of the family: "Various branches got into trouble through frivolity of their own fault or morally sank."[34] Leonore Davidoff and Catherine Hall make the point that "intermarriage and a wide kinship network implies that some may be chosen and others quietly forgotten or actively defied."[35]

Many conflicting forces drew kin together and drove them apart. A competent, active businessman like Georg von Siemens, however close he remained to his

30 Spethmann, *Franz Haniel*. A similar point is made throughout von Treskow's study, "Adel in Preussen." See also Kocka, "Familie, Unternehmer und Kapitalismus," pp. 113–5; Hansjoachim Henning, "Soziale Verflechtungen der Unternehmer in Westfalen 1860–1914," in *Zeitschrift für Unternehmsnsgeschichte*, 23 (1978): 1–30; Michael Stürmer, Gabrielle Teichmann, und Wilhelm Treue, *Wägen und Wagen: Sal. Oppenheim jr. & Cie. Geschichte einer Bank und einer Familie*, 2d ed. (Munich, 1989), pp. 67, 86, 117; Hartmut Zwahr, "Zur Klassenkonstituierung der deutschen Bourgeoisie," in *Jahrbuch für Geschichte* 18 (1978): 21–83, here 34.

31 The phrase comes from Meyer Fortes, "Kinship and the Axiom of Amity," in *Kinship and the Social Order: The Legacy of Lewis Henry Morgan* (Chicago, 1969), pp. 219–49. See the remarks by Budde, *Weg ins Bürgerleben*, pp. 263–72.

32 Gabriele Reuter, *Vom Kinde zum Menschen: Die Geschichte meiner Jugend* (Berlin, 1921), p. 173.

33 Bansa, *Lebensbild in Briefen*, p. 210.

34 Focke, *Briefe Focke*, pp. 246–51.

35 Leonore Davidoff and Catherine Hall, *Family Fortunes: Men and Women of the English Middle Class, 1780–1850* (Chicago, 1987), p. 32.

cousin Werner and the Siemens firm, found it necessary to plot his own life. As his son-in-law and biographer Karl Helfferich pointed out, Werner saw Georg as the hoped-for savior of the dynasty, but Georg found it awkward to be in business with relatives.[36] On the other hand, it was precisely the solidifying of his own independent position that allowed him to support his relatives so successfully in the long run: by the end of the century, as director of the Deutsche Bank, he was a key figure in the financial operations of the house firms founded by Werner and his brothers. Throughout the nineteenth century, a similar dynamic was to be found among growing, expansive families of entrepreneurs and merchants. Such families offered frequent opportunities for this or that son to make himself independent. But when, for example, Franz Haniel separated from his brother Gerhard in 1809, he did so calling on the financial support of a large group of relatives – independence and dependence were relative matters. A whole set of closely allied relatives, Haniels, Noots, and Jacobis, all went their own ways and devoted their energies to founding independent firms, a wise strategy in an expanding field of opportunity and risk. But then they intermarried. Franz's sister married Gottlieb Jacobi, a former partner. His brother Wilhelm married into the Noot family, also with a long history of business partnership. In 1837 Franz's son Hugo married Gerhard's daughter Bertha. The history of these allied families over more than a hundred years describes a succession of reorganizations, mergers, personal initiatives, alliances, autonomous foundations, mutual investments, and bitter, sometimes irreconcilable, splits.[37] Marriage alliance and business alliance moved on two planes, constantly tracking each other, creating connections on one level that frequently transformed those on the other. One lesson to be learned from a close study of familial relations is that the kinship business required labor, time, and investment to bridge differences, coordinate energies, combat indifference, and counteract competing desires.

It must be emphasized here that the kinship system that developed during the last half of the eighteenth century and emerged in full blossom in the nineteenth was a transformation – I am searching for a good way to express *Aufhebung* – of an earlier one. Many of the same elements continued to pattern expectations and practices but were rearranged in quite new configurations. Both the clientage system of the sixteenth and seventeenth centuries and the new kinship system that emerged from it in the course of the eighteenth century involved intense networking and the building of political and economic relationships with and around kin. But since endogamy was precluded for all but a small minority of the population in the earlier period, any long-term relationships between families tended to be constructed as asymmetrical clientage networks, perhaps with ritual kinship creating bonds over generations that precluded marriage exchanges. As

[36] Helfferich, *Georg von Siemens,* vol. 1, p. 165.

[37] Brigitte Schröder, "Weg zur Eisenbahnschiene," describes a bitter conflict over the desire of Ferdinand Remy to develop independence (p. 117). On the other hand, his new companies were funded by relatives. And Franz Haniel broke with his brother-in-law Heinrich Huyssen; Spethmann, *Franz Haniel,* p. 93. See Kocka on Krupp, "Familie, Unternehmer und Kapitalismus," p. 117.

Volker Press pointed out, clientage relations could associate two noble and burgher families over many generations without there ever being any question of connubium.[38] I cannot detail all the differences between the two systems and the two periods, for the spade work to chronicle that shift has not yet been done. Peter Moraw rightly says that what we are after is usually too close to basic assumptions to be subject to explicit comment in the sources and requires the patient reconstruction of complicated practices.[39] The crucial differences seem to lie in the nature of alliance construction (clientage versus affinal networks), the relative importance of succession and alliance (cultivation of landed estates, guild monopolies, and merchant oligarchies versus an expanding industrial and trading economy), the practical exigencies of support for kin (conflation of private ownership and public office versus promotion by merit and the rise of a bourgeois public sphere), and the center of gravity in kinship practices (protection of a patrimony versus socialization, education, and strategic support for careers).[40]

Despite the fact that marriage among kin during the nineteenth century brought together families of equal station, a coordinated kin-group – the dynasty, lineage, or clan – was never composed of equals. The Siemens family is instructive in this regard. Werner Siemens interacted with a set of family members of about 200 persons.[41] He also maintained a strong sense of family dynasty, as already mentioned. Everywhere one looks in the firms he was associated with or led, one finds relatives – as chemists, engineers, managers, auditors, salesmen, and stockholders. But within the family there was considerable social differentiation. Werner kept a large and open household establishment, entertaining the political, social, and economic leaders of Berlin and Imperial Germany.[42] A second cousin in the chemical laboratory was simply not a social equal (although he might become one). Kinship and class follow along on different tracks, continually interconnecting and supporting the progress of one another. And there is no question that the cultivation of family sentiment made possible very different access to family resources and certainly is part of the story of any analysis of expropriation.[43]

38 Volker Press, "Patronat und Klientel im Heiligen Römischen Reich," in Antoni Maczak, ed., *Klientelsysteme in Europa der frühen Neuzeit,* Schriften des historischen Kollegs, Kolloquien, 9 (Munich, 1988), pp. 19–46, here p. 20.

39 Peter Moraw, "Ueber Patrone und Klienten im Heiligen Römischen Reich des späten Mittelalters und der frühen Neuzeit," in Maczak, *Klientelsysteme,* pp. 1–18, here p. 7.

40 Davidoff and Hall, *Family Fortunes,* p. 33, chronicle a similar shift in England from vertical to horizontal ties. A very important new work on the kinship system of the seventeenth and eighteenth-century German nobility is Christophe Duhamelle, "La noblesse d'église. Famille et pouvoir dans la chevalerie immediate rhenane xviie–xviiie siècles," Thèse d'histoire, Université de Paris-1 (28.11.1994), mss. See his discussion of inheritance of office (p. 157), marriage prohibitions (p. 231), inequality (p. 217), group solidarity based on exogamy (p. 234), the beginnings of endogamy in the eighteenth century (p. 255), new forms of stratification (p. 305).

41 J. D. Scott, *Siemens Brothers 1858–1958: An Essay in the History of Industry* (London, 1958), p. 29.

42 Helfferich, *Georg von Siemens,* vol. 3, p. 232.

43 A very useful anthropological analysis of kinship dynamics and a family corporation is by E. Leyton,

The usefulness of kin

Kin helped and supported one another in many ways, but there seems to be more information in biographical and autobiographical literature about the use of kin for obtaining an education than about anything else – getting a place in a school or Gymnasium, receiving a scholarship or free board (*Freitisch*), arranging for lodging, or helping out with expenses. To some degree, this impression comes from the conventions of biography itself. Men in the nineteenth century characteristically divided the accounts of their lives into two quite distinct parts – an early childhood and schooling and perhaps young adulthood surrounded by kin and family and a period of adult success based upon individual achievement, with the "private" side rigidly suppressed. Ludwig Wiese, the educational administrator, is a case in point. In the long account of his career (written in two full volumes), he mentioned only in passing having married. He did once pause, excusing himself to the reader in the process, to make an expressly "private" aside: to blame *his wife* for not providing him with children.[44] Gustav Freytag once remarked that a history of German literature and culture in the nineteenth century would be the account of family connections among the educated bourgeoisie, yet the *Allgemeine deutsche Biographie* systematically erases all traces of kinship in its articles, all of which are written to celebrate individual achievement.[45] But even if writers were less guarded when chronicling their early years and therefore acknowledged more readily the help of kin during their formation, the impression remains that education of all their young (men) was indeed the central concern of extended kin groups.[46]

The theologian Bernhard Rogge (b. 1831), son of a Silesian pastor, obtained a place at Schulpforta through the intercession of his older sister's husband, the later minister of war, von Roon. Von Roon subsequently offered him an opening in his regiment, which another brother later took up. Rogge's oldest brother became chaplain of von Roon's division.[47] *Emil Lehmann (b. 1823) tells how his brother Heinrich accompanied their uncle August Leo to Paris in order to study painting. His younger brother later went to study with the older brother. When Emil in turn went to Berlin to study, he ate midday meals with an uncle.*[48] *Wilhelm Appuhn (b. 1804) was sent to the Gymnasium in Halberstadt because of so many family connections. He ate meals*

"Composite Descent Groups in Canada," in C. C. Harris, *Readings in Kinship and Urban Society* (Oxford, 1970), pp. 179–86.

[44] Ludwig Wiese, *Lebenserinnerungen und Amtserfahrungen*, 2 vols. (Berlin, 1886), vol. 1, pp. 54, 151. On the other hand, he found his joy in raising his orphaned godchild.

[45] Freytag, cited in Zunkel, *Rheinische-Westfälische Unternehmer*, p. 83 (*Bilder*, ser. 2, vol. 7, pt. 4 [Leipzig, 1928], p. 320). Karin Hausen brought the suppression of family matters in the AdB to my attention.

[46] And that was one of the expressed purposes for the founding of family associations during the 1870s and after. See Haupt, "Männliche und weibliche Berufskarrieren," p. 158.

[47] Rogge, *Sieben Jahrzehnten*, pp. 54, 113.

[48] Lehmann, *Lebenserinnerungen*, pp. 13, 27–8, 121.

in rotation at the homes of three different uncles while lodging with one of them.[49] *Friedrich Von Raumer (b. 1781) went as a schoolboy to the Joachimstaler Gymnasium in Berlin where he lived with his uncle (FZH), President Gerlach. His mother's bother was one of his professors at the Gymnasium. When he entered the Prussian bureaucracy, he started under his uncle Gerlach, who helped write his probationary essay.*[50] *Karl Hase (b. 1800), another pastor's son, went to live with his godparent after his father's death. During early schooling he lived with an uncle (FB). At the Gymnasium in Altenburg, he ate by turns at houses of relatives, including a cousin, and later he received financial support from other cousins to study.*[51] *The historian Pauli (b. 1823) was sent to an uncle in Berlin to study at the Gymnasium. School vacations were spent with other relatives.*[52] *Louise Otto called this practice of schoolboy visits to various relatives during vacation going on the "cousin road [Vetternstrasse]."*[53] *Ludwig Wiese (b. 1806) got into a garrison school at the recommendation of a relative. His mother traveled to Berlin to arrange with a distant relative for a scholarship at a higher school.*[54] *Charles Kestner, son of Karl, left Strasburg to go to school in Frankfurt/Main because his uncle Theodor and cousins were there.*[55] *The Remy family and its allied branches traded children back and forth between their various merchant houses for apprenticeship training over many generations during the eighteenth and nineteenth centuries – up and down the Rhine and back and forth between Germany and Holland.*[56] *In a letter to her mother, the 23-year-old Annette von Droste Hülshoff reported on all the schooling needs of relatives and how each one was being paid for.*[57] *After Gabriele Reuter's father died and her mother liquidated the bankrupt Egyptian merchant house, an aunt paid for Gabriele's schooling. She was sent to an uncle in Mecklenburg for catechism instruction and confirmation.*[58] *The politician and university rector Hermann Hüffer (b. 1830) was sent to Bonn because his mother's family was there.*[59] *Paul Deussen from a Rhenish parsonage (b. 1845) mentions that his mother was sent to an uncle for schooling in 1830. In the 1850s he and his brothers were sent to the same relatives for their schooling.*[60] *The novelist Levin Schücking (b. 1814) attended school in Osnabrück, where he lived with an aunt (FZ).*[61] *Wolfgang Zorn*

[49] L. Walther, ed., *Erinnerungen aus Wilhelm Appuhns Leben, aus seinen Aufzeichnungen zusammengestellt* (Gotha, 1885).

[50] Friedrich von Raumer, *Lebenserinnerungen und Briefwechsel,* 2 Teile (Leipzig, 1861), T. 1, pp. 12, 46–7.

[51] Karl Hase, *Ideale und Irrthümer: Jugend-Erinnerungen,* 2d ed. (Leipzig, 1873), pp. 1–3, 9–11, 160.

[52] Reinhold Pauli, *Lebenserinnerungen,* pp. 1–24.

[53] Louise Otto, *Frauenleben im deutschen Reich: Errinerungen aus der Vergangenheit mit Hinweis auf Gegenwart und Zukunft* (Leipzig, 1876), p. 3.

[54] Wiese, *Lebenserinnerungen,* vol. 1, pp. 7–9.

[55] Kestner-Köchlin, *Briefwechsel Kestner,* pp. 114–5.

[56] Schröder, "Weg zur Eisenbahnschiene," pp. 19–21, 40, 47, 55–67. See also Kocka, "Familie, Unternehmer, und Kapitalismus," pp. 103–5.

[57] Annette von Droste-Hülshoff, *Historisch-kritische Ausgabe, Werke, Briefwechsel,* edited by Winfried Woesler, vol. 8, 1: *Briefe 1805–1838,* ed. Walter Gödden (Tübingen, 1987), pp. 41–6.

[58] Reuter, *Vom Kinde zum Menschen,* pp. 174–6, 194, 207–8.

[59] Hermann Hüffer, *Lebenserinnerungen,* ed. Ernst Sieper (Berlin, 1912), p. 23.

[60] Paul Deussen, *Mein Leben,* ed. Erika Rosenthal-Deussen (Leipzig, 1922), pp. 4, 58.

[61] Levin Schücking, *Lebenserinnerungen,* 2 vols. (Breslau and Leipzig, 1886), vol. 1, p. 85.

in his account of Swabian merchants and banking families offers example after example of relatives providing apprenticeships for the young men of allied families.[62] *Ottilie Wildermuth sent her daughter to her godparent in Switzerland for her education.*[63] *Cleophea Bansa offers many examples of apprenticeships and first positions for family members through family connection.*[64] *Robert von Mohl sent both his daughters to his brother in Paris for their socialization and education.*[65] *In the petit-bourgeois Fricke family, children were sent to relatives for schooling, who all chipped in to help with the finances.*[66] *Carl Zeiss got his start in Jena through the support of his sister.*[67] *In the account of the Warburg family by Rosenbaum and Sherman, the nineteenth century is filled with numerous examples of sons receiving apprenticeship training or positions in other banks through family connections.*[68] *Three of the Siemens brothers boarded with an uncle (MB, who later adopted their sister) during their education. Children were constantly exchanged between branches of the family for training. Werner gave his cousin Georg his first start. He also trained a third cousin, Alexander, who was sent to London where he was subsequently adopted by Werner's brother William and became his successor.*[69] *In his account of the administrative class in Westphalia, Wegmann points out that candidates for the position of Landrat frequently were supported over the long period of waiting by relatives and friends.*[70]

In the scattered evidence offered here, kin offer strategic support for one another above all in the development of careers. Boys received apprenticeship training at the hands of relatives or through their intercession, or they found schooling, Gymnasium education, or university education through family assistance – scholarships, lodging, or board. Daughters, too, were sent to relatives, often to learn household management, writing skills, music, and general deportment in their households. But both young and older women were also frequently exchanged between families in times of need. They could live together for years with elderly family members or with young mothers busy with household chores, with sick or widowed friends and relatives. It is difficult to underestimate the

[62] Wolfgang Zorn, *Handels- und Industriegeschichte Bayerisch-Schwabens 1648–1870: Wirtschafts-, Sozial-, und Kulturgeschichte des schwäbischen Unternehmertums,* Veröffentlichungen der schwäbischen Forschungsgemeinschaft bei der Kommission für Landesgeschichte, Reihe I: Studien zur Geschichte bayerischen Schwabens (Augsburg, 1961).

[63] Bernhardine Schulze-Smidt, ed., *Ottilie Wildermuths Briefe an einen Freund: Mit einer Lebensskizze* (Bielefeld and Leipzig, 1910), pp. 38–9.

[64] Bansa, *Lebensbild in Briefen,* passim.

[65] Ellen von Siemens-Helmholtz, ed., *Anna von Helmholtz: Ein Lebensbild in Briefen* (Berlin, 1929), pp. 15–35.

[66] Friederike Fricke, ed., *Aus dem Leben unserer Mutter: Familienbriefe für die Familie* (Göttingen, 1929), pp. 19–38, 85.

[67] Willam, *Carl Zeiss,* p. 13.

[68] E.g., Rosenbaum and Sherman, *Warburg,* p. 40.

[69] Werner von Siemens, *Personal Recollections,* trans. W. C. Copland (London, 1893), pp. 27–9; J. D. Scott, *Siemens Brothers,* p. 69.

[70] Dietrich Wegmann, *Die leitenden staatlichen Verwaltungsbeamten der Provinz Westfalen, 1815–1918.* Geschichtliche Arbeiten zur westfälischen Landesforschung, wirtschafts- und sozialgeschichtliche Gruppe, vol. 1 (Münster, 1969), p. 205.

importance of those family members, especially women, who were consistently called upon during stressful or crisis periods in a family's development.

Bernhard Rogge remembered that his mother's sister lived with his parents, whose parsonage was the center of constant hospitality, with his mother frequently feeding and caring for 40 people a day. That aunt lived for years at a time with whatever family was in particular need of help.[71] *Agnes Kayser-Langerhanss moved in successively with two sisters after she herself became a widow, and she acted as nurse for a long time for a nephew wounded in 1871.*[72] *The Berlin Eberty family utilized extended kin for stressful periods.*[73] *Gabriele Reuter's mother had been sent to help out her sister after the latter's marriage. She herself was sent to accompany an aunt who had decided to settle in Weimar.*[74] *After Carl Friedrich Siemens's divorce, his sister took over the burdens of the household.*[75] Unmarried girls, spinsters, and widows of closely allied kin in many instances became central figures in extended families through their charitative labors. Charlotte Kestner moved to Alsace in order to help a brother and his wife raise their considerable family.[76] After Charlotte's death, Henriette Feuerbach wrote: "In the large circle of family and way beyond, Aunt Lottchen was providence itself. One turned to her in joy and pain, at every uncertainty, in every difficulty and found, if not always help, then always smart and sober advice and heartfelt sympathy."[77] Carlota Sieveking played a similar role in her widely dispersed family, both as correspondent and as governess.[78] After Doris Focke died in 1818, her husband's niece took over the household and raised the children.[79] There are too many examples of relatives living with families to chronicle. In many autobiographies, writers refer to uncles, aunts, and grandparents in the households, who in many cases were there to help with the running of the household or business.

In addition, relatives, often distant ones, were frequently called upon as godparents. But friends, too, could become ritual kin and in turn play strategic roles for a family. The theologian Bernhard Rogge cemented his relationship with

[71] Rogge, *Sieben Jahrzehnten,* p. 28.

[72] Agnes Kayser-Langerhanss, *Erinnerungen aus meinem Leben* (Dresden, 1894).

[73] Felix Eberty, *Jugenderinnerungen eines alten Berliners* (Berlin, 1878), p. 120. A distant relative of her grandfather, together with her mother and siblings, considered herself a client of the family and was always ready to jump in when needed. "Such persons were then found everywhere in the entourage of every respectable house, to which they felt bound through all kinds of favors and assistance. They found pride to be counted in a larger sense among the relatives. It was a kind of vassal relationship, not unlike the one which perhaps existed between a large landholder and the family of his administrators. Along with the so-called good old days, such relationships, which had their very agreeable [*gemütliche*] side, appear pretty much to have disappeared [*zu Grabe gegangen*]."

[74] Reuter, *Vom Kinde zum Menschen,* pp. 22, 220.

[75] Georg Siemens, *Carl Friedrich von Siemens: Ein grosser Unternehmer* (Freiburg, 1960), p. 254.

[76] Kestner-Köchlin, *Briefwechsel Kestner,* pp. 12–13.

[77] Kestner-Köchlin, *Briefwechsel Kestner,* pp. 350–1.

[78] Rebensburg-Reich, *Tante Carlotas Nachlass,* pp. 10, 23, 34–5, 135.

[79] Wilhelm Olbers Focke, ed., *Briefe von Doris Focke geb. Olbers an ihren Bruder, für die Familie als Manuscript gedruckt* (Bremen, 1886), pp. 187ff.

Ritschl by making him godfather (along with his brother-in-law von Roon) for his firstborn.[80] Emil Lehmann's father had called on his cousin August Leo to be godfather to his daughter. The same cousin later took Emil's brother with him to Paris to study art. August sent his daughter back to Hamburg to become governess for the Heine family, which was intimately (*innig*) bound to the Lehmanns.[81] Ludwig Wiese raised his orphaned godchild.[82] The factory worker Richter found his early training in the establishments of his two godparents, a smith and a barrel maker.[83] The godfather of the future pastor Otte (b. 1808) was appointed as his guardian. The godmother provided lodging for the widowed mother and children and eventually made the family heir to her property.[84]

Also crucial for the coordination of middle-class family life was the office of guardianship. Guardians administered property, provided for education, and frequently took their wards into their own households. After his father died, Mörike went to live with his uncle-guardian Eberhard von Georgii.[85] Annette von Droste-Hülshoff mentioned in a letter that one of her relatives died leaving seven small children, who were all taken in by other relatives.[86] Carlota Sieveking discussed the establishment of a family foundation for a related orphan, with one of the solicitor uncles acting as legal guardian.[87] Marchtaler makes the point that because Johann Arnold Günther, the Hamburg senator, had no children, he became active as an uncle-guardian for many wards. Orphans in these circles were always taken in by relatives. Many household heads were legal guardians for young relatives or acted as foster parents.[88]

The relationship between kinship and capital formation is a complicated one, and although many historical monographs point out the importance of family-supplied capital for the course of German economic development in the nineteenth century, there is no overview of the process and no consideration of the way kinship and capital may have helped structure each other over time, except for the inspiring but neglected study by Jürgen Kocka.[89] During the first half of the eighteenth century, some merchant houses began to expand on the basis of pooled capital and cross-investment between firms founded by different branches of related families. Schröder's monograph on the Remy family offers an outstand-

[80] Rogge, *Sieben Jahrzehnten,* p. 139.

[81] Lehmann, *Lebenserinnerungen,* pp. 12–13, 29.

[82] Wiese, *Lebenserinnerungen,* vol. 1, pp. 151–2.

[83] Otto Richter, *Lebensfreuden eines Arbeiterkindes: Jugenderinnerungen* (Dresden, 1919), p. 26.

[84] Christian Heinrich Otte, *Aus meinem Leben* (Leipzig, 1893), pp. 2–3, 8.

[85] *Deutsches Geschlechterbuch.*

[86] Droste-Hülshoff, *Briefwechsel,* vol. 8, 1: pp. 81–5.

[87] Rebensburg-Reich, *Tante Carlotas Nachlass,* pp. 103–4.

[88] Hildegard von Marchtaler, *Aus althamburger Senatorenhäusern. Familienschicksale im 18. und 19. Jahrhundert,* Veröffentlichung des Vereins für hamburgische Geschichte, 16 (Hamburg, n.d. [1958]), pp. 38, 130, 163, 170, 191, 193.

[89] Kocka, "Familie, Unternehmer und Kapitalismus." See also the important leads offered by Hartmut Zwahr in his study of the Leipzig entrepreneurs and industrialists, "Zur Klassenkonstituierung der Bourgeoisie."

ing example. Another stage was reached between 1780 and 1800 when many banking and merchant houses were established, with the foundation of industrial firms following hard on their heels.[90] According to Friedrich Zunkel, the economic growth from the later eighteenth century onward was closely related to the search for marriage alliances in order to provide capital for entrepreneurial activity. Most entrepreneurs emerged from rooted, well-established families, which were crucial in the difficult period of finding sufficient financial resources to expand.[91] Beginning in the 1840s and 1850s, the problems of accumulating capital led to the foundation of joint-stock companies, although many of these enterprises were in fact still family holdings. As late as the turn of the century, Siemens and Halske under the prodding of Georg Siemens from the Deutsche Bank became a joint-stock company, but the shareholders were all from the family.[92] Even in the early phase of industrial development, says Friedrich Zunkel, capital demands often led to family firms to bring in partners and eventually break up the firm.[93] Here, he probably underestimates the importance of long-term alliances. What looks like a foundation by entrepreneurs from different families turns out frequently to be one made by men from different branches of families allied in many different ways, often over several generations. Because of the marriage politics of industrialists, Zunkel himself pointed out, "leading entrepreneurial families of the industrial and merchant cities of Rhineland-Westphalia [were] mostly related by marriage to one another, frequently even many times."[94] During the second half of the nineteenth century, middle- and upper-class groups solidified their internal structure and maintained boundaries through marriage politics.[95] Toni Pierenkemper argues that the strong tendency to endogamy within various strata during the second half of the century probably continued to have a great deal to do with access to capital.[96] By the end of the nineteenth century, joint-stock companies had slowly whittled away at the familial character of capital accumulation.[97] What finally broke the connection between

[90] Manfred Pohl, *Hamburger Bankengeschichte*, p. 29; Schröder, "Weg zur Eisenbahnschiene," p. 53; Rosenbaum and Sherman, *Warburg*, pp. 1–20; Spethmann, *Haniel*, pp. 78–112.

[91] Zunkel, *Rheinisch-Westfälische Unternehmer*, pp. 9–23. See also Schröder, "Weg zur Eisenbahnschiene," pp. 50–5, 109–19; Spethmann, *Haniel*, pp. 110–12. The same point is made by Zwahr, "Zur Konstituierung der Bourgeoisie," pp. 26–34.

[92] E.g., Schröder, "Weg zur Eisenbahnschiene." In 1873, H. W. Remy & Consorten became a joint-stock company, the Rasselsteiner Eisenwerksgesellschaft. The shares were widely scattered among the larger family (*Grossfamilie*). It was soon bought up by Otto Wolff, although the technical and commercial management remained in the hands of the Remy family until the 1930s. See also Spethmann, *Haniel*, pp. 280–93. Also Volker Wellhöner, *Grossbanken und Grossindustrie im Kaiserreich*, Kritische Studien zur Geschichtswissenschaft, vol. 85 (Göttingen, 1989), pp. 216–26.

[93] Zunkel, *Rheinisch-Wesfälische Unternehmer*, pp. 72–3.

[94] Zunkel, *Rheinisch-Westfälische Unternehmer*, pp. 94–5.

[95] See Zwahr, "Zur Klassenkonstituierung der Bourgeoisie," Kocka, "Familie, Unternehmer und Kapitalismus," and Henning, "Soziale Verflechtungen."

[96] Toni Pierenkemper, *Die Westfälischen Schwerindustriellen, 1852–1913: Soziale Struktur und unternehmerischer Erfolg*, Kritische Studien zur Geschichtswissenschaft, vol. 36 (Göttingen, 1979).

[97] Kocka, "Familie, Unternehmer und Kapitalismus," p. 130, describes tensions within the Siemens family about paying out shares, and Zwahr, "Zur Klassenkonstituierung der Bourgeoisie," p. 41, argues that the foundation of limited liability companies lessened the importance of family alliance

capital and family alliance, says Marion Kaplan, was post–World War I inflation, which wiped out savings and forced the children from many formerly independently wealthy families into the workforce.[98] Other factors in the decline of kinship endogamy and the intense interaction among extended families after World War I were the changes in capital markets and in the way careers developed.

Marriage alliance and social status

Until World War I various groups were open or closed to one another depending on the way in which transfers of capital and property were directed – with distinct tendencies toward hypergamy.[99] Most historians have examined this issue in terms of frequency distributions of marriage partners by occupation and status, but the larger picture is about familial dynamics over time. Bernard Rogge's autobiography shows coordinated kinship alliances between pastoral families, university professors, and the military aristocracy; the Kestner correspondence, between Bildungsbürger, merchants, industrialists, and officials; the Siemens family history, between industrialists, scientists, professors, and estate owners.[100]

The details of how class was regulated through marriage are lost in the hundreds of unstated assumptions surrounding negotiations between individuals, their friends and peers, and their families.[101] Property, as von Stein pointed out, lay at the foundation of social existence and social difference.[102] Whatever limitations one might want to put on this generalization, one cannot deny that marriage involved substantial property transfers and was too important in that regard to be left unattended. Dowry was one of the great social regulators in the nine-

for capital concentration. But counterexamples abound. See e.g., Walther Däbritz and Carl Schmöle, *Geschichte der R. & G. Schmöle Metalwerke Menden/Kreis Iserlohn 1853 bis 1952: Zugleich ein Beitrag zur Industriegeschichte des märkischen Sauerlandes in drei Jahrhunderten* (o.O., 1953).

[98] Kaplan, *Making*, p. 85.

[99] An excellent analysis of marriage of daughters upward is found in von Treskow, "Adel in Preussen." The same point is made for the high bourgeoisie by Zwahr, "Zur Klassenkonstituierung der Bourgeoisie," p. 41. Given my findings about nineteenth-century endogamy among small landholders in Neckarhausen, I would suggest that hypergamy was a central feature of propertied classes during the nineteenth century, that it was a major way for capital transfers to move upward in the status hierarchy (a classic case of Bourdieu's point about real capital and symbolic capital being fungible), and that it made possible such openings between classes as we observe between industrialists and nobility at the end of the century. Werner Mosse, *German-Jewish Economic Elite*, pp. 161–85, goes beyond what I can offer here on different models of family alliance and on shifts and changes throughout the nineteenth century. He shows how different Jewish families went through different phases over time, although whether newcomers recapitulated certain stages depending on when they emerged is an open question. In any event, Mosse provides the basis for analyzing the patterns of alliance over time. On hypergamy among silk weavers, see Peter Kriedte, *Eine Stadt am seidenen Faden: Haushalt, Hausindustrie und soziale Bewegung in Krefeld in der Mitte des 19. Jahrhunderts*, Veröffentlichungen des Max-Planck-Instituts für Geschichte, vol. 97 (Göttingen, 1991), p. 220.

[100] Rogge, *Sieben Jahrzehnten*; Kestner-Köchlin, *Briefwechsel Kestner*; Hermann W. Siemens. "Ueber das Erfindergeschlecht Siemens," *Archiv zur Rassen- und Gesellschaftsbiologie* 12 (1916–18): 162–92.

[101] For the most recent discussion, see Budde, *Weg ins Bürgerleben*, pp. 58–72.

[102] Lorenz von Stein, *Die Frau auf dem socialen Gebiete* (Stuttgart, 1880), pp. 23–5.

teenth century. In fact, it appears that dowries became ever more substantial for the middle class and played an ever greater role in determining which groups and individuals were open to each other at any particular time. Wolfgang Zorn reckons that from the eighteenth to the early nineteenth century the average dowry rose on the order of 3,000 fl to 50,000 fl among the merchant families he studied.[103] And Marion Kaplan, who has analyzed dowries and the marriage market for middle-class Jews during the Imperial period, argues that dowries grew in importance for Germany as a whole after 1890.[104] There seems to have been a constant inflation throughout the nineteenth century, making the dowry ever more useful for underlining class differences and as a regulator for providing social access, integration, and differentiation.

The Freiherr von Schaezler from Augsburg (writing about events in the early nineteenth century) gave an instructive account of his marriage strategy and negotiations.[105] As a young merchant living far from home in Aachen, he wrote to a cousin (FBS) in Augsburg to find him a suitable party. He was soon invited to join the firm of Baron Liebert, whose youngest daughter was in love with an inappropriate candidate. (Von Schaezler's current employer, not wishing to lose him, offered to find a rich prospect among his own relatives.) Von Schaezler, however, preferred Baron Liebert's older daughter, who fell in love with him at first sight. For the father, this arrangement seemed suitable, and the two men drew up a contract involving the exchange of a substantial dowry and the obligation of the young man to work for the firm for a set number of years. The young couple was also to live in the Baron's house and take their meals together with him each day.

The middle classes made a great deal out of love as the foundation of marriage. Von Schaezler had no problem with falling in love quickly and decisively, nor did he see any contradictions in his account of marriage founded simultaneously on love and business.[106] As Zunkel pointed out, the emergence of capable young men of industry and trade in the early stages of industrial growth took precisely this route.[107] But their access to business and property was closely regulated by calculation and contract. Clearly as this case shows, the system depended on women following their inclination and sentiment. Just because they were "free" to choose, they had to be hedged in by pressure and steered in the right direction. With her acid wit, the alienated countess Franziska zu Reventlow described formalities at the other end of the century. Daughters of her aristocratic circle spent "all their time reading about love" and were watched all the more anxiously in the company of men.[108] The situations in which contacts were made were carefully "choreographed" – the ball season providing one of the most important

[103] Zorn, *Handels- und Industriegeschichte*, p. 266.
[104] Kaplan, *Making*, pp. 106–10. See Mosse's comments, *German-Jewish Economic Elite*, pp. 93ff.
[105] Printed in Zorn, *Handels- und Industriegeschichte*, pp. 310–22.
[106] On courtship, see Mosse, *German-Jewish Economic Elite*, pp. 98–127.
[107] Zunkel, *Rheinisch-westfälische Unternehmer*, p. 20.
[108] Else Reventlow, ed., *Briefe des Gräfin Franziska zu Reventlow* (Munich, 1929), pp. 22–3.

stages for negotiation. "While the unfortunate victims innocently amuse themselves, their mothers sit in long rows around the floor, observing with eagle eyes who courted whom, and do their best to make matches. What they accomplish in one ball season is unbelievable."[109]

The new alliance system developed step by step with the opening up of the economy.[110] The most intensive early examples that I have found involve families like the Remys and Hoffmanns who were rapidly developing trade networks between Holland and the Rhineland before the mid eighteenth century.[111] Zunkel puts the roots of the great expansion in the last third of the eighteenth century and provides evidence to show that the systematic use of marriage to create trading networks, to concentrate capital, and to attract able young men from the right families to a firm expanded at the same time.[112] Biographies of such early nineteenth-century figures as Franz Haniel offer rich examples of the proliferation of economic activity and the intensified practices of the care of kin.[113] Pohl's account of the Hamburg merchant houses points to 1780–1800 as the period in which the great houses were established, and part of the process involved the creation of a dense network of family connections through systematic and planned marital strategies.[114] It is hard to avoid the conclusion that the work that went into the new kinship system was related to a new kind of economy – this was the fundamental insight of Gérard Delille. The old system was occupied in maintaining a patrimony, while the new acceded to a much more open and flexible way of managing and creating opportunity.[115] And this worked for the old nobility as well. Heinz Reif has contrasted a tight inheritance-driven system in the ecclesiastical territories of eighteenth-century Westphalia with the creation of a regional elite through marriage alliance and the cultivation of emotional social networks after secularization.[116] In the earlier period, the nobility monopolized office by virtue of their status and purity of blood. "Private" families exercised their right to "public" office. In the conditions of the nineteenth century, office had to go to its incumbent through merit, and nepotism could no longer operate as an openly acknowledged system of recruitment to position. Nonetheless office-holding families spawned officeholders. With the growth of government to

109 Reventlow, *Briefe Reventlow,* p. 23.

110 A point emphasized by Kocka, "Familie, Unternehmer und Kapitalismus," esp. p. 126. On development of the economy and forms of alliance, see Mosse, *German-Jewish Economic Elite,* pp. 161–85.

111 Schröder, "Weg zur Eisenbahnschiene," pp. 18–27. See also Zwahr, "Zur Klassenkonstituierung der Bourgeoisie."

112 Zunkel, *Rheinisch-westfälische Unternehmer,* pp. 20–5, 77–8, 94–6, 103–10.

113 Spethmann, *Franz Haniel,* pp. 44, 50–1, 65, 70, 76, 87–98.

114 Pohl, *Hamburger Bankengeschichte,* pp. 29–30, 39–41.

115 Kocka, "Familie, Unternehmer und Kapitalismus," p. 126, reflects on industrial bourgeois families this way: "these families represented *something new* in a *new environment.* They did not carry on a preindustrial craft economy or a peasant farm based largely on subsistence; rather, they had to do with a functioning, expanding, centralized industrial enterprise according to its own internal capitalist (or even not at all capitalist) logic."

116 Heinz Reif, *Westfälischer Adel 1770–1860: Vom Herrschaftsstand zur regionalen Elite* (Göttingen, 1979). And now see Duhamelle, "Noblesse d'église."

keep pace with the economy, here too was a growing field of opportunity. The whole system performed in the fashion of Lévi-Strauss's "generalized exchange." Rather than maintaining a particular right to a particular property or office, families gave up, or were forced to give up, such claims with the expectation that what they gave in one place, they would receive in another. But such politics involved cultivating intensively and extensively narrow and extended groups of kin. And the whole game had to be played differently with the family's relationship to institutions recast. It now became important for allied kin to see that their youth got proper educations, that daughters were provided with dowries, that capable and enterprising young men were backed with capital. The circulation of goods and services was redirected in a new system of exchange.

People of the nineteenth century had to learn to manage quite different kinds of networks, and part of the issue in this delicately choreographed system involved the presentation of each family and its members according to the rules of the particular stratum and cultural sphere in which they wished to operate. The private house and its activities were intricately articulated with a larger network of social connections and aesthetic assumptions.[117] The education of both men and women to open and fluid systems where couples had to cooperate in tasks of social representation required protracted drill in taste, morality, sentiment, and style. Many a middle-class man was anxious that his future wife might cause embarrassment in their public functions or might create tensions in the family at points most crucial for his business and social interests. Love and sentiment and emotional response or their expected development were built into the very nature of familial circuitry. They were the software necessary to direct the course of all the hard-wired conductors. There were, of course, many different ways of falling in love. Some people first chose a suitable family by visiting, dining, walking, and playing cards together in the evening, and others did it by correspondence. Some looked for friendly faces among relatives while others latched onto families where their careers were directed. Some followed the wishes and advice of their parents and siblings, and some bravely struck off for themselves. But love always determined the flow of capital, access to office, the course of a career – and everyone knew it.[118] Some people made very bad mistakes, as did Carl Friedrich Siemens, who came home with a quite unsuitable bride.[119] The family had to hire detectives and present him with evidence that she was not of the right station. His mother and sister declared him socially dead and cut off all relations until he meekly followed their lead and never saw his wife again.

[117] See the important work on this subject by Budde, *Weg ins Bürgerleben*, pp. 89–102, 124–43, 173–90, 317–22.

[118] Davidoff and Hall, *Family Fortunes*, p. 219, emphasize that "free choice" of marriage partners was exercised in a "carefully controlled context of mutual values."

[119] Georg Siemens, *Carl Friedrich von Siemens*, pp. 27–9. Eduard Harkort was disinherited by his widowed mother for marrying a carpenter's widow: Hartmut Zwahr, *Proletariat und Bourgeoisie in Deutschland: Studien zur Klassendialektik* (Cologne, 1980), p. 89.

Middle-class endogamy

From the current statistical literature on endogamy (see Chapter 21), it appears that Germany operated well within European parameters. Before 1700, there were few if any marriages between recognizable blood kin, and given what is known about the horror felt and the controls exercised in the seventeenth century concerning marriage with a close relative of a deceased spouse, it is safe to say that direct, repeated alliances between families through marriage across generations were not central to social relationships in Germany at that time. But the new endogamous alliance system instituted around 1740 flowered into a continuous effort to develop and maintain alliances across generations lasting until after World War I. Although endogamous marriage is clearly only one indicator of a shift in the way family and kinship worked, it still is a powerful indicator and one aspect most accessible to examination. There has never been a good statistical study of middle-class endogamy for Germany on the order of that done by George Darwin for England. This section provides some impressionistic evidence about marriage and kinship in the German middle class, although the examples are so abundant that there is space for only a small selection here. I have read through a large number of autobiographies, biographies of industrial and business figures, and a few histories of firms and industry branches. Not many of these works make family connection an explicit theme, so the problem is to work out a portrait from disparate materials and unsystematic accounts. I have tried to scan material concerning shopkeepers, merchants, industrialists, bureaucrats, educators, artists, literary figures, and scholars to get a sense of the general practices of a disparate and multilayered class.[120]

The following paragraphs describe repeated alliances between families, most notably cousin marriages. Attention is also given to marriages with two sisters, sibling exchange, and similar forms, and also cases of families allied through business, politics, or social friendship who strengthened their ties through the exchange of marriage partners.[121] *One particularly interesting case is that of Berhard Rogge (b. 1831), who has already been mentioned in this book several times. The son of a pastor from Silesia, he became a theologian in turn. According to Rogge, his family had close social ties with Hofrat Schneider, the two families visiting back and forth over the years. Rogge's brother married Schneider's niece and foster daughter. Rogge's grandmother was a von Roon, and his older sister continued the alliance with a marriage to a von Roon. That sister had become close to the Thielen family, and Rogge eventually married their daughter. The daughter of one of his closest friends married his son. A second friend had courted Rogge's younger sister, while a third*

[120] See also Budde, *Weg ins Bürgerleben,* pp. 263–4; and Mosse, *German-Jewish Economic Elite,* pp. 161–85.

[121] Davidoff and Hall, *Family Fortunes,* p. 279, commenting on sibling and cousin marriages in England: "It may be argued that free choice marriage controlled in this way provided a form of security in binding together members of the middle class in local, regional and national networks, a guarantee of congenial views as well as trustworthiness in economic and financial affairs."

actually married her. Her daughter and his son married, making his sister mother-in-law to his own son and "co-grandparent" of his grandchildren.[122] *Emil Lehmann (b. 1823), whose father was a miniaturist, describes a constant interactivity among related families. His father and father's cousin, August Leo, married sisters. Heinrich Leo (another cousin of his father) married his father's sister. Emil himself married his cousin, Amalie Leo. Emil's brother worked for Julius Oppenheimer, and this connection led to the marriage of their sister to Julius's brother Adolph in New York.*[123] *Professor Pauli fell in love with a daughter from a house in Bremen (the merchant family Ulrich) close to his own family, but he decided to marry her sister (his parents were very pleased with the alliance with this family). Unfortunately, she died within a short period of the marriage, and he went off to the archives in London to recover: "I am feeling a bit better; the incomparable virgin treasures, in which I am working, exercise their charms once more."*[124] *Not long afterwards, he married the other sister, the one he had first been in love with. Mörike's genealogy provides a south German example of continual alliances between pastors, officials, scholars, and poets. Both his mother and mother's mother were Beyers. Her mother's brother married a Mörike as she did (a cousin), who after his death married another brother. His mother's sister married an Abel, who later married her cousin. His uncle-guardian-foster parent von Georgii married a niece. During the rest of the nineteenth century, there were repeated marriages between Mörikes, von Georgiis, and Abels.*[125] *Johanna Thiersch, the daughter of Justus von Liebig, commenting on the generation marrying in the 1860s through the 1880s, pointed out that her father had been close to a set of interrelated families: Volhard–Hofmann–Kekulé. Two cousins Thiersch married a von Hofmann and a Kekulé. She was on intimate terms with Cora Kekulé (who had married a von Hofmann cousin, and whose mother had also married a cousin). Cora's daughter married Johanna's son and another daughter married Johanna's sister's son.*[126] *Cleophea Bansa married within a tight group of friendly families – her father and her husband's father had been close friends. Her mother's sister had been an intimate of her husband's mother, and her uncle's father had been her husband's godfather.*[127] *The Rothschilds were obviously only at one end of a spectrum of family endogamy, and I do not support the thesis that the Jewish middle class was more endogamous than the rest of the middle classes.*[128] *Of the 58 marriages of the descendants of Meyer Amschel in the nineteenth century, one-half were with first cousins. His son married his own niece. This was not just a matter of knitting together five European capitals by marriage within the line. There were also systematic alliances with the Montefiore family, among others.*[129] *When*

[122] Rogge, *Sieben Jahrzehnten*, pp. 28–42, 113, 121, 139, 189, 206.
[123] Lehmann, *Lebenserinnerungen*, vol. 1, pp. 12–13, 27–8, 73–5, 96, 242.
[124] Pauli, *Jugenerinnerungen*, p. 204, also 198, 219.
[125] *Deutsches Geschlechterbuch.*
[126] Von Harnack, *Thiersch Briefe*, pp. 3–6.
[127] Bansa, *Lebensbild in Briefen*, pp. 5–22.
[128] Kaplan, *Making*, pp. 114–5.
[129] Battersea, *Reminiscences*, pp. 3–8. Lady Battersea thought that the extreme endogamy had to do with a combination of class and religious commitment; Germaine Tillion, *The Republic of Cousins: Women's Oppression in Mediterranean Society*, trans. Quinten Hoare (London, 1983; first published

the Rothschilds created a connection through marriage with the Behrens in the 1850s, the Warburgs felt outflanked. It was a brother-in-law of Aby Warburg, Paul Schiff, trained in the Behrens bank, who forged the relationship with the Rothschilds. Aby's son Felix married Frieda Schiff in the next generation, which also brought connections to Kuhn and Loeb in New York. Subsequently Paul Warburg married Nina Loeb.[130] *The Siemens family was not dissimilar to the Rothschilds in its international connections and in its family-centered economy. There were also similar marriage strategies, although since several of the brothers of Werner's generation produced no children, various opportunities were missed. The Siemens family had developed repeated alliances with other families in the eighteenth century, utilizing cousin marriages several times. By the end of the century, several Siemens had married women whose grandmothers or great-grandmothers were Siemens. During the first half of the nineteenth century, several of the lineage marriages were with spouses who had the same great-grandparents. Following out any particular line demonstrates systematic connections. For example, the one established by Carl Georg and Adolph involved two brothers marrying two sisters. Carl Georg's son went off to Berlin to work for Werner, and Werner eventually turned to the daughter for his second wife. One of Werner's sons, Wilhelm, married Werner's niece, the son of his brother Ferdinand, a large estate owner in East Prussia. The case of Werner's childless brother William is also interesting. William had become friendly with Lewis Gordon after Gordon married a Hanoverian woman, the sister of another woman who had married a Siemens. Wilhelm subsequently married his friend's sister. Gordon's nephew by marriage (WZS), Alexander Siemens, was sent to Berlin to be trained by Werner, and then to London to join the firm there. He was eventually adopted by William and succeeded him.*[131] *The family history can be spun out to find many more such alliances, but I will stop there. The family of Friederike Fricke, née Pfannkuchen, offers a petit bourgeois example of repeated alliances. Figure 22.1 shows the repeated marriage alliances of Pfannkuchen.*[132] *Many more endogamous family connections are mentioned in the autobiographies and correspondence of the Wiggers, Ebrard, Kussmaul, Hase, Bartsch, Parthey, Stahr, Lewald, Reuter, Otte, Hüffer, Heitefuss, Schücking, Focke, and Hunnius families. But the point can also be documented somewhat further from genealogical records and family studies that are somewhat more systematic.*[133]

in French, 1966), p. 104. The statistics are from Frederic Morton, *The Rothschilds: Family Portrait* (New York, 1962), pp. 57–8.

[130] Rosenbaum and Sherman, *Warburg,* pp. 31–41, 93–5, 99–100.

[131] Hermann W. Siemens, "Ueber das Erfindergeschlecht Siemens," pp. 162–92; J. D. Scott, *Siemens Brothers,* pp. 31, 69; Georg Siemens, *Carl Friedrich von Siemens,* p. 14; Herbert Goetzeler und Lothar Schoen, *Wilhelm und Carl Freidrich von Siemens: Die zweite Unternehmergeneration* (Stuttgart, 1986), p. 15; Helfferich, *Georg von Siemens,* pp. 6–13; Werner von Siemens, *Personal Recollections,* pp. 5, 132–3, 207, 337, 352, 382.

[132] Friederike Fricke, ed., *Aus dem Leben unserer Mutter, Familienbriefe für fie Familie* (Göttingen, 1929). The father opened a tobacco shop in Göttingen in 1876 after retiring as steward of an estate.

[133] Other commentators are beginning to note cousin marriages and repeated alliances among the nobility and entrepreneurial classes: von Treskow, "Adel in Preussen," p. 354. Von Treskow argues that such marriages brought a "strong familial cohesion." Zwahr, "Zur Klassenkonstitui-

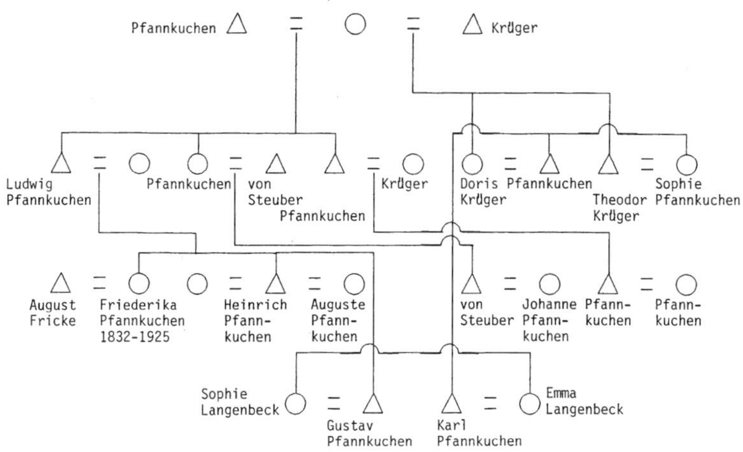

Figure 22.1

I have already mentioned the wonderfully full genealogy for the Delius family.[134] Since the principles on which it is built have to do with tracing through the male-transmitted surname lines, many alliances are difficult if not impossible to trace from the evidence presented, although the author of this genealogy has frequently followed allied surname lineages for several generations. She has broken the family into seven branches, which originated in the early eighteenth century. To condense matters, one can look at the small but typical section of a branch beginning with the seven children of Anton Henrich Delius (1724–89) and Marie Elisabeth Schlichtebrede (he and his brother-in-law founded a firm in Bielefeld together). (1) *Their first daughter married a* Schrader. *One of their daughters married a* Hagedorn *in 1796, six years after his brother had married her* Delius *aunt (1790). In 1817 she married for the second time – a* Delius *cousin (his FxBDD). From the 1790 Hagedorn–Delius marriage, a daughter married a* Delius *in 1823. In that same generation two Delius siblings married two* von Laer *siblings. (2) A second daughter (1761–1817) married a* Wilmanns *(a family allied to the Deliuses nine times). (3) A son (who took over the business started by his father and uncle) married a* Delius *(1792), his FBD. Their son married a woman adopted by a couple, the wife of which was a* Wilmanns. *In turn, their daughter married a* Wilmanns *(his FZ(D)D). The grandson of the Delius–Delius marriage of 1792 married a* Delius *in Mexico in 1863 (FFBSSD). (4) We are not able to follow the line of the fourth daughter. (5) A daughter married a cousin* Delius *(his FFBSD). His son from another marriage married their son's daughter in 1849 (his xBD). (6) A daughter, like her older sister, married a* Hagedorn. *Two of their daughters (1823*

erung der Bourgeoisie," p. 36, argues that on the basis of such marriages: "A network of social ties, dependencies, and mutual influences arose as elementary preconditions for the development of stable class connections."

[134] *Deutsches Geschlechterbuch,* vol. 193.

and 1828) married Delius *brothers (FFFBSDD). A third daughter married a* von Laer, *who had earlier been married to a sister of the two Delius brothers. (7) A final sister married into the aristocracy.* Between 1790 and 1828, this genealogical segment contains six marriages between descendants of the original couple and closely related Hagedorns. There were several Delius–Delius marriages and a repeated alliance with the Wilmanns. A family such as von Laer crops up several times over several generations. In many cases, I cannot trace the links with families such as the Schraders, which shows up in the published genealogy 11 times. There are constellations of related lineages such as Schrader–Hagedorn–Delius: a Hagedorn daughter with a Delius mother marries a Schrader, in turn closely related to the Delius family. Many names crop up repeatedly in the Delius genealogy: Bertelsmann 13, Bosch 6, Hagedorn 9, Hildebrand 7, Hofbauer 8, Kisker 7, Meyer 16, Möller 6, Müller 8, Nolting 6, Schmidt 10, Steinmann 7, Tilemann 8, Velhagen 5, Wilmanns 9.

The Remy family, which is also mentioned frequently in this volume, provides further examples of alliances.[135] Taking again only one small segment of their genealogy, generation 1 has a Freudenberg–Remy marriage; generation 2 (1756–67), two more plus two Freudenberg–Hofmann marriages; generation 3 a Freudenberg–Remy and a Freudenberg–Hofmann (MBD); generation 4, two Freudenberg–Hofmann (first cousin, second cousin) and a Freudenberg–Remy. Other branches show other alliances between the same families. In the five genealogical diagrams at the end of the study, besides the almost 20 percent Remy–Remy marriages pointed out earlier, there are many sibling exchanges, marriages of siblings with two cousins, marriages with a man and two sisters (sororate), and marriages between first cousins of different patrilines (MBD, FZD).[136]

Familial intercourse

Festivals, birthdays, anniversaries, and family days provided many opportunities in the nineteenth century for family members near and far to come together,

[135] Schröder, "Weg zur Eisenbahnschiene."

[136] Exactly the same kinds of alliances have been traced by Wolfgang Zorn in Bavarian Swabia for the von Rad, Hösslin, von Stetten, and Süsskind families; see the article by Eggel on Kaufbeuren: Eberhard Eggel, "Die Textilkaufleute Heinzelmann in Kaufbeuren und ihre Verwandtschaft," in *Archiv für Sippensforschung* 32 (1968): 574–91. Spethmann has looked at the Haniel family from 1679 onward. He finds continual renewed alliances between the Haniels, Sombarts, Noots, Jacobis, and Huyssens. By Franz Haniel's generation, his and his siblings closed a whole set of circles: his sister married a Jacobi (1800), his brother a Noot and then a Sombart, and he a Huyssen. Zunkel points out that the Krefeld silk manufacturers von der Leyen built business connections systematically by planned marriage policies with the Cologne banking family Herstatt. The Bönninger and Rath families cemented six marriages in two generations. He confirms other findings with regard to Franz Haniel, who systematically built ties with other leading industrial families, while reintegrating his own – one son married his niece, a son and daughter married Cockerills, and three other children were married to Böcking, de Greiff, and Leibrecht; Zorn *Handels- und Industriegeschichte.* Zwahr gives similar examples for Leipzig families, "Zur Klassenkonstituierung der Bourgeoisie."

sometimes for many weeks at a time.[137] Families typically set a specific time in the year when they gathered in a particular place or at the home of a central person. Before the advent of the railroad, such travel was arduous enough to warrant relatively long stays. Professor Wiggers (b. 1811) recalled that all his relatives gathered at a village parsonage near Rostock every Easter (at his MFB, who had married his FZ).[138] For the Luthardts, Christmas provided the occasion for meeting.[139] During the fall weeks and in the early year, the four von Mohl brothers met together with the rest of the clan at Robert's house each year.[140] All the Focke family came together each October.[141] The first two generations of the Rothschilds celebrated the Jewish holy days in Frankfurt at the paternal grandmother's.[142] The Droste-Hülshoff clan visited annually at Bökendorf.[143] Werner Siemens mentions meeting with his brother William twice a year.[144] The family associations formed from the 1870s onward tended to meet in groups of 40 to 50 every two to five years.[145]

Christenings, confirmations, birthdays, anniversaries, and funerals occasioned more or less extended celebrations. Emil Lehmann describes how people came from Berlin, Paris, and London to Hamburg to celebrate the twenty-fifth anniversary of his parents.[146] For a full two weeks, the house was open in the evening for guests. The uncles, aunts, and cousins danced, ate, and walked together during this time of intense family intercourse. Karl Hase (b. 1800) described a similar gathering for a family golden anniversary in Altenburg.[147] In this case, he met and fell in love with a cousin, who rejected him but remained his life-long passion. Gabriele Reuter describes a Nathusius silver wedding anniversary at Althaldensleben in the Prussian Province of Sachsen, where the mass of guests were put up in the cells of what had once been a nunnery.[148] Among the clan of the Kurland Hunnius family, birthdays could bring together 40 relatives.[149] The editor of the Kestner correspondence says the family made a cult out of birthdays, although they were so dispersed between Hannover, Frankfurt, Alsace, Rome, Bourdeaux, and Sicily that the great family gatherings could take place only every

137 An important new work on the subject is Budde, *Weg ins Bürgerleben*, pp. 89–95, 262–73.
138 Wiggers, *Aus meinem Leben*, pp. 11–12.
139 Christian Ernst Luthardt (b. 1823), *Erinnerungen aus vergangenen Tagen*, 2d ed. (Leipzig, 1891).
140 Helmholtz, *Lebensbild*, p. 15.
141 Wilhelm Olbers Focke, ed., *Briefe von Doris Focke geb. Olbers an ihren Bruder, für die Familie als Manuscript gedruckt* (Bremen, 1886). Doris Focke was born in 1786.
142 Constance de Rothschild Flower Lady Battersea, *Reminiscences* (London, 1922).
143 Clemens Heselhaus, *Annette von Droste-Hülshoff: Werk und Leben* (Düsseldorf, 1971), p. 68.
144 Werner von Siemens, *Personal Recollections*, p. 122.
145 Besides the example of the Delius family mentioned earlier, see Kocka, "Familie, Unternehmer und Kapitalismus," p. 123, for the Siemens Family Association, which brought together more than 50 people each time they met.
146 Lehmann, *Lebenserinnerungen*, p. 55.
147 Karl Hase, *Ideale und Irrthümer: Jugenderinnerungen*, 2d ed. (Leipzig, 1873), pp. 160–93.
148 Reuter, *vom Kinde zum Menschen*, pp. 173–4.
149 Monika Hunnius, *Briefwechsel mit einem Freunde*, ed. Sophie Gurland (Heilbronn, 1935), pp. 110–12.

four or five years.[150] Carlota Sieveking related that the family always provided an elaborate festival when any member returned.[151] As late as the 1870s, they were still operating with elaborate skits, declamations, and living pictures, acting out Goethe's turn-of-the-century portrait of domestic cultural life in *Elective Affinities.*

Many families lived close to one another – whole clans together in Hamburg, Berlin, Darmstadt, or Königsberg. This allowed for a dense, elaborate winter season of balls, card playing, musical and literary evenings, or weekly get-togethers of aunts, uncles, and cousins for meals, walks, and conversation. The Remy family, for example, developed an intense interchange between Frankfurt and Bendorf.[152] Whenever a family was rich in cousins coming up to marriage age, social life intensified for a period of years. Cleophea Bansa describes such a nonstop period during the years preceding her own marriage.[153]

Georg Gottfried Gervinus came from a family of leather and wine merchants in Darmstadt.[154] Two of his father's brothers boarded with them, while another lived across the street. His mother's brother and sister both lived near the market. His early life was lived around cousins. Felix Eberty in Berlin also lived cheek by jowl with relatives.[155] His great-grandmother and two aunts lived in the house with them. His father worked in his grandfather's bureau near two maternal great-grandfathers. The whole family met for dinner several times a week in the rooms of the great-grandmother. After she died, a great-aunt became the central figure. But just because he had no cousin of his own age, until he was eight or so he had no one except his sister to play with.[156] Christian Ernst Luthardt (b. 1823), who became an academic theologian, describes the life of his family in Schweinfurt – where his father, a customs officer, was born.[157] There were about 50 cousins, "all bound in familial love with each other," all of whom have "maintained a common family spirit." "The circles have broken up and have closed themselves off independently in new relationships – still the cohesion has even today not dissolved and forms a common cultural disposition [geistige Naturboden], which profits the individuals as much as an ancestral estate [Erbgut]."[158] Fanny Lewald described how all the branches of the Oppenheim family in Königsberg dined at the father's house three times a week.[159] Gabriele Reuter related that her mother's cousin Luise Gatterer married the industrialist Nathusius in Magdeburg and that consequently several other Gatterer daughters settled in the region.[160]

150 Kestner Köchlin, *Briefwechsel Kestner,* pp. 52, 117, 192, 326–9.
151 Rebensburg-Reich, *Tante Carlotas Nachlass,* p. 74.
152 Schröder, "Weg zur Eisenbahnschiene," pp. 76–93.
153 Bansa, *Lebensbild in Briefen,* pp. 10–12.
154 Georg Gottfried Gervinus, *Leben von ihm Selbst. 1860* (Leipzig, 1893), pp. 8–13.
155 Eberty, *Jugenderinnerungen,* pp. 95–106.
156 Jürgen Schlumbohm, " 'Traditional' Collectivity and 'Modern' Individuality: Some Questions and Suggestions for the Historical Study of Socialization: The Examples of German Lower and Upper Bourgeoisies Around 1800," *Social History* 5 (1980): 71–103.
157 Luthardt, *Erinnerungen,* pp. 8–10.
158 Luthardt, *Erinnerungen,* p. 9.
159 Lewald, *Lebensgeschichte,* vol. 1, pt. 2: p. 62.
160 Reuter, *Vom Kinde zum Menschen,* pp. 16, 173, 194.

The estate at Althaldensleben became a center of lively interchange between cousins. During Gabriele's youth after her father died, she and her mother lived on the neighboring estate of Neuhaldensleben with other relatives. The heir to the central estate married his cousin, Gabriele's maternal aunt. Clara Heitefuss (b. 1867) grew up within an intense set of family relations. At her birth, her grandmother, two aunts, and an uncle lived in the house – centered on the colonial and ironware trade. Every Sunday her grandmother, mother, and aunts brought everyone together for coffee. In the nearby Itter Valley, three of her mother's brothers had settled, providing the opportunity for steady family commerce. "When a girl in our Corbach became engaged, one knew the suitor, knew his parents, and their extended kindred [Sippe]."[161] *Marchtaler makes the point that in Hamburg, family members were frequently not only business associates but members of the same clubs and Vereine. Sisters might see each other daily.*[162] *Emil Lehmann's playmates for many years were six cousins living in the neighborhood.*[163] *Julius Wiggers also only played with cousins until he went to school at age 15.*[164]

Whenever families lived close to one another, opportunities for regular commerce presented themselves. Hüffer, Eberty, Kestner, Bansa, and many others point up the centrality of music for familial sociability.[165] For the von Droste-Hülshoff family and the Sievekings, reading together was a central activity.[166] Marion Kaplan has pointed to the importance of "cousin circles" in the Jewish middle class at the end of the century, but these were widespread among the middle classes throughout Germany.[167] The effects of such intensive intercourse is summed up by the teacher, Johannes Schmarje (b. 1845), from rural Schleswig-Holstein: "With the strongly marked feeling for the kindred (*Sippe*), social intercourse was mostly family intercourse. To the family in the larger sense . . . belonged the distant members, so that relations among relatives from Clasholm and Trinamellersch could no longer be counted on the fingers and for strangers went beyond their capacity for understanding [*Begriffsvermögen*]."[168]

This intense family life – whether urban or rural, centered on clubs, houses, or casinos, or celebrated in the still of *Kaffeekränzchen* or the more rambunctious activities of sledding or balls – was central for the creation of cultural understanding and practice. Such social intercourse, as Zunkel points out, was crucial for the formation of social (*Schichten*) consciousness. "Each self-conscious social

161 Clara Heitefuss, *An des Meisters Hand. Lebenserinnerungen* (Schwerin, 1939), pp. 11–13.

162 Marchtaler, *Hamburger Senatorenhäusern,* pp. 95, 193.

163 Lehmann, *Lebenserinnerungen,* pp. 12–13.

164 Wiggers, *Aus meinem Leben,* p. 12.

165 Hüffer, *Lebenserinnerungen,* p. 123; Eberty, *Jugenderinnerungen,* p. 131; Kestner-Köchlin, *Briefwechsel Kestner,* p. 5; Bansa, *Lebensbild in Briefen,* p. 36.

166 Heselhaus, *Annette von Droste-Hülshoff,* p. 69; Rebensburg-Reich, *Tante Carlotas Nachlass,* pp. 54–6, 74.

167 Kaplan, *Making,* p. 83; Bansa, *Lebensbild in Briefen,* pp. 31, 48, 51–5; Focke, *Briefe Focke,* pp. 37–9, 47–50, 254–7; Gustav Parthey, *Jugenderinnerungen,* ed. Ernst Friedel, 2 Teile (Berlin, 1907), T. 1, p. 227.

168 Johannes Schmarje, *Lebenserinnerungen eines schleswig-holsteinischen Schulmannes* (Altona, 1925), p. 21.

stratum tended to consider its specific values and modes of behavior as superior and to raise claims for their general validity in the society."[169] "In cities and industrial areas, clans (*Sippenkreise*) formed out of entrepreneurial families of similar rank, which mostly belonged to the same economic branch, which agreed with each other in their social and political opinions, and which cooperated in the pursuit of their economic interests."[170]

Many families over time were dispersed across Germany or Europe or even across continents. Correspondence and visiting played central roles in knitting their extended families together. Bernhard Rogge pointed to the considerable correspondence that tied their father's parish to far-flung family members.[171] Friedrich von Raumer among many others noted the importance of older female members – his aunt, a *Stiftsfräulein,* and his grandmother – for carrying on the family's correspondence.[172] Ludwig Wiese remarked that the inhabitants of the Harz mining town of Clausthal where he first taught carried on a very large correspondence with relatives from all over.[173] This may explain how mining engineers and officials across Germany seem to have composed one large family.[174] Fanny Lewald first got to know an aunt and her cousins in Baden-Baden through letters, before she went to live with them for several years.[175] The Remy family knit together Bendorf and Frankfurt through steady correspondence as well as regular visits.[176] Felix Eberty developed close relations with an aunt in Düsseldorf through letters.[177] Marchtaler points out that Hamburg patrician daughters were trained in the skills of letter writing precisely in order to carry on the important labor of familial networking.[178] Indeed, the many volumes of published correspondence from the period attest to the centrality of letter writing as fundamental kinship work.

Visiting – often for long periods of time – was a regular form of contact. In the late eighteenth century, when relatives of the Remy/Hoffmann/Freudenberg clans in Bendorf came together, they played games, held balls, took boat trips, and commissioned commemorative paintings, poems, and books.[179] Emil Lehmann describes constant visiting between Hamburg, Berlin, Paris, and London.[180] But this was by no means a matter only for business elites and the wealthy. Karl

169 Zunkel, *Rheinisch-westfälische Unternehmer,* p. 82.

170 Zunkel, *Rheinisch-westfälische Unternehmer,* p. 82. See also, Hans-Ulrich Wehler, "Vorüberlegungen zur historischen Analyse sozialer Ungleichheit," in *Klassen in der europäischen Sozialgeschichte* (Göttingen, 1979), pp. 9–32, here p. 21.

171 Rogge, *Sieben Jahrzehnten,* pp. 13–14.

172 Von Raumer, *Lebenserinnerungen,* pp. 12ff.

173 Wiese, *Lebenserinnerungen,* pp. 61–5.

174 Walter Serlo, ed., *Bergmannsfamilien in Rheinland und Westfalen,* Rheinisch-Westfälische Wirtschaftsbiographien, vol. 3 (Aschendorff, Münster, 1974).

175 Lewald, *Lebensgeschichte,* vol. 2, 1: pp. 33, 87–100, 138, 152, 167.

176 Schröder, "Weg zur Eisenbahnschiene," p. 76.

177 Eberty, *Jugenderinnerungen,* pp. 108–10.

178 Marchtaler, *Althamburger Senatorenhäusern,* p. 47.

179 Schröder, "Weg zur Eisenbahnschiene," pp. 21–2.

180 Lehmann, *Lebenserinnerungen,* passim.

Bartsch from a surveyor family (b. 1832) described frequent visits of extended relatives.[181] Ottilie Wildermuth, wife of a Gymnasium teacher in Tübingen, described a constant stream of visitors, many of whom stayed for several months at a time. She and her family traveled each year on vacation "from uncle to uncle [*herumonkeln*]."[182] One might expect a central university town like Tübingen to attract visitors, but even an out-of-the-way parish such as the one Bernhard Rogge grew up in in Silesia became a magnet for relatives. He wrote that his mother regularly dealt with as many as 40 guests each day.[183] During the 1790s, the Remys got into a veritable "travel fever."[184] Zorn describes a similar phenomenon for Bavarian Swabia for the same period.[185] Carlota Sieveking, whose extended family eventually became centered around the Basel mission, noted that distant cousins frequently visited and took part in family life.[186] The Kestner family changed its style once the railroad speeded up travel and made visiting less arduous. Previously they had seen each other less often but for longer periods of time.[187] Many like the Hunnius family in Kurland (Monika Hunnius, b. 1858) sent children off to live with uncles and aunts for longer or shorter periods of time where they were able to build intensive relationships with their cousins.[188] Carlota Sieveking's sister-in-law Mary wrote to her (1868): "It's a joy to see with how much sincere love the children hang on their two cousins . . . , we must strive to renew this connection so that the love between us siblings will continue to live in their children."[189] In many instances such visiting brought together families scattered across different countries (von Mohl, Rothschild, Kestner, Bansa, Siemens, Reuter, Sieveking). Urban areas were constantly brought into relation with small towns and the countryside (Zeiss, Reuter, Hüffer). With or without constant commerce between relatives, people felt bonds and an ease of relationship that went beyond friendship. Relationships with relatives did not *have* to be constantly cultivated (even if they often were) and could be picked up quickly after considerable neglect. Annette von Droste-Hülshoff mused on the difference between family and friends in this way: "Since relatives remain close to us even if they live hundreds of miles away, we can go see them anytime. Everyone finds that natural and motivates (*animirt*) us to do it. To the contrary with friends of the same sex there needs to be pressing reasons. With the relatives there is no such need at all – thus a separation of ten miles lasts a year or can easily become life-long."[190]

[181] Karl Bartsch, *Aus der Kinderzeit. Bruchstück einer Biographie* (Tübingen, 1882), pp. 22–3.
[182] Bernardine Schulze-Smidt, ed., *Ottilie Wildermuths Briefe an einen Freund: Mit einer Lebensskizze* (Bielefeld and Leipzig, 1910), p. 56: "It's a very comfortable way to travel," pp. 64–70.
[183] Rogge, *Sieben Jahrzehnten,* p. 28.
[184] Schröder, "Weg zur Eisenbahnschiene," p. 76.
[185] Zorn, *Industriegeschichte Bayerisch-Schwabens,* p. 280.
[186] Rebensburg-Reich, *Tante Carlotas Nachlass,* p. 56.
[187] Kestner-Köchlin, *Briefwechsel Kestner,* p. 153.
[188] Hunnius, *Briefe,* "Einleitung," p. 19. See Kaplan, *Making,* pp. 84, 123.
[189] Rebensburg-Reich, *Tante Carlotas Nachlass,* p. 96.
[190] Droste-Hülshoff, *Historisch-kritische Ausgabe,* vol. 9, 1: *Briefe 1839–42,* ed. Walter Gödden and Ilse-Marie Barth (Tübingen, 1992), pp. 105–9.

Cousins often were, as I have pointed out, the first playmates young children had, and they often provided the chief circle of friends during the period of entering society and courtship (Lewald, Gervinus, Reuter, Remy, Sieveking, Focke, Hunnius, Bansa, Lehmann, Pauli, Hase, Deussen).[191] Cousins also frequently were packed off to school and Gymnasium together – or, as noted earlier, boys sent off to school often boarded with their uncles and aunts. Summer vacations brought together cousins, uncles, and aunts, adult siblings, and wider networks of family (Lehmann, Wiggers, Ebrard, Gerok, Pauli, von Schaezler, Wildermuth, Focke, Hunnius).[192] In the correspondence of Doris Focke, née Olbers, with her much-loved brother, she describes a deep rift in the family occasioned by the problematic relationship with her sister-in-law (HBW): "A thousand strands thread between the distant sisters; will that fabric, which love weaves, also bind them together at last? If it were not so impossible in itself, I would consider it to be inevitable."[193] The dynamics of kinship often brought pain and conflict – there is no end to the examples – but many people considered the lack of an extended family to be a more serious deficit. It brought dependence, coldness, and an extreme sense of alienation for the upwardly mobile. Adolf Stahr (b. 1805) describes his father, a Prussian regimental chaplain, as a "homo novus." He came "out of poverty," and was proud of lifting himself up. He had not known the "blessings of a father's house" and had to "go early among strangers."[194] The very fact of having no kin around brought the continuous humiliation of seeking favors from nonrelatives, of building obligation on an artificial foundation.

From the other end of the social scale, Cleophea Bansa, surrounded by friends and kin, thought there was an important dialectic between "society" and family. She argued that intense emotional activites in a family gave a young person training in certain kinds of social attachment, while activities in larger social spheres with people of the right station taught one to mask one's true feelings in order to negotiate easily among strangers, freeing one from the kinds of discomfort Stahr's father had felt. Writing to her son in England, she argued:

> It is continually proven that nothing surpasses the circle of true friends built around ourselves from youth. What develops later is never so open and sincere for us, and such intercourse remains always stuck with flattery, which shows us its artificiality. Le jargon du monde is still something else again, to which flattery necessarily belongs as a master key. When I feel myself in such a circle, I always find that I do not play such a bad comedy and that I declaim my role prima vista, also con amore. Still such stiff evil also has its place, and I wish that you might find occasion to practice this innocent game. The everyday world would nauseate us without this completely expedient throwing ourselves into the thing – which we (can more easily rank as) can call dissimulation [*Verstellung*]. I

[191] See also Kaplan, *Making*, pp. 82–4, 122–6.
[192] See also Kaplan, *Making*, pp. 83–4, 122–4.
[193] Focke, *Focke Briefe*, pp. 122–3.
[194] Adolf Stahr, *Aus der Jugendzeit. Lebenserinnerungen*, 2 vols. (Schwerin, 1877), vol. 1, pp. 10–11.

would like, like Uncle Conrad, to be able to lunch with the King of Prussia without loosing face or letting myself be embarrassed.[195]

Many families developed a particular focal point over time. For several decades, the central lineage holding of the families connected to the Nathusius estate in Althaldensleben treated it as their social center: "Visitors from all over Germany streamed together there." In the 1870s and 1880s, after the death of her husband, old Madame Nathusius took over and ran the four large estates and the industrial complex, raising five sons and two daughters in the bargain. Reuter described this "Stammesmutter" as a center of pilgrimage for family members who came to her for advice.[196] For the aristocratic family von Droste-Hülshoff, the *Stammgut* at Bökendorf also became a central focus of familial life.[197] Carl Zeiss was one of many whose familial life was oriented toward a rural parish.[198] Among Fanny Lewald's kin, Aunt Simon in Breslau was the central attraction.[199] The center of the Kestner family shifted to wherever Charlotte moved, since she kept all of the strands of the family together through her correspondence.[200] This was also the case for Carlota Sieveking.[201] For the larger Siemens clan, a widowed aunt, for the von Mohls, a grandmother, acted as the integrating element.[202] In some families activities intensified around a generation of cousins growing up. Cleophea Bansa described the interchange of a group of cousins who met alternately at the houses of their mothers and aunts.[203] For some of the writers I have cited, families became integrated around a particular figure, estate, or business, others, around a generation of siblings or cousins who closely coordinated their activity. With the passing of time, individual families had to regroup, some able to achieve new cohesion. Each generation, however, had different materials to work with – space, servants, unmarried resident relatives, numbers, generational coherence, religion, institutional allegiance, transportation, and skilled correspondents. Davidoff and Hall warn against conceiving of an essential middle-class family: there were only families, flexible, permeable, and in constant formation and reformation.[204]

Interaction in nineteenth-century middle-class families resulted in strong identification with family and schooling in specific forms of behavior and attitude. In 1819 Cleophea Bansa received a letter from her Aunt Moser: "The number of your relatives is so great that when you are all together it makes for a considerable society. There the hearts understand each other and there is no need for trite

[195] Bansa, *Lebensbild in Briefen,* p. 146.
[196] Reuter, *Vom Kinde zum Menschen,* pp. 20, 210–11.
[197] Heselhaus, *Annette von Droste-Hülshoff,* p. 117.
[198] Willam, *Carl Zeiss,* pp. 73–4.
[199] Lewald, *Meine Lebensgeschichte,* vol. 2, pt. 1: pp. 86–7.
[200] Kestner-Köchlin, *Briefwechsel Kestner.*
[201] Rebensburg-Reich, *Tante Carlotas Nachlass.*
[202] Werner von Siemens, *Personal Recollections,* p. 7; Siemens-Helmholtz, *Anna von Helmholtz,* p. 15.
[203] Bansa, *Lebensbild in Briefen,* pp. 51–4.
[204] Davidoff and Hall, *Family Fortunes,* p. 31.

subjects of conversation."[205] Yet Cleophea remarked on several occasions that coordinating clans was a matter of purposeful labor. She wrote to her son in 1838: "A cheerful individual . . . maintains peace without being noticed even in large families where there are usually many opinions to be reconciled. You will always find that when it comes to a decision en famille, my agreement takes place with dispatch because one cannot think and act harmoniously enough in the Schmidt and Bansa circles in order to promote a happy union."[206] The experience of clan life could appear at times to be too constraining. Fanny Lewald eventually broke out of her clan through a series of steps – rejection of a suitor and the role of wife and mother, conversion, a writing career, and a late marriage to a fellow writer. She saw clearly that family and social class were intimately bound up together. Reflecting on the "Brahmin-like family spirit [*Geist*]," from which she tore herself free (although ironically she continued to visit, support, travel with, and write to a large circle of kin), she wrote: "Out of this familial arrogance originates that notion about the solidarity of family members which can become virtual shackles for particular individuals. Although we universally call for equality of classes (*Stände*) and know how to talk splendidly about human rights, most families cultivate in themselves a caste spirit, which is less suitable for the free opinions of the nineteenth century than for the ancient laws of the Hindus."[207]

A German Galatea

In the early 1840s, Jacob Henle, a professor of anatomy in Zürich, picked up a seamstress on the street and after a few months decided he was in love with her.[208] After he accepted a call to Heidelberg, he dropped his plan to set her up as his mistress and decided to marry her. The problem was that she did not speak or move gracefully enough to represent him as his wife, so he devised a plan with the aid of his brother-in-law (Mathieu) to send the 22-year-old woman to a finishing school for girls for a year and then integrate her into the Mathieu household so that Henle's sister could operate a kind of forced-action socialization in a short period (make her into a cousin, as it were). In fact, the family made up a story about Elise being a distant cousin who had come to live with them. The unfolding of this German Pygmalion/Galatea story is very much one of family socialization. Mathieu, when he first met Elise, wrote to Henle that she moved awkwardly and conversed hesitantly, pointing thereby to two attributes essential to middle-class family culture, manners trained into the body and developed in crucial years through games, parties, dancing, and everyday family exchange.[209] Henle's sister Marie was aware of the great difficulties of a marriage among unequals, but gamely agreed to take on the task assigned to her. But first

205 Bansa, *Lebensbild in Briefen,* p. 90.
206 Bansa, *Lebensbild in Briefen,* p. 164.
207 Lewald, *Meine Lebensgeschichte,* vol. 3, pt. 1: p. 175.
208 Paula Rehberg, ed., *Elise Egloff: Die Geschichte einer Liebe in ihren Briefen* (Zürich, 1937).
209 Rehberg, *Elise Egloff,* p. 45.

Elise was shunted off to a girls' school (Pension) (where she was a 22-year-old among 14- and 15-year-olds). Henle wrote to Mathieu: "I want nothing more than that the Pension will bring her far enough that you can take her into your house without embarrassment and hear that she accompanies you in society and on walks."[210] She was to learn enough history, French, and mythology to follow a conversation without giving herself away, but Mathieu found other difficulties: "Mostly it is her manners, her way of carrying herself, of walking, of conversing, which betrays her earlier class (*Stand*) and which will be all the more difficult for her to change, since she does not always feel why she should not let herself completely go."[211]

Eventually Elise was presented to Henle's father, who wrote: "it appears to me that she is physically too strong and mentally [*geistig*] still too weakly formed [*gebildet*] to meet your standards."[212] Henle took the advice of a few friends at the same time. One had hoped he would bring a well-educated lady of the right class (*standesgemässen, feingebildeten Dame*) into their social milieu. But another thought it might be an advantage to have a "girl from a class in which the sufferings and perversities of our culture have not yet penetrated."[213] Henle finally wrote down exactly how he saw the situation and how class socialization and family socialization overlapped:

> The first act of education, without which the second would be impossible, consists in bringing E. so far that I and you can appear among friends and acquaintances without having to betray her origins. That was the external part, the one which we owed the world – I consider that as completed. Your pupil leaves nothing in this regard for me to desire further. Even if her bows are a little stiff, and if her laughter a little too hearty, people can find that just quite as amusing as many other departures from form. They will consider it fitting for a Swiss girl; indeed I don't want to have her quite finished in these matters.
>
> There follows now in the second part of the education – the inward – which can be reckoned as *my* particular area, in which I myself can assist, that which, if I am not mistaken about her natural talent will not be all that difficult, but indeed if I am wrong, quite impossible. I mean the education [*Bilding*], which is necessary to while away an evening with acquaintances and relatives comfortably, those with whom one can discuss everything and with whom one does not tend to discuss the usual *topic's der Conversation,* to show an interest in interesting facts without showing off what one knows and without reservation about disclosing weak points, a cheerful, affectionate judgment with possibly a little mockery over beloved friends [*Nächsten*], a need for exchange about what one has experienced and about plans, a devotion to those whom one recognizes as friends, above all to a wonderful picture of a little wife [*Weibchen*] – on whose shoulder a man can lay his head in the evening, weary from work.[214]

[210] Rehberg, *Elise Egloff,* p. 84.
[211] Rehberg, *Elise Egloff,* p. 86.
[212] Rehberg, *Elise Egloff,* p. 113.
[213] Rehberg, *Elise Egloff,* p. 136.
[214] Rehberg, *Elise Egloff,* pp. 137–8.

He went on to write his sister that Elise had many of those qualities already, but it would be some time before one could really make a judgment. A while later Marie was in despair. She said it was a great mistake to have thought that the manner of feeling – or at least talking in an appropriate way about feeling – could as easily be cultivated as external things. Marie apparently had thought that she could act as trainer, overseer, reporter, and judge and at the same time elicit an openness and intimacy with Elise. She was quite furious that Elise would not tell her all her thoughts and concluded that she lacked depth: "I now believe less than before that she can develop very much more than has been the case up to now."[215] After a few exchanges of letters and emotional scenes, Marie finally decided that Elise "indeed thinks and feels more than one can at times perceive."[216] The education completed, the engagement and marriage followed, and the couple lived for three years in blissful matrimony until Elise's death in childbirth.

Kinship and aesthetics

Louise Otto, one of the sharp observers of family life, writing in the 1870s, underscored the point that Henle and his family learned in practice: "Everything that in this connection [speaking of aesthetic education] is neglected in the earliest age can never later be completely recovered or replaced. . . . The whole atmosphere which dominates [in the home] is crucial for the development of every noble instinct."[217] Such observers pointed up continually that class was a matter of moving, carrying oneself, speaking, and acting in a certain way. These practices were worked into the flesh in a continual set of everyday exercises.[218] Ernst Brandes, the sharp-eyed misogynist, at the beginning of the century already made it clear that since families could no longer force girls into marriage, they had to train them to recognize the right man from the right class (*Stand*): "The power of physical impressions is there, however, above all only then really there, where it is internalized (*hineintragt*) in the girls, where the mothers put great store in social charm (*Annehmlichkeit*)."[219] The manners one learned at home created the instinctive foundations for boundary patrolling, the implicit recognition of who belonged and who remained outside. Bonnie Smith describes this process for northern France during the second half of the century: "Within each social oc-

215 Rehberg, *Elise Egloff*, p. 161.

216 Rehberg, *Elise Egloff*, p. 177.

217 Louise Otto, *Frauenleben im deutschen Reich: Erinnerungen aus der Vergangenheit mit Hinweis auf Gegenwart und Zukunft* (Leipzig, 1876), p. 219.

218 Pierre Bourdieu, "What Makes a Social Class? On the Theoretical and Practical Existence of Groups," *Berkeley Journal of Sociology*, 32 (1987): 1–17, here 5, argues that familial socialization inscribes social differences in the body and that "objective differences tend to reproduce themselves in the subjective experience of distance."

219 Ernst Brandes, *Betrachtungen über das weibliche Geschlecht und dessen Ausbildung in dem geselligen Leben*, 3 vols. (Hannover, 1802), vol. 2, p. 114.

casion lay the possibility that some outsider would betray with an untoward gesture that he or she did not belong."[220]

Brandes had in fact observed relations of class and family in great detail. Much of what Henle was after in practice was described by Brandes in grand generalized apodicta. He pointed out that "a great part of the reputation of the higher classes [*Stände*] rests on external cultivation [*Bildung*]."[221] The body projects propriety and rank (*Würde*). Just as Henle expressed the matter, it was not necessary for a woman to be learned, but she ought to have read enough in order to be able to understand her husband and speak sensibly in public.[222] It would be very uncomfortable for a husband to have his wife look bored as he and his friends conversed. What Marion Kaplan says of the Jewish middle class goes for the middle and upper classes as a whole: children were prepared for the class they were born in at home and in the give and take of extended families. It was there that high culture and the "ideas and customs of the classes they aspired to" were learned – above all, that bodies expressed class and gender boundaries.[223]

Over and over, observers stressed carriage, grace, and style as crucial for successful negotiation in everyday social, economic, and political life. Deportment and gesture contained clues and codes that everyone read in contemplating marriage alliances. Louise Otto was one of many who underlined the importance of aesthetics in early socialization.[224] And to be successful, education had to lead to internalized skills, savoir faire, and a mimetic incorporation of gesture. As Lorenz von Stein put it, the social and cultural aspects of marriage choice were decisive: "since for a man the woman of his future house represents all his social pretensions."[225] Through a succession of governesses, teachers, and finishing schools, young women were taught social skills: bearing, conversation, dress, and manners – "so that an appropriately cultivated girl appears suitable for the future status [*Stand*] of her husband."[226] Both Louise Otto (1875) and Ernst Brandes (1802) accented grace and style, the outcome of training in music, dancing, and drawing. Dancing cultivated grace in bodily carriage, the art of presenting oneself, and the avoidance of unpleasant movement. Music developed a feeling for harmony, rhythm, and measure. Painting gave a sense of form.[227]

Social and familial endogamy were embedded in a system of adaptable, re-

[220] Smith, *Ladies of the Leisure Class,* p. 130. Kocka, "Familie, Unternehmer und Kapitalismus," p. 125, puts it this way: "On the basis of an educational process which was so interwoven with the family and on the basis of such carefully selected marriage connections, with a tendency toward endogamy, 'kinship' means very much more than today: the same confession, similar value orientation, similar lifestyle, usually also similar lineage membership." See also for Germany and England, Budde, *Weg ins Bürgerleben,* pp. 180–92.

[221] Brandes, *Betrachtungen,* vol. 2, p. 232.

[222] Brandes, *Betrachtungen,* vol. 2, p. 471.

[223] Kaplan, *Making,* pp. 54–60.

[224] Otto, *Frauenleben,* pp. 218–20.

[225] Lorenz von Stein, *Die Frau, ihre Bildung und Lebensaufgabe,* 3d ed. (Berlin and Dresden, 1890), p. 24.

[226] Von Stein, *Die Frau,* p. 24.

[227] Otto, *Frauenleben,* pp. 221–30; Brandes, *Betrachtungen,* vol. 2, pp. 227–36.

sourceful, and versatile alliance politics. The way a body was trained to move had everything to do with how capital was concentrated and property transferred.[228] Families and clans provided the soil for the nursing of tender plants – in their protective environment, people were trained in style, tone, desire, and boundary marker recognition. Friedrich Zunkel found that the large extended families of the industrial Rhineland offered a cultural and social stage upon which desires, values, and interests could be coordinated. In the voluminous correspondence of a Westphalian aristocrat like Annete von Droste-Hülshoff, the practices of intense family exchanges can be pieced together into a dense mosaic capable of showing us many of the details of schooling in class behavior. The same goes for the extensive correspondence of the Frankfurt merchant family Bansa. Although Lorenz von Stein was wedded to the sociological tools at his disposal – above all the distinction between public (production) and private (reproduction), he frequently offers the most direct route to understanding the different forces that went into constructing class. Most of what we have been considering in our argument up to here, the dynamics of family life, socialization, and marriage alliance, fits into that part of class forming and structuring that he called "social feeling."[229] He argued that similar forces produce similar attitudes and feelings. Many different families and clans developed analogous traditions, secrets, and habits of self-recognition: what appeared to be due to individual cultivation of a particular style and behavior was conditioned by similar social arrangements.[230] Family was connected to class as one of the most important sites of coordination.

> A class is a community of equals, achieved in the consciousness of similarity in their social conditions. Wherever such a similarity appears, which holds good for a mass of personalities different in and of themselves, there it is certain that the similarity no longer rests on that which the one or the other does or believes or wants. In such a case, it cannot be constituted arbitrarily at all and even less be arbitrarily prevented. Rather, it is the result of similarly effective forces exercised continually, which exert a common effect on the individuals in that community. There is no doubt that this all happens there where we speak of a class [*Classe*] of society.[231]

Thus far, the discussion in this book has dealt with propertied classes. And not much attention has been given to the notion of class consciousness. Instead the emphasis has been on practices that give coherence to groups below the level of articulated response. As the Comaroffs put it, "Consciousness is not found in the explicit statements of common predicament on the part of a social group, but

[228] Kocka, "Familie, Unternehmer und Kapitalismus," p. 195: "The connections established through marriage reflected and furthered the formation of the bourgeoisie as a class."

[229] Lorenz von Stein, *Die Frau auf dem socialen Gebiete* (Stuttgart, 1880), p. 63.

[230] Von Stein, *Frau auf dem socialen Gebiete,* pp. 22–5. Von Stein comes closer than any other nineteenth-century writer to the position developed by Pierre Bourdieu. See "What Makes a Social Class?" and "The Social Space."

[231] Von Stein, *Frau auf dem socialen Gebiete,* p. 47.

in the implicit language of symbolic activity."[232] That appears to be the principal point in von Stein's analysis of property and class. Property acts like a "relational idiom," mediating relationships between people, giving regularity to their conduct, connecting and disconnecting them as they strike alliances and maintain distance.[233] Two aspects of both class and kinship strike me as crucial. Both are lived and experienced "locally" and both give rise to practices that continually force choice on people.[234] Social class is always constantly being generated, and kinship ties are always constantly being negotiated.[235] There are no hard and fast boundaries to either. As Kathleen Canning puts it, the "boundaries of class are seldom fixed – class formations and the exclusions on which they were based were continually contested and transformed."[236] And if the boundaries are not fixed, neither is class unified at the core but rather is made up of a multiplicity of different milieus. Class in formation in the nineteenth century was a process of making connections across localities and regions, between more or less well-articulated milieus, neighborhoods, clans, and strata, and among occupational, professional, and craft groups with strong traditional practices of exclusion.

There has not yet been much analysis of kinship and class formation among the propertyless or property-poor classes. Note once again that the emerging group of construction workers in Neckarhausen developed their own system of cousin marriages and godparentage a generation after landed proprietors did. Their kinship connections tended to connect people across a larger region than those of the small-holding peasantry. Jürgen Schlumbohm in a recent analysis of a north German parish has found a growth in kinship integration among landless laborers (*Heuerlinge*) during the nineteenth century:

> The changes which we can establish over time definitely contradict the idea of a linear development such that in the course of the transition from a so-called "traditional" peasant society to a "modern" one, kinship ties became ever more loosened and weakened and that the "nuclear family" became ever more strongly "isolated" from the network of kin. To the contrary, in order to master the economic and social problems of "modernization" – one could say – kinship connections in the nineteenth century were more strongly activated than ever before, between peasant land holders and their "poor relatives," but above all inside the propertyless stratum itself.[237]

[232] John and Jean Comaroff, *Ethnography and the Historical Imagination* (Boulder, 1992), p. 157.

[233] The term is Esther Goody's and was used by Hans Medick and David Warren Sabean, "Interest and Emotion in Family and Kinship Studies: A Critique of Social History and Anthropology," in Medick and Sabean, eds., *Interest and Emotion: Essays on the Study of Family and Kinship* (Cambridge, 1984). The argument was picked up by Davidoff and Hall, *Family Fortunes,* p. 32.

[234] Bourdieu, "What Makes a Social Class?" and "Social Space and the Generation of Groups" provide theoretical support for the way I have been arguing throughout this chapter. See also his *Zur Soziologie der symbolischen Formen* (Frankfurt, 1970), esp. pp. 63–71.

[235] Rheinhard Bendix and Seymour Martin Lipset, "Karl Marx's Theory of Social Classes," in *Class, Status, and Power: Social Stratification in Comparative Perspective* (New York, 1966), pp. 6–11, here p. 9.

[236] Canning, "Gender and Class Formation," p. 744.

[237] Jürgen Schlumbohm, *Lebensläufe, Familien, Höfe. Die Bauern und Heuerleute des Osnabrückischen*

Hartmut Zwahr has undertaken a detailed analysis of the proletarian class in Leipzig in the nineteenth century. The thrust of his work had been on the use of godparents and the slow extension of marriage relations out of traditional, craft-based milieus to encompass the larger group of skilled and unskilled factory workers. He maintained that kinship, both ritual and "real," provided an essential set of practical ties to constitute workers as a "social class." In his treatment of the issues, Zwahr emphasizes that the political opposition between the middle classes and workers is essential to the way workers reconfigured neighborhood, associational, and kinship ties among themselves. In Neckarhausen, if I am right, the propertied groups in the village first withdrew from the property-poor by no longer standing as godparents for them or developing marriage alliances among them. They recast their ties toward their own political associates and fellow property owners in an endogamous system at once based on kinship and class. Connubium lay at the heart of policing social boundaries, and no doubt at the heart of class formation. Zwahr has described a similar process for the much larger and more complicated society of urban Leipzig. He has shown how carefully the multilayered middle classes sought to construct ties with their fellows and maintain distance especially from those they considered their inferiors. The process of class formation among workers developed partly in reaction to exclusion from above and partly in the experiences of creating new bonds on the basis of common work and neighborhood experiences. Zwahr's argument runs this way: "Essential for the formation of class ties was the unfolding class antagonism between proletariat and bourgeoisie. Above all, the exploited workers under capitalist conditions began to develop intensive communal ties. For this, personal connections such as marriage and the selection of godparents among other things formed an essential condition. In turn, they fostered and shaped the emergence of proletarian class solidarity and norms of behavior."[238]

Recent thinking about class and class formation has almost exclusively concentrated on the proletariat, partly because it failed to fulfill the historic role many observers had hoped or expected.[239] The debates are too complicated to go into here, but the most promising tendency in the research is to emphasize the development of five or six broad milieus within the German working class of the nineteenth century. Josef Mooser has emphasized the crucial importance of kinship in the construction of each of these milieus, and it seems that the time is ripe to research kinship more seriously in a detailed way and to begin to compare kinship dynamics across milieus, strata, and classes.[240]

Kirchspiels Belm in proto-industrieller Zeit, 1650–1860, Veröffentlichungen des Max-Planck-Instituts für Geschichte, vol. 110 (Göttingen, 1994), p. 595.

238 Zwahr, *Proletariat und Bourgeoisie,* p. 147.

239 See the remarks by Peter Kriedte, *Stadt am seidenen Faden,* p. 231, on the role of kinship as a "structuring principle" for the class of silk workers.

240 Besides the literature cited in footnote 2, see Mooser, *Arbeiterleben in Deutschland*; Jürgen Kocka, *Lohnarbeit und Klassenbildung: Arbeiter und Arbeiterbewegung in Deutschland 1800–1875* (Berlin and Bonn, 1983), esp. pp. 11–30; Kocka, *Traditionsbindung und Klassenbildung: Zum sozialhistorischen*

The obvious question that now arises is this: if kinship took on a new urgency for all classes in the nineteenth century, and if endogamy was such a crucial aspect of this, why was there so little sociological analysis of kinship dynamics and so little comment on the fact and the social implications of consanguineal marriage? Here the reason has to do with how observers construed the political. Kathleen Canning has put her finger on the problem: the private/public dichotomy, she suggests, conceptualizes the public as the essential space where political life takes place and thereby depoliticizes the private sphere.[241] Kinship, marriage, and family became uninteresting for male observers, whose attention was fixed on what counted for them – the political in its public guise. Turning one's attention to kinship opens up a vast arena of women's political activity. As Chapter 23 shows, women were the ones who policed the social boundaries most fiercely by training bodies, inculcating norms of behavior and expression, establishing elaborate networks of like-minded friends, constructing the social space in which men and women met, and guarding the entry and exit points to class by intensive concern with marriage alliance.

Ort der frühen deutschen Arbeiterbewegung, Schriften des historischen Kollegs, Vorträge 8 (Munich, 1987), esp. pp. 7–31.

[241] Canning, "Gender and the Politics of Class Formation," p. 740.

23

Kinship and gender

It should come as no surprise now that during the nineteenth century the dynamics of kinship in Neckarhausen came to be governed by women. Widows married less frequently and seldom gave up their property until they were old and feeble. In the life of the village, older, propertied, and resident women grew more powerful as they learned to control fundamental resources: land, agricultural equipment, buildings, and credit. They also became important in negotiating marriages and were at the center of an alliance system that stressed mutual reciprocity between lines rather than patriarchal authority – as can be seen in the choice of godparents and in naming practices. With the gender balance of the village tipped radically in favor of women (100 adult women to 85 adult men), and with agriculture demanding more of their labor, they negotiated a central place in the productive structures of the village and in the consumption decisions of their households. If formal offices remained in the hands of men and if the early Verein movement took up most of their energies, women came to find a parallel field for political and social activity in caring for kin, negotiating networks, brokering alliances, and maintaining the viability of agriculture and flax production. Although there is no prima facie reason to expect that women from different classes in the course of the nineteenth century would play similar roles or develop equivalent social and familial functions and strategies, that is in fact what happened. The reconfigured kinship system examined in the concluding chapters was largely the result of the activities and work of women. Kinship provided a vast – and today largely unexplored – area of political activity for women. This contention can be documented from middle-class sources and shown to be a variation on a theme played all across the villages, towns, and cities of nineteenth-century Germany.

Little research has been done on the development and maintenance of kinship networks for any period of German or, indeed, European history. Patterns of interaction changed considerably over time, and even for a restricted period like the nineteenth century it is too early to be able to chronicle the structural shifts in familial interaction and to get a clear sense about milieu, periodization, and cultural practices. Marion Kaplan, writing about German-Jewish middle-class families at the end of the century said her task was to show how "women maintained extensive kin and social networks and hence consolidated interfamilial and class relations."[1] She is one of the few people to recognize that the coordination of kinship ties greatly affected the ways in which class relations were constructed – and that *women* were at the center of the work. Kaplan's observations about Jewish women could well apply to all women: they "took responsibility for family networks . . . for the moral and material support, the continuity and organization, of an often geographically dispersed family system."[2]

A recent book to take up the same issues Kaplan deals with concerns rural and urban kinship networks in German-speaking Switzerland.[3] Elisabeth Joris and Heidi Witzig show, first, that kinship networks were reconfigured in the nineteenth century, and second that they became more and more an area of women's care and concern.[4] The conceptual split between private and public, which associates politics (and until recently also history) with the public sphere, has obscured this whole area of intense social activity of women. If the construction of class was central to the political dynamics of the nineteenth century, then this work has to be brought conceptually into the framework of the "political." Recent explorations into practice by such people as Pierre Bourdieu, Michel Foucault, and Michel De Certeau, who shift attention away from formal ideology and party political struggles to the construction of discourse, everyday behaviors, and aesthetics – to the fine networks of social interaction and the locations (always in these thinkers there is an underlying sense for geographical place)[5] of social imagination and reciprocities – shed light on how to do this. Joris and Witzig provide a detailed examination of everyday relations and exchanges between family members, an account of the sites, in which and from which classes were created out of social strata.[6] Groups with similar values (*gleichgesinnte*), they argue, were constructed through the constant work of women, not through some

[1] Marion Kaplan, *The Making of the Jewish Middle Class: Women, Family, and Identity in Imperial Germany* (New York, 1991), p. 20.

[2] Kaplan, *Making,* p. 83.

[3] Elisabeth Joris and Heidi Witzig, *Brave Frauen, aufmüpfige Weiber: Wie sich die Industrialisierung zur Alltag und Lebenszusammenhänge von Frauen auswirkte (1820–1940)* (Zurich, 1992).

[4] Joris and Witzig, *Brave Frauen,* pp. 239–40. The latest author to deal with the issues is Gunilla-Friederike Budde, *Auf dem Weg ins Bürgerleben: Kindheit und Erziehung in deutschen und englischen Bürgerfamilien 1840–1914* (Göttingen, 1994). This is the most systematic account of gender and family in Germany I know. It offers considerable detail on how women organized networks of family members.

[5] See Jacques Rancière, *Die Namen der Geschichte. Versuch einer Poetik der Geschichte,* trans. Eva Moldenhauer (Frankfurt, 1994), pp. 93–112; Michel Foucault, *Power/Knowledge: Selected Interviews and Other Writings 1972–1977,* ed. Colin Gordon (New York, 1980), pp. 63–77; Michel de Certeau, *The Practice of Everyday Life,* trans. Steven Randall (Berkeley, 1988), pp. 91–130.

[6] Joris and Witzig, *Brave Frauen,* pp. 252–62.

magical relation between class position and class interest. At least this is one side of the issue. They also point to the new male clubs (*Vereine*) that developed in the nineteenth century as places for constructing social networks and suggest that women's cultivation of family connections can be seen as either parallel to, or as compensation for, the Verein movement.[7] The temporal as well as the reciprocal interaction of the two spheres needs to be worked out – which goes beyond the scope of this volume – but there is growing evidence that kinship played a central but still scarcely understood role in nineteenth-century society and that women were responsible for maintaining the necessary contacts for the system to work. "All information converged on them. They were in a position to shape (*gestalten*) relationships and to profit over the long run from them for themselves and their families."[8]

Autobiographies and published correspondence from mostly middle-class sources in nineteenth-century Germany lead in the same direction as a whole as the material offered by Kaplan and Joris and Witzig. The dense network of the Gatterer, Nathusius, and Reuter families near Magdeburg were structured and maintained by a series of powerful women.[9] The story Gabriele Reuter tells supports the observation of Joris and Witzig that networks were "matrilinear," composed of mother/daughter and sister/sister core relations, built on emotion and sentiment.[10] Although it is true that the networks were usually put together and cultivated by women, there is ample evidence for the first half of the nineteenth century at least that the brother/sister dyad frequently provided the tightest emotional bond. The Kestner family provides one example that can be buttressed with many more.[11]

Fostering networks

At the beginning of the nineteenth century, the Hannoverian bureaucrat and Göttingen university administrator (and champion of women in the home), Ernst Brandes, observed that the work of maintaining the far-flung connections between near and distant kin fell largely to women: "The most important thing for women, who feel themselves fitted for small, narrow household relationships, is the cultivation of kinship, the whole kindred. Life in the wide world is not conducive to bringing narrow family ties closer to the heart and to bind them tighter. But most women believe that the chief purpose for their husbands' find-

[7] Joris and Witzig, *Brave Frauen,* pp. 239–40.

[8] Joris and Witzig, *Brave Frauen,* pp. 240–1.

[9] Gabriele Reuter, *Vom Kinde zum Menschen. Die Geschichte meiner Jugend* (Berlin, 1921).

[10] Joris and Witzig, *Brave Frauen,* p. 248.

[11] Hermann Kestner-Köchlin, ed., *Briefwechsel August Kestner und seine Schwester Charlotte* (Strassburg, 1904). See also the remarks by Heinz Reif, *Westfälischer Adel 1770–1860: Vom Herrschaftsstand zur regionalen Elite* (Göttingen, 1979), pp. 266–7. Also David Warren Sabean, "Fanny and Felix Mendelssohn-Bartholdy and the Question of Incest," *Musical Quarterly,* 77 (1993): 709–17.

ing themselves in important state service is to take care of their relatives."[12] He, too, argued that family and class were two sides of the same configuration: "Next to the inclination to cultivate kin – and sometimes even more pronounced – the idea of real or imagined prerogatives of status (*Stand*) determines the actions of most women and is spread by them in mixed social gatherings."[13]

Family networks were only part of the activity of network construction, but family always remained the core, or the two were inextricably intertwined. Carlota Sieveking's correspondence, for example, shows how much the family centered its activities around the Basler Mission or the Sieveking foundation in Hamburg (always run by a woman).[14] The intense interaction of uncles and aunts, cousins, and extended kin, whether gathered together for a time (reading religious literature to one another, playing games, singing, or playing music) or corresponding, continually shaded off into charitative, business, and political activity. Sieveking women were constantly active in reaching out from the family but always with the firm foundation of family behind them. In the history of the self-conscious Siemens family, particular women such as Elise Görz, the wife of Georg Siemens, were crucial for developing the social networks on which the men depended.[15] Other examples of the close interconnections between social (here literary, religious, regional, and political) networks and family networks is documented continually in the correspondence of the aristocratic writer and poet, Annette von Droste-Hülshoff, the upper-middle-class Kestner family of entrepreneurs and officials, and the academic family of Anselm and Henriette Feuerbach.[16]

There are many ways in which women acted as mediating figures or go-betweens in families. When, for example, Carl Friedrich von Siemens as head of the clan faced rebellion in the 1920s by younger members who wanted to pull their capital from the firm, he wrote to his sister Anna to deal with the issue. She was the one who "understood" all of the familial dynamics and who was capable of exercising "influence" in the situation.[17] Schubert argues that women were an integrating element in criminal organizations and gangs. In such groups

[12] Ernst Brandes, *Betrachtungen über das weibliche Geschlecht und dessen Ausbildung in dem geselligen Leben,* 3 vols. (Hannover, 1802), vol. 2, p. 37. Karin Hausen brought Brandes to my attention.

[13] Brandes, *Betrachtungen,* vol. 2, p. 41.

[14] Luisa Rebensburg-Reich, ed., *Aus Tante Carlotas Nachlass. Familienbriefe Sieveking/Cramer aus Hamburg, Basel, Genf, u.a.* (Hamburg, 1937).

[15] Karl Helfferich, *Georg von Siemens: Ein Lebensbild aus Deutschlands grosser Zeit,* 3 vols., 2d. ed. (Berlin, 1923), vol. 1, p. 236.

[16] Annette von Droste-Hülshoff, *Historisch-kritische Ausgabe,* vol. 8, pt. 1, vol. 9, pt. 1, vol. 10, pt. 1 (Tübingen, 1987, 1993, 1992); Kestner-Köchlin, *Briefwechsel Kestner*; Hermann Ahde-Bernaÿs, ed., *Henriette Feuerbach. Ihr Leben in ihren Briefen* (Berlin/Vienna, 1912).

[17] Georg Siemens, *Carl Friedrich von Siemens: Ein grosser Unternehmer* (Freiburg, 1960), pp. 183–4. E. Leyton discusses a similar function within a large extended Canadian family during the 1950s: "If an individual attempts to sever relations with the composite descent group, considerable pressure is also brought to bear . . . [A student attempted this in 1962]: in the twelve-month period following his attempt he received weekly phone calls and visits from family negotiators and censure and persuasion from friends of the family." See "Composite Descent Groups in Canada," in C. C. Harris, *Readings in Kinship in Urban Society* (Oxford and New York, 1970), pp. 179–86, here 184.

marriages were stable and women provided the essential skills of mediation to keep the groups cohesive.[18]

In many instances women were called upon for the delicate phases of marriage negotiations. Justus Liebig's daughter was wooed by several suitors, all of whom mobilized their sisters to open negotiations through her sister.[19] Annette von Droste-Hülshoff offers many examples in her correspondence of women as key figures in marriage negotiations. They were mobilized to survey the possibilities, corresponded with each other about the suitability of particular families, called on potential spouses to check on their characters, manners, and carriage, and initiated inquiries and saw through negotiations at each stage. Annette's sister Jenny, who lived on the Lake of Constance, asked Annette to look closely at two sisters (related to the Droste-Hülshoff family by marriage) as potential partners for her son. Annette mobilized her entire (considerable) network to find out every detail.[20] Marion Kaplan shows for late nineteenth-century Jewish families the same kind of informal brokering through familial and friendship networks.[21]

Ernst Brandes with his jaundiced eye was an acute observer of clan dynamics. He thought that women were responsible for all of the mediating activities in families and that they tended to widen the circles of their influence because they were limited to kinship activities. It is often difficult to sort out his observations from his prescriptive recommendations, yet he can usefully be called in as a witness about conditions among the Hannoverian Bildungsbürger at the beginning of the nineteenth century. Women, he thought, developed as go-betweens because they were used to fostering intense personal relations.[22] "Women cherish and foster family ideas in the circles in which they dominate, and the vanity of men easily follows along each of their thoughts."[23]

Doris Focke had a very difficult marriage, which stemmed from the fact that her sister-in-law (HBW) had been in love with her husband. The relationships between the two houses were strained and over a 10-year period full of conflict. In correspondence with her lawyer brother, Focke detailed the everyday conflicts between those two and many other related houses. What becomes apparent throughout her letters is the strong imperatives for the households to coordinate many activities, not the least because the brothers had business dealings with each other and lived across the street from each other. In Chapter 22, I quoted one letter in which in a moment of deep despair she talked about the thousand threads that bound the households together. Over the whole period, related

[18] Ernst Schubert, *Arme Leute, Bettler und Gauner im Franken des 18. Jahrhunderts,* Verein der Gesellschaft für fränkischen Geschichte, Reihe 9, Darstellungen, Band 26 (Neustadt a. d. Aisch, 1983), pp. 275–6.

[19] Ernst von Harnack, ed., *Johanna Thiersch, geborene Freiin von Liebig. Briefe aus ihren Jugendjahren 1848–1855: Für die Familie zusammengestellt zum Gedächtnis ihres 100. Geburtstages* (Berlin-Zehlendorf, 1936), pp. 35–6.

[20] Droste-Hülshoff, *Briefe,* 9, pt. 1, pp. 10–27, 233–45, 300–307.

[21] Kaplan, *Making,* p. 89.

[22] Brandes, *Betrachtungen,* vol. 1, p. 91.

[23] Brandes, *Betrachtungen,* vol. 2, p. 39.

women acted as go-betweens. They kept each side completely informed about all of the activities of the other side and took on the task of carrying out fundamental tasks such as bringing the children of the households together.[24]

Correspondence

One of the chief ways by which women developed and maintained a network of kinship ties was through letter writing.[25] Of course, many men in the nineteenth century carried on a wide correspondence, especially with family. Werner von Siemens is a good example here. But Joris and Witzig, after surveying considerable published and unpublished correspondence for German-speaking Switzerland, came to the conclusion that the task of carrying on familial correspondence shifted during the late eighteenth century from men to women. A German example is offered by the Voss family, in which the husband wrote most of the letters up to 1782. By 1792 his wife had taken over this central family function.[26] Ernst Brandes, always anxious to disparage the literary activities of women, noted: "A literary talent in which women quite certainly surpass us is in the act of writing letters. . . . The best of the genre offered by women has always been those not interested for publication or the wider public but only written for their friends and acquaintances without intending that their letters would ever be put before the eyes of the world."[27] Brandes's strict division of labor between private and public points to a realm of activity of women that was never static and was in fact growing at the time that he wrote. And it was an important area that had once been dominated by men. Marchtaler points out that the education of middle-class Hamburg daughters in this period was centered among other things on writing, and that these women became extraordinarily skilled in letter writing.[28] There has been a great deal of ambivalence in recent historical writing about the private/public distinction.[29] Although, on the one hand, historians want to bring women as they actually lived back into the historical narrative and to revise the judgment on their everyday activities in the domestic realm, on the other, they also implicitly or explicitly judge the public realm to be superior and in any case more interesting. By no means all but much of the history of women has centered on their purposeful exclusion from the

[24] Wilhelm Olbers Focke, *Briefe von Doris Focke geb. Olbers an ihren Bruder für die Familie als Manuscript gedruckt* (Bremen, 1886), pp. 9–10, 92–4, 101–4, 122–3, 135–7, 173, 220–4, 278–81, 284.

[25] See Budde, *Weg ins Bürgerleben,* pp. 66, 86, 99, 103–4, 156–7, 255, 344–45.

[26] Ludwig Bäte, ed., *Vossische Hausidylle. Briefe von Ernestine Voss an Heinrich Christian und Sara Boie (1794–1820)* (Bremen, 1925), p. 16.

[27] Brandes, *Betrachtungen,* vol. 3, p. 18.

[28] Hildegard von Marchtaler, *Aus Althamburger Senatorenhäusern. Familienschicksale im 18. und 19. Jahrhundert,* Veröffentlichung des Vereins für Hamburgische Geschichte, vol. 16 (Hamburg, n.d. [1958]), p. 47.

[29] There is an excellent discussion of the problem in Leonore Davidoff and Catherine Hall, *Family Fortunes: Men and Women of the English Middle Class, 1780–1850* (Chicago, 1991), pp. 13, 32–4. See also the recent summing up by Kathleen Canning, "Gender and the Politics of Class Formation: Rethinking German Labor History," *American Historical Review* 97 (1992): 736–68.

public sphere, their attempts to gain access to it, or unusual or unknown examples of their public activities as artists, writers, entrepreneurs, and leaders in social or religious causes. Their correspondence, largely unintended for publication, was a many-layered activity not easily analyzed in public/private categories but frequently conceptualized as private and not examined either in terms of the work of kinship or as an area of important literary or political expression. Charlotte Kestner, who moved to the Strassburg area to raise the children of her widowed brother Karl, took over all of the business correspondence for his chemical firm as well as the recordkeeping. All communication between him and his family, friends, and business associates passed under her pen.[30]

Joris and Witzig have described many of the essential aspects of women's letter writing in the nineteenth century. Because the extensive contacts with kin went through women, they were in position to shape relationships. For the middle and upper classes, letters were a means of communication beyond the local.[31] Letters circulated among kin like *samizdat* publications. Through this activity, women were able to manipulate the whole communication network inside a family. "Writing letters as an area of women's activity became quasi-ritualized. Despite the mass of news, it was not a question primarily of transmitting the latest events but rather of maintaining communication in and for itself."[32]

Unfortunately, the published correspondence of women from the nineteenth century is usually truncated. The fairly large volumes of letters between August and Charlotte Kestner are only a small part of Charlotte's extensive network of communication. Henriette Feuerbach, herself at the center of a vast network of correspondence, wrote in Charlotte's obituary that she was the key figure in a widespread correspondence with friends and relatives, "tying together near and far."[33] Because of her importance as a poet and writer, the entire extant correspondence of Annette von Droste-Hülshoff has been published (she frequently made copies of her letters for her own records). With her writing, the ritualized aspect pointed out by Joris and Witzig grew more and more important with time. As she entered her 40s, she became an ever more central figure in mediating among family members. In a typical letter (1843), she took up each of the family residences in turn – Rüschhaus, Hülshoff, Böckendorf, Hinnenburg, Herstelle, Arnswaldt, Husen, Erpernburg, and Stapel – and then went into details about 26 other people.[34] She explicitly expected her sister to circulate the letter, which took on the dimensions of a family newspaper. Fanny Lewald even got started as a writer because a cousin published a letter of news she had written to his

[30] Kestner-Köchlin, *Briefwechsel Kestner,* pp. 17, 114.

[31] Joris and Witzig, *Brave Frauen,* p. 240. This was also the case for petit-bourgeois families in Germany. Friederike Fricke, living in Fallingbostel, connected Hannover, Vienna, Neukloster, and Bremerhaven in her extensive correspondence with family members; Friederike Fricke, ed., *Aus dem Leben unserer Mutter, Familienbriefe für die Familie* (Göttingen, 1929).

[32] Joris and Witzig, *Brave Frauen,* p. 240.

[33] Kestner-Köchlin, *Briefwechsel Kestner,* p. 350.

[34] Droste Hülshoff, *Briefe,* 10, pt. 1. pp. 16–32.

mother in his journal.[35] The easy shift between letter writing and essays and novels meant for a public is also demonstrated by Monika Hunnius.[36]

In many bourgeois families the husband was seldom in fact at home, which gave a woman opportunity to determine and develop a considerable social life, at first, usually by capitalizing on a familial network already in place. Anna (née Mohl) von Helmholtz's correspondence suggests that her husband never spent much time with her – which may be one reason why she developed into such a formidable and interesting character. He spent long hours pursuing science, traveled incessantly, hung out at the club, and spent his vacations mountain climbing apart from his family. Not only did Anna organize her intellectual and social life around familial correspondence, she also seems to have communicated to her husband largely through letters.[37] A rather different example is provided by the Levysohn family. Wilhelm was a journalist, publisher, and book dealer and a delegate to the Frankfurt Parliament, who had to sit out a year in prison for his political activities. Even though he was a journalist, he was quite a miserable letter writer. His wife had to carry on all the correspondence, and when he went off to pursue his political calling, she took over the entire business, publishing the newspaper and bringing order into his papers.[38] There are enough hints in what I have read so far to show that women frequently played the role of bookkeeper and correspondent for many businesses. What Marion Kaplan says about behind-the-scenes activity of bourgeois Jewish women can be generalized for German nineteenth-century family business as a whole.[39]

Patterns of reciprocity

Part of the reciprocities knitting kin together involved the constant exchange of gifts. Joris and Witzig point to the central importance of women giving their friends and relatives objects they frequently made, which mediated a particular emotional force.[40] The correspondence of Annette von Droste-Hülshoff is full of discussions about gift-giving strategies, and she frequently offered advice to a cousin or niece about an appropriate gift for a relative. When her uncle presented her with some music he had composed (she often sent poems as gifts), she thought the proper gesture of return would be to commit the piece to memory and surprise him with it. Discovering another uncle's interest in coins brought a life-long stream of presents to him as she sought out rare and unusual examples on her travels.[41] The correspondence of women abounds with examples of anticipated gifts and comments on gifts already exchanged.[42]

[35] Fanny Lewald, *Meine Lebensgeschichte,* 3 pts. in 6 vols. (Berlin, 1861–2), pt. 2, vol. 2, pp. 154–8.
[36] Monika Hunnius, *Briefwechsel mit einem Freund,* ed. Sophie Gurland (Heilbronn, 1935).
[37] Ellen von Siemens-Helmholtz, ed., *Anna von Helmholtz: Ein Lebensbild in Briefen* (Berlin, 1929).
[38] Monty Jacobs, ed., *1848: Briefwechsel zwischen Wilhelm und Philippine Levysohn* (Grünberg, 1906).
[39] Kaplan, *Making,* pp. 18–19, 26. On this point, compare Davidoff and Hall, *Family Fortunes.*
[40] Joris and Witzig, *Brave Frauen,* pp. 244–7.
[41] Droste-Hülshoff, *Briefe,* 8, pt. 1, pp. 38–40, 41–6, 48–51, 57–9, 64, 105–9, 162–4, 199–204.
[42] Two examples are Jacobs, *Briefwechsel Levysohn,* pp. 212–13; and Focke, *Briefe Focke,* p. 137.

Women were responsible for taking care of family members in illness, old age, and crisis, and they were crucial for raising the many orphans that nineteenth-century society produced.[43] There are too many examples of this kind of thing to try to document at any great length.[44] Young women frequently were sent to help out their sisters, especially during the stressful years of raising children. Joris and Witzig give the example of a woman who abandoned her own marriage plans at the death of her mother in order to provide support for her married sister.[45] Both future ministers Bartsch and Rogge recalled that their busy mothers were aided for many years by their own sisters.[46] Charlotte Kestner in 1808 left Hannover at the request of her recently widowed brother Karl to settle in Alsace to care for and raise his children. By 1822, she had moved to Basel with one of the nieces she had raised to help with her new family. (In 1848, she left for several years to tend a dying brother in Frankfurt.)[47] Ottilie Wildermuth sent her younger daughter to Holstein to assist the older daughter busy with a young family.[48] Carlota Sieveking in 1858 left Hamburg to go to Basel to help her sister raise her children.[49] At the end of the century (1896), the Lieder singer and writer Monika Hunnius at the age of 38 joined her aunt to help raise her cousins.[50] Ottilie Wildermuth recalled the visit of one guest: "After that a cousin came for eight days, a charming guest, one of the peaceful, self-sacrificing souls, who sacrifice the energy of youth and the quiet of later days for others, a night violet whose value we only recognize when the night of suffering descends on a house – to us she came this time not as a help in need, but in order to enjoy a few peaceful days with a small, languishing foster child."[51]

Households frequently had problems dealing with children at certain phases of development. After Carl Zeiss was widowed, he sent his son Roderich to his sister to be taken care of. After he married again, the new wife never really became much of a mother to Roderich, and he was sent off to another of Carl's sisters from time to time.[52] Cleophea Bansa was the oldest child of a fairly large

[43] This is a point emphasized by Marion Kaplan for German Jewish women; *Making,* p. 239. And Budde, *Weg ins Bürgerleben,* pp. 100–109, 265–9, offers much new detail on the subject.

[44] Paul Deussen, *Mein Leben,* ed. Erika Rosenthal-Deussen (Leipzig, 1922), pp. 4–5; Brigitte Schröder, "Der Weg zur Eisenbahnschiene. Geschichte der Familie Remy und ihre wirtschaftliche und kulturelle Bedeutung," *Deutsches Familienarchiv. Ein genealogisches Sammelwerk,* 91 (Neustadt an der Aisch, 1916): 3–158, here p. 81; Focke, *Briefe Focke,* p. 7; Monika Hunnius, *Wenn die Zeit erfüllet ist. Briefe und Tageblätter,* ed., Anne Monika Glasow (Heilbronn, 1937), pp. 210, 215, 331.

[45] Joris and Witzig, *Brave Frauen,* p. 250.

[46] Bernhard Rogge, *Aus Sieben Jahrzehnten. Erinnerungen aus meinem Leben* (Hannover and Berlin, 1897), p. 28; *Karl Bartsch, Aus der Kinderzeit. Bruchstück einer Biographie* (Tübingen, 1882), p. 4.

[47] Kestner-Köchlin, *Briefwechsel Kestner,* pp. 12, 15–17, 110, 126, 193, 287, 342.

[48] Bernardine Schulze-Smidt, *Ottilie Wildermuths Briefe an einen Freund. Mit einer Lebensskizze* (Bielefeld and Leipzig, 1910), p. 176.

[49] Luisa Rebensburg-Reich, ed., *Aus Tante Carlotas Nachlass. Familienbriefe Sieveking/Cramer aus Hamburg, Basel, Genf u.a.* (Hamburg, 1937), p. 23, 35.

[50] Hunnius, *Briefwechsel,* pp. 276–319.

[51] Schulze-Smidt, *Wildermuths Briefe,* p. 68.

[52] Horst Alexander Willam, *Carl Zeiss 1816–1888,* Beiheft 6, *Tradition: Zeitschrift für Firmengeschichte und Unternehmerbiographie* (München, 1967), pp. 69, 72, 74.

family. She was sent to her childless aunt to be raised along with two cousins, one of whom was orphaned.[53] Annette von Droste-Hülshoff's mother took over the tasks of educating the children of a very extended set of kin. It was Annette's task to provide instruction.[54]

A central way of connecting households was to send a daughter from one to the other for a time. Daughters were frequently sent to stay with a lonely grandmother or aunt for a period of years until their households had to be given up, and, of course, they were often called upon to act as nurse for chronically or terminally ill relatives.[55] But the exchange of daughters was often the equivalent of sending sons off to school. The aunt or cousin who took them in provided the finishing touches to an education. It was a way of cementing relations between sisters or cousins who exchanged their children. Marion Kaplan underlines the importance of exchanging cousins for developing and maintaining kinship networks.[56] The fact of living in the house of an aunt together with cousins for several years provided the basis of life-long intensive contacts through correspondence, traveling, crisis aid, and even marriage. For a young woman like Amalie Schoppe, going to become the teacher of a cousin at 18 was at the same time a matter of leaving home and entering into the adult world.[57] Fanny Lewald had had to take over all the responsibilities of her parents' considerable household at the age of 17 for a few years. That experience is probably what led her to become a writer. In the crisis years as she was unwilling to enter an arranged marriage and was negotiating with her father over beginning a writing career, she was sent to an uncle and aunt in the Rhineland to live for a few years. She subsequently spent some time with a great aunt and cousins in Breslau.[58] Such visits were part of strategies to relieve stress at certain points in extended kin relations and to develop and strengthen ties at other points. Young Johanna von Liebig at 14 went to stay for a time in Darmstadt with a godmother aunt. That is where her mother had such intense family and friendship relations. There she developed a lifelong friendship with a cousin, and years later their children married.[59] Among the four von Mohl brothers, relationships were extraordinarily close. They met together each year for several weeks. A formative experience for Robert's daughter Anna, and before her her older sister, was the several years she spent in Paris in the house of her uncle, where her aunt ran one of the most important Parisian salons for many years.[60] In the tense relationships between Doris Focke and her sister-in-law, sending children

[53] Otto Bansa, ed., *Ein Lebensbild in Briefen aus der Biedermeierzeit. Zur Geschichte der Family Bansa in Frankfurt a. M.* (Frankfurt, 1914), pp. 31–50.

[54] Clemens Heselhaus, *Annette von Droste-Hülshoff: Werk und Leben* (Düsseldorf, 1971), pp. 68–9.

[55] See Kaplan, *Making,* p. 82.

[56] Kaplan, *Making,* p. 123.

[57] Amalie Schoppe, geb. Wiese, *Erinnerungen aus meinem Leben* (Altona, 1838).

[58] Lewald, *Lebensgeschichte,* pt. 1, vol. 2, p. 36; pt. 1, vol. 1, pp. 57, 86.

[59] Von Harnack, *Thiersch Briefe,* pp. 3–4.

[60] Von Siemens-Helmholtz, *Helmholtz Lebensbild,* pp. 15–34.

back and forth between the households provided openings for reconciliation, while withdrawing them exacerbated the splits.[61]

Local, regional, and transregional networks

Reading through autobiographies and volumes of correspondence gives one an impression of German families dispersed over a considerable landscape. Despite the fact that they frequently had an acknowledged center, the trading, entrepreneurial, and bureaucratic families encountered here – such as the Bansas (Frankfurt), Kestners (Hannover), Sievekings (Hamburg), Nathusiuses (Saxony/Magdeburg), Deliuses (Bielefeld), Remys (Bendorf), or Siemens (originally from Goslar) – were scattered across Europe, and sometimes the Middle East and North and South America. Correspondence and the exchange of children was crucial for holding them together, but visiting, often for considerable lengths of time, could also be important. The fact that women traveled a great deal to see each other was a crucial instrument for knitting relations among the Jewish bourgeoisie of Imperial Germany.[62] Frequently such visits took an annual form, organized and planned by women.[63] Annette von Droste-Hülshoff described in 1840 a typical summer and fall of constant traveling back and forth of relatives to her and she to relatives in every direction.[64] Fanny Lewald described how her great aunt in Breslau functioned as the center of family pilgrimage – many kin who could not visit one another found themselves together in their periodic visits to her.[65] Charlotte Kestner visited Hannover from Alsace, bringing her nephew and niece along to see the relatives. Her trip took her by way of Frankfurt and another brother where all the cousins got to spend several weeks together. Henriette Feuerbach in her obituary of Charlotte noted that her house was never free of friends and relatives.[66] Louise Otto, looking back over her life in 1876, remembered that visitors during the 1830s and 1840s often came for weeks and months at a time and suggested that with the development of the railroad that was no longer the case.[67] But there is ample evidence that families experienced an ebb and flow of intensity and that no such generalization can be made. The railroad may have made it possible for people to move more freely and with less investment, but many families continued to experience visitors who came for many months at a time. Ottilie Wildermuth described in a letter a stream of visitors to Tübingen during the spring and summer of 1862.[68] An orphaned relative came

[61] Focke, *Briefe Focke*, pp. 131–6.
[62] Kaplan, *Making*, p. 84.
[63] Joris and Witzig, *Brave Frauen*, p. 244.
[64] Droste-Hülshoff, *Briefe*, 9, pt. 1, pp. 105–9.
[65] Lewald, *Lebensgeschichte*, pt. 2, vol. 1, pp. 86–8.
[66] Kestner-Köchlin, *Briefwechsel Kestner*, pp. 77–84, 351.
[67] Louise Otto, *Frauenleben im deutschen Reich: Erinnerungen aus der Vergangenheit mit Hinweis auf Gegenwart und Zukunft* (Leipzig, 1876), p. 3.
[68] See the similar account in Budde, *Weg ins Bürgerleben*, pp. 254–55.

for a visit, then a cousin with her foster child for eight days, the husband of a close friend and his second wife, followed by the son of one of her correspondents for a few days over Easter. Her oldest brother turned up in May, sick, for 13 weeks, visited frequently by his wife. A cousin – a pastor – and his wife dropped in for several weeks in the meantime. "There was often such large assemblies of relatives, of cousins and aunts, that our rooms hardly had enough space." An elderly woman from Basel collecting for a mission stopped for four days with her servant. A Swiss friend of her daughter joined them for eight days. Ottilie and her husband traveled to Bad Boll to meet relatives from Schleswig. By July a cousin and her husband – "very dear guests" – came from Schleswig. After that came a cousin who had been orphaned early and had been a half foster child of her parents. She, incurably sick, stayed several weeks. A couple of student cousins came from Denmark – "very Danish" – at the same time as an uncle and aunt from Holstein. They all stayed for two months. A Baronin von Knöbel-Doberitz from Pomerania, who she had corresponded with, came "like a ray of sun" with her sister. She was followed by a woman, a friend from youth, now running a girl's pension in Holland – the supporter of her whole family – "a new gratifying demonstration of how much power God has put into the apparent weakness of the female nature." After that came many other guests, including a cousin like a sister. She herself took a short vacation trip with her husband to siblings and friends. By the late fall, she was flooded by new students, all of whom had been recommended to them.[69] Such constant visiting can be illustrated from the correspondence of many other women, good examples being the Biedermeier family of Cleophea Bansa centered on Frankfurt and the late nineteenth-century Baltic family of Monika Hunnius.[70]

Just as visiting back and forth across Germany or Europe knit dispersed families together, so weekly and daily visiting integrated people from the same locality.[71] Zunkel pointed out that it was the custom among entrepreneurial families in the Rhineland to meet once a week.[72] And Marchtaler gives examples of daily visiting of sisters and sisters-in-law in Hamburg.[73] Typically, some families gathered on Sunday afternoon for coffee and cake, the central figures always being mothers and daughters, grandmothers, aunts, and female cousins.[74] Other women chose a particular evening or afternoon to hold a Kaffeekränzchen – a "Tuesday

[69] Schulze-Smidt, *Wildermuths Briefe*, pp. 64–70.

[70] Hunnius, *Briefwechsel*; Bansa, ed., *Lebensbild in Briefen.*

[71] See Budde, *Weg ins Bürgerleben*, pp. 89–95.

[72] Friedrich Zunkel, *Der Rheinisch-Westfälische Unternehmer 1834–1879. Ein Beitrag zur Geschichte der deutschen Bürgertums im 19. Jahrhundert*, Dortmunder Schriften zur Sozialforschung, vol. 19 (Köln, 1962), p. 73.

[73] Hildegard v. Marchtaler, *Aus Althamburger Senatorenhäusern. Familienschicksale im 18. und 19. Jahrhundert*, Veröffentlichungen des Vereins für hamburgische Geschichte, vol. 16 (Hamburg, n.d. [1958]), p. 95.

[74] Johannes Schmarje, *Lebenserinnerungen eines schleswig-holsteinischen Schulmannes* (Altona, 1925), p. 21; Clara Heitefuss, *An des Meisters Hand. Lebenserinnerungen* (Schwerin, 1939), pp. 12–13.

Society" for example.[75] Vacations provided another opportunity for women to plan and organize familial gatherings.[76]

Characteristic of women's activities in building networks were "cousin circles" or groups of sisters and sisters-in-law who coordinated family news and information and configured larger networks of kin. Marion Kaplan points to the centrality of Kusinenkreise for Jewish middle-class women at the end of the century.[77] Gabriele Reuter noted that at crucial periods of the Nathusius clan, sets of sisters or cousins formed the core of social relations between houses.[78] Monika Hunnius spent her adolescence and young adulthood among a set of cousins known in the family as the "clique." As an adult, she participated in a ring of correspondence and visits with cousins, and as an old woman, with her nieces and the children of her cousins.[79] Doris Focke took part in a meeting once a week (*Dienstaggesellschaft*) with nearby cousins and sisters-in-law. She and a series of cousins corresponded and planned common activities together. In the several years before her early death, she met every two weeks with her cousins to read together.[80] Cleophea Bansa was raised with two cousins in the household of her aunt. The three of them, together with another cousin connected Paris, Hamburg, Frankfurt, and Stuttgart in a round-robin French correspondence. Locally during the phase of raising her own children, she met periodically with three cousins and another relative together with their 30 children on regular occasions to play cards, read to one another, and engage in other social past times. Before she was married, she and her three sisters got together every Thursday with the four sisters of her future husband and with three or four other relatives and friends – the core for later social exchanges.[81]

Of course, much of the family visiting involved men, even if most of the planning and organization was carried on by women. All of the work of cooking, cleaning, washing up, directing the household servants, nursing, and the like was carried on by women. Quite central to the dynamics of kinship cultivation was the hospitality provided by wives, sisters, and daughters. Ottilie Wildermuth noted that her husband enjoyed visits by both his and his wife's relatives but reserved the right to withdraw to his study, which he frequently did.[82] Bernhard Rogge described how his father's parsonage was the center of a rich social life, but he was clear on the fact that it was his mother and aunt who managed the smooth hospitable environment, which frequently involved a household, as I have

[75] Gustav Parthey, *Jugenderinnerungen,* ed., Ernst Friedel, pts. 1 and 2 (Berlin, 1907), 1, pp. 204–5; Focke, *Briefe Focke,* pp. 254–62, 278–93; Bansa, *Lebensbild in Briefen,* pp. 144–6.

[76] Kaplan, *Making,* pp. 83–4, 123–4; Focke, *Briefe Focke,* pp. 186–7; Felix Eberty, *Jugenderinnerungen eines alten Berliners* (Berlin, 1878), pp. 118, 120; Hunnius, *Briefwechsel,* "Einleitung," pp. 45–52.

[77] Kaplan, *Making,* pp. 82–4, 122–6.

[78] Reuter, *Vom Kinde zum Menschen,* pp. 16, 20, 163, 205, 213.

[79] Hunnius, *Briefwechsel,* pp. 72, 149, 292, 320, 384–7, 413.

[80] Focke, *Briefe Focke,* pp. 37–9, 47–50, 121–2, 186–7, 201–7, 225–9, 254–63.

[81] Bansa, *Lebensbild in Briefen,* pp. 31, 44–5, 48, 51–5, 105–6, 140, 146.

[82] Schulze-Smidt, *Wildermuths Briefe,* p. 70.

pointed out before, of 40 people.[83] The fact that Georg von Siemens was able to sit at the center of a large circle of kin and Kaiserreich power brokers derived from the fact, according to his son-in-law, that his wife was skilled at developing social networks.[84] Joris and Witzig, after examining the histories of many Swiss families, came to the conclusion that hospitality provided by women as well as their planning activities was at the heart of integrating extensive kinship networks.[85] Charlotte Kestner provides an excellent example of a woman whose household was open to family, artists, and literati.[86] Lorenz von Stein saw the role of wives as central to the ability of their husbands to create social networks. He put the issue abstractly in terms of "social thought" (male) and "social feeling" (female), another way of glossing the public/private distinction. The connection between the two spheres was configured by women who represented all the ambitions of their husbands and who provided the environment in which all of their social networks were constructed.[87] Louise Otto is one of the few writers to offer a specific discussion on the work load involved in the task of providing house-centered sociability.[88] Brandes at the beginning of the century had distinguished between public and private spheres but defined a mediating sphere in which men and women met on an equal basis, an area he called "Geselligkeit" or "society." In such mixed society everything turned around women – largely it seems because they framed the space in which such gatherings took place as well as the forms of the interaction.[89] Henriette Feuerbach, whose music room became the center of intellectual life in Heidelberg, captured some of the ambivalences in the realm of brokering social relations, providing hospitality, and maintaining familial ties: "I find myself on the margins of the proper female spheres of activity, stuck between two rich fields, neither of which I can reach. On the one side, household business pulls me, although I have no real love for it. On the other side, art and study (*Wissen*) attract me, but for them I have no real calling. Thus I am nothing in either."[90]

Matrifocality

Many families and kin networks were organized around a key older woman. Werner von Siemens, for example, pointed to an aunt who had been widowed at an early age and who "formed at that time the acknowledged centre of our

[83] Rogge, *Aus sieben Jahrzehnten,* p. 28.
[84] Helfferich, *Georg von Siemens,* 3, pp. 232–46.
[85] Joris and Witzig, *Brave Frauen,* pp. 239–44.
[86] Kestner-Köchlin, *Briefwechsel Kestner,* p. 351.
[87] Lorenz von Stein, *Die Frau auf dem socialen Gebiete* (Stuttgart, 1880), pp. 62–3, and *Die Frau, ihre Bildung und Lebensaufgabe,* 3d ed. (Berlin, 1890), pp. 24, 27.
[88] Otto, *Frauenleben,* pp. 7–16.
[89] Brandes, *Betrachtungen,* vol. 1, pp. 76–83, 91; vol. 2, pp. 27–8; 3, pp. 172ff.
[90] Ahde-Bernaÿs, *Feuerbach Briefen,* p. 63. On this whole subject, see Budde, *Weg ins Bürgerleben,* pp. 180–92.

family."[91] Marion Kaplan found that among Jewish middle-class families, "the oldest woman orchestrated family events until she was no longer able."[92] Such a person could provide a central place to which others pilgrimaged periodically. Lady Battersea referred to her Rothschild paternal grandmother to whom everyone made their way for the Jewish holy days. But she was also an active person, whom Battersea described as "authoritative," someone who "managed all the members of her family."[93] The fact that Battersea and Siemens left these descriptions vague is disappointing. But one can imagine that such women mediated among family members in dispute with one another and were final arbiters in conflicts. It does seem clear that such women were crucial for coordination and cohesion among relatives – in both these cases, scattered across a very large territory.

Joris and Witzig argue that because of the centrality of women and a key older woman as the emotional pole for kin, family relations were stronger with the mother's family of origin.[94] Other observers such as Lorenz von Stein thought that women progressively became integrated into the families into which they married.[95] It seems that they did two things at once. They fostered lineal ties, ties to a surname group, to those related to each other by blood. Siemens's aunt seems partly responsible for his own concern to make the Siemens clan as famous and cohesive as he thought the Fuggers had been. Many such figures lived long lives as widows or never themselves married – Carlota Sieveking and Charlotte Kestner and Monika Hunnius are all good examples. Nonetheless, what was crucial for the nineteenth century was the systematic interaction between two or more patrilineally defined groups. Joris and Witzig stress the emotional bonds provided by the core women and think of them as "matrilineal" – pointing to key dyads of mother and daughter and sister and sister. But such ties also existed between many brothers and sisters such as Charlotte and August Kestner and Doris Focke and Georg Olbers, whose language of affection sometimes borders on the erotic. For the most part they capture a key element in the system, namely that the dynamic center of a clan or allied kin devolved in the course of time onto another woman or, finding no such heir, broke up, to be reconfigured around other dynamic centers. An allied group of women could give considerable stability over several generations. Joris and Witzig describe how the hometown could act as a center for dispersed family members: "The family was dispersed because of the brothers working in England and France, but it was held together primarily through women in Männedorf."[96] In this particular case – the Spörri family – the kin-group maintained cohesion from this central place over five generations. Many a network cultivated by a mother was inherited by a daughter: "It was a

[91] Werner von Siemens, *Personal Reflections,* trans. W. C. Coupland (London, 1893), p. 7.
[92] Kaplan, *Making,* p. 82.
[93] Constance de Rothschild Flower Lady Battersea, *Reminiscences* (London, 1922), p. 8.
[94] Joris and Witzig, *Brave Frauen,* p. 248.
[95] Von Stein, *Die Frauen, ihre Bildung,* p. 27.
[96] Joris and Witzig, *Brave Frauen,* p. 249.

self-evident duty and corresponded to her nature that after the death of her mother she cultivated all of the extraordinarily extended family and friendship connections."[97]

This phenomenon occurs too often in autobiographies to document at length, and the considerable correspondence of women attests to their assuming the task of developing and maintaining social ties among people. One can see, for example, in the correspondence of Annette von Droste-Hülshoff that as she entered her 40s still unmarried, her letters got ever longer, ritualized greetings became ever fuller, and the news of far-flung relatives took on the dimensions of a small newspaper. She advised, intrigued, mediated, and entertained. She helped provide for orphans, encouraged the old and sick, brokered marriages, and spun a net among a culturally cohesive regionally based Catholic elite.[98]

Gabriele Reuter described her aunt Nathusius at Althaldensleben in similar terms as the center of a large web – a "Stammesmutter." She was one of those strong characters to whom everyone came for advice.[99] Fanny Lewald's great aunt in Breslau was described in the same way.[100] Family members old and young "pilgrimaged" to such women, and their birthdays could be the occasion for annual family festivals.[101]

At two crucial periods in the Remy-Hofmann alliance, widows lived for a very long time after the deaths of their husbands and became the figures around which family dynamics were organized.[102] It may well have been the case that older unmarried women and widows were particularly suited for the work of kinship network construction. Certainly, the old notion of the pitied spinster underestimates the nature of politically effective, flexible, strategically negotiated ties, organized around interest and emotion at once. I have quoted from parts of Henriette Feuerbach's obituary of Charlotte Kestner, but it would be useful here to offer a larger portion of it to see the many criss-crossing elements which could combine to create for a centrally placed woman an effective area of social, cultural – and I would argue, political – operation. "In friendly reciprocity her hospitable house was almost never empty of relatives and friends, from scholars and artists. . . . In the large family network, however, and also way beyond it, Aunt Lottchen was Providence itself. Everyone turned to her in joy and sorrow, at any time of despair, in every difficulty and found even if not always material help then always wise and sober advice and heartfelt comfort."[103] The ecology of a well-connected Bildungsbürger family made the unusually extensive and culturally important network of Charlotte Kestner possible even if it was her particular personality

97 Joris and Witzig, *Brave Frauen,* p. 250.

98 Droste-Hülshoff, *Briefe,* vol. 8, pt. 1; vol. 9, pt. 1; vol. 10, pt. 1.

99 Reuter, *Vom Kinde zum Menschen,* pp. 210–11.

100 Lewald, *Lebensgeschichte,* pt. 2, vol. 1, pp. 69–100.

101 Heitefuss, *An des Meisters Hand,* pp. 8–13: her grandmother was the central figure. She was very much like Reuter's aunt at Althaldensleben, who ran four large and complex estates and the industrial enterprise, while raising five children.

102 Schröder, "Weg zur Eisenbahnschiene," pp. 107–8, 119.

103 Kestner-Köchlin, *Briefwechsel Kestner,* p. 350.

and energy that put it together. Henriette Feuerbach was able to appreciate Charlotte because she was part of the Kestner network and herself the center of another one. Carlota Sieveking's activity around Protestant missionary activity seems a parallel case for the next generation.[104] Joris and Witzig offer evidence to show that peasant families with a mobile set of emigrant relatives could function in similar ways even if not at the same level of cultural attainment.[105] Friederike Fricke provides a German petit-bourgeois example – her mother was at the center of a far-flung, European-wide exchange of correspondence and gifts.[106]

The business of business

In the public/private distinction, it was always assumed that women did not have a public function, especially in business. A number of historians and others have remarked upon the occasional women who apparently without any prior experience sprang in after their husbands died to take over a business successfully.[107] The success of these brilliant naïves goes unexplained. Louise Otto arguing in 1876 for women's competence shares the myth: "The businessman is in doubt [about women's capacities] despite the fact that in this sphere it has happened a hundred times that even a mere widow has learned a business only through *experience* without any *preparation* and brought new prosperity to what her husband has perhaps largely destroyed."[108] I have no doubts about women's competence, just about the idea of their lack of experience. I doubt if Charlotte Kestner, who handled the business correspondence and managed the records of her brother's firm, was so unusual.[109] Some women, of course, moved into areas in which they had a great deal of learning to do. The editor of the correspondence of the provincial publisher Wilhelm Levysohn and his wife Philippine left out "some boring business matters," but there is enough in their correspondence to see that with a young wife (30) and six children, he found no problem leaving her with the business to go off to the Frankfurt Parliament and jail.[110] It does seem true that she had to take over his part of the work – where she discovered a total lack of good organization – but since this newspaper editor was incapable of writing a straightforward letter in a legible hand, his wife must already have been carrying on the business correspondence. At any event, she expanded her

[104] Rebensburg-Reich, *Tante Carlotas Nachlass.*
[105] Joris and Witzig, *Brave Frauen,* pp. 248–50.
[106] Fricke, *Aus dem Leben unserer Mutter.*
[107] See most recently, Budde, *Weg ins Bürgerleben,* pp. 100–109.
[108] Otto, *Frauenleben,* p. 168.
[109] Kestner-Köchlin, *Briefwechsel Kestner,* p. 17. Compare Davidoff and Hall, *Family Fortunes.* Also the important work of Bonnie G. Smith, *Ladies of the Leisure Class: The Bourgeoises of Northern France in the Nineteenth Century* (Princeton, 1981). See also Heinz-Gerhard Haupt, "Männliche und weibliche Berufskarrieren im deutschen Bürgertum in der zweiten Hälfte des 19. Jahrhunderts: Zum Verhältnis von Klasse und Geschlecht," *Geschichte und Gesellschaft* 18 (1992): 143–60.
[110] Jacobs, *Briefwechsel Levysohn.*

area of competence quickly to run the bookstore and biweekly newspaper. She complained steadily, as many women must have done, that his incompetence had created an impossible situation and that his political work was a flight from reality, only made possible because he could dump the whole thing on his far more orderly and capable wife.

Marion Kaplan points out that because men in theory were supposed to carry on all the business affairs and support their families, women, who frequently were active in their husbands' enterprises, had to go to elaborate lengths not to appear to do so.[111] I suspect that this was often the case. Furthermore, there was a structural aspect to families that set women up with a good deal of property, authority, and independence. Men began to look around for wives after they had earned enough or become well enough established to marry someone of the right station – frequently much younger than themselves.[112] Many of these women were widowed when they were relatively young and left with young children. It was not always the case that they had to spring in to take over from their deceased husbands. They now had considerable property in their hands and simply asserted their rights. The well-known cases of Bertha Krupp, Sara Warburg, and Charlotte Oppenheim are good examples, but there are many lesser-known ones.[113] The four large estates and business agglomeration of the Nathusius family fell into the competent hands of the young widow.[114] According to Wolfgang Zorn, it was quite normal for widows in Swabia to take over the functions of their husbands, but it was not always just a matter of stepping into the breach because the role of wives in entrepreneurial activity was, as he notes, frequently important.[115] One has to make do with these kinds of observations in lieu of any systematic study of this phenomenon. One can imagine that Clara Heitefuss's grandmother, who ran the family colonial and ironware business for 17 years, was already active in it before her husband died.[116] But even if she did suddenly spring in, the kind of family negotiating and network building that such women were used to doing, coupled with ownership or usufructary rights over property, gave them a solid foundation for entering the world of trade and commerce.

There were many small entrepreneurial establishments that women ran on their own in the first place – boardinghouses are the most familiar. Some of them

[111] Kaplan, *Making,* p. 26.

[112] Wolfgang Zorn, *Handels- und Industriegeschichte Bayrisch-Schwabens 1648–1870: Wirtschafts-, Sozial-, und Kulturgeschichte des schwäbischen Unternehmertums,* Veröffentlichungen des schwäbischen Forschungsgemeinschaft bei der Kommission für bayerische Landesgeschichte, Reihe I: Studien zur Geschichte des bayerischen Schwabens, vol. 6 (Augsburg, 1961), pp. 286–74; Zunkel, *Rheinisch-Westfälische Unternehmer,* p. 95; Siemens, *Personal Reflections,* pp. 132–3. Fontane's *Effi Briest* makes the same point.

[113] E. Rosenbaum and A. J. Sherman, *M. M. Warburg & Co. 1798–1938: Merchant Bankers of Hamburg* (New York, 1979), pp. 30–1. Manfred Pohl, *Hamburger Bankengeschichte* (Mainz, 1986), p. 67.

[114] Reuter, *Vom Kinde zum Menschen,* pp. 210–11.

[115] Zorn, *Handels- und Industriegeschichte,* p. 280.

[116] Heitefuss, *An des Meisters Hand,* pp. 10–12.

expanded the practice of exchanging cousins into full-blown *Pensionen*, finishing schools for young girls.[117] Ottilie Wildermuth refers in one of her letters to a visiting cousin who ran a "Töchterpension" who was the "Schutz und Stütze" of her whole family.[118] Setting up such an establishment was something relatively easy for a rural pastor's wife to do, since a parsonage could be roomy, the educational level of the family high, and in some cases payments in kind from parishioners could form the foundation of a boarding system.[119]

Kinship and style

Women were crucial for other aspects of class formation. For one thing, they set the tone and rules of respectability. Marion Kaplan formulated the situation well for Jewish families, but her observations can be generalized well beyond the period and group she deals with.[120] Her point is that Jewish women controlled the style of the way of life. They contributed to the "tranquility" and "steadiness" of the bourgeois family – established the aura of *Gemütlichkeit* and controlled the manners and pretensions of families.[121] All of the large literature of the nineteenth century that coded this aspect of women's work as "aesthetics," "form," "rhythm," "style," or "grace" point in the same direction. Brandes brought the issue down to socializing women, who were no longer simply movable as pawns, into making class-conformable decisions about marriage. As far as he was concerned it came down to aesthetic preferences and training in recognizing equals by the way they moved and talked. "The power of physical impressions is there, but only really particularly there, when they are embedded in the girls, when a mother puts a very high premium on social charm."[122]

Lorenz von Stein later on in the century dealt with the same issues as Brandes. His notion of "social feeling" encompassed the same area of aesthetics that Brandes was concerned about. But he thought that too much emphasis was placed on those aspects that prepared daughters to make the right alliance choice and not enough on the large set of competencies called into play once married.[123] Louise Otto thought that the socialization provided by mothers worked toward both goals. She also stressed aesthetic categories.[124] Among many writers, words like "beauty" (*Schönheit*) and "harmony" were central categories of their analysis.[125]

[117] Deussen, *Mein Leben*, p. 21.

[118] Schulze-Smidt, *Wildermuths Briefe*, pp. 68–9.

[119] Deussen's mother being a good example; *Mein Leben*.

[120] See Budde, *Weg ins Bürgerleben*, pp. 181–96.

[121] Kaplan, *Making*, pp. 9–10.

[122] Brandes, *Betrachtungen*, vol. 2, p. 114.

[123] Von Stein, *Die Frau, ihre Bildung*, pp. 24–6; Ulrike Henschke was a critic of this kind of education and wanted to stress practical competence. Again, she is a witness to a social form; *Die Bedeutung des Vereinsleben für die Frauen* (Lissa, 1866), p. 17.

[124] Otto, *Frauenleben*, pp. 216–21.

[125] Carl Edward Vehse, *Ueber die gesellige Stellung und die geistige Bildung der Frauen in England, Amerika, Frankreich und vornehmlich in Deutschland* (Dresden, 1842), p. 30, also stressed "harmony."

Women set the style of cleanliness and order that lay at the foundation of respectability. "Thus the mother has the high task . . . to supply the child – cleanliness, fresh air and sunshine, movement, nourishing food, comfortable clothes suitable to the seasons – in and with all these things [and] thereby at the same time to lay the foundation for the aesthetic education of her child."[126] Otto went on to say that "everything in this regard which is neglected in the earliest age can never fully be recovered or replaced."[127] I see this kind of text less interesting from the standpoint of ethical theory than as witness to the social dynamics that such writers observed. These texts help us understand how class style and self-recognition were constructed. What Louise Otto tells us is what the relatives of Paul Henle told him when he thought about reconstructing his "fair lady."[128]

A pastor like Bogumil Goltz captured the erotic and titillating side to properly brought up girls and displayed the interplay between form, grace, eroticism, and class-based alliance.

> Even in the muscles and angular movements of men, nature expresses the sharp accents of their character, just as in the soft flowing forms of the female body and in its waving motion it expresses the melodic disposition and grace of women – *whoever has understood that will perceive in love and marriage a still deeper law, a more sublime economy and sufficiency, than the reproduction of the human race.*[129]

* * *

This book began with a consideration of the eighteenth-century political debate over nepotism (Vetterleswirtschaft). Central to the attack on corruption was a careful distinction between things public and things private. Reform was on the agenda during the first three decades of the nineteenth century at every level of political instance, from village to princely court. Advancement by merit and a polity free from corruption forced property holders throughout the social hierarchy to develop flexible sets of networks of people beholden to one another. Whether the problem was managing a rapidly developing market for land or "capitalizing" on opportunity for business investment or providing paths of advancement for promising young men through a landscape where the signposts seemed to direct only men who traveled alone, everyone needed to be supported by people who felt strong obligations to them or recognized in them others who understood the same code. The new networks were constructed through a newly fashioned alliance system. Those with property frequently preferred repeated exchange and strong bonds; those without, spread their networks over a larger "landscape," relying on more distant kin and the intensive use of godparents. The rise and fall of consanguinity correlated closely with the formation of class,

[126] Otto, *Frauenleben,* p. 218.

[127] Otto, *Frauenleben,* p. 219.

[128] See Chapter 22 in this volume; Paul Rehburg, ed., *Elise Egloff: Die Geschichte einer Liebe in ihren Briefen* (Zurich, 1937).

[129] Bogumil Goltz, *Zur Charakteristik und Naturgeschichte der Frau* (Berlin, 1863), p. 32. See another man's opinion on "grace," "form," "beauty," "proportion": Christian Gottfried Körner, *Für deutsche Frauen* (Berlin and Stettin, 1824), pp. 6, 12, 21, 23.

its integration during the central and later decades of the nineteenth century, and the breaking up of coordinated class milieus in the twentieth. Kinship responded to formal exigencies and utilized classic and inventive principles of exchange. But the work and the political effort fell during the nineteenth century largely on the shoulders of women. This book has explored some of the dark corners of a relatively uncharted terrain. It has attempted to force a convergence of three conceptual tools of social analysis: kinship, which has fallen on hard times during the last decades of anthropological neglect; class, whose political relevance and analytical power have evaporated over much the same period; and gender, whose strength may yet develop the power to reinvigorate and give new direction to them both.

Appendix

Contents

Appendix

A. Construction of genealogies

A systematic study of kinship networks cannot proceed without genealogical information. That information must be broad enough to test the limits of genealogical knowledge and practice. It is common enough for people in primitive or "traditional" societies to have a considerable genealogical memory and to be able to locate most of their acquaintances somewhere on its coordinates. The methodological difficulty arises as soon as one wants to study more than a handful of people, for constructing a genealogy is a time-consuming, complex business. Theoretically, at least, its dimensions can be overwhelming. Assume, for example, a family size of four children who eventually marry. Tracing back three generations from an individual and then forward one generation beyond him or her would produce a genealogy well in excess of 4,000 individuals. To carry out the same exercise for the marriage partner would, of course, double the number of people traced. In actual fact, genealogies constructed on the basis of Neckarhausen records are never of this size, although the longest by far that I have constructed for a married couple has between 1,500 and 2,000 individuals in it. A typical long genealogy has 700–900, the average around 500–600. Genealogies of this dimension include those children who died young or who never married. Tracing just individuals who attained adulthood or who can be shown to have married reduces the size considerably, although not the complexity. Even then, the systematic use of genealogical information is time-consuming. To give one example, I constructed by hand an interlocking genealogy of 20 individuals from the 1780s who had been active in the village land market. Working from the family files of a completed family reconstitution, I diagrammed the relationships back three generations and, where relevant, forward one generation, retaining only those individuals who eventually married. The genealogy became 10 yards wide, contained more than 1,000 individuals, and took about two months to construct. Clearly, the investigation of several cohorts and different kinds of networks – godparents, guardians, land buyers, marriage partners – takes on considerable dimensions.

The investigation of kinship networks in this book is based on two separate procedures. All of the systematic tables were developed from computer-generated genealogies of individuals, although each genealogy was checked by hand to make up for missing information or ambiguities. By contrast, most of the family histories discussed in this book were constructed by hand. Both procedures used completed family files of a family reconstitution based on parish registers from 1558 to 1869. All of the baptism, marriage, and burial records for a man and his wife and all of their children have been brought together into a single file.[1] A

[1] Here I followed standardized procedures developed by Louis Henry and Etienne Gautier and adapted and discussed by Anthony Wrigley. The baptism, marriage, and burial registers are found in the parish office (*Pfarramt*) in Neckarhausen. I worked from a microfilm copy (signature S2405/KB429 and 430), provided by the Landeskirchlichesarchiv in Stuttgart. The baptism register begins with 25 September 1558; burials, December 1574; marriages, 23 August 1562. Between the begin-

genealogy can be generated by computer by following the location of particular documents. For example, given a particular family, the computer matches the baptism record of a husband/father with one in which the same person occurs as a son. That locates the "family of origin" and provides all the baptismal records of his siblings and parents. By matching and following the branches, in principle at least, one can build a genealogy of any depth and breadth. A problem arises when a baptism form is missing, either because of a gap in the record or because a person was born outside the village. The marriage record or burial record could be used to make linkages, but serious complications arise when one tries to trace the steps by computer using all of the records. This is where linkage by hand became necessary. I have not yet completed what specialists call "Family Reconstitution Forms," which would involve trading information from the individual baptism, marriage, and burial forms to standardized (computerized) family files. With such uniform dossiers, pointers between families could be made more efficient, simple, and consistent. However, I decided to use the material in its present form so as not to delay the analysis for another year or so. Nonetheless, the computer-generated genealogies as they now stand provide an important means of investigating kinship networks. Once a genealogy for a person has been constructed, it is a simple matter to search the disk-held computer file for the baptism or marriage record of any person with whom he or she transacted business. For example, to find out if people sold land to kin and to which sort of kin, one has simply to generate a sufficient sample of land sellers or buyers and search their files for their customers. The manipulation of the genealogical data was carried out in Göttingen on an IBM mainframe computer between 1983 and

ning dates and 1869, there were 8,746 baptisms, 6,533 burials, and 2,437 marriages. I filled out coded forms between June 1971 and October 1974. All the forms were keypunched onto holerith cards and verified at the University of Pittsburgh by Sandy Dumin, Elwin Green, Laura Jacobs, and Lena Crnovic. During 1975, the cards were all transferred to magnetic tapes, printed out, and edited by myself. I moved to the Max-Planck-Institut für Geschichte in Göttingen in 1976, where during 1979–81, the files were reformatted into the system "Kleio" developed by Manfred Thaller. Files were proofread and updated in light of linkages between 1980 and 1982 by myself and entered by Cornelia Menne. I had a "Family Register" containing 1,017 entries to hand to supplement the reconstitution. These registers, which included all vital dates for each living family, started at the beginning of the nineteenth century, with information reaching back well into the eighteenth century. They were kept up to date through the nineteenth and twentieth centuries. I was able to use information from this register to supplement the family reconstitution, which ended in 1869. The forms were completed by Eva Savol and keypunched by Elwin Green, Laura Jacobs, and Lena Crnovic. Between 1980 and 1982, I linked all the parish registers by hand to reconstitute individual families, obtaining a computer printout of the results. Before I left the Max-Planck-Institut in 1983, Manfred Thaller provided me with about 200 computer-generated genealogies, the basis for the study of kinship and marriage. In subsequent years, he provided another 200 or so for the study of land sales, guardianship, godparentage, and the like. See Etienne Gautier and Louis Henry, *La population de Crulai, paroisse normande: étude historique,* Institut national d'études demographiques, travaux et documents, cahier 33 (Paris, 1958); Louis Henry, *Manuel de demographie historique,* Hautes études médiévales et modernes, 3 (Geneva, 1967); D.E.C. Eversley, Peter Laslett, and E. A. Wrigley, *An Introduction to English Historical Demography from the Sixteenth to the Nineteenth Century* (New York, 1966); E. A. Wrigley, ed., *Identifying People in the Past* (London, 1973).

1985. It involved considerable computer time and an enormous bulk of paper. I have not experimented with the use of a personal computer.

B. Godparents

The investigation is based on five cohorts selected every forty years between 1700 and 1870: 1700–1709 (I), 1740–9 (II), 1780–9 (III), 1820–9 (IV), 1860–9 (V). For each cohort, I began with 10 individuals who were married during the decade and appeared in the tax register at the end. They were distributed equally in the four tax quartiles, and half were "Bauern" and half artisans. (Since there are no tax registers between 1731 and 1789, I could only use occupation as a guide for Cohort II.) In order to investigate patterns among siblings and to expand the sample to a suitable size, I then expanded it to what is often called a "snowball" sample by including all the marriages of all the siblings of the original group. In each instance, I ended up with between 35 and 40 married couples who had produced children. This expansion of the sample added marriages contracted before and after the decade being studied, so that reference to the cohort of 1700–1709, for example, includes marriages contracted, and, of course, children born outside of that period. In fact, the largest number of children born to each cohort is in the decade subsequent to the starting point. Here, as in each of the other relationships I studied, I generated a genealogy back from an individual to his great grandparents and from them and their siblings down to the generation following "ego." I also worked sideways to investigate in-laws – out to the siblings of marital partners of ego's siblings, their marital partners, and their siblings and marital partners (e.g., ZHZHZH), as well as to the same connections through ego's wife (e.g., WZHZHZH).

Table A.1. *Godparents: number of families and children in samples.*

Cohort	Number of families	Number of children baptized
1700–9	40	164
1740–9	36	146
1780–9	33	177
1820–9	35	175
1860–9	35	121

Table A.2. *Godparents: decade of birth of legitimate children in samples.*

Cohort	1670s	'80s	'90s	1700s	'10s	'20s	'30s	'40s	'50s	'60s
1700–9	0	5	13	19	55	45	19	1	3	4
1740–9							11	28	50	35
1780–9								2	8	17
	1770s	'80s	'90s	1800s	'10s	'20s	'30s	'40s	'50s	'60s
1740–9	17	5								
1780–9	20	35	49	30	13	3				
1820–9					5	44	63	48	13	2
1860–9							1	16	43	61

Table A.3. *Godparents identifiable as kin.*

Cohort	N godparents	N identifiable as kin	%
1700–9	106	21	19.8
1740–9	98	64	65.3
1780–9	91	54	59.3
1820–9	101	74	73.3
1860–9	84	69	82.1

Table A.4. *Age difference in years between parents and godparents.*

Cohort	Mean age older than father	Mean age older than mother
1700–9	6.29	10.15
1740–9	5.88	9.27
1780–9	5.74	7.20
1820–9	- 0.17	0.09
1860–9	0.58	4.37

Table A.5. *Tax quartiles of godparents.*

Cohort	I	II	III	IV	NG[a]	% IV of I+II+III+IV
1700–9	0	4	17	46	39	68.7
1740–9	—	—	—	—	—	—
1780–9	2	10	20	32	27	50.0
1820–9	3	5	25	49	25	59.8
1860–9	2	8	15	37	22	59.7

Note: In ascending order.
[a]Not given.

Table A.6. *Godparents from the village notability.*

Cohort	Pastor	Schoolmaster	Rat and Gericht	Schultheiss	N godparents with occ given	Percent from notability
1700-9	9	1	25	15	87	57.8
1740-9	2	10	37	10	98	60.2
1780-9	0	2	23	2	87	31.0
1820-9	0	0	8	3	95	11.6
1860-9	0	0	9	0	75	12.0

1. Cohort I (1700–1709)

Table A.7. *Cohort I: Parents' and godparents' tax quartiles.*

	Godparents' tax class[a]								
Parents' tax class[a]	Total	I	II	III	IV	Pastor	Richter/Rat[b]	Schultheiss[b]	Nonvillage
I	19	0	0	4	8	4	(5)	(1)	3
II	10	0	0	1	7	1	(2)	(2)	1
III	28	0	1	7	15	3	(12)	(5)	2
IV	31	0	2	6	13	0	(6)	(4)	10

[a]In ascending order.
[b]Included under tax-class figures.

Table A.8. *Cohort I: Parents' and godparents' occupations.*

	Godparents' occupations							
Parents' occupation	Total	Bauer-shepherd	NG[a]	Bauer/weaver	Publican[b]	Artisan	Pastor	Schult-heiss[c]
Bauer/shepherd	33	8	12	0	4	8	1	3
NG	11	2	4	0	2	1	2	2
Bauer-weaver	6	0	2	0	0	2	2	0
Publican[b]	—	—	—	—	—	—	—	—
Artisan	32	6	17	0	0	5	4	7

[a]NG = not given but Neckarhausen resident.
[b]Innkeeper, butcher, baker.
[c]Also counted under relevant occupation.

Table A.9. *Cohort I: Godparents' relation to parents.*

Husband		Wife	
1. BWZH(2)		10. ZHB(1)	
2. BWH(3)		11. ZHBW(1)	
3. BWHB(1)		12. ZHZHW(1)	
4. BWM(1)		13. ZHZHD(1)	
5. FBW(1)		14. FZH(3)	
6. FBWZH(1)		15. FZSW(1)	
7. FBDH(3)			
8. WHB [1W1HB](1)			
9. MMZSD(1)			
Godfathers	11	Godfathers	4
Godmothers	3	Godmothers	4
Total	14	Total	8

2. *Cohort II (1740–9)*

Table A.10. *Cohort II: Parents' and godparents' occupations.*

	Godparents' occupation								
Parents' occupation	Total	Bauer/Shepherd	NG[a]	Bauer/ Bauer-Weaver	Publican[b]	Artisan	Pastor	Schultheiss[c]	Richter/Rat[c]
Bauer/Shepherd	46	28	8	7	1	1	1	6	20
Bauer-Weaver	6	2	0	0	3	1	0	0	4
Publican[b]	—	—	—	—	—	—	—	—	—
Artisan	32	15	4	1	5	7	1	6	12

[a]NG = Not given, but Neckarhasuen resident.
[b]Innkeeper, baker, butcher.
[c]Also counted under relevant occupations or NG.

Table A.11. *Cohort II: Godparents' relation to parents.*

Husband		Wife	
F	1	F	1
M,xM	3	xM	3
B	1		
Z	1	Z	9
FB	1	FB	1
FZH	1	FZH	2
		FBW	1
xMB	1		
MZH	1		
FBD	1		
FZS	1		
FZD	1		
		MBSW	1
		MZS	1
		MZD	2
		FBDD	1
FZDD	1	FZDD	1
FZDDH	1		
FFBSW	1	FFBDH	1
FMZSW	1		
FFBDSW	1		
FFBDDH	1		
FMBDS	3		
BW,xBW	2	BW	2
BWZS	2		
xBWHZH	1	xBWHZH	1
		ZH	1
		ZHB	1
ZHFBD	3		
Godfathers	15	Godfathers	9
Godmothers	15	Godmothers	20
Total	30	Total	29

3. *Cohort III (1780–9)*

Table A.12. *Cohort III: Parents' and godparents' tax quartiles.*

	Godparents' tax class							
Parents' tax class	I	II	III	IV	Nonvillagers	NG	Total	Magistrates[a]
I	0	0	2	1	1	9	13	(1)
II	0	1	6	12	4	7	30	(6)
III	1	3	3	13	1	4	25	(12)
IV	0	1	6	6	2	0	15	(4)

[a]Schultheiss, Gericht, Rat: included in tax-class figures.

Table A.13. *Cohort III: Parents' and godparents' occupations.*

	Godparents' occupation				
Parents' Occupation	Bauer/ Shepherd	Bauer-Weaver	Publican[a]	Artisan	Day-laborer
Bauer/Shepherd	31	4	1	0	0
Bauer-Weaver	5	0	0	0	0
Publican[a]	—	—	—	—	—
Artisan	22	2	1	5	0
Day-laborer	2	0	0	2	1

[a]Innkeeper, butcher, baker.

Table A.14. *Cohort III: Godparents' relation to parents.*

Husband		Wife	
F	1	F	1
M	1		
		B	1
Z	2	Z	1
		FB	3
		FFS	1
		FxBW,FBW	2
		FZHW	1
		MB	1
		MBW	2
FZS	1	FZD	2
		FBDH	1
MBD	1	MBS	1
MZS	1	MBD	2
MZD	1		
MZDH	1	MZDH	1
MZSW	1		
FFBD,FFxBD	2	FBDDH	1
FFxBDD	1	FFxBSW	1
FFBSS	1	FFWBDH	1
FFBSWBS	1	FFxBSWHW	1
FFxBSSWB	1	FFWBSDH	1
FFxBSDD	2	FFWBDS	1
FFxBSDDHW	1	FMBDH	1
FFxBSDSW	1	FMBSW	1
FFBSDHS	1		
FFxBSWBSW	2		
FFxBSDHW	1		
FFZSDH	1		
FMZDH	1		
MFZDH	1	MFBS	1
MMBS	1	MFBD	1
BW	1	BW	3
ZH	2	ZH	1
BSW	1	FFWH	1
1WMBS	1	1HMB	1
1WFB	1	1HMBS	1
1WFxBW	1		
1W1HMBS	1		
1WFZHW	1		
Godfathers	17	Godfathers	20
Godmothers	20	Godmothers	16
Total	37	Total	36

4. *Cohort IV (1820–9)*

Table A.15. *Cohort IV: Parents' and godparents' tax quartiles.*

	Godparent's tax class							
Parents' tax class	I	II	III	IV	Nonvillage	NG	Total	Magistrates[a]
I	0	0	0	0	2	0	2	0
II	2	0	8	8	7	2	25	2
III	1	1	13	15	6	1	37	2
IV	0	4	4	21	2	1	33	7

[a]Included under tax-class data.

Table A.16. *Cohort IV: Parents' and godparents' occupations.*

	Godparents' occupations				
Parents' occupations	Bauer/shepherd	Bauer/weaver	Publican[a]	Artisan	Day-laborer
Bauer/shepherd	17	1	2	6	0
Bauer-weaver	5	0	1	7	0
Publican[a]	1	0	1	0	0
Artisan	13	6	1	23	0
Day-laborer	1	1	0	3	2

[a]Innkeeper, butcher, baker.

Table A.17. *Cohort IV: Godparents' relation to parents.*

Husband		Wife	
B	6	B	9
Z	8	Z	3
FZ	1	FB	1
		FZH	1
		MZ	1
FBDH	1	FxBS	1
FZS	1	FBD	1
FZSW	1	FBDH	1
FZD	1	MBS	1
MBS	1	MxBD	1
MBSW	1	MBDH	1
MBD (MxBD)	5	MZSW	1
MBDH	2	MZD	2
MxBDD	1		
FMBDH	1	FMZSS	1
MMZD	1	MFBSW	1
		MFBSS	1
FFBSS	1	FFZDSW	1

Husband		Wife	
FFZSS	1		
FMBSS	1		
FMBSD	1		
FMBDS	1		
FMZDSW	1		
FMZDDH	1		
FFFBSSW	1		
MMFBSDD	2		
BW	5	BW	1
ZH	3	ZH	3
BWZD	1	BWZ	1
ZDH	1	MZHW	1
ZDHZ	1		
		1HMBD	1
		1HMBDD	1
Godfathers	21	Godfathers	20
Godmothers	31	Godmothers	16
Total	52	Total	36

5. *Cohort V (1760–9)*

Table A.18. *Cohort V: Parents' and godparents' tax quartiles.*

	Godparents' tax class							
Parents' tax class	I	II	III	IV	Nonvillage	NG	Total	Magistrates[a]
I	0	0	1	1	0	0	2	—
II	2	4	5	10	4	1	26	4
III	0	2	4	6	6	3	21	2
IV	0	2	5	18	1	3	29	3

[a]Included in tax-class figures.

Table A.19. *Cohort V: Parents' and godparents' occupations.*

	Godparents' occupations				
Parents' occupation	Bauer/shepherd	Bauer-weaver	Publican[a]	Artisan	Factory worker
Bauer/shepherd	25	3	3	3	0
Bauer-weaver	3	3	0	2	0
Publican[a]	0	0	0	1	0
Artisan	5	2	3	5	4
Factory worker	4	3	0	4	0

[a]Innkeeper, baker, butcher.

Table A.20. *Cohort V: Godparents' relation to parents.*

Husband		Wife	
M	1	M	1
B	4	B	12
Z	9	Z	4
MZ [FBW]	1		
ZS	1		
FBW	1	FBW	1
FBS	4	FBS	1
FBD	2	FBD	1
FZS	1	FZS	1
MBS	1	FZD	1
MBD	2		
MZS	1	MZS	2
MZD	2	MZD	1
MBDH [ZHB]	1		
		1HMZD	1
FMBDH	1		
FMBSD	2		
FMBDS	2		
FMZDS	1		
BW	2	ZH [HMZDH-1]	4
Not found, probably husband's side:		*Not found, probably wife's side:*	
Village		*Village*	
Male	1	male	2
Female	2	female	2
Not village		*Not village*	
male	—	male	1
female	3	female	3
Godfathers	18	Godfathers	23
Godmothers	27	Godmothers	15
Total	45	Total	38

C. Marriage with kin

As before, I have developed the statistics on the basis of five cohorts, although each sample spills out over the boundaries of the particular decade under discussion. In each instance, the sample began in principle with 20 couples married during the particular decade. However, for the decade 1700–1709, given the size of the cohort and the quality of the information, I was able to locate only 14 suitable cases (some of them siblings). As I noted in the description of the study of godparentage, I expanded each sample in "snowball" fashion by adding the sibling group of each husband and including all marriages from the larger cohort, giving a total of 67 marriages to study. Naturally the group then involved marriages outside the decade from which I took my departure, but, for example, just short of two-thirds (40) took place in the period 1690–1719 (a sample of 28.4 percent of all marriages in the three decades).[2] Table A.31 details the distribution by decade.

In tracing out the relationships of the selected sibling groups, I also examined by hand all the marriages of the sibling groups linked to these, which provide a larger sample as a control group for testing observations.[3] I systematically followed the genealogies of this control group to the depth of two generations, and whenever clues through surnames were offered, I traced possible links to three and occasionally four generations. For example, for the first cohort, there were 11 selected sibling groups involving 67 marriages. In the "second sample" (see Table A.33), altogether about 195 couples were examined for kin links. In this group there are 24 more kin-linked marriages. It is important to note that studying the control group was a rather rough-and-ready procedure and does not have statistical significance in itself. However, I have no doubt that a systematic computer search of all the genealogies would end with the same percentage of kin-linked marriages as the original sample offered. The value of this operation is to see whether the kin-linked marriages here were of the same type as I encountered in the first sample. For each cohort, I have offered both an original "snowball" sample and a second "rough-and-ready" sample as a check. In each case, the second sample shows the same kind of kin chosen as godparents.

I have dealt with the problems of specifying occupation in Volume I on Neckarhausen.[4] In the tax lists from 1710, 1720, and 1730, the crafts exercised by individuals were mentioned only sporadically. By searching all of the parish registers (baptisms, marriages, and deaths), one can recover most handicrafts, although there are still many men who were never assigned an occupation. Most of these appear to have carried on farming and for this reason are put together in the first tables with other agriculturalists (Bauern, shepherds, day-laborers [of

[2] The 14 from 1700 to 1709 account for 36.6 percent of all marriages for the decade.

[3] Many marriages occur more than once in the sample since it is constructed relationally.

[4] David Warren Sabean, *Property, Production, and Family in Neckarhausen, 1700–1870* (Cambridge, 1990), Appendix F.

which there were very few in this early period]). With the various occupations grouped in broad categories, it is still possible to make an initial assessment of succession between fathers and sons and fathers- and sons-in-law.[5]

Table A.21. *Surname matches at marriage, 1560–1869 (by decade).*

Decade	Match	No match	Total	Percent	Names
1560s	0	20	20	0	
1570s	0	32	32	0	
1580s	1	47	48	2.1	Schmohl-1
1590s	0	46	46	0	
1600s	0	31	31	0	
1610s	1	70	71	1.4	Sterr-1
1620s	1	35	36	2.8	Schmid-1
1630s	0	38	38	0	
1640s	0	19	19	0	
1650s	0	20	20	0	
1660s	0	20	20	0	
1670s	0	33	33	0	
1680s	0	56	56	0	
1690s	0	36	36	0	
1700s	0	34	34	0	
1710s	1	51	52	1.9	Hentzler-1
1720s	0	52	52	0	
1730s	0	43	43	0	
1740s	4	43	47	8.5	Hentzler-3 Häfner-1
1750s	3	72	75	4.0	Hentzler-3
1760s	0	66	66	0	

[5] In these tables, I have simply taken each groom and matched his occupation against those of his father and father-in-law. Some sons therefore appear more than once because of multiple marriages, and since I am working with sibling groups, the fathers and fathers-in-law are repeated.

1770s	6	62	68	8.8	Hentzler-5
					Sterr-1
1780s	3	81	84	3.6	Hentzler-3
1790s	4	80	84	4.8	Hentzler-3
					Bauknecht-1
1800s	7	84	91	7.7	Hentzler-7
1810s	7	71	78	9.9	Hentzler-5
					Bauknecht-1
1820s	10	101	111	9.0	Hentzler-7
					Bauknecht-1
					Waldner-1
					Schach-1
1830s	8	138	146	5.5	Hentzler-4
					Häfner-1
					Hörtz-1
					Holpp-1
					Falter-1
1840s	5	167	172	2.9	Hentzler-3
					Bauknecht-1
					Falter-1
1850s	5	124	129	3.9	Hentzler-4
					Haussmann-1
1860s	4	183	187	2.1	Hentzler-4

Table A.22. *Frequency of surname match at marriage, 1560–1869 (by surname).*

Bauknecht	4	Schach	1
Falter	2	Schmid	1
Häfner	2	Schmohl	1
Haussmann	1	Simon	1
Hentzler	52	Sterr	2
Holpp	1	Waldner	1
Hörtz	1		

Table A.23. *Frequency of marriages with partners over 29 (by cohort).*

	Cohort				
Partner	I	II	III	IV	V
Men					
N 30–34	3	7	8	18	16
% total	6.9	9.7	12.3	18.8	23.5
N 35-39	2	0	3	5	7
% total	4.7	—	4.6	5.2	10.3
N 40+	0	0	2	2	1
% total	—	—	3.1	2.1	1.5
% over 29	11.6	9.7	20.0	26.0	35.3
Women					
N 30-34	3	5	7	16	12
% total	5.8	7.5	8.9	14.8	16.2
N 35–39	2	1	7	16	3
% total	3.8	1.5	8.9	14.8	4.1
N 40+	0	0	8	4	3
% total	—	—	10.1	3.7	4.1
% over 29	9.6	9.0	27.8	33.3	24.3

Table A.24. *Average age at marriage (by cohort).*

	Cohort				
	I	II	III	IV	V
Men					
Mean age 1st marriage	25.5	24.8	26.6	27.8	28.6
Median age 1st marriage	24	25	26	26	27
Mean age 1st marriage, kin-linked	23.6	24.3	24.3	28.4	28.0
Median age 1st marriage, kin-linked	23	24	23	27	26
Women					
Mean age 1st marriage	24.0	23.3	26.4	27.2	26.1
Median age 1st marriage	23	22	23	25	24
Mean age 1st marriage, kin-linked	24.2	22.3	23.5	29.8	25.2
Median age 1st marriage, kin-linked	25	22	20	27	24

Table A.25. *Consanguineal and affinal marriages in Neckarhausen.*

N Sample	Number in sample	Kin-related	%	Affinal	%	Blood	%	1st cousin	%	2nd cousin	%	3rd cousin	%
Cohort I: early 18th century	67	17	25.4	17	25.4	0	0.0	0	0.0	0	0.0	0	0.0
Cohort II: mid 18th century	100	39	39.0	31	31.0	8	8.0	1	1.0	5	5.0	0	0.0
Cohort III: late 18th century	101	29	28.7	17	16.8	12	11.9	2	1.9	2	1.9	1.9	1.9
Cohort IV: early 19th century	122	32	26.2	18	14.8	14	11.5	2	1.6	4	2	1.6	1.6
Cohort V: mid 19th century	83	41	49.4	13	15.7	28	33.7	2	2.4	7	9	10.8	10.8

1. Cohort I (1700–1709)

Table A.26. *Cohort I: Intergenerational continuity of occupation (summary).*

Occupation	F/S	F/S-in-L
Agriculture/agriculture	25	29
Agriculture/handicraft	13	21
Handicraft/agriculture	14	10
Handicraft/handicraft	15	7
Total	67	67

Table A.27. *Cohort I: Intergenerational continuity of office-holding.*

Occupation	F/S	F/S-in-L
Magistrate/magistrate[a]	6	3
Magistrate/agriculture	3	8
Magistrate/handicraft	7[b]	8[c]
Agriculture/magistrate	7	8
Handicraft/magistrate	—	1
Total	23	28

[a] Schultheiss, Bürgermeister, Richter, Rat.
[b] Includes 2 weaver/Bauer.
[c] Includes 1 weaver/Bauer.

Table A.28. *Cohort I: Intergenerational continuity of occupation by sibling group.*

Father's occupation	Number of sons who follow	Number of sons-in-law who follow
Bauer	1 of 3	3 of 4
Bauer	—	2 of 2
Bauer	2 of 4	0 of 1
Bauer	0 of 3	—
Bauer	2 of 4	1 of 2
Weaver	0 of 2	0 of 1
Weaver	0 of 1	—
Tailor	2 of 3	0 of 1
Smith	2 of 4	—
Smith	2 of 2	0 of 5
Carpenter	1 of 2	—

Table A.29. *Cohort I: Intergenerational continuity of office holding by sibling group.*

Fathers	Sons	Sons-in-law
Magistrate	1 of 4	—
Magistrate	1 of 2	1 of 5
Magistrate	0 of 2	0 of 1
Magistrate	0 of 3	—
Bauer	1 of 3	0 of 4
Bauer	1 of 4	0 of 1
Bauer	—	1 of 2
Bauer	1 of 4	0 of 2

Table A.30. *Cohort I: Intergenerational continuity of occupation.*

	F/S	F/S-in-Law
Agriculture/agriculture	25	29
Agriculture/tailor	1	1
Agriculture/weaver	7	4
Agriculture/smith	1	9
Agriculture/cooper	1	1
Agriculture/carpenter	3	4
Miller/agriculture		1
Weaver/agriculture	3	2
Weaver/weaver		1
Weaver/cobbler	1	
Weaver/cooper	1	
Tailor/agriculture	3	
Tailor/tailor	3	1
Tailor/weaver	1	1
Cobbler/agriculture		1
Cobbler/tailor		1
Cobbler/cooper		1
Carpenter/agriculture	3	
Carpenter/carpenter	1	
Cooper/agriculture		1
Smith/agriculture	5	4
Smith/weaver		2
Smith/cobbler		1
Smith/smith	8	
Butcher/agriculture		1
Baker/tailor		1

Table A.31. *Cohort I: Distribution of marriages in sample by decade (kin-related).*

Sequence	1660s	'70s	'80s	'90s	1700s	'10s	'20s	'30s	Total
H/W1	1	3(1)	6(1)	7(1)	11(2)	8(3)	1	0	38(8)
H2+/W1	0	0	2	2	2	1	7(5)	2(1)	16(6)
W2+/H1	0	0	1	2	2(1)	2	2	0	9(1)
H/W 2+	0	0	0	2(1)	0	1(1)	1	1	5(2)
Total	1(0)	3(1)	9(1)	13(2)	15(3)	12(4)	11(5)	3(1)	67(17)

H=Husband; W=Wife; 1= first marriage; 2+ = second and subsequent marriages

Table A.32. *Cohort I: Distribution of kin-related marriages (counting from a male ego).*

1. BWBD	10. ZHBD
2. BWBSWZ	11. ZHBWBD
3. FSWBWZ (xBWBWZ)	12. ZHZHBWD
4. BWBWHBW	
5. BWBWBWZ	13. FBDHZ
6. BWFBD	14. FBDHFD
7. BWFBSWZ	15. FBWZHW
8. BWFZHD	
9. BWFZHD	16. MHBD
	17. WFDHZHZ (WxZHZHZ)

Table A.33. *Cohort I: Distribution of kin-related marriages (second sample).*

BWBD	ZDHZ	FBDHZ
BWFBD	ZHZHZ	FBDSWZ
BWBWMSW	ZHBWHZ(3)	FBDHZ
BWBWFZ	ZHWZD	FBWZ
BWHZHZ	xZHFBD	FBWHBWD
xBWHWZ		
		FZDHBWZ
		FZSWZ
	WFDHZHZ	xFBD(MHBD)
		xMBD(FWBD)
		FFBSD

2. Cohort II (1740–9)

Table A.34. *Cohort II: Intergenerational continuity of occupation (summary).*

	F/S	F-/S-in-L
Bauer/Bauer[a]	57[bc]	50[bd]
Bauer/artisan	9	11
Artisan/Bauer	3[bd]	11[ebc]
Artisan/artisan	19[f]	16
Weaver–Bauer/Bauer	1	-
Bauer/weaver–Bauer	3	3
Weaver–Bauer/artisan	-	2
Artisan/weaver–Bauer	4	2
No information	4	5
Totals	100	100

[a]Includes 1 shepherd.; [b]Includes 1 Bauer–day-laborer.; [c]Includes 1 day-laborer.; [d]Includes 1 Bauer–field guard.; [e]Includes 1 Bauer–forest guard.; [f]Includes 1 tailor–village servant.

Table A.35. *Cohort II: Intergenerational continuity of office holding.*

Occupation	F/S	F-/S-in-L	F/F-in-L
Magistrate/magistrate[a]	17	5	9
Magistrate/Bauer	14	10	18
Magistrate/artisan	4	6[b]	7
Bauer/magistrate	5	10	10
Artisan/magistrate	5	7	4

[a]Schultheiss, Bürgermeister, Richter, Rat.
[b]1 weaver-Bauer.

Table A.36. *Cohort II: Intergenerational continuity of occupation by sibling group.*

Father's occupation	N sons who follow	N sons-in-law who follow
Bauer	2 of 2	1 of 1
Bauer	2 of 2	1 of 3
Bauer	3 of 3	1 of 1
Bauer	1 of 2	0 of 1
Bauer	1 of 1	0 of 1
Bauer	3 of 4	3 of 4[a]
Bauer	4 of 4	4 of 5[a]
Bauer	2 of 2	2 of 2
Bauer	1 of 1	—
Bauer	1 of 1	3 of 3
Bauer	1 of 1	3 of 3[a]
Bauer	1 of 1	6 of 6
Weaver	2 of 2	0 of 1
Weaver	1 of 1[a]	0 of 3
Cobbler	2 of 3	0 of 2
Cooper	1 of 2	—
Smith	1 of 2	0 of 1
Baker	0 of 2	0 of 2

[a]1 weaver-Bauer.

Table A.37. *Cohort II: Intergenerational continuity of office holding by sibling group.*

Occupation of father	N sons in the magistracy	N sons-in-law in the magistracy
Schultheiss	3 of 4	0 of 5
Bürgermeister	1 of 2	0 of 1
Richter	1 of 3	1 of 1
Richter	1 of 2	0 of 1
Richter	1 of 1	—
Richter	1 of 1	0 of 4
Bauer	1 of 2	1 of 1
Bauer	0 of 2	0 of 3
Bauer	0 of 1	0 of 1
Bauer	1 of 4	0 of 3
Bauer	0 of 2	0 of 2
Bauer	0 of 1	—
Bauer	0 of 3	0 of 1
Bauer	0 of 1	1 of 3
Bauer	0 of 1	0 of 6
Weaver	1 of 1	0 of 3
Cobbler	1 of 3	1 of 2
Cooper	0 of 3	—
Smith	1 of 2	1 of 1
Baker	0 of 2	1 of 2

Table A.38. *Cohort II: Intergenerational continuity of occupation.*

	F/S	F-/S-in-L
Bauer/Bauer	56	49
Bauer/day-laborer	1	1
Bauer/weaver-Bauer	3	3
Bauer/weaver	8	10
Bauer/cobbler		2
Bauer/smith		1
Bauer/wheelwright	1	
Shepherd/Bauer		1
Weaver–Bauer/Bauer	1	
Weaver/weaver–Bauer	4	
Weaver/Bauer	1	3
Weaver/weaver	6	
Weaver/tailor		2
Weaver/cobbler		1
Weaver/ropemaker		1
Weaver/smith		1
Weaver/cooper	1	1
Tailor/Bauer		1
Tailor/tailor	2	
Tailor/weaver		1
Cobbler/Bauer		2
Cobbler/weaver–Bauer		2
Cobbler/weaver		2
Cobbler/cobbler	3	
Smith/Bauer		4
Smith/weaver		4
Smith/smith	2	
Smith/wheelwright		1
Cooper/weaver	4	
Cooper/cooper	2	
Baker/Bauer	2	1
Baker/cooper		1
NG/Bauer		1

Table A.39. *Cohort II: Distribution of marriages in sample by decade (kin-related).*

Sequence	1720s	1730s	1740s	1750s	1760s	1770s	1780s	1790s	1800s	Total
H1/W1	4(2)	14(4)	16(7)	18(5)	2(2)	1	—	—	—	55(20)
H2+/W1	—	1(1)	3	2	5(1)	3	—	—	—	14(2)
H1/W2+	1	1(1)	5(4)	4(3)	4(2)	2(1)	2	—	2(1)	20(12)
H2+/W2+	1	—	—	2(1)	2(2)	2(1)	2	—	2(1)	11(5)
Total	6(2)	16(6)	24(11)	26(9)	13(7)	8(2)	4	—	4(2)	100(39)
All marriages	67	57	59	96	82	82	98	88	103	

Table A.40. *Cohort II: Frequency of kin-related marriages by sibling group.*

N kin marriages in sibling group	Frequency
0	6
1	8
2	7
3	0
4	3

Table A.41. *Cohort II: Kin-related marriages by occupation of husband.*

Occupation	Kin-linked	Non–kin-linked	Total	Percent
Bauer	22	29	51	43.1
Artisan	12	20	32	37.5
Magistrates[a]	13	6	19	68.4

Note: The statistics include individuals in a series of marriages only once but count all marriages in assessing whether there was a kin-linked marriage.
[a]Included in the above occupational statistics.

Table A.42. *Cohort II: Kin-related marriages by occupation of father and wife's father.*

Occupation	Kin-linked	Non–kin-linked	Total	Percent
Bauer	55	83	138	39.9
Artisan	23	33	56	41.1
Magistrates[a]	30	26	56	53.6

[a]Magistrates included in the above occupational statistics.

Table A.43. *Cohort II: Distribution of kin-related marriages.*[a]

1	FBD (Consanguinität 2. Grad)
2	FWHBSSW [xFBSSW]
3	FFSSD [FxBSSD]
4	FFSDD [FxBDD]
5	FFBSD
6	FFBSWD [FFBSxD] (Verwandtschaft)-2
7	FFZSD (Freundschaft)
8	FMBDD (nähe Verwandtschaft)
9	MFZSD
10	MFZSSW
11	FWMBDD [xMMBDD] (freundschaft)
12	BWZ [also:WMZSW]
13	BWZD [also:BWFFBSD]
14	BWBD [also: FFSDD, BWFBSD]
15	FSWBW [xBWBW; also: FWSWBD, xMSWBD]-2
16	BWBWZHZ-2
17	FSWHWZHSW [xBWHWZHSW]-2
18	MDHMD [xZHxZ]-2
19	ZHFBD-2
20	ZHFBD [also:BWHBD]
21	FDHMZD [xZHMZD]
22	MDHFBSD [xZHFBSD]-2
23	ZHSWZ
24	ZHFBW
25	FZHZD-2
26	FZHBW
27	MFFSWBSD [MFxBSWBSD]-2
28	WFBSD (Affinität 3. Grad) [also:ZHBD]
29	WHSWZ (xSWZ; also: WHZHBW]

[a]I have noted whenever a dispensation was remarked in the marriage register.

Table A.44. *Cohort II: Distribution of kin-related marriages (second sample).*

FBD [Consanguinität 2. Grad]
FFBSD
FBZSD [Freundschaft]
MFBSD [Consanguinität]
nähe Verwandtschaft (4 cases)
Verwandtschaft (2 cases)
Freundschaft (2 cases)
Consanguinität
BWZ (2 cases)
BWMZ
xBWZD
xBWHZHZ
xBWHWZHSW
BWFBD
ZHFBD
xZHMZD
ZHBWHWZ
FZHBW
FZSWHW
FxBDHZ
MZSW
WMBD
WMZSW

3. *Cohort III (1780–9)*

Table A.45. *Cohort III: Intergenerational continuity of occupation (summary).*

	F/S	F-/S-in-L
Bauer/Bauer[a]	48	38
Bauer/artisan	12	10
Artisan/Bauer	4	11
Artisan/artisan	18	10
No information	10	11
Not included	9[b]	21[c]

[a]includes 1 vintner, 4 shepherds; [b]1 weaver–Bauer, 3 day-laborers, 4 innkeepers, bakers, butchers, 1 soldier; [c]7 weaver–Bauer, 2 village servants, 1 soldier, 7 day-laborers, 3 innkeepers, bakers, butchers, 1 schoolmaster.

Table A.46. *Cohort III: Intergenerational continuity of occupation by sibling groups.*

Father's occupation	Sons	Sons-in-L
Bauer	4 of 4	—
Bauer	3 of 4	1 of 3
Bauer	3 of 3	1 of 1
Bauer	3 of 3	—
Bauer	2 of 2	—
Bauer	2 of 2	2 of 2
Bauer	2 of 2	1 of 2
Bauer	1 of 2	0 of 1
Bauer	1 of 1	—
Bauer	1 of 1	—
Bauer	1 of 1	—
Bauer	1 of 1	5 of 6
Bauer	0 of 1	—
Bauer	—	1 of 1
Bauer–innkeeper	0 of 3[a]	0 of 1[a]
Shepherd	1 of 2	0 of 3
Shepherd	0 of 1	—
Weaver	1 of 2	—
Weaver	0 of 1	0 of 1
Weaver–soldier	0 of 1[b]	0 of 1
Tailor	1 of 1	0 of 1
Smith	2 of 4	0 of 4
Carpenter	2 of 3	—

[a]all Bauer; [b]Soldier.

Table A.47. *Cohort III: Intergenerational continuity of occupation.*

	F/S	F-/S-in-L
Bauer/Bauer	39	31
Bauer/Shepherd	—	2
Bauer/Bauer–day-laborer	5	3
Bauer/Bauer–policeman[a]	—	1
Bauer/Bauer–trader[b]–day-laborer	1	1
Bauer/weaver–Bauer	1	1
Bauer/weaver	2	1
Bauer/cobbler	2	1
Bauer/tailor	3	2
Bauer/carpenter	—	1
Bauer/brickmaker	—	1
Bauer/wheelwright	1	2
Bauer/soldier	—	1
Bauer/baker	1	—
Bauer–fieldguard[c]/brickmaker	—	1
Bauer–forestguard[d]/smith	—	1
Bauer–innkeeper/Bauer	2	1
Bauer–innkeeper/policeman[a]	1	—
Day-laborer/Bauer	—	1
Day-laborer/wheelwright	—	1
Day-laborer/carpenter	—	1
Shepherd/shepherd	4	—
Shepherd/Bauer	—	1
Shepherd/Bauer–day-laborer	—	1
Shepherd/carpenter	—	1
Shepherd/cooper	1	—
Shepherd/baker	—	1
Shepherd/brickmaker	3	—
Shepherd/soldier	—	1

Weaver–Bauer/Bauer	—	2
Weaver–Bauer/brickmaker	—	1
Weaver–Bauer/smith	—	1
Weaver–Bauer/wheelwright	—	1
Weaver–Bauer/day-laborer–weaver	—	1
Weaver–day-laborer/day-laborer	—	1
Weaver–forestguard[d]/day-laborer	1	—
Weaver–forestguard[d]/day-laborer–weaver	1	—
Weaver/Bauer	—	5
Weaver/shepherd	1	2
Weaver/weaver	1	2
Weaver/smith	—	1
Weaver/wheelwright	3	—
Weaver/potter	—	1
Weaver/soldier	1	—
Tailor/tailor	2	—
Tailor/carpenter	—	1
Tailor/day-laborer	—	2
Tinker/carpenter	1	—
Smith/weaver	1	1
Smith/Bauer	1	1
Smith/smith	5	1
Smith/Bauer–day-laborer	—	1
Smith/shepherd	—	1
Smith/day-laborer	1	—
Smith/tailor	—	2
Mason/carpenter	—	1
Potter/potter	1	—
Cooper/cooper	—	1
Cooper/baker	—	1
Carpenter/carpenter	3	—
Carpenter/weaver	1	—
Wheelwright/tailor	—	1
Miller/Bauer	—	1
Schoolmaster/Bauer	—	1

[a]Fleckenschütz; [b]Händler; [c]Güterschütz; [d]Waldschütz.

Table A.48. *Cohort III: Age at first marriage.*

Parameter	Men	Women
N	65	79
Range	18-43	17–52
Mean	26.6	26.4
Median	26	23
Mode	23	20

Table A.49. *Cohort III: Age at first marriage where kin-related.*

Parameter	Men	Women
N	21	26
Range	18-36	17–44
Mean	24.3	23.5
Median	23	20.5
Mode	23	20

Table A.50. *Cohort III: Distribution of marriages in sample by decade (kin-related).*

Sequence	1740s	1750s	1760s	1770s	1780s	
H1/W1	3	5(1)	3(1)	14(3)	17(6)	
H2+/W1	—	—	—	4	5(1)	
H1/W2+	1	1	1	1	1	
H2+/W2+	—	2	—	1(1)	1	
Total	4	8	4	20	24	
All marriages	59	96	82	82	98	
	1790s	1800s	1810s	1820s	1830s	Total
H1/W1	19(7)	3(2)	2(1)	—	—	66(21)
H2+/W1	2(2)	2	2	3(1)	1(1)	19(5)
H1/W2+	—	2	1	—	—	8
H2+/W2+	1	2(2)	—	1	—	8(3)
Total	22	9	5	4	1	101(29)
All marriages	88	103	86	119	160	

Table A.51. *Cohort III: Frequency of sibling groups with kin-related marriages.*

Number	Frequency
0	10
1	6
2	4
3	2
4	1
5	1
Total	24

Table A.52. *Cohort III: Kin-related marriages by occupation of husband.*

Occupation	Kin-linked	Non–kin-linked	N	Percent
Bauer/shepherd	15	23	38	39.5
Artisan	6	16	22	27.3

Table A.53. *Cohort III: Kin-related marriages by occupation of husband's father and wife's father.*

Occupation	Kin-linked	Non–kin-linked	N	Percent
Bauer/Shepherd	48	75	123	39.0
Artisan	12	48	60	20.0
Magistrates[a]	14	22	36	38.9

[a]Included in occupational figures.

Table A.54. *Cohort III: Couple's tax quartile in kin-related marriages.*

Tax class[a]	Kin-related	Non–kin-related	N	Percent
I	2	15	17	11.8
II	4	9	13	30.8
III	9	10	19	47.4
IV	2	3	5	40.0

[a]In ascending order.

Table A.55. *Cohort III: Distribution of kin-related marriages.*

1. FZD [also: FWHD (xMHD, xFD)] (consang. 3. Grad)
2. FZD (consang. 2. Grad)
3. FBDHD [=FBDxD]
4. MHFBWD [=xFFBxD] (consang. 3. Grad)
5. MFZDD [also: MFFZSSD] (consang. 3 grad)
6. MMBSD [also: MFFFFFBSSSSSD, FFFFFBSSSSSD]
7. FWFBDD [=xMFBDD]
8. FBWHFWHD [=FBxFxD?]
9. FFMBSD
10. FMBSSD
11. FFBWHBSSD [=FFBSSD]
12. FMBDSD [also: FMFFFBSSSSSDD, FMFFFBSSSDDD]
13. MFBSDD [also: MFMBDSD]
14. FFFBSDD
15. FMFBSSDD
16. FWFFBWSDDD [=xMFFBxSDDD, also: FWFFFBSSDD, FWFFBWBDSD]
17. FFFFFFBSDSSD
18. FFFFFBSSSSSD
19. BWMFBSD
20. BWBWZHZ
21. ZHZ
22. ZHSWZ [=ZxSWZ]
23. FDHSD [=xZxSD]
24. FWHDHMFBDD [=xZHMFBDD]
25. FDDDHZ [=xZDDHZ]
26. FBDDHZ
27. FFBWHBSSD
28. MFBDHBSD [also: MFFBSWBSSD]
29. MZHFWDHZ [=MZHxZHZ]
30. WZ (1. Grad)
31. WMFBDD

Note: Dispensations are noted.

Table A.56. *Cohort III: Distribution of kin-related marriages (second sample).*

FBD (consang.)

MBD (consang. 2. Grad)
Consang. 2. Grad

MFBD

Consang. 3. Grad
Consang. 3. Grad
Consang. 3. Grad
Consang. 3. Grad
Consang. 3. Grad
Consang. 3. Grad (also: ZHZ)
Consang. 3. Grad (Also: BWZ and ZHZ)

Verwandt.
Consang.

BWFD
BWFD
FSWBW (=xBWBW)
BWZHZHZ

ZHZ
ZHZHZHZ
ZHBWBWZ
ZHZHMHSD [=ZHZHxBD]

FFSWSWZ [=FxBxSWZ]
FFSWHWFSWZ [=FxBWxBWZ]

MBWBW

WZ
2. Grad [W's cousin]

4. Cohort IV (1820–9)

Table A.57. *Cohort IV: Intergenerational continuity of occupation (summary).*

	Son			
Father	Bauer	Artisan	Publican	Laborer/ village servant
Bauer	33	18	4	1
Artisan	7	31	2	3
Publican	—	2	1	—
Laborer/village servant	—	8	—	6
	Son-in-law			
Father-in-law	Bauer	Artisan	Publican	Laborer/ village servant
Bauer	30	21	5	3
Artisan	6	24	4	5
Publican	2	1	—	—
Laborer/vilage servant	—	9	1	—

Note: Bauer = bauer, shepherd, vintner; laborer = all day-laborers/agriculture combinations; artisan = all artisans and any combinations with artisans; publican = innkeepers, bakers, butchers; village servants = village servants in all combinations.

Table A.58. *Cohort 4: Intergenerational continuity of occupation by sibling group.*

Occupation of father[a]	Number of sons follow	Number of sons-in-law follow
Bauer	2 of 3	1 of 3
Bauer	2 of 5	0 of 3
Bauer	3 of 4	2 of 4
Bauer	1 of 2	1 of 1
Bauer	2 of 3	0 of 1
Bauer	1 of 1	—
Bauer	2 of 3	3 of 6
Bauer	0 of 1	—
Bauer	0 of 2	1 of 2[b]
Bauer/day-laborer	1 of 1	0 of 2
Shepherd	1 of 3	0 of 3
Weaver	0 of 2	—
Weaver	1 of 4	1 of 1
Weaver	4 of 4	2 of 3
Weaver	2 of 2	0 of 2
Weaver	2 of 2	—
Day-laborer	2 of 3	0 of 2
Day-laborer	0 of 3	—
Cooper	0 of 1	1 of 6

[a]Took dominant occupation.
[b]Other son-in-law not given.

Table A.59. *Cohort IV: Intergenerational continuity of occupation.*

Occupation	F/S	F/S-in-L
Bauer/Bauer	31	26
Bauer/shepherd	1	1
Bauer/Bauer–day-laborer	—	1
Bauer/day-laborer	1	1
Bauer/day-laborer–weaver	—	2
Bauer/weaver-Bauer	6	4
Bauer/weaver-Bauer-publican	2	1
Bauer/weaver	3	—
Bauer/weaver-paver[a]	—	2
Bauer/cobbler	—	1
Bauer/smith	1	—
Bauer/tinker	1	—
Bauer/brickmaker	1	—
Bauer/mason	—	1
Bauer/cooper	—	2
Bauer/publican	1	—
Bauer/cooper-Bauer-publican	—	1
Bauer/butcher	—	2
Bauer/baker	2	—
Bauer/baker-Bauer	—	1
Bauer/wheelwright	1	4
Bauer/NG	1	1
Bauer-day-laborer/Carpenter	—	1
Bauer-day-laborer/NG	—	1
Bauer-day-laborer/Mason	—	2
Bauer-day-laborer/day-laborer	3	—
Bauer–village servant/day-laborer–village servant	1	—
Shepherd/Bauer	—	2
Shepherd/shepherd	1	—
Shepherd/weaver-Bauer	1	—
Shepherd/day-laborer–village servant	—	1
Shepherd/cobbler	2	—
Shepherd/weaver	—	1
Vintner/Bauer	1	—
Vintner/vintner	—	1
Vintner/weaver	—	2
Vintner/NG	1	—

Table A.59 (cont'd.)

Day-laborer/day-laborer–Bauer	1	—
Day-laborer/day-laborer–weaver	4	—
Day-laborer/day-laborer–village servant	1	—
Day-laborer/weaver	3	1
Day-laborer/cobbler	—	1
Day-laborer/nailsmith	—	1
Day-laborer/carpenter	—	1
Day-laborer/brickmaker	1	—
Day-laborer/weaver-Bauer-publican	—	1
Weaver/Bauer	2	2
Weaver/Bauer-day-laborer	1	1
Weaver/day-laborer–vintner	1	—
Weaver/vintner	1	—
Weaver/day-laborer	—	2
Weaver/day-laborer-weaver	1	—
Weaver/day-laborer–village servant	—	1
Weaver/weaver	4	7
Weaver/weaver-Bauer	—	3
Weaver/tailor	1	—
Weaver/cobbler	—	1
Weaver/carpenter	5	—
Weber–Day-laborer/weaver	3	—
Weaver–Day-laborer/mason	4	—
Weaver–day-laborer–Bauer/Bauer	—	1
Weaver–day-laborer–Bauer/weaver–Bauer	1	—
Weaver–day-laborer–Bauer/weaver–day-laborer	—	2
Weaver–day-laborer–Bauer/weaver	1	1
Weaver–day-laborer–Bauer/weaver–paver[a]	2	—
Weaver–day-laborer–Bauer/butcher	—	1
Tailor/day-laborer	1	—
Tailor/Bauer	1	—
Cobbler/day-laborer–vintner	—	1
Cobbler/weaver-Bauer	1	—
Cobbler/joiner	1	—
Carpenter/weaver	—	1
Mason/cobbler	1	—

Cooper/Bauer	2	3
Cooper/cooper-Bauer	—	1
Cooper/cobbler	—	1
Cooper/baker	—	1
Cooper/publican	—	1
Cooper/cooper-Bauer-publican	1	—
Cooper-Bauer/cooper	2	—
Publican/Bauer	—	1
Baker/Bauer-baker	1	—
Butcher/shepherd	—	1
Butcher/Bauer	—	1
Butcher/weaver-Bauer	—	1
Smith/smith	—	1
Nailsmith/nailsmith	1	1
Smith/wheelwright	—	1
Smith/butcher	1	—
Potter/baker	—	1
Tinker/tinker	—	1
Wheelwright/Bauer	1	—
Wheelwright/weaver-Bauer	—	1
Wheelwright/tailor	—	1
Wheelwright/cooper-Bauer	1	—
Wheelwright/mason	—	2
Wheelwright/wheelwright	2	—
Wheelwright-publican/wheelwright	2	—
Village servant/weaver	—	1
Village servant/weaver–day-laborer	—	1
Village servant/joiner	—	1
Schoolmaster/Bauer	—	1
NG/Bauer	1	—
NG/day-laborer	—	2
NG/cobbler	2	—

[a]Pflästerer.

Table A.60. *Cohort IV: Age at first marrriage.*

Parameter	Men	Women
Number	96	108
Range	21–43	19–56
Mean	27.8	27.2
Median	26	25
Mode	25	23

Table A.61. *Cohort IV: Age at first marriage where kin-linked.*

Parameter	Men	Women
Number	23	29
Range	23-43	21–56
Mean	28.4	29.8
Median	27	27
Mode	25	24

Table A.62. *Cohort IV: Distribution of marriages in the cohort sample by decade (kin-related).*

Sequence	1790s	1800s	1810s	1820s	1830s
H1/W1	6(2)	7(3)	13(2)[a]	31(9)[b]	25(5)[c]
H2+/W1	—	1	1	5(1)[d]	2(1)[e]
H1/W2+	—	—	—	2	—
H2+/W2+	—	—	—	—	5(1)
Total	6(2)	8(3)	14(2)	38(10)	32(7)
All marriages	88	103	86	119	160

Sequence	1840s	1850s	1860s	Total
H1/W1	11(2)	—	—	93(23)
H2+/W1	6(3)	1(1)	—	16(6)
H1/W2+	1	—	—	3(0)
H2+/W2+	1	3(1)	1(1)	10(3)
Total	19(5)	4(2)	1(1)	122(32)
All marriages	194	111	187	

Duplicates: [a]2(0); [b]4(2); [c]2(1); [d]1(0); [e]1(1).

Table A.63. *Cohort IV: Frequency of sibling groups with kin-related marriages.*

Number of kin-related marriages	Frequency
0	2
1	8
2	5
3	3
4	1
Total	19

Table A.64. *Cohort IV: Occupation of husband in kin-linked marriages.*

Occupation	Kin-linked	Non–kin-linked	Total	Percent
Bauer	11	30	41	26.8
Artisans	15	45	60	25.0
Publicans	2	7	9	22.2
Labor/village servant	3	7	10	30.0
Not given	1	1	2	
Totals	32	90	122	26.2

Table A.65. *Cohort IV: Occupation of husband's father and wife's father in kin-linked marriages.*

Occupation	Kin-linked	Non–kin-linked	Total	Percent
Bauer	31	89	119	26.1
Artisans	16	68	84	19.0
Publicans	3	4	7	42.9
Labor/village servant	10	18	28	35.7
Not given	4	1	5	
Totals	64	180	244	26.2

Table A.66. *Cohort IV: Husband's tax quartile in kin-related marriages.*

Quartile	Kin-linked	Non–kin-linked	Total	Percent
I and II	4	15	19	21.1
III	12	18	30	40.0
IV	12	26	38	31.6
NG	4	31	35	11.4

Table A.67. *Cohort IV: Tax quartile of husband's father and wife's father in kin-linked marriages.*

Quartile	Kin-linked	Non–kin-linked	Total	Percent
I and II	16	29	45	35.6
III	17	47	64	26.6
IV	21	43	64	32.8
NG	9	62	71	12.7

Table A.68. *Cohort IV: Distribution of kin-related marriages.*

FBD (2. Grad)
MZD (2. grad)
FFBSD (consang. 3. grad)-2
MMZSD (3. Grad)
FWHFZD [=xFFZD]
3. Grad
MFFBSD
MFBSDD
FFFBSDD
FMMMBDSD
FFWDDSD [=FFxDDSD]
MMFBSSSD [also: MBWZDHWZ (illeg.)]
MFFBSSD
MMFBSSSD
FBWBD
FBWZD
FZSWHD [=FZSxD]
MBSWHD
MZSWZ
FFWxBD
FFWBDSD
MBSWHD [=MBSxD]
MZSWZ
BWFD [BWxZ]
BWFBD
ZHMZD
FFFBSWHFBSSSD
WZ-2
WZ (1. Linea)
WZ (1. Grad)
WBWZ
WFWHBD

Note: Dispensations noted.

Table A.69. *Cohort IV: Distribution of kin-related marriages (second sample).*

FBD (2. Grad)
FZD
FZD [also: BW]
Consang. 2. Grad
2. Grad
2. Grad
FMBD (consang. 3. Grad)
Consang. 3. Grad
Consang. 3. Grad
Consang. 3. Grad
Consang. 3. Grad
Consang. 3. Grad [also: ZHZ]
Consang. 3. Grad [also: ZHZ, BWZ]
3. Grad
3. Grad
3. Grad
3. Grad
ZHZ
ZHZ
ZHZHFDHZ
MSWZ [xBWZ]
BWZHBW
BWBWMD
FZSWZ
MZSWZ
MFZDHBWZ
MBWZDHWZ
MZHBWZ
1. Grad (WZ)
1. Grad (WZ)
WBWBD
WBWZ

5. Cohort V (1860–9)

Table A.70. *Cohort V: Age at first marriage.*

Parameter	Men	Women
Number	68	74
Range	22–48	19–47
Mean	28.6	26.1
Median	27	24
Mode	26	20, 24

Table A.71. *Cohort V: Age at first marriage where kin-linked.*

Parameter	Men	Women
Number	32	33
Range	23–48	20–37
Mean	28.0	25.2
Median	26.5	24
Mode	25, 26	20

Table A.72. *Cohort V: Distribution of marriages in sample by decade (kin-related).*

Sequence	1820s	1830s	1840s	1850s	1860s	Total
H1/W1	2	11(6)	14(9)[a]	20(10)[b]	14(6)[c]	61(31)
H2+/W1	—	1	2(1)	12(4)	—	15(5)
H1/W2+	—	—	3(2)	2(1)	1(1)	6(4)
H2+/W2+	—	—	—	—	1(1)	1(1)
Total	2	12(6)	19(12)	34(15)	16(8)	83(41)
All marriages	119	160	194	111	187	

Duplicates: [a]2(2); [b]4(3); [c]1(1).

Table A.73. *Cohort V: Frequency of kin-related marriages by sibling group.*

Number of kin marriages	Frequency
0	4
1	1
2	2
3	2
4	1
5	1
6	1
7	2

Table A.74. *Cohort V: Kin-related marriages by occupation of husband.*

Occupation	Kin-linked	Non–kin-linked	Total	Percent
Bauer	23	18	41	56.1
Artisan	15	13	28	53.6
Publican	1	4	5	20.0
Day-laborer	1	1	2	50.0
Factory worker	0	6	6	0
Not given	0	1	1	—
Totals	40	43	83	48.2

Table A.75. *Cohort V: Occupation of husband's father and wife's father in kin-related marriages.*

Occupation	Kin-linked	Non–kin-linked	Total	Percent
Bauer	49	46	95	51.6
Artisan	18	26	44	40.9
Publican	3	4	7	42.9
Day-laborer	7	2	9	77.8
Total	77	78	155	49.7
Not given	1	10	11	9.1
Magistrates[a]	22	18	40	55.0

[a]Included in above statistics.

Table A.76. *Cohort V: Husband's tax class in kin-related marriages.*

Tax category	Kin-linked	Non–kin-linked	Total	Percent
II	2	11	13	18.9
III	19	9	28	67.9
IV	13	15	28	46.4
Total	34	35	68	50.0
Not given	6	8	14	42.9

Table A.77. *Cohort V: Tax quartile of husband's father and wife's father in kin-related marriages.*

Tax category	Kin-linked	Non–kin-linked	Total	Percent
I and II	10	3	13	76.9
III	10	18	28	35.7
IV	51	41	92	55.4
Total	71	62	133	53.4
Not given	9	25	34	

Table A.78. *Cohort V: Distribution of kin-related marriages.*

FZD (2. Grad)-2
FBSW

FMBD (3. Grad)
MBDD (3. Grad)

FMBSD [also: FBWBD]
FMZSD
MFZDD-2
MFZDSW
MFBDD (3. Grad) [also: BWMZxD]
MMZDD
Verwandt (wife from another village)

FFBDSD

FFFZSSD [also: MFFZDSD]
FFFZDSD [also: FFMBSSD]
FFMxZDSD
MFFBSD
MFFZSDD
MFMBSDD-2
MMFBDDD [also: MFMZDSD]

FFFFFZDSSD [also: FFFFMBSSSSD, FFFFMBSSSDD]
FFFFBSDSD
FFFFZSDSD
FFFFZSDSD [also: FFFFFZSSSD]
FFMFxBSDSD
FFMxZDSD
FFMFMBSSSD
MFFBSDSD

BWZHZ
FBSW-2
ZHD [ZxD]-2
xZHZ-2
ZHMZD [also: MFMBSDD]
MFZDSW

MBDHZ

WZ (1. Grad)-2
WZ (1. Grad) [also: ZHD (ZxD)]
WZ (1. Linea)

Note: Dispensations noted.

Table A.79. *Cohort V: Distribution of kin-related marriages (second sample).*

FZD
MBD
MBD [also: BW]
MBD
FBSW

FMBD

FMBSD

Verwandt
Verwandt
Verwandt
Verwandt
3. Grad
3. Grad
3. Grad

BW
BWZHZ

ZHZ
ZHZ
ZHBW
ZHWZ

WZ
WZ

WBWZ

D. Kinship Naming Practices

I have studied the same five cohorts examined for godparents, using the same set of families and genealogies.

1. Cohort I (1700–1709)

Table A.80. *Cohort I: Number of times information is missing, 41 families.*

FB/FBW	3	MB/W	18
FZ/FZH	3	MZ/H	18
FF	0	MF	3
FM	2	MM	18
FFB/W	25	MFB/W	30
FMB/W	15	MMB/W	30
FFZ/H	25	MFZ/H	30
FMZ/H	15	MMZ/H	30
FFF	19	MFF	28
FFM	26	MFM	30
FMF	5	MMF	19
FMM	14	MMM	31

Table A.81. *Cohort I: Closest kin match for sons.*

Relation	Birth order						Relation	Birth order					
	1	2	3	(3+)	4+	tot		1	2	3	(3+)	4+	tot
GODF	3[a]	5[b]	1	(2)	1	10							
F	14	5	2	(6)	4	25							
FB	9	4	5	(7)	2	20	MB	1	5	2	(2)		8
FZH	1		1	(2)	1	3	MZH	1					1
FF	3	2	1	(1)		6	MF	1	2				3
FFB							MFB						
FFZH	1					1	MFZH						
FFF							MFF						
FMB							MMB		1				1
FMZH							MMZH						
FMF							MMF						
NO MATCH	1	2	4	(7)	3	10	TOTAL	35	26	16	(27)	11	88

[a]+3 overlap with father. [b]+1 overlap with father.

Table A.82. *Cohort I: Closest kin match for daughters.*

Relation	1	2	3	(3+)	4+	tot	Relation	1	2	3	(3+)	4+	tot
GODM	10[a]	4	3[b]	(6)	3	20							
M	13	2	4	(5)	1	20							
MZ	3	1	1	(2)	1	6	FZ	4	3	2	(2)		9
MBW							FBW	1	2	1	(1)		4
MM	1		1	(1)		2	FM	2	3				5
MFZ							FFZ	1					1
MFBW							FFBW						
MFM							FMM						
MMZ							FMZ						
MMBW							FMBW						
MMM							FMM						
NO MATCH	2	7	3	(5)	2	14[c]	TOTAL	37	22	15	(22)	7	81

[a]2 overlap with mother. [b]+1 overlap with mother [c]2 names created from 2 adult kin.

2. Cohort II (1740–9)

Table A.83. *Cohort II: Number of times information missing, 35 families.*

FB/W	1	MB/W	6
FZ/H	1	MZ/H	6
FF	0	MF	1
FM	1	MM	7
FFB/W	8	MFB/W	12
FMB/W	19	MMB/W	16
FFZ/H	8	MFZ/H	12
FMZ/H	19	MMZ/H	16
FFF	1	MFF	8
FFM	9	MFM	11
FMF	6	MMF	9
FMM	18	MMM	16

Table A.84. *Cohort II: Closest kin match for sons.*

Relation	1	2	3+	total	Relation	1	2	3+	total
GODF	7[a]	9	3	19					
F	15	3	3	21					
FB	1	1	6	8	MB	1	3	4	8
FZH					MZH				
FF			2	2	MF	1		1	2
FFB					MFB			1	1
FFZH	1			1	MFZH				
FFF					MFF				
FMB					MMB				
FMZH					MMZH				
FMF					MMF				
No Match	2	3	8	13[b]	Totals	28	19	29	76

[a]Three overlap with F. [b] Three names created from two adult kin.

Table A.85. *Cohort II: Closest kin match for daughters.*

Relation	1	2	3+	total	Relation	1	2	3+	total
GODM	8[a]		5	13					
M	14	4	3	21					
MZ		2	3	5	FZ			1	1
MBW			2	2	FBW			1	1
MM	2	2	1	5	FM		2		2
MFZ					FFZ		2	1	3
MFBW					FFBW				
MFM					FFM				
MMZ					FMZ				
MMBW					FMBW				
MMM					FMM				
No Match	6	7	6	19[b]	Totals	30	19	23	72

[a] Three overlap with mother. [b]Thirteen names created from two adult kin.

Table A.86. *Cohort II: Creation of new girls' names.*

M+		GODM+		MZ+		FM+	
GODM	6	FM	1	MZ	1	MM	1
FM	1	—	1				
MZ	1						
—	1						

3. Cohort III (1780–9)

Table A.87. *Cohort III: Number of times information missing, 34 families.*

FB/W	3	MB/W	9
FZ/H	3	MZ/H	9
FF	0	MF	0
FM	2	MM	4
FFB/W	7	MFB/W	9
FMB/W	17	MMB/W	20
FFZ/H	7	MFZ/H	11
FMZ/H	17	MMZ/H	21
FFF	3	MFF	10
FFM	7	MFM	10
FMF	3	MMF	11
FMM	14	MMM	17

Table A.88. *Cohort III: Closest kin match for sons.*

Relation	1	2	3+	Total	Relation	1	2	3+	Total
GODF	8[a]	4[a]	10[b]	22					
F	5	7	10	22					
FB	7	5	15	27	MB	2	3	2	7
FZH			1	1	MZH			1	1
FF	3		1	4	MF	1		3	4
FFB					MFB				
FFZH					MFZH				
FFF			1	1	MFF				
FMB					MMB				
FMZH					MMZH				
FMF					MMF				
No Match	3	3	6	12[c]	Totals	29	22	50	101

[a]One overlap with father. [b]Two overlap with father. [c]Three names created from two adult names

Table A.89. *Cohort III: Closest kin match for daughters.*

Relation	1	2	3+	Total	Relation	1	2	3+	Total
GODM	7	9	6[a]	22					
M	10	5	10	25					
MZ	1		5	6	FZ	3	3	3	9
MBW	1			1	FBW				
MM	2		2	4	FM		1	2	3
MFZ					FFZ				
MFBW					FFBW			1	1
MFM					FFM				
MMZ	1			1	FMZ		1		1
MMBW					FMBW				
MMM					FMM				
No match	5	4	4	13[b]	Total	30	23	33	86

[a]One overlap with mother. [b] Thirteen names created from two adult names.

Table A.90. *Cohort III: Creation of new girls' names.*

M+		GODM+		FZ+		MZ+	
FZ	1	MM	1	FZ	1	MZ	1
GODM	5	FM	1				
MM	1	—	2				

4. *Cohort IV (1820–9)*

Table A.91. *Cohort IV: Number of times information missing, 35 families.*

FB/W	0	MB/W	5
FZ/H	0	MZ/H	5
FF	0	MF	0
FM	0	MM	0
FFB/W	7	MFB/W	11
FMB/W	12	MMB/W	14
FFZ/H	7	MFZ/H	12
FMZ/H	12	MMZ/H	13
FFF	0	MFF	5
FFM	0	MFM	5
FMF	0	MMF	5
FMM	1	MMM	7

Table A.92. *Cohort IV: Closest kin match for sons.*

Relation	1	2	3+	Total	Relation	1	2	3+	Total
GODF	16[a]	6	3	25					
F	7	6	6	19					
FB	3	3	5	11	MB		1	5	6
FZH			1	1	MZH				
FF		4	3	7	MF			1	1
FFB			1	1	MFB				
FFZH	1			1	MFZH				
FFF					MFF				
FMB					MMB				
FMZH					MMZH				
FMF					MMF				
NO MATCH	3	5	8	16[b]	TOTAL	30	25	33	88

[a]One overlap with F. [b]Fourteen names created from two adult names.

Table A.93. *Cohort IV: Closest kin match for daughters.*

Relation	1	2	3+	Total	Relation	1	2	3+	Total
GODM	13[a]	3[b]	7	23					
M	9	7	2	18					
MZ	1	1	2	4	FZ	2	1	4	7
MBW					FBW	2		2	4
MM			3	3	FM		2		2
MFZ					FFZ			2	2
MFBW					FFBW				
MFM					FFM				
MMZ					FMZ				
MMBW					FMBW				
MMM					FMM		1		1
NO MATCH	5	6	14	25[c]	TOTAL	32	21	36	89

[a]Four overlaps with M. [b]One overlap with M. [c]Twenty-one names composed from two adult names.

Table A.94. *Cohort IV: Creation of new boys' names.*

F+		GODF+		FB+		MB+	
GODF	1	FB	1	FB	2	—	2
FB	3	FF	1	MB	1		
—	1	MB	1				
—	1						

Table A.95. *Cohort IV: Creation of new girls' names.*

M+		GODM+		FZ+		MZ+		FBW+		FM+	
GODM	7	FZ	1	FZ	1	—	2	—	1	MM	1
MM	1	MZ	1	—	1						
FZ	2	—	2								
—	1										

5. *Cohort V (1860–9)*

Table A.96. *Cohort V: Number of times information missing, 34 families.*

FB/W	2	MB/W	6
FZ/H	2	MZ/H	6
FF	0	MF	1
FM	0	MM	1
FFB/W	3	MFB/W	11
FMB/W	5	MMB/W	7
FFZ/H	3	MFZ/H	11
FMZ/H	5	MMZ/H	7
FFF	3	MFF	7
FFM	2	MFM	6
FMF	2	MMF	6
FMM	2	MMM	6

Table A.97. *Cohort V: Closest kin match for sons.*

Relation	1	2	3+	Total	Relation	1	2	3+	Total
GODF	8[a]	1	1	10					
F	8	5	3	16					
FB	1	1	1	3	MB	1	3	2	6
FZH			1	1	MZH	1			1
FF					MF		1		1
FFB					MFB				
FFZH					MFZH				
FFF		1		1	MFF				
FMB					MMB		1		1
FMZH					MMZH				
FMF					MMF				
No match	10	7	20	37[b]	Totals	29	20	28	77

[a]Three overlap with F.
[b]Twenty-one names created from two adult names.

Table A.98. *Cohort V: Closest kin match for daughters.*

Relation	1	2	3+	Total	Relation	1	2	3+	Total
GODM	9	2	2	13					
M	5	1	1	7					
MZ	1	2	2	5	FZ	3		2	5
MBW		1		1	FBW	2			2
MM					FM		1		1
MFZ		1		1	FFZ				
MFBW					FFBW				
MFM					FFM				
MMZ			1	1	FMZ			1	1
MMBW					FMBW				
MMM					FMM				
No match	9	10	6	25[a]	totals	29	18	16	62

[a]Twenty-four names created from two adult names.

Table A.99. *Cohort V: Creation of new boys' names.*

F+		GODF+		FB+		MB+	
GODF	2	FB	5	FB	1	FZH	1
FB	1	MB	1	—	2	—	1
MB	3	MZH	1				
—	2						

Table A.100. *Cohort V: Creation of new girls' names.*

M+		GODM+		FZ+		MZ+		MM+	
MM	2	MZ	3	MZ	1	MZ	1	—	1
GODM	4	FZ	1	—	1	MBW	1		
FZ	2	—	2			—	1		
MZ	1								
—	3								

E. Use of kin

1. Guardianship

For each cohort, I attempted to locate 20 Pfleger in the records, although this was not possible for the cohort 1700–1709.

Table A.101. *Frequency of related guardians by cohort.*

Cohort	Number of Pfleger	Number related	Percent related	Ratio F/M kin
1700–9	11	7	64	4:3
1740–9	20	16	80	3:5
1780–9	20	17	85	8:9
1820–9	20	17	85	10:7
1860–9	20	15	75	8:7

Table A.102. *Guardians' occupations by cohort.*

	Cohort				
Occupation	I	II	III	IV	V
Schultheiss	1			1	
Bürgermeister	3	3		1	
Richter	1	2	1	4	
Rat					1
Bauer	2	5	12	7	10
Bauer-weaver		2			
Shepherd			1		
Weaver		5	2	5	1
Tailor		2			
Cobbler		2			
Smith	1				
Cooper	1		1		
Cobbler			1		1
Wheelwright			1		
Carpenter				1	1
Baker			1	1	
Baker-innkeeper					1
Policeman					1
Forest guard					1
Not given	2	1			

Table A.103. *Relation of guardian to ward.*

	Cohort				
	I	II	III	IV	V
Number	11	20	20	20	20
Number related	7	16	17	17	15
B				1	
F		1	1		3
FB	3	1	4	1	3
FWB					1
FZH	1			1	2
FZHB		1			
FZHZH				1	
FFZH				1	
FMZH		1			
FZDH		1		1	
FWFB				1	
MB	1	8	3	1	3
MZH		1	1	1	2
MF		1			
MHB	1				
MMB			1		
MMBS				1	1
MMZH			1		
MZHZS			1		
MZHZH				1	
FBS			1	1	
FZDH					
FMBS			1		
FFBDH		1			
MFBS			1		
MFZS				1	
FFMBS				1	
FMFBSS			1		
FMFZDS				1	
MFFBDS				2	
MHBWHB	1				

2. Kriegsvogtschaft

For Cohort I (1700–1709), eight Kriegsvögte were identified.

Table A.104. *Occupations of Kriegsvögte.*

	Cohort			
Occupation	I	II	III	IV
Schultheiss	1			1
Bürgermeister	1	5		1
Richter	3	4	7	2
Rat		2		1
Schoolmaster			1	
Bauer	1	4	2	10
Bauer-weaver		2		
Day-laborer			1	
Weaver		2	2	2
Tailor		1		
Smith			1	
Cooper				1
Brickmaker				1
Not given	1			

Table A.105. *Relation of Kriegsvögte to Kriegsfrauen.*

	Cohort			
Relation	I	II	III	IV
Number	8	20	20	20
Number related	5	11	12	16
F				1
B, xB	2		1	2
ZH				2
FB		2	3	
FZH				2
FZS			1	1
MZH	1	1		
MZDH			1	
BWF		1		
FBS		2		
MZS		2		
FFBS		1		
FFBDS				1
MMBSD				1
MMZDH				1
HB	1			
HBWF			1	
HFB	1			
HMBS				1
HWF			1	
HFZH				1
HFBDH		1		
HFFBDDH			1	
HMMBS				1
HMMZDDH			1	
HZHZH			1	
HMBWZH			1	

3. Pledging

I could find only three cases of Bürgschaft in the records for the eighteenth century. In no instance were the two parties related to each other, and there was no godparentage connection. These data are not a great deal to go on, and I am sure that in many cases of pledging two brothers went surety for each other and fathers guaranteed the debts of sons. However, until some better source becomes available, such relationships must remain unclear.

For each of the last two cohorts, I searched for 20 examples of pledging (*Bürgschaft*). In some cases there were more than one guarantor.

Table A.106. *Kin-relations of pledgers to principals (Cohorts IV and V).*

Relation	IV	V
F		5
B	5	4
ZH	2	4
WB	1	3
WZH	1	1
HZH	1	
FB	2	
MB	3	
FZH	4	
BS	1	
FBS	1	1
FZS	2	
No relation established	5	2
Total	28	20

F. Sales of real estate

These tables are taken from *Property, Production, and Family in Neckarhausen*, Chapters 15 and 16.

Table A.107. *Frequency of real estate sales to women.*

Period and status	Arable	Meadow	Garden[a]	Buildings	Mixed/ more 1	NG/ other [b]	Total	Percent of sales
1700–9								
Widowed	—	—	—	—	—	—	—	
Married	—	—	—	—	—	—	—	
Single	—	—	—	—	—	—	—	
NG	—	—	—	—	—	—	—	
Total	0	0	0	0	0	0	0	0
1740–9								
Widowed		-	—	3	—	—	3	
Married	—	—	—	—	—	—	—	
Single	—	—	3	1	—	—	4	
NG	—	—	—	—	—	—	—	
Total	0	0	3	4	0	—	7	2.0
1780–9								
Widowed	8	3	1	2	—	—	14	
Married	—	—	—	1	—	—	1	
Single	3	1	1	3	—	—	8	
NG	—	—	—	—	—	—	—	
Total	11	4	2	6	0	0	23	3.9
1820–9								
Widowed	7	—	1	2	—	—	10	
Married	4	—	—	1	1	—	6	
Single	33	2	11	9	1	—	56	
NG	7	—	2	—	—	—	9	
Total	51	2	14	12	2	—	81	9.9
1860–9								
Widowed	6	1	—	5	1	—	13	
Married	2	3	—	2	—	1	8	
Single	6	6	1	3	1	—	17	
NG	—	—	1	—	1	—	2	
Total	14	10	2	10	3	1	40	8.1

[a]Includes gardens, flaxlands, and vineyards.
[b]NG = not given.

Table A.108. *Arable land market from selected decades.*

Market feature	1700–9	1740–9	1780–9	1820–9	1860–9
Total arable (Morgen)	1028.9 (1728)	1028.9 (1728)	1028.8 (1769)	1028.8 (1769)	927.3 (1846)
N arable plots sold	132	199	392	522	275
N arable pl. transacted[a]	193	264	392	522	275
Total arable sold (M)[b]	121.61	146.2	269.31	309.57	148.93
Total arable transacted	183.25	192.33	269.31	309.57	148.93
Price/Morgen (fl.)[c]	30.77	53.60	109.16	126.74	564.25
Percent arable sold	11.82	14.21	26.18	30.09	16.06
Percent arable transacted[a]	17.82	18.69	26.18	30.09	16.06
Mean population/decade	340	455	516	738	924
Amount arable sold/head (M)[b]	.358	.321	.522	.419	.161
Amount arable trans./head[a]	.539	.423	.522	.419	.161
N Buyers[d]	41	102	135	232	198
N buyers/% of mean population	12.1	22.4	26.2	31.4	21.4
Mean size arable plot (M)[b]	.95	.73	.69	.59	.54
Largest accum. purchase[e]	11.63	13.49	8.78	11.21	4.46
Mean accum. purchase[e]	3.13	1.60	2.06	1.41	.94
Median accum. purchase[e]	2.63	1.03	1.19	1.05	.69
Percent arable and meadow purchased by top 10%	26.0	32.9	34.4	34.0	26.9
Percent arable and meadow purchased by bottom 50%	22.5	21.0	17.3	20.5	24.0
Mean age sellers	49.4	41.6	43.1	50.3	52.6
Mean age buyers	42.2	36.6	33.4	37.0	41.8
Percent arable sold of expected inheritance	35.5	42.6	78.5	90.3	48.2

[a]Sold or traded. [b]Morgen. [c]Florin, gulden. [d]The number of individual buyers active in the land market during the decade. [e]Of arable and meadow, in Morgen.

Table A.109. *Kin-related sales by cohort (percent).*

Category	1700–9	1740–9	1780–9	1820–9	1860–9
Kin	64.4	81.8	64.5	63.1	67.1
Nuclear family	62.1	40.7	26.1	52.8	47.3
Cousins	8.6	39.5	50.0	36.0	34.5
Affines	29.3	19.7	23.9	11.2	18.2

Cohort I (1700–1709)

Table A.110. *Kinship relations between buyers and sellers, 1700–9.*

Buyer's relation to seller	N	%
Nuclear family	36	40.0
S, DH (14, 2)[a]	16	17.8
B, xB, ZH (10, 3)[b]	12	13.3
WB, WZH (4, 3)	7	7.8
WF	1	1.1
First cousins, nephews	5	5.6
xBS[a]	1	
WFZS	3	
WFBDH	1	
FBSDH	1	
Affines	17	18.9
DHB	1	
WZHB	1	
FBWxZH	1	
MBDDHB	2	
WBWZHB	1	
BWZHB	1	
BWZHBWB	1	
BWBWZHB	1	
BWZHZHB	3	
BWHBWZH	1	
MBWZHB	1	
FZHFZD	1	
WZHBWZHZH	1	
WBWBWZHB	1	
No established relation	32	35.6
Total	90	100.1

[a]One purchased by a xBS and DH together.
[b]One purchased by a B and ZH together.

Table A.111. *Kinship relations between exchange partners, 1700–9.*

Category	N	%
Nuclear family	3	10.7
B/B	2	
B/Z	1	
First cousins	5	17.9
WFBDH/WFBDH	1	
MBDH/WFZS	1	
MBDS/MFZS	1	
MBDDH/WMFZS	2	
Second cousins	1	3.6
WMMZSS/FMZDDH	1	
Affines	8	28.6
ZHB/BWB	1	
WZH/WZH	1	
ZHZH/WBWB	2	
MZHB/BWZS	1	
BWZHZHB/BWBWZHB	1	
BWHBWBWB/ZHZHBWHB	1	
BWHWFBSWH/WHFDHWHB	1	
No established relation	11	39.3
Total	28	100.1

Table A.112. *Sales and exchanges: kinship relations 1700–9.*

Category	N	%
Nuclear family	39	33.1
Cousins	11	9.3
Close in-laws	25	21.2
No established relation	43	36.4

Note: In addition, there were two gifts. No relation can be established between the parties.

Table A.113. *Sales and exchanges between parties linked through godparents, 1700–9.*

Status	Sales	Exchanges
Total	32	13[a]
Number linked	18	10
Percent linked	56.3	76.9

[a]Includes the two most extended affines from the table

Cohort II (1740–9)

Table A.114. *Kinship relations between buyers and sellers, 1740–9.*

Buyer's relation to seller	N	%
Nuclear family	33	32.4
S, DH (3,7)	10	9.8
B, ZH, xZH [FWHDH] (3, 5, 1)	9	8.8
WB, WZH (10, 1)	11	10.8
F, WF (1, 1)	2	2.0
DS	1	1.0
First cousins, nephews, nieces	21	20.6
xZDH [FWHDDH]	1	
WZS	1	
FZS	1	
MBDS	2	
WMBS	3	
WMZS	1	
WFBS	3	
WxFBS	1	
WFBDH, WHWHFBDH	2	
FFBDH	1	
MHWBDS	1	
WMMBS	3	
WxFBSDH	1	

Table A.114 (cont'd.)

Second cousins	11	10.8
FFZSS	1	
FFBDDH	2	
FMBSDH	1	
WFFZSDH	3	
WFFZSWBS	1	
WFMZSS	1	
WFFZSDH	1	
WMFZSDH	1	
Affines	16	15.7
BWH	1	
BWZS	1	
BWBDH	1	
ZHB	1	
ZHZH	1	
ZHFBS	1	
DHZH	1	
HWHBWH	1	
WFZHB	2	
MZHZHB	1	
MFZHBD	1	
WFBSWZH	1	
WBWBWFBS	1	
xDHBWxB	1	
FBSWMZH	1	
No established relation	18	17.6
No information	3	2.9
Total	102	100.0

Table A.115. *Kinship relations between exchange partners, 1740–9.*

Category	N	%
Nuclear family	4	23.5
B/B	3	
xDH/WxF	1	
First cousins	2	11.8
MFZS/MBDS	1	
WHFBS/FBSWH	1	
Second cousins	1	5.9
FMZSDH/WFMZSS	1	
No established relation	6	35.3
No information	4	23.5
Total	17	100.0

Table A.116. *Sales and exchanges: kinship relations, 1740–9.*

Category	N	%
Nuclear family	37	31.1
Cousins	35	29.4
Affines	16	13.4
No relation established	24	20.2
No information	7	5.9
Total	119	100.0

Table A.117. *Cousin connections between buyers and sellers, 1740–9.*

Buyer to seller	Frequency	Seller to buyer
FBS	4	FBS
FBD	2	FBS
FZS	1	MBS
MBS	3	FZS
MZS	1	MZS
FBSD	1	FFBS
FFBD	1	FBSS
MBDS	3	MFZS
MMBS	3	FZDS
FFBDD	2	MFBSS
FFZSS	1	FMBSS
FFZSD	4	FMBSS
FMBSD	1	FFZSS
FMZSS	1	FMZSS
MFZSD	1	FMBDS

Table A.118. *Sales and exchanges between parties linked through godparents, 1740–9.*

Status	Sales	Exchanges
Total	24	11
Number linked	19	8
Percent linked	79.2	72.7

Cohort III (1780–9)

Table A.119. *Kinship relations between buyers and sellers, 1780–9.*

Relation	N	%
Nuclear family	37	15.8
S, xS (11), xDH (4)	15	6.4
B, xB (10), ZH (7), xBWH (1)	18	7.7
WB, WZH (2,2)	4	1.7
First cousins,[a] *nephews, uncles*	48	20.5
BS	5	
xBDH	3	
WBS	1	
ZS	1	
ZHDH	1	
WZSS	2	
WZSDH	1	
WZSSS	1	
WHDS	1	
WHDDH	1	
MB	1	
MZH	3	
FBS, FxBS	2	
FZS	5	
WFZS	1	
WFBDH	1	
MBS	4	
FWHS	1	
FBWHBS	2	
FFBS	1	
FBSDH	1	
HFBSS	2	
WFZSS	1	
WFxZDH	2	
MBSS	1	
WMBSS	1	
MZDS	2	

Second cousins[b]	23	9.8
FFBSS, FFxBSS	2	
WFFxBSS	2	
FMBSS	6	
FMHSDS	2	
MFZDS	1	
HMMBSS	1	
FFZSSS	1	
WFFBSDS	1	
FFBSSDH	1	
WFFZSDSW	1	
MFFWHSS	2	
MMFBSDH	1	
WHFMBSS	1	
WHWFBSS	1	
Affines	34	14.5
xBWZH	1	
BWxZH	1	
xBWHF	1	
BWBS	2	
xZHB	1	
MZDHB	1	
MZSWF	2	
WZHB	4	
WZHBS	1	
ZHF	2	
HZH	1	
WZDH	1	
BDHZH	1	
BDHMZS	1	
WZHBSS	1	
WZHZSS	3	
WZSDH	1	
WZHBS	1	
MZDHBS	1	
HFBWFBS	2	
HxZHSDH	1	
WHFZHZHZ	1	
WHZDDHM	2	
WZHBWH	1	
No relation established	78	33.3
No information	14	6.0
Total	234	99.9

[a]Includes first cousins once removed. [b]Includes second cousins once removed.

Table A.120. *Cousin connections between buyers and sellers, 1780–9.*

Buyer to seller	Frequency	Seller to buyer
FBS	4	FBS
FBD	1	FBS
FZS	6	MBS
MBS	4	FZS
MBD	1	FZS
FFBS	1	FBSS
FBSD	1	FBSS
FBSS	2	FFBS
FBDS	2	MFBS
FZSS	1	FMBS
FZSD	2	FMBS
MBSS	2	FFZS
MZDS	2	MMZS
FFBSS	4	FFBSS
FMBSS	6	FFZSS
MFZDS	1	MMBDS
MMBSS	1	FFZDS
FFZSSS	1	FFMBSS
FFBSDS	1	MFFBSS
FFBSSD	1	FFFBSS
FFZSD	1	FMBSS
MMFBSD	1	FFBDDS

Cohort IV (1820–9)

Table A.121. *Kinship relations between buyers and sellers, 1820–9.*

Relation	N	%
Nuclear family	47	30.9
M	1	.7
S, DH (19, 7)	26	17.1
B, ZH	9	5.9
WB, WZ, WZH (8, 1, 2)	11	7.2
First cousins, uncles[a]	13	8.6
FZS	1	
HFBDH	1	
MBD	1	
MZS	1	
WMZS	2	
FFBS	1	
WMFZDH	1	
WFBSS	2	
WHFBDS	1	
MBSDH	1	
MBDDH	1	
Second cousins[b]	19	12.5
WFFZSS	1	
WFMBSDH	1	
WFMZSS	1	
WFMZSDH	3	
WFMZDDH	1	
WMFZSS	2	

Table A.121 (cont'd.)

Second cousins[b]	19	12.5
MFZSS	1	
MMZSS	1	
FFFBSDH	2	
WMFBDSS	1	
WMMZSDDH	1	
FFBSSS	1	
WFFBSDS	1	
FMBSDS	1	
FMBDDDH	1	
Affines	10	6.6
SWZ	1	
DHB	1	
ZHBS	1	
FFWBS	1	
WBWB	1	
WBDH	1	
WSWZH	2	
WHSWBS	1	
WZHZSDH	1	
No established relation	52	34.2
No information	11	7.2
Total	152	100.0

[a]Including first cousins once removed.
[b]Including second cousins once removed.

Table A.122. *Cousin connections between buyers and sellers, 1820–9.*

Buyer to seller	Frequency	Seller to buyer
FBD	1	FBS
MBD	1	FZS
MZS	3	MZS
FFBS	1	FBSS
MFZD	1	MBDS
FBSS	2	FFBS
FBDS	1	MFBS
MBSD	1	FFZS
MBDD	1	MFZS
FFZSS	1	FMBSS
FMBSD	1	FFZSS
FMZSS	1	FMZSS
FMZSD	3	FMZSS
FMZDD	1	MMZSS
MFZSS	2	FMZSS
MFZSS	1	FMBDS
MMZSS	1	FMZDS
FFFBSD	2	FFBSSS
MFBDSS	1	FMFBDS
MMZSDD	1	MFMZDS
FFBSSS	1	FFFBSS
FFBSDS	1	MFFBSS
FMBSDS	1	MFFZSS
FMBDDD	1	MMFZSS

Cohort V (1860–9)

Table A.123. *Kinship relations between buyers and sellers, 1860–9.*

Relation	N	%
Nuclear family[a]	26	30.9
S, D, DH, WDH[b] (1, 1, 7, 2)	11	13.1
B, Z, ZH, xZH (3, 1, 2, 1)	7	8.3
WB, WZH, WBW, HZH (2, 2, 1, 1)	6	7.1
SS, DS (1, 1)	2	2.4
First cousins, nephews[c]	15	17.9
MB	2	
BS	1	
ZS	4	
WZD	1	
FBS	1	
FZS	1	
MBDH	1	
WFZS	1	
WMZDH	2	
WMZDS[d]	1	
Second cousins[e]	4	4.8
MFZDS	1	
MMBDDH	1	
MZDSDH	1	
MFZDSDH	1	
Affines	10	11.9
BWB	1	
HBWB	1	
WBWB	1	
WZHB	1	
BWZH	2	
DHFZD	1	
WMBWWZH	1	
WZHZDH	1	
WMHWHW	1	
No established relation	27	32.1
No information	2	2.4
Total	84	100.0

[a]Including linear descendants. [b]Also BDH. [c]Including first cousins once removed. [d]Also WBWDH. [e]Including second cousins once removed.

Table A.124. *Cousin connections between buyers and sellers, 1860–9.*

Buyers to sellers	Frequency	Sellers to buyers
FBS	1	FBS
FZS	2	MBS
MBD	1	FZS
MZD	2	MZS
MZDS	1	MMZS
MFZDS	1	MMBDS
MMBDD	1	MFZDS
MZDSD	1	FMMZS
MFZDSD	1	FMMBDS

Table A.125. *Sales to sons, sons-in-law, brothers, and brothers-in-law.*

Buyer	1700–9	1740–9	1780–9	1820–9	1860–9
S	14	3	11	19	1
B	10	3	11	3	3
D, DH	2	7	4	7	10
Z, ZH, WB, WZH	10	17	11	17	9
Percent S/B	66.7	20.0	62.9	47.8	17.4
Percent B-in-law	27.8	56.7	31.4	37.0	39.1
Percent S-in-law	5.3	23.3	10.8	15.2	43.5

Bibliography

Manuscript Sources

Gemeindearchiv Neckarhausen (NH)

Feld- und Waldrugungsprotocolle (1789–1870).
Gemeindepflegerechnungen (1710, 1720, 1730, 1795–1870).
Gerichts- und Gemeinderatsprotocolle, 18 vols. (1746–1870) (*Gericht*).
Inventuren und Teilungen, 1-3356 (1727–1871) (IT).
Kaufbücher, 19 vols. (1653–1870) (KB).
Schultheissenamtsprotocolle, 3 vols. (1839–70) (*Schultheissenamt*).
Skortationsprotocolle, 1 vol. (1822–69) (*Skortationsbuch*).
Vogtruggerichtsprotocolle (*Bescheid- und Recessbuch*), 2 vols. (1747–1906) (*Vogtruggericht*).

Pfarramt Neckarhausen

Taufregister (Microfilm from LKA: S2403-5/KB429-431).
Eheregister (Microfilm from LKA: S2403-5/KB429-431).
Todtenregister (Microfilm from LKA: S2403-5/KB429-431).
Familienregister (1828–73).
Kirchenkonventsprotocolle, 4 vols. (1727–1848) (*Kirchenkonvent*).

Stadtarchiv Neckarhausen

Gerichtsprotocolle, 52 vols. (1586–1841) (*Nürtingen Stadtgericht*).

Dekenatsamt Nürtingen

Pfarr- und Übersichtsberichte (1821, 1832, 1840). Akten I/3,4.

Bibliography

Stadtarchiv Laichingen

Ruog-Gerichts-Protokolle. 1734–43.

Hauptstaatsarchiv Stuttgart (HSAS)

Malifizsachen, A209, Bü 35.

Commissionsberichte, A214, Bü 184, Bü 276, Bü 479, Bü 481, Bü 517, Bü 518, Bü 550, Bü 551, Bü 559, Bü 739, Bü 740, Bü 743, Bü 921, Bü 925, Bü 926, Bü 930, Bü 1023, Bü 1037, Bü 1059, Bü 1061, Bü 1114.

Steuerrevisionsakten, A261.

Staatsarchiv Ludwigsburg (STAL)

Oberamtsgerichtsprotocolle Nürtingen, 21 vols. (1802–1891). *In causis fori mixti.* 1801–12. F190 Band 9; *In causis civilibus.* 1812–17. F190 Band 10–11; 1817–23. F190II Band 257–59; *Oberamtsprotocolle.* 1822–91. F190II Band 260–74.

Landeskirchlichesarchiv Stuttgart (LKA)

Synodus Protocolle

Pfarrbericht (1828). A39, 3060.

Secondary Sources

Abelson, Andrew. "Population Structure in the Western Pyrenees: Social Class, Migration and the Frequency of Consanguineous Marriage, 1850–1910." *Annals of Human Biology* 5 (1978): 167–78.

"Population Structure in the Western Pyrennes: II. Migration, the Frequency of Consanguineous Marriage and Inbreeding, 1877 to 1915." *Annals of Human Biology* 12 (1980): 92–101.

Ahde-Bernaÿs, Hermann, ed. *Henriette Feuerbach. Ihr Leben in ihren Briefen.* Berlin/Vienna: 1912.

Alström, Carl Henry. "First-Cousin Marriages in Sweden 1750–1844 and a Study of the Population Movement in Some Swedish Subpopulations from the Genetic-Statistical Viewpoint: A Preliminary Report." *Acta Genetica* 8 (1958): 295–369.

Ammon, Christoph Friedrich. *Ueber das moralische Fundament der Eheverbote unter Verwandten.* 3 Abhandlungen. Göttingen: 1798, 1799, 1801.

Anderson, Nancy Fix. "Cousin Marriage in Victorian England." *Journal of Family History* 11 (1986): 285–301.

Anderson, Robert T. "Changing Kinship in Europe." *Kroeber Anthropological Society Papers* 28 (1963): 1–48.

Bansa, Otto, ed. *Ein Lebensbild in Briefen aus der Biedermeierzeit. Zur Geschichte der Familie Bansa in Frankfurt a. M.* Frankfurt: 1914.

Barnes, J. A. *Three Styles in the Study of Kinship.* London: 1971.

Barth, D. "Das Familienblatt – Ein Phänomen der Unterhaltungspresse des 19. Jahrhunderts." In *Archiv für Geschichte des Buchwesens* 15 (1975).

Bartsch, Karl. *Aus der Kinderzeit. Bruchstück einer Biographie.* Tübingen: 1882.

Bäte, Ludwig, ed. *Vossische Hausidylle. Briefe von Ernestine Voss an Heinrich Christian und Sara Boie (1794–1820)*. Bremen: 1925.

Battersea, Constance de Rothschild Flower, Baroness. *Reminiscences*. London: 1922.

Beck, Ulrich. "Jenseits von Stand und Klasse? Soziale Ungleichheiten, gesellschaftliche Individualisierungsprozesse und die Entstehung neuer sozialer Formationen und Identitäten." In *Soziale Welt*, Sonderband 2: *Soziale Ungleichheiten*, edited by Reinhold Kreckel, pp. 35–74. Göttingen: 1983.

Becker, Peter, and Werner, Thomas. *Kleio. Ein Tutorial*. Halbgraue Reihe zur historischen Fachinformatik. Series A: Historische Quellenkunde, vol. 1. 2d ed. St. Katharinen: 1991.

Bedenken über die Frage ob die Ehe mit des Bruders Witwe erlaubt sey? Frankfurt: 1758.

Bedenken über die Frage Ob die Ehe mit des Bruders Wittwe erlaubt sey? Samt derselben umständler Widerlegung. Frankfurt: 1758.

Bell, C. H. "The Sister's Son in the Medieval German Epic: A Study in the Survival of Matriliny." *University of California Publications in Modern Philology* 10 (1920): 67–182.

Bell, Julia. "A Determination of the Consanguinity Rate in the General Hospital Population of England and Wales." *Annals of Genetics* 10 (1940): 370–91.

Bendix, Rheinhard, and Lipset, Seymour Martin. "Karl Marx's Theory of Social Classes." In *Class, Status, and Power. Social Stratification in Comparative Perspective*, pp. 6–11. New York: 1966.

Berger, Peter A., and Hradil, Stefan. "Die Modernisierung sozialer Ungleichheit – und die neuen Konturen ihrer Erforschung." In *Soziale Welt*, Sonderband 7: *Lebenslage, Lebensläufe, Lebensstile*, edited by Peter A. Berger and Stefan Hradil, pp. 3–24. Göttingen: 1990.

Bloch, Maurice. "The Long Term and the Short Term: The Economic and Political Significance of the Morality of Kinship. In *The Character of Kinship*, edited by Jack Goody, pp. 75–87. Cambridge: 1973.

Bohnenberger, Karl, ed. *Volkstümliche Ueverlieferungen in Württemberg: Glaube – Brauch – Heilkunde*. Stuttgart: 1980; original 1904ff.

Böök, J. A. "The Frequency of Cousin Marriages in Three North Swedish Parishes." *Hereditas* 34 (1948): 252–5.

Böök, J. A., and Måwe, C. E. "The Incidence of Cousin Marriages in a West-Swedish Rural Community." *American Journal of Human Genetics* 7 (1955): 426–9.

Bourdieu, Pierre. *The Logic of Practice*. Translated by Richard Nice. Stanford: 1990.

Outline of the Theory of Practice. Translated by Richard Nice. Cambridge: 1977.

"The Social Space and the Genesis of Groups." *Theory and Society* 14 (1985): 723–44.

"What Makes a Social Class? On the Theoretical and Practical Existence of Groups." *Berkeley Journal of Sociology*, 32 (1987): 1–17.

Zur Soziologie der symbolischen Formen. Frankfurt: 1970.

Bourgoin, Jacqueline, and Khang, Vu Tien. "Quelques aspects de l'histoire génétique de quatre villages pyrénéens depuis 1740." *Population* 33 (1978): 633–59.

Brandes, Ernst. *Betrachtungen über das weibliche Geschlecht und dessen Ausbildung in dem geselligen Leben*. 3 vols. Hannover: 1802.

Brenk, Hermann. "Ueber den Grad der Inzucht in einem innerschweizerischen Gebirgsdorf." *Archiv der Julius Klaus-Stiftung für Vererbungsforschung, Sozialanthropologie und Rassenhygiene* 6 (1931): 1–39.

Buchholtz, Christoph Joachim. *Pro matrimonio principis cum defunctae uxoris sorore contracto. Responsum juris collegii JCTorum in academia Rintelensi.* Rinteln: 1651.

Budde, Gunilla-Friederike. *Auf dem Weg ins Bürgerleben: Kindheit und Erziehung in deutschen und englischen Bürgerfamilien 1840–1914.* Göttingen: 1914.

Burguière, André. "Endogamie et communauté villageoises: Pratique matrimoniale Romainville." *Annales de démographie historique* (1979): 313–36.

Calderon, R. "Inbreeding, Migration and Age at Marriage in Rural Toledo, Spain." *Journal of Biosocial Science* 15 (1983): 47–57.

Canning, Kathleen. "Gender and the Politics of Class Formation: Rethinking German Labor History." *American Historical Review,* 97 (1992): 736–68.

"Christoph Nellmanns zweiter Zuruf an die Gemeinds-Deputierten zu Lauffen." In *Der Württembergische Volksfreund. Ein Wochenblatt für Recht und bürgerliche Freiheit.* Stuttgart: 26 March 1818.

Claverie, Elisabeth, and Lamaison, Pierre. *L'impossible mariage. Violence et parenté en Gévaudan, xvii*e, *xviii*e, *xix*e *siècles.* Paris: 1982.

Collier, Jane Fishburne, and Yanigisako, Sylvia Junko. "Introduction." In *Gender and Kinship. Essays towards a Unified Analysis,* edited by Jane Fishburne Collier and Sylvia Junko Yanigisako, pp. 1–13. Stanford: 1987.

Comaroff, John. "*Sui genderis*: Feminism, Kinship Theory, and Structural 'Domains'." In *Gender and Kinship. Essays towards a Unified Analysis,* edited by Jane Fishburne Collier and Sylvia Junko Yanigisako, pp. 53–85. Stanford: 1987.

Comaroff, John, and Comaroff, Jean. *Ethnography and the Historical Imagination.* Boulder: 1992.

Crognier, Emile. "Consanguinity and Social Change: An Isonymic Study of a French Peasant Population, 1870–1979." *Journal of Biosocial Science* 17 (1985): 267–79.

Crognier, Emile, Bley, Daniel, and Boetsch, Gilles. *Mariage en Limousin. Evolution séculaire et identité d'une population rurale: Le canton de Chateauponsac (1870–1979).* Paris: 1984.

Däbritz, Walther, and Schmöle, Carl. *Geschichte der R. & G. Schmöle Metalwerke Menden/Kreis Iserlohn 1853 bis 1952. Zugleich ein Beitrag zur Industriegeschichte des märkischen Sauerlandes in drei Jahrhunderten.* n.p.: 1953.

Dahlberg, Gunnar. "On Rare Defects in Human Populations with Particular Regard to In-breeding and Isolate Effects." *Proceedings of the Royal Society of Edinburgh* 58 (1937–8): 213–32.

Darwin, George H. "Marriages between First Cousins in England and Their Effects." *Fortnightly Review* 18 n.s. (1875): 22–41.

"Marriages between First Cousins in England and Their Effects." *Journal of the Statistical Society* 38 (1875): 153–84.

Davidoff, Leonore. "Where the Stranger Begins: The Question of Siblings in Historical Analysis." In *Worlds Between: Historical Perspectives on Gender and Class,* pp. 206–26. Oxford: 1995.

Davidoff, Leonore, and Hall, Catherine. *Family Fortunes: Men and Women of the English Middle Class, 1780–1850.* Chicago: 1987.

de Certeau, Michel. *The Practice of Everyday Life.* Translated by Steven Rendall. Berkeley: 1988.

de Heusch, Luc. *Why Marry Her? Society and Symbolic Structures.* Translated by Janet Lloyd. Cambridge: 1981.

Dehlinger, Alfred. *Württembergs Staatswesen in seiner geschichtlichen Entwicklung bis heute,* 2 vols. Stuttgart: 1951, 1953.

Delille, Gérard. *Famille et proprieté dans le royaume de Naples (xve–xixe siècle).* Bibliothèque des écoles françaises d'athènes et de rome, vol. 259. Rome: 1985.

Deraemaeker, R. "Inbreeding in a North Belgium Province." *Acta Genetica* 8 (1958): 128–36.

Deussen, Paul. *Mein Leben,* edited by Erika Rosenthal-Deussen. Leipzig: 1922.

Deutsches Geschlechterbuch. Genealogisches Handbuch bürgerlicher Familien, vol. 193; also published as *Westfälisches Geschlechterbuch,* vol. 7. Prepared by Uta von Delius. Limburg an der Lahn: 1987.

Droste-Hülshoff, Annette von. *Historisch-kritische Ausgabe: Werke, Briefwechsel,* edited by Winfried Woesler. Vol. 8, 1: *Briefe 1805–1838,* edited by Walter Gödden. Vol. 9, 1: *Briefe 1839–42,* edited by Walter Gödden and Ilse Marie Barth. Vol. 10, 1: *Briefe 1843–48,* edited by Winfried Woesler. Tübingen: 1987, 1992, 1993.

Dubisch, Jill. "Gender, Kinship and Religion: 'Reconstructing' the Anthropology of Greece." In *Gendered Identities: Gender and Kinship in Modern Greece,* edited by Peter Loizos and Evthymios Papataxiarchis, pp. 29–46. Princeton: 1991.

Duby, Georges. "In Northwestern France: The 'Youth' in Twelfth Century Aristocratic Society." In *Lordship and Community in Medieval Europe,* edited by F. L. Cheyette, pp. 198–209. New York: 1968.

The Knight, the Lady, and the Priest: The Making of Modern Marriage in Medieval France. Translated by Barbara Bray. New York: 1983.

Duden, Barbara. *The Woman beneath the Skin: A Doctor's Patients in Eighteenth-Century Germany.* Translated by Thomas Dunlop. Cambridge, Mass.: 1991.

Eberty, Felix. *Jugenderinnerungen eines alten Berliners.* Berlin: 1878.

Eder, Klaus. "Jenseits der nivellierten Mittelstandsgesellschaft. Das Kleinbürgertum als Schlüssel einer Klassenanalyse in fortgeschrittenen Industriegesellschaften." In *Klassenlage, Lebensstil und kulturelle Praxis. Beiträge zur Auseinandersetzung mit Pierre Bourdieus Klassentheorie,* edited by Klaus Eder, pp. 341–92. Frankfurt: 1989.

Egenter, Arnold. "Ueber den Grad der Inzucht in einer Schwyzer Berggemeinde und die damit zusammenhängende Häufung rezessiver Erbschäden." *Archiv der Julius Klaus-Stiftung für Vererbungsforschung, Sozialanthropologie und Rassenhygiene* 6 (1931): 1–39.

Eggel, Eberhard. "Die Textilkaufleute Heinzelmann in Kaufbeuren und ihre Verwandtschaft." *Archiv für Sippensforschung* 32 (1968): 574–91.

Elderton, Ethel M. *On the Marriage of First Cousins.* London: 1911.

Ellis, Walter S., and Starmer, William T. "Inbreeding as Measured by Isonymy, Pedigrees, and Population Size in Törbel, Switzerland." *Human Genetics* 30 (1978): 366–76.

Eversley, D. E. C., Laslett, Peter, and Wrigley, E. A., eds. With contributions by W. A. Armstrong and Lynda Overall. *An Introduction to English Historical Demography from the Sixteenth to the Nineteenth Century.* London: 1966.

Feinberg, Richard. "Kindred and Alliance on Anuta Island." *Journal of the Polynesian Society* 88 (1979): 27–48.

Fischer, Hermann. *Schwäbisches Lexikon.* 6 vols. Tübingen: 1904–36.

Flandrin, Jean-Louis. *Families in Former times: Kinship, Household and Sexuality.* Translated by Richard Southern. Cambridge: 1979.

Focke, Wilhelm Olbers, ed. *Briefe von Doris Focke geb. Olbers an ihren Bruder, für die Familie als Manuscript gedruckt.* Bremen: 1886.

Fortes, Meyer. "Kinship and the Axiom of Amity." In *Kinship and the Social Order: The Legacy of Lewis Henry Morgan,* pp. 219–49. Chicago: 1966.

Web of Kinship among the Talensi: The Second Part of an Analysis of the Social Structure of a Trans-Volta Tribe. Oxford, 1949.

Fox, Robin. *Kinship and Marriage: An Anthropological Perspective.* Harmondsworth: 1967.

Foucault, Michel. *History of Sexuality.* Vol. 1: *An Introduction,* translated by Robert Hurley. Harmondsworth: 1978.

Power/Knowledge. Selected Interviews and Other Writings 1972–1977, edited by Colin Gordon. New York: 1980.

Freeman, J. D. "On the Concept of the Kindred." *Journal of the Royal Anthropological Institute* 91 (1961): 192–220.

Fricke, Friederike, ed. *Aus dem Leben unserer Mutter. Familienbriefe für die Familie.* Göttingen: 1929.

Friedl, John, and Ellis, Walter S. "Inbreeding as Measured by Isonymy and by Pedigrees in Kippel, Switzerland." *Social Biology* 23 (1976): 158–61.

"Inbreeding, Isonymy, and Isolation in a Swiss Community." *Human Biology* 46 (1974): 699–712.

Froeschle, Hartmut. *Ludwig Uhland und die Romantik.* Köln and Wien: 1973.

Gailey, Christine. *Kinship to Kingship. Gender Hierarchy and State Formation in the Tongan Islands.* Austin: 1987.

Gautier, Etienne and Henry, Louis. *La population de Crulai, paroisse normande: étude historique.* Institut national d'études demographique, Travaux et Documents, Cahiers 33. Paris: 1958.

Gedde-Dahl, Tobias, Jr. "Population Structure in Norway: Inbreeding, Distance and Kinship." *Hereditas* 27 (1973): 311–32.

Geertz, Hildred, and Geertz, Clifford. *Kinship in Bali.* Chicago, 1975.

Gellner, Ernest. "The Concept of Kinship, With Special Reference to Mr. Needham's 'Descent Systems and Ideal Language.'" *Philosophy of Science* 17 (1960): 187–204.

Gervinus, Georg Gottfried. *Leben von ihm Selbst 1860.* Leipzig: 1893.

Ginzburg, Carlo. "Microhistory: Two or Three Things That I Know about It." *Critical Inquiry* 20 (1993): 10–35.

Goodenough, Ward H. "Personal Names and Modes of Address in Two Oceanic Societies." In *Context and Meaning in Cultural Anthropology,* edited by Melford E. Spiro. New York: 1965.

Goody, Jack. *The Development of the Family and Marriage in Europe.* Cambridge: 1983.

"Evolution of Kinship." Edinburgh Lectures, ms. n.d.

The Expansive Moment, The Rise of Social Anthropology in Britain and Africa 1918–1970. Cambridge: 1995.

"Marriage Prestations, Inheritance and Descent in Pre-Industrial Societies." *Journal of Comparative Family Studies* 1 (1970): 37–54.

The Oriental, the Ancient, and the Primitive: Systems of Marriage and the Family in the Pre-Industrial Societies of Eurasia. Cambridge: 1990.

Production and Reproduction. A Comparative Study of the Domestic Domain. Cambridge: 1976.

Goetzeler, Herbert, and Schoen, Lothar. *Wilhelm und Carl Freidrich von Siemens. Die zweite Unternehmergeneration.* Stuttgart: 1986.

Goltz, Bogumil. *Zur Charakteristik und Naturgeschichte der Frau.* Berlin: 1863.

Gouesse, Jean-Marie. "L'endogamie familiale dans l'europe catholique au xviiie: première approche." *Mélanges de l'école française de Rome. Moyen âge. Temps moderne* 89 (1977): 95–116.

"Epouser les deux soeurs." *Annales de Normandie,* numéro special (1982) [Réceuil d'études offert en hommage au doyen Michel de Boüard, vol. 1]: 253–67.

"Mariages de proches parents (xvie–xxe siècle). Esquisse d'une conjoncture." In *Le Modèle familial européen: Normes, déviances, contrôle du pouvoir,* pp. 31–61. Actes des séminaires organisés par l'école française de Rome, vol. 90. Rome: 1986.

Grob, Walter. "Aszendenzforschungen und Mortalitätsstatistik aus einer st. gallischen Berggemeinde." *Archiv der Julius Klaus-Stiftung für Vererbungsforschung, Sozialanthropologie und Rassenhygiene* 9 (1934), pp. 237–64.

Habermas, Jürgen. *The Structural Transformation of the Public Sphere. An Inquiry into a Category of Bourgeois Society.* Translated by Thomas Burger. Cambridge, Mass.: 1991.

Hareven, Tamara. "The History of the Family and the Complexity of Social Change." *American Historical Review* 96 (1991): 95–124.

Harnack, Ernst von, ed. *Johanna Thiersch, geborene Freiin von Liebig. Briefe aus ihren Jugendjahren 1848–1855: Für die Familie zusammengestellt zum Gedächtnis ihres 100. Geburtstages.* Berlin-Zehlendorf: 1936.

Harris, C. C. *Readings in Kinship in Urban Society.* Oxford and New York: 1970.

Hart, Donn V. *Compadrinazgo. Ritual Kinship in the Philippines.* DeKalb: 1977.

Hase, Karl. *Ideale und Irrthümer. Jugend-Erinnerungen.* 2d ed. Leipzig: 1873.

Hasselhorn, Martin. *Die altwürttembergische Pfarrstand im 18. Jahrhundert.* Veröffentlichungen der Kommission für geschichtliche Landeskunde in Baden-Württemberg. Series B: Forschungen, vol. 6. Stuttgart: 1958.

Haupt, Heinz-Gerhard. "Männliche und weibliche Berufskarrieren im deutschen Bürgertum in der zweiten Hälfte des 19. Jahrhunderts: Zum Verhältnis von Klasse und Geschlecht." *Geschichte und Gesellschaft* 18 (1992): pp. 143–60.

Hegel, G. W. F. *Elements of the Philosophy of Right,* edited by Allan W. Wood. Translated by H. B. Nisbet. Cambridge: 1991.

"Ueber die neuesten innern Verhältnisse Württembergs besonders über die Gebrechen der Magistratsverfassung" (1798). In *Hegels Schriften zur Politik und Rechtsphilosophie,* edited by Georg Lasson. Vol. 7, *Sämtliche Werke,* pp. 150–4. Leipzig: 1913.

"Verhandlungen in der Versammlung der Landstände des Königsreichs Württemberg im Jahre 1815 und 1816." In *Hegels Schriften zur Politik und Rechtsphilosophie,* edited by Georg Lasson. Vol. 7, *Sämtliche Werke,* pp. 157–281. Leipzig: 1913.

Heitefuss, Clara. *An des Meisters Hand. Lebenserinnerungen.* Schwerin: 1939.

Helfferich, Karl. *Georg von Siemens: Ein Lebensbild aus Deutschlands grosser Zeit.* 3 vols. 2d ed. Berlin: 1923.

Henning, Hansjoachim. "Soziale Verflechtungen der Unternehmer in Westfalen 1860–1914." *Zeitschrift für Unternehmensgeschichte,* 23 (1978): 1–30.

Henry, Louis. *Manuel de démographie historique.* Hautes études medievales et modernes, vol. 3. Geneva: 1967.

Henschke, Ulrike. *Die Bedeutung des Vereinsleben für die Frauen.* Lissa: 1866.

Héritier, Françoise. *L'exercice de la parenté.* Paris: 1981.

Heselhaus, Clemens. *Annette von Droste-Hülshoff: Werk und Leben.* Düsseldorf: 1971.

Hochangelegene und bisshero vielfältig bestrittene Gewissens-Frage/ Ob Jemand seines verstorbenen Weibes Schwester/ sonder Ubertrettung Göttlicher und Natürlicher Gesetze/ in wiederholter Ehe zu heuratten berechtigt? Durch auff dem in der Fürstlichen Residenz zu

Oettingen den 10. October. Anno 1681. gehaltenen Colloquio Ergangene Wechsel-Schrifften/ Responsa und hochvernünftige Judicia; Nach höchstes Fleisses überlegten beyderseitigen Rationibus, und hierüber gefassten Grund-Schlüssen Erörtert: und als ein Curiöses und ungemeines Zweiffel-Werck/ zu eines jeden gnugsamen Unterricht Truck aussgefertigt. Frankfurt: 1682.

Holy, Ladislav. *Kinship, Honour and Solidarity: Cousin Marriage in the Middle East.* Manchester: 1989.

Hölzle, Erwin. *Das alte Recht und die Revolution. Eine politische Geschichte Württembergs in der Revolutionszeit 1789–1805.* München: 1931.

Howell, Signe, and Melhuus, Marit. "The Study of Kinship; The Study of Person; A Study of Gender." In *Gendered Anthropology,* edited by Teresa del Valle, pp. 38–53. London: 1993.

Hradil, Stefan. "System und Akteur: Eine empirische Kritik der soziologischen Kulturtheorie Pierre Bourdieus." In *Klassenlage, Lebensstil und kulturelle Praxis. Beiträge zur Auseinandersetzung mit Pierre Bourdieus Klassentheorie,* edited by Klaus Eder, pp. 111–41. Frankfurt: 1989.

"Die Ungleichheit der 'Sozialer Lage'," in *Soziale Welt,* Sonderband 2: *Soziale Ungleichheiten,* edited by Reinhold Kreckel, pp. 101–18. Göttingen: 1983.

Hüffer, Hermann. *Lebenserinnerungen,* edited by Ernst Sieper. Berlin: 1912.

Hunnius, Monika. *Briefwechsel mit einem Freunde,* edited by Sophie Gurland. Heilbronn: 1935.

Wenn die Zeit erfüllet ist. Briefe und Tageblätter, edited by Anne Monika Glasow. Heilbronn: 1937.

Jacobs, Monty, ed. *1848. Briefwechsel zwischen Wilhelm und Philippine Levysohn.* Grünberg: 1906.

Jerusalem, J. W. F. *Beantwortung der Frage ob die Ehe mit der Schwester-Tochter, nach der göttlichen Gesetzen zulassig sey.* Braunschweig: 1754.

Jolas, Tina, Verdier, Yvonne, and Zonabend, Françoise. "Cousinage, voisinage." In *Echanges et communications, Mélanges offerts à Claude Lévi-Strauss,* pp. 169–80. Paris: 1970.

" 'Parler famille.' " *L'homme* 10 (1970): 5–26.

Joris, Elisabeth, and Witzig, Heidi. *Brave Frauen, aufmüpfige Weiber: Wie sich die Industrialisierung zur Alltag und Lebenszusammenhänge von Frauen auswirkte (1820–1940).* Zurich: 1992.

Jussen, Bernhard. *Patenschaft und Adoption im frühen Mittelalter: Künstliche Verwandtschaft als soziale Praxis.* Veröffentlichungen des Max-Planck-Instituts für Geschichte, vol. 98. Göttingen: 1991.

Kaplan, Marion A. *The Making of the Jewish Middle Class: Women, Family, and Identity in Imperial Germany.* New York: 1991.

Kaschuba, Wolfgang, and Lipp, Carola. *Dörflisches überleben: Zur Geschichte materieller und sozialer Reproduktion ländlicher Gesellschaft im 19. und frühen 20. Jahrhundert.* Untersuchungen des Ludwig-Uhland-Instituts der Universität Tübingen, vol. 56. Tübingen: 1982.

Kayser-Langerhanss, Agnes. *Erinnerungen aus meinem Leben.* Dresden, 1894.

Kestner-Köchlin, Hermann, ed. *Briefwechsel August Kestner und seine Schwester Charlotte.* Strassburg: 1904.

Kettner, L. Friedrich Ernst. *Grundliche Untersuchung der hochangelegenen und bissher vielfältig bestrittenen Gewissensfrage: Ob jemand seines verstorbenen Weibes leibliche Schwester nach Geist- und Weltlichen Rechten heyrathen darff?.* Quedlinburg: 1707.

Khang, Jacqueline Vu Tien, and Sevin, André. *Choix du conjoint et patrimoine génétique. Étude de quatre villages du Pays de Sault de 1740 à nos jours.* Paris: 1977.

Khera, Sigrid. "An Austrian Peasant Village under Rural Industrialization." *Behavior Science Notes* 7 (1972): 29–36.

Kocka, Jürgen. "Familie, Unternehmer und Kapitalismus. An Beispielen aus der frühen deutschen Industrialisierung." *Zeitschrift für Unternehmergeschichte* 24 (1979): 99–135.

Lohnarbeit und Klassenbildung: Arbeiter und Arbeiterbewegung in Deutschland 1800–1875. Berlin: 1983.

Traditionsbindung und Klassenbildung. Zum sozialhistorischen Ort der frühen deutschen Arbeiterbewegung. Schriften des historischen Kollegs, Vorträge 8. Munich: 1987.

Köhler, F. A. *Nehren: Eine Dorfchronik des Spätaufklärung,* edited by Carola Lipp, Wolfgang Kaschuba, and Eckart Frahm. Untersuchungen des Ludwig-Uhland-Instituts der Universität Tübingen, vol. 52. Tübingen: 1981.

Körner, Christian Gottfried. *Für deutsche Frauen.* Berlin: 1824.

Kreckel, Reinhard. "Klasse und Geschlecht. Die Geschlechtsindifferenz der soziologischen Ungleichheitsforschung und ihre theoretischen Implikationen." In *Leviathan. Zeitschrift für Sozialwissenschaft* (1989): 305–21.

"Klassenbegriff und Ungleichheitsforschung." In *Soziale Welt,* Sonderband 7: *Lebenslage, Lebensläufe, Lebensstile,* edited by Peter A. Berger and Stefan Hradil, pp. 51–79. Göttingen: 1990.

Kriedte, Peter. *Eine Stadt am seidenen Faden. Haushalt, Hausindustrie und soziale Bewegung in Krefeld in der Mitte des 19. Jahrhunderts.* Veröffentlichungen des Max-Planck-Instituts für Geschichte, 97. Göttingen: 1991.

"Kritik des Verfassungs-Entwurfs der württembergischen Stände-Versammlung." *Württembergisches Archiv* 2 (1817): 27–8.

Kühn, Arthur. "Inzucht und Auslese in zwei Eifeldörfern." *Archiv für Rassen- und Gesellschaftsbiologie* 31 (1937): 482–505.

Kuper, Adam. *The Invention of Primitive Society: Transformations of an Illusion.* London: 1988.

Lamaison, Pierre. "Les stratégies matrimoniales dans un système complexe de parenté: Ribennes en Gévaudan (1650–1830)." *Annales ESC* 34 (1979): 721–43.

Larson, Carl A. "The Frequency of First Cousin Marriages in a South Swedish Rural Community." *The American Journal of Human Genetics,* 8 (1956): 151–3.

Laqueur, Thomas. *Making Sex: Body and Gender from the Greeks to Freud.* Cambridge, Mass.: 1990.

Leach, Edmund. *Pul Eliya: A Village in Ceylon.* Cambridge: 1961.

Rethinking Anthropology. London School of Economics Monographs on Social Anthropology, vol. 22. London: 1961.

Lehmann, Emil. *Lebenserinnerungen.* 3 vols. Kissingen: [1885]–95.

Leinsberg, Gottfried von. *Das Paradies meiner Kindheit 1825–1840.* Lübeck: 1909.

Le Roy Ladurie, Emmanuel. "Family Structures and Inheritance Customs in Sixteenth-Century France." In *Family and Inheritance. Rural Society in Western Europe, 1200–1800,* edited by Jack Goody, Joan Thirsk, and E. P. Thompson, pp. 37–70. Cambridge: 1976.

Lévi-Strauss, Claude. *The Elementary Structures of Kinship.* Rev. ed. Translated by James Harle Bell, John Richard von Sturmer, and Rodney Needham, editor. Boston: 1969.

The Savage Mind. London: 1966.

Lewald, Fanny. *Meine Lebensgeschichte.* 3 parts in 6 vols. Berlin: 1861–2.

Leyton, E. "Composite Descent Groups in Canada." In *Readings in Kinship and Urban Society,* edited by C. C. Harris, pp. 179–86. Oxford: 1970.

List, Friedrich. "Die Ackerverfassung, die Zwergwirtschaft und die Auswanderung (1842)." In *Friedrich Lists kleinere Schriften,* edited by Friedrich Lenz, pp. 437–554. Jena, 1926.

Loizos, Peter. *The Greek Gift: Politics in a Cypriot Village.* Oxford: 1975.

Luebke, David. "Terms of Loyalty: Factional Politics in a Single German Village (Nöggenschwihl, 1725–1745)." In *Infinite Boundaries: Order, Disorder, and Reorder in Early Modern German Culture,* edited by Thomas Robisheaux and Max Reinhard. Sixteenth-Century Studies: forthcoming (1997).

Luthardt, Christian Ernst. *Erinnerungen aus vergangenen Tagen.* 2d ed. Leipzig: 1891.

Luther, Martin. *Vom ehelichen Leben* (1522). In *Luthers Werke in Auswahl,* edited by Otto Clemen, vol. 2, pp. 335–59. Berlin: 1950.

Marchtaler, Hildegard von. *Aus Alt-Hamburger Senatorenhäusern. Familienschicksale im 18. und 19. Jahrhundert.* Veröffentlichung des Vereins für Hamburgische Geschichte, vol. 16. Hamburg: n.d. [1958].

Masterson, J. G. "Consanguinity in Ireland." *Human Heredity* 20 (1970): 371–82.

Mauss, Marcel. *The Gift: Forms and Functions of Exchange in Archaic Society.* Translated by Ian Cunnison. London: 1966.

Maybury-Lewis, David. *Akwe-Shavante Society.* New York: 1974.

Medick, Hans. "Village Spinning Bees: Sexual Culture and Free Time among Rural Youth in Early Modern Germany." In *Interest and Emotion: Essays on the Study of Family and Kinship,* edited by Hans Medick and David Warren Sabean. Cambridge: 1984.

Weben und überleben in Laichingen, 1650–1900. Lokalgeschichte als Allgemeine Geschichte. Veröffentlichungen des Max-Planck-Instituts für Geschichte. Göttingen: 1996.

Medick, Hans, and Sabean, David Warren. "Interest and Emotion in Family and Kinship Studies: A Critique of Social History and Anthropology." In *Interest and Emotion: Essays on the Study of Family and Kinship,* edited by Hans Medick and David Warren Sabean, pp. 9–27. Cambridge: 1984.

Merzario, Raul. "Land, Kinship, and Consanguineous Marriage in Italy from the Seventeenth to the Nineteenth Centuries." *Journal of Family History* 15 (1990): 529–46.

Michaelis, Johann David. *Abhandlung von der Ehe-Gesetzen Mosis welche die Heyrathen in die nahe Freundschaft untersagen.* Göttingen: 1755.

Mira, Joan F. "Mariage et famille dans une communauté rurale du pays de Valence (Espagne)." In *Etudes rurales* 42 (1971): 105–19.

Mitterauer, Michael. *Ahnen und Heilige. Namengebung in der europäischen Geschichte.* Munich: 1993.

"Christianity and Endogamy." *Continuity and Change* 6 (1991): 295–333.

Moltmann, Günter, ed. *Aufbruch nach Amerika. Friedrich List und die Auswanderung aus Baden und Württemberg 1816/17: Dokumentation einer sozialen Bewegung.* Tübingen: 1979.

Mooser, Josef. *Arbeiterleben in Deutschland 1900–1970.* Frankfurt: 1984.

Moraw, Peter. "Ueber Patrone und Klienten im Heiligen Römischen Reich des späten Mittelalters und der frühen Neuzeit." In *Klientelsysteme in Europa der frühen Neuzeit,* edited by Antoni Maczak, pp. 19–46. Schriften des Historischen Kollegs, Kolloquien, vol. 9. Munich: 1988.

Mosse, W. E. *The German Jewish Economic Elite 1820–1935: A Socio-Cultural Profile.* Oxford: 1989.

Morton, Frederic. *The Rothschilds: Family Portrait.* New York: 1962.

Murdock, George P. *Social Structure.* New York: 1949.

New Catholic Encyclopedia. 17 vols. New York: 1967–89.

Nitzsch, Carl Ludwig. *Neuer Versuch über die Ungültigkeit des mosaischen Gesetzes und den Rechtsgrund der Eheverbote in einem Gutachten über die Ehe mit des Bruders Wittwe.* Wittenberg: 1800.

Nolte, Paul. "Gemeindeliberalismus: Zur lokalen Entstehung und sozialen Verankerung der liberalen Partei in Baden 1831–1855." *Historische Zeitschrift* 252 (1991): 57–93.

Nutini, Hugo V. *Ritual Kinship: Ideological and Structural Integration of the Compadrazgo System in Rural Tlaxcala,* vol. 2. Princeton: 1984.

Oexle, Otto Gerhard, Conze, Werner, and Walther, Rudolf, "Stand, Klasse," in *Geschichtliche Grundbegriffe,* edited by Otto Brunner, Werner Conze, and Reinhard Koselleck, vol. 6, pp. 155–284. Stuttgart: 1990.

Orel, Herbert. "Die Verwandtenehen in der Erzdiözese Wien," *Archiv für Rassen- und Gesellschaftsbiologie* 26 (1932): 249–78.

Ortner, Sherry. "The Virgin and the State." *Feminist Studies* 3 (1978): 19–35.

Osiander, Andreas d. ä. *Gesamtausgabe,* edited by Gerhard Müller, with Gottfrid Seebass. 8 vols. Gütersloh: 1975–90.

Otte, Christian Heinrich. *Aus meinem Leben.* Leipzig: 1893.

Ottenheimer, Martin. "Lewis Henry Morgan and the Prohibition of Cousin Marriage in the United States." *Journal of Family History* 15 (1990): 325–34.

Otto, Louise. *Frauenleben im deutschen Reich. Errinerungen aus der Vergangenheit mit Hinweis auf Gegenwart und Zukunft.* Leipzig: 1876.

Panse, Friedrich, and Krings, Josef. "Die Häufigkeit der Blutsverwandten-Ehen der katholischen Bevölkerung in der Erzdioziöse Köln von 1898–1943." *Rheinische Vierteljahrsblätter* 14 (1948): 148–56.

Parthey, Gustav. *Jugenderinnerungen,* edited by Ernst Friedel. 2 parts. Berlin: 1907.

Pastner, Carroll. "Cousin Marriage among the Zikri Baluch of Coastal Pakistan." *Ethnology* 18 (1979): 31–47.

Pauli, Reinhold. *Lebenserinnerungen nach Briefen und Tagebüchern,* edited by Elisabeth Pauli. Halle a. S.: 1895.

Perthes, Clemens Theodor. *Politische Zustände und Personen in Deutschland zur Zeit der französischen Herrschaft.* 2d ed. Gotha: 1862.

Peters, Emrys Lloyd. "Aspects of Affinity in a Lebanese Maronite Village." In *Mediterranean Family Structures,* edited by J. G. Peristiany, pp. 27–80. Cambridge: 1976.

Pierenkemper, Toni. *Die Westfälischen Schwerindustriellen, 1852–1913: Soziale Struktur und unternehmerischer Erfolg.* Kritische Studien zur Geschichtswissenschaft, vol. 36. Göttingen: 1979.

Pinto-Cisternas, J., Zei, G., and Moroni, A. "Consanguinity in Spain, 1911–1943: General Methodology, Behavior of Demographic Variables, and Regional Differences." *Social Biology* 26 (1979): 55–71.

Pitt-Rivers, Julian. *The Fate of Schechem or the Politics of Sex: Essays in the Anthropology of the Meditteranean.* Cambridge: 1977.

"Ritual Kinship in the Meditteranean: Spain and the Balkans." In *Mediterranean Family Structures,* edited by J. G. Peristiany, pp. 317–34. Cambridge: 1976.

Plakans, Andrejs. *Kinship in the Past: An Anthropology of European Family Life 1500–1900.* Oxford: 1984.

Pohl, Manfred. *Hamburger Bankengeschichte.* Mainz: 1986.

Press, Volker. "Patronat und Klientel im Heiligen Römischen Reich." In *Klientelsysteme in Europe der frühen Neuzeit,* edited by Antoni Maczak, pp. 19–46. Schriften des historischen Kollegs, Kolloquien, vol. 9. Munich: 1988.

Radcliffe-Brown, A. R. *Structure and Function in Primitive Society. Essays and Addresses.* London: 1952.

Rancière, Jacques. *Die Namen der Geschichte. Versuch einer Poetik der Geschichte.* Translated by Eva Moldenhauer. Frankfurt: 1994.

Ranke, Leopold von. *Zwölf Bücher zur Preussischen Geschichte.* 2d ed., vols. 3 and 4. In *Sämmtliche Werke.* 3d ed., 54 vols. Leipzig: 1867–1900.

Raumer, Friedrich von. *Lebenserinnerungen und Briefwechsel.* 2 Teile. Leipzig: 1861.

Realencyklopädie für protestantische Theologie und Kirche. Leipzig: 1898.

Rebensburg-Reich, Luisa, ed. *Aus Tante Carlotas Nachlass. Familienbriefe Sieveking/Cramer aus Hamburg, Basel, Genf, u.a.* Hamburg: 1937.

Reddy, William M. *Money and Liberty in Modern Europe: A Critique of Historical Understanding.* Cambridge: 1987.

Rehberg, Paula, ed. *Elise Egloff. Die Geschichte einer Liebe in ihren Briefen.* Zürich: 1937.

Reif, Heinz. *Westfälischer Adel 1770–1860: Vom Herrschaftsstand zur regionalen Elite.* Göttingen: 1979.

Reuter, Gabriele. *Vom Kinde zum Menschen. Die Geschichte meiner Jugend.* Berlin: 1921.

Reutlinger, Wilhelm. "Ueber die Häufigkeit der Verwandtenehen bei den Juden in Hohenzollern und über Untersuchungen bei Deszendenten aus jüdischen Verwandtenehen." *Archiv für Rassen- und Gesellschaftsbiologie* 14 (1922–3): 301–5.

Reventlow, Else, ed., *Briefe des Gräfin Franziska zu Reventlow.* Munich: 1929.

Reyscher, August Ludwig, ed. *Vollständige, historisch und kritisch bearbeitete Sammlung der württembergischen Geseze.* 19 vols. Stuttgart and Tübingen: 1828–51.

Richter, Otto. *Lebensfreuden eines Arbeiterkindes. Jugenderinnerungen.* Dresden: 1919.

Rivers, W. H. R. "The Genealogical Method of Anthropological Enquiry." *Sociological Review* 3 (1910): 1–12. Repr. in *Kinship and Social Organization.* London School of Economics Monographs on Social Anthropology, 34. London: 1968.

Robisheaux, Thomas. *Rural Society and the Search for Order in Early Modern Germany.* Cambridge: 1989.

Rogge, Bernhard. *Aus sieben Jahrzehnten. Erinnerungen aus meinem Leben.* Hannover: 1897.

Roper, Lyndal. *The Holy Household: Women and Morals in Reformation Augsburg.* Oxford: 1989.

Rosenbaum, E., and Sherman, A. J. *M. M. Warburg & Co. 1798–1938: Merchant Bankers of Hamburg.* New York: 1979.

Rudolph, Richard L. "The European Peasant Family and Economy: Central Themes and Issues." *Journal of Family History* 17 (1992): 119–38.

Sabean, David Warren. "Aspects of Kinship Behaviour and Property in Rural Western Europe Before 1800." In *Family and Inheritance: Rural Society in Western Europe, 1200–1800,* edited by Jack Goody, Joan Thirsk, and E. P. Thompson, pp. 96–111. Cambridge: 1976.

"Exchanging Names in Neckarhausen around 1700." In *Theory, Method, and Practice in Social and Cultural History,* edited by Peter Karsten and John Modell, pp. 199–230. New York: 1992.

"Fanny and Felix Mendelssohn-Bartholdy and the Question of Incest." *Musical Quarterly* 77 (1993): 709–17.

"Household Formation and Geographical Mobility: A Family Register Study for a Württemberg Village 1760–1900." *Annales de démographie historique* (1970): 275–94.

Power in the Blood. Popular Culture and Village Discourse in Early Modern Germany. Cambridge: 1984.

Property, Production, and Family in Neckarhausen, 1700–1870. Cambridge: 1990.

"Social Background to Vetterleswirtschaft: Kinship in Neckarhausen." In *Frühe Neuzeit – Frühe Moderne? Forschungen zur Vielschichtigkeit von Übergangsprozessen,* edited by Rudolf Vierhaus and Mitarbeitern des Max-Planck-Institut für Geschichte, pp. 113–32. Veröffentlichungen des Max-Planck-Instituts für Geschichte, vol. 104. Göttingen: 1992.

"Soziale und kulturelle Aspekte der Geschlechtsvormundschaft im 18. und 19. Jahrhundert." In *Handbuch für die Rechtsgeschichte der Frau,* edited by Ute Gerhard. Beck Verlag. München: forthcoming [1997].

"Unehelichkeit: Ein Aspekt sozialer Reproduktion kleinbäuerlicher Produzenten. Zu einer Analyse dörflicher Quellen um 1800." In *Klassen und Kultur. Sozialanthropologische Perspektiven in der Geschichtsschreibung,* edited by Robert Berdahl et al., pp. 54–76. Frankfurt: 1982.

"Verwandtschaft und Familie in einem württembergischen Dorf 1500 bis 1870: einige methodische überlegungen." In *Sozialgeschichte der Familie in der Neuzeit Europas,* edited by Werner Conze, pp. 231–46. Stuttgart: 1976.

"Young Bees in an Empty Hive: Relations between Brothers-in-Law in a South German Village around 1800." In *Interest and Emotion: Essays on the Study of Family and Kinship,* edited by Hans Medick and David Warren Sabean, pp. 171–86. Cambridge: 1984.

Saugstad, Letten Fegersten. "Inbreeding in Norway." *Annals of Human Genetics* (London) 40 (1977): 481–91.

"The Relationship between Inbreeding, Migration and Population Density in Norway." *Annals of Human Genetics* (London) 30 (1977): 331–41.

Saugstad, Letten Fegersten, and Ødegård, Ørnulv, "Predominance of the Extreme Geographical Proximity of the Spouses of Heirs to Independent Farms in a Mountain Valley in Norway between 1600 and 1850." *Annals of Human Genetics* (London) 40 (1977): 419–30.

Schlegel, Karl August Moriz. *Kritische und systematische Darstellung der verbotenen Grade der Verwandtschaft und Schwägerschaft bey Heirathen.* Hannover: 1802.

Schlumbohm, Jürgen. *Lebensläufe, Familien, Höfe: Die Bauern und Heuersleute des Osnabrückischen Kirchspiels Belm in proto-industrieller Zeit, 1650–1860.* Veröffentlichungen des Max-Planck-Instituts für Geschichte, 110. Göttingen: 1994.

" 'Traditional' Collectivity and 'Modern' Individuality: Some Questions and Suggestions for the Historical Study of Socialization The Examples of the German Lower and Upper Bourgeoisies around 1800." *Social History* 5 (1980): 71–103.

Schmarje, Johannes. *Lebenserinnerungen eines schleswig-holsteinischen Schulmannes.* Altona: 1925.

Schmoller, Gustav. "Der deutsche Beamtenstaat vom 16. bis 18. Jahrhundert." In *Untersuchungen zur Verfassungs-, Verwaltungs- und Wirtschaftsgeschichte,* pp. 289–313. Leipzig: 1898.

Schneider, David M. *A Critique of the Study of Kinship.* Ann Arbor: 1984.

Schoppe, Amalie (née Wiese). *Erinnerungen aus meinem Leben.* Altona: 1838.

Schröder, Brigitte. "Der Weg zur Eisenbahnschiene. Geschichte der Familie Remy und ihre wirtschaftliche und kulturelle Bedeutung." In *Deutsches Familienarchiv. Ein genealogisches Sammelwerk,* vol. 91, pp. 3–158. Neustadt an der Aisch: 1986.

Schücking, Levin. *Lebenserinnerungen.* 2 vols. Breslau and Leipzig: 1886.

Schubert, Ernst. *Arme Leute, Bettler und Gauner in Franken des 18. Jahrhunderts.* Verein der Gesellschaft für fränkische Geschichte, Reihe 9: Darstellungen, vol. 26. Neustadt an der Aisch: 1983.

Schulte, Regina. *The Village Court: Arson, Infanticide, and Poaching in the Court Records of Upper Bavaria, 1848–1910.* Translated by Barrie Selman. Cambridge: 1994.

Schulze-Smidt, Bernhardine, ed. *Ottilie Wildermuths Briefe an einen Freund. Mit einer Lebensskizze.* Bielefeld and Leipzig: 1910.

Scott, J.D. *Siemens Brothers 1858–1958: An Essay in the History of Industry.* London: 1958.

Seeger, von. "Vortrag des Abgeordneten v. Seeger die lebenslängliche Dauer der Gemeinde-Aemter betreffend" (1824), pamphlet. n.p.: n.d.

Segalen, Martine. *Fifteen Generations of Bretons: Kinship and Society in Lower Brittany 1720–1980.* Translated by J. S. Underwood. Cambridge: 1991.

"Parenté et alliance dans les sociétés paysannes." *Ethnologie Française* 11 (1981): 307–9.

Segalen, Martine, and Richard, Philippe. "Marrying Kinsmen in Pays Bigouden Sud, Brittany." *Journal of Family History* 11 (1986): 109–30.

Sehling, Emil, ed. *Die evangelischen Kirchenordnungen des XVI. Jahrhunderts.* 15 vols. Leipzig: 1902–13; Tübingen: 1955–77.

Serlo, Walter, ed. *Bergmannsfamilien in Rheinland und Westfalen.* Rheinisch-Westfälische Wirtschaftsbiographien, vol. 3. Aschendorff, Münster: 1974.

Serra, Angelo. "Italian Official Statistics on Consanguineous Marriages." *Acta Genetica* 9 (1959): 244–6.

Serra, Angelo, and Soini, Antonio "La consanguinité d'une population. Rappel de notions et de résultats. Application trois provinces d'Italie du Nord." *Population* 14 (1959): 47–72.

Service, Elman R. *A Century of Controversy: Ethnological Issues from 1860 to 1960.* Orlando: 1985.

Siemens, Georg. *Carl Friedrich von Siemens: Ein grosser Unternehmer.* Freiburg: 1960.

Siemens, Hermann W. "Ueber das Erfindergeschlecht Siemens." *Archiv zur Rassen- und Gesellschaftsbiologie* 12 (1916–18): 162–92.

Siemens, Werner von. *Personal Recollections.* Translated by W. C. Copland. London: 1893.

Siemens-Helmholtz, Ellen von, ed. *Anna von Helmholtz. Ein Lebensbild in Briefen.* Berlin: 1929.

Simmel, Georg. "Die Verwandtenehe." In *Aufsätze und Abhandlungen 1894–1900,* pp. 9–36. Frankfurt: 1992.

Smith, Bonnie G. *Ladies of the Leisure Class: The Bourgeoises of Northern France in the Nineteenth Century.* Princeton: 1981.

Smith, Daniel Scott. "Child-Naming Patterns and Family Structure Change: Hingham, Massachusetts 1640–1880." *Newberry Papers in Family and Community History,* Paper 76–5. Chicago: January, 1977.

Smith, Raymont T. *The Negro Family in British Guiana: Family Structure and Social Status in the Villages.* London: 1956.

Spethmann, Hans. *Franz Haniel, sein Leben und seine Werke.* Duisburg-Ruhrort: 1956.

Spindler, Adolf. "Ueber die Häufigkeit der Verwandtenehen in drei württembergischen Dörfern." *Archiv für Rassen- und Gesellschaftsbiologie* 14 (1922–3): 9–12.

Spittler, Ludwig Timotheus von. "Entwurf einer Geschichte des engern landschaftlichen Ausschusses" (1796). In *Sämmtliche Werke,* edited by Karl Wächter, 13 vols. Stuttgart and Tübingen: 1837. Vol. 3: *Vermischte Schriften über deutsche Geschichte, Statistik und öffentliches Recht,* pp. 16–156.

"Geschichte des württembergischen Geheimen-Raths-Collegiums." In *Sämmtliche Werke,* edited by Karl Wächter, 13 vols. Stuttgart and Tübingen: 1837. Vol. 3: *Vermischte Schriften über deutsche Geschichte, Statistik und öffentliches Recht,* pp. 279–452.

Stahr, Adolf. *Aus der Jugendzeit. Lebenserinnerungen.* 2 vols. Schwerin: 1877.

Stein, Lorenz von. *Die Frau auf dem socialen Gebiete.* Stuttgart: 1880.

Die Frau, ihre Bildung und Lebensaufgabe. 3d ed. Berlin: 1890.

Strathern, Marilyn. *After Nature: English Kinship in the Late Twentieth Century.* Cambridge: 1992.

"Parts and Wholes: Refiguring Relationships in a Post-Plural World." In *Conceptualizing Society,* edited by Adam Kuper, pp. 75–104. London: 1992.

Stürmer, Michael, Teichmann, Gabrielle, and Treue, Wilhelm. *Wägen und Wagen: Sal. Oppenheim jr. & Cie. Geschichte einer Bank und einer Familie.* 2d ed. Munich: 1989.

Sutter, Jean. "Fréquence de l'endogamie et ses facteurs au xixe siècle." *Population* 23 (1968), pp. 303–24.

Sutter, Jean, and Goux, Jean-Michel. "Evolution de la consanguinité en France de 1926 à 1958 avec des données récentes détaillées." *Population* 17 (1962): 683–702. Excerpted in *Eugenics Quarterly* 11 (1964): 127–40.

Sutter, Jean, and Lévy, Claude. "Les dispenses civiles au mariage en France depuis 1800." *Population* 14 (1959): 285–303.

Sutter, Jean, and Tabah, Léon. "Fréquence et répartition des mariages consanguins en France." *Population* 3,4 (1948): 607–30.

Teschner, Manfred. "Was ist Klassenanalyse? Ueber Klassenverhältnis, Ausbeutung und Macht." In *Leviathan. Zeitschrift für Sozialwissenschaft* (1989): 1–14.

Thiersch, Heinrich W. J. *Das Verbot der Ehe innerhalb der nahen Verwandtschaft, nach der heiligen Schrift und nach den Grundsätzen der christlichen Kirche.* Nördlingen: 1869.

Tillion, Germaine. *The Republic of Cousins: Women's Oppression in Mediterranean Society.* Translated by Quintin Hoare. London: 1983.

Titzmann, Michael. "Literarische Strukturen und kulturelles Wissen: Das Beispiel inzestuöser Situationen in der Erzählliteratur der Goethezeit und ihre Funktionen im Denksystem der Epoche." In *Erzählte Kriminalität. Zur Typologie und Funktion von narrativen Darstellungen in Strafrechtspflege, Publizistik und Literatur zwischen 1770 und 1920,* edited by Jörg Schönert, with Konstantin Imm and Joachim Linder, pp. 229–81. Studien und Texte zur Sozialgeschichte der Literatur, vol. 27. Tübingen: 1991.

Trawick, Margaret. *Notes on Love in a Tamil Family.* Berkeley: 1990.

Treskow, Rüdiger von. "Adel in Preussen: Anpassung und Kontinuität einer Familie 1800–1918." *Geschichte und Gesellschaft* 17 (1991): 344–69.

Twiesselmann, Fr., Moreau, P., and François, J. "Evolution de consanguinité en Belgique de 1918 à 1959." *Population* 17 (1962): 241–66.

van Velson, J. *Politics of Kinship: A Study in Social Manipulation among the Lakeside Tonga.* Manchester: 1964.

Vernier, Bernard. "Emigration et déreglement du marché matrimonial." *Actes de la recherche en sciences sociales* 15 (1977).

"Putting Kin and Kinship to Good Use: The Circulation of Goods, Labour, and Names in Karpathos (Greece)." In *Interest and Emotion: Essays on the Study of the Family and Kinship,* edited by Hans Medick and David Warren Sabean, pp. 28–76. Cambridge: 1984.

Verschuer, O. Freiherr von. "Neue Befunde über die Häufigkeit von Blutsverwandtenehen in Deutschland." *Zeitschrift für Morphologie und Anthropologie* 46 (1954): 293–6.

Walker, Mack. *German Home Towns: Community, State, and General Estate 1648–1871.* Ithaca: 1971.

Walther, L., ed. *Erinnerungen aus Wilhelm Appuhns Leben, aus seinen Aufzeichnungen zusammengestellt.* Gotha: 1885.

Waugh, Scott. *The Lordship of England: Royal Wardships and Marriages in English Society and Politics 1217–1327.* Princeton: 1988.

Wegmann, Dietrich. *Die leitenden staatlichen Verwaltungsbeamten der Provinz Westfalen, 1815–1918.* Geschichtliche Arbeiten zur westfälischen Landesforschung, wirtschafts- und sozialgeschichtliche Gruppe, vol.1. Münster: 1969.

Wehler, Hans-Ulrich. "Vorüberlegungen zur historischen Analyse sozialer Ungleichheit. In *Klassen in der europäischen Sozialgeschichte,* edited by Hans-Ulrich Wehler, pp. 9–31 Göttingen: 1979.

Wellhöner, Volker. *Grossbanken und Grossindustrie im Kaiserreich.* Kritische Studien zur Geschichtswissenschaft, vol. 85. Göttingen: 1989.

Wiese, Ludwig. *Lebenserinnerungen und Amtserfahrungen.* 2 vols. Berlin: 1886.

Wiggers, Julius. *Aus meinem Leben.* Leipzig: 1901.

Wikman, K. Robert von. *Die Einleitung in die Ehe: Eine vergleichend ethno-soziologische Untersuchung über die Vorstufe der Ehe in den Sitten des schwedischen Volkstums.* Aabo: 1937.

Willam, Horst Alexander. *Carl Zeiss 1816–1886.* In *Tradition. Zeitschrift für Firmengeschichte und Unternehmerbiographie,* Beiheft 6. Munich: 1967.

Wrigley, E. A., ed. *Identifying People in the Past.* London: 1973.

Wulz, Gustav. "Ein Beitrag zur Statistik der Verwandtenehen." *Archiv für Rassen- und Gesellschaftsbiologie* 17 (1925–6): 82–95.

Yalman, Nur. *Under the Bo Tree: Studies in Caste, Kinship, and Marriage in the Interior of Ceylon.* Berkeley, 1967.

Young, Michael, and Willmott, Peter. *Family and Kinship in East London.* Harmondsworth: 1962.

Yver, Jean. *Egalité entre héritiers et exclusion des enfants dotés: Essai de geographie coutumière.* Paris: 1966.

Zonabend, Françoise. "Le très proche et le pas trop loin: Réflexions sur l'organisation du champ matrimonial des sociétés structures de parenté complexes." *Ethnologie française* 11 (1981): 311–18.

Zorn, Wolfgang. *Handels- und Industriegeschichte Bayerisch-Schwabens 1648–1870: Wirtschafts-, Sozial-, und Kulturgeschichte des schwäbischen Unternehmertums.* Veröffentlichungen der schwäbischen Forschungsgemeinschaft bei der Kommission für Landesgeschichte, Reihe I: Studien zur Geschichte bayerischen Schwabens. Augsburg: 1961.

Zunkel, Friedrich. *Der Rheinisch-Westfälische Unternehmer 183· –1879. Ein Beitrag zur Geschichte des deutschen Bürgertums im 19. Jahrhundert.* Dor munder Schriften zur Sozialforschung. Köln: 1962.

Zwahr, Hartmut. *Proletariat und Bourgeoisie in Deutschland: Studien zur Klassendialektik.* Köln: 1980.

"Zur Klassenkonstituierung der deutschen Bourgeoisie." *Jahrbuch für Geschichte,* 18 (1978): 21–83.

General index

General index

General index

Index of villagers

Key: e = emigrated to; i = immigrated from; b = born (date and/or place, or maiden name); m = married; d = died; h = husband(s). Dates in parentheses indicate that a baptismal or burial record is not available but that a date is given in another record or can be reckoned from an age attribution. Orthographic problems make such dates less reliable.

Index of villagers